"Richard Eager"
A Pilot's Story
from Tennessee Eagle Scout
to General Montgomery's "Flying Fortress"

"Richard Eager"

A Pilot's Story
from Tennessee Eagle Scout
to General Montgomery's "Flying Fortress"

Colonel Richard Ernest Evans
and Barbara Evans Kinnear

"Richard Eager"
A Pilot's Story from Tennessee Eagle Scout
to General Montgomery's "Flying Fortress"
Colonel Richard Ernest Evans
and Barbara Evans Kinnear

Printed in the United States of America.
July 2021
Soft cover: ISBN: 978-1-7333518-7-4
Hard cover: ISBN: 978-1-7333518-8-1

Kieran Publishing
www.kieranpublishing.com
P.O. Box 3683, Santa Barbara, CA 93130
kieranpublishing@gmail.com

Book/Cover Design & Layout: Anna Lafferty/Lafferty Design Plus

DEDICATION

This book is dedicated to dads...
mine in particular.

My dad was a bespectacled, scholarly gentleman who smiled a lot. It was a genuine smile. William Ernest Evans or "Pug" Evans, as he was called in Knoxville, Tennessee, was a happy, contented man. At Knox High, Dad taught chemistry for one year before becoming the school principal and self-appointed assistant football coach for the next forty-one years.

I was twenty and in my third year at the University of Tennessee, when orders arrived from the War Department directing me to report to Love Field, Dallas, Texas, for active duty in the Army Air Corps. It was October, 1939. Hitler had invaded Poland in September. The Second World War was thirty days old... and I was still in civvies.

My mother said, "You won't have to go, Dick. You're not of age; all I have to do is just not sign these papers."

"But, Mom," I pleaded, "You know I have thought about the Air Corps for a long time, and feel I should join up. And, Mom, if I wait until I'm twenty-one, the flying school quotas will be filled. Then they'll draft me into the infantry, Mom."

"You won't have to go anywhere right now if I don't sign these papers, Dick; and I'm not signing anything."

Dad had been listening in the hallway. He had let Mom do the talking as he often did. But, when Mom said she wouldn't sign my papers, Dad stepped into the doorway and, in a soft voice, said, "That's all right, Helen. I'll take the responsibility. I'll sign Dick's papers."

Mom was speechless, a rare condition for my spirited mother. Dad had taken her off the hook by saying he would take the responsibility. But Mom knew what Dad had done; he had crossed her in front of one of her sons.

I remember watching my confident and determined mother as she pushed her chair back, stood up, then leaned over our dining room table, the table where our "important family discussions" had always taken place. Mom started to speak but stopped short; then she dropped her head and just sat back down. I was sure Mom had noticed the points of light reflecting off the tears that had formed behind Dad's glasses; the lens had made the tears look larger.

After a moment, my father, a man at peace with himself, who had never savored victory over his wife or any of his sons, said, "Helen, peace can be a very precious thing; it may even be worth fighting for."

I will never forget that moment. Mom then looked up at Dad; now tears were in Mom's eyes, too. She stood up, took a step toward Dad and put her head on his shoulder.

I left the room without a word. I knew what Mom and Dad were thinking: Besides me, they had three more sons to go....

Colonel Richard Ernest Evans, 1993

TABLE OF CONTENTS

AUTHOR'S PREFACE

The author declares and avows, with respect to intent, this book is not autobiographical. He hopes a gracious readership will accept his personalized treatise as a collection of boyhood stories and war stories, in which he was a participant along with thousands of his contemporaries.

It will become evident to adventurous readers that this book cannot be construed as the life story of anyone; such tedium has been eliminated by starting in the middle, then occasionally flashing backward and forward, describing challenging, exciting and heart-breaking experiences. Through these flashbacks, Richard Evans interrupts his personalized telling of war to recall youthful, developmental years with family and friends and as a Boy Scout in the Smoky Mountains.

Perhaps this book might be thought of as an anthology: a collection of tales describing the experiences of many young Americans who, in their late teens and early twenties, took the war to their country's enemies in B-17s, B-24s, B-25s, B-26s, B-29s and A-20s, P-47s and P-51s. "Richard Eager," as this author was nicknamed by his flying school peers, joined the war early and flew all these aircraft.

In 1939, while a junior at the University of Tennessee, Richard Eager began to think he was fated for war and that this war, hovering on his horizon, offered the jarring promise of becoming the greatest of wars, but also the deadliest war of all times. Richard Eager feared that this new war would strike his generation directly and would have an even greater impact on its participants than did "The Great War", which had ended just 68 days before Richard Eager was born.

Despite these fears, young Richard Eagar also hoped that, for the first time in history, the targets of war might not be the peoples of adversarial nations but rather their tools and their weapons that start wars and keep them going. Perhaps, he hoped, wars might be fought with the intent to disarm, rather than to wantonly kill and destroy.

"What is this 'Richard Eager' business?" his mother asked when she was on hand in San Antonio, Texas, for his graduation from flying school.

"Mother," he responded, "my classmates started calling me 'Eager' when I was appointed Captain of my class because they thought your son to be too eager."

"It means, Helen," his dad interjected with his characteristic grin, "our son is erring on the positive side."

It is with this view, that of the optimistic, young Richard Eager, that I share these stories.

Conceived as the Twentieth Century is coming to an end, this book is written for interested and concerned young people, anxious to understand and to reflect upon the kind of world they are inheriting. It is also for older folks: those who, while they may be fading, find joy and pride in recalling the young people they once were.

Colonel Richard Ernest Evans, 1993

CO-AUTHOR'S PREFACE

This is a story of reflection, one my father wanted to tell and one my family and I felt compelled to preserve. What follows is a true tale, not a tall tale, of a young boy from Knoxville, Tennessee, who spread his wings, quite literally, to fly throughout the world in the service of the US Army Air Corps during World War II. It is the story of a close family told lovingly by one of its five sons, four of whom would live to serve in and survive the Second World War. It is also a glimpse of Middle American lives through small windows of time, reflecting the nineteen twenties, thirties, and forties.

This is a firsthand account of a young man coming of age just as the Second World War erupted. For Richard Ernest Evans, and for many other young men and women, this was a harrowing and life-changing time to be alive. In the service of their country, average citizens became professional soldiers and had experiences that movie producers can only dream about. As they performed their duties, they met, served, and protected illustrious and prominent leaders, who are today recognized in the pages of history, but they themselves are not.

Captain Richard E. Evans was an American B-17 *Flying Fortress* pilot. He flew 55 combat missions and during that time was also chosen to fly British Field Marshal Bernard L. Montgomery to wherever the General needed to be throughout North Africa and Italy. Evans and "Monty" traveled together during a particularly dangerous phase of the war, when the Allied forces were just beginning to turn back the brutal Axis armies that had invaded North Africa and were closing in on Egypt in an effort to gain control of the strategically vital Suez Canal. Over the deserts of Tunisia, Libya and Egypt, a rocky but honest and respectful friendship formed between the young American pilot, Captain Evans, and his British commander, Field Marshal Montgomery, later to become 1st Viscount of Alamein.

Captain Evans retired to the Air Force Reserves months after the Japanese surrendered, returning home to his wife and young daughter. He was asked to fly again when the Korean War began. He continued in the Air Force flying the B-47, B-52, and he became the B-58 Test Squadron Commander before retiring from the Air Force in 1959 as a Command Pilot and full Colonel.

Throughout my childhood, my brother and I would listen to our father's accounts of his flying and travels. In my adulthood, his stories took on greater detail as he revisited memories and friendships long past and recounted his childhood and upbringing with fondness. He was a wonderful storyteller. So, in the early 1990s, with the encouragement of his family, retired Colonel Richard E. Evans began to set his memories down into writing.

Colonel Evans wrote in his own words. His sense of duty, his sense of humor, his humility and his love for family illuminate the pages. A paragraph within a most descriptive letter to his father back in Knoxville, dated June 19, 1943, reveals the essence of his character: "These experiences with the brass hats are unusual, Pop, and as such, interesting. But know ye, they are not the real thing! I am these days in the company of generals, air marshals and kings only because of circumstances, not because of anything meritorious that I have accomplished." (Appendices letter: 6.19.43, page 3, "Flying Through Flak.")

This book is organized with the military chapters in chronological order, but with family stories interspersed in between. As Colonel Evans wrote his narrative, some memories easily led to others. Some memories came crashing in while others lingered in the corners of his consciousness to be slowly teased out and revealed. In this fluid, personal manner, my father committed his family stories and overseas adventures to the page, researched them for background detail, and began organizing them for publication. Colonel Evans passed away in 2006 before he could make his final edits. I vowed to publish my father's work.

Scattered across computer hard drives, family filing cabinets, floppy disks and notepads, my father's chapters awaited their assembly. Working closely with my family, I gathered the twenty-one finished and nearly finished chapters, along with much of the background research. But, then, in November 2008, my home burned to the ground in a disastrous wildfire. All of my father's written work was lost. Or so we feared.

In 2009, while cleaning out a small storage unit that belonged to my father, my daughter and I found a treasure trove of earlier drafts and original photographs. A small selection of intact chapters provided a basis for hope. And to fill in the gaps, we tracked down countless manuscripts that had been shared amongst extended family over the years. This was enough, we believed, to finish my father's book.

Although Colonel Evans died having never seen his book in print, he did believe he had written stories filled with compassion, courage, humor, humility and history – poignant anecdotes of early life in Tennessee, US Army Air Corps training, B-17 bombing missions over Africa and Italy and German-held parts of Europe, and, of course, enlightening accounts describing the times he spent with Monty on long flights and at Monty's headquarters.

To provide greater context and color to Colonel Evans's experiences, I have included in this book much research and additional archival materials, including: a chronology of his life's milestones and Second World War details; a glossary of war terms, many defined with his usual humor and wit; an appendix of original family letters, V-Mail, commendations and interesting documents, all primary sources that shed light on his fears, reflections and important personal and professional relationships; photos of his young years in Tennessee and his years in military service; and maps, illustrating the lands and seas over which he flew. An epilogue detailing his work after the Second World War is also included.

Throughout the book chapters, glossary terms and names are highlighted in bold print and their definitions can be found in alphabetical order in the Glossary. The Dedication, Author's Preface and Introduction are compiled from Colonel Evans' own notes.

In this book, Richard Eager's words have been rediscovered. My family hopes his stories will add a bit to history and encourage others to tell their stories as well.

Barbara "Bobbie" Evans Kinnear
Co-author & Editor
September 12, 2020

INTRODUCTION

This book is about growing up, tripping up and starting over again. The pages tell of youthful failure and disappointment, but also of second efforts resulting in some successes and a few out-and-out victories.

The tales told are true, spanning the quarter-century beginning when Richard Earnest Evans was born in January 1919, two months after the First World War ground to an inglorious end in the trenches of France, through September 1945, when the Second World War ended abruptly in August 1945 after a fire-bombing and nuclear bombing of Japan. The Second World War formally ceased on September 2, 1945, with Japan's unconditional surrender aboard the *USS Missouri* sitting in Tokyo Bay.

These tales commence in July 1943, shortly after Army Air Corps Captain, Richard Earnest Evans, (fondly called "Richard Eager" by his Air Corps comrades since flying school days in 1939), lands his B-17 in Marrakech, Morocco, en route to England. He is proud to be flying a brand-new Boeing B-17 *Flying Fortress* across the Atlantic and proud for having volunteered for his new assignment. Also, he feels a slight chill and some foreboding when he considers what could lie ahead.

Richard Eager's 99th Bomb Group had flown the southern route from the United States to the MTO (Mediterranean Theater of Operations), flying from Florida to Puerto Rico to Georgetown, British Guiana (now Guyana), to Belem, Brazil, and to Natal, Brazil, before crossing the Atlantic Ocean to Yundum Field, Bathurst, Gambia, then continuing on to Marrakech and finally England. However, upon reaching Marrakech, the 99th is abruptly reassigned to Jimmie Doolittle's 12th Air Force and directed to fly to an airfield in northern Algeria.

Captain Evans's B-17 touches down at Marrakech about three weeks after Winston Churchill and Franklin Roosevelt conclude the first of a series of meetings that they will hold over the course of the war. During the Casablanca Conference, they agreed on a strategy to drive the Axis invaders out of North Africa, to free the Mediterranean and expose the "soft underbelly of Europe," and finally to attack mainland Europe. History reports that they also agreed to delay their returns to London and Washington for a few days, affording them more time to get to know one another and to formulate an over-riding strategy for the conduct of the war.

While in Algeria, North Africa, Richard Eager receives orders from "Ike", General Dwight Eisenhower, through General James Doolittle, directing him to fly a B-17 to Tripoli and report for duty to General Bernard Law Montgomery, Commander, British 8th Army. "Monty," as this general suddenly came to be known throughout the world, had just defeated General Erwin Rommel, Hitler's favorite Field Marshal, the fabled "Desert Fox," at the decisive Battle of El Alamein.

This B-17 pilot has his reservations about flying around North Africa with top brass aboard. The weight of the responsibility is not lost on him. Had he responded to his new situation in the vernacular of youths of the 1990s, he might have shouted, "No way! I'm outa here!" However, what this well-trained and possibly over-disciplined youth of the 1940s says as he salutes is, "Yes, sir." But, in only a few hours, he actually is out of there and on his way to Tripoli.

Often with Monty in the skies over North Africa, Sicily and Italy and at Monty's forward battle camps during the following months, Captain Richard Evans has some good moments and some bad moments with the General. "A great experience," he writes to his folks in Tennessee, "when Monty introduced me to a genial King George VI." But "not that great an experience," he writes when, in Palermo, he finds himself suddenly uncomfortably juxtaposed betwixt an agitated General Montgomery (who moments earlier, thought his life was ending) and a petulant General George Patton who thinks Monty's pilot had been grandstanding when, in fact, he had deliberately ground-looped Monty's suddenly brakeless *Flying Fortress* to keep it within the bounds of Palermo's under-sized airdrome.

Returning later to "combat ops" to complete the required 50 missions, the Captain becomes a Major and a Squadron Commander. On one of those missions, he is the leader of a 37-plane B-17 formation, charged with the safety of 370 flight crew members, and armed with a total of 148 tons of high-explosive bombs.

After completing 54 missions in Europe, Richard Eager returns to America and is trained as a B-29 *Superfortress* heavy bomber pilot and becomes Assistant Director of Training at Army Air Base Alamogordo, New Mexico. Some months later, he is again on his way overseas, this time to the Pacific. As an advance man for Colonel Thomas J. DuBose, Commander of the 316th Bomb Wing, part of General Doolittle's 8th Air Force (which had been shifted from England to Okinawa), Richard Eager stops off at Tinian and Saipan to fly a few B-29 missions over Japan.

While flying over Japan, Richard Eager is witness to the virtual end of the Second World War. In Europe, German fighters had attacked his B-17s at 25,000 feet. In Japan, the fighters are also at 25,000 feet; his B-29, however, is at 35,000 feet. "This war isn't winding down," he said to himself, "It is essentially over. Hitler is dead and Hirohito can't lay a glove on us. His flying machines can't get themselves up to our new operating altitude." After a moment, he smiles to himself, "Thank you God; thank you Boeing; thank you Rosie the Riveter."

While in the PTO (Pacific Theater of Operations), Richard Eager also visits Guam to familiarize himself with the mission-control setup on the island and to meet Major General Curtis LeMay, the legendary Second World War bomber commander.

General LeMay is present at the 21st Bomber Command's Mission Control Room late one night to receive the strike reports from B-29s over Japan as they return from their first of a series of low-level, firebombing raids on Tokyo. Richard Eager waits through the night with the General, the General he would again serve under in a future war, the Cold War, and with whom he would enjoy a life-long friendship.

Preliminary damage assessment that fateful night, sourced from still-damp B-29 strike photos, evidenced success beyond anything previously thought possible. Clearly, the firebombing raids on Tokyo marked the beginning of the end of the Second World War.

With the explosion of two atomic bombs within three days, the greatest and certainly the worst of wars to assault the planet finally grinds to a halt. At the end, Richard Eager is again serving under his old commander, General Doolittle, in Okinawa.

This is the story of an American flyboy's experience in the Second World War over North Africa, Europe and the Pacific. Between periods of elevated activity, Richard Eager allows his thoughts to reflect and ruminate on earlier times. With intermittent flashbacks to what he calls his "pre-paring years" in Knoxville, Tennessee, and the Great Smoky Mountains, and to the camps and flying fields of the pre-war Army Air Corps, Richard Eager brings to life stories that illuminate the common experiences of many of America's youth of the 1930s and 1940s, thereby allowing the reader to appreciate the early life this American boy is coming from as he faces the realities of war.

The years leading up to and encompassing the Second World War were filled with fear and hope. Nonetheless, it was a period of time during which the United States proved itself, matured as a nation and, indeed, became a leader among nations. Richard Eager also came of age during these pivotal years and was fortunate to live to share his personal story.

Colonel Richard Ernest Evans, 1993

M-1 *Captain Richard E. Evans keeps his own record of his Atlantic Ocean*
crossing to North Africa and his first 25 MTO missions

MAPS OF ROUTES & OPERATIONS
INVOLVING CAPTAIN RICHARD EVANS

These maps show some of the Second World War airfields and cities that Captain Richard E. Evans flew to between 1943 and 1944. The dots indicate the airfields, towns and cities mentioned in this book. They include:

- Map of South Atlantic Air Ferry Route to Africa for the 99th BG

- Map of Mediterranean Locations Involved During the Mediterranean Theater of Operations, 1943–1944

- Map of Allied Airfield Locations During the Major African Campaign, 1940–1943

- Map of Captured Japanese Airfields in the South Pacific, 1944–1945

Map of South Atlantic Air Ferry Route to Africa for the 99th BG

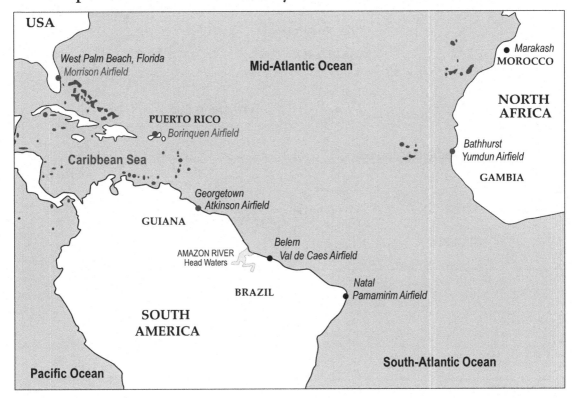

Map of Mediterranean Locations Involved
During the Mediterranean Theater of Operations, 1943–1944

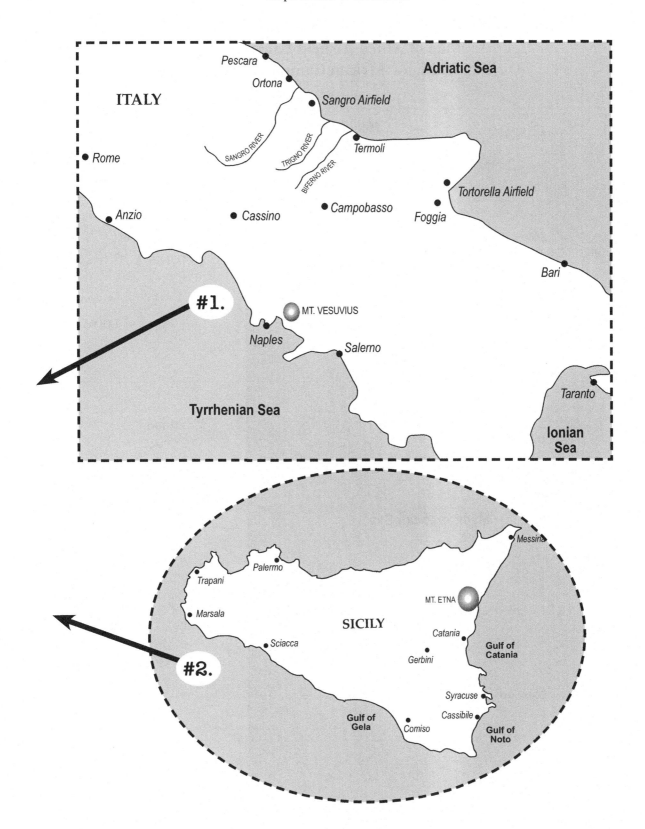

Map of Allied Airfield Locations
During the Major African Campaign, 1940–1943

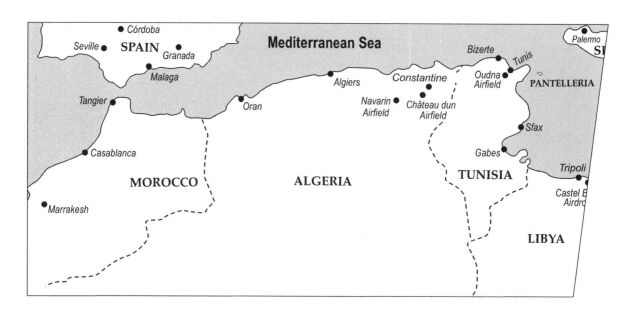

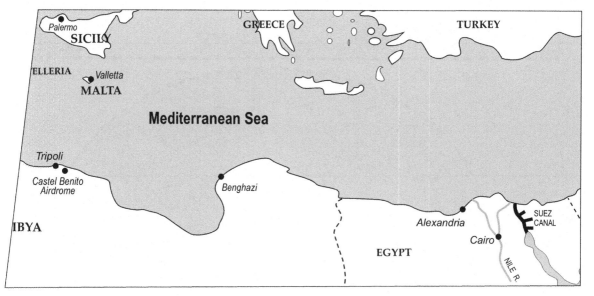

Map of Captured Japanese Airfields in the South Pacific, 1944–1945

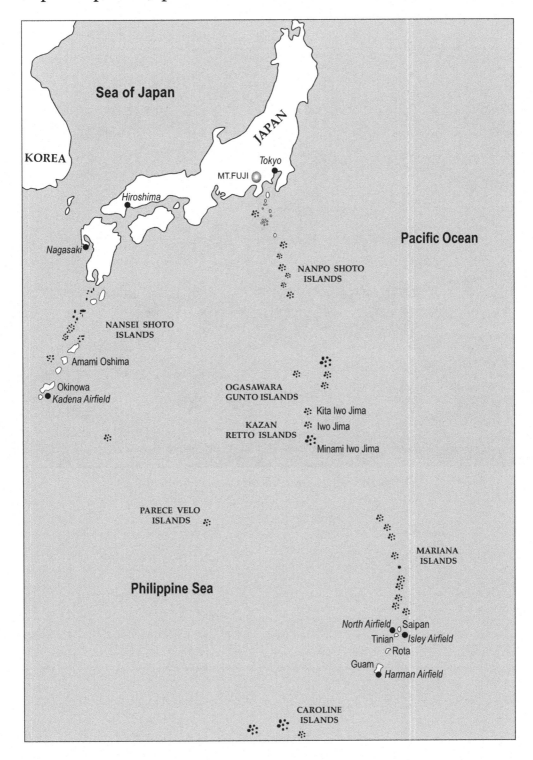

1.1 *B-17s cross the great Atlantic Ocean to North Africa*

CHAPTER 1
ORDERS FROM IKE

There is a tide in the affairs of men
Which, taken at the flood, can lead to fortune.
Ignored, the voyage of our lives
May be bound in the shallows.
We must take the current when it serves,
Or we must lose our ventures.

Julius Caesar
(Act 4, scene iii, lines 214-223)

This story begins not by the parting of a curtain on a Shakespearean stage but by the parting of a flap on a tent, a GI tent pitched atop a hill in Algeria. This tent looked out upon a broad valley, stretching 400 miles from the low Aures Mountains that formed the Tunisian frontier in the East to the snow-capped High Atlas Range that formed the Moroccan frontier in the West.

It was spring 1943, when this tent flap parted. It was 0600 hours. It was chilly but not cold. I had washed up as well as one could with a GI helmet as a washbasin. Coffee was brewing on my jury-rigged, aviation-fuel-powered stove. No combat missions were scheduled. Colonel Upthegrove's 99th Bomb Group of Major General Doolittle's 5th Wing of General Eisenhower's African Theater was standing down to let some weather pass through and give our ground crews time to bring our B-17s up to combat-ready status.

Warrant Officer House rapped on my tent ropes and called out, "Captain Evans, Colonel Upthegrove wants to see you... his tent at 0730 hours." The Commander of the 99th Bomb Group usually started his day higher up the command hierarchy, first a Colonel or Lieutenant Colonel, and then a Major. "Uppie", as his 500-man bomb group warmly called him, might get around to a Captain by noon.

Stepping from my tent, I stretched and looked out across our 99th Bomb Group tent city, which was just beginning to stir. Shadows from tents, jeeps and trucks, elongated by the low, flat, morning light, reached out like giant fingers in the direction of my gaze. As the sun rose behind me, these shadowy fingers visually contracted, appearing to rake the green fields towards me.

Then, for a few seconds with interest approaching awe, I watched a distant line between dark and light make its way up one side of a tree, over the top and down the other side, then slip across the ground, and then up another tree as it worked its way towards me across the mile-wide orchard.

I vowed to never tell anyone about the time I got all worked up about the sun causing a shadow to glide quickly up one side of a tree and then just as quickly down the other side. After all, perhaps a million people have stood atop a tall New York building and watched the "shadow of the night," chased by the sun, run up one side then down the other of one skyscraper after another in Manhattan. In North Africa, one had to use a distant orchard and one's imagination. Actually, I've never seen anything like this racing shadow since that day in 1943.

To my left, I could see our 5,000-foot airstrip and our hardstands where our B-17s slouched their wings in repose. Our taxiways, hogged out of mud-red earth, appeared as great slashes cut by a giant saber, harsh cuts in a spring-green countryside.

"To the sun-darkened people who inhabit this timeless agrarian valley," I mused, "our 99th Bomb Group, with its noisy airplanes and anxious, restless crews, must be thought a gross intrusion. Small wonder, that the people of this land appear not to see us as they pass us by on their ancient, time-worn roadways."

Relaxing on their hardstands and without the speed of the wind to support their wings, our dusty, olive drab B-17s appeared to slump over their landing gears. The great and terrible power of sixty B-17s was stilled for a time; they awaited their crews in silence.

In my mind's eye, I watched our ground crews arrive, followed by our aircrews. I observed them, tumbling from their jeeps in high spirits. If they were shrill and their excitement showed, it was forgivable; for on any given day, there would be some who would not return.

For a while, both the flight crews and the ground crews would appear to mill about as flight gear, maps, checklists and lunches were stowed aboard the B-17s and final inspections were completed. Then, in a short while, the flight crews would climb aboard to stay, and the doors and hatches would be buttoned down behind them. The silence would then return.

Finally, a single Wright Cyclone R-1820-97 engine would chug, fire, then whir to a higher pitch. Others would follow and quickly this timeless, spring-green valley would be filled with a great and, until recently, unfamiliar sound, the resonating roar of a hundred engines. Like a great orchestra, the 99th Bomb Group would be tuning up for another live performance.

This pageant, which would become a permanent part of my memory, would not, however, be reenacted on this day. No missions had been laid on: the mighty 99th was standing down. The action this day would be a few test-flights for aircraft, which had just received major repair. There might also be a few checkout flights for replacement crews arriving from the States. And, on this particular morning, my Group Commander was summoning me. "Colonel Uppie" had sent word, "suggesting" that I report to his Command tent promptly at 0730 hours.

To the northeast behind my tent, the sun was still breaking through white, billowy, cumulus clouds hanging low over the eastern-most extension of the African Atlas Mountains. The ancient village of Constantine, named for the Roman Emperor, was up there in those mountains in the sun, as was our 12th Air Force headquarters and its Commander, Major General James H. Doolittle.

Smiling, I said to myself, "Fitting, isn't it, that the first light of dawn should come streaming down to warm us from our Air Force Headquarters high up in those beautiful, cool, green mountains... where Jimmie Doolittle and the Red Cross girls live."

In a short time, approaching Colonel Upthegrove's Command Tent, I could see my boss striking his open palm with a piece of rolled up paper. The "Old Man," I thought to myself, "still thinks he has a riding crop there. And, he appears to be less pleased than I am with the prospects of the morning."

An "Old Man," a group commander or higher in the Army Air Corps of the late 1930s and early 1940s, was usually in his early 30s, his commissioned air-crewmen were in their early twenties, and his non-commissioned airmen were in their late teens!

I wondered what my group CO had for me. Maybe orders sending me home? Not likely. In fact, it was most unlikely, for I had flown just twenty-seven missions. Even less likely, my promotion to Major. I wasn't a professional soldier; I wasn't "regular army." I was a reserve officer, dedicated to serving in the Air Corps of the US Army "for the duration" of the war.

In a moment, within a few feet of my Commander, I stopped, came to attention and saluted. I enjoyed saluting "Uppie." I thought him a man of honor, with good humor and integrity, an experienced airman, and a discerning, in-control and under-control B-17 Combat Group Commander. Also, Colonel Upthegrove was an honest, gentle, hard-working man–like my dad.

I will always remember my first meeting with my Group Commander, which happened the day after my 24th birthday, January 19, 1943. It was the night before his 99th Bomb Group was scheduled to take off from Salina Air Base in Kansas, headed for the ETO (European Theater of Operations) to join up with the 8th Air Force in England. I had learned that one of Colonel Upthegrove's pilots had suddenly come down with something, a hernia I was told, and that he had just been consigned to the base hospital.

I had felt self-conscious and off-balance when I approached Colonel Upthegrove. Understandably, he was very busy on the eve of his departure for the air war in Europe, which at the time was just getting underway. I could feel my hand shaking as I saluted. And I could feel perspiration on my brow that normally wouldn't be there in January. I suggested quickly, too quickly, that with the shortage of pilots, might he need a replacement pilot... for the trip he was planning to the ETO, the European Theater of Operations... in England, in the UK? (I remember thinking, "That's a run-on sentence, you jerk... settle down.")

I had learned that the Colonel's newly formed 99th Bomb Group would be the first full group to fly the southern route to the ETO: starting from West Palm Beach, Florida, southeast across the West Indies and the Caribbean, to Georgetown, British Guiana (Guyana), continuing southeast to the mouth of the Amazon, to Belem, Brazil, then to Natal, on the eastern-most tip of Brazil. Then, after a thorough inspection of the B-17s, the 99th would make a 90-degree change in course to the northeast and fly directly across the South Atlantic to Bathurst, Gambia, located on the western tip of Africa.

This "air armada" of thirty-five B-17s would then refuel and turn north towards Casablanca. Finally, on its sixth leg and seventh day, Colonel Upthegrove's 99th Bomb Group would continue on a northerly route, heading to a base in England, for assignment to the 8th Air Force. This would be the first fully organized group to make the trip in mass. Others would follow.

A B-17 commander named Curtis LeMay was already in England, starting to emerge as one of the great leaders of the War. I would personally meet General LeMay near the end of the Second World War on Guam in the middle of the Pacific and would meet him again following the Korean War. I would serve under him on the General's Strategic Air Command staff and command the Mach 2 B-58 Test Force Squadron. I would come to know General LeMay as a commander and friend for the rest of the General's life, and even be on hand when "Curt" and his wife, Helen, were put to rest at the Air Force Academy in Colorado.

After articulating my proposal to Colonel Upthegrove, my Combat Group Commander just looked at me with what I guessed to be embarrassed silence. I decided that I should simplify my request. "Colonel Upthegrove," I said, "I would like to make the trip to England with you, which I have just this day learned about. I understand that you are taking off at 0600 hours tomorrow morning. Also, you have a pilot in the hospital in sickbay. Colonel, Sir, I am packed and ready to go, right now if you need a replacement pilot... if you think I might fill the bill."

For thirty seconds or so, Colonel Upthegrove just looked at me like he hadn't understood. Then, quickly, he started asking questions for three or four minutes. He wanted to know when had I graduated from flying school? How much flying time did I have? How much in the Boeing B-17? Was I checked out in the B-17? What other aircraft had I flown? How much time did I have in some of the others? How much bad weather flying had I had? Why in hell did I want to go to combat? And had I said anything about this to my present boss? Also, would my boss release me without a big fuss?

After I had answered the Colonel's questions and had assured him that my current boss, Colonel "Bunny" Dawson, the top foul weather instructor pilot in the Army Air Corps, had already said that he would release me, Colonel Upthegrove again just stared at me.

Finally, he shrugged his shoulders and said, "Okay, Captain, you've got yourself a job. Meet Warrant Officer Fogle at 0500 hours tomorrow morning here at Base Ops with your gear packed in a B-4 bag and a parachute bag. Mr. Fogle will give you the tail number of your B-17. It will be your aircraft. It's brand new, arrived from Boeing yesterday; so, let's don't be busting it up right away. Mr. Fogle will bring a crew around for you. See you take command immediately. We don't have time for discussion. I'll catch up with you at the Breakers. This okay with you?"

I gulped, said it sure was okay with me. I was aware that the pounding in my chest was my heart. But why was it beating like a tom-tom? I wasn't a kid anymore, or was I? Hadn't I finally become a man? I thought I had. Wasn't this what I had been trained to do? And, what I had told myself I should do? Or had I assumed it was too late to get aboard when I made known to Colonel Upthegrove my interest in his trip across the South Atlantic to the war zone in Europe?

And hadn't I actually been relieved when on two prior tries to get overseas assignments I had been turned down? Yes, I had been. But, no matter now, Colonel Upthegrove had called my hand! I was on my way... overseas... to the European Theater of Operations, purportedly the toughest air-combat theater in the war at the time.

I admitted to myself that I wasn't eager to have people I didn't know shooting machine guns at me... not on the ground and certainly not while I was flying around in the sky at 25,000 feet where outside air temperatures run fifty-five degrees below zero and where there's enough oxygen in the air to sustain consciousness for sixty whole seconds. I had thought that, once committed, I could relax. I was committed all right; Colonel Upthegrove had called my hand. But, I didn't feel relaxed.

Raising my hand to salute my new boss, I noticed that he was looking, not at me, but at my hand. "Damn, damn, damn," I shouted silently to myself. "Look at you, Richard Eager, your hand is shaking like a leaf and Colonel Upthegrove, busy as he is, feels he must stand there and wait for it to stop!"

My new Group Commander of a very few minutes did not raise his arm to return my salute. He just shoved out his hand, pointing it towards mine. "Welcome to the 99th Bomb Group, Captain," he said. Then he shook my hand slowly and firmly, while looking straight at my serious eyeballs. I guessed the Colonel's eyes were smiling, just a tad, but the rest of him, however, sure wasn't.

Later, I would say to myself, "You jerk! Colonel Upthegrove wasn't smiling at you. How could he have been smiling? The man was bone-weary getting 35 B-17s and some 350 or more air crewmen and their equipment ready to go to war. And, very likely, the Colonel had just trained and dispatched 500 or so ground personnel who would be making the trip by boat from Staten Island across the Atlantic to Oran, Algeria."

That night in January 1943, when Uppie and I first met, seemed like yesterday. That following morning, I took command of my B-17 and my skeptical crewmen. I had made the first of what would be three Atlantic crossings and later three Pacific crossings during the course of the war. I had not, however, joined up with General Doolittle in England as planned.

On that first crossing, the 99th B-17 Bomb Group was halted at Marrakech in Morocco. General Doolittle, and a non-flying Army General called "Ike," had already come down from the UK. Did they come down to welcome the new 99th? No, they had just implemented a tough but successful invasion of French North Africa, Operation Torch. And they had new orders for the 99th. We were not flying to the UK, we were flying to support the Allied invasion of North Africa, Sicily and Italy, the underbelly of the Mediterranean and Europe. We were there to back the British Army as they chased Rommel out.

We, in the 99th, had not been invited, but President Franklin D. Roosevelt and Prime Minister Winston Churchill, about three weeks before our arrival, had just finished the "Casablanca Conference" on the African coast at Casablanca, French Morocco, only 137 miles north of us.

We stayed put almost the entire week at Marrakech while the great Allied generals spent time together, getting acquainted and planning a War. We got word on the QT that they had just moved to a local sultan's more-than-ample digs close by our hotel in Marrakech. We didn't mind the delay at all. We reconnoitered both at the "Arabian-Nights-like" town of Marrakech and in the surf of the Casablanca beaches.

Our Moroccan hotel was great, as was the food, as was Casablanca, only a short jeep ride into the setting sun. That same setting sun dipped into the Atlantic Ocean across from which was home. So far, it wasn't a bad war.

Even so, we were in combat before a fortnight had passed. Though I wanted to, I didn't jump out of my B-17 when German Me-109s flew straight at me and then flashed by a few feet above my head or below my plane's nose. I'll admit I was transfixed at times when smoke from flak (ack-ack) would boil up directly in front of me and then flash past my window. It was a while before we realized that the close-by smoke, which one could see, couldn't hurt us. The lethal message was already delivered by the time we could see the smoke.

Flying away from the sun, the flak that bursts in front of us resembled white puffs of cotton. Flying into the sun, these miniature thunderheads were backlit by "ominous, little black clouds, black being a more fitting color," I recall observing to myself.

When returning from a mission under those real war conditions, I often wondered if I felt "eager" as my good friend, Flying Cadet Frank Roberts, used to call me? Richard Eager was the name he pinned on me at Randolph Field because he thought I was excessively gung-ho. I took that as a compliment and considered the name quite fitting.

Frank and I met at Love Field, Dallas, for primary flight school, and continued our friendship during basic training at Randolph Field, San Antonio, the "West Point of the Air," and throughout advanced training at Kelly Field, also in San Antonio.

Those were action-packed days. Our instruction was extremely rigorous with flying, physical drills, classes and then more flying. There were aircraft accidents and there were deaths. During the primary flight school days, we were a class of about one hundred at the beginning, reduced to thirty-two by the heavy "wash-out" rate back in 1939 and 1940. With feelings of relief and pride, a smaller group of us were graduated to Randolph Field. Frank and I, with two other cadets, rented a small home near the base. Those were confident but tense times. We studied together, flew together and relaxed together.

Frank and I were promoted to Advanced Flying School at Kelly Field. We chose the bombardment division so we could fly the bombers. Other instruction options were observation, attack and pursuit. We had more freedom, as senior flying cadets, but the reality of our training became powerful and apparent. We learned to use the airplane as a weapon.

I do remember when Frank named me Richard "Eager." He commented, "Richard Eager, you are trying too hard; you must loosen up. I fear our Flight Surgeon has shot you in the ass with an excessive dose of zeal." Then, with the very distinctive grin I have remembered for half a century, Cadet Roberts added, "But I do take note, Richard Eager, that you have just been named our Flying Cadet Commander, Class 40-E." Frank was my witty, laid-back friend who understated everything having to do with himself. But he never failed when asked to put everything he had to give on the line.

I got a couple dozen missions under my belt very quickly, and, by my choice, had flown every position in the combat formation, starting in the "Tail-end-Charlie" position below and behind the trailing squadron. I felt very young and a tad terrified the first time I got up there where the air-war was going on. I remember thinking, "This is no picture-show, Richard Eager. This is the real thing. And, keep your wits about you, this 'flak' business could get you killed."

I began to understand that, very likely, everyone up there on both sides was frightened out of his wits at some time or another. The trick was to not shut your eyes and, as we liked to put it, "just go ahead and do the job you were trained to do, flying about up there in the blue with a B-17 strapped to your ass." Old timers (with a half-dozen missions under their belts) would tell new replacement crews from the States, "Plan to be afraid later on when you get back on the ground and have time to give the matter some deep, serious thought."

I was beginning to gain confidence in what I was learning to do five miles up in the sky over enemy-held territory. And others were beginning to accept and follow my lead both in the air and on the ground. Colonel Upthegrove was teaching me by example how to take command of my men. He would often say, "Don't forget, Captain, your men aren't looking to you for 'leadership'; they're looking to you, depending on you, to get them back home."

————————————

When I arrived at 0730 that morning at my Group Commander's tent, Uppie did not return my salute nor did he bother to say, "Good morning! "He just pushed toward me the rolled-up paper with which he had been whopping his left palm. Uppie usually smiled when he was greeting one of his Captains at an early morning hour at the beginning of a new day. But the prospects for a smile this morning didn't appear to be that great.

Quickly, I unrolled the paper, which was thrust into my hands and let my eyes scan down the page. I read near the bottom, by order of General Eisenhower's Supreme Allied Headquarters, Algiers, through General Doolittle's 12th Air Force Headquarters, Constantine, Algeria, North Africa."

My eyes then jumped quickly to "Captain Richard E. Evans, AO-397378, 99th Bombardment Group, 12th Air Force, North Africa, ETO, is hereby relieved of his current duty assignment, is transferred to the British 8th Army and is directed to report without delay to The Army Commander, General Sir Bernard Law Montgomery."

I glanced at my Group Commander, and I'm afraid my mouth dropped to the full-open position. A second paragraph stipulated, "A combat-ready B-17 with full ammo and combat aircrew will be assigned to Captain Evans for the period of this duty."

After a moment of silence, Uppie spoke first. This was our custom since that night at Salina when he and I first met, when I had haltingly advised Colonel Upthegrove that I was looking for work, and he had hired me on the spot.

"Dick, dammit," he asked after a moment, "What do you know about this boondoggle? You related to Ike, or Jimmie Doolittle, or somebody up the line whom I don't know about? Level with me." Colonel Upthegrove, I had learned, was a gentle man. I had also learned that, characteristically, Colonel Uppie got right to the point, not always taking the time to smile.

I stated that I had no knowledge of this boondoggle. And my family had never suggested that we were related to the "Eisenhowers nor the Doolittles either," I volunteered. I was thinking, as I looked at my recently acquired boss, "Uppie didn't bother to return my salute when I reported to him; and now, he isn't returning my smile, either."

I then remained silent for what seemed quite a long time while my Group Commander continued to eyeball me. Finally, he sighed and said, "Well, Captain, you had better pull a crew together and get yourself over to Château dun. Work with Major Lowery, your Squadron Commander, and line up the men you need from your 346th Squadron. And, you'd better get on your horse. I'm told an aircraft has already been serviced and is awaiting your arrival at 301st Group

Ops... even now."

Colonel Upthegrove then speculated, "I doubt you're going to be dropping any bombs with General Montgomery aboard, Captain. You just might, however, be shooting at some German fighters, particularly if word gets out whom it is you've got up there, chasing about in the sky with you.

"I'm told you are being issued a full combat-load of ammo. That makes it clear to me somebody has some right serious plans for you that they haven't bothered to let me in on nor Ike, if I can reach him before you get off the ground!"

Colonel Upthegrove was then silent for a full sixty seconds. Finally, he said, "If I sound a tad irritated, Dick, it's because I wasn't brought in on your deal early on. But I can see you're as surprised as I was when I got this TWX; I know you didn't go over my head. Good luck, Captain. See you keep your head about you. It can get a little rough up there as I think you know. There are some people on this side of the ocean who would like to see us all dead and they are trying very hard to bring this condition about. You're aware of this, aren't you?"

I smiled and said I was aware there were some unfriendly people in the area. Then I saluted my Group Commander and turned to go. I was touched by Uppie's poorly-disguised, genuine concern for one of his Captains.

Châteaudun-du-Rhumel, abbreviated as Château dun, was an Algerian village on the Algiers-to-Constantine rail line, also on Algeria's principal east-west country road. Château dun was home base for our sister B-17 groups, the 97th and 301st, both of which had been transferred from the 8th Air Force in England to General Doolittle's new, soon-to-be activated 12th Air Force in North Africa. Our newly-formed 99th Bomb Group, assigned to the 8th Air Force when we left the ZI, was now reassigned to the 12th Air Force just a few days following our arrival in Marrakech.

General Doolittle, accompanying General Eisenhower from England at the beginning of "Operation Torch," had been named by Ike to be the first Commander of our new 12th Air Force. In a few months, the 12th would become the Tactical Air Force in North Africa and would eventually become the new 15th Strategic Air Force Command.

As I saluted and again turned to go, Colonel Upthegrove added, "And, Dick, don't let those British chaps talk you into something if you don't like the odds. I'm sure Monty and his English ground-pounders know their business very well. I doubt they know very much about daylight, strategic bombing, however. You're in command of your B-17 and your men at all times. Remember that and see that you get that flying machine back here with its wings still on and with ten men still inside it."

Uppie continued with a change of mood and a grin, "And, not to worry, Captain, there will still be plenty of missions for you to fly when you complete your TDY with General Montgomery. I'll find something to keep you busy."

Again, I started to leave, but Uppie added, "And, Dick, let's not be busting Monty's butt in that US flying machine. It would be a black mark on your service record. I doubt you'd ever make Major. You might not even make it back to the States. And, sure as sin, Churchill would want to know how it happened and Ike and Doolittle would pass the job on to me of having to hand-carry your accident report to Whitehall in London."

Then Uppie, who was becoming a second father to me and to others as well in his 99th Bomb Group, ignored my salute, smiled warmly and extended his hand.

Major Leon Lowery, the 346th Squadron Commander and my good friend and tent mate, said he would assemble a flight crew for me and send them along ahead to check out my aircraft. "Do you have any special requests, Captain?" he asked. "Colonel Uppie has instructed me to give you anybody and anything you wish from our 346th Squadron." "Yes," I said, "I would like the men who helped me get my B-17 over from the States; I have flown most of my combat missions with them, you know."

"Fine," Major Lowery said, "you've got 'em. I'll round them up and send them along ahead of you so they can be preflighting your B-17 while you're getting your flight clearance. Anything else?"

"No, Major Lowry, I can't think of a thing. But I would like to thank you, Leon, for letting me come aboard. Thank you for making room for me in your squadron at Salina and in your tent here at Navarin." Then, I added with a grin, "It's been a great trip, so far." My friend, tent-mate and Squadron Commander then shook hands with me.

I put a spare flying suit and freshly hand-washed but unpressed uniform in my B-4 bag, scooped up my toilet kit, towels, shoes, socks, and shorts, and dropped this gear into an extra parachute bag and was on my way. Packing for a trip was a greatly simplified procedure in those old, high-pressure, hurry-up days.

I hopped in a jeep and drove north for five minutes, turned east onto the Algiers-to-Constantine main road, which connected with the Château dun roadway. Then, I settled down a bit and took a moment to focus on my new situation.

"My God, Richard Eager, what's going on here?" I asked myself. "Ike, Jimmie Doolittle or somebody at Theater Headquarters has picked you to be Monty's pilot for a spell. Not that I will miss flying combat all that much, but why me? Maybe somebody had a look at my file and noticed all the weather flying I've been logging in recent years. And, how do you suppose Monty sweet-talked Ike out of a *Flying Fortress* in which to buzz him around North Africa and, very likely, up to the UK?"

I had seen General Montgomery's picture on the cover of a recent *Time* magazine, probably early February 1943, just as we were departing from the States. He was wearing a Tank Commander's beret at a jaunty angle that had become his signature worldwide. General Montgomery had just defeated General Rommel, a German hero of the First World War, at El Alamein. General Rommel was said to be one of Hitler's most-favored Generals.

The Battle at El Alamein was the turn-around battle of the African campaign and had been fought in the Egyptian desert along the coastal desert region bordering the Mediterranean. The German easterly advance towards Cairo and the Suez was stopped cold at the small village of El Alamein, a short 150 miles from Cairo. Commencing at midnight on October 23, 1942, the battle for El Alamein was the first clear Allied victory in the field during the Second World War.

I had asked myself, "Why wouldn't General Montgomery, the first Allied British Commander to defeat an Axis army in the field, just order up a British aeroplane and flight crew to fly him about in the war zone? Why did he think it necessary that he con Ike out of a B-17?" I had no answers to my questions and some time would pass before I would have a clue... as to why Ike was sending Monty a combat-ready B-17... and me.

I was expected at Base Ops at Château dun, our sister airfield ten or twelve miles east of my base at Navarin, Algeria and was told immediately where my aircraft was parked. My flight-crew was on hand, conducting a pre-flight inspection, and a local ground crew was standing by to help us get fired up and on our way.

I took a moment to check the weather at my destination, RAF Castel Benito Airport and was not surprised to read, "Clear, with blowing sand." I said to myself, "Big deal, that has been the prognostication for Libya since the beginning of time." I had filed a few hundred flight-clearances to a few hundred places, but I had never before filed for Tripoli, Libya. In a moment, the Base Operations Officer pushed a second form in front of me and asked me to sign one more time... this time for my B-17.

Now this was a new experience. I had flown forty or fifty military aircraft but had never been required to take title to a US flying machine before they'd let me take it off the ground. I wondered if they planned to take it out of my salary for the next thirty years if I banged it up a tad.

It was a short, quick trip in the Base Ops jeep out onto the field to my aircraft. I noticed, as I approached, that my flight crews were on their feet, lined up and standing "at ease." As I climbed out of the jeep, Lieutenant Johnson called them to attention. This formality had not been a regular practice when we had met before at our aircraft preparatory to starting engines for a combat mission. Nor had the expectant, broad, ear-to-ear grins that were greeting me been a part of our pre-mission experience. Most of the crew who traveled over the Atlantic with me were present, except the navigator and bombardier. The new fellas, Second Lieutenants, Carver and Beringsmith, seemed to be grinning, too.

I stopped in front of my smiling men, eyeballed them with a half-grin for a few seconds, and then said, "All right, men, stand at ease and listen up. I can see you have the right idea. We are not going on a combat mission this day. But you do understand, do you not, that we are being given a right significant assignment. This is not just fun and games... this is a serious business trip. If we screw-up this job, Generals Eisenhower and Doolittle and Colonel Uppie will, all three, have a piece of each one of us. No one, no one will escape."

In a few minutes, I had completed a "walk-around pre-flight inspection" of our B-17 with Technical Sergeant Dale Owens, my able, soft-spoken, senior non-commissioned in-flight engineering officer and top-turret gunner. Sergeant Owens was a dedicated, very supportive, useful young man; and he gave me more respect than I felt I actually merited. Also, Sergeant Owens gave me his friendship. In a very few minutes, we were all aboard, had stowed our gear, had cranked up our flying machine and had taxied out onto the active runway.

While taxiing to the takeoff end of the field, we were cleared by the tower for "immediate takeoff." In a few short minutes with plenty of ammo but without the usual 6,000-pound load (of 12 500-pounders), we were quickly up, up and away.

All of my crew were pleased and proud, as was I, to be selected to fly Monty about the combat theater for a while. We understood that, when we returned to our Combat Group, we would still be required to complete a full "combat tour" of fifty or sixty missions.

On clearing the ground, I immediately dropped my left wing and started a slow climbing turn. In a few minutes, I rolled out onto a southeasterly heading, heading us for Tunisia. In a short time, we broke out in the clear above a thin layer of clouds. I glanced down to watch the eastern extension (Aures Mountains) of the Saharan Atlas Mountain Range drop away below... and behind us. This part of the Atlas Range, lower and less spectacular than the High Atlas Range in Morocco, formed a natural boundary between northern parts of Algeria and Tunisia.

A short time later, now over Tunisia, I glanced out my left window and looked northeast toward the Mediterranean Sea. I took note that on this day no Me-109s from Bizerte were climbing to greet us, and no flak bursts were darkening the skies over the ancient city of Tunis, as had been the case on recent combat missions flown in the North African "Theater of War."

The harbors and airfields of Bizerte and Tunis, Tunisia, now coming into view on the northeastern horizon, had been on our target list only weeks earlier. Now, both of these Tunisian cities were free of Germans and Italians and were loaded to the gunnels with Britishers, South Afrikaners, Aussies, and Canadians. Finally, our British Allies must have thought, some Yanks were at last also on hand in respectable numbers and the word was out that more were on the way.

I said to myself, "Richard Eager, you aren't able to know just how this is going to turn out; but this is a very nice beginning to what could turn out to be a very nice day. Why knock it? Thank you, Ike; thank you, Jimmie Doolittle; thank you, Uppie. And, thank you, Monty, for your victory over Hitler's General Rommel at the battle of El Alamein; I look forward to meeting you, Sir."

I then relaxed a "tad," as we liked to put it back in those days, and I allowed my thoughts to flash back to Château dun where I had picked up my newly-assigned aircraft, an "E" Model B-17 that looked like all the rest: olive drab, dusty and well used. We would soon get more "F" models and still later, "G" models with "chin" turrets, each equipped with twin .50-caliber M-2 machine guns.

On takeoff without the typical three-ton bomb load, we were "wheels up" within the first third of the field. We had gotten off quicker and shorter than I had expected; and in a very few minutes we were straight and level, on-course and holding at 10,000 feet. White, billowy, cumulus clouds swirled around us as we slashed through them. I thought to myself, "Don't knock it, Richard Eager; just go along with it. This job isn't all that bad. Monty can't be as tough as they say he is."

I then reset the throttles, prop-pitch and fuel-mixture controls for cruise. We were embarking, not on a regular combat mission, but on a different kind of adventure with a very different kind of man. I would learn that Monty had suddenly become known throughout the world. Also, I would learn that this was just fine with Monty.

As a thoughtful third son of Mrs. Evans, I would accept Monty as a challenge and would work quite hard to understand and fully appreciate this rather complex human being, who at this very moment in time was being heralded throughout the world as "General Sir Bernard Law

Montgomery, the Victor at El Alamein." At that moment, El Alamein was the first and only Allied victory of the Second World War. Before Alamein, the Anglo-American Allies had not won a major battle; post Alamein, the Allies would never lose a major battle.

Settling in for the flight, I recalled noticing during my pre-flight check that my new B-17 was a quite old B-17E named *Theresa Leta*. I recall saying to myself, "Well, *Theresa Leta*, I don't know whether you've been named for a French saint or for some B-17 jock's girlfriend. Whatever. In the days ahead, I'm thinking that you and I had best take care to look out for one another."

I never did know for sure, and I did not think it very important, but I had heard the *Theresa Leta* was the B-17 Air Corps General Carl "Tooey" Spaatz had flown down from the UK to North Africa during the invasion of North Africa by the Allies. Colonel Upthegrove's 99th Bomb Group was entering the combat theater from the south, flying up from Gambia to Marrakech. Our new boss was "meeting us halfway." Monty was coming north-to-south from the UK at the same time. The 97th and 301st B-17 Groups, ahead of us, had also come down from England. We would all meet at Châteaudun-du-Rhumel, near ancient Constantine.

Monty, I would learn, did indeed covet the B-17. I would learn that Monty thought it only reasonable that the world's greatest Army Commander be flown about in the world's greatest flying machine! I remember thinking, "I don't have a problem with this." And I didn't until Jimmie Doolittle, my Wing Commander, and others, put the word out that the Army Air Corp was very reluctant to spare any B-17s.

Later I was told that Lieutenant General William Gott, who was returning to Cairo from the battle area in a British Bristol Bombay transport plane, was intercepted and shot down by two pair of German *Messerschmitt* Bf-109 fighters. The British transport crash-landed successfully after both engines were knocked out, but a third pair of German fighters pursued the crippled plane, strafed the fuselage, killing most aboard including General Gott. Gott was to command the 8th Army. Monty was chosen by Prime Minister Winston Churchill and General Sir Alan Brooke to replace Gott. Monty was determined to evade that perilous situation of flying in dangerous skies. He felt the *Flying Fortress* would even his chances.

I respected General Doolittle as a very real aviation pioneer and decided that my position should be that I would go along with anything he might be able to work out with Ike, Monty or Monty's boss, King George VI, who Uppie had told me as we parted, would be looking in on Monty in Tripoli.

GO FOR IT

Time does seem to fly,
And the good times past
Seem seldom, if ever, to last.
But the Bard has suggested
That we must each seize our tide,
And while holding fast to the mast,
Enjoy our ride!

Richard Eager

1.2 Richard first trains in PT-3, Love Field, Dallas

1.3 *Roosevelt and Churchill meet at the Casablanca Conference* (Imperial War Museum)

1.4 *General Fay Upthegrove, 99th BG Commander*

1.5 *Ground crewmen load the bombs for a mission* (99th Bomb Group Historical Society)

1.6 *B-17s roll out on steel Marsden Matting in Tunisia, 1943* (National Archives and Records Administration)

1.7 *Flying cadets, Frank A. Roberts, left end of third file, "Richard Eager" far right with sword, Randolph Field, TX*

1.8 *Frank Roberts is left of flying cadet roommates, Kelly Field, TX*

1.9 *Flying cadet "Richard Eager" buys his first car*

1.10 *Pilot training in Boeing "Stearman" biplane*

1.11 *Consolidated PT-3 "Husky" is the first primary flying school trainer built in quantity*

1.12 *AT-6 training maneuvers*

1.13 *Flak looks like white puffs of cotton when reflecting the sunlight*

1.14 *Flying into the sun, flak is backlit and looks like ominous black clouds* (99th Bomb Group Historical Society)

1.15 *B-17s fly in combat formation to drop their bombs* (99th Bomb Group Historical Society)

1.16   *"Theresa Leta" is Monty's future B-17* (Imperial War Museum)

2.1 *Tight B-17 formations fly through storm clouds* (99th Bomb Group Historical Society)

CHAPTER 2
FORCED LANDING IN AFRICA

INVICTUS

Out of the darkness that covers me,
Black as the pit, from pole to pole,
I thank whatever gods may be
For my unconquerable soul!

In the fell clutch of circumstance,
I have not winced nor cried out aloud.
Under the bludgeoning of chance,
My head is bloody, but unbowed.
Beyond this place of wrath and tears
Looms but the horror of the shade,
And yet the menace of the years
Finds, and shall find, me unafraid.

It matters not how strait the gate,
How charged with punishments the scroll,
I am the master of my fate.
I am the captain of my soul.

William Ernest Henley

En route to my first meeting with Monty, a glance to the north brought to mind combat missions flown against enemy shipping and air-transport facilities at the air and water ports of Bizerte, Tunisia, 35 miles north and west of modern Tunis and ancient Carthage. I recall a picture, ever seared into my memory, reminding me of disturbed bees buzzing angrily about their hives. These "bees" were German fighters, Me-109s and **Fw-190s**, attacking our sister bombardment groups, the 97th and 301st just ahead of us. We had a good view of these bees buzzing around our comrades and a good mental picture of them starting to work us over. We were next in line.

However, by the time our 99th BG reached the target area and Colonel Upthegrove was leading our run in, the fighters must have been back on the ground refueling. They were gone and not missed.

We got only "light-to-moderate flak" that day, and we came off the target with no B-17s smoking. There would be a silent concert of sighs among the 200 flight crewmen aboard the 20 B-17s that made up our 99th BG formation that spring day back in May 1943.

However, we had not dropped our bombs! Our sister groups attacking ahead of us had radioed that the target was obscured by broken clouds. They had dropped their bombs and thought they might have gotten them down okay. Our 99th BG had followed and Colonel Upthegrove made two passes; however, our lead bombardier, Lieutenant Beringsmith, was unable, on either run, to pick up the target in his bombsight.

Colonel Upthegrove had then elected to abort the mission because a greater problem was starting to develop that could jeopardize the safe return to base of his entire force of B-17s and crewmen.

En route to our target, **Bizerte**, Colonel "Uppie" had altered course repeatedly in order to maneuver our formation around some magnificent but ominous thunderheads building up along the Mediterranean coastline. We had never seen weather like this in North Africa.

Coming off the target on a southerly heading, Uppie had delayed making the 90-degree right turn to the west towards our bases. Clearly his hope was to get us south of the massive cloud buildups we had all observed forming as we were flying east toward our Tunisian target.

I had been assigned to fly on Colonel Upthegrove's right wing, an honor I was pleased to accept. This placement in a four-squadron, 24 to 28 aircraft group was reserved for the **Deputy** air-commander, who could quickly slide into the lead-position should the leader be forced to abort.

I was anxious to demonstrate that the pig-in-a-poke captain, whom Colonel Uppie had picked up in Salina, Kansas, the night he was packing to leave the States, might work out okay. So far, I had done a tolerable job of staying "tucked-in," behind and below Uppie's right wing, my only responsibility unless Colonel Upthegrove should be forced to abort. Then, the responsibility of the entire group of 24 to 28 B-17s would be mine.

In a short time, Colonel Upthegrove made the expected 90-degree right turn, putting our Group formation on a westerly heading toward our base at Navarin. Continuing a slow letdown, we were hoping to remain clear of the clouds and get beneath them. But, as we descended, the massive cloud formation was no longer to our right. I remember thinking, "This is unreasonable weather for North Africa." But no matter that, the ominous clouds were now **dead ahead** with the tops seeming to rise higher and the base clouds growing darker and more foreboding.

At the time, I noted our position on my map; we were still in Tunisia, east of the Algerian border with the Tebessa rail line in view angling off to our southwest. I made a mental note that my "last-resort plan" would be to return to this area and attempt a wheels-down landing on an open field down there below us.

Also, I gave some thought as to just what my first move might be should Uppie suddenly be forced to pass the formation-lead to me.

The overcast above us had become solid and darker and below us ever lower, forcing Uppie to continue a slow descent as we approached the eastern extension of the Atlas Range, now dead ahead and at right angles to the course that would take us home.

Here I am in Algeria in the spring, not at a motion picture at Knoxville's Strand Theater. This is for real. This is happening and I had best be giving some "deep serious thought" to my options before "I'm in deep trouble up to my eyeballs."

My primary task, I reminded myself, was to get my B-17 and crew back home on the ground with their skins intact. Uppie was now being forced to make sharper turns than would normally be made by a formation leader. Turning sharply again and again, Uppie would not be able to avoid dragging his wingmen through the darkening clouds that were beginning to close in around us.

Our formations were built around "**elements**" of three B-17s, an element leader and two wingmen forming a triangle. Two elements, one behind the other with the second stepped down at a lower elevation, constituted a squadron of six planes. On max-effort missions, a seventh aircraft might "fill in the box," i.e., fly behind and below the trailing 3-ship element.

Four 6-to-7 aircraft squadrons constituted a group, aggregating 24 to 28 B-17s. The right squadron in a group formation would be "stepped up," with respect to the lead squadron. The left stepped down. This could be reversed should the sun placement be a factor, which on this day, it certainly was not.

Squadrons might also be arranged "in-trail": six, three-ship elements, one behind the other and stepped-down to the rear, for easier maneuverability and better control. This was our formation as Uppie led us through the cloud build-ups forming along the eastern extension of the Atlas Range.

We had not seen the sun since leaving Bizerte. But we had had been getting sufficient reflected light to see each other well enough to hold our positions in the formation as we brushed through the clouds. Now, however, the sun was lower, and we were losing light very fast.

Again and again, individual aircraft flying the positions on their element leaders would be forced to brush through the darkening clouds, not seeing the plane just ahead of them. Their visibility with respect to each other would at times suddenly be reduced to zero for a few seconds. The pilots for those short periods would suddenly be "in the dark," figuratively and literally.

As our ceiling continued to lower and become more ragged, Uppie was forced to lose altitude, bringing our formation ever closer to the Atlas Mountain range... now dead ahead and between us and our base at Navarin.

I had our position pegged at twenty miles east of **Telergma Airfield, Algeria**. I knew that we were getting very close to home; but would we have sufficient visibility to stay clear of the mountains, and of each other, and actually get home?

Because of the clouds, rain and now the onset of nightfall, our visibility continued to deteriorate. It was becoming increasingly more difficult for each of us to maintain visual contact with the single B-17 ahead of us, which was our vital link to the formation.

I was okay for the time being, "tucked in," as we liked to say, flying behind, down, and to the right of the Colonel's B-17. However, for short periods my lateral visibility would be reduced to zero and Uppie's B-17 would then disappear in the clouds for a few seconds. Suddenly, this unsettling condition was beginning to occur with more regularity.

I had given thought to this kind of problem before and had decided that one might fly in reasonable safety without visual reference to the specific airplane on which he was dependent for contact with the formation, for ten seconds, which can seem a very long time. After ten seconds, he should then pull up and turn away from the formation. A collision forward in the formation, particularly with bombs aboard, could result in a colossal disaster, effecting an entire group's aircraft.

Suddenly, I found myself in precisely this situation: Uppie's B-17 had disappeared. The darkening clouds had swallowed it up! I was flying on instruments alone with my commander's right-wing tip only feet from my left-wing tip.

In a moment, my ten-second-tolerance expired. I remember that I froze, but also that I thawed very quickly. In a few quick movements practiced before in clear skies, I pushed all sets-of-four engines: fuel-mixture, prop-pitch, and throttle-controls to "the **firewall**," as far forward as I could push them.

Then, immediately, I eased the control column back to climb quickly, but not too steeply, while letting my right wing drop slightly, to turn me away from the formation. As a precaution, I then dropped partial flaps to lower my stall speed.

I had, of course, already "gone on the gauges," our expression for flying by reference to the aircraft flight instruments only. I well-remember that I had self-doubts and that I had acknowledged to myself that I was excited. But I did not come undone... not completely. Not yet.

Early on, I had taken time to think through the actions I might quickly take to forestall a possible disaster should visual contact with other aircraft in a large formation be suddenly lost. I had told myself that I should commit to a course of action, before the fact, which might not solve my problem completely but would increase my distance from immediate danger. This would give me time to think a bit before having to react.

When my arbitrary time limit ran out, quickly I put my B-17 into a steep, climbing right-hand turn, shooting me up and away from the formation. While still flying "blind" on the gauges, I slowly effected a 180-degree turn. I then rolled out, leveled off and reset my flight controls for cruise.

I was still **in the soup**, but I knew where I was relative to our other B-17s: I was above our air group, heading in the opposite direction. I wasn't going to be crashing into my friends, but where was I planning to have my evening meal?

Then suddenly, I was in the clear again, out of the clouds for a few seconds actually between cloud layers. I had not expected to see the ground, nor other B-17s, and I did not. I remember thinking, "Okay, Richard Eager, you've been in tough situations before; take a moment to catch your breath, settle down, and rethink your options. You have bought yourself some time and you have fixed it, so you won't be crashing into any of your fellow-airmen right away. On the other hand, they are heading for home, but you've taken up a course that will take you to the German lines."

I was taking deep breaths and shaking my head to settle myself down when a calm voice came on our aircraft **intercom** line. It was Technical Sergeant Morris, my radio operator. Morris had a good excuse for becoming disoriented because we kept him strapped in back there, **aft** of the **bomb bay** with the smallest window, effectively in the dark. And yet, this quiet young man always knew who he was, where he was, and just what it was that he, by damn, was planning to do next. I had acknowledged to myself that Morris was one of my favorite crewmen. "Radio to pilot," he had called out, "anything I can do to help, Captain?"

Clearing my throat and allowing my heart a couple more beats before pressing the intercom switch, I said, "Pilot to Radio Operator, thanks for the offer, Sergeant Morris. Have you received any transmissions from Colonel Upthegrove's plane?"

The familiar voice that answered was, as always, calm and self-assured, "Radio operator to pilot, Sir; I have received no transmissions from the Group Commander's aircraft; is there anything else that I might check into for you, Captain?"

I have remembered for half a century as I write this story that it was Sergeant Morris's quiet response to my inquiry that helped settle me down. I guessed that Sergeant Morris had a calming effect on all his crew members. Also, I remember thinking, "Why shouldn't Morris be restrained and self-assured: most of my crewmen back there are eighteen... Morris, for God's sake, is nineteen."

I pressed my mic button and answered, "No, Sarge... can't think of anything right away." Then I asked, "Are you hearing anything from other aircraft in our Group? Again, I asked, how about Colonel Upthegrove? Have you gotten any transmissions from our boss?"

"No, nothing from the Colonel," Morris reported, "And, nothing specific between aircraft. I can tell though, Captain, some of our pilots are getting a little edgy out there."

"Okay, Morris," I responded, "I hear you loud and clear. We're all a little tensed-up; keep listening for me; and let me know if you get any specific directives from Colonel Upthegrove's aircraft or any advisories from Navarin or Château dun."

I then turned to our copilot and said, "Get everybody on the intercom, Johnson, I want to let them know what we're up against and what I'm planning to do about it."

In a moment, Johnson touched my elbow, nodded, and said, "Okay, Captain, everyone's online."

"All right, men, listen up." I said into my mic, "Here's our situation. The weather's a complete surprise... we are not supposed to have low ceilings like this in North Africa and heavy rain to boot all at the same time for God's sake.

Now, some of you know that I'm supposed to be a hot-shot, foul-weather pilot; but I'm not planning to show off for you tonight. As you have noticed, it's starting to get dark, very dark, very fast. Our ground-control operators are still learning their jobs, like the rest of us. And, frankly, with three groups (72 B-17s) buzzing in and out of the rain and dark clouds around our two bases and with night-time closing in, I'm afraid our young ground-control operators could be overwhelmed.

I'm getting our butts back to a clear area with some good-sized flat fields, which I saw and which I marked on my map, back on the Tunisian side of the mountains. We'll be there in twenty-five minutes, before it gets dark. I'll get this machine down for you, which is all we're interested in right now.

"I didn't predict this weather, but earlier when we turned west and faced that solid line of thunderstorms, I started looking for flat places to land an airplane should things suddenly go to hell in a hand-basket. I saw a couple of likely spots and noted their positions on my map. And that's where I'm taking us right now.

"**Don't sweat it**," I continued. "I'll get this baby on the ground for you, and on its wheels." Then I added, "I may feel like some kind of jerk tomorrow finding that everybody but us got back home; but that's my problem. You just relax back there as best you can; keep someone on the intercom at all times, and I'll keep you posted on how we're doing up front here."

A youthful, up-beat voice from the State of Virginia that always cheered me up came online as others were clicking off. "Whatever you say, Captain, we're fine back here." It was Staff Sergeant Eldon Austin, my always-smiling, be-freckled, redheaded ball-turret operator. I never got around to telling Austin how his confidence in me bolstered my confidence.

In a short time, I was over the area that I had marked earlier on my map. I circled wide, had a good look and alerted the crew to my intention to land.

Suddenly, the bombardier, who was new to this crew, let it be known that he thought me something of an "iron-ass," and appeared behind me on the flight deck. "Captain," he sneered (this character couldn't just talk, he had to sneer), "ya-think we should land with our **bombs** still armed?"

"Of course not," I said, irritated; then added, "Check to see that the pins are in (which prevent the bombs from exploding on impact), and I'll salvo all twelve immediately." After a moment, he reported the pins in, and I pulled the salvo control.

When the bombs left the bomb bay, I could feel the B-17 leap up, as if we had just dumped three tons of dead weight, which, of course, is exactly what we had done. But then, in a second, we heard a muffled explosion, and felt a shock wave slam against the underside of our aircraft.

Clearly, one or more bombs had exploded a scant two to three hundred feet beneath our B-17. And, clearly, all the safety pins were not in. I didn't swear much in those days, was never able to free myself completely from the effects of Mom's early training and Dad's often-referenced "exemplary example." I would compensate, however, by swearing to myself when I deemed it absolutely necessary. This seemed like the perfect time. Indeed!

When I heard and felt the explosion beneath us, I mused, "I'm going to have that fat-assed, fowl-mouth's butt one of these days!" (This didn't satisfy my inner anger, but I well remember it helped.)

I called the **Ball Turret** gunner on the intercom and asked him to duck down into the ball turret to survey the underside of the fuselage, engines and wings. In delaying our **approach** to the field to make an unplanned visual check of our B-17's under-belly, following the detonation, I found that I had used up more of the landing area than I had intended. We circled back around and again began our descent.

After extending the gear and dropping the flaps, I lined up the plane with the over-grown flat field, brought the throttles back, and took a deep breath. We were losing light faster than I had expected and I was beginning to get a tad edgy.

I remember that I was excited as I flared, leveling off to land on this field, which I could see intermittently buried as it was beneath a heavy cover of wild grass. I found it hard not to be excited with my heart pounding like it might be doing damage to my chest wall. "But, what the hell," I mused, "how many times does a Tennessee boy get a chance to test his training and put a *Flying Fortress* down in an open field in Tunisia, in a field where, for God's sake, he can't see all the ground? Back in the States, we were well-trained by the best-experienced pilots for such emergency landings, but you never get comfortable.

A loud "whump" was the sound I recall hearing when we landed in a full stall, squarely on all three wheels. We bounced hard. I was conscious of our rising up out of some taller grasses, then making a second and final landing. "Oh my," I said to myself, "it's great to be on the ground and rolling, albeit up to our knees in patches of pampas-like grasses."

Then quickly, the grass thinned, and the terrain ahead looked to be rougher than it had appeared to be from above and with stubby trees not too far ahead. Also, I noticed a sharp rise to my right clear of obstacles. Immediately, I came down hard on the right brake, while pushing the left out-board throttle full forward "to the fire-wall." The B-17 hesitated; then in an abrupt, left-skidding, ninety-degree right turn, it headed straight up that hill. I knew in a flash that at last we had it made. We were down, we were decelerating quickly, and we were in one piece.

Boeing's stalwart B-17 flying machine, negotiating a steeper grade than it had ever seen before, decelerated like a small boy grabbed by the seat of his pants. My sharp turn up hill had stopped our forward momentum, but had I created another possible problem? "Oh God," I thought, "what if my brakes don't hold? What if this baby decides to slide back downhill... tail first?"

While I still had momentum, I turned one more time. This time, I applied left rudder and full right out-board throttle, momentarily heading our machine back to the left, intending that the aircraft end up at right angles to the slope. I wanted to get cross-wise to the grade, but I definitely did not want to overshoot and get pointed back downhill with possibly insufficient braking power to keep us from sliding back down into the trees that I had swerved uphill to avoid.

This time, that great forgiving Boeing product, which a Seattle reporter, observing the initial roll out in 1937, had reported, "looked like a flying fortress," suddenly made an abrupt, skidding, turn to the left, across the top of the hill and stopped cold.

Then in my mind's eye, my steady steed, which I had wrestled to the earth, then snorted, pawed the Earth and tossed his head back and forth. I smiled to myself, inwardly but possibly outwardly as well.

Strange images in my head were not strangers to me in those heady days. I remembered imagining a cartoon of Boeing's great B-17, snorting and pawing the ground, with me astride the top-turret.

In my fantasy, I was Tom Mix, and my B-17 was Tom's pony, Tony. I had slowed, stymied and stopped Tom's stomping steed, and now I visualized him, with his head down and his legs apart, blowing steam all over the place.

"Yippee," I shouted, "My wheels are on the ground and I'm not rolling backwards downhill. My flying machine is in one piece and my crewmen are alive. We're all alive!"

Then my psyche plummeted from euphoric heights to dismal depths, and a poem from school days, came to mind, " ...black as the pit from pole to pole." Then, I remembered William Ernest Henley's last verse, " ...It matters not how strait the gate / How charged with punishments the scroll / I am the master of my fate / I am the captain of my soul."

Then I shouted to myself, "Thank you, Mr. Henley. Thank you for your *Invictus* that you wrote many years before I was born" and that my idealistic father once suggested I "put in my memory bank for future use."

Then, with more control, I said to myself, "And, thank you, Dad, for your suggestion. I did what you suggested. I did indeed memorize *Invictus*. And it came to mind in Africa at its darkest in 1943. Fate has dealt kindly with me, Dad. I am on the ground; my crewmen are safe, and my B-17 is in one beautiful piece. And I am the luckiest, most blessed man on Planet Earth. Thank you, thank you, thank you, Dad."

Recalling my trials on that particular mission over North Africa, I later wrote my own quatrain intending a modest tribute to Mr. Henley and my dad:

A FLYBOY'S "INVICTUS"

When courage takes a powder
And fear comes swaggering in,
There's a need to reach down deeper,
And take account of what has been:
"How have I prepared for my moment of trial?
What are my options now?
Do I have a plan to answer?
What? Which? When? Where? And How?"
"Or have I simply sat on my thumbs,
And given no thought to disaster?
My moment has come; will I just succumb
And go to meet my master?"

Richard Eager

After a moment, I scolded myself. I said, "Okay, okay, so you're on the ground, Richard Eager. Yes, but your flying machine is balanced precariously on the side of a good-sized hill; and my God, man, you are congratulating yourself and reciting poetry to yourself, but you're supposed to be at an airport in Algeria where your fellow combat jocks have no doubt landed, had a shower, and are enjoying their evening meal!"

Then, the thought I had resisted… persisted. "What if our base at Navarin was in the clear just around the next mountain as Uppie approached with his 99th Bomb Group intact, except for one lone B-17 driver who might have become an Air Group Leader today. What if all three B-17 groups had gotten down in good shape, except for one single, slow-witted loner who thought he had a better solution."

I remember the moment very well. I felt drained and a tad ill. I said to myself, "My God, Richard Eager, you stupid ass; you're about to throw up and damned if you aren't reciting "Invictus" to yourself."

I climbed out immediately to make use of the remaining light to check over my B-17 and face my crew. I was weary of surprises, but I had one to go. My crewmen had not divined in their collective psyches the fearful thoughts that had crept into mine. They weren't hissing at their pilot as I approached. As we liked to say in French North Africa in the '40s, *"au contraire."* Most were on their knees, jokingly rocking back and forth and kissing the ground. And their faces were greeting me with happy, confident smiles.

And, oh My God, was I ever grateful and proud of my men! There wasn't a whimper out of the lot of them; how sweet it was. We had become a good team with every man working full time to improve his knowledge and do his part… well, almost every man.

With my feet back on the ground, I had some other thoughts, "But, how do you think those faces are going to look tomorrow, Richard Eager, when you come flying home to Navarin in triumph a tad late for breakfast?"

Sergeant Owens wasted no time in producing tie-down ropes from an emergency kit he had thoughtfully assembled and stowed aboard our aircraft. He and his men were already hard at work securing our B-17 to the side of my landing hill.

And a strange sight it was. Walking back down that quite steep hill, taking a couple of backward glances over my shoulder, I saw our great Boeing flying machine back-lit by the rays of a gloriously yellow-red setting African sun, which suggested to me a tilting, Dutch windmill silhouetted against a beautiful, flaming, yellow-red, evening sky. Everyone glanced back and looked up at it and no one could resist a smile. Then, as if on cue, everybody laughed out loud, quite loud from relief, I guessed.

Perhaps they laughed because our now-tamed flying machine, strapped to the top of that hill, looked so wild and so unreal with its downhill wing almost lost in the lengthening shadows and its top-of-the-hill wing pointing towards the now-darkening African sky.

We were all just beginning to relax when suddenly we heard a familiar sound: the heavy, droning beat of four Wright Cyclone engines. Another B-17 was suddenly overhead, circling our position. Staff Sergeant Chuck Ward, our hustling, gung-ho, tail gunner said, "He followed us here, Captain. We went by him right after we broke out of the overcast. He was heading south; I watched him as he turned around and caught up with us."

This was a real lift. At least one other fly-boy thought it smart to get clear of the formation and clear of that weather for the evening, but he seemed to be delaying; I was concerned, thinking he might be in trouble.

But, in a moment, we could see his landing lights, letting down towards a field near ours. Except for his tail fin, he too almost disappeared in the scrubby brush and patches of tall grass. As he rolled to a stop, my crowd let out a discordant cheer for our side. I was feeling better. I had; after all, led a formation today albeit of just two B-17s. I had, led them back towards our target instead of a course that would have taken us home.

The drone of our sister B-17 and the cheers from my crew when both our airplanes were safely on the ground were the only sounds that we had heard since arriving in Tunisia. Then suddenly there was a loud crack, followed closely by a flash of light in the eastern sky.

"Artillery, I hope it's British," I said, recalling some modest firing training, which I had received at the ROTC training camp at Fort McClellan, Alabama, during the summer of '39. I was at Fort McClellan studying warfare just 30 days before Hitler attacked Poland on September 1st. On that very day, I had received orders from the War Department advising me of my acceptance in the Army's then new, fledgling Flying Corps.

I motioned to Sergeant Owens and suggested he send a couple men over to the area where the field guns were firing. "Tell your men to approach with caution, Sarge, in case I've put us down on the wrong side of the German lines." Then I added: "And, you might send a couple of men over to our sister B-17 to see who has been following us and find out if they need anything from us."

Sergeant Owens, responding characteristically, said, "Right away, Captain," and he was off. In a few minutes I could see our two scouting parties making their way through the tall scrubby trees and tough grasses. The thought went through my mind that I had doled out assignments like this in my Boy Scout days in the Smokey Mountains. "Maybe Baden-Powell's Boy Scout program really did help get me moving in some right directions," I mused, "as Dad said it would."

Actually, Dad had said it might! "Thank you, Dad, for staying the course with me; and thank you Baden-Powell for inventing Boy Scouts in England in time to help me make some right turns in the US. And thank you Mr. Hoffeld for shaming me into returning to Scouting, after quitting, enabling me to pass Life Saving, to make Eagle Scout, and in the same week, to save a young boy from drowning and to gain some confidence in my own life."

In a short time, my runners returned with word that we were closer to the German lines than I had thought but that "we were not actually behind their lines." I was sure we weren't behind their lines, but I was very pleased to get some third-party substantiation.

The Germans, we would confirm, were 20 miles north and east of us and were presumed to be withdrawing in the direction of Tunis. It was also nice to confirm that a local British artillery brigade had been responsible for the dramatic streaks of light we had observed. These streaks were long-range artillery, taking off on a north-easterly heading from a point a quarter-of-a-mile from where we had tethered our B-17 to the top of her own hill.

The brigade commander of the British sector in which we had landed sent word that he "would like it very much if the *Flying Fawtress* Commander who blithely landed in his firing sector would join him for an evening meal, alfresco."

Accompanying my response with a grin and raised eyebrow, I said, "I accept, Sarge, and not-to-bother, I'll deliver my acceptance in person. And, if invited, I might just stay the night and find out if I have any lost cousins from the Evans or Stewart clans in their Brigade. This okay with everyone?"

All agreed that my plan was **hunky-dory**, also that they could survive the night without their Captain. I indicated that I thought their enthusiasm for my departure from camp was a little more than absolutely necessary.

While making the ten-minute hike to the British Army camp in failing light, I located a good, straight run to which we could taxi our B-17 in the morning. I didn't see our other B-17 that evening but learned from my men that the pilot was Captain Orrance from another squadron in our 99th Group who happened also to be a classmate of mine during the period when we were Army Air Corps Flying Cadets at Randolph Field in San Antonio, Texas.

I found the British camp and was afforded a very warm welcome. I was invited to share some excellent food: piping-hot, baked in the ground Boy-Scout-style, fresh corn borrowed from the local Arabian economy. We dined alfresco around a warming and very pleasant empty ammo box fire.

My British hosts were most gracious, and I did indeed get invited to climb into a spare sleeping bag. I told my British counterpart where our 99th Navarin airbase was located and invited him to bring his men and drop in on me sometime. I indicated that, with little warning, I could arrange a B-17 hop if his men were interested. He put the question to them while we were roasting the corn. All indicated they thought my offer smashing.

After our stand-up dinner around the ammo box fire, the British artillery commander took me on a short tour of his gun positions. Some units were standing down; the men were cleaning their weapons, policing their areas and getting some rest. A few of their units were firing but at what, I guessed to be, a modest rate. I guessed the objective that blustery spring evening in western

Tunisia was harassment... keeping the Germans mindful that as they retreated elements of the British Army were close on their heels.

I reminded myself that the Germans and Italians had both had their turn at harassing large population segments of Europe and Africa and that "turn-about was fair play."

My British friend, after apologizing for the relative inactivity of his unit, said, "I say, Captain, I know this is a bit dull for you what with your regular flights up to France, Germany and Austria where the big air war is going on. I feel we have not shown you much real sport now, have we? Actually, if you would not mind a bit of slithering along on your tummy, I could arrange for you to move up to where we have some scouts posted. You wouldn't be in any real danger, unless, of course, you happened to pop your head up... a spot too high, you know."

Attempting to match my youthful host's straight face, I thanked him warmly, said his offer was inviting, was something I had always wanted to do, but since the hour was late and he and his men were quite likely quite weary, I said I would not wish to keep any one up late and would decline.

"Oh my, oh my," he said, "I am very sorry, Old Chap, a misunderstanding. Actually, we had no intention of accompanying you. You see, we have all seen this sort of thing a time or two or didn't you know?" He didn't laugh aloud, but I thought I should be able to hear his broad smile. His men evidenced great enjoyment, however, in the sport he was having at the expense of the visiting Yank fly-boy.

In the British camp at 0500 hours the following morning, we were up and into our "warmies" quickly, enjoyed "a spot of hot tea" around a new fire and said our good-byes. My comrades-in-arms assured me that the German and Italian Armies would soon be driven from North Africa. They didn't say it would be "a pice of cike." They did offer their opinion that in very short order Hitler would be doing his jig to a different tune.

My fellow commander observed as I turned to go, "I say, Captain Evans, if you Yanks plan to continue to land helter-skelter here about in North Africa, we Britishers had better damn well get these Nazis and I-tie fellows out of our area, wouldn't you say?"

I smiled, chuckled and stuck out my hand. "I agree, a good plan," I said. Then added, "Lefftenant, I shan't forget this night. You have been a generous and gracious host; I am very obliged to you. And, please, do remember me to the Evans and Stewart clans when you get back to England. Tell them, if you will, that I am proud of my British roots. And, please, do stop by our base at Navarin; we are only a few miles south of the Constantine-to-Algiers highway, near Châteaudun-du Rhumel Airfield."

"We might flight-test a B-17 coming out of engine overhaul and fly it up to **Bone** and have a look at the blue-green Mediterranean," I continued. I said that I had found the Med particularly beautiful when viewed from our British-American hospital located on the heights above the surprisingly blue sea 400 feet or more straight down from a surprisingly flat plateau.

I mentioned that on a recent trip to Bone, on the Med, I had been surprised and pleased to find Britishers, Yanks, Italians and Germans all being treated alike at the British-American Bone Hospital. "A flight in the B-17 might be a nice break," I suggested, "from the scorching sands and the tough duty which you and your commander, Monty, have undertaken and are undertaking for our side.

———————————

The black storm that had been so menacing had departed in the night. The B-17, now front lit by the low, morning sun, brought me out of my reverie. It really did look like a Dutch windmill up there with one wing pointing skyward, the other pointing towards the valley. Sergeant Owens had spotted me and was walking towards me. I greeted him with a smile and said, "Good morning, Sarge. I see our machine hasn't slid down the hill. Did you have a good night?"

"I've never had a better night in my entire life," he answered quickly, then smiled.

"Great," I said with a matching smile. "Why don't you start up our engines and check them out while I'm having some conversation with our crewmen; I'd like to hear how they feel about camping out in North Africa in the spring of '43."

In short order, we were aboard our B-17, had fired up our engines, checked them out, and were easing our great Boeing machine down off its hill-with-a-view very carefully. From the top, I had my men chocking the left wheel while I gunned the right outboard engine to turn us completely around and across the steep grade. When we would reach a point cross-wise to the hill, I would stop, ask them to shift and now chock the right wheel.

I would then **gun** the left outboard engine, again turning us back across the downhill centerline. In this manner, we were able to zigzag down the quite steep hill with almost no use of the brakes and, more to the point, without fear of losing control at some point and sliding all the way back down into those scraggly trees.

Austin and Ward put their hands on the brake drums and signaled up to me that the brake pucks were not getting hot at all. In fifteen minutes, we were off the steep grade and approaching the broad, flat overgrown field, which we were about to make an "instant Army Air Corps flying field."

When we got over to the flat, I had my men walking out ahead of the B-17 searching the tall grass for hidden obstacles. When we got to the end of our field, I taxied back the full length of our "marked-in-the-grass" runway with my men still walking out in front of me, double-checking for obstacles. Our trip down and back made a track through the grass, which would provide good directional reference for my takeoff run.

After confirming that everyone was aboard, I checked the gauges and pushed our four throttles "to the fire-wall" (as we liked to say). We quickly, nervously at times, raced strangely through the bunched native grasses. I was forced to use the directional instruments to maintain a constant heading on this field with uneven visibility. I was surprised to find that it was not difficult at all to maintain directional control using "blind flying" techniques.

It was a little sporty for a minute or so with the varied pampas-like grass flashing by our waist side windows. But then in a moment, the wings started to take hold of the air and the grass quickly dropped away below us. Suddenly, we were "up, up and away."

The sky was clear; the dark clouds, so menacing the night before, had departed with the arrival of a beautiful sunrise. I smiled to myself and said to myself as tears rushed to my eyes momentarily blurring my vision, "Oh my, oh my, it's great to be alive. Thank you, Boeing, and please tell your **Rosies**-Who-Rivet, who put this great flying machine together, that I love them and will never, ever, forget them." (More than half-a-century has passed... and I haven't forgotten them, yet.)

Forty minutes after rising up out of the deep African grass in Tunisia, we were over-flying our home field at Navarin in Algeria in bright sunlight. As I approached the familiar layout of our flying field and our adjoining tent city, I thought to myself, "Man, is this ever a great feeling. I'm back, I got home, the sun is shining, my men are all alive and well, and my aircraft is in one piece. If Orrance and I were the only ones who didn't make it back to base for the evening meal, then that's just too damn bad. We did what we thought we had to do."

I didn't rate my performance at 100 percent, but I was pleased that I had not just hung in there awaiting divine guidance. I had taken charge with my heart pounding in my chest and my throat. I had looked hard at my problem and the odds. And, I had taken actions which I thought would give my crew and me our best shot at staying alive and returning to base.

In a short time, I was circling our field at Navarin, near Constantine, in North Africa, and the sun was shining brightly. I was checking for local traffic, when suddenly my heart skipped a beat! "Oh my God," I shouted silently to myself, "what am I seeing down there? Look at all those empty hard stands! Where are our 99th Bomb Group's B-17s?"

Suddenly, it was clear. It really had been a terrible night. Others had had their problems too. I called our 99th Bomb Group tower, identified my aircraft, requested landing instructions, and then asked how many of our 99th Group aircraft had been able to weather the storm and return to base.

I was told that none had returned to base, that the unexpected, unseasonably heavy rains had reduced the visibility at Navarin to zero and had made a quagmire of our flight **strip**. Also, that our 99th had lost some B-17s, as had our sister groups, the 97th and 301st, but that a full accounting hadn't been made yet.

Subsequently, I learned that most, after a long delay, had been able to get into our Château dun airfield. After hours of orbiting above the range at night in blinding rain with their nerves shot, most had finally gotten down. It was suggested that I also land at Château dun, that our field at Navarin was a sea of mud and was not yet safe to land on, and finally that ground transport back to base would be standing by for my crew and me when we got on the ground.

Since my crew and I had come through unscathed and we had learned that there had been fatalities and aircraft losses, I decided that I had been fortunate indeed and didn't press for details regarding others' experiences. I guessed that, with time, most of the stories would come out and most did.

The number of aircraft lost was a half dozen or so. I never pressed for a full accounting. I didn't want to draw attention to my good fortune nor appear critical of others' misfortunes. In most cases where B-17s were lost, crews had continued to circle above the clouds over the marker-beacon for most of the night hoping for a break in the unusual weather.

Then, when they did not get the break, they so desperately needed with their fuel too low for further tries at **GCA** landings, some were forced to climb back up to a safe altitude and bail out into the black, lightning flashing and storming night. Most who had parachuted had been located, picked up and trucked back to their base, sans their B-17s. A few, not yet accounted for, were still out there some place on the African landscape.

One crew, all good friends of mine, had a particularly difficult and harrowing experience. The pilot had made a number of unsuccessful GCAs. On final approach to the runway, he would reach the minimum altitude without breaking clear of the low clouds; then he would get a "**wave-off**" (borrowed Navy term) or a "**go-around**" from the ground operator and would be directed to abort his landing attempt, return to an assigned altitude and get in line for another GCA. He had made four "missed approaches."

Finally, with fuel enough for one, final effort after which he would be forced to bail out his crew as others had done, this pilot set up his B-17 for one, last, radar-controlled descent. It would be his last approach and final shot at the airfield.

After a few minutes, he reported to the tower, "This is B-17 213; we are in heavy rain and clouds; our gear is down and locked; we have half flaps; our fuel mixture is full rich; engine power is 2100 **rpm**; airspeed is being reduced to 150 mph; rate of descent is holding nicely at 500-feet-per-minute."

Things were going very well in the pilot's cockpit of B-17 213. After a few minutes the GCA operator, transmitting to the pilot, said, "Air Corps 213, I have you on my scope, you're lined up, you're cleared to start your final descent to the runway."

In a moment, he continued, "Good, 213, I see you are now on glide path, on course, and holding good position. Now, you are about to pass through 500 feet; reduce your rate-of-descent to 200 feet-per-minute. Very good, 213; now bring your air speed down to 140 miles per hour."

Then suddenly, the tone of the controller's voice changed: "Pull up, 213; pull up. You're dropping below glide path. Do you read me, 213? Do you read me?" The blip on the ground controller's scope had been on course to the runway and was holding steady on the desired rate-of-descent and glide path. Then, suddenly, the blip representing the B-17 had disappeared from the operator's radar screen apparently lost in "ground-clutter."

On board B-17 213, the flight engineer had been standing on the flight deck between the pilot and co-pilot's seats in position to observe both pilots and also the B-17 instrument panel. So positioned, the flight engineer would have a clear view not only of the pilot's and co-pilot's in-strument panels, but also, upon breaking out below an overcast, he would be able to see out over the nose of the B-17 with a clear view of the runway.

In a moment, 213's on-board flight engineer was also shouting to the pilot, "Pull up, pull up, Major; I have a clear view of the runway; I can see out over the nose; you're in the clear, but you're letting down into a slight rise ahead of the runway.

And you are angling off to your right, Major; you're not aligned with the runway you are drifting right. You're too close to the rise, Major... pull up... pull up!"

The tower, too, was saying, "Pull up; pull up, 213. I do not have you in sight; you are not in view at the approach end of the field. I repeat: 213, pull up!"

But B-17 213 continued to move slowly towards the slight rise on the approach, which by now had blanked out the radar operator's view of the B-17 blip on his screen. Both the B-17 pilot and co-pilot were apparently "on the gauges," as indeed they had been for most of the night. Clearly neither pilot had realized that they had broken out of the overcast and could now get off the gauges and complete the landing visually. They may not have raised their seats back up, after lowering them to make the long periods of instrument flying more comfortable.

Aboard 213, only the flight engineer, standing between and slightly above the eye-level of the two pilots, was able to see forward over the B-17s nose and observe that 213 on its last possible pass had broken out of the overcast. Across the top of the rise, he was able to see down the length of the runway.

But the rise, as B-17 213 continued to descend, was itself now rising up, directly in front of the flight engineer's line of sight of the runway.

It was reported, post-flight, that the flight engineer after shouting a second time that "he could see out over the nose and that he had the field in sight" had then reached for the pilot's control column and at the very last instant had pulled the coupled, control columns back into the laps of the two pilots.

The aircraft descended in landing configuration with both its landing gear and, flaps down, and struck the top of the rise wheels first. Then it bounced nose-high into a partial stall. Then, in seconds, it slammed down hard off to the right side just before reaching the runway.

The landing gear was crushed on impact; the right wing and engines had struck the ground very hard and were partially crushed; but the B-17 had remained in an upright position. Skidding on its belly and engine nacelles a hundred feet or so on the right side of the runway, B-17 213 finally came to a stop.

There was no fire. There was no fuel to burn. B-17 213's tanks were bone dry. The aircraft was effectively destroyed.The crew members, understandably, were severely "shaken up." All were able, however, to climb out and walk away from their B-17.

There were other near misses that dreadful night resulting in severe emotional stress and trauma for many crewmen. Some would not recover immediately. They would just disappear from camp; their bunks would be quickly emptied and, just-as-quickly, refilled by replacement crewmen.

Many would tell of the anxiety and the terror of having to circle and wait... circle and wait... during the stormy night as their fuel gauges crept lower and lower. Finally, some would be forced to **"crack silk,"** jump from their B-17s into a black void into the cold rain and sleet, at night over Africa... at its darkest.

Ironically, the only deaths that would occur that night in the entire Air Division would be from drowning. One pilot had elected to fly north to the Mediterranean, hoping the storm might end before his fuel supply did! He put his money on the hope that he would eventually be able to let down through the low clouds on instruments at night over the Mediterranean. And, then fly visually just above the waves toward the lights of Bone, a seaside Algerian town known for its exceptional Allies Military Hospital atop a 400-foot cliff.

Bone also had an airport jointly operated by the British Royal Air Force and the US Army Air Corps, which was in the process of being enlarged and improved. Specifically, runways and over-runs were being widened and extended and minimal night lighting, rated only marginally adequate for B-17 operations, was being renovated and brought to British and American standards.

It was reported that the pilot who put his money on Bone continued well into the exhausting, endless night trying to descend on the radio range down through the overcast and break out below the clouds in time to visually pick up the Bone airfield and land his B-17.

Finally, with his fuel supply all but exhausted, this pilot let down through the clouds one more time. This last time his intent was to ditch his B-17 in the Med; his target was not the Bone airfield but the small harbor at Bone.

He was able to ditch his B-17 in the Mediterranean close enough to see the lights of Bone. But it was said the plane landed about fifteen miles offshore, and he had difficulty getting his emergency five-man life rafts inflated and launched clear of his sinking B-17.

His crewmen were able to inflate only two (of five) of the five-man rafts stowed on their B-17 for its eleven-man crew. Both rafts were over-loaded with some crewmen being forced to remain in the cold water holding on to the sides of the two rafts for their lives. In a short period, it was perceived that one of the two floating rafts was leaking and that, in the confusion following the night-water-landing, the emergency hand-pump and the rubber patching materials had not been off-loaded from the sinking B-17.

In a very short while, there was only one of the two, five-man rafts still afloat with the same four passengers in this single, surviving raft. Seven exhausted men were in the chilling waters, holding on to the hand-ropes on this raft for their lives. After another terrible hour, the dawn finally broke.

The seven men, who were forced to remain in the water for the entire period, were no longer holding on to the sides of the single remaining raft. Several tried to swim ashore and were not seen again. Others, their strength gone, let go their desperate hold to the raft, and to life. And they silently sank below the surface of the Mediterranean Sea.

Only the original four who had remained during the entire ordeal in the single, usable raft were still alive. Three of five of the original rafts had failed; seven of eleven crewmen had died from drowning. All who had parachuted into the night had landed safely and were all picked up by mid-morning the next day.

The four men who had remained in the single, surviving raft for the entire period, who had not taken a turn in the chilling waters of the Med, finally floated into shallow waters, and waded to shore, as the dawn was breaking. As I recall, none of these men were returned to Navarin.

Lessons were learned; equipment and operating procedures were studied and modified; and, survivors, many still in their teens, were toughened and tempered by the tragic experience.

CORNERS TO BE TURNED

Busy are our lives, beset with corners, which must be turned.
We are told to look first to our right and then to our left.
We must check both ways ... taking care ... to not get "burned"!
But often we are beset with choices, difficult to make!
We are told: "Forward, onward and upward we must venture,"
And that some of life's risks ... we must take.
Taught we were when we were all quite youthful
That life, at its best, must have zest! Also, that
Life's turns, as quests for the best, can be fruitful.

Richard Eager

2.2 *B-17s fly tucked in elements of three in formations* (99th Bomb Group Historical Society)

2.3 *B-17 looks like a windmill in the dark*

3.1 *General Montgomery is the Victor of Alamein*

CHAPTER 3

MONTY, THE VICTOR AT ALAMEIN

Alamein would not be just a battle
To protect Cairo and the Suez from the Hun.
Alamein would be the turning-point battle
That would set the Hun on the run!

Richard Eager

For a while we saw no land. Then, quickly Tripoli Bay and the City of Tripoli was seen on the horizon. As we approached, I descended to 200 feet above the water so that my crewmen and I might have a closer look at what the British Navy had done to the harbor facilities and the Axis warships trapped there and to catch a glimpse of the frenetic urban activity along this historic waterfront. I remember thinking that the frenzy I observed in the streets below was probably never long-interrupted, even when a war was passing through this timeless, major, metropolitan city in North Africa.

I circled back and delayed for a few minutes to observe a nautical graveyard. British sea and air attacks had caused a dozen or more Italian vessels to settle upright on the bottom of this shallow bay, their decks awash and only their masts projecting above the waves. I remember taking a look around to see if any had left their flags flying. None had. (Interesting the minutiae that surfaces in one's mind when one's thoughts are allowed to range back, even over half a century.)

In a moment I lowered my right wing towards the water and pulled the B-17 up a few hundred feet, heading us inland towards the center of Tripoli, Libya's principal city and one of its two capital cities; its alternate capital, Benghazi, was 400 miles to the east of us, across the Gulf of Sidra. Within the week, I would be selecting Benghazi as an emergency landing field and Monty would be very upset with me.

Faces darkened by centuries of harsh sunlight turned to watch us fly by. These Tripolitans gazed at us with apathetic eyes; they had seen warplanes before, Italian, German, British, and now, finally a few American B-25s. This would be their first viewing of a *Flying Fortress*. They seemed not to be impressed.

At first the streets of Tripoli seemed a twisting, tortured maze without pattern. But as we raced along a few hundred feet overhead, star-shaped intersections would quickly materialize, each boasting a small fountain or a statue at its center. Then, just as quickly, these small constellations would dissolve in the swirling mist behind us.

A dark, steamy haze hung over this ancient Arabic metropolis. It appeared so thick, I thought, at times, that it might somehow seep into our cockpit. I remember drawing a deep breath through my nose, half expecting to experience again the odors of the Casbahs of Casablanca, Oran, Marrakech and Algiers: always pungent, exotic and wondrous and not always unpleasant. I could detect only the familiar, acrid odor of oil at work protecting and lubricating moving, metal parts. There was no romance to be found in the smells in a B-17 *Flying Fortress*.

In a flash, we were over the suburbs of Tripoli. A few arterial streets began to take shape out of the maze and haze, suggesting spokes in a great flat wheel pointing the way out of town. At the end of one such southerly-pointing spoke, our destination materialized out of the floating sands that blurred the southern horizon. Then quite suddenly, **Mussolini**'s Castle Bonito Airdrome came into sharp focus. Below us and beyond, stretching south into the sun, lay the vast, endless Sahara.

Only a few weeks had passed since Monty's 8th Army had passed through Tripoli. Overnight, this Axis airfield had ceased to function as the principal supply and communications link connecting Rome and Berlin, particularly Rome, with North Africa. As we flew closer, shattered big guns, tanks, trucks and aircraft could be seen strewn about the airfield. These twisted, rusted, grotesque remnants of Axis power had been shoved together without ceremony, forming hastily bulldozed burial mounds. I recall symbolizing this jumble of twisted, rusty, metal as the decaying body parts of deceased Fascism.

Few structures remained standing. A control tower on the far south side of the field seemed to rise up and stand tall and alone among the rubble. I guessed that the cheery British accent giving me landing instructions was being transmitted from this tower. Resembling a coastal lighthouse, out-of-place on the northern edge of the Sahara Desert, this battered monument to fascist power was now transmitting the King's English rather than Italian and German. "A favorable sign of the times," I mused.

Close by this tower, the skeletal remains of the only other structure breaking the southern horizon appeared. It had once been a large hangar. Now, its entire roof and much of its side covering were gone, "missing in action," I thought. Substantial portions of its concrete floor, however, had withstood the blasts, and resourceful British mechanics had wasted no time in getting an aircraft maintenance and repair operation underway on this lone, surviving, hard, flat surface.

Touchdown at Tripoli was "uneventful," as we liked to say back in those days. But, as the weight of our B-17 shifted from its wings to its wheels, the entire aircraft began to lurch and shake, protesting the tortured condition of the patched and re-patched, steel-planked runway.

Quickly a British lorry appeared off our left wing. Bucking and bouncing along on the mangled steel planking, it gained on us as *Theresa Leta* decelerated. The driver, in British desert khakis and showing unabashed exuberance, waved and then pulled ahead and beckoned us to follow. It was a warm welcome to Tripoli by our British allies.

As we continued to lose speed and the lurching and bouncing subsided, I noticed again the rusted remains of the wrecked trucks, tanks and aircraft, which I had observed from the air. In sharper focus now, it was still difficult to identify individual vehicles and war machines in their crippled and contorted conditions. It was clear enough, however, that they were of Italian and German design (red and black meant German, green meant Italian).

I had seen pictures in *Life* magazine and on Paramount News reels of the Axis partners when they had paraded as conquerors in Ethiopia, Albania, Austria, Czechoslovakia and Poland.

I observed to myself, employing an accent I guessed my new British partners would deplore: "By Jove, I say. These bloody machines were jolly well in better condition when last I viewed them on the British Pathé News at Knoxville's Strand Theater. These Nazi chaps, who have been terrorizing the world, are finally jolly well having problems of their own, wouldn't you say now?"

The lorry leading us suddenly spun about, stopped, and quickly gave birth to a diminutive dust devil. Leaping up, the tiny whirlwind made me mindful of a whirling dervish as it swirled away across the sandy airfield. The smiling British Tommy who had been leading us jumped to the ground and threw his arms overhead and quickly pulled his right finger across his throat, the universal signal to "park your aircraft and cut your engines." I brought the B-17 to a stop, set the parking brakes and pulled the four mixture-control levers to their off positions. I then watched the four-engine manifold pressure and rpm gages grind down to zero. Finally, I flipped the ignition and radio switches to their off positions, then glanced at Sergeant Owens out front. "Chocks in place," he signaled.

Then I turned battery power off, released the brakes, unbuckled my seatbelt and pushed myself up and out of the B-17 pilot's position. With practice, one could shut down Boeing's flying machine in under sixty seconds.

In those days, I was sure that most B-17 pilots enjoyed starting up all that power; we thought it considerable. Also, I guessed that most, particularly on returning from combat missions, found it quite satisfying to shut down all that power one more time. I never tired of either experience.

A British staff car could now be seen bearing down on our position in the middle of Mussolini's Castle Bonito Airdrome. A trail of fine suspended sand was rising to reflect in the sky the staff car's course on the ground. This over-sized, spiraling dust devil brought to mind accounts I had read in *The Stars and Stripes* of British and German tank formations racing to outflank one another in recurring death struggles along the 1,200-mile Mediterranean seaboard from Alamein (140 miles northwest of Cairo) across Libya and Tunisia to Tunis, the modern capital city built near the sites of ancient Utica and Carthage.

I watched this single plume of flying sand rising from the staff car as I reflected on the stories of death, told many times, when a few hundred such whirling dervishes would levitate from the desert floor, springing skyward from tanks and motorized-infantry vehicles as their British and German drivers frantically maneuvered for their lives. These battles had taken place only a few weeks before my arrival in western Libya, called "Tripolitania" by its citizens.

Quickly the staff car pulled up and stopped. I called my crew to attention, a little early I decided. The driver jumped out, opened the rear door and a tall, very distinguished, very British-looking officer dismounted. I smiled and raised my hand in salute, also a little early while this officer was still some distance away. He returned my smile, but not my salute.

But then, in a moment when he was directly in front of me, up came his right bare knee preparatory to stomping the ground. At the same instant his right arm sprang from its position at his side. Then, in a flash, the fingertips of his right hand were touching his right temple, his palm facing forward. In this position, his thumb was very close to being in his right ear. As this flawless example of the formal British hand salute was being completed, the entire hand-wrist-arm mechanism continued to vibrate for a few seconds, providing a splendid finish.

Realizing that a very senior and very friendly British General was spoofing me by demonstrating the exaggerated, formal British salute, I said to him, "Sir, I am Captain Evans of the 99th Bomb Group, US Army Air Corps. My crew and I are pleased and proud to be assigned to the victorious British 8th Army." Then I added, "And, General, I am pleased to salute you, although I fear my Yank salute is no match for the demonstration which you have just provided us."

The General gave me a broad smile, then laughed pleasantly, and said, "Ask your men to, please, stand at ease, Captain Evans. Actually, we are rather informal out here. I am **General Sir Francis de Guingand**, Chief of Staff, 8th Army; you may hear Monty call me "Freddy." The Army Commander has asked me to welcome you to Tripoli and to the 8th Army. I am pleased to do so."

Pointing beyond the B-17, he continued, "Tents and **mess hall** have been provided for your men just over there. Monty would like you to be quartered in Tripoli, accessible to him and to his senior staff. You may park your aircraft hereabout, as you wish. There are very few taxiways in good repair, as you have probably observed; the desert floor, however, is quite firm and unyielding, if a bit rough."

I smiled and volunteered that these were precisely my observations on landing.

"Monty has asked," he continued, "that I bring you straight away to his field headquarters, just over there. You will find him making plans for a victory celebration, which he hopes you and your men will attend. Most of the 8th Army and our King will be on hand, you know."

I had not known, but I was pleased to learn that my crew and I were on the invitation list for a get-together, the prospects of which seemed pleasant, indeed. I was flattered by the General's mock-formal, overtly friendly welcome; also, I was beginning to think I might be getting special attention, intended for someone else. I wondered if Jimmie Doolittle might have misspelled the name, he sent down to Colonel Upthegrove.

But what was I to say? I decided on, "Sir, my crew and I have nothing planned for the 'morrow; we would be pleased and honored to attend your victory celebration."

"Then it is settled," General de Guingand said, "We must go along; we shan't keep Monty waiting, you know."

I liked this man, about the age of my father I guessed, and I vowed to serve him and his boss with courtesy and to the very best of my ability. I could not know then that General de Guingand would often be an intermediary between his commander and me. Nor did I know that an even greater problem would arise between General Montgomery and me that would involve General Patton as well. There would be just two Allied Army Commanders in the North African Mediterranean Theater during the summer months of 1943. Both had reputations of being endowed with excessive zeal and monumental egos. And I was destined to screw it up with both.

I turned to my co-pilot and said, "Take over."

Lieutenant Johnson's response was prompt, rendered smartly and to the point. "Yes, sir."

Then, as an afterthought, Lieutenant Johnson came to attention, and saluted me for just the second time in his life.

During the drive across the dusty airdrome between rows of pyramidal tents numbering perhaps a thousand, the General alone in the rear seat appeared lost in his own thoughts. I took the opportunity to try to fix his name in my memory. Dale Carnegie, author of the book, *How to Win Friends and Influence People*, lecturing at Knoxville High when I was a student there in the mid to late '30s, had pointed out that "memory is aided by association with humorous events already fixed in one's psyche."

"For example," Mr. Carnegie said, "If you should meet someone named 'Butterfield', you might picture him in a field of butter. The more ridiculous the scene you conjure up in your mind and associate with Mr. Butterfield the greater the likelihood should you meet again that you would be able to bring to mind, first the ridiculous scene, then Mr. Butterfield."

I ran a quick scan to see if I had anything on file, which had the same meter and might also be associated with "Guingand" and out popped "**ying-yang**." "Not a perfect match," I thought, "but close enough." I had learned the term "ying-yang" from my older brother when I was a much younger brother (and had no idea what he was talking about). For many years, back in those days, I listened to and believed everything my mother, father, scoutmaster, YMCA coach and older brother had to say to me.

But even as this definitive, evocative and memorable term came to mind out there in Tripolitania, it also came to mind that I should reject it. Granted, "ying-yang" was etched in the cortex of my brain for all time and might be counted on to nudge "Guin gand" to the surface, I feared that my psyche, under pressure at some unpropitious moment, might arc across an extraneous circuit prompting me to blurt out, "Good morning, General de Ying Yang, sir."

General de Guingand stirred and gestured towards a scene just coming into view. Ahead were the Army Commander's two caravans and his headquarters tent. There was no mistaking it; the British Jack and some corps banners flying out front were good clues.

And there was no mistaking the slight figure of the Army Commander himself standing close by his flags. Monty, looking as he had looked in the pictures, which had quickly spread across the US and around the globe following his victory at El Alamein, was standing alone with his own thoughts. I presumed he was taking a moment to stretch and reflect, with some satisfaction, on recent events. It was as pleasant as mid-day gets in Tripoli and recent events had been pleasant indeed for the Commander of the victorious British 8th Army. Fortunately, for me I would not have to depend on Mr. Carnegie's mnemonic memory devices with Field Marshall Bernard Law Montgomery's name.

While taking part in the war, an American flyer could not always be appraised of developments in other theaters. However, if he read *The Stars and Stripes* and was able to make periodic trips to higher headquarters, he could stay reasonably well abreast of the progress of the war. I had top-secret clearances and made frequent trips to higher headquarters in both Algeria and Tunisia. When I was about to meet Monty for the first time, some of the great General's recent history quickly came to mind.

Hitler had sent four Army Commanders against Monty in Egypt. General Georg Stumme (an older General Officer well overdue for retirement) was in command while General Rommel was hospitalized at Wiener Neustadt. Stumme had presumably died of a heart attack and was found in the track of his armored car on the Alamein battlefield. It was on the afternoon of the first day of the Battle of El Alamein when the unfortunate General Stumme's (very probably once-stout) heart gave out.

A second Army Commander, General Wilhelm Ritter von Thoma, was taken prisoner while personally participating in a tank battle at El Alamein. For his troubles, General von Thoma was rewarded with a private dinner with Monty himself. Dinner was served alfresco on the sand in front of Monty's caravan the evening following the afternoon of General von Thoma's capture.

It was reported that while General von Thoma got a very nice meal out of Monty, the 8th Army Commander was unable to get anything at all out of General von Thoma.

When Winston Churchill was told of this dining-out on the Sahara sands, the Prime Minister is quoted as saying, "Poor von Thoma; I know how he felt. I too have eaten at Monty's table."

In a short time, I would have my own experiences with respect to eating at Monty's table. One dinner meal in particular, at Monty's bivouac in Sicily on the heights above the plains of Catania, would be unforgettable. But it would help me to understand this implacable, inexplicable, popular and very useful man, called "Monty."

Following Monty's victory at the battle at Mareth, Rommel, Hitler's "Desert Fox" and favorite General, had flown out of Tunisia in the night to Rome and on to Hitler's field headquarters at Rastenburg, Poland in a small, single-engine **Storch** aircraft. General Rommel would never return to North Africa. He would avoid surrender and prison camp in North Africa and later he would serve in France. But the Desert Fox would never again lead his tanks in battle.

Later, I would learn that Hitler (suspecting correctly that Rommel was one of a number of his Generals giving thought to his assassination) would send SS officers to the Rommel home near Ulm in the Black Forest of southern Germany where the General was at home on sick leave. Hitler's assassins would be instructed should Rommel refuse the poison that they would deliver to him, to shoot General Rommel, his wife and his son.

Rommel would bid his wife and son goodbye, then drive away with the SS officers. The car would be seen going over a rise. It would then pull off the road near some trees. Rommel would be handed a single pellet. Germany's most popular Army Commander, knowing well the routine, would place it under his tongue. It was reported that within three seconds, General Rommel was dead by Hitler's order, whom Rommel had faithfully served until he died on this road.

Manfred Rommel, the General's son, on leave from his unit in France, would witness the arrival of the green sedan from Berlin; he would be afforded only a few minutes with his father before the green sedan, with his father in the rear seat, would pull away.

Years later, he would describe the circumstances of his father's death to the renowned British military tactician and historian, B. H. Liddell Hart. Of interest, Rommel's son would select this distinguished Englishman to be the editor and publisher of his famous father's personal papers.

Thus, Hitler did demonstrate his dedication to high purpose. Also, his brutal efficiency and his special brand of loyalty towards German officers, who at the beginning sought only to serve faithfully... their country, and their Führer.

Two other Axis Army Commanders, Germany's General Hans-Jürgen von Arnim and Italy's General Giovanni Messe would also oppose Monty in Tunisia. For their efforts they would both be taken prisoner near Enfidaville, a small town forty miles southeast of Tunis where the Axis's African campaign would grind to a halt. Hitler would promote Von Arnim and Mussolini would promote Messe, both very late in their military careers; so late in fact that each General would add his fifth star and receive his Field Marshal baton the very same day that he would be forced to surrender his army to the Allies.

Of all the Allied and Axis Field Commanders directly involved, Monty alone was alive, free and in command, with high hopes that Winston Churchill might soon promote him to Field Marshal five-star rank. Monty had good reason for thinking himself a contented man until he met his new US Army Air Corps pilot that spring day in 1943 in front of his 8th Army command tent at Mussolini's Castle Bonito Airdrome.

I was still in the dark about the B-17 and my assignment to the 8th Army, but I would soon learn that Monty and Ike had made a bet having to do with the timing of the end of the war in North Africa. Monty had understood, I was told, that his reward if he won would be a *Flying Fawtress* complete with pilot and crew.

I would learn, too, that General Eisenhower would be unable to recall having made such a bet. Nevertheless, General Ike did direct Jimmie Doolittle to send along to Monty a B-17 with a combat-ready flight crew to transport Monty around the Mediterranean Theater of Operations. I reckoned this was an effort to keep the peace in the not-always-so-peaceful Anglo-American Officers' alliance that General Eisenhower commanded.

In a short time, the British staff car taking General de Guingand and me to Monty's HQ at Mussolini's erstwhile Castel Benito Airdrome came to a stop. Following General de Guingand's lead, I dismounted quickly and approached the first Allied Army Commander to achieve victory over an Axis Army Commander in the field. Monty had licked not just one but all four of them.

I was confident and proud to snap to attention when I came before him. And I was proud to salute Great Britain's great Army Commander. I noted that he was slight of frame and not quite as tall as I was; I liked him immediately. I was aware in those days that I tended to like men who were not quite as tall as I was.

I was not, however, prepared for what would follow. The Commander of the 8th Army did not come to attention when I did; but then I thought quickly, "Why should he?" Neither did he return my salute. Now, this was a new experience for me.

Even so, I recovered quickly and said to myself, "Well, what the hell, why should Montgomery of Alamein, as history would call him, take time from his busy day to salute Professor Evans's third son, Dick, from The Great Smoky Mountains and the Tennessee Valley? Why, indeed."

General de Guingand, sensitive to the awkwardness in progress, allowed Monty's new pilot a moment to recover his composure and get his saluting arm out of the air and stowed again at his side. Then he said in a manner suggesting some experience with awkward beginnings, "Monty, this is Captain Evans; Ike has sent him 'round to fly you about in an American *Flying Fawtress.*"

I remember feeling very obliged to General de Guingand from the beginning for his courtesy to a US Army captain, also for what I presumed to be some considerable courage under the circumstances. My composure returned quickly but I would promptly lose it again. The Army Commander did not respond in any way to General De Guingand's pleasant introduction; instead, he fixed a pair of uncomprehending, disbelieving eyes on me.

This reaction caused me some concern. I was at a loss to understand what it was about me that the Commander of the 8th Army could neither comprehend nor believe. Later developments would suggest that Monty was thinking. "My God, Ike really is upset with me; he's sent some green kid out here to try and get me killed."

General de Guingand must have been aware of the disputed Eisenhower wager, which I hadn't yet been filled in on. He quite suddenly decided that there was some place elsewhere he wished to be. He took his leave with a quick look in Monty's direction and no look at all in mine.

The Army Commander, however, continued to look directly at me with his head cocked slightly to one side, possibly in an effort to frighten me away, I thought. Then quickly and without a word or a look, he turned and walked directly by me in the direction of his command tent.

Moments before, Monty had resisted any impulse he might have had to return my salute; then he had stared down his nose at me for what I guessed to be a full sixty seconds. Finally, as he moved by me missing me by inches his gaze directed elsewhere, son-of-a-gun if he didn't almost run me down. Clearly, the Army Commander considered it my responsibility to be out of harm's way, should he suddenly decide to come roaring through.

General de Guingand had told me that Monty was very much looking forward to meeting me. I was beginning to wonder how things might have turned out had he not been anticipating my arrival with such pleasure. It was beginning to get through to me that it was very possible Monty had been expecting someone else besides me to show up with Ike and Jimmie's flying machine.

Dad had often counseled me when he sensed I was not moving in a "forward direction." "Dick, my boy," he would say with his puckish grin and smiling eyes, "you must understand that you can never win every time. And, Son, there will be times in your life when you will be sure that you have won, only to discover that in reality, you just lost. But don't stop to worry about it," my dad would say. "Just keep on plugging away. And give it some time. Given time, things often work out quite well."

As I turned to follow General Montgomery into his command tent, it hit me that this was, for sure, one of those times that Dad had so clearly foreseen in my future. There was no question that I was not winning, nor that I was at a total loss to understand why I was losing before I had gotten started.

I wasn't in lock step with the General as he moved to enter his command tent, of course not, but neither was I very far behind. Even so, I was not able to make it through the tent opening before the flap-door closed behind General Montgomery and directly in front of me. Of course, this put the Army Commander clearly inside and Colonel Upthegrove's unsettled B-17 pilot clearly outside.

Halfway through the doorway, I hesitated. In my peripheral vision, I could see the dust rising from General de Guingand's transport. "No help there," I said to myself; "no help from General de

Ying Yang, err... Ging Gand."

Many times, when I would find myself in trouble, I would think of my dad. "What would Dad do?" I would ask myself. Then I would try to answer my own question. This time the answer came quickly. I said to myself, "You knucklehead, Dad wouldn't know what to do with General Montgomery either. Dad knows how to run a high school, but he doesn't know any more about British Generals than you do, Richard Eager. Now, why don't you just screw up your courage a tad and get your butt into that 8th Army command tent, invited or not, and plan to hang around a spell and just see what develops?"

This bit of self-direction straightened me up a tad. And that is just what I did: I pushed open the tent flap and walked without invitation into the Command Tent of the British Commonwealth's 8th Army, knowing of course that The Army Commander himself was lurking about in the dim light in there someplace.

And he was, indeed; he was seated at the center of the head table writing. I hoped he couldn't hear my heart thumping the way it still was. The tent was good-sized, like the sideshow tents I had seen years before at Knoxville's Knox County Fairs. Tables and chairs were set up in a "U" shape recalling to mind Dad's Kiwanis Club luncheons. General Montgomery was sitting as expected at the base of the "U."

I decided that I should be pleasant but should probably forgo a second try at saluting. The Army Commander, writing on a clipboard, did not look up; he did, however, point toward an empty seat. A few minutes passed in silence except for the loud scratching of his pen.

Then, quite suddenly, Monty pushed back his clipboard and looked up, straight at me. I remember the moment very well, indeed. He just blinked a few times, and he didn't say anything.

Then suddenly, he was smiling at me. There could be no doubt about it. There was no one else in the tent. And that's all he did for a few seconds: he just sat there and smiled at me.

And what did I do? I'm not really sure as I think of it now. Most likely, I just smiled right back, which is what people did in Tennessee. Mom would say, "When in doubt, Dick, just show those nice white teeth, which you're blessed with." And that's exactly what I did. I showed Monty my white teeth.

I remember thinking that the General and I would have felt rather silly, if someone had walked into that tent while we were both sitting there, grinning silently at each other. It's hard to believe that it really happened that way.

Then, finally, as if there had been no earlier meeting between us, General Montgomery said, "I am very pleased to meet you, Captain Evans. I say, could you fly me to Cairo within the week? Our Embassy is there, we do our planning work there, and I would be pleased to show you our Embassy. It is very old."

I answered, "Of course, sir." The promptness of my response didn't mean that I was getting myself under control. "Of course, sir" was a knee-jerk response, which I learned at my father's knee and practiced assiduously, sometime before my first days in the Army Air Corps.

I said that I would be honored to see his embassy in Cairo, and he continued, "Excellent, but before we fly to Cairo, I would like to introduce you to my King. He's quite a nice chap, you know, and he is coming to Tripoli; perhaps General de Guingand has spoken to you of our King's visit? He is coming here to Tripoli on the morrow, Captain Evans."

As I listened to Monty referring to his King as a "nice chap," I was sure that he was being anything but flippant; it was clear that Monty both respected and liked his King very much. "Yes sir, General Montgomery," I said, "General de Guingand has mentioned your King's visit... as we drove over from the B-17. He said that you wished my crew and me to attend. I told General de Guingand that my crew members and I would be very proud to greet your King, sir."

"Splendid," Monty almost shouted and then he beamed without restraint. "Now, I must push off," he said. "Would you mind very much awaiting my return, just here for a short period?"

I said that I would of course be pleased to await his return, and quite suddenly Monty of Alamein was on his feet and on his way with a nod and a smile in my direction. I was also on my feet promptly but saluting again didn't seem the way to go as his backside was already disappearing through the tent door. I recall thinking, "By George, when Monty thinks it's time to **move out**, one might take pains to estimate his intended course and try very hard not to be on it."

I could hear Monty's staff car pull up, stop, then quickly drive away. I had moved toward the tent door and allowed the flap to swing open just far enough to let me observe the Army Commander's departure. As his staff car sped away and disappeared among a thousand tents, it was quickly lost from my view. Its course on the ground, however, was still reflected in the sky by one of those tenacious Saharan dust spirals that one could never quite escape.

I thought to myself, it must be rough-going indeed, when one is trying very hard to evade lethal pursuit in the desert, as was Rommel during his 1200-mile race with Monty from El Alamein in Egypt to Mareth in Tunisia. When a giant dust devil attaches itself to you in North Africa, there is no place to hide for all, for miles around, can divine your track on the ground from your sandy reflection in the sky.

When I had first walked into the 8th Army Command Tent, it was empty, except for Monty. Now it was again empty, this time, except for me. I sat down in a chair next to the one that I guessed was reserved for Monty and decided that I was a tad tired. Dad had cautioned me on numerous occasions about feeling sorry for myself. But, on this day in the 8th Army Command tent in North Africa, I was beyond Dad's reach, if not his influence. I smiled to myself and said, "Well what the hell, Richard Eager; if there ever was a time to just sit on your butt and feel sorry for yourself this has got to be it. Enjoy."

I placed my chair in front of a sturdy, well-set tent pole. Then, I sat down, leaned back against the pole and propped my feet up on Monty's table. It struck me that quite a few months had passed since I had been able to take the time to just sit back, prop my feet up, and contemplate the nothingness of the ceiling of a tent and here I was....

On our combat missions, we had struck targets in North Africa, then crossed over the Med and attacked in Sicily, Italy, the Balkans and southern France. Also, we had started over-flying the Swiss, Italian and Austrian Alps, extending our attacks into Austria and southern Germany.

We were going deeper into Axis territory with almost every mission. We were Doolittle's "12th Air Force" at the beginning; we would become General Twining's "15th Air Force" by the war's end.

The 15th would be born in North Africa and I would later be proud to have been on hand at its birthing.

We understood that General Curtis LeMay's B-17s, flying out of bases in the UK, were catching the brunt of the German fighter and anti-aircraft defenses in Western Europe. We knew that it was part of our job to draw off and destroy as much of the German defense forces as we could to assist our harder hit 8th and 9th Air Force friends flying out of the UK.

We were all hit by the same German units flying out of southern Germany and Austria, but the England-based 8th and 9th Air Force units were under attack, going and coming from the English Channel to their targets and back. Our attackers in southern Germany would usually withdraw when we would over-fly the Alps, on a heading for North Africa. They rarely followed us very far out over the Mediterranean.

In my reverie and still gazing at the ceiling of Monty's tent, those brightly-colored fighters and dully-colored flak bursts would flash again in my mind. I thought for a while that the scenes of air-combat that I was on hand to see and feel would never quite go away.

But they did. Looking back, it all seemed quite unreal, as if we hadn't really been up there and were only watching motion pictures of ourselves flying headlong into the flak bursts.

After another moment, my thoughts drifted back still farther to 1939 and early 1940 when I was at Randolph and **Kelly Fields**, the training fields in San Antonio of the then-fledgling Flying Corps of the US Army. I remembered how happy I had been when it began to look like I was not going to be washed out of the flight-training program. I remember very well that I stumbled more than once before I learned to fly.

On graduation day at Kelly Field, I was awarded my Silver Wings and was commissioned a second lieutenant in the US Army Air Corps. Also, I was made an instructor-pilot, "effective immediately upon graduation," right there at Kelly Field. I thought that I had never been so happy.

One day I was a cadet. The next day five students were assigned to me, and I was told that it was now my job to teach them everything that I had just learned. The washout rate was high in the Primary Training phase as over half of our comrades were sent home. In the next level, Basic Training phase at Randolph Field, only 10-to-15% of us were bounced.

In the Advanced Training phase at Kelly and Brooks Fields, the latter only a few miles west and south of San Antonio, very few were eliminated. The survivors of Basic Training would buy their officers' uniforms and, for most, their first automobile with impunity, while they were completing the advanced (and final) phase of the Army Air Corps Flying Training programs.

My earlier fears were behind me. I had understood, that when fellow cadets called me "Eager," they were thinking, "this character's too bloody eager." I knew that I was generally thought to be over-zealous and even "a tad square."

When I related this state of affairs to my dad and told him that "square" and "eager" had special meanings in the Army Air Corps and that his son was thought by contemporaries as being both, Dad wrote back, "That's great, Dick; no one hits the target in the center every time. You're just erring on the positive side. As I have heard you say a few times, all you need do is to 'hang in there.' Which, I presume, means to keep trying."

I could hear Dad's laugh as I read. Dad would often laugh when I wasn't sure the subject was all that funny. But, I remember, too, that Dad would laugh just as hard when the joke was not on one of his sons or Mom, but on him.

Letting my thoughts drift back even farther, suddenly I could see my dad towering over me. I was a little kid, and I was in big trouble with my dad. I was frightened, but also, I was ashamed; I had done something very bad and I had let my dad down.

From the very first, I had always... well, most always tried hard to make my dad proud of me. And I never, ever wanted him to be ashamed of me. I remember once when, as the expression went back then, I really "ripped it."

As perceived in my mind, a very large lady loomed up out of the mist! She was a neighbor of ours. It was in the mid '20s. She was looking down at me and she was really mad at me. From where I was looking up at her, she looked very big and very mad.

I had finally done something especially bad, and I knew that I would have to pay. I will never forget that very large and very mad lady that I did something really bad to! She lived in the same block that we did. Only she was on the street just behind us. I will never forget her; her name was Mrs. Oglesby....

3.2 *General Francis de Guingand stands in front of one of Montgomery's caravans* (Imperial War Museum)

3.3 *B-17 contrails alert the enemy to their presence* (World Conflict Images)

3.4 B-17s join with other flights for a long mission (Captain Joseph J. Merhar Jr. Collection, AFHRA)

3.5 *99th BG B-17s fly over the Swiss Alps*

3.6 *Contrails fill the sky as a 99th BG squadron of B-17s flies toward their mission*

3.7 *Captain Richard Evans teaches navigation students*

4.1 *Big brother, Stewart, and Dick, second from left, sit with their mother and brothers, Tom and toddler John, in front of their home, 306 Magnolia Avenue, Knoxville, TN, during the 1920s*

CHAPTER 4

"I'M SORRY, MRS. OGLESBY"

When I was a little boy, even before my mom called me "a little man," I remember my dad saying, "We remember good things very well, Dick, but bad things are never forgotten." I probably wouldn't have remembered Dad had said that if it hadn't been, that a really bad thing really did happen to me when I was little. Dad said that I remembered this bad thing very well because I was in it up to my eyeballs!

This bad thing happened on Linden Avenue, the street behind Magnolia Avenue where we lived. Dad sure was right. I don't just remember that something bad happened on Linden Avenue, I remember exactly what it was that happened, how it happened, where it happened, who it was that did it, and who it was that put me up to it. It was a long time ago; I was about seven and a half years old.

I believe it was probably late October 1926. My brother Stewart's chums were standing around one afternoon down on Linden Avenue when I walked up to them. They asked me right off if I had heard about Butch. I said, "No, I hadn't heard about Butch." I added, however, that I did know who Butch was. I knew that Mr. Butcher, a neighbor who lived behind us on Linden Avenue, had a bulldog that he had named "Butch." I remember thinking that I thought it was clever of Mr. Butcher to name his dog "Butch," him being in the Butcher family... and all.

My big brother's friends then went on to tell me about Butch. They said that Mr. Butcher had come home from work the day before and had unchained Butch so that Butch could run around in his yard and other people's yards to get some exercise.

Well, there was an older couple, the Oglesbys, who lived across the street from the Butchers. The Oglesbys didn't like Butch, probably because the Oglesbys didn't have a dog or any children who might have wanted a dog. What the Oglesbys had, instead of a dog, were a lot of nice flowers. What old Butch had was a bad habit of playing in the Oglesbys' flowerbeds. Also, Butch would dribble some on Mrs. Oglesby's nice roses. Everybody knew Mrs. Oglesby liked to water her roses herself.

My big brother's friends then told me that yesterday when Mr. Butcher turned old Butch loose, Butch made a beeline for the Oglesbys' front yard. They said Butch first sniffed some flowers to wet on and dirt to scratch on; then he sniffed out a bone. Butch then brought the bone back over to his yard and sat down to chew on it for a while. Afterwards he decided he would take a nap.

After a little while, Mr. Butcher called Butch, but Butch didn't wake up and come to him. So, Mr. Butcher came around from behind his house to find Butch and wake him up. Mr. Butcher found old Butch, but Butch wasn't just asleep. Butch was dead.

I couldn't believe that Butch could really be dead; I hadn't heard that Butch was even sick. That's when my brother's friends told me the rest. Butch wasn't sick at all. Mrs. Oglesby had poisoned old Butch!

I couldn't believe my ears; that was the very worst thing I had ever heard about in my whole life. I couldn't believe that somebody would poison somebody else's dog just because their dog had to go right away, right when he just happened to be looking around in somebody else's flowers.

My brother's friends went on to tell me that the meat, which Butch had picked up in the Oglesbys' front yard, was "found to contain strychnine." I had never seen strychnine but heard it was a really bad poison. I remember thinking that a bottle of strychnine would probably have a skull and cross-bones on it like the old iodine bottles did.

I wondered if the Oglesbys had maybe broken one of the Scout Laws when they poisoned old Butch. I hadn't learned all twelve laws yet so I couldn't be sure. But I figured that the Oglesbys probably didn't know about the Scout laws anyway; so, I guessed the laws wouldn't count for them, or for Butch either.

Still, I couldn't get what the Oglesbys had done to Butch out of my head. I decided there must be some real laws against poisoning a neighbor's dog that had just scratched around some while he was wetting somebody's flowers. I was really upset, and I started thinking that something should be done to the Oglesbys to "pay them back" for what they had done to poor old Butch.

When I told my brother's chums what I thought, they said they were in "complete agreement" and that they had already come up with a "proper course of action." I couldn't wait to hear what my brother's chums had planned for the Oglesbys.

Well, as it happened, they couldn't wait to tell me about their plan either, and they went on to describe a plan, which I knew my dad would say was "ingenious." They said they knew where they could get some tar, which, if warmed up would easily drip from a can onto the Oglesbys' sidewalks. It would be sure to stay there for a very long time, maybe forever. This would not just be punishment for the Oglesbys, it would also warn other people who might be planning to poison some other dogs that had dribbled on their flowers.

Remembering how much Mrs. Oglesby liked her flowers and being what Dad called "a perfectly normal kid," I thought my brother's friends' plan was great. I was very excited when I asked them when was it going to be done and could I watch?

They said it should be done on Halloween to make it look like pranksters did it, and that Halloween was "tomorrow night." Then, they all slapped me on the back to show me how much they liked me. They said I could not only watch, but, in fact, I could be the one to pour the tar!

In those days, I slept in a double bed with my big brother, Stewart. I could tell he was getting a good night's sleep that night; his eyes were shut. I could tell his were shut because mine were open. Mine stayed that way the whole night.

As I lay there, I tried to sort out just what had happened. I figured that something had come up, which was going to give me a chance to show that I was a big boy. But I had not thought that my chance was going to turn out the way it did. I decided that my brother's friends, who had said they were my friends, too, must have decided that I really wanted to help a whole lot because I hadn't told them that I wasn't anxious to help that much. They had said, as they pounded me on my back that they would meet me with the "tools" I would need to carry out my mission. They would meet me same time, same place, tomorrow night.

I couldn't remember going to school the next day but my friends told me I was there but said I was acting funny. I made sure that I was right where my brother's friends told me to be the next night. I even got there early so I could tell them I had decided not to take them up on their offer before they went to a lot of trouble melting the tar and all.

But I wasn't early enough. When I got there, the tar was already at the right temperature and it was already in two buckets. No brush was required they told me. All I would have to do was to walk up and down in front of the Oglesbys' house and tilt the buckets so that the tar would run out in a nice stream onto Mrs. Oglesby's sidewalks. I might make some wavy lines and circles if I wanted to, they added.

I wasn't sure how I got there but suddenly I realized that I was standing in the dark, under a tree, in front of the Nichols' house, with my arms being straightened out by the weight of two buckets of warm tar. I was told where to stand and someone had pointed me down the sidewalk towards Mrs. Oglesby's house. Without moving my feet, I turned and looked over my shoulder, thinking I should run through the plan one more time. I was too late; my new friends were gone. They were running towards the empty house across Linden Avenue. I knew that the old house would give them a good view of me tarring the Oglesbys' sidewalks.

To this day, I don't know why but I just started walking. My heart was pounding so hard in my chest I thought I would be able to see my sweater popping in and out if I looked down. Honor-bright, I did look down but I couldn't see my sweater pounding the way my heart was. I started walking straight ahead. The Oglesbys' house was in the middle of a double lot with flower gardens on both sides of their house. In a moment, I arrived at the place on the sidewalk that lined up with their hedge which I knew was the start of their two lots.

I tilted the buckets just a little bit and kept on walking. In a minute, I looked back over my shoulder at the two black lines dogging me. They were thin, straight lines. I tilted the buckets and started swinging them to make the lines wider and wavy. I was thinking about my friends in the empty house and was sure they would like my lines better if they were wider and wavier.

I walked past the house to the hedge at the other end of the Oglesbys' double lot. Then I turned around and started back, being careful not to step in the wet tar. Looking back up the Oglesbys' sidewalk, I could see where my thin lines ended and my heavy, wavy lines began. Soon I arrived again in the middle of the Oglesbys' sidewalk and without stopping turned and walked right up to their front porch.

Their house was darker than I thought it would be. The other houses in the block were dark too. I couldn't see anyone but I remember thinking they couldn't see me either. I was afraid of the dark, but I thought the dark was better than having someone come up and ask me what I thought I was doing there.

Then suddenly, I felt better. "This is a cinch; this is a cinch," I shouted silently to myself, "this will show the Oglesbys." Then I shouted again to myself, "The Oglesbys killed a dog. They killed poor old Butch. It serves them right."

At the Oglesbys' steps, I turned around and headed back towards Linden Avenue. I felt better; my buckets were getting lighter. This was fun! I decided I should make some circles, and some Xs since I was right in front of the Oglesbys' house. I was sure my brother's friends would be watching and would think my making some Xs was a good plan.

In a minute the tar just stopped; I was surprised that it was all gone. Then, I got afraid all over again and I didn't know why. I darted across the street to the empty house, my buckets flying behind me, empty but dripping the last of the tar. I couldn't wait; I knew my brother's friends would be pounding me on the back, which would make me feel a lot better.

In a moment, I was on the front porch, peering through a broken window at an empty room. It was dark inside, but I could tell no one was in there. That's when I remembered... it was Halloween!

I remember thinking, too, that these were all really good reasons why I should be someplace else. I took off across Linden Avenue once more and cut through the Nichols' side-yard toward our common alley. I dumped my buckets, still dripping tar, into the Nichols' trashcan. I can still remember thinking that the Nichols would be mad at me because I had spilled some tar inside their clean trashcans. (Many times, I've thought it's funny how one can remember things like that after half a century but not remember where one parked one's car a half hour before.)

I then ran up the alley to our garage, raced across our back yard, took our high outside steps two at a time, opened our back door, and then took our inside steps two at a time, too.

In a flash, I was upstairs inside my room with my bedroom door closed very quietly behind me. I immediately sat down on the edge of my bed to catch my breath. My heart was pounding like it might bust right out of my chest. It was really dark in my room, and it stayed really dark. I didn't turn the lights on that whole night.

I have no memory of what happened next. I can't remember going to bed or getting up or going to school the next morning. I wasn't able to remember anything that happened at school or when I got home after school.

On the other hand, I can remember hearing Dad very clearly when he came home from High School. He looked around for me right away and found me. I was sitting on our back steps holding my knees. Without looking at me, Dad said he would see me in my room, which meant that he would be up there in a hurry and that I had better be there.

In a moment, I was sitting on the edge of my bed. And I was starting to think about how Dad had played varsity basketball at Oberlin College in Ohio during his entire college career. I remembered that in his senior year, Dad wasn't just the captain of his team; he was the coach. Oberlin had won their regional championship every year that Dad was there. Dad's college pictures showed that he had lots of muscles back then, and I knew he still liked to stay in shape even though he was now a professor. While I was waiting for him in my room, I was thinking about Dad being in good shape.

Also, I got to thinking about the old-fashioned, worn-out razor strap that Dad kept over the top of the door in the room that my brother and I slept in. That strap was already old-fashioned when I first saw it, but Dad pointed out "it was worn out only with respect to its original purpose." Dad didn't use the strap to sharpen razors anymore; he said he used it on my big brother and me to sharpen us up a little. Also, I should say that while my dad used this wide leather strap on Stewart and me a few times, he never left any scars. And we were always okay the next day. My brother and I knew Dad never really liked having to actually do it, which is just what, Dad would always say after he had actually done it.

Suddenly, I heard Dad's footsteps coming up the stairs. In seconds, he was in the room and had closed the door behind him. I could tell he wasn't looking at me as he walked past where I was sitting on the edge of my bed even though I was not looking up but looking mostly at the floor. I could tell, too, when Dad turned around and leaned against the desk where my brother Stewart and I did our homework. I could see his feet move. Then Dad folded his arms on his chest (which I knew was a bad sign). Then he turned around and looked at me for a whole minute. Finally, Dad said, "What am I going to do with you, Dick?"

I didn't think Dad sounded so mad and he really didn't look like he was that mad either at first. It was when Dad noticed that I had gotten the razor strap down from its place above the door and had put it on the old iron bed beside me that Dad got really mad. Dad had never looked that mad at me before; I couldn't understand why he got so mad so fast. It would be a few years before I would learn that Dad thought I had gotten the razor strap down and put it on the bed beside me, figuring Dad would feel sorry for me and wouldn't whap me so hard. That was why Dad got madder at me than he ever had before.

But that wasn't what I was thinking at all. I knew I had done the wrong thing and I knew I should get a spanking, and a hard one. I had thought that if I got the strap down, Dad would know that I knew I had done the wrong thing, was sorry and expected to get "a good, hard spanking." I didn't understand for years how a "hard spanking" could ever be a "good spanking."

Dad just looked at me for another whole minute after he saw the strap on the bed. He would look at the strap then back at me. Years later Dad would laugh and say, "I didn't know what I should do, Dick, with you or the strap."

Many times, my thoughts have wondered back to that distant but unforgettable day. It has always seemed to me that maybe Dad saw in my eyes that I knew I had done something really bad this time, and that I was trying to tell him how sorry I was by getting the strap down.

I remember Dad just kept on looking at me; then finally he got up and walked towards me. When he leaned over my bed, I thought my heart would stop; it had been pounding so hard for two days. But Dad didn't even touch me and he didn't tell me to get up and bend over either. He just picked up the strap, walked over to the door and put it back up on top of the door in its special place where my brother and I could always see it. Then, with his back to me, Dad took out his handkerchief and started wiping off his glasses. And he blew his nose. That's when I knew that Dad was crying, too!

Finally, Dad walked back towards me and stood in front of me. I had slid off my bed and was on my knees, on the floor, looking at the floor. I really was. I couldn't look at Dad because I was so ashamed. I just looked at Dad's shoes.

Then, I felt my dad's hand on my head. "Dick," he said, "I'm sure you didn't do this alone; and

I'm not going to ask you to tell me who was involved with you. But I must know one thing. You were the one who actually poured the tar, is that right?"

I said, "Yes sir; I was the one. I poured the tar. That's right, Dad."

Dad didn't say anything for a minute but then he said, "Well then, look at me, Son. I want you to know that you're not alone in this. I will stand with you."

I couldn't understand; I knew I had done the wrong thing. But my dad had said he was "going to stand with me," that "I wasn't alone." I remember holding on to my dad's pant legs because I didn't want him to see me crying; but then I realized that my tears were getting Dad's pants wet. I looked up and I was afraid all over again. But Dad didn't seem to mind very much that I had gotten his pants legs wet.

At first, I guess I cried because I felt so afraid and so alone. Then, I believe I kept on crying because I was so ashamed. I had let my dad down. Finally, I guess I kept on crying because I loved my dad so much, and because he had said that he would stand with me. That's when I started wondering where it was that Dad and I were going to be standing together.

"Now, Dick," Dad finally said, "straighten up and look at me. Here's what we must do. You must apologize to Mrs. Oglesby. You are going to have to go down to her house and tell her that you are sorry for what you did. I will come along but I will stay out on the sidewalk. You must walk up to her door and tell her yourself. You must apologize, Son, for what you did to Mrs. Oglesby's sidewalks. Do you understand what I am saying to you?"

I said I understood, but I don't think I really understood. The full gravity of having to face Mrs. Oglesby after tarring her sidewalks hadn't sunk in yet. Also, a full understanding of the kind of father I had hadn't sunk in either.

When I had gotten to bed that night after pouring the tar, I had tossed and turned. Mom used to say, "we toss and turn" when we can't get to sleep because we have something on our minds. After Dad left me in my room, I thought to myself that Dad had fixed it so that I was going to be tossing and turning two nights running.

The next afternoon before supper time, Dad and I walked down to the Oglesbys' house. We didn't cut through the alley the way I always did. We walked down Castle Street and turned right on Linden Avenue, which took longer, which was okay with me. I noticed that the fall leaves were on the Nichols' lawn as we passed. I noticed, too, that there weren't any leaves on Mrs. Oglesby's lawn.

As we came closer to the Oglesbys' house, my heart started pounding again. I didn't look down at my sweater like I had done before; I was already looking at Mrs. Oglesby's flowers. I noticed for the first time ever just how nice Mrs. Oglesby's flowers looked.

My tar had gone dry. It looked like it couldn't ever be scraped off. I thought Mrs. Oglesby's house would never look nice again. That's when I remembered what Mom had told me once. "Dick, Mrs. Oglesby can't have any little boys or girls. She just has her nice house and her pretty flowers to keep her company."

Dad stopped in front where the sidewalks came together. Then he turned towards the

Oglesbys' house. He could see tar on one side of him and tar on the other side, also tar in front of him. Dad shook his head from side to side like he couldn't believe all that tar.

I walked on up to the Oglesbys' front steps the way Dad said I had to. I hadn't noticed before how the blue-grey paint on the Oglesbys' front porch looked newer and nicer than the paint on the other porches in our neighborhood. I climbed up the high, wide steps and knocked on the door. Then, I looked up at the door and waited for it to open. I could feel my heart pounding against my sweater again, but I didn't look down at it. I just looked up at where Mrs. Oglesby would come out.

But no one came right away. Then, when I raised my arm to knock again, the door squeaked and opened really slow. All I could see in the doorway was Mrs. Oglesby's apron. Mrs. Oglesby always wore her great big apron, whether she was working on her flowers or not.

Then, I looked up at Mrs. Oglesby like Dad said I had to. But she didn't look down at me at all. She was looking straight out over my head at Dad. Then she and Dad kept looking at each other for a long time and I didn't know what to do. I thought neither of them looked too mad though and they hadn't said anything to each other, either.

Finally, I heard my own voice saying, "I'm sorry, Mrs. Oglesby." Dad had said I had to say I was sorry, and I had finally gotten it out.

Not 'til then did Mrs. Oglesby drop her head and look down at me. I thought she looked at me kind of funny though and for a very long time. But maybe it just seemed like a long time. Then, she did something, which I didn't understand. She didn't look like she was really mad at me. Mrs. Oglesby looked like she was surprised to see me, like she didn't even know that I was "the little Evans boy," which is what everyone called me back then. Then, she looked like she was going to cry.

Mrs. Oglesby kept looking at me for maybe a whole minute. Finally, she said very quiet-like that she was sorry too.

After that, she didn't look at Dad or me anymore. She just backed up into her house and closed the door without slamming it.

I didn't know what I was supposed to do. Turning my head as far around as I could without moving my feet, I looked back out towards the sidewalk and towards Dad. I hadn't known before that I could turn my head that far around without moving my feet. I knew I looked funny with my head turned that far, but I didn't know what else to do.

In a minute, Dad said, "Come along, Dick." Only half-turned around, I turned the rest of me around and walked back down Mrs. Oglesby's high, wide steps and out her tarred sidewalk towards Dad. I thought as I walked that I didn't have to mind where I put my feet; the tar wasn't sticking to my shoes at all. It was just sticking to Mrs. Oglesby's sidewalk, and I could tell somehow that it was going to stay stuck there for a very long time.

Dad took my hand and we walked back up Linden Avenue together. Dad didn't look like he was too mad but he didn't look down at me either. I didn't say a word. When we reached the corner and turned up Castle Street towards Magnolia Avenue, I remember thinking that my heart had finally stopped pounding so hard. That's when I said, "Dad, why did Mrs. Oglesby look surprised to see me? And why did she say she was sorry too?"

Without looking down at me, Dad said, "I think Mrs. Oglesby was surprised, Dick, when she saw you. I think she was sorry too, very sorry. I believe Mrs. Oglesby thought that you were going to be a much bigger boy, Son. I believe when she got a good look at you, she realized that she had done something wrong, too." Dad took a deep breath and looked at the ground like he felt truly sad. Then, he said, "But you know, Son, I believe you may have even helped Mrs. Oglesby."

Then we turned onto Magnolia Avenue toward where we lived. I was looking down at my feet again, but I could tell my dad was looking down at me. And somehow, I knew my dad was smiling.

That's when Dad said to me, "But, please, Dick, don't ever, ever help anybody that way again."

4.2 *A Knoxville home like Mrs. Oglesby's* (McClung Historical Collection)

5.1 *Stewart and baby Bobby, Dick's elder brothers, play with their parents in the yard*

CHAPTER 5
SMOKY MOUNTAIN LOGGING TRAIN

I didn't know what was happening; it wasn't clear in my mind. Actually, I'm not sure I had a real mind yet; I was just two years old and I was still really little. I had heard my mother and my dad say that I wasn't even a toddler yet, that I was a lap baby.

I knew I was little because my mother and dad said that my brother was "a bigger boy." I had learned very early what "big" meant; it meant my big brother got a head start on me that would keep him ahead of me always. I didn't think that was fair. My brother's name was Stewart; he was named after our grandfather, my mother's father.

My name was "Dickybird"; somehow, I knew I wasn't named after anybody. One time after I had gotten a little older, I asked Dad how come I wasn't named after somebody.

Without looking up from his paper, Dad said, "What are you talking about, Dick? You were named after millions of people. You were named after everybody who was born before you."

Dad would often answer us kids this way to make us think and to make a little joke at the same time. "You know what I mean, Dad," I said "You and Mom named Stewart, after Grandpa Stewart. But you didn't name me after anybody. How come, Dad, and if Stewart has Grandpa's name why is he called 'Pug' sometimes?" Dad did respond to the nickname question, "Why, Dick, don't you notice a family resemblance of pug noses as he pointed to his own?" The pug nose seems to be a family trait that runs with the men."

I remember one time when my mother was holding me on her lap when we were going to the Smoky Mountains on the train. She never held Stewart on her lap that way. Stewart could run around between the seats in the passenger car and he didn't need anybody to hold him. I heard Mom say on one trip that I couldn't even "toddle" very well.

Looking back, I would guess it was the summer of 1924 or 1925, even before my dog "Judge" came to our house, looked around and then stayed the rest of his life.

Dad's school where he was the principal had let out, and there was a lot of excitement as our family got ready to go to Elkmont, a tiny, little town with only one store, way back up in the Smoky Mountains above Gatlinburg near Wonderland Park.

Stewart wanted to ask the conductor if he could get out on the logging cars that we could see behind our car; but Dad said even if the conductor was crazy enough to let Stewart ride out there, he wasn't. Dad told Stewart that he didn't have a crazy father.

There was only one passenger car on the logging train. We had to climb up steep steps to get into that car. Dad hurried us up because he would get really embarrassed; he said he didn't like to hold other people up while he was loading all the things Mom insisted on taking to Elkmont.

Dad said the horse-drawn streetcar that went by our house on Magnolia Avenue was "the first leg of our all-day journey to the mountains" and that it was fifty-five whole miles up to Elkmont from our house.

Early in the morning, Dad would put our things in cardboard boxes and set them out on the sidewalk at the corner where the streetcar would stop. He would then make three trips from our house to the corner with our boxes. Then, when the horse-drawn streetcar finally came and stopped in front of our pile, Dad would pile our things and all of us into the streetcar as fast as he could.

Dad was always embarrassed to hold up other people while he was piling our things and us into something. The motorman would hit a bell that clanged to get Dad to hurry it up. This would make Dad's face turn red. Mom thought it was funny, but I could tell that Dad didn't think it was funny at all.

It took our streetcar maybe two hours or so to get to the train station. Dad said our horse moved along pretty well as long as he was headed for the car barn where the horses lived; but that "after we passed their barn, they would always slow down, and they weren't in a hurry anymore."

When we finally got to Gay Street, which was our main street in Knoxville where the Southern Railroad depot was, we had to climb down out of the streetcar and pile all our things on the sidewalk by the curb. Then we had to walk a whole block back to the Southern Railroad Train Station where the logging train was smoking and getting ready to take us up into the Great Smoky Mountains.

When we came to the Gay Street viaduct, we walked halfway across so that we could look right down on top of the Smoky Mountain logging train. The smoke from the engine came right up at us. I still remember how excited I was having the smoke come right up at me like it would hit me and maybe hurt some. It didn't hurt though; it just swirled all around us all without making any noise at all. Dad held me up so that I could look over and see the train down below and watch the smoke come right up at me. It might have been the very first time in my life that I got really excited. It was just wonderful, I thought, how the smoke seemed so big like thunderclouds but didn't hurt at all when it came up and swirled all around me.

Dad had to make two trips to get all our stuff and us from the Gay Street Bridge to the Southern Railroad ticket office. Then he had to make two more trips to move our boxes and us to the tracks where we could climb up into the passenger car on the Elkmont train. Dad liked to spring words we didn't know on us. He said, "This family is going to 'portage' me to death getting us from our house to the train even before we get on our train and start our train ride to the Smokies."

We were not allowed to climb up into the passenger car or hand our things up 'til a man that Dad said was called "the conductor" yelled out, "All aboard. All aboard for the Great Smoky Mountains; all aboard that's a goin' aboard for Alcoa, Maryville, Townsend, Walland and Wonderland Park." After the conductor said all those names, everybody crowded together so that they could get on the train first and try to get a seat next to a window. Dad told Mom to go ahead of him and try to get us some seats and that he would wait until everybody was on the train. Then he would load all our stuff on to the passenger car.

After we had scrambled, found seats and Dad had loaded all our things, Dad sat down beside Mom and said, "Whew, I'm sure glad to get that over with." I couldn't talk yet, but I knew what it was that Dad was glad to get over with; I had heard him say that he was "sick and tired of hauling around, all day long, all the things that Mom thought she would need up in the Smoky Mountains."

After a little while, the train jerked hard and started puffing; then we started chugging very slowly out of Knoxville's nice Southern Railway Station. It was very exciting. The man Dad said was "the conductor" shouted from the front of our car: "Next stop, Alcoa and Maryville, Tennessee; next: Walland; final stop: Wonderland Park, in the heart of the Smoky Mountains."

Dad said, "At last we're on our way. It's fifty-two miles to Elkmont and it will take the rest of the day to get to our cottage. But all our things are aboard, we're moving, and I'm sitting down." We had just passed under the Gay Street Bridge, which we had been standing on earlier, when Dad said, "When are we going to eat something, Hellie?" Dad called our Mom "Hellie" because her name was Helen.

Mom then told Dad, "I packed a picnic lunch, Ernest. It's with our things in the baggage car; we'll get it out and have lunch after we have made the stop at Marysville."

Dad said, "Okay, Hellie, whatever you say." I noticed that Mom always set our eating schedule and that Dad never argued with Mother. Actually, Dad didn't argue with Mother on any subject. I heard him tell Stewart one time that he didn't like to "ruffle Mother's feathers" or do anything that would "cause her to get her dander up." This was before I knew what "ruffle," meant and I still don't know what "dander" is, or how you get it up.

It was a long ride from Knoxville to Elkmont back in those days; I didn't know how far fifty-five miles was, but Dad said it was way back up in the heart of the Smokies, "at the confluence of Little River and Jakes Creek." He told Mom it would just be getting dark when we would finally get to our cottage, way back up there on Jakes Creek in the Smoky Mountains.

Later when I woke up, I could hear Mom talking to Dad. She was talking like I had been on the train before, but I couldn't remember ever riding that train before. It was so rough and so noisy 'specially when we were getting started and getting stopped each time that I thought that I would never forget riding to the Smokies on that old logging train.

After a while, our train started to slow down and the conductor yelled out, "Next stop, Maryville, Tennessee; all off for Maryville and Alcoa." When the train stopped some people got off. Then quickly new ones got on. Suddenly, we were on our way again, hugging and jerking along the way.

Our car, which was right behind the engine and the coal car, would be jerked forward, then we would jerk the baggage car, and then the baggage car would jerk the first logging car. When the jerks got all the way back to the last logging car, the train would start moving very slowly. Then each car, starting from the back, would bang back into the car ahead of it until the baggage car hit us in the back, and then we would hit the coal car. Mother held me tight while the cars kept banging into us, first, in the back, and then in the front until we finally got going.

I heard Dad say that he could see the empty logging cars behind us when we went around curves. He said we would unhook the logging cars at Walland and go on up to Wonderland Park without them. Then, when the train came back, the cars at Walland would already be loaded with logs and ready for us to hook onto them again and pull them back to Knoxville where they would be sawed into boards to make things.

Dad said, "Our final destination was our cottage near the Appalachian Club House at the confluence of Jakes Creek and Little River." The train, however, would stop down in front of the new

Wonderland Park Hotel, the end of the line for the Elkmont train in those wonderful old days. A mule-pulled wagon would take the family the last three miles to Elkmont. Dad always called our days together up in the Smokies "those wonderful old days."

I fell asleep again in Mom's lap, but I woke up when we came along side Little River. I could see lots of big rocks in the water. With water splashing over the rocks the way it did, it made the water look white and sparkly in the sunshine. Mom held me, and she started holding me too tight. Then she started crying, very soft and quiet like.

Mom and dad had been talking about my brother, Bobby, but I hadn't seen him get on our streetcar, or our train either. Mom put her head down so that her cheek was touching mine and she got my cheek wet. I knew Mom was crying. I knew what crying was; I did some myself. Dad had put his arm around my Mom's shoulder, and he looked like he was quite sad, too. I would get afraid when Mom cried but I liked it when my dad put his arm around my mom.

I didn't know where my big brother Stewart was, but I had seen him running up and down the aisle. I knew he wanted to get up in front with the engineer since Dad wouldn't let him get out and ride on a logging car in the back. Stewart was six or seven then I think. I couldn't count yet, so I wasn't sure.

After a while, it started getting a little dark as we chugged around the turns in "Little River Valley." Finally, Mom stopped crying and Dad got some sandwiches out of our things in the baggage car. Mom wiped her eyes with her handkerchief and took charge of dishing out our food.

When we got off the train at Wonderland Park, the sun had gone down behind the mountains, but it wasn't dark yet.

Dad found our wagon driver and asked him to bring his wagon over to our pile of things. Dad helped Mom climb up beside the driver; then he handed me up to Mom. Dad and the driver then piled our boxes and things into the back of the wagon and tied ropes around them. Finally, Dad and Stewart climbed up in the back and sat on some of our boxes. I didn't see my other big brother, Bobby, get on but I didn't think about him then because Mom and Dad weren't talking about him anymore.

Our family would stay at Elkmont all summer long, everybody but Dad. Dad would teach summer school during the week and he would have to ride up and back on the logging train on weekends. Sometimes he would bring friends with him to swim and hike and play horseshoes.

The thing I remember most about those "wonderful old days" was getting baths in a sink that was right next to a big window that stretched across the back of our cottage. Like the windows, the sink was big too, bigger than we needed for washing our hands and faces. Mom would wash clothes in our big sink... also little kids.

I remember that I sure liked how the warm water felt in the sink and how the sunlight coming through the window made me feel when I got a bath. Mom would let me soak, and I could look out the windows that went all the way across the back of our cottage, and I could see Jakes Creek in the windows. The creek ran right behind our cottage, three floors below the windows. Stewart would often be down there in the creek making dams with a buddy while I was up in the warm sink water soaking.

I believe I really do remember my baths in that nice, warm water, in the sun, looking down on that splashing, "crystal-clear mountain stream." It was back in the early '20s; I thought things were ever so nice "way back in the early '20s."

But, when I think about it now, I don't believe that it was the good view that I got of Jakes Creek or the view of my brother and his friends down there playing that I liked so much while I was getting my baths and soaking in that warm water. I think it was probably the good view that I got of my cousin Marion. Aunt Gene would plop Marion in the warm water beside me and let us both soak for a while.

It was on one of those early train rides going back to Knoxville when I first started to understand why my brother Bobby seemed to always be around somewhere, but I never got to see him. Mom had started to cry again and after a while she handed me over to Dad. That's when I heard Mom say, "Oh, Ernest, how can I ever get on this train without remembering that ride back to Knoxville with our little boy wrapped up in that small cardboard box back there all by himself in the baggage compartment? Why did our dear little Bobby have to die like he did? What did we do so wrong?"

I didn't understand. I hadn't heard about "dying" yet. I didn't know what that meant, but I was afraid because Mom was afraid. I'm not sure when I finally did understand that Bobby had come after Stewart but ahead of me and that my brother Bobby had already gone away before I came to live with my Mom and Dad.

I remember that, during the early part of my life, Bobby was always a presence in our family like he was somewhere, but that I didn't know where to look for him. Mom and Dad couldn't ever forget Bobby. I guessed later that they really didn't want to forget him. I think they blamed themselves that Bobby died, and they couldn't ever forgive themselves.

A number of years passed before I finally understood what happened to him. Dad told me that they had taken Bobby up to Elkmont before his second birthday and that he got sick with "the colic," an acute infection in the lower intestine, especially associated with babies back in those days. "There were only a few automobiles in Knoxville back then," Dad said, "and not too many roads outside of Knoxville. No roads had been cut through the mountains to Elkmont yet."

The logging train was the only way to get into the Smokies and the only way out. When my brother, Bobby, got the colic, the next train due out of Elkmont was three days away. But the colic killed my brother, Bobby, in two days.

Dad finally told me years later. After Bobby died, the family had to wait another whole day and night before he and Mom and my brother, Stewart, could ride back to Knoxville in the passenger car on the logging train. Dad told me, as he looked at me through misty glasses, that Bobby had made his last ride back to Knoxville behind the passenger car on a shelf in the baggage car. "Your other big brother that you never got to know," Dad said, "had to make the trip back to Knoxville in a small box."

"He was too little to have to die," Dad told me one time when I older. "When your brother Bobby got sick, your mother and I had nowhere to turn. We could only watch him. We had done everything we knew how to do. He had never been sick like that in Knoxville. We were helpless, trapped up there in our wonderful cottage in our Smoky Mountains."

"We thought he was getting better when we finally went to bed. It was 3 o'clock in the morning when your mother finally shut her eyes. She was so afraid; she just shook in my arms like she was so cold and couldn't get warm. I just held her close, trying to make her warm. My heart was breaking because I couldn't do anything for her or our little boy."

"I woke up suddenly right at 4:30 in the morning," Dad said, "and I very quickly slipped out of our bed to take a look at your brother in his crib. He was on your mother's side and I started around the foot of the bed, but I could tell before I reached his crib that our little boy was gone. He was cold and dead."

"Your mother had finally fallen asleep. I didn't know how to tell her. I just sat there in a chair beside the crib with a blanket wrapped around me. And I just watched her, dreading the moment when she would awaken. I felt so guilty that I hadn't been able to do anything at all for our son."

Dad then looked right at me and said, "Your mother slept almost two hours before she stirred. Then suddenly she sensed that I wasn't beside her. She bolted upright and looked at me. I was still sitting beside the crib."

"Then she screamed, and she couldn't stop... and I didn't know how to help her. I was terrified and I felt ashamed that I didn't know how to help her."

*5.2 Dick, left, at the age of his first trip to the Smokies
with his mother and older brother, Stewart*

5.3 *Engine 105 takes families to the great Smoky Mountains* (McClung Historical Collection)

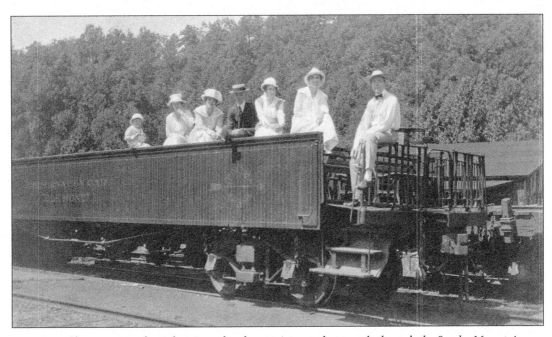

5.4 *Dick's parents, to the right, sit on the observation car that travels through the Smoky Mountains*

5.5 *Bath in the big sink is a special memory at "Osocozy"*

5.6 *Dick's mother, left, and his Aunt Marian enjoy the front porch of "Osocozy"*

5.7 *Dick, left, and friends play in Jakes Creek*

6.1 *General Montgomery talks with Captain Richard E. Evans and his B-17 crew,*
Castel Benito Airdrome, Tripoli, Libya

CHAPTER 6

THE KING AND I

King George VI on Tripoli did land,
General Montgomery, of El Alamein, his visit had planned.
His Highness, from Ike had flown that day...
A night with Monty in Tripoli to stay.

On the morrow, he would fly to Malta for a visit.
To this blue, green and white isle in the Med, exquisite!
His mission... to bestow on a people, most brave,
A medal of honor for the lives they gave.

Malta, a palette of brilliant blues, greens and whites,
Had resisted the Nazis through the days and the nights.
The King George Cross must have seemed little to give
To those who no longer had their lives to live.

Richard Eager

It was the morning of my third day in Tripoli, the day that King George VI would stop by to pay tribute to his victorious 8th Army. Up at 0600 hours, I had breakfasted at the Tripoli British-American Officers Club. By 0730 I was winding my way in a jeep through the streets of Tripoli. I had asked Lieutenant Johnson and Technical Sergeant Dale Owens to meet me at the B-17 at 0900. As I drove through the baroque gate of Mussolini's Castel Benito Airdrome, I could see my men standing by our B-17 across the field.

We had performed some minor maintenance and had flight-tested *Theresa Leta* the previous day. **Lieutenant John W. Poston** wanted to go along with us, and we were pleased to have him aboard. He said it was his first ride in a B-17. John had become General Montgomery's aide-de-camp after Churchill ordered Monty to Cairo to assume command of the 8th Army. John, I guessed to be both Monty's aid and a liaison officer, i.e., a communications contact between the 8th Army's administrative and tactical headquarters.

John, I learned, had developed some considerable driving skills in motorcars and was anxious to try his hand at the controls of the B-17. I was pleased to oblige. He was a natural. He thought our machine "cornered" very well and he delighted in flying it across Tripoli Harbor at 500 feet, at 200 mph.

Previously, Monty had driven out on the Tripoli airfield with me to note where the King would be standing while the 8th Army band and the troops did their march-past. Monty thought the B-17 should be part of the show. I agreed. He picked a spot in front and to one side of a bombed-out hangar and battered tower and asked, "Would this be satisfactory?" I answered that it would, indeed, and that I would arrive with my crew early, dust off the B-17 and taxi it into a position where it could easily be seen by the deployed British 8th Army and by the arriving King George VI of England.

The next morning, Technical Sergeant Owens stood by the fire extinguisher while Lieutenant Johnson and I started the engines. Then Sergeant Owens led the way in his jeep as I taxied *Theresa Leta* to her spot of honor where the King could not miss her.

I was told that essentially all of His Majesty's troops remaining in Tripoli would be on hand for their king's visit, scheduled for 1100 hours. These troops started flowing through the battered entry to the airfield in British lorries at about 0800. Quite a few tanks and pieces of heavy artillery were also rumbling and trundling onto the airfield with these Brits.

This preliminary parade lasted an hour and a half. It took that long to get the British 8th Army onto the airfield. The plan seemed to be to park the heavy transport and big guns along the periphery of the field, leaving the center clear for the march-past planned for His Majesty, the King of England.

When the rest of our crewmen arrived, I suggested we drive to the main gate where we could observe, close-up, the march-past of the 8th Army's military vehicles and big guns as they entered Mussolini's Castel Benito Airdrome. It was a great day to be in Tripoli.

Truckload after truckload of British Commonwealth fighting men drove through that ornate, battered gate giving us friendly cheers, jeers and salutes as they passed. Not to be outdone, I lined up my crewmen and ordered them to stand at ease. Then, when an enthusiastic group of Britishers, Australians, Scottish Highlanders, South Afrikaners or Canadians approached, I would call up my group of eight, face about, and salute our allies. Clearly, both sides enjoyed the pleasant and genuine exchange.

When Staff Sergeant Chuck Ward, my 19-year-old tail-gunner, spotted a truckload of High- landers dressed, not for battle, but for a parade in their kilts, he could not resist a low whistle. For his efforts, he was rewarded with a first-rate, Scottish moon job. Observers from both hemispheres thought this an appropriate response to Sergeant Ward's gesture. Any question about the Scottish myth that suggests a disdain by the Scots for undergarments was dispelled with finality. We were shown the bare facts.

As I stood there with all that military machinery and humanity flowing about me, a scene from the First World War motion picture "The Big Parade" came to mind. In that mid '20s movie, which I had seen in the old Strand Theater in Knoxville, long lines of trucks, loaded with uniformed English, French and American young men could be seen moving slowly towards a distant, darkened horizon where rapier-like flashes from gunfire slashed the sky.

In that old '20s movie, a second line of trucks on that same road could be seen moving in the opposite direction, escaping the storm, and heading for the place from whence the first trucks had come. No sounds could be heard from the trucks returning from the flashing sky. Red Crosses on their sides were silent heralds, making clear the sad nature of their missions.

Years later, I would realize that in addition to the parades exiting south towards the Somme and Marne rivers, there were also parades, the same in character exiting north and east from those historic killing-fields. The youth of Germany were the silent occupants of these north and eastbound vehicles.

These "big parades" were continuous through the days and the nights during the fall of 1918. Finally, they came to a halt, late in the year, on November 11th. I would be born just ten weeks later in mid-January 1919. Years later, I would ask my dad about those World War One parades. He would understand that I feared I might be in such a parade in a second, even fiercer and desperate, World War.

The haunting memory that I have nursed for a lifetime has been that those young men, who fought along the Somme and the Marne Rivers west and east of Paris, had no control over their lives. As I was coming to life, they were being slaughtered. They did not have "a fighting chance." I vowed early on that I would do everything I could to give myself a fighting chance. I was sure that many of my generation thought as I did.

The parade that I was watching in Tripoli was a different kind of parade. No one was coming from the battlefield. The battles had been fought, the deadly contests won and lost. The trucks marked with red crosses had made their last trips to what I would hear Monty call "the killing fields." I would see no Red Cross trucks in this parade. This parade in Tripoli in the spring of 1943 was different. This was a victory parade, celebrating the first decisive Second World War Allied victory in North Africa. This was Monty's victory at El Alamein over Hitler's elite and favorite Army Commander, General Erwin Rommel, The Desert Fox.

But the jubilant mood of the celebration would not be reflected in the faces of all who passed. There would be unfilled spaces in the trucks, and there would be some on hand for the victory celebration who had escaped the killing fields but who had not had time to heal and forget.

Shortly after 1000 hours over by the battle-worn hangar and tower, I lined up my flight crew in front of the *Theresa Leta*. I had seen half a dozen dusty staff cars across the field heading in our direction. This I guessed to be Monty, the Victor at El Alamein. But it wasn't. It was a group of British general officers. I recognized General de Guingand immediately, but none of the others. These generals, I was sure, would include Monty's three Corps Commanders and members of his tactical staff. They would, of course, be on hand to pay their respects to their supreme commander, their King, who was coming to North Africa to thank them for service rendered to their home and country.

Lieutenant John Poston was heading our way with the largest of these Generals. "Here comes a General," I thought, "who looks like he is in command when he is still fifty yards away." I guessed that he was six feet-six and would weigh 240 pounds. Lieutenant Poston would tell me that this General was indeed about six-six but weighed only 17 stones. This was close enough for me since the British measure of weight, 17 stones, equaled 238 pounds. As the two men approached, I called my crew to attention. John and the jumbo-sized general stopped in front of us and I saluted.

I admit that in those days I enjoyed saluting people whom I had reason to admire and respect. I was aware also that junior officers who actually liked saluting their seniors risked being classified as "apple polishers" or worse. No matter; I was proud to salute this towering man, whom I didn't know anything about, except what I was told by his insignia and what I thought I could read in his large, pleasant, open face.

Poston spoke first, "General, this is Captain Richard Evans. General Eisenhower has sent him over to fly Monty about in a B-17; perhaps you have heard."

The General had heard all right; his broad smile made this clear. Besides, I was wearing a strange-looking uniform and standing directly in front of a foreign aircraft. I would very soon learn that this over-sized General was General Eisenhower's British **deputy** and that he would replace Ike as Allied Commander in North Africa when Ike would subsequently be transferred to the UK to take command of "**Operation Overlord**," the invasion of Europe.

Lieutenant Poston would have completed my introduction, but it wasn't necessary. The General, returning my salute in the manner of a man who savors time, had his hand up, down, and outstretched well before he came to a stop in front of me. I had to get my hand up quickly and back down from my forehead and into his. I mused, "Richard Eager, you don't want to keep a man as big as this one waiting." This greater-than-life Englishman grasped my hand, shook it vigorously, and said, "Captain Evans, I am General Maitland Wilson; I am very pleased to meet you. And please ask your men to stand at ease for a few minutes. I would like to take you over and introduce you to my fellow officers all around." He was already turning to return to the group of officers who had accompanied him to the airdrome, confident that I would be smart enough to catch up to him.

I glanced over my shoulder in the direction of Lieutenant Johnson, pointed a cocked finger at him indicating that he was in charge, and moved out quickly in an effort to catch up with this impressive, pleasant General and to see if I could get in step with his giant stride.

In a moment, General Wilson commenced my introduction to the principal members of Monty's tactical staff. It was clear that he was putting on a little show, a pleasant, hands-across-the-ocean sort of thing. "Captain Evans," he said, "this is Lieutenant General Brian Horrocks of 13 Corps, who faced General Rommel in the south between the Alam Halfa ridge and the **Qattara Depression** (the Qattara Canyon), sometimes called the Grand Canyon of Africa." Continuing, General Wilson said, "Possibly, you know, Captain, that El Alamein, an otherwise inauspicious Arab town, is strategically located between the Mediterranean in the north and the Qattara in the south, and sits astride a land-bridge which, militarily speaking, is the only entry from the west into Cairo, Alexandria, the Nile Delta and the Suez. Rommel attacked three times at El Alamein; and three times he was driven back by the forces of General Brian Horrocks. When "The Desert Fox" hightailed it from Alam el Halfa, it was his first decisive defeat and, though not immediately perceived as such, it was the beginning of the end for the Desert Fox and Hitler in North Africa."

I was pleased to smile and salute General Horrocks, whose slight frame and sharp features belied the inner strengths, which he must have mustered at Alam el Halfa.

"And this, Captain Evans, is Lieutenant General Oliver Leese of 30 Corps, who was the first to move forward through the coastal mine fields west of El Alamein and who, for twelve endless nights and days, continued to apply pressure that finally and inevitably resulted in the breakout to the west."

I saluted and shook hands with General Oliver Leese, handsome, youthful, smaller in stature, and clearly the youngest of the select group. He would serve again with Monty in Sicily and Italy, and he would assume command of the 8th Army when Monty would be summoned to England to prepare for the invasion of France.

"And this, Captain Evans," General Wilson continued, "is Lieutenant General Herbert Lumsden of X Corps, our 'fleet corps de elite' whose task it was to back up General Horrocks and General Leese along the entire 30-mile line, during the twelve-day battle for El Alamein. When the Italian lines in the north near the sea started to crumble, our corps de elite, equipped with scores of your splendid Sherman Tanks, forced an opening beyond the mine fields and through the lines of the Axis Armies. From that moment, The Desert Fox would be on the run, as you might say, for good."

I saluted and shook hands with General Lumsden. I would later learn that General Lumsden and Monty did not hit it off; I would learn too, that this would prove unfortunate for General Lumsden, who had not wished to return so soon to the pleasant but unrewarding service life in India, or In'ja, as Brits called it.

I was enjoying the tongue-in-cheek formality and the brief review on El Alamein. I understood that I was not entitled to the level of military courtesy being extended me, and I was sure my new friends knew I knew.

For a short moment in time, a Yank Army Air Corps Captain was the ranking representative of the U.S. Armed Forces in Tripolitania. My country's ally was making pleasant use of the time saluting its ally. My British friends were also bragging a bit and had need of a good listener. Listening was one of my good subjects. I had learned about listening from Dad. One time Dad said, "Dick, you really are a quite good listener. Why, sometimes you take on a look that suggests you really are interested. That's a fine trait, Son."

General Wilson turned and spoke to me. "And, Captain Evans, I understand that you have already met General Sir Francis de Guingand. Freddie, here, is Monty's Chief of Staff; and the way Monty operates, which is effective if unorthodox, Freddie wears two hats, functioning as Chief of Staff, as well as Monty's Chief of Operations. Monty reflects in his caravan on the entire situation; then with minimum assistance, draws up our battle plans, our important training plans and our vital logistic plans. General de Guingand must then see that the battle directives are properly drawn up, distributed, and executed. General de Guingand is kept quite busy changing hats and charging back and forth between Monty and his Corps Commanders."

Then I saluted and shook hands once again with my friend of a few days, General de Guingand. I looked at his face and again thought that, in his polite and warm manner, this man appeared to be almost shy. Yet, to his comrades-in-arms, he must have been the embodiment of courage and loyalty.

General Wilson, turning to his men, then said, "Captain Evans is already acquainted with Lieutenant Poston, General Montgomery's Aide-de-camp. I understand Captain Evans 'checked out' our Lieutenant in his B-17 yesterday. Is that not right, John?"

John was smiling and shaking his head from side to side, but I was moving mine up and down. I said, "You're absolutely right, General Wilson. It took Lieutenant Poston all of five minutes to find the handle on our machine. He is a natural pilot. And, John, by the way, has promised to check me out in his racing cars when I visit him in England after the war. I have been hearing that he drives quite fast, also that he holds the official record for most 8th Army vehicles smashed on the Sahara."

Everyone laughed; modest John, enjoying the attention, smiled. I thought I had not met a more pleasant group of men. And why shouldn't they be pleasant and even a tad jubilant? They had come from behind and had been victorious on the battlefield at El Alamein. And their King was coming to town to thank them on behalf of their countrymen at home. These countrymen themselves had responded with courage, putting out the home fires, which Hitler and Göring had rekindled nightly for nine terrible months while I was still going to flying school in San Antonio, I reminded myself.

These Englishmen had met at their doorsteps all that Hitler was able to hurl at them, but it wasn't enough to bring them to their knees. I well understood that their brave resistance gave us Yanks, 2000 miles from the Battle of Britain, time to equip ourselves and to learn to use our flying machines as fighting machines. I had practiced for war flying over Texas. These Brits, whose heritage I shared (my great-grand-parents were Welsh, Scottish... and German) had sharpened their swords over the English Channel and also at their workplaces and at homes. Sitting in on their victory celebration was something I certainly did not take lightly.

General Wilson then pulled me aside and said, "I suppose that you realize, Captain Evans, that Monty will be introducing you to our King."

"No, General" I answered, "General Montgomery hasn't mentioned introducing me to your King. We did discuss moving the B-17 over here to a position where the King might have a look at it if he liked. I was pleased to move it earlier this morning. Has General Montgomery said anything to you about introducing me to your King, General?"

"Actually, no," General Wilson responded, "but he will be. Monty won't be able to resist. You see, you are a prize that Monty feels he has won, you know. Or did you know, Captain Evans?"

"General Wilson, I'm no prize," I said, "but I do understand what you are telling me."

Relaxing his smile, General Wilson then asked, "Have you ever been presented to royalty before; have you ever met a king or a queen, Captain Evans?"

"No, sir, I've never met a king nor, for that matter, a queen before," I responded.

"Do you know what you are going to say to our King? You will have a private audience, you know. Monty will introduce you, then he will step back so that you and the King may talk about whatever pleases you. I presume you have heard of an audience with a king, have you not?" he asked with a smile.

"Yes, sir," I said, "I have heard, General Wilson, but I have yet to have my first audience with a king; is there some protocol which you might tell me about? I'll do my best."

"I'm sure you will. And, no, there isn't really any protocol to worry about; your meeting will be quite informal, actually. But I thought you might like some warning and might wish to give some thought to what you might like to say to His Majesty." Then, continuing, he said, "You wouldn't think it, but our King is quite shy, and it is not easy to talk with him. It would be a bit awkward, you know if you both just stood there in front of the entire 8th Army looking at each other for a few minutes without a sound emanating from either of you. There are a lot of people here today who are going to be watching both the King and you, Captain." General Wilson then raised his eyebrows as he dropped his head, then smiled warmly once again.

"I have noticed the people, General Wilson" I responded quickly. "And it is thoughtful of you to alert me. As you have guessed, I have had limited experience with kings to date, sir."

Again, Monty's over-sized Deputy Theater Commander smiled and raised his eyebrows, which I took to mean, "Well, Captain, it's your problem." Then he turned to go and meet a staff car that was just pulling up and which he appeared to recognize. As a matter of fact, everybody seemed to recognize this car; and while I couldn't see who was in it, I could make a good guess.

I had met only one man in Tripoli who would delay his entry until all the guests had found their places. I decided it was time I found my place over by my airplane and crew. As I pointed myself in the direction of *Theresa Leta* and moved out, I thought, "This is where Ike, Jimmie Doolittle and Colonel Upthegrove would all wish me to be."

When Monty climbed out of his staff car, three Generals were holding the door for him. He acknowledged their greetings with what I presumed to be characteristic geniality, a nodding of his head in recognition, without smiling. Almost immediately, I saw General Montgomery's eyes move in the direction of the B-17; only then he smiled.

Theresa Leta was center stage for the show that was about to commence. She looked a little dusty as a consequence of having to spend her nights on the edge of the Sahara Desert. Even so, in those days, she was an impressive looking lady. She and her kin were getting a reputation throughout the world for holding their own against the best that Hermann Göring and Admiral Yamamoto could throw at them.

It occurs to me today, as I write and as I recall those times, that a quick review of often used military commands might be in order at this juncture while everyone is awaiting His Majesty's arrival. Very soon I would be running my small flight crew through the entire "close order drill." It would be the first time in months that my men had done anything "military." Flying combat missions had kept them adequately occupied.

"Attention," as most know, means to stand straight, eyes to the front, chin in, chest out, stomach in, shoulders back, arms reaching for the ground, buttocks rolled forward slightly, legs together, heels together and feet turned out. It is a simple, straightforward command.

"Stand at Ease" means to snap one's left foot smartly to the left while clasping one's hands behind one's back. Since one is not supposed to move about when standing "at ease," one clearly is not at ease when he assumes this position.

"At Ease" means that one can do anything one likes, so long as he remains on his feet, does not talk and keeps one foot "in place." Clearly, one is simulating being chained to an invisible stake when one is standing "at ease."

"Rest" is a straightforward command that means one is not required to stand at attention, but neither is one allowed to depart the area, where one might expect to find a more suitable place to actually rest. Also, when one is "at rest," it is not intended that one look as if one is at rest: "a soldier must always look alert."

"Fall Out" means that one is permitted to leave wherever it is that one happens to be. This command, as I think of it, now has nothing at all to do with "falling," and even less with "falling-out" of something.

While his Generals were welcoming Monty, I turned towards my crew and said, "Fall In," which as I think of it, is an important command, which I just neglected to cover. "Falling In," of course, is simply the opposite of "Falling Out."

Then, I called out, "Right Dress," which I have also neglected to cover. On this command, each man puts his left hand on his own left hip and turns his head smartly to his right with the single exception of the man on the right end. This end man puts his left hand on his left hip like the others but does not turn his head to the right since there is no one on his right to look at. Everyone else shuffles their feet, left or right, until they all just nudge the left elbow of the man on their right excepting, of course, the end man who has no one on his right.

Some have difficulty with this command, but it is easier to do than to describe. Its purpose is to get everybody in a straight line and an "elbow-length" apart. While it seems a bit over-engineered, it actually is quite easy to learn and works quite well.

As soon as my crewmen were lined up and had spaced themselves properly, I gave the command "Stand at Ease." I then did an "About Face" and stood at ease myself. I was just in time because I could see that Monty was now heading in our direction.

So, I then did a second "About Face," called my crew to "Attention," then followed with a third "About Face" so that I would once again be facing Monty, who was now only ten feet or so away.

In a moment, I executed "The Hand Salute" and thought to myself, "Now, General Montgomery, what are you going to do? You're dealing with the winner of the **Morgan Medal** and the former Cadet Commander of the Knox High ROTC Battalion, Class of '37... also the Cadet Commander of Company 'C', Class of '40-E, at Randolph Field, The Army Air Corps' "West Point of the Air." Now, I know what I'm supposed to do. I also know what you're supposed to do, General; it is called "military courtesy." Now, are you going to ignore my salute before ten thousand witnesses? This time, it's not just the two of us alone in front of your command tent, General."

General Montgomery then demonstrated how a man, bucking for Field Marshal, salutes when he feels good. As he approached, he had in his saluting hand a small "baton" to which was attached hair from a horse's tail, an item which clearly had more utility in the old horse-cavalry days than it could possibly have had in the more recent tank corps times.

Observing my salute while still a few paces away, Monty transferred his baton to his free left hand and then brought his right hand up to a position about where General de Guingand had positioned his. This put Monty's right thumb in alignment with his right ear. But, while General de Guingand's saluting fingers were stiff and straight and even slightly arched, Monty's were actually curved forward, as if he was expecting a baseball a scant few inches off his right ear.

And, while General de Guingand had stopped the forward motion of his body and had stamped the ground with great force, an integral part of the classic British salute, General

Montgomery had started his salute early and had just kept on coming, his arm and hand still positioned as if to catch stray baseballs.

While I admit these kinds of thoughts did course about in my head in those days, they certainly weren't transmitted to just anyone who might be passing by or just hanging around. If I allowed myself a little private humor, it didn't mean that I went about being some kind of jerk who had to make a joke out of everything. Actually, I think it was my way of getting control of myself when I felt I was on the spot and a tad nervous.

The part about Monty's salute is accurate. He did look like he was expecting a baseball a few inches off his right ear. And he was, indeed, bent forward in the manner of someone walking into a stiff breeze.

"Good morning, General," I said and brought my arm down. I could see that he was in good spirits. And I was finding it pleasant to be around The Army Commander when he had found a reason to be pleasant. I didn't have a problem with this. Monty, I was learning, was a very interesting, inspired and hardworking man, but one who was just thrifty with pleasantries.

"I see you have brought your aircraft over, Captain Evans. Excellent," he said. "We have received a signal from **Maison Blanche Aerodrome,** the airfield at Algiers, you know, and we are advised that the King's departure has been delayed. He has been visiting with Ike. I should say he would be along on the half hour. Would you like to put your men at ease and join the rest of us over by the airdrome tower?"

Monty was looking at my men who were standing rather rigidly at attention and who looked freshly laundered, if unpressed, in their hand-washed khakis. I turned about and said, "At ease, men. This is General Montgomery." I thought this sounded a little stiff, so I added, "I believe you all know who he is."

With that, Monty's B-17 crewmen smiled broadly and so did the 8th Army Commander himself. This was indeed turning out to be a nice day. Lieutenant Poston had just joined us, and he was now taking pictures of Monty and his American flight crew.

Looking directly at my crewmen, this man who had addressed the few hundred thousand men who constituted the 8th Army just before they went into battle at El Alamein and had told them that contingency plans for falling back towards Alexandria and Cairo had been canceled and that they would stand together or die together at El Alamein, now clasped his hands behind his back and rocked slightly on the balls of his feet. Then he said to my men, "I hope you are being made to feel comfortable here in Tripoli. If you should need anything, anything at all, please just signal Lieutenant Poston here."

Lieutenant Poston, not expecting to be singled out, quickly allowed his arms to drop to his side. His camera, seemingly suspended in mid-air for a moment, then fell the distance allowed by its neck strap. This young Englishman, whom I was beginning to like very much, then brought his heels together without a sound and leaned forward slightly at the waist. Poston's eyes seemed to convey that following his commander's wishes was the single thing in life bringing him the greatest joy.

Poston's interpretation of standing at attention suggested that he wasn't a regular officer. This soft-spoken, pleasant young man, I guessed, was not a full-time career soldier; probably he had simply stepped forward because he thought his country had need of his service.

My crewmen, assured by Monty's example (that on this special day it was okay to smile), were indulging themselves. Staff Sergeant Ward, whose trousers I noticed failed to reach his shoe-tops and whose cap clung precariously to one side of his head (whose voice on the intercom, coming from the tail gunner's position, had always been steady when yellow-nosed fighters were diving through our formation) had on this day been smiling without interruption. I reckoned that this might be the first time Sergeant Ward would meet an Army Commander and a King in the same day. (My inner-self then quickly quipped, "Watch yourself, Richard Eager, it's a first for you, too.")

I noticed that Staff Sergeant Ward's trousers failed to reach his shoes, not because of a sizing problem, but because Staff Sergeant Ward had simply rolled his trousers up. He had rolled them up to make it easier for the casual passerby to see the shine on his GI shoes, right? Wrong. Sergeant Ward wasn't wearing GI shoes. It appeared that Sergeant Ward had rolled up his trousers so that a casual observer might have an unobstructed view of a pair of finely crafted, hand-sewn, ankle length boots which the Sergeant had acquired in Natal when we were making the journey from the States to the Combat Zone.

What could I say? I said to myself, "this 18-year-old has got to have some space and he has found some great looking boots there. If someone tries to make a problem out of this, I'll just tell them my tail gunner took on some shrapnel in his foot over Germany and that the flight surgeon ordered him to wear these special boots."

General Montgomery then trooped the line, stopping and leaning forward slightly to have a few words with each man. He made no move to shake hands, however. During my time with the General, I would observe that he was not an eager observer of the handshaking ritual.

I would experiment and find that if one pointed his hand directly at Monty's belt buckle under circumstances where one might reasonably expect to shake hands, Monty might take the proffered hand. But, after the experience, one could not readily recall whether he had felt Monty's hand in his or not. Clearly, Monty was saving himself for the big one.

But who was I to judge? Monty knew what he was doing. My men were pleased with his welcome greeting and I don't believe they expected him to stop and shake hands with each one of them. Staff Sergeant Austin, our youngest (not yet twenty, I guessed) who routinely crammed his slight frame into our ball-turret when we crossed over into enemy territory, was delighted; Eldon could look eye-to-eye with General Montgomery.

Monty motioned to me to come along with Lieutenant Poston and the three of us rejoined his 8th Army senior staff. Word had come down and quickly spread around the field that the King's transport was approaching. In a few seconds, twenty thousand eyes were searching the sky, in most cases, for their first look at a king.

When I picked up the King's aircraft, it was just touching down at the far end of the field. Moments later, it stopped about mid-field and was immediately met by three staff cars. Very quickly, these staff cars picked up their passengers, turned about, and were now speeding in our direction. I was aware that I was excited along with everyone else. "He's just a king," I said to myself; "what's your problem, Richard Eager, you never met a king before?" Answering my own question, I said, "Of course, I've never met a king before; you know I've never met a king before."

"Careful, you're losing it, Sport," I continued, "You had better start thinking of something intelligent to say in case this King of England should happen to drop by and want to chat."

I had thought of something to discuss with the King right after General Wilson made his suggestion. Something about King Georgie in a field of barley, but what about the field of barley? What would Dale Carnegie have said about barley? Now, it seemed I had misfiled my subject. Trying to snap out of it, I decided that this was no time for the usual joking with myself.

"Come on, get serious, Richard Eager," I said, "This is not something to be taken lightly. Think hard. Now, just what were you planning to talk to the King about? What did General Wilson suggest you do when the King first arrived?" Nothing came.

I was beginning to panic. The staff cars had stopped in front of Monty and I thought I had seen all the doors on all three cars open at once. I had not. Actually, one rear door on one of the cars had remained closed. Three men on the outside, however, had located this door and were making an uncoordinated effort to get it open.

Then, suddenly, this last door virtually flew open. Still, no one got out immediately. "Of course," I said, continuing my conversation with myself, "Kings take their time. Why, indeed, should a king be in a hurry to get out of a staff car, for God's sake? The King surely knows that Monty and his 8ᵗʰ Army aren't going any place."

Monty, however, must have been surprised when no one stepped out immediately; he leaned down quickly and took a look inside. I'm not suggesting that they actually butted heads (Monty and the King), but it must have been close. I have no idea what Monty expected to find in there, other than a king. But my new boss sure jumped back in a hurry. And finally, out came His Royal Highness, His Majesty, King George VI, King of England and the British Empire.

A warm, clearly friendly and prideful roar arose from the 10,000 gathered at Castel Benito Airdrome that day. I recognized the King immediately and said to myself, "Of course, he's the one who took the top job, right after his older brother had to disqualify himself; something about a problem with a lady from Baltimore." I remember thinking that King George was thinner than I expected a king might be, what with free rations and all.

"He's wearing khakis like the rest of us but he's not wearing any rank or medals," I observed. "He is wearing a British officer's cap with the red band reserved for General Officers and up," I guessed. "Also, he is carrying one of those special horsehair fly swatters like Monty has."

The band, standing in the bombed-out hangar next to the bombed-scarred tower was practically on top of the visiting party and making much too much noise, I thought. "But then, maybe, the band members were excited, too. And why shouldn't they be? Why, indeed?" I said to myself.

Thinking back, I don't know what I expected. I was sure they would all line up and have a ceremonial salute for somebody or something. I remember thinking that perhaps the King would award some decorations. "Why not make good use of his time while he's in town?" But that didn't happen either; nothing formal was taking place. Everybody around the King was talking and laughing.

Suddenly I felt like an outsider, as if I were hanging around somebody else's party. Of course, Monty had invited me to the party, but now that it had gotten underway, I felt out of place. I was at the edge of the welcoming group, so it was easy for me to rejoin my men over by the B-17. Also, I figured that this is where Ike, Jimmie and "Uppie" would all expect me to be.

As I approached, Lieutenant Johnson called our crew up. "At ease," I said, then added so that only they could hear me, "What the hell, they're all at ease, and having a good time. Why shouldn't we be at ease and just watch for a while?" Everybody agreed that this was a good plan. And everybody thought they were on a holiday, and some holiday it was.

Invariably, under these circumstances back in those days, someone would always observe, "This sure beats the hell out of flying combat missions." For example, if the chow is particularly bland, someone would always chortle, "Damn, this stuff's worse than horse meat, but it sure beats hell out of flying combat!"

Staff Sergeant Austin, my redheaded, freckle-faced, all-American ball-turret gunner, catching a lull in the excitement, raised his hand as if he were still in attending school.

"Captain?" he said.

I said, "Yes, Staff Sergeant Austin?" (On our combat missions, Staff Sergeant Austin would routinely be tamped down into the cramped quarters of his ball turret, bolted to the underside of the B-17; then later, when we were back out of the combat zone, he would be lifted out of his personal torture chamber by his fellow-gunners. Then, after a while, he would thaw out and be okay.) I repeated, "I hear you, Staff Sergeant Austin, what do you have on your mind?"

This cheery, boyish gunner whose eyes seemed to always be smiling, grinned at me and said, "These sure beats hell out of flying combat, missions, doesn't it, Captain?"

I answered with a smile as big as his, "It most certainly does, Staff Sergeant Austin, and I'm mighty glad you are here to enjoy it with me."

Then Lieutenant Beringsmith, my steady, unflappable bombardier, while looking at me said, "Captain," then tilted his head in the direction of the "royal party." I turned quickly, expecting to see a couple lines of men standing at attention with the King and Monty out in front giving out some medals or new batons or something. But it was not to be. This was not a formation; this really was a party. And, as we Yanks would often put it back then, "everybody was having a ball."

Then I saw what Lieutenant Beringsmith had observed. Two members of the royal party had broken away from the pleasant, happy group and had started walking in the direction of *Theresa Leta* and her crew. It was Monty... and the Guest of Honor.

As the 8th Army Commander and the King approached our position by the B-17 on this special day in Tripoli in the late spring of '43, I noticed that Monty had a different look about him. The victor at El Alamein was excited, too. This was Monty's respected boss, whom Monty was bringing over to show off the prize that he had won, a prize awarded to him by General Eisenhower, The Theater Commander. Also, this was the American crew that Ike had sent over to Monty... to fly him about... in his very own *Flying Fortress*.

The King looked pleasant and interested, but he wasn't smiling. Like Monty, he too walked a little bent over; unlike Monty, who had a good tan, the King looked quite pale. I thought to myself, "His Majesty doesn't look as if the flight from Algiers agreed with him."

When the King and Monty were about ten paces away, I faced about, called my crew to attention, and then I faced about again facing the front. In a moment without hesitating, I rendered the hand salute to General Sir Bernard Law Montgomery, Commander, 8th Army, of El Alamein, and to His Majesty, King George VI, the Reigning Monarch of the British Commonwealth, which had for three years been standing pretty much alone against the premeditated armed might of Germany and Adolph Hitler.

Remembering that Monty had not returned my salute on our first meeting, I wondered if both the King and Monty would now ignore me. I had been saluting upper levels of command for some time but had gained no experience with royal levels. I thought, "Well, what the hell. As Dad would suggest, I'll err on the positive side. For sure, I don't want to find myself in a position where it would be incumbent on me to be returning His Majesty's salute in front of 10,000 witnesses."

That day, it would be the British, I told myself, who would be slouching about, having a good time while their American visitors would be lending a little class to their show. Up came my arm, and I figured on holding it there until somebody else's followed suit.

My fears were unwarranted. Monty was pleased as punch. He smiled bigger than I had seen him smile and bigger than I was destined to see him smile in our times together. Very quickly, he brought his cupped right hand up to his right ear.

The King, however, was taken aback; I wondered for a moment if His Majesty was looking for me to bow or something. The King glanced at Monty and then he, too, was greeting me with the English Officers' off-the-right-ear baseball-catcher salute.

"Hot Ziggity; going well," I said to myself as I brought my arm back down and stowed it at my side.

As the King and General Montgomery came to a stop before me, Monty said, "Sir, this is Captain Richard Evans of the United States Army Air Corps. Ike has sent Captain Evans over to fly me about in this remarkable *Flying Fortress* aircraft. I can fly wherever I wish without need of fighter escort. And these, Sir, are Captain Evans' fine crewmen."

The King nodded in the direction of my crew, then quickly pushed his hand towards mine, afraid, I guessed, that I would start the saluting all over again. I reached out and grasped the King's extended hand and smiled as I had been taught to smile in Tennessee when meeting a nice person.

Monty then backed up a few steps. "His protocol, not mine," I said to myself; then I got serious. "This is it; this is what General Wilson was telling me about. I'm about to have an audience with His Majesty, King George VI, Reigning Monarch of The British Commonwealth. And, Oh God! What was the subject I had decided to talk to him about?"

But the King spoke first. "I am very pleased to meet you, Captain Evans. Are you taking good care of our Monty?" After these words, His Majesty was silent and waiting.

I answered promptly, "Yes, sir." Then, following the King's lead, I was silent and waiting.

When after a few seconds the King was still silent and still waiting, I said to myself, "Oh my God, Richard Eager, you're going to look like a plain damn fool. You haven't had Monty off the ground yet and you've just told his boss that you're taking good care of him."

His Majesty then tried a different tack, "How are you enjoying Tripoli, Captain Evans?"

Oh Boy, an easy one, I thought and said, "Very much, sir, a very nice city. The harbor and boulevard along the waterfront are particularly nice." Then there was mutual silence again.

But, after a moment, the King agreed that the harbor and the boulevard were indeed, very nice. Then he asked, "Have you flown combat missions over Europe, Captain Evans?"

Bingo. This was one I could answer. And I did. I said, "Yes, sir, I sure have."

After waiting a moment for a more circumspect response to his question, the King then asked, "Have you encountered any **Messerschmitts** over Europe, Captain Evans?"

Had I seen any Messerschmitts? Of course, I had. After the first one, you don't really want to see any more. I had dreams about those yellow-nosed fighters coming straight at me. Since I had started flying Group and Wing leader, I thought a couple times that those bastards were going to ram my B-17 head on.

I forced my mind to return to the King's question and said, "Yes sir, I've seen lots of Messerschmitts and Focke-Wulf 190s, too, quite close up, sir. Sometimes you can read the numbers on the German fighter planes as they flash by your window. Most, but not all, have painted yellow noses."

Gaining confidence and some momentum, I added, "Sir, you're surprised that you can't always hear them coming in, but you hear them clearly after they have flashed by. I think it may be that it's because our combined closing speeds, relative to each other, exceed the speed of sound, sir. You think that you hear one of them zinging into you; then you realize that you just saw him flashing by. I have thought that, on a number of occasions, I caught a glimpse of the German pilot's face, Sir."

When I have looked back and recalled my conversation with King George VI, I've wondered how this man could have been so patient with me. I have thought that I must have looked like a plain damn fool. I didn't feel that I was afraid of him; I just couldn't concentrate while the whole 8th Army was waiting for me to clam up so they could get on with their march-past. My show was about to end, I was quite sure. I was absolutely certain I had not distinguished myself with His Majesty. Or, perhaps, I had. Perhaps the King of England was thinking, "This has got to be the dumbest Yank I've met yet on either side of the Atlantic."

With one final effort to make a conversationalist out of me, this pleasant, soft-spoken man said with a warm smile, "And, how has your health been... out here in North Africa, Captain Evans? You've been well have you?"

I thought quickly, "Hot Ziggity, I can handle this one," and I quickly said, "Fine, Sir; just fine." And, without realizing what I was doing, I went over onto the offensive. I asked King George VI, "And, how has your health been, Sir?" And, of course, I smiled.

But then it hit me the minute I made that inane inquiry into His Majesty's private life. I said to myself, "You blew it, you Ninny, you blew it. You could have guessed, that if his Majesty has complaints, he sure isn't going to be sharing them with you, Richard Eager. A king's state of health is his own damn business. He isn't obliged to tell every commoner he runs into whether he's ailing or not. And, if he has picked up a case of the trots, sure as hell it isn't likely that he would be anxious to share this kind of information with you."

But King George VI wasn't your average King. After taking a look over his shoulder to check Monty's position and confirm that he was out of earshot, King George leaned forward. I leaned forward, too, certain that one should meet a King halfway. His majesty then practically whispered into my ear. "Captain Evans, I am not a well man; I am a very sick man," he said. "I believe... I'm as sick as I have ever been... in my entire life."

I could see that the King was serious; for sure he was not trying to make jokes. And I remember thinking that when I first saluted him; I had thought he looked a little green. But, of course, we hadn't met before and I had no idea how he usually looked. Suddenly, I felt very comfortable in his presence. I was, of course, flattered that his highness would discuss the state of his health with me. More at ease now and with rising confidence, I said, "Sir, I am very sorry. May I just ask what seems to be your problem, Sir?"

When His Highness again leaned forward to speak, I again figured that one should meet a king halfway. As I did so, I caught a glimpse of Monty over the King's shoulder. And a glimpse was all I needed to see that some of the joy of the morning had departed the face of the victor at El Alamein. Clearly, Monty was being left out of the King's protracted discussion with his (Monty's) *Flying Fortress* pilot.

His Highness certainly wasn't whispering in my ear, but neither was he very far away when he answered my question. He said in a quite low voice, "Captain Evans, I have dysentery."

I recall clearly that I was struck dumb for a second or two. I couldn't believe my ears; I said to myself, "Oh my God, His Majesty's got the trots! To gain time, I said, "Sir, have what?"

Again, he glanced back in Monty's direction; then leaned forward in my direction and repeated, "Captain Evans, I have dysentery."

Now, suddenly all fear left me. I was on solid ground at last. And my confidence returned in a flash. This was a subject on which I was a minor authority. I had learned about "lower stomach" difficulties very early in life. Additionally, I had broadened my knowledge after leaving Mom and Dad and had gained substantial field experience while serving out in the open in North Africa.

I took a small step towards his highness, leaned forward at the waist and practically whispered into his ear, "Sir, you are not alone."

"What exactly do you mean, Captain Evans?" was the King's startled response. I thought the King might smile, but he seemed not to be in the mood. I was smiling, but since he wasn't, I decided I should wipe mine off and promptly did.

On a new tack, I said, "Sir, everybody in North Africa has dysentery. Just look around you. There are 10,000 of us out here today and all of us have dysentery in various stages, Sir. It is not a distinction, you know. And, Sir, it is not something one need be ashamed of." It was becoming clear that I wasn't making it with the King of England; he hadn't thought my comments relevant, constructive or amusing.

His Majesty responded, "Yours is not a comforting thought for me, Captain Evans. It is not that I am ashamed; it is just that it is well, so annoying and so very inconvenient. And, I do not usually have this kind of problem in England; I just want somebody to tell me how I can rid myself of this plague! Just what exactly does one do about this sort of thing down here in Africa, Captain Evans?"

My recall will sound like an exaggeration; it isn't. It might sound as if His Majesty was joking with me. He wasn't. I believe His Highness, the King of the United Kingdom, was being dead serious with me. Suddenly, I felt better. I was under control. Dad would be proud of his third-born son. I was about to become an advisor to a King, the King of England, and the British

Commonwealth. "Sir," I asked, "May I speak frankly?"

"By all means, Captain Evans," was his prompt response, and I noted that the eyes of the Reigning Monarch of the United Kingdom had the look of a man who could not have been more sincere.

I was being singularly honored. I spoke slowly and I chose my next words with great care.

"Sir," I said, "Dysentery is indigenous to this region. There really is no known cure. So long as you remain in North Africa, it is likely that you will be afflicted. However, you can be free of this dread condition, Your Highness. You need only to depart these shores."

Smiling, I continued, "Sir, I suggest that you return to England at once and you will be whole again. Go home; do not delay; do not hesitate." I could not resist the picture in my twisted mind of King George VI, on his knees before me, with my hand resting on his head as I delivered this gentle man from the pestilence that gripped North Africa in the spring of 1943.

For sure, I did not laugh, but I was beginning to enjoy my audience with a candid, friendly, although discomforted king. I did smile just a tad. His Majesty, however, did not... not right away.

But, in a moment he let himself go.

I had heard that monarchs practice restraint with respect to smiling and that rarely would one actually laugh and almost never in public. I will never forget being on hand, on a very special day, in Tripoli, in July 1943, when a very pleasant King George VI laughed quite hard indeed in the presence of his entire 8th Army, including its newly famous Army Commander, Monty, the Victor at El Alamein.

I remember that when the King laughed, he leaned forward slightly at the waist and appeared to be looking at the ground. And, then he slapped his right thigh a number of times, as his laugh became a chuckle.

Finally, His Majesty, recovering from his mirth, said to me, "Captain, Evans, you make a quite good point, and I am going to act on your advice. I am scheduled to fly to Malta, perhaps you have heard. I am going so I may personally award a medal of high honor to those gallant people on that small, but no longer beleaguered, island. But I shan't tarry I assure you. I shall return to England before the week is out."

Smiling broadly, his Royal Highness added, "I hope, Captain Evans, that you will serve Monty as ably as you have served me this day. I will remember our meeting quite a long time. If you should be in England during the war or after the matter is settled, perhaps you would look in on me sometime. You might just "check in" as you say at Whitehall. Just tell the orderly that "Monty's B-17 Pilot" would like a word with me.

Clearly, the King was having fun, too, despite his discomfort. Still chuckling, he reached for my hand a second time. After a moment, he released it and then smiled less broadly with returning restraint. King George VI then took a step backward to where Monty was waiting.

I decided another try at saluting wouldn't be the way to go. I came to attention and smiled the way we smiled in Tennessee when we had enjoyed a very nice talk with a very nice person.

TO A STRAIGHT-FORWARD KING

When Richard Eager met The King of Britain,
His Majesty proclaimed that he had been stricken!
"I am ill," he said; then he inquired outright:
"Might Monty's pilot shed some light?"
Spake the King: "I came to these shores as well as might be.
Why has this pestilence been thrust upon me?"
"Never in my lifetime have I been so ill...
Surely, by now... there is some kind of pill."
Emboldened in time, Monty's pilot did speak,
His courage returning, no longer was he weak.
"Sir," said he, "The problem we have here... can be beat.
I suggest to England... straight-away, you retreat."

Richard Eager

6.2 *Captain Evans meets General Maitand Wilson, Castel Benito Airdrome,*
Tripoli, Libya (National Archives and Records Administration)

6.3   *Captain John Poston, far right, is the Aide-de-Camp to General Montgomery, North Africa* (Imperial War Museum)

6.4   *General Montgomery waits for King George VI to land at Castel Benito Airdrome*

6.5 *Captain Evans is introduced to King George VI by General Montgomery*

6.6 *King George VI is introduced to the B-17 "Theresa Leta" crew by Captain Evans*

6.7 *King George VI greets the British troops* (Imperial War Museum)

7.1 *Judge, Dick's childhood companion*

CHAPTER 7

DOG FINDS BOY

The joys of finding can make one sad,
When you're the lad of a principled dad!

Richard Eager

I can't remember exactly when Judge came to our house. I might have been around seven or eight years old. But I remember begging, "Let me keep him, Dad; oh please, please, Dad, let me keep him. I'll take good care of him, Dad."

Judge was sitting on our front porch when I got home from school, looking at me like I was the visitor. Dad would tell me he was a Boston terrier. He wasn't black and white though; Dad said he was "brindle." Also, he was a little bigger than the Boston bull dogs I had seen; they were always black and white, and they never stopped yapping.

Judge was alert. His clipped ears were always up. And he didn't yap at all. Sometimes he looked like he was smiling. Judge and I became friends right off. I got a dish of milk, which he lapped up in a hurry. He didn't have much tail to wag; but when he felt good, which turned out to be most of the time, he would wag his whole back end. Also, he was a little sway backed, causing his short tail and rear end to stick up in the air.

Sometimes Judge would wag both his tail and rear end so hard that his hind legs would seem to vibrate on the floor. He had a pug nose and a drooping muzzle. And he arched his neck like a racehorse, pushing his pointed ears up and bringing his muzzle in towards his chest. His neck and his chest were white, making it look like he had a napkin hanging down around his neck.

When Judge would sit at attention like I taught him, I thought he looked like a cartoon of a soldier dog; he would pull his chin in, push his chest out and pull his elbows back. I had seen pictures of soldiers who stood at attention that way; I didn't think I wanted to be a soldier. Dad said, "That's good, Dick; I'm not anxious for you to be a soldier either."

When Dad got home from work, at Knoxville High, and looked at Judge's big eyes, wrinkled brow and drooping jowls, he said, "Dick, your dog looks like a solemn judge." Then, while he looked straight at me, Dad said that, of course, we would have to inquire around and see whose dog he really was and that some little boy like me was probably very unhappy right now.

I had already thought some little boy like me might be missing his dog, but I suggested to Dad that a little boy exactly like me was going to be really unhappy if someone came and took my dog away. Dad looked at me without changing his expression.

I knew that when Dad looked at me like that, it was time for me to stop doing whatever it was I was doing. Dad said lots of times, "Dick, you should try talking less and listening more."

Two days dragged by. Every time the telephone rang, my heart started pounding in my chest. But no little boy called to ask about Judge. Then on the third day, Dad came home from school and said, "Okay, Dick, I've been thinking; here's what we must do. We'll place an ad in the paper. If it isn't answered in three days, we'll cancel it. But, Dick, if a little boy like you comes around to our house, say within a couple weeks, and your dog jumps all over him and licks him, would you let Judge go without a big scene?"

I said, "I guess so, Dad. "What else could I say?" Dad really was a very nice man, but he said it was his responsibility to the family to be firm. He was always saying to me, "Remember, Dick, somebody has to be responsible and some day it will be your turn."

Many years later, I would hear President Truman say, "The Buck stops here" on the radio, which would always remind me of Dad.

But, back in those days, I thought my dad was inclined to go overboard on the side of fair play. Finally, he said one day, "Okay, Dick, I'll help you write the ad, and you can call it in." I didn't know what "calling it in" meant, but I knew Dad was getting ready to "teach me a lesson" or "further my education"; this kind of thing happened a lot at our house.

Dad was always the teacher. Mom said if Dad stopped teaching every day when he left Knox High, he picked up again the minute he got home in the afternoon. Dad got a pencil and some paper, sat down at our dining-room table and asked, "What shall we say, Dick?"

I answered, "You write the ad, Dad; I don't feel like writing an ad today. Besides, you know I've never written an ad before; and, Dad, I don't even know what an ad is. I haven't even learned to write yet either, Dad."

My dad gave me a long look and then quickly said, "Okay, okay, I know you can't write yet but it's never too early to start." I'll bet Dad said that at least once every week while my brothers and I were growing up, "It's never too early to start."

"Let's see now; we'll make it short," Dad mumbled, and he wrote a few lines on the paper. Then he motioned to me to follow him to Mom's sewing machine, which was also in the dining room.

When our sewing machine wasn't sewing for Mom, it was a stand for our telephone. Dad picked up our telephone with his right hand and held the receiver to his ear with his other hand. The phones in those days looked like black sticks with a horn on one end to talk into. The receivers looked like skinny bells; they were black, too, and had a wire on them. I knew a lady called "Central" would come on at the other end when Dad picked up the receiver and put it up to his ear. She would always say, "Number, please?"

Dad gave the "Central" lady the number he had looked up and, in a moment, he said, "Knoxville Journal? Yes, would you give me your want ad department please?" After another moment, Dad said, "Yes? This is Mr. W. E. Evans; my son, Dick, would like to place an ad in your want ad section." Then, he handed the phone over to me.

I heard a nice lady say, "Is this Dick? "I said, "Yes, ma'am."

Then she said, "Please go ahead with your message, Mr. Evans."

I looked at Dad; then as he read from his paper, I repeated the message to the lady on the phone. "Found, bull terrier, medium sized, brindle with white chest, white paws and clipped tail. Call W. E. Evans, Hemlock 4221."

The lady's voice said, "We will print your ad starting tomorrow morning, Mr. Evans. Just give me a call when you want us to stop it." She didn't hang up right away and I didn't either; in a few seconds, she said, "Good luck, Dick."

I thought I had done okay with my first want ad, but I knew my heart wasn't in it. Mom would often say to me, "I can see what you're doing, my Dickie bird; you're doing what I asked you to do, I guess. But your heart isn't in it." If Mom wasn't there, then Dad would say, "You must do more than just go through the motions, Dick; you should always put your heart in it."

Suddenly I couldn't hold back how I felt. I handed our phone to Dad, and then ran through our kitchen and out the back door. Dad didn't follow me.

I ran across our big back porch wide as our house. Then I ran down our wide steps to our back yard. Judge was spread out under our two big maple trees that shaded most of our back yard. They also kept the grass from growing good in the middle. I remember thinking that Judge had moved right in. Why should I have to throw him out if he liked our place better than where he came from? Why couldn't I just hide him in my room or in the garage for a few days?

When Judge relaxed, he would put his chest flat on the ground, push his front legs forward, and draw his rear legs up under him. This would push his rear end up and make his stub tail higher than his head. He would put his muzzle flat on the ground between his front paws; then he would have to roll his eyes up so he could see whatever it was he wanted to look at. In this position, Judge's clipped ears and clipped tail would be pointing straight up. When he was happy his tail would make little circles in the air.

Judge was relaxing this way under our maple trees when I ran out of the house. As the screen door slammed behind me, he jumped to his feet and stood at "attention" chin in, chest out, ears up, back arched, tail up, too, and making those circles in the air. I noticed that Judge's tail-circles were getting smaller and slowing down; Judge knew something was wrong. I picked him up and he licked my face. I didn't like it when he licked my face, but I didn't want him to know I didn't like it. My mom would always say, "Animals have feelings, too, my Dickie bird. Be nice to them."

Then, the longest days of my life dragged by. Dad would come home from school and say, "Dick, did anyone call today?"

And, I would answer, "No, Dad. Nobody called today, Dad."

Then, Dad would say, "Well, Dick, we better let your ad run another day or so."

"My ad," as Dad called it, had run, not three days like Dad had said we had to run it, but six days. Finally, one day, Dad asked, "Still no calls, Dick?"

I said, "No, Dad. Nobody's called at all; it's been a whole week now, Dad." Okay, Son, we'll stop our want ad," he said. "But remember what we agreed to do. If a little boy still comes by and we can see that Judge knows him, we must let Judge go... and without a lot of whooping and hollering. Is that right?"

I nodded my head up and down but I was thinking, "No, it isn't right but, yes, I do understand."

In a couple weeks, school finally let out. The Family Studebaker was packed, and the family climbed up into our car. When we finally backed out and got going, Dad announced, as he had done on previous summers, "Here we go again; Helen Wilhelmina Stewart Evans, her four sons and her great husband are once again heading out for their cottage in the Great Smoky Mountains. They will be travelling in their new 1925 Studebaker, averaging almost 20 miles per hour. They will be heading for Elkmont, in the heart of the Smokies, going through Sevierville, Gatlinburg and Wonderland Park. If the Evans boys behave themselves, we might just stop at the Wonderland Park Hotel for ice-cold lemonade."

While Dad was making his annual announcement, I was thinking to myself, the only telephone at Elkmont is at our Appalachian Clubhouse, a good quarter of a mile from our cottage. I sure wasn't planning to hang around our clubhouse waiting for phone calls from Knoxville.

I wasn't around yet when they did it, but I was told that Dad and Grandpa built our cottage in the Smokies with their own hands. They built it on a steep hill right next to Jakes Creek, which Mom described as a "lovely mountain stream with crystal-clear water, bounding over rough granite rocks, making big and little water falls and forming pools, which tired mothers could wash their hair in and put their feet in and little boys could play in."

Mom had a nice, low voice that Dad called "contralto," which you could hear every Sunday in Knoxville's First Methodist Church. Actually, you could hear Mom if you were outside walking by our church. Dad said one time; "Your mother's remarkable skills in music are very likely the reason her literary skills have remained quite dormant." Dad would make jokes about Mom, but you could tell my Dad really loved my Mom a lot.

When Mom would say all those things about Jakes Creek, Dad would say, "All the things your mother puts into a run-on sentence about Elkmont and Jakes Creek are worth running on about and some of them are true." I would always smile when Dad would talk about Mom this way; I knew he was kidding. I was a lot older when I told Dad one time that I thought he shouldn't make fun of my mother!

Dad's eyes laughed and he came right back at me, "That's very funny, Dick; you're a chip off my old block!"

We had a sign over our two-or-three steps up onto the front porch of our cottage. I had looked at this sign many times, but I didn't know what it meant. One day I asked Dad about our sign.

Dad came back at me with a quick question. "You don't know what that sign over our door says, Dick?" Then Dad pointed his finger at the sign, smiled and spelled out what the sign said, "0-s-o-c-o-z-y."

I had already tried to figure it out and I shook my head from side to side. "No, Dad," I said, "I don't know what it means; what does it mean"?

"Dick, My Boy," he said, "that sign hanging over the welcome mat of our home in the Smokies has two meanings: one is American, one Russian." Pointing at our sign, Dad said, "You see the way you would say our sign in Russian puts the accent on the second syllable, like this, 'Oh-SO-coh-zee'. Now, you say it."

I said, "Oh-SO-coh-zee."

"Good boy," Dad said. "Now in Russian that means, 'some lucky kid's dad has built a great house here in the Smoky Mountains.'" Dad looked to see if I was paying attention, then went on, "Now listen carefully, Dick. In English, the pronunciation is, not 'Oh-SO-coh-zee'; it's 'OH-so-coh-zee', which means 'what a wonderful, warm, nice place Professor Evans built with his own hands... to bring his best girl and his four sons up to!'"

I said, "Da-ad, you are always playing tricks on me; why didn't you grownups spell it the right way? Besides, you know I can't spell in Russian. I can't even spell in American yet, Dad."

Dad leaned over like he was going to tell me a big secret and whispered in my ear, "Actually, I think your mother made that sign and painted the letters on it while I was building the dam up on Jakes Creek and setting the pipes to bring the water down to our house." Then Dad raised his eyebrows and grinned and looked back at me while he walked into our cottage.

I looked at the back of my dad's head as he walked away from me and noticed that it was getting a little bald and that Dad had some grey hairs, too. I had heard Mom say that Dad was almost 39; I hoped Dad wasn't getting old. I remember thinking that I would just die if anything ever happened to my dad.

Mom had her head over on Dad's shoulder as our Studebaker passed through Sevierville and headed out for Pigeon Forge; I knew that the road would take us alongside Pigeon River for a while and hit Gatlinburg next. Then, after a few minutes, the road would get steeper and we would start climbing up into the Smoky Mountains.

I pulled my dog up close and rolled down the window so he could stick his nose out into the wind and look up the road.

I was sure that no little boy would be able to find Judge and me in the mountains even if he happened to find out that Dad had taken us up there after school let out. Anyway, the little boy's dad would probably have already gotten him another dog by the time we got back to Knoxville.

I can still remember how happy I was when I fell asleep in the car. How could I ever forget the time when Judge and I escaped to the Smokies? Oh boy, was I happy! I had my very own dog!

When I dozed off with my arms around Judge, I think I dreamed about the first time our family went up to the Smokies in an automobile. It was a few years earlier on the very first day the new "River Road" was opened. Unlike the old logging train, the River Road went through Gatlinburg instead of Maryville. From Gatlinburg you could drive over "The Lookout" above Gatlinburg and get all the way back into Wonderland Park and to Elkmont where our cottage was located on Jakes Creek. On this first trip on the River Road, we were all in Grandpa Stewart's brand new 1926 Durant motorcar with Grandpa at the wheel.

We didn't have seat belts in those days, but no one was hurt when Grandpa swerved to miss a car that he said was coming right at us. We were packed in so tight that we didn't have room to bounce around, so no one was hurt very much. Our car bounced though and the back-end banged into the ditch and kept bouncing off the side of the mountain until Grandpa could get us stopped.

Then, Grandpa jumped out really fast to take a good look. In a minute, he reported that everything looked okay except that we had bent the right rear wheel and maybe the rear axle, too.

Grandpa Stewart was a great big Scotsman with a large red nose like Santa Claus. I thought he was always happy and very nice; Grandma said Grandpa was often too happy and not very nice at all when he would come home late from the Elks Club.

Dad said Grandma told everybody in Knoxville that one night Grandpa was coming home from Knoxville's Elks Club late and was climbing up the high, front steps to his house when all of a sudden, he decided to go to sleep right there on his own steps. Dad wanted to tell us one time at breakfast how Grandpa had cut his head over his eye, had bloodied his big, red nose and had gone to sleep on the steps, but Mom wouldn't let Dad tell us this story about Grandpa.

I remember Mom got up from our breakfast table one time and said, "All right, all right, everybody out, out. You're going to be late to school." Funny thing, I remember that that's exactly what Grandpa said right after he drove his new car into a ditch at the "Lookout Turn" between Gatlinburg and Wonderland Park. He said, "All right, all right, everybody out! Everybody out and start pushing."

"The Lookout" was a high place in the road to Elkmont where you could look out and get a good view of Mt. LeConte, and The Chimneys, too; also, the grape vineyards running all the way down the steep hill to where the Pigeon Forge River turns to go toward Gatlinburg.

Everybody did get out, and we silently looked at Grandpa's car in the ditch; we also looked with long faces, as Dad would say, at the long drop to the valley on the other side of the road. Dad said, "Down there someplace is where we would have stopped rolling if we had been going home to Knoxville, rather than coming up to our cottage at Elkmont." Dad shook his head from side to side and didn't smile.

Grandpa said the only damage done was to our right rear wheel, which he said got bent. He said we should all push while he gunned the engine on his new Durant Motorcar. I remember to this day how proud I felt being asked to help push with "the adults." When we all pushed together, Grandpa's new car slowly wobbled up out of the ditch and back onto the road. Dad said our right rear wheel was making motions like an Arab belly dancer in a Cairo casbah.

Mom said, "Hush, Ernest, the children." I remember that Mom said that a lot. My brother, Stewart, thinking Mom's scolding Dad was even funnier than Dad's jokes, laughed as hard as he could. Dad said, "Okay, okay, that's enough; stop that, Stewart. Mom's right: it wasn't that funny."

Then we started wobbling slowly along on our damaged wheel for the last ten miles to Wonderland Park. Dad said, "That wheel looks like a pretzel." Also, so that Grandpa could hear him, he added, "We are now averaging a very respectable five miles per hour, considering the shape we're in." Dad was giving it to Grandpa because Grandpa wouldn't let Dad do any of the driving in his new car. It was still a long time before Dad got our very own family Studebaker for us.

As we wobbled along on that brand new, one-day-old, dark, narrow, muddy road, which Grandpa said, had finally been cut through the gap that very day, a long line of cars started lining up behind us. It was getting dark and I could see the headlights of eight or ten cars flashing on the pine trees on each side of the road as we went around curves.

It had started to rain but not too hard. Some of the drivers were blowing their horns because they wanted to get around Grandpa. Dad explained so that Grandpa could hear him that Grandpa was afraid, if he pulled over to the side of the road to let folks pass by him, he would not be able to get wobbling again. Dad acted like he thought this was very funny, but Grandpa didn't laugh at Dad's joke.

Finally, we came wobbling into the straightaway in front of the new Wonderland Park Hotel that sat back up on a hill off to our left. We could see a lot better with the hotel lights shining down on us. Dad said we were leading a parade "of a couple dozen very slow, very unhappy autos."

As they all sped up and passed us on the straight part of the road in front of the hotel, most of the drivers waved their arms and smiled as they passed us. Dad said that some of them weren't waving their arms at us; they were waving their fingers at Grandpa. Dad thought this was very funny, but Mom said it was crude and obscene. Grandpa didn't laugh. I guessed he probably agreed with Mom.

It was dark and blustery when we finally pulled up in front of "Osocozy." The ride from Wonderland Park had taken more than an hour, Dad said, as all of us piled out of Grandpa's brand new, wet, and very muddy and wobbly Durant motorcar.

But we all thought we were like pioneers or something; everybody was a little excited. I remember I was a lot excited! "The Loop," from Knoxville to Sevierville to Elkmont and back to Knoxville by the "river route" through Townsand and Maryville, had just been completed that very day. I was excited and repeated what Dad had told me earlier; I said, "Dad, we can say that we were in the first group of cars to drive through The Gap to the Smokies, can't we Dad?"

Dad's eyes looked really bright when he answered me, "That's right, Dick. And, we can say we were the first, ever... to wobble all the way through the gap to Elkmont."

I never learned whether Granddad saved our lives that day or just over-corrected and almost got us killed. But it sure was o-so-cozy when we finally got to our cottage in the Smokies. Dad told Stewart that he could carry our things in while he got the fire going. I sure loved Elkmont when it was cold, and Dad got the fire going in our big stone fireplace that my dad had built himself out of a lot of big rocks he got out of Jakes Creek.

And, this time, it was better than ever; it turned out that Judge liked fires as much as we did. He would curl up beside me and put his chin on the rug and watch the fire burn. Every time the fire would pop, Judge's ears would twitch. Then we would all laugh at Judge. Judge would then look like he was smiling back at us. I think Judge knew that we all really liked him when we would all laugh at him like that. Afterwards, he would walk around to each of us and try to lick us on the face to get us to laugh at him some more. When one of us fell off to sleep, we'd wake back up because we could feel Judge licking our face. When this happened, everybody else would laugh like crazy.

Judge would know that when we laughed like that, we liked him a whole lot and he would smile while letting his tongue hang out of one side of his mouth.

After that cold, rainy night, I don't think we ever made another trip up to "O-so-cozy" in the Smokies that Dad didn't tell us how lucky we were. Dad was on the couch in front of the fire with his arm around Mom; Judge and I were down on the rug as close to the fire as we could get. When I looked back at my dad, I could see the fire reflecting in his glasses. Dad would smile and say, "What did I tell you, Dick, aren't we a lucky family?"

I would look at Judge and say with my ear-to-ear grin, "Yes, Dad, we are a lucky family." Many years later I understood that we weren't just lucky, that both Mom and Dad worked hard to make us a happy family. A fond memory for me was to look over at my folks on the couch when the oil lamps were turned off. The dancing reflections from the fire showed my dad with his arms way around my mom.

7.2 *Dick's mother, Helen, is ready for a drive in the family Studebaker*

8.1 *Montgomery's 8th Army enters Sfax, Tunisia, before the US Army and wins the bet with Eisenhower for a B-17* (Imperial War Museum)

CHAPTER 8
"THIS ENGINE HAS STOPPED!"

Tripoli, in western Libya, where I picked up Monty, is 1,000 miles from Cairo. The pyramids are on the southwestern edge of Cairo, as is Payne Airfield, the **RAF** airdrome where we planned to land and deliver Monty and his staff. The Army Commander would then proceed by motor car to the British Embassy.

Averaging 175 miles-per-hour in our B-17, our flight time would be 5 hours, 45 minutes. We would touch down at Payne Airfield at 1515 hours, Cairo time. Long shadows extending north-east from the pyramids would be pointing the way to Shepheard's Hotel where I planned to check in and sit out the war for a few days.

It was the end of spring, 1943: it would be unlikely that we would see a single cloud in the sky as we overflew the Gulf of Sidra in the Libyan Mediterranean and continued along the northern rim of the Sahara in Libya and Egypt towards Cairo. Nor did we expect to run into any Axis fighters; they were becoming extinct in North Africa.

After a few days with Monty's staff, I was beginning to articulate my thoughts in the language of my new British friends. I released the brakes, pushed the four throttles against the stops and said to myself, "The likelihood of an uneventful flight is high, indeed." Then I added, "And, Richard Eager, you don't know why you're here but **don't sweat it**. This could turn out to be a pleasant diversion from combat ops; why not just give in to it?"

In Eastern Algeria at Châteaudun-du-Rhumel Airfield near Constantine, we had outfitted Monty's "Flying Fawtress" with a combat crew, no bombs, but a full load of ammo. Instead of having to "**sweat-out**" getting off the ground before running out of flying field, the usual primary concern of bomber crews when taking off with full combat loads of fuel, guns, ammo and bombs, on this flight with Monty, his staff and guests aboard, I would find myself happily **airborne** with half the airfield still out ahead of me. When we could leave the usual three tons of bombs on the ramp, the B-17 was a joy to fly. It was often said in those days, "she climbs like a homesick angel." On this flight, as with others that would follow, instead of bomb loads, we would onload substantial numbers of British brass. Even then, she'd climb like an **HSA**, a homesick angel.

Following General de Guingand's example, the men constituting Monty's staff were a hard-working, pleasant, confident group, the epitome, I thought, of the oft-used expression, "officers and gentlemen." It occurred to me that I should not be accepting pay for the pleasant, adventuresome work that I was doing at this time. I did not, however, bring the matter up with my 99th Bomb Group paymaster.

With Monty securely strapped into his bolted-down chair in his specially built, comfortable but windowless "flying office" in our modified bomb bay, my B-17 started down the clattering steel-matted runway at Castel Benito Airdrome, setting off on my first flight with the Army Commander. As we lifted off, I raised our flaps and landing gear and adjusted our **rpm** and mani-fold pressure controls for the climb-out. As the gear retracted, I rolled the stabilizer control wheel forward a tad to hold the aircraft nose on a point slightly above the horizon.

In a moment, I started the flaps up, dropped the right wing slightly and commenced a slow, climbing turn back to the east, affording *Theresa Leta's* crew and high-ranking British passengers a close-up view of life in the streets of Tripoli. As before, the city flashed by with the same faces, squares and fountains that had greeted us on our arrival... the faces now observing our departure with unchanged expressions.

Continuing to hold a slow rate of turn through 180 degrees, we were soon over the Tripoli Harbor, heading east with an excellent view of the city and its beautiful, blue harbor taking shape out our co-pilot's window and out our right **waist-gun** opening in the back. Rolling out on an easterly heading, we looked directly into a morning sun, which heightened the whitewashed colors below.

Tripoli Harbor, with its fleet of a dozen or so half-sunken German and Italian ships, was now just off our right wing. General de Guingand and another British general, looking out the window behind the co-pilot's position, were taking note of the wreckage in the harbor and attempting to reconstruct the most likely scenarios that would explain the positions and conditions of these battered and broken Axis ships of war.

The largest of our British officers, General Maitland Wilson, Ike's Deputy Theater Commander, who had been so very considerate and reassuring when Monty presented me to the King, gave me a smile and a thumbs up. I took his pleasant gesture to mean that he was pleased, indeed, that the takeoff had been "accomplished without incident," an often-used tongue-in-cheek expression employed in the US Army Air Corps of the period with intent to glorify the moment of flight.

At other times, when fighters had been zinging through our formation in the sub-strato-sphere of southern France, Austria, Germany and Italy, Technical Sergeant Owens would be spinning around in his **top turret**, blasting away with his twin 50-caliber guns at Me-109s, Fw-190s and an occasional Me-110. I would hear and feel the spine jarring thumping of Sergeant Dale Owens' guns firing above and behind my head. I would think my top non-com was getting a better view of the air-battle than I was. But Sergeant Owens' guns were silent right now, and he was standing in the aisle beside me, ready to assist in any way he might.

"Captain Evans," he said in a tone showing a little more deference and formality than had been our custom on combat missions, "our passengers are grouped around the waist-gunner's windows which I have opened so they can enjoy the view and get some fresh air." Continuing, he reported that Sergeant Charles "Chuck" Ward, our handsome, youthful tail gunner, quickly identified by his hand-made-in-Natal, Brazil, leather boots, had persuaded General de Guingand to crawl back into his tail-gun position with him.

Staff Sergeant Eldon Austin, our smiling, redheaded, freckled-faced, all-American boy, was trying without success to persuade a smaller General to crawl down into the cramped quarters of his ball turret. Technical Sergeant Francis Morris, our modest, thoughtful, soft-spoken radio operator at his station, aft of the bomb bay and forward of the waist-gunners, would be busy, I was sure, being modest and speaking only when spoken to. I was proud of my non-commissioned officers, not one of whom had yet celebrated his 20th birthday. A couple hadn't made nineteen.

Obliged to Technical Sergeant Owens for his unsolicited report, I glanced at this slender, blond, serious-minded young man and could see that he was uncomfortable with all the British brass aboard. I caught his eye and said, "Sarge, have you been assuming the duties of head hostess on our super-class, top-brass, transport service?"

Observing the color rising in his face and realizing I had overdone it, I quickly added, "Sarge, I appreciate the initiatives you are taking upon yourself back there. Please do what you think appropriate to make things as pleasant as you can for our British guests. And, be assured, Sarge, when you're back there, you're in charge."

All on board were pleasantly occupied, except Monty. It seemed to me that The Army Commander, the title that Monty most enjoyed, appeared to be apprehensive most of the time. It also struck me that this man had tremendous responsibilities and ambitions to match. "So what," I thought, "if it didn't suit Monty's concept of decorum to go about grinning at just anybody before they had proven themselves to the Army Commander?"

General de Guingand had counseled me about Monty the day that we were all awaiting the arrival of the King. "Do not take Monty's disinclination to smile as necessarily negative," the General suggested with a fatherly smile. "Actually, you will find that Monty can be a most pleasant fellow. Indeed, when Monty tells you a story which casts Monty in a favorable light, it will strike you that you have not met a more pleasant fellow."

When General de Guingand told me that tale, I glanced quickly at this very-correct, strict-but-pleasant Englishman and noted no trace of rancor accompanying his smile. I thought to myself, "This man trusts me in a way that is very flattering; he has known me for only a short period of time, yet he feels he can joke with me about his Army Commander, assured that I share the feelings of respect and affection that this very special Englishman from South Africa holds for his Army Commander."

Monty was busying himself with some writing in his small but comfortable "office" in our B-17 bomb bay. There were no windows in the bomb bay. An over-sized chair had been bolted to the supporting structure and an attractive brass lamp had been clamped to a very ample desk. I would learn that Monty took time out of each day to chronicle in longhand the events of that day so that History, I conjectured, might recount the greatness of his life.

I asked myself, "Richard Eager, you don't have a problem with this, now do you?" The thought came to mind that if my dad had been along with us, he would have added, "Avoid a critical posture, Dick; just do your job, keep your eyes and ears open and if possible, your mouth shut." Dad would often pop up and counsel me in this manner no matter where on the globe I might happen to be.

Tripoli Harbor slid silently behind us as I rolled out on an easterly heading. Still low and paralleling the beach to enjoy the sights, I pulled up a few hundred feet to have a look at whatever might be seen farther inland from the shore of this mystical land. I was surprised to find some areas beyond the beach were very green. Those must have been the farmed patches of agriculture. Otherwise, it was quite lifeless. (I remember that it struck me that I was beginning to punctuate with "quites," quite like my new English friends quite often did.

Then, as I pulled in closer to shore and flew along the beach, I wondered if this might be the "Shores of Tripoli" that our US Marines once landed on and now sing about. I couldn't recall whether our brave Marines had run into some trouble here or had just stopped by to enjoy a swim in the blue Mediterranean Sea. I swam in the Med near Tunis, in Tunisia, and at the large military hospital at Bone, in Algeria, and found the warm water to be clean and delightful.

The picture of the beach east of Tripoli that has remained with me after half a century is one of unexpected beauty and solitude: an empty, silent beach located a few miles from the frenetic congestion that was then and may still be Tripoli. I thought to myself, "In Tripolitania, roughly the western half of Libya, civilization ends abruptly at the city limits."

"Life is hard in this parched, sun-drenched land," I mused. "With each day's struggle to live, balanced precariously on the southern edge of the Mediterranean and the northern edge of the Sahara, there would be little time left for Tripolitanians to go walking on their beautiful beach."

Letting my eyes wander from the beach, I saw striking bands of color. I saw the deep, cobalt blue of the deep water directly beneath my B-17, the yellow green of the shallows closer to shore, the snow-white froth at the surf, and then the tan sand of the beach. Looking further inland, I saw the mottled, light-and-dark-green of the low, chest-high undergrowth at the edge of the beach; and finally, I saw the brown and grey dust of the ever-blowing Sahara sands blurring the southern horizon beyond.

Tripolitania borders one of the world's greatest sand piles, extending south from the southern boundary of its capital city's metropolitan area a thousand miles to a west-to-east line, extending from Senegal to Sudan. This grandfather of all sand piles is three thousand miles wide from the Atlantic to the Red Sea.

Holding an easterly course across the Gulf of Sidra, I watched the land turn away from us towards the south. I then leveled off at 8,000 feet, activated the **autopilot**, and took a few minutes to note our en-route position, the time of day, our power settings and engine-instrument readings.

Everything was normal in the cockpit. Nope, it wasn't normal, not quite. Actually, the No. 3 engine oil-pressure indicator was not in alignment with the other indicators. "We are losing oil pressure," I noted mentally, "but we're still in the green; I'll check again in 20 minutes." I glanced at my watch and noted the time on the corner of my map.

A quick scan of the B-17 pilot's panel was all that was required to locate an aberrant instrument reading. It could then be related to other readings to assess the magnitude of a potential problem. B-17 pilots as a group were agreed that they owed much to the first-rate Boeing engineering and flight-test teams that designed, tested and built the B-17. The B-17 pilot's panel would be the starting point for the design of many future panels for almost all large, multi-engined aircraft that would follow.

It was clear at the beginning that the pilot's panel could not accommodate instruments for seven engine-performance parameters for each of four engines. That would require twenty-eight instruments. The problem, however, was quickly resolved: instead of one pointer per instrument, why not two pointers per instrument... like hands on a clock? Label the two pointers "No. 1" and "No. 2," and wire them up so they would provide readings for Engines 1 and 2 on the left wing.

Then do the same thing for Engines 3 and 4 on the right wing. In this way, the need for twenty-eight instruments on the B-17 pilot's panel would be reduced to fourteen, leaving space for flight and navigation instruments. That is just what Boeing did.

Also, it was decided at Boeing that all performance instruments would be rotated and mounted to the instrument panel so that the needles would be pointing straight up to the 12 o'clock position when all engines were operating within the normal cruise operating ranges. An aberrant reading could be picked up by a quick glance across the entire panel. A second, closer look at a particular instrument out of alignment with the others would indicate the location and severity of a potential problem. Wonderful.

To delineate ranges of safe and unsafe operation, green and red bands were painted on the instrument faces to indicate safe and unsafe operating regimes. Not every pilot would be able to immediately recall all the pressure and temperature limits; a bright orangutan, however (with an Air Corps scarf), could tell whether these readings were inside or outside these delineating red and green bands.

The bright, interested British Generals aboard my B-17 were soon checked out on Boeing's straightforward system. To demonstrate their interest and understanding, they would often return to the flight deck after an earlier briefing and inquire in perfect Yank dialect, "How're we doin', Captain? Everything hunky-dory?"

I would answer, "Everything's in the green, General," whereupon they would go away happy and assured with respect to, not only the prospects of our reaching our destination, but to the continuance of cordial, pleasant relations within the British American wartime partnership.

Suddenly, a voice with a British accent acquired in South Africa, which I was beginning to differentiate from other voices, came on the intercom, "Tail-gunner to pilot, this is de Guingand, here, reporting that the enemy is not in sight, praise the Lord, and that the view here about is absolutely mah'velous! I say Captain, would you happen to know where we are? Over."

"Pilot to tail-gunner," I responded, "Thank you for your report. As it happens, I do know where we are. Over the Mediterranean and having departed the Gulf of Gabes, we are at this time entering the Gulf of Sidra. As you know, these waters are contiguous areas of the Mediterranean lying off the coast of North Africa. I am pleased to report that enemy action in this region is expected to be light to non-existent for perhaps the next half century, a condition for which we are obliged to you and your boss, who by the way, is still at work at his desk in our bomb bay."

"Excellent, Captain. And would you happen to know our position with respect to Surt? It is a small town on the coast of Libya. I visited there recently, perhaps you know it?"

I smiled inside, enjoying the very pleasant, special Englishman from South Africa, who was close to my father's age. "Yes," I answered, "I did, indeed, hear that you were in Surt recently, a couple fortnights ago was it not, sir? As I understood, at the time, you and your esteemed boss and your 8th Army were hard on the heels of the great two-war, German Army Commander and worthy foe, Erwin Rommel, as you motored along this beautiful, albeit a tad warm, coastline."

"And" I continued, "We're coming up on a position north of Surt and west of Benghazi, Libya's alternate capital city. I understand you cut across the desert south of Derna and Benghazi as you and your Army Commander were chasing the Desert Fox out of Cyrenaica, the rather lyrical name of the eastern Libyan Sahara."

"I should say we are about 65 miles northwest of Surt, Libya, Sir, and about 180 miles from landfall, where we will be entering Cyrenaica just south of Benghazi. Our altitude is presently 7,500 feet. Would that be quite all, General?"

"Smashing," my happy passenger exulted in good fun. "But could you tell me why I am not able to see the coastline to the south from this rather respectable height? Are you quite sure, Captain, that you know where you are?"

"Certainly, I know where I am, General, at all times. But even if I should forget, I need only to call my navigator down in the nose of our flying machine. For a period of most of a year, I was a navigation instructor, General. I would teach seven navigation students at a time in a specially equipped twin-engine Beach aircraft. I make it a practice in our B-17 to work the navigation problems up here on a map in my lap."

"My navigator is doing the same thing in his nose compartment on his nice flat desk in his comfortable, well-lit office. We regularly compare notes over the intercom. Should we find a disparity in our positions or ETA's, we simply check with one of our teen-age gunners, who at times will have a better view outside than we have up here in our two front offices. And what was your other question, General de Guingand?"

My very pleasant, new, South African friend chuckled, as he asked, "Why am I not able to observe the coastline?"

"But of course, General," I responded. "That would be the airborne Sahara sands. We have a condition our meteorologists call an obscuration, which inhibits our viewing of the horizon and on occasions, can prohibit our viewing of the coastline."

Continuing, I said, "I understand, General, that a couple of armies recently drove along the coast road bordering the Gulf of Sidra, marking their passage through to Tunisia with a cloud of sand and dust that for weeks obscured the sun from the ground; and even today a couple weeks later, it still blurs the horizon and the coastline when one is up here in the sky, tooting about in a flying machine as we are."

After a short break, I said, "One could say, General de Guingand, that the dust from your recent, history-making activities has yet to be settled in the physical sense. On the other hand, I would venture that, in the military and political sense, you and your respected Army Commander have very likely settled, for perhaps another century, the issues being contested in North Africa."

"Yes, yes; you are right" my pleasant, 3-star British General friend responded. And, after a moment, discarding the mock roles we had been playing and enjoying, he added, "We did, indeed raise a bit of dust down there didn't we, Captain?"

"You did indeed, General, and the world was watching. I got regular reports at Alamogordo," I said. "And, Sir, I am sure the matter of North Africa has been cleared up for years to come with much thanks to you, your boss, and your courageous 8th Army. We Yanks realize that we are in your debt, General."

"Thank you, Captain," General de Guingand said with a "smile" that I could hear over the intercom. "For a Yank, as you say, you're quite a decent chap," he responded with a chuckle. Then after a moment, he added, "I believe I shall get out of here now if Sergeant Ward will give me a hand: I'll just stretch my legs a bit and look in on Monty. Do you have a message which I might pass along to him, Captain?"

"Yes, I do," I said quickly. "Please tell the Army Commander, if you will, that I would be pleased if he would care to join me up here on our flight deck any time that he is not busy and might like to come up and have a look around. I note that he is often occupied, but sometimes I think he appears to be quite lonely, tucked away in our window-less bomb bay."

"You might tell him that the view from up here is superior to what we are able to provide in his special, 'air-born' office." General de Guingand said that he would be pleased to deliver my message. And, he added that he would check in with me when he came forward.

I had continued to take periodic readings on our No. 3 engine oil pressure while General de Guingand and I were having our pleasant conversation. It had dropped a bit but was still in the green. Also, I asked Lieutenant Johnson to go back and look out the right waist-gunner station to see if he could see oil escaping from our No. 3 engine, and if oil was collecting on the leading edge of our right horizontal stabilizer that extends into the slipstream aft of our right **inboard** engine.

"And, Johnson," I added, "take pains not to get those nice people back there energized unnecessarily; yawn a little, look bored and happy while you're checking the situation for us. And as I think of it, while you're back there, check for oil on the left stabilizer, as well, behind our No. 2 engine."

While Johnson was having a look out back for me, I measured the loss of pressure, calculated the rate at which it was falling, and estimated the pressure we could expect to have upon reaching Cairo. I judged that we had a good chance of making Cairo without having to shutdown No. 3 engine.

Johnson returned to the flight deck and reported that our right horizontal stabilizer did indeed have an oil build-up on its leading edge, and as a matter of fact, so did our left stabilizer.

My eyes quickly flashed to the left oil pressure indicator; and sure enough, our No. 2 pointer appeared to have fallen off very slightly. Oil on both horizontal tail fins was a clear indication that engine oil was escaping through the exhaust manifolds from both inboard engines. Clearly, we were slowly pumping engine oil overboard from two and possibly four of our engines. There was no immediate cause for alarm. However, I now had two engines to keep an eye on. "Of course, you also have two eyes, Richard Eager," I said to myself, "What's the big deal?" I remembered that Dad would often make silly remarks, as I had just made to myself, during periods of mounting tension when some situation was starting to get a little "irksome," as Dad would put it.

As the coast of Cyrenaica, the eastern third of Libya, broke the horizon dead ahead, I thought I might use the time to try to think through just why I happened to be out here buzzing around North Africa with General Montgomery in my bomb bay instead of my more common load of twelve, 500-pounders.

I had been in Tripoli just about four days when King George VI had dropped by to pay his respects to the 8th Army and its Commander. While there, I was billeted in a nice set of quarters on the attractive, palm-lined avenue bordering Tripoli Harbor. This street, paralleling the waterfront, ran generally east and west. At one point, however, it turned 90 degrees north towards the harbor then quickly 90 degrees back to the east again. It then continued right on out of town toward Benghazi and Cairo where we were headed.

My assigned apartment sat squarely on this turn facing, not the harbor, but the center of downtown Tripoli. From my balcony on the fifth floor, I had a great view of the coastal boulevard as I looked west towards the center of Tripoli. A tall spire dominated the view. Atop this single column, the Italian mother wolf with her suckling twins, the mythical Romulus and Remus, founders of Rome, was rendered in marble. It was a strange rendering to a Yank, but it was beautifully executed.

I remember wondering to myself why the Italians, the creators of so much beauty and art in the world through the ages, ever allowed a rough, artless fellow like Mussolini to take control of their beautiful country and to instigate brutal fights with neighboring nations throughout Europe and across the placid Mediterranean and Adriatic Seas.

Tripoli Harbor, with its warm, blue-green, Mediterranean waters lapping its long, uninterrupted, sandy beach, was a beautiful sight from my apartment atop one of the white buildings that lined the beach. The beach wasn't wide and there was no surf. However, it stretched to the east as far as one could see. Farther out in the Mediterranean at right angles to the coastline, the water was a beautiful cobalt blue. (I know, I know, I use that term often, but the Med isn't just blue, it has a depth of color that is beautiful and special.)

There were a dozen or more half-sunken Italian ships sitting upright on the bottom of this shallow bay, which was bordered by clean, white, well-kept buildings along the bay road. The view from my balcony was outstanding. I mused, "Thank you Monty, thank you Ike, thank you Jimmie and thank you Uppie."

It was a beautiful sight, and I remember thinking that it was nice to have a few minutes during a war to relax and enjoy the spectacle of an exciting, ancient city with colorful environs like Tripoli in Tripolitania.

One morning, I walked out onto my balcony to observe a British military parade as it marched directly toward me from downtown Tripoli, then turned 90 degrees to the left toward the bay directly under my balcony, then turned back onto its easterly course. This daily, early-morning, British "march-past" would march directly past and under my balcony. I would watch it every morning for most of a week.

The Union Jack was always conspicuous, as the troops would come marching down the coast road. I was moved as I observed it moving in and out of the shadows of the palm trees that lined the avenue as far as I could see looking back toward the center of town. It crossed my mind that Yank soldiers preceding me had fought against that flag a century and a half before. When it turned the corner beneath me, I came to attention and saluted the flag of my country's first major enemy but its current ally. I thought the second arrangement better.

As I stood watching the marching men with a sampling of trucks, tanks and artillery pieces moving beneath my balcony, I recalled an incident that had taken place just a few days before. I had just finished lunch at the British Officers Club in Tripoli and some friendly British officers were helping me fill in a missing bit of **info** regarding the recent transfer of a US B-17 to the British 8th Army's equipment list.

I was being told that a personality clash had occurred between General Montgomery and

General Eisenhower. I had countered that it seemed reasonable to me to presume that Ike, being Monty's boss, might have the advantage in such a confrontation. Locals at this predominantly British Allied Officers Club grinned and suggested that I should not be too sure of that.

A group of new British friends had made me feel very welcome in this Club. Actually, it was an Allied Officers Club but there were only a dozen or so B-25 pilots and one B-17 pilot and members of their crews around to wave the Stars and Stripes. The flag of choice very much in evidence in the bar area of the club was the Union Jack.

The matter of "the *Flying Fortress* bet" came to a head one day when I was enjoying the downtown Tripoli club. The scuttlebutt was that Monty had started letting it be known around the various military headquarters in North Africa, including nice spots like the Tripoli Officers Club, that he had won a bet with Ike and that the prize was a B-17! However, there was also a backlash to the effect that Ike could not recall having made such a bet.

It seems The Supreme Theater Commander then sent out some signals of his own to the effect that he could not recall making bets with any of his commanders. And, as a matter of fact, he really didn't approve of bets among his top officers.

General Eisenhower was also broadly quoted as having observed that **General Doolittle** did *not* have surplus B-17s sitting around idle on his bases. It was suggested, however, by my new friends in Tripoli's British Officers Club that the matter was about to escalate to the Churchill-Roosevelt level, when it was learned that a solution had in fact, been worked out. This was, of course, interesting listening for me. Clearly, I was a part of that solution and it appeared that I was about to hear how my TDY assignment to Monty had come about.

A liaison officer whose job was to make regular trips and deliver packets between Ike's headquarters at the Saint George's Hotel in Algiers, Algeria, and Monty's headquarters, presently on the Tripoli water-front close to my digs, stated that a solution had been found and that orders had simply been cut (printed) at Ike's HQ and forwarded through Doolittle's HQ to one of the B-17 Groups under his command.

"And?" I said, taking note that most of the British Officers now collected in the spacious bar area were alert, interested, and gathering around to hear just why Monty had been assigned a Yank airplane with a Yank pilot and crew. It was clear to everyone present that the American officer enjoying breakfast and dinner at their club for the past few days was, indeed, the Yank who had been given this cushy assignment. I smiled as I stood up so that all present could hear my words and see my smile.

I asked, "And, what exactly did the military orders directing the transfer of a B-17 to General Montgomery specify?"

"These orders," my British informant, with a broad smile that suggested he was savoring the moment, stated "that some turkey down in Doolittle's Wing who knew how to get a B-17 off the ground and back down again should be directed to strap one of those big birds to his arse, high-tail it to Tripoli, and, upon arrival, report for duty to General Sir Bernard Law Montgomery, the Victor at El Alamein. A smashingly clean arrangement!"

My dad had said that laughter can be contagious, and he was right. There was no Anglo-American rivalry in the Tripoli Officers Club on that quite warm but pleasant summer day in 1943.

I had sensed what was coming down and upon whom it must inevitably land. It was clear to all who were on hand that I was enjoying the attention, as well as the friendly joking that was being leveled at me.

It was very funny the way the British Major told his story. He had accentuated his own British accent for my benefit, which wasn't often done by British officers. But many of his words were very good US GI jargon. And it was evident that while these British officers were certainly laughing at me, they were also smiling with me with open, easily read, friendly faces.

As their laughter subsided, I got to my feet, clicked my heels and rendered the hand salute. Then I said, "Major, clearly you are an outstanding liaison officer, a credit to your trade. Without your report, I would never have guessed that so much care had gone into my selection as Monty's pilot." Then they all laughed quite heartily. From the day of my first meeting with Monty and his splendid staff, I remembered most British adverbs were preceded by "quite," which was quite right with me. Quite!

"And, Major," I continued, "may I commend you on your excellent grasp of the American GI dialect currently in fashion in the US Army Air Corps?" Then, they laughed again. (The British laughed quickly, and then cut it off quite quickly. I liked it, thought it was a good way to go.)

I heard a lot of war stories at the Tripoli British Officers Club; some were probably true. I learned that Monty was defensive on the subject of the bet, and I guessed that he was probably guilty of something. I suspected that Monty knew he had conned Ike out of the B-17, thinking that Ike would not go public on the matter. Then, I guessed that when Monty didn't hear from Ike right away, he probably didn't know how to back away from the strife that he was creating for himself.

But Monty was enjoying his royal carriage and I was enjoying driving it about for him in North Africa.

But why had Ike gone along with Monty's effort to con him out of a combat aircraft for the use of an albeit world-acclaimed war hero, which Monty most certainly was? Monty was the first and only Army Commander who at the time had prevailed in a do-or-die struggle with an Axis Army. He had been the architect of the first allied victory over Axis Armies in North Africa. Later in regard to the North African Campaign, Winston Churchill would say, "Before Alamein we never had a victory. After Alamein we never had a defeat."

Even so, wouldn't Monty have guessed that Ike might be thought irresponsible if he pulled a combat aircraft and crew off the line for the private use of one of his commanders? One could easily presume this to be the case.

"But, no," I said, continuing my conversation with myself, "quite the opposite might be the case. Monty would have thought it nothing but logical that the world's greatest general be provided the world's greatest flying machine to fly about the combat theater regardless of where it happened to have been manufactured."

I said to myself, "Richard Eager, you don't have a problem with this now, do you?" I answered my own question promptly with a quite British "Of cau'se not."

The next day at lunch, my British liaison officer friend filled me in. The "bet" had to do with the timing of the expected pullback of the Axis Armies from the Mareth Line to Sfax, a coastal town south of Tunis. Defeating the Germans at Mareth would prevent pressure on the right flank of the American Armies, which were then driving towards Bizerte and Tunis.

Monty told me once in confidence that he did have an agreement with Ike about a B-17, but that it really should not be characterized as a bet. He said that he had told Ike that he would free Sfax by 10 April and that "it would be splendid, if he (Ike) would then send around a B-17 for him to fly about in."

On a flight we made together over the **El Alamein** battlefield, with Monty enjoying the view from the co-pilot's seat, he abruptly announced that he had written out for me why Ike had given him a Flying Fawtress and me. Handing me a three-page letter in longhand, he said, "You can give this to your grandchildren someday."

I had never pressured Monty for the details of his deal with Ike, but he wanted me to know his version. The following is Monty's "statement" which he wrote out for me in long hand, in some detail, in his airborne office, in our B-17 bomb bay, during one of our flights together.

MONTY'S DISCLAIMER

"The Fortress aircraft was given to me by General Eisenhower in April '43, after I had captured SFAX. He came to visit me at my Army HQ shortly after the Battle at Mareth; it was April 2nd and I was busy preparing to attack the Akarit position, and then to burst through the GABES Gap out onto the plains of Central Tunisia.

I told General Eisenhower that when I had captured SFAX there would be need for considerable coordination between the Allied armies in Tunisia, and this might mean a good deal of traveling about for me. I asked him if he would give me a Fortress; the splendid armament of the aircraft makes escort quite unnecessary, and I would be able to travel at will and deal easily with enemy opposition. I said I would make him a present of SFAX by mid-April, and if he would give me a Fortress it would be magnificent. He agreed.

I captured SFAX on 10 April and the Fortress was sent over to me a few days later. I have traveled many miles in it, and it has saved me much fatigue. I have no hesitation in saying that having my own Fortress aircraft so that I can travel about at will has definitely contributed to the successful operations of the 8th Army. I cannot express adequately my gratitude to General Eisenhower for giving it to me; he is a splendid man to serve under. It is a pleasure and honor to be under his command.

The crew of my Fortress are a fine body of officers and men; their comfort and well-being is one of my first considerations. It is a great honor for a British General to be flown about by an American crew in an American aircraft and I am very conscious of this."

B. L. Montgomery
General, 8th Army

A few years would pass before I would learn that Ike's Chief of Staff, the American General, Bedell Smith, had also played a role having to do with Monty's "bet" with Ike. There were many written variations of Monty's B-17 story. Nigel Hamilton wrote one fairly complete account. He published his book in 1984, *Master of the Battlefield,* Monty's War Years, 1942–1944. Within the researched pages, Chapter 7, Part Two, is the entire story. The chapter describes conversations, memos and letters about the incident, in which many top generals had their "say." The chapter is inaccurate, however, in that it states that the B-17 in question (*Theresa Leta*) crashed in July 1943, which is not true since I continued to fly her. *Theresa Leta* served her country well and was written off inventory in June 1945.

General Smith would add that Monty proposed the bet, not to Ike but to himself, adding that Monty suggested the bet at a most awkward time when General Smith was on his feet but still quite busy with the task in hand in the officers' **latrine**! "Beetle," as contemporaries called General Bedell Smith, would relate that he thought Monty was joking and had not expected to be taken seriously.

In any event, orders would come down through General Doolittle's HQ to Colonel Upthegrove's 99th Bomb Group Headquarters, directing that Captain Richard E. Evans be placed on TDY to General Bernard Law Montgomery, and that he be directed to pick up a B-17 named *Theresa Leta* at Châteaudun-du-Rhumel Airfield, Algeria, fly it to Tripoli, and report on arrival to The Commander of the British 8th Army.

Now, the question that I was beginning to mull over in my mind while continuing to Cairo was, "Is it just possible that Ike, thinking he had **been had**, was so upset he sent word to General Doolittle to send a '**hangar queen**' (a worn-out, war-weary airplane taking up space in a hangar) to Monty?"

As I continued to consider the possibilities, it was clear that my orders had come from Ike's Supreme Command HQ, through Doolittle's 12th **AF** HQ; and that while it might be presumed that Ike might not have known one B-17 from another, General Doolittle certainly would. Everyone knew that Doolittle, an early racing and barnstormer pilot, had led the B-25 raid on Japan. One presumes that Jimmie knew one aircraft from another and very likely also knew what was going on between Ike and Monty. I had met General Doolittle, but not General Eisenhower. I thought I was beginning to get the picture.

Also, in my thinking, I was getting down to Group level where I considered myself reasonably informed. If neither of the higher command levels had specified anything more definitive than "a B-17 type aircraft" and if the choice of B-17s is left to a Captain or Major in charge of Group Maintenance, what would his decision be: to fuel up his best aircraft and turn the keys over to a pilot from a competing, sister group? Not likely. I reached this point in my thought process about the time that *Theresa Leta*, above the limitless sands, crossed over the invisible boundary separating Libya to the West from Egypt to the East.

"You idiot," I said to myself, "if the choice of flying machines was made at Group level, of course, they gave you a hangar queen; that's what they are trained to do. *Theresa Leta*, an older B-17E, was delivered to the USAAC, Geiger Field, Spokane, WA, April 7, 1942. According to her aircraft logbook, she was assigned to the 8th Air Force and arrived in England the first week of June 1942. In July she was transferred to the 97th Bomb Group and had flown many missions before landing in Africa in November 1942. She deserved to be a Hanger Queen.

The Boeing engineers were rapidly improving the B-17s as battle experiences showed them where improvements could be made. When I flew with the 99th Bomb Group from Salina, Kansas, across the Atlantic to Bathurst, Gambia, I piloted a new B-17F (42-5477 *Able Mable*). This bird had numerous internal changes to improve the effectiveness, range, and load capacity, but it didn't have adequate defensive protection when attacked from the front. This defense problem was solved with the improved guns in the "chin turret" built under the nose of the B-17G, which entered the war summer of 1943.

But ultimately, the *Theresa Leta* was chosen to be Monty's taxi because she already had a small office built in her bomb bay, perfect for the Field Marshal of the British 8th Army.

There was, however, constant pressure from higher headquarters to "get more aircraft into the air," and keep the experienced bomber crews in the air as well. This was the prerequisite first step "to getting more bombs on the target." There was a period, when these two directives were the only words routinely passed from on high down to us at group level, from Jimmie's Wing Headquarters up in the Atlas range where the Red Cross girls lived high above the much more arid valley below.

I was, of course, surprised when I got the Monty assignment. Also, when I took off for Tripoli from Château dun Airfield, I was pleased to observe out on the field the rather large group of flight crews and maintenance crews who had stopped their routine activities for a few minutes to watch us get airborne.

I was getting close. In a few seconds it hit me, "Of course. These people at Château dun, who were watching with such interest when I took *Theresa Leta* into the air for our first flight, weren't paying tribute to the pilot selected to fly Monty of El Alamein about in the sky; they were on hand to see if that 'hangar queen' could still get off the ground!"

It was becoming very clear to me that my selection for this temporary duty assignment had not come from Ike. It also cleared up the question of my family possibly being related to the Eisenhowers.

I thought to myself, "I will pass this information along to Colonel Upthegrove at the earliest opportunity, if I survive."

Whatever the circumstances, I decided that *Theresa Leta*, bless her heart, was very likely one of the early arrivals in the North African Theater, ahead of me by a few days, and that it would be a good bet she had done honorable service operating from **Biskra**, before being towed or perhaps trucked up the highway to Château dun where we were destined to meet.

Biskra was a small Arab town, south of the Eastern Algerian Atlas Range and, more to the point, situated on the northern edge of the Sahara. Biskra, 225 miles south of the Mediterranean, was located just the other side of the mountain range that marked the northern limit of the Sahara. This put Biskra about 1,300 miles north of Algeria's southern border with nothing in between save 1,300 miles of Saharan sands.

At Biskra, aircraft engines did not wear out; a thirsty desert consumed them. When taxiing on the ground or flying low during take offs and landings, sand would be drawn into aircraft engines, resulting in a grinding action quite like that used in the shaping of diamonds.

As pistons moved up and down in their cylinders, the pistons, the piston rings and the cylinder walls that contained the pistons would all be shined to a high gloss by the grinding action of the high-grade Saharan sands. As a consequence, all of the exposed surfaces would become shinier and also thinner, increasing the space between them.

In time, engine oil, in increasing quantities, would seep through these spaces between the moving parts of the engines. Some of this oil, escaping through these spaces into the airstream, would attach itself to the horizontal stabilizers directly behind the inboard engines.

Lieutenant Johnson had reported oil behind on, not one of the inboard engines, but both. The horizontal tail fins did not extend far enough laterally to collect oil that might be escaping from the outboard engines. An idea was beginning to form in my mind. I didn't think it likely, but it was possible that I could soon be having problems with all my engines.

With clear indications of oil problems in two engines, I began to look at my options with growing interest. I thought that I might make Cairo without having to **feather an engine**, but I couldn't be sure.

I could return to Tripoli, but this might trigger an international incident; Monty might get wind of my conversation with myself about *Theresa Leta* being a hangar queen and might accuse Ike of sending him a worn-out, desert-weary B-17. Putting aside the lives involved and the likely strain on the British-American alliance, this sequence of events, I demurred, could have deleterious effects on my military career.

On this occasion, I did not think, "What would Dad do?"

Dad had built a cottage in the Great Smoky Mountains, dammed up a stream above it and piped running water to our cottage. Dad knew about dams, electrical wiring, piping and toilets, but I didn't think Dad knew much about flying machines, particularly B-17s that had done time at Biskra on the northern rim of the vast Sahara.

It was beginning to get through to me that while the political implications of my 8th Army TDY were not my concern, the flying safety implications arising out of receding engine oil pressure on two engines and possibly more to come, were very much my business.

After thinking through several possible eventualities, I decided that I would not return to Tripoli immediately but would continue beyond Benghazi to Tobruk before deciding to abort the balance of the flight to Cairo. It also crossed my mind that my military career would not be enhanced should Monty be forced to negotiate the last few miles across the African desert by camel.

Benghazi, an American Air Base and Headquarters for the 9th **Air Force**, was equipped with 4-engine **B-24s**. If I decided to drop in at Benghazi, I might be able to talk them out of a B-24 for a few hours. (I was a certified IP instructor pilot in B-24s as well as B-17s.) I could borrow a B-24, fly Monty and his staff to Cairo before dark, drive the B-24 back to Benghazi that night and promptly the next morning get on the job of getting *Theresa Leta's* cylinders working again.

Then a better idea came to me that I hadn't recalled seeing in the B-17 Flight Manuals. It seemed strange at first but with a few minutes thought it made sense to me: "Why not **feather** our sick No. 3 engine right now, which would keep it from losing oil in the air. To compensate for that loss of power, increase our No. 1 and No. 4, still good outboard engines, with the expectation of restarting No. 3 when we have Cairo in our sights? This would give us balanced power on landing and, more importantly, enough power for a "go around" should we get an unexpected "**wave-off**" from the tower as we approached for landing.

Lieutenant Johnson looked startled when I told him what I had decided to do. He asked, "What if we can't get No. 3 going?"

"Then we'll land at Cairo with unbalanced power very carefully," I said. "And we'll try hard to get our limping bird on the ground in one pass. I intend to draw power for the balance of our trip from our stronger engines, bringing our ailing engine back online for the finish where ideally we would like to have balanced power, particularly if we got an unpredicted wave-off from the tower."

"When we have Payne Field in our sights, I'll just bring our sick engine back online for the landing. We'll be saving No. 3 for the finish, so to speak, where the situation could become critical should we start losing oil pressure on still more engines."

I reached forward, pressed the feathering button on No. 3 engine and observed the prop outside Johnson's window as it slowed down, feathered and ground to a halt. I had shut down engines in flight before but couldn't remember it ever being a fun experience. It wasn't fun this time either, looking at the propeller turned edge first to the air stream so as not to cause drag when it should be turned at right angles to drive the air backwards and produce thrust. I thought it a proper hedge against the possibility of more serious problems that might develop in one or more of the other engines.

After a moment, I pulled the mixture control on No. 3 back to the off position. Then, I suggested to Lieutenant Johnson that he select, with great deliberation, the No. 3 ignition switch and turn it off. He did and I then set the outboard engines at slightly higher power settings and rolled the stabilizer back a notch or two. *Theresa Leta*, a hangar queen, or not, you performed like a stout lady. Apparently, three engines were OK with her.

One thing for sure we had to do after this trip. With engine three badly leaking and the others losing oil in varied quantities, all engines would need an over-haul at Payne Field. There were sufficient skilled ground crew at this field and there might even be sufficient B-17 engine parts available to rebuild Monty's four engines for his *Theresa Leta*.

Lieutenant Johnson, thinking ahead, asked, "What shall I tell our passengers?"

"Tell them nothing for the present," I said. "Someone may notice after a while that No. 3 isn't turning over. Indeed! If so, we will tell our passengers about our problem and what we're doing about it, just as if we did this sort of thing every day. We could add that Boeing has given us so much power in our flying machine that we sometimes just shut an engine down, to let it rest.

Or we might get lucky and have No. 3 back online before someone notices that we decided to let it rest for a spell," I added. "You're the boss," my loyal co-pilot said.

"Make no mistake of it," I answered, with a grin intended to take some of the edge off our not-yet-too-serious situation. A short time later, I told Johnson that he was in charge for a few minutes, and I got up to walk to the rear of the plane.

Our passengers in the back were lounging on the mattress pads that we had brought along for them. I looked at Monty as I came back by his position and he looked up at me. I think we both nodded without smiling. I was convinced that no one in the back had yet noticed the feathered No. 3 engine.

After passing Monty, I stopped, screwed up my courage and said, "General, we're abeam El Agheila. We will soon make landfall over Cyrenaica. We will be 30 miles or so south of Benghazi.

If you would like to join me up front, I would suggest to Lieutenant Johnson that he get a little rest in the back end on one of our air mattresses back there."

General Montgomery smiled; it was a breakthrough. He then asked if it would be all right. I assured him that it would, indeed, be all right. Returning to the front, I explained the new seating arrangement to Johnson who proceeded happily to the rear to find an unoccupied mattress.

I was sure General Montgomery must know about autopilots; but as I watched him climb into the seat beside me, I noticed that he could not take his eyes off the unattended pilot and co-pilot controls. He was careful not to bump the co-pilot's controls as he sat down beside me. I gave him a moment to settle in and become more relaxed.

As he gazed at the instrument panel in front of him, he turned slightly towards me with a half-smile. He asked, "I say, Captain Evans. Did you know I've been flying about in this B-17 since the middle of April? My first pilot was First Lieutenant Frank B. Evans. Remarkable, are all of your B-17 pilots named Evans?" I was surprised when hearing this and responded, "That is an amazing coincidence, sir. I hope this Evans will do as good a job as the last."

On a hunch, I asked General Montgomery what it was like to be in a tank. I thought he might unwind a bit if I could get him onto his subject and off mine for a while. He wanted very much to be responsive, but it was clear that he was uncomfortable and embarrassed in this unfamiliar environment. I diverted my attention to the instrument panel for a few minutes to give him a more time to get settled in. Then I started on a new tack.

"General," I said, "Are you familiar with the *Stars and Stripes*? It is our GI overseas newspaper."

"Yes," he said, "I have seen copies when I have visited at Ike's headquarters in Algiers, quite good, quite good, indeed."

"Perhaps you know then that your campaign against General Rommel has had very good coverage in our *Stars and Stripes*. We Yanks are very conscious of the fact that you have carried the load for us for some time now and have given us time to get ourselves trained, equipped and in position over here where the war is going on. I understand that at Kasserine Pass, we Yanks learned that we still have a few things to learn about battle tactics."

I was sincere but I was taking a chance; General Montgomery might take my remarks as apple-polishing. I could have saved myself the concern; because as Monty and I became better acquainted, I would learn that it was not possible to embarrass him with flattery. Monty would believe anything nice you might have to say about the Commander of the 8th Army. In fact, he would pump you for details.

"Is that so? What did you learn about me in the *Stars and Stripes*?" the Army Commander asked. "Well, let's see. I learned that you wore a beret and that it was the headpiece of choice among the men of your tank corps. Actually, I already knew that because I had seen your picture on the front of *Life* magazine wearing a beret. That was just after your victory at El Alamein a few weeks before I left the States. You also wore the South African campaign hat at times, festooned, I understood, with the badges of the various corps which you have commanded."

"Wonderful," he said with a rare, unguarded smile and eyes that were beginning to relax.

I could see that Monty was, indeed, starting to enjoy the flight. No question, I had found his frequency. "Where did you say we are?" He asked, noting that the land jutting into the

Mediterranean just ahead of us was beginning to move toward us at a quickening pace.

"Sir, we are approaching the coast of Cyrenaica," I answered. "That is Benghazi off to our left. I can't make out anything in the haze, but El Agheila is down there on our right in the far corner of the Gulf of Sidra. I am aware that you are familiar with these small towns that rim the Gulf of Sidra, General."

He turned immediately to see if he could make out El Agheila, an Arab town that was both a coastal and a desert town. There was no separation between the sands of the desert and the sands of the sea at El Agheila. This was the place from which Rommel had launched his first attack against the British forces under the command of General Claude **Auchinleck**.

Upon arriving at El Agheila via Tripoli, as indeed we were doing ourselves at that very moment, Rommel, within a few days of his initial arrival in Africa, was personally conducting midnight missions, reconnoitering tank sorties behind the British positions on the uncharted 300 miles of desolate desert between El Agheila and the Libyan-Egyptian border, 300 miles east of our landfall. Rommel, on one such occasion, accompanied only by a second, trailing tank, completely circumnavigated the British Army's position in total darkness. I thought this remarkable.

Rommel had chased the British forces 400 miles across the Cyrenaican desert and another 250 miles along the Mediterranean coastline to El Alamein. An inauspicious Arab town on a single, east-west rail line connecting Libya with Alexandria, Cairo and the Nile Delta, El Alamein had no significance except that it was located within a few miles from the Mediterranean to the north and less then forty miles from the Qattara Depression to the south. Beyond the Qattara, which we Yanks might dub "the Grand Canyon of North Africa," the Libyan-Saharan Desert extended further south by another thousand waterless miles.

El Alamein marked the location of a land bridge less then forty miles wide, which an army travelling east towards Cairo and the Nile Delta would necessarily have to cross to stay out of the Mediterranean to the north and the Qattara to the south.

Rommel, adequately supplied by Hitler at the onset and with space to maneuver in Libya, had to this point, deftly driven back the British forces. But now, he was delayed and then stopped in the narrows at El Alamein between the Qattara Depression and the Mediterranean Sea. As Rommel's supplies from the north were beginning to be diverted, out of necessity, to Hitler's ill conceived, poorly timed, and now desperate on-going struggle in Russia, Monty, the new Commander of the 8th Army, decided that he was in no hurry. Time was on his side. At a later time in a different clime, we could have said that Monty was "playing it cool" on the northern rim of the desperately hot Sahara sands.

Lend-lease materials of war produced in the US had at last started leaving US port cities on the Atlantic and the Gulf of Mexico and were now, on a regular basis, making their way across the South Atlantic, around the Cape of Good Hope, up through the Mozambique Channel, across the Indian Ocean to the Arabian Sea, into the Gulf of Aden, and up the Red Sea to the Mediterranean Port of Alexandria.

When the Battle of El Alamein commenced on the night of October 23, 1942, Monty's resources for battle in all essential categories – men, tanks, aircraft, trucks and petrol – were almost twice those of the Desert Fox.

I was aware, as, indeed, was the entire world, that General Montgomery had repulsed Rommel at El Alamein and had driven him backwards out of Egypt across 500 miles of desert to El Agheila, Rommel's starting place in North Africa. El Agheila was beginning to take shape out of the haze that had been blocking Monty's view. It had been presumed by most that Monty would move to close the trap and wrap up the eastern desert campaign, probably at El Agheila.

But it didn't happen that way. Monty interrupted his pursuit of Rommel at El Agheila to let his own supply trains catch up and to regroup. And, in so doing, Monty allowed his desperately wounded Desert Fox to withdraw from El Agheila to the west towards Surt and Tripoli. Feeling some compassion, I guessed that Monty looked down on El Agheila with mixed emotions, but I did not pry.

I wanted to tell the Army Commander that I was certain I understood his tactics and that they would have certainly been mine, had I been in command of the 8th Army at El Agheila. I think Monty's response very possibly could have been, "Son, do you have any idea to whom you are gratuitously offering your opinions?"

Monty might have said to himself, "Let the Desert Fox run; let him exhaust himself on the northern rim of the Saharan sands. He's starved for ammo, fuel, water, food and medical supplies but Hitler can't help him. Hitler, at last, had his own problems in Russia. And Monty probably thought, "Why shouldn't I let Rommel run right into the arms of the Yanks and let them get a few shots in and shed a little blood."

The sun, now overhead, was desert bright but its rays were refracted by a few billion particles of dust that still hung in the sky along the coastline of Cyrenaica. Monty would not be able to see very much down there but he continued to stare through the desert haze at El Agheila. I did speculate as to what might be on the Army Commander's mind as we flew along but I had no thought of interrupting his reverie.

I did not know then, but one day I would learn that Field Marshal Erwin Rommel, who contemporary German writers would say, "was like a son to Hitler," would be destroyed. Destroyed, not by Englishmen or Americans, but by Hitler himself. And Hitler would destroy Rommel twice.

Hitler had turned a deaf ear to his "Desert Fox's" pleas for reinforcements, fuel, engine parts, tanks, and air support with which to reconstitute his "Afrika Korps." Without Hitler's support, the Desert Fox would certainly die on the African desert.

But what could Hitler do? Hitler by then was holed up in his "Wolf's Lair," the name he called his field headquarters in East Prussia just 60 miles from the half-frozen Baltic. The winds of war and the winds of winter had blown bitter cold for Adolph Hitler.

Hitler's Army was never able to take **Leningrad**. The best he could do was to put Russia's first capital city under siege for a protracted period and starve millions of people.

Hitler's Army reached **Moscow**, but the Russian winter also reached Moscow at the same moment in time. A few German patrols penetrated the Russian capital, but they were unable to get a foothold. They were forced out into the snow and the ice and the sub-zero cold. And, come the spring that comes late in central Russia, the German survivors huddling around their tanks and field guns could no longer be called an Army.

Early on, Hitler's army had put **Stalingrad** under siege but, in so doing, it had allowed itself to be surrounded in an unexpected second stage of the battle. Hitler's army was then defeated, and German prisoners were summarily rounded up and marched off to Siberia, with no trace left for others to see that they had ever existed.

When the greatest tank battle in history at **Kursk** (July 5-16, 1943) finally ground to a halt after eleven days and eleven nights of fighting, there were survivors but no victors. There was only mutual decimation and death at Kursk. Hitler was now exhausting military resources, which he could not replace on the steppes of Russia. The battle was the final strategic offensive that the Germans were able to launch on the Eastern Front.

His quadruple defeats at Leningrad, Moscow, Stalingrad and Kursk have been recorded in the history books of Germany in the blackest and bleakest of inks. Hitler could send no support to Rommel in Tripoli; suddenly he had nothing left to spare for his favorite General and perhaps his surrogate son.

Rommel's fate in North Africa was probably sealed at the "bend of the Don," at the place in southern Russia where the Don River flowing southeast towards Stalingrad suddenly makes a sharp ninety-degree right turn to the southwest. At this place, the Russian 62nd Army, under the command of Marshal Georgi Zhukov, and assisted by Communist Party Representative, General Nikita Khrushchev, began Operation Uranus, a plan to break out from Soviet positions and encircle and destroy General Friedrich Paulus' 6th Army. They were successful.

With only a small part of the blood and the resources of war that Hitler squandered when he refused to let General Paulus affect an orderly withdrawal from Stalingrad, Rommel might have been supported in North Africa for a much longer period. But Rommel was forced to continue the fight along the southern coast of the Mediterranean, walking backwards from El Alamein to El Agheila, to Surt, to Tripoli, to Sfax, over a thousand miles without adequate support. The end of the Afrika Korps finally came in Tunisia in May 1943. At that time, I was in the area, just across the hills that separate Tunisia from Algeria.

Was Rommel so clever in eluding Monty in Tripoli, or was Monty less than anxious to engage the Desert Fox even when the Fox was crippled and abandoned by his commander at El Agheila? Had Monty been content at El Alamein to sit tight and build up his forces? And, if so, wasn't he right? Supplies had started coming through the Suez Canal regularly, including Sherman tanks and heavy artillery fresh from assembly lines in the USA. A complete B-25B Bombardment Group arrived from the States in time to support Monty at Alamein.

When the attack at El Alamein finally came, at midnight, October 23, 1942, Monty's strength versus Rommel's, in essentially all categories – men, tanks, artillery and planes, was two-to-one. Also, the British had obtained, through the heroism of Polish and British patriots, a copy of a German coding-decoding machine, called **Enigma**. The device, the size of a small typewriter, was spirited out of Poland under the very noses of the early Nazis. A team of skilled and highly motivated British scientists and engineers had then worked tirelessly to first learn the German system for encoding messages through the machine, then use the critical information thus obtained without tipping their hand to the Germans that they had broken their secret codes.

The prime military intelligence produced by the British at Bletchley Park was code-named

Ultra. Messages would be encoded at Rommel's headquarters in North Africa into an Enigma machine, then transmitted by conventional radio to Hitler's "Wolf's Lair" in East Prussia. When messages were being received and decoded in East Prussia, an identical Enigma machine at Bletchley Park, England, was spelling out Rommel's battle plans in English… for Monty!

Monty was always apprised of Rommel's battle plans. Right? Wrong. Over time, Hitler's demands became so unrealistic that Rommel was obliged to re-modify the modified plans that he had in hand one more time after they had been returned from Hitler's headquarters in East Prussia, to Rommel… through Bletchley Park, in rural Buckinghamshire.

Early on, Hitler had become dissatisfied with first one, then another of a series of Chiefs of Staff. By 1942, he had taken unto himself overall command of the *Wehrmacht*, the German high command. Ignoring his General Staff, Hitler would personally develop battlefield plans in detail and then send specific instructions directly to his Army Commanders in the field. Of course, these battle directives were also received at Bletchley Park, where they were decoded, then "re-coded" and sent directly to British and American field forces. There is no clear evidence that Hitler ever knew that the Allies were looking down his throat.

Still, Monty did not always have a pat hand going into battle. He would find that Rommel, as his situation became more desperate in North Africa, would take it upon himself to re-modify Hitler's plan: back to something that would more-closely match reality… the reality that General Rommel had to face daily at the front in North Africa.

After twelve days and nights of struggle at El Alamein in the first week of November 1942, Monty's X Corps finally broke through, and a sick and dispirited Rommel then pulled back and fought, and continued to pull back and fight, again and again, until he was once more back at El Agheila, his starting point. Why did Monty, many wondered, not just finish off the trapped Desert Fox?

Why did Monty delay and regroup at El Agheila, allowing Rommel time to escape to the west? What was Monty thinking as he and I flew east into Egypt in Ike's B-17, paralleling his recent westerly pursuit of The Desert Fox? And what was Monty thinking as we continued to fly towards El Alamein, the Qattara Depression and Cairo?

For a long time, The Army Commander peered off into the haze that hung over El Agheila where he had stopped only weeks before to reorganize his forces, giving Rommel time to escape to the west, time to bind his wounds and fight again.

———————

Suddenly Monty's hand grasped my shoulder with unexpected force and a frightful, rasping sound came from his throat. I turned and was alarmed to see the fear in General Montgomery's face. He got his breath in a moment and half shouted, half choked, "It's stopped! It's stopped! The engine stopped… it's not running!"

General Montgomery's left hand clutched my shirtfront. As I turned toward him, his right arm, thrown back toward the window on his side, was pointing toward No. 3 engine. He was trying to say something, but no sound was coming from him; he couldn't get it out.

My eyes quickly came to focus on that prop blade, pointing straight up – still as death framed by the co-pilot's window and Monty's face. "Oh, My God," I shouted to my inner-self, 'how could you have not warned General Montgomery, how could you have forgotten that you had feathered the No. 3 engine? You were so busy showing off Boeing's great *Flying Fortress*, you clean forgot that you had feathered that bloody engine."

I remember thinking to myself that I was swearing to myself. My parents would never let me swear out loud when I was growing up; I was not allowed to develop the habit. Somehow, I knew that I was missing out on a form of self-expression that could certainly prove comforting to one's self, if not always persuasive to someone else's self.

"You only swear to yourself," I said to myself. "You never let it all out; you keep it bottled up. And look what you've done to this poor man; you've humiliated him. And, oh my God, he's the top military man in the British Commonwealth. You're a blinkin' idiot, Richard Eager!"

I had released my seat belt and was now standing in the aisle that separated the pilot and copilot's seats, leaning over in front of the General. The autopilot was flying the airplane. With my left hand I grasped Monty's right shoulder; my right palm was open and directly in his face. I was trying to get him to focus his attention on something, anything. I said, "General Montgomery, it's okay. It's okay, sir. The engine did not just stop running; it did not turn itself off.

I could see that he was beginning to settle down and come out of it. He had been pushing up against his seat belt, which, incidentally, was doing its job. There was an emergency in the cockpit and it hadn't let go of him. Then, quite suddenly, he just fell back exhausted and drained. It was over I thought; I could now explain what I had done. I opened my mouth to speak…

But General Montgomery was ahead of me and he asked a very good question. In an unexpectedly strong voice, he asked, "Why, in God's name, would you just turn it off?" He was looking directly into my eyes for the first time during our few days together. I wondered if he saw the terror, which I was sure they must have been reflecting. I was terrorized, I confess, not by the airplane, but by Monty.

"Sir, I turned that engine off myself. I feathered No. 3, which means I shut it down and changed the angle of the propeller blade, so the edges cut through the wind and not put drag on the plane. The engine was leaking too much oil, sir, and I needed to preserve the engine in case I needed it for our landing. Feathering an engine is done all the time in flight if the engine needs a rest. These B-17 air ships are built to fly with three engines, and if needed, two engines."

The Commander of the British 8th Army, the only general of the Allied cause to defeat an Axis Army in the field, "Monty, the Victor at El Alamein," was looking at me as if he would like to have me shot. "Oh, God" I thought, "He just might be able to pull it off." I decided it was my turn to be terrified.

I remember my dad telling me one time that everybody is afraid of something at some time or another, and it's not something one need be ashamed of. "But to recover quickly," Dad had said, "there are some things one must learn to do. For example, Dick, humor loosens the grip of fear."

"That's it," I thought. "Dad was right. I've got to get the Army Commander to laugh at something." Quickly, I managed to say to General Montgomery, "If you please, General, sir, I am sorry to have alarmed you. I was enjoying our conversation so much I honestly forgot for a moment that I had shut down our No. 3 engine. And I realized too late how that dead engine must have looked to you more than several feet from your face."

The General was calming down now, and I was reassured. I thought, "Here's where I will introduce some humor to 'loosen the grip of fear.'"

"General Montgomery," I said as calmly as I could manage, "the first public viewing of the B-17 occurred at the Boeing Plant in Seattle in our state of Washington. Back then the B-17 seemed much larger than it does today.

"A reporter from the *Seattle Times*, searching for words to describe how he felt when the B-17 was first rolled out from its hangar with machine guns pointing up-and-down, for-and-aft, and right-and-left, gleefully said to himself and subsequently wrote in the Seattle newspaper, 'It looks like a flying fortress.' And, as you know, General Montgomery, it has been called "The *Flying Fortress*" since the moment of that initial roll-out."

Continuing, I said, "General Montgomery, Boeing gave us so much power in this machine..." and, I repeated, "we sometimes shut an engine down to let it rest." And I gave General Montgomery my best Tennessee grin that my mother loved so much.

After 30 seconds, during which General Montgomery did not smile at all and, indeed, allowed no sound to emanate from him, it was getting through to me that my light humor had failed. As I watched the backside of the world's first clear winner for the Allied Cause making his way aft toward his special bomb bay office, I fell once again to swearing to myself.

"Damn, damn, damn, Richard Eager," I said to myself, "You have for sure ripped it now. How could you have been so stupid? And just how are you planning to explain this to Jim Doolittle? And what are you going to do when General Jim tells you to go tell your story to Ike? And where do you suppose Ike will send you?"

Momentarily shaken from the surprise reaction from the General, I realized the need to get back to the real problem at hand, the safe landing of our B-17. I called Lieutenant Johnson back to the front and we formulated a plan for landing. More than four hours into the flight we were now within safe reach of Payne Airfield near Cairo. We determined the oil levels in the three operating engines would be sufficient under their leaky circumstances to bring us in without restarting engine No. 3. Nevertheless, as we made our approach to the landing strip, I was again breathing normally for the first time in hours.

We landed without incident, and as we parked the *Theresa Leta*, a group of newsmen with cameras swarmed in as close as they dared to the three decelerating props. It seemed there were always cameras present when the General was present.

Securely on the ground at Payne Airfield near Cairo, I found I had sufficient strength to stand by the side of this great man and receive his gracious thanks for a "splendid trip down" and the smoothest landing etc., etc. in front of a news camera and flashing bulbs.

8.2 *General Montgomery meets "Theresa Leta" near Gabes, Tunisia* (Imperial War Museum)

8.3 *Lieutenant Frank B. Evans, first "Theresa Leta" pilot to fly General Montgomery,*
introduces his crew to the general (Imperial War Museum)

8.4 *Lieutenant Frank B. Evans shows General Montgomery the waist gunner's
.50-cal machine gun* (Lieutenant Frank B. Evans)

8.5 *General Montgomery talks with flight and ground crewmen* (Imperial War Museum)

8.6 *Captain Richard E. Evans, second "Theresa Leta" pilot, gives a flying lesson to General Montgomery* (Captain James W. Hudson)

8.7 *"Monty" the pilot* (Captain James W. Hudson)

8.8 *Montgomery's airborne B-17 "office"* (Captain James W. Hudson)

8.9 *Norden Bomb Sight is placed in the nose of a B-17* (Alamy Stock Photo)

8.10 *The well-designed B-17 cockpit* (World Conflict Images)

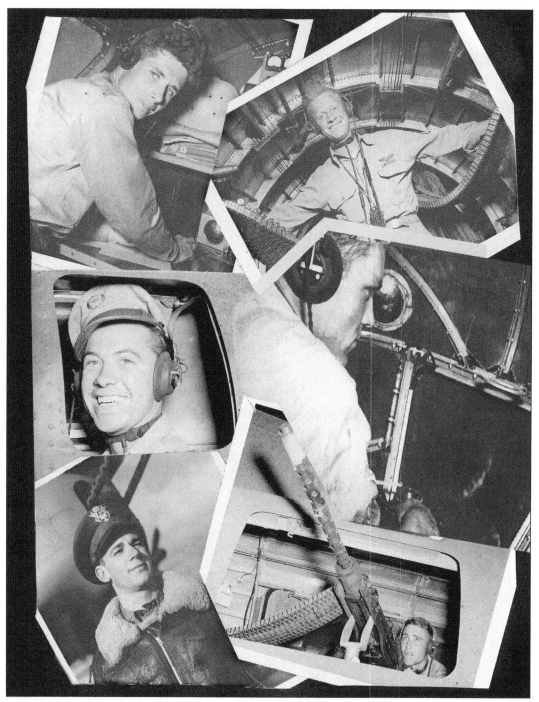

8.11 *"Theresa Leta" B-17E crew: From top left corner, clockwise, Technical Sergeant Francis R. Morris, Staff Sergeant Eldon B. Austin, Second Lieutenant Albert L. Beringsmith, Staff Sergeant Victor J. Kennedy, Second Lieutenant Thomas H. Carver and Staff Sergeant Charles W. Ward* (Captain James W. Hudson)

Photos 8.11 and 8.12 are copies from Colonel R. E. Evans' memory book made for his wife, JoAnn.

8.12 *"Theresa Leta" B-17 crew: From top left corner, clockwise, Second Lieutenant Fred L. Johnson, Staff Sergeant Dale E. Owens and unknown* (Captain James W. Hudson)

8.13 *General Montgomery and Captain Evans stand in front of feathered #3 engine, Payne Field, near Cairo, Egypt* (Captain James W. Hudson)

8.14 *Ground crewmen replacing a B-17 engine* (World Conflict Images)

8.15 *"2nd Patches" is a B-17G from the 346th Squadron, 99th* (World Conflict Images)

9.1 *Don't cross the street, Magnolia Avenue* (McClung Historical Collection)

CHAPTER 9
LIFE AND DEATH ON MAGNOLIA

I was probably four or five when my dad asked me, "What are the first words you remember, Dick?" Mom looked up from her sewing. I recall the looks on both my parents' faces; they were smiling and waiting. Sure of myself, I matched their smiles with one of my own and answered, "Don't step off that curb." Both of my parents' smiles faded fast. I would learn that the words they were expecting to hear were "Mother" or "Dad" or both.

Dad looked really surprised and said, "Don't what?"

"The first words I ever remember, Dad, were 'Don't step off that curb.' You remember Dad, you and Mom didn't want me to get out in the street and get hurt. You said Magnolia was a thoroughfare and that folks drive like crazy on thoroughfares."

I can still see my dad standing over me and pointing down at that curb in front of our house, a half-century ago. Dad's look made me think that if I stepped off that curb and wasn't hit by a car, I might get a whap or two from Dad's old razor strap.

Mom and Dad made a convincing case back then. Dad said, "It helped keep you alive, Dick, during a critical period in your development." Maybe so, but a time soon came when I would understand that Dad, being the principal of Knoxville High School, would be at Knox High from 8-to-6 on weekdays, and Mom, being what Dad called "a gifted lady with a powerful contralto voice" would be at the weekly meeting of the 'Knoxville Ladies' Tuesday Morning Musical Society. Actually, Mom would often stay with the Tuesday morning musical ladies most of the day. They would always plan to "have a little lunch" after their regular Tuesday Morning Musical Society meeting and "do a little shopping" at Miller's down-town department store afterwards.

Dad would always say, "Dick, your mother has never really done a little shopping." It so happened that Mom's Tuesday activities in downtown Knoxville coincided with "the iceman's" regular ice deliveries on Magnolia. Assured that Mom was away, I decided one time that I was old enough to step off the curb just a few steps and swipe ice out of the back of the ice wagon with a good chance that neither Mom nor Dad would find out about it.

The time period was the mid '20s; the place was East Tennessee. While we kids "of modest circumstances," as Dad described us, had modest experience with ice cream back then, we did enjoy the cooling effects of plain ice. Also, we developed special skills for getting ice out of the back of ice wagons.

My friends John Lea, Dick Wayland and I learned to work as a team. Two of us would rush the ice wagon from the rear while the other one would run along the sidewalk beside the horse. He would be our lookout man. We got the idea from motion-picture cowboys, Tom Mix, Ken Maynard and Buck Jones. They always had a lookout man.

If our lookout man saw the horse getting a funny look, maybe even raising his tail a bit, he would holler "lookout" to warn us. Then, we would all "take corrective steps," as Dad would say, and run on the sidewalks or the grass until the horse got through.

———————————

Every Saturday we watched our cowboy heroes ride their horses. It cost us 22 cents, 10 cents for the show and 6 cents each way for the rides on the Park City street cars. Horses pulled these cars at first; later the horses were replaced by "modern" electric trolley cars.

All our cowboy-movie cowboys rescued girls. They never went steady or married any girls, however. And they never ever kissed girls at the end of their movies either; the kissing endings came later. At first, the old cowboys, as I well remember them, would just ride off "into the sunset." Then the organ would get louder and louder. We thought these were nice endings back in those days, even in black and white.

I was beginning to think the parts about the girls were okay, but I didn't tell John Lea or Dick Wayland or Fred Ford. I didn't tell my big brother, Stewart, either. But he told me that he "went around with girls a whole lot" and that "they were a lot more fun when they got a little older."

This was way back in the twenties, I think, when the movies were just one-kiss-movies. The kissing would always start near the end when the bandits were tied up and the girl was untied. This would be the last scene. And, as the organ got louder, the "The End" flashed on.

One night after dinner, I told dad that I thought Buck Jones had the prettiest girls and that Ken Maynard didn't seem to like girls the way Buck did. Also, that Tom Mix didn't seem to notice the girls at all. I said Tom probably liked his pony, Tony, best of all. Dad showed he agreed with me by nodding his head up and down. Then Dad looked at me but kept on reading his paper.

In a minute, he said, "That's nice, Dick," but he didn't bring his paper down like he would when he wanted to talk. I turned to go upstairs to my room but just then dad looked over the top of his paper and said, "I'm sorry, Dick; what did you say?"

I turned back around and told Dad again about how Buck liked girls more than Ken did and that Tom mainly liked Tony, his pony. Dad got his paper way down this time and I could see that he had a big grin on his face.

I remember that I knew when Dad was grinning with me, or at me, because all of a sudden, my face got really hot. I knew that meant my face would be getting red and that Dad would know that it had gotten hot, and he would smile at me. (Later on, I realized what a nice man my dad was. Dad would smile at me lots of times, but he never did really laugh at me.)

That time, Dad leaned back in his chair still smiling, which made his glasses sparkle. Then he said, "Well, well, well."

Dad looked at Mom, who was sewing at our dining room table, and said, "Hellie, what do you make of this? I think our son, Dick, here would like to take a ride on Tom Mix's pony, Tony, and would also like to take Buck Jones' girl away from him. What do you make of this?"

Mom looked up from her sewing. She was smiling, too, but not like Dad was. She looked at me and quickly said, "Leave the boy alone, Ernest." Then she turned toward me and said, "Don't pay any attention to your father, Dick. It's okay to like girls a little bit; someday you will like them a lot. I'm a girl; you like me, don't you?" Then Mom started smiling funny, too.

I said, "Mom, I love you; but you're different; you're my mother."

When I finally fessed up to Dad how we ran behind the ice wagon, he said that he thought this was "excellent judgment on our part and that while we were running, we could think we were running around left end, like in football." After we got the idea of one of us being the "lookout man," we had a perfect record. Never were we hit by a car, the horse or our parents.

Magnolia Avenue was a real wide street. First, it had two-way horse traffic pulling wagon loads of vegetables, which Mom could go out and buy off the back of the wagon. Later, we had two-way horse-drawn streetcars, and still later, in the early '20s, electric trolley cars took the place of the horses, which weren't needed anymore.

On Halloween, when the new electric street cars stopped at our corner, my big brother, Stewart, and his friends Herman Wayland, Jim Murdock and Bill Smythe would run up behind a car and yank down on the rope at the back. This would pull the trolley wheel off the cable that was running down the middle of the street. The motorman would then have to go around to the back of the car and put the trolley back on the cable. This always made us boys laugh as we ran away.

Sometimes while the motorman was putting the trolley back on the cable, Dick Wayland, John Lea, and I would come out of our hiding places and dump trash cans full of leaves through the front door of the streetcar left open to let the motorman back in. When the motorman came back around front and saw all the leaves in his car, we thought this was very funny; so, we laughed while we were running away.

The motorman usually wouldn't laugh though; sometimes he would wave at us while he was touching the end of his nose with his thumb. This made Stewart, Jim, Herman and Bill laugh even harder; but John and Dick and I didn't know about thumbing our noses yet. We were always making sure that we were running fast enough to get away from the motorman.

We had great fun playing tricks on the iceman and the motorman; however, we had to give up some of our fun when we joined the YMCA, the Young Men's Christian Association, and the Boy Scouts of America. I remember that Dad said, "Dick, there are some inconsistencies in your program which require resolution." Dad would talk like this so we wouldn't forget he was the Principal of Knoxville High School.

On Friday afternoons after school, we went to "Scout Meetings" at our church and got to stay up late. On Saturday mornings, some of us would go to the YMCA. At the "Y," we all swam naked in the indoor pool. After the first time, you didn't get embarrassed anymore about looking "different"; everybody seemed to understand that the new members would be getting some hair before too long anyway.

We also learned how to climb ropes and do other things to build muscles. I got so I could go hand-over-hand all the way to the ceiling of the gym, starting from a sitting position on the floor. Our coach taught me to keep my legs stiff and straight out in front all the way up and all the way back down.

Another way to climb the rope was to pump your legs going up, making it look like you were running up the rope; then you would come back down with your legs stiff, and pointed straight out like you were sitting down.

It was real hard climbing hand-over-hand with your feet out in front of you in a "sitting" or "jack-knife" position, but Dad said he knew why I was working so hard on the rope: he said, "Dick, you're trying to out ape Tarzan." I didn't always get Dad's jokes back then, but Dad would always explain his jokes and keep repeating them until I got them. Sometimes I would laugh for Dad, even when I didn't know what was funny.

I knew that "Tarzan" was a new comic strip in the *Knoxville News Sentinel*, coming after "Jigs," "Barney Google" and the "Katzenjammer Kids." Tarzan was about a fellow who thought he was a monkey because his mother was one. Dad said he thought that "was a logical conclusion to draw." Tarzan never saw his father while he was growing up, though I guessed his father was probably an ape, which was a bigger monkey. I found out that Tarzan's dad was named "Lord Greystoke," which I thought for a long time was one crazy name for an ape, or even a large monkey.

Joining the Boy Scouts was another thing that nice boys did back in those days besides going to the YMCA. Dad said it was particularly important that school principals' sons be nice boys.

Knoxville's Boy Scout Troop 12 met in the basement of the First Methodist Church where my Mom sang in the choir. The Boy Scout laws still come to mind; that's because they came to my mind every Friday afternoon for about three years running back into the '30s. When Troop 12 lined up to start the scout meeting, we all stood at attention and recited all twelve of the Scout laws together.

We all liked and respected our 5-foot, 6-inch scoutmaster, Melvin Hoffeld, who also went to our church. We would all have liked Mr. Hoffeld even if our parents hadn't insisted on our liking him. Every boy in Troop 12 was pretty sure he would soon be topping 5 feet 6 inches and could then say he was taller than his scoutmaster.

I will never forget those scout laws; I can recite them even now: "A Scout is trustworthy, loyal, helpful, friendly, courteous, kind, obedient, cheerful, thrifty, brave, clean and reverent." My dad never actually told me to stop dumping leaves in streetcars or to quit stealing ice off the back of ice wagons. He did, however, suggest that I might want to become an Eagle Scout someday when I grew up, if I ever grew up.

My mom once said to me, "Dick, your dad has a way of putting things. But, when he puts it to you, he will most of the time already be smiling."

"A good rule of thumb with Dad," Mom suggested, "was to be sure Dad was smiling, before you started smarting off with him."

At one point, I gave some thought as to just how the "decision process" (as Dad often put it) worked in our family. That's when I came up with the idea that Mom had more than one vote when "critical family decisions" were being made. For example, Mom thought Scouting was great—not because she liked snakes and potatoes baked in mud—but because being a Scout would require my being at The First Methodist Church, not just once a week but two times a week, Sunday School and Church on Sunday mornings and Scout meetings on Friday nights.

Mom tried to use "man" talk with me, like Dad did, and one time she said that going to Scouts and Sunday school at First Church was "doubling the odds" on my becoming a nice boy. I don't recall that my mom ever did tell me that I was a "nice boy"; the best I ever got when I had behaved "within reason" was "keep that up, my Dickie bird, and some day you may become a nice boy."

After three-quarters of a century, dear Mother, I'm still working on it.

———————————

One Tuesday, when Dad was at school and Mom was at the Tuesday Morning Music Society, a streetcar ran into a man who was walking across Magnolia. I was by myself and I saw the car hit the man. It knocked him up in the air and he hit the curb with his head, across the street, real hard. Then, he went limp! I decided quickly that this was to be a very special day "in my development into young manhood." Dad had said many times, "There is a good chance, Dick, that you just might develop into a man someday."

I decided that I should stop at the curb, "look both ways," and then I should run across Magnolia Avenue real fast, so I could join the people starting to run towards the man and maybe help some way. I remember thinking how grown up I must have looked to the others, being the first one to get to where the man was, which gave me a front-row view of him.

Very quickly a crowd was standing around the man and me. I knew that I was excited, but since I had gotten there first, I stayed right out in the middle with the man. Studying him closely, I noticed that his eyes were open, but that they weren't blinking at any of us who were watching him.

His head was broken open, just like an eggshell; I could see the bone, and I remember that I was surprised that there wasn't more blood, on the bone, on his head. There was a little blood in his hair, but I could see that none of it was running out on the street. Being on the front row, and being shorter than everybody else, I could tell that I was getting a much better view than anybody else of this man's broken open head.

Actually, I was getting a good view inside his head, and I had never had a view like that before. A large piece of bone with skin and hair on it was knocked loose from his head. And the skin on his head was twisted so that the bone was hanging upside down and inside out, over his ear. I remember thinking that this bone looked like a broken door, swinging on one hinge; a barn near our cottage in the Smokies had a door that hung open just like this man's head did.

I knew if Dad had been there, he would have said, "Dick, the streetcar has opened a door into this poor man's mind." Dad was always trying to help us understand things like our brains, by making little jokes.

It's funny what you think about when you're little and what you remember after you're grown up. I have always remembered that Dad said, "We all need more brains than we've got." I was sure Dad was right, and that this must be why our brains are all wrinkled up the way they are, being jammed into our heads so tight. This man's brain really was wrinkled up; I figured he must have been real smart before the streetcar hit him. I also decided after a while, that since he hadn't blinked his eyes at all, he must be dead. And, it was exciting, I decided, to see your first real dead man, with his head open.

Although I hadn't seen a dead man before, still I wasn't afraid at all. I figured that probably all grown-ups had seen at least one dead man, but probably had never seen inside like I was seeing, on my first ever broken head. I remember thinking that I had seen my first open head, and I had gotten a good view inside, and I was ten years old, still just a Tenderfoot Scout.

I waited until after supper, when dad was busy reading his paper in front of our coal fire in our living room, to tell him about the man who had gotten his head broken and had died. I was afraid to bring up the subject to Dad, about the man and his head, and me being out there in the middle of Magnolia Avenue. But I was even more afraid that somebody else would bring it up to Dad ahead of me.

I started out by telling Dad how I had seen a man's brain; then I started asking a lot of questions about our brains, hoping that Dad wouldn't ask me how come I got such a good view of this man's brain. Dad always liked to teach, and in this case, I was really anxious to learn.

Dad said he had heard about the accident, and that the man had died immediately without any pain. Also, that our family didn't know him. Then he put the paper back up in front of his face.

Dad was always teaching us boys; so, I figured there was a lesson in there someplace. I thought about it for a while, and then I said to Dad, "I've got it, Dad, if a man gets killed and our family doesn't know him, we don't have to worry about him anymore. Have I got it right, Dad?"

The paper came down quickly and Dad said, "Now, wait just a minute, Dick. I didn't mean it quite like that. We're sorry when someone gets hurt, but we can't do very much about it, after it's all over. And, of course, we didn't know this man either."

Dad and I talked in front of the fire for a long time that night, way after my bedtime, and Mom didn't send me off. Once she came out of the kitchen and stood in the hall and listened to Dad talking. Dad was telling me that probably what I saw was the poor man's cerebrum; that's when Mom said, "Dick saw the poor man's what?"

I had just started to feel better, and think I was off the hook with Dad (about being out in the street) when Mom got into it. But Dad turned toward Mom and said, "Hellie, Dick and I were just having some man-to-man talk. Dick had some questions about the brain, and I was describing the somatotopic organization of the cerebrum. Dick really is quite interested in these heady things, Hellie."

I didn't understand Dad's "heady" pun back then, but I did realize that "heady-things-Hellie" sort of rhymed, which I figured made it real funny. Anyway, I laughed like crazy, thinking that Dad was helping me out with Mom, and things were working out really well.

Dad's eyes shined bright as he went on and said, "I was just about to shift to the base of the brain and tell Dick what the medulla oblongata does for us. Would you like to join us, Hellie?"

I took it that Mom didn't really want to join Dad and me. She just turned away without saying "good night" to either one of us. Then we could hear her walk down the hall to our downstairs bathroom and close the door. Dad's eyes were bright behind his glasses, when he smiled again and said, "I guess it's our bedtime too, young man. We'll talk some more about the human brain another time. Give me a hug and get on up the stairs."

Dad would tell me "we have to keep the girls a little off balance, Dick." I remember thinking, a few years later, that Dad might have been trying to get Mom off balance, that night after I saw my first broken head.

After I had hugged Dad and had turned to head up stairs, he said, "Oh, Dick, just one more thing. You are getting to be a pretty big boy now, and before long you will be wanting to help your big brother, Stewart, with his paper route. It will then be necessary for you to walk across streets." I thought to myself, "Oh, oh, here it comes."

Dad, however, just kept on going and said, as he looked me straight in the eyes, "Dick, I don't believe you need to stay right on the curbs anymore, Son, but don't forget to always look both ways." I know you don't want folks looking at your cerebrum, now do you? And, right out there in the middle of Magnolia Avenue? I doubt yours has even started to wrinkle yet, Dick, what do you think?"

I told Dad that I agreed that mine probably wasn't very wrinkled yet, that I sure didn't want people to see it all smooth and all, and that I would look both ways. Then, I slipped down the hall heading for the stairs, being careful not to make any noise when I went by the bathroom where the light was still on. But I didn't get by Mom. As I started up the steps, I heard her singing in a low voice, "I'm on to you, Dickie Bird, my brainy boy; see that you always walk across the streets. Don't run."

Looking back, I have thought that that special day in my life, made even more memorable by my thoughtful dad, must have been a watershed day in my development. Dad told me the next day that my "horizons were expanding." I had already thought that if I could cross Magnolia without permission, I could walk up to Fifth Avenue, and see what John Lea and Dick Wayland were doing… just anytime I wanted to.

In fifteen or sixteen years, John, Dick and I would all be pilots in the Army Air Corps. In another 30 years, John and I would get on the telephone (like the telephone ads on TV) and talk and remember: we would remember our early days on Magnolia and Fifth Avenue and the days that followed in the war, the war that we always thought was coming. We would recall that we had told each other that a Second World War for our generation would be "our common destiny." And, of course, it was.

John and I wouldn't be able to call our friend Dick Wayland. Dick would die flying out of England. So would A.C. Murphy, whose mom was my mom's close chum. And we wouldn't be able to reach Fred Ford either, or I.C. Hewgley. None of these boyhood chums would get to come back home from the war after it finally ended in September 1945.

My brothers (Stewart, Tom and John) and I joined the Army Air Corps. All four of us would be active flyers: three pilots and one navigator. All of us became Officers in the then new US Army Air Corps: Pilot Captain Tom Evans and navigator First Lieutenant John Evans would fly in A-26s and B-25s in the CBI (China-Burma-India) Theater; Pilot Lieutenant Colonel Stewart Evans would fly B-29s in the Pacific Theater out of Guam; Major Richard Evans would fly B-17s in the European Theater out of Africa, Italy and England, B-29s in Pacific Theater out of Guam and Okinawa. (After the Second World War Colonel Richard Evans would fly B-47s, B-52s and the B-58 in the United States Air Force.)

Who would have the toughest war? Mom, of course, with Dad a close second.

9.2 *The Evans family, 1940, William ("Pop"), Dick, Tom, Stewart,*
Helen ("Mom") and John (front center)

9.3 *Dick and Stewart, Alamogordo Air Base, NM, 1942*

9.4 *Dick and older brother, Stewart Evans, fly a North American AT-6 at Biggs Field Army Air Base, TX*

9.5 *Lieutenant Tom Evans flies the B-25J, "Mitchell" named "Sunday Punch"*

9.6 *Dick's younger brother,*
Tom Evans, USAAC,
12th BG, 81st Squadron

9.7 *Lieutenant Tom Evans pilots the A-26, "Invader"*

9.8 *Dick's youngest brother, John Evans, USAAC, WWII Navigator*

9.9 *John, furthest right, back row, is navigator for this B-24 "Liberator" crew*

9.10 *Dick and John in Guam, South Pacific*

10.1 *Park City Lowry School* (McClung Historical Collection)

CHAPTER 10

SCHOOL DAZE

My formal training began at the Park City Lowry School in Knoxville, Tennessee, when I was 5½. I was excited that first day of school and would have been even more excited if my mom hadn't come along. Nobody else brought his or her mother.

I was expecting a nice young teacher, but Mrs. Dickerson looked like she might have started to work at Park City when the old school first opened up. Also, I thought I was starting in first grade, but as it turned out I was standing in line for kindergarten.

I don't remember very much that happened in my first three months of formal training. Then, something happened which I have remembered for over half a century. I remember cutting a piece of folded paper along a dotted line with some scissors. Then Mrs. Dickerson unfolded my paper in front of the class and there before all our eyes, was not just one rabbit but also four of them holding hands. It seems my classmates had been given the same task with varying results, some winding up with missing rabbit parts and others with whole rabbits missing. I admit I was pleased with the commotion I caused, until the next day when I looked up and saw my mom talking excitedly with Mrs. Dickerson. If someone had told me back then that my dexterity with scissors would be cause to reconsider what grade I should be in, I would have had some doubts about what Mom and Dad called my "formal training."

Before that week was out, I found myself in a new room, seated at a new desk in Mrs. Fielding's first grade class. I was right behind Gladys Kennedy. Gladys didn't notice that I was behind her, but she was all I noticed my last half of the first half of first grade.

In particular, I noticed that when it was hot, Gladys would sweat. Her wet hair would form little ringlets on the back of her neck, which would affect me in a way I didn't understand; in fact, I still don't fully understand it.

Once I tried to discuss with dad how Gladys would sweat, and I would watch. Then, Dad tried to explain it back to me. "It has to do with chemistry," he said. That didn't help me either, but I knew Dad knew. I knew my Dad taught chemistry at Knox High before he became principal.

"But, Dad, you know I'm not old enough to take chemistry," I said. "I'm a long way from chemistry, Dad."

"You're closer than you think, Richard, my boy," Dad laughed, and his eyes sparkled behind his glasses. In a moment, he had to take off his glasses and wipe them off. When Dad laughed while I was telling him about Gladys, my face would get hot; I never knew why it did that. I just remember it had something to do with Gladys.

Gladys and I looked at each other a lot, but we never talked. I mentioned this to Dad while he was reading our *Knoxville News Sentinel* one night before my bedtime. Without looking up from his newspaper, Dad asked, "Why don't you and Gladys talk, Dick?"

I replied, "Because when I see her, I can't think of anything that I think she would like to talk about, Dad."

I waited, but Dad didn't answer. "Dad," I continued, "I don't think Gladys can think of anything to talk to me about either. That's the other reason Gladys and I don't ever talk."

Dad finally dropped his newspaper down and looked over the top of it. He didn't say anything because I think he was trying to remember what I had just said to him. Then, he remembered, "Oh, I see, those are all good reasons for not talking, Dick. When neither you nor Gladys can think of anything to talk about, that's a good time to not talk." Then Dad's paper went back up over his eyes again.

After a few minutes passed and I was quiet, Dad dropped the *Sentinel* again and looked at me for maybe a whole minute. Mom had said Dad was never rude, not even to little kids. Then, he quickly folded his newspaper up and looked thoughtful, "Well now, let's see, Dick, I don't suppose you would want to change your seat? It's hard to talk to somebody when they are directly behind you. I see your head moving so that means you don't want to change your seat, right? Well, okay then. Why don't you ask Gladys, to walk out on the playground with you at lunchtime? Yeah, why don't you try that ploy, Dick?"

"Dad," I said, "I don't know what a ploy is; besides all the boys would laugh at me. We all have to chase each other at lunchtime and try to knock each other down on the cinders without using our hands. You know, Dad, we wouldn't be able to talk to the girls while we're chasing each other. And the girls are all over at their table. They talk to each other at lunch while we're all chasing. Besides, the girls would all giggle if any of us came over to their tables."

"Well, Son," Dad look concerned, "you've got a real problem there. And, problems, real problems like yours, must be studied with great care. Let me think about your problem, and you think about it, too. You go to bed now and we'll talk about it tomorrow when I get home from school. Fair enough? Good, give me a hug and kiss your Mom and get on up the stairs."

The very next day at lunchtime, Gladys walked right up to me out on the playground. The boys, whom I always ran with, stopped running and looked at us. Gladys still didn't say anything and just handed me a note. I opened it and looked at it, but I didn't know why I was looking at it. I already knew I couldn't read, and so did Gladys. Gladys must have remembered that she had never heard a sound coming from the seat behind her during the entire time she was in First Grade.

Then, I guess Gladys saw how my face had gotten hot again. She laughed, "It's for your mother."

After school, I took Gladys' note home to Mom. She opened it and looked up, "It's for you, my Dickie Bird."

"But Gladys told me it was for you, Mom,"

"Well actually, it is to me, but it is for you. It is from Mrs. Kennedy. Mrs. Kennedy says that she is having a birthday party for Gladys and Gladys wants you to come. Would you like to go?"

The family always laughed a lot about the way I seemed to blush more than other people. I could feel the heat rising from my neck all the way up to my forehead. But this time Mom didn't laugh. She said, "Would you like me to help you pick out a birthday present for Gladys, Mr. Richard Evans?"

I said, "I sure would," and ran out of the house.

The party was just great. We had all kinds of chocolate things to eat and lots of lemonade to drink. But I didn't see much of Gladys. I kept ripping around outside with some of the boys, hoping that Gladys would look out the window and see how fast I could cut corners. I learned that all the girls were clustered together somewhere in the house and were all talking to each other at the same time, while we boys were out cutting corners and falling on the ground.

When word got into the house that I had cut a corner too sharp and had torn a large hole in my pants and a smaller hole in my knee, all the girls came outside to see how much blood there was. Gladys' mother arrived very quickly with gauze and iodine. I recognized that iodine bottle right off with its skull and cross-bones picture on the side. (Warning labels were more forthright back in those days.)

Mrs. Kennedy put a towel on a sawhorse and asked me to pull my trousers up and put my knee across the sawhorse. I was enjoying seeing the faces in the circle around the sawhorse and me until Mrs. Kennedy touched my knee with that iodine! I already knew that iodine hurt, but this iodine almost threw me off the sawhorse. But, with Gladys standing there, I didn't make a sound. I did start to sweat though and that reminded me of how I would watch Gladys sweat in class. I felt a little better.

Always before, when I looked to see if Gladys was looking at me, I would start looking too late; she would already be gazing some other way when I started looking at her. But this time, after the iodine stopped hurting some, I looked right at Gladys, and I could see she was looking right back at me. And she kept on looking back at me. I got that hot-face feeling again, but I thought it was probably from the iodine. Gladys still looked like she wanted to say something to me, and I was awfully interested to hear what she wanted to say. Finally, she looked me right in my eyes and called me by my name. She said, "Dick, does iodine always make you sweat like that?"

I knew of course that we studied "our ABCs" in first grade. But, when I got there, Mrs. Fielding was already teaching the others "their LMNs." The "primer" which first graders studied in those days was called "Baby Ray." My classmates were already halfway through Baby Ray's life story before I heard about his book. During my first grade in school, I have to say that I really did have a lot of trouble. I couldn't get first grade, Baby Ray or Gladys sorted out in my mind.

I could have saved myself some of the worry. I was destined to have a second shot at Baby Ray, starting with the next semester. Dad said, "That's okay, Dick. If you catch up, you can have another shot at Gladys Kennedy."

It was a few years before I understood what an embarrassment, I had been to my dad what with him being the Principal of Knox High and me, his kid, flunking out of both kindergarten and first grade during my first semester in school.

Dad didn't mind at all. When I said I was sorry, he just laughed and put his hand on my shoulder, "It's a distinction, Son; I don't think it's ever been done before."

———————————

That night it was hot up in my room and I couldn't get to sleep. I heard Mom and Dad talking downstairs. I slipped out and sat on the top step to listen. My mom's unhappy voice, winding its way from our dining room, down our hallway, and up our stairs, suggested that Mom and Dad were having a "family discussion." Incidentally, a "family discussion" at our house was anything but a family discussion; actually, Mom and Dad were the only members of the family invited to family discussions.

Dad had said that the one thing that I had going for me in those days was "intellectual curiosity." That's probably why I had gotten out of bed and was sitting on the top step with my ear pushed through the banister.

I had figured out that Dad called Mom "Hellie" when he was trying to make her feel better, which was what he was calling her during this particular family discussion. I could hear Dad say, "Hellie, you know that you and Mrs. Dickerson shouldn't have pulled Dick out of kindergarten like that and shoved him into first grade in the middle of the term. The only thing he learned during the entire semester was that Gladys Kennedy sweats a lot."

"He learned what?" Mom mumbled.

"Never mind. We can discuss it later," Dad tried to console.

Mom sounded like she was almost crying, or maybe trying to cry. "I was doing it for you, Ernest," she whispered, "and for my Dickie Bird," she added. I could tell even from the top step in our hallway that Mom wasn't getting her point across to Dad.

Finally, Dad said, "Well, Hellie, why don't we go along to bed now, and we can talk about it in the morning." I had learned that when Dad would say in the morning, "We'll talk about it tonight," that was bad news (for whomever of us he was talking to). But, when Dad would say to Mom at night, "We'll talk about it in the morning, Hellie," that was good news for Mom. They always sounded like they had made up and weren't unhappy at all anymore.

10.2 *William Evans ("Pop") is always the professor*

11.1 *Dick at the age when he restored Judge's health*

CHAPTER 11
NO ONE TO TURN TO

My dog, Judge, and I were walking someplace but I don't remember just where. Normally, Judge would be our leader, looking back over his shoulder to see where I was taking him. This time, however, Judge really had passed the lead over to me and was taking more and more time with every tree or fence we passed. "Come on, Judge," I called out to him. He would catch up again.

After a while, though, he fell behind and stayed behind. When we got home, I scolded him, "What's the matter with you, Judge? Are you getting lazy or just old? Don't you know you're too young to be old?" Judge tilted his head to one side and looked at me with those big, round sad eyes, as he had done many times before. "It's not going to work this time, Old Boy," I said. "Okay, go to your box if you have to sulk. I think you're just getting lazy."

I watched my dog turn and climb our wide back stairs, eight or ten steps up to our back porch. Then he crawled into his box on the porch and put his muzzle on his front legs and rolled his eyes up at me. "I'm not impressed. I think you're getting old, Judge," I said, as I reached down, patted his head and then went into the house.

The next day after school, I went to the "Y" and didn't see Judge until that evening after dinner. I took him a plate of leftovers that he just looked at and then he looked up at me. "I didn't think dinner looked that great either, fellow," I said. "Maybe you'll get hungry later on." Then I left him and went back into the house to help Mom with the dishes to put off having to do my studies.

The following afternoon I came home right after school. My elementary school was Park City Lowry on Linden Avenue and usually I stayed on Linden until I got to our block. Then I would cut through the Nichols' side yard to our alley and then head across our back yard and up our back steps. Judge would usually be standing up on our back porch, making circles in the air with his stubby tail waiting for me to get home.

Somebody asked me once, "Are you saying your dog really makes circles with that sawed-off tail of his; doesn't he just wag it back and forth?"

I said I thought that he really did make circles; but in my mind, I wasn't sure. The next time I saw him wagging, I stood up over him and looked straight down at his tail. He looked over his shoulder at me but didn't stop his tail. He looked so funny I laughed out loud. His tail wasn't making big circles, but it sure wasn't just going side-to-side. I used to tell folks that I probably had the only "tail-circling" dog in Tennessee.

But nothing was circling when I got home from school that day. Judge wasn't around to greet me. I called him but couldn't raise him. I checked his favorite spots, in the house, on our back porch and in the garage. That's where I found him... in our old garage, lying on some rags. Only his big round eyes acknowledged my arrival. "What's the matter with you, Judge? Are you really getting old, you getting sick or something?"

Then it hit me. Of course, Judge was sick. He'd been sick for the last three days, maybe four. I hadn't paid much attention to him. I stroked the top of his head and his back and said, "You're going to be all right, fellow; Dad will be here in a little while and he'll know what to do. That's right, give me your paw, Judge."

When Dad got home, I took him to the garage and said, "Look at Judge, Dad; I think he's sick, real sick." My dad bent down and stroked Judge's head and his back the same way I had done. Dad agreed that Judge probably was really sick. He said, "We better give Judge a couple Sergeant's de-wormer Sure-Shot capsules, Dick. You stay here with Judge; I'll go get the bottle."

I stroked my dog some more and was relieved my dad was on hand to take charge. When Dad got back, he dumped two capsules into my hand and said, "Here, put them on Judge's tongue, Dick, all the way back. That's it. Now hold his mouth shut and rub his throat. That's right: you know how to do it."

I followed Dad's instructions and Judge choked down both pills. Dad said, "He'll feel better in the morning." I smiled weakly at that familiar phrase. When Dad found it "absolutely necessary" to whack one of us "for general recalcitrance and behavior unbecoming a decent growing boy," as Dad often put it, he would never leave one of us without some word to show that he wasn't really mad at us. He would say, with one eyebrow raised, "You will feel a lot better in the morning, Dick, my boy." I never smarted off to Dad, but I used to think to myself, "Why does Dad always say that? How else does he think I would feel in the morning?" I always felt awful right after Dad whacked me.

The next morning before heading out on my paper route, I looked in on Judge. I had moved his box into the garage because it looked like rain. Judge was sick all right, hadn't jumped out of his box to greet me and his head was still resting on his front paws. Dad was up when I got back from my morning paper route. "Dad," I said, "Judge doesn't look any better; please come out to the garage and take a look at him."

Dad walked to the garage, stooped down and put his hand on Judge's head. "If he isn't better when I get home from school tonight, we'll get a vet to take a look at him, Dick. Okay?"

I said, "Okay, Dad." But I didn't feel okay. Judge's eyes were looking straight at mine and I thought Judge didn't think it was okay either.

When "the final bell" rang at our school, I was the first out the door. I was by the fire station in the 2300 block of Linden Avenue before my classmates even started to pile into the street. In two or three minutes, I had already run a whole block – five more blocks to go. I had never run a whole mile without stopping; but our house, Dad had said, was exactly a mile from school. He drove it once just to show me.

I was still running when I passed Uncle Bob's house in the 2700 block and wasn't too tired. I thought to myself, "It will be flat from here on, no more hills," I felt stronger. I kept repeating out loud, "I can run a mile. I can run a mile."

At the end of the 2900 block, I turned up towards our alley. In a minute, I was barreling along, going full speed up our alley. Then I turned into our driveway, off our alley, and right away I pulled open one of our garage doors. Judge was in the back corner in his box; he looked like he hadn't moved since Dad and I left him that morning. I noticed that Judge's eyes didn't look up to see mine, even a little bit.

I lifted his head up with my hands under his muzzle and looked at him. His eyes looked so sad; Judge's eyes always looked sad because they were kind of droopy, but now they looked even sadder. I thought maybe Judge thought he might die, if he knew what "die" meant. I didn't know exactly myself, but I knew that I was starting to get afraid. All of a sudden, some tears filled up my eyes and started running down my cheeks. I knew Judge couldn't talk and probably couldn't listen, but all of a sudden, I heard myself sob, "Oh, Judge; oh, Judge, don't die; please, please don't die."

As a kid, I had never panicked, or hadn't thought I had. But now, I was running for the house, yelling as loud as I could, "Mother, Mother," but knew she wasn't there. Then I yelled "Eddie May, Eddie May;" even though I knew she had probably finished her house-keeping chores for my mother and had already gone to her home on Holston Hills Pike. I remember I thought that probably I was panicking, and just that thought helped me calm down.

I knew that Dr. and Mrs. Smith, our next-door neighbors, were out of town and that Mrs. Galyon, on the other side of the street, was always away in the late afternoon. "I'm all by myself and Judge maybe dying," I said to myself. "Judge is looking at me like he thinks I should know what to do."

I raced back to the garage, knowing that there would be no change in Judge, but I didn't know where else to go or what else to do. I picked up my dog and held him in my arms like I had held my little brothers, Tom and John, when they were born and real little. Judge didn't move at all; he was too weak. And his eyes didn't look like they were seeing mine.

I knew that I was standing in our garage, holding my dog; but I remember thinking that I was watching me stand there. I heard my own voice sobbing, "Oh Judge, please don't die. Oh, please don't die." I remember thinking to myself, "Your heart really does ache when you're real sad. I can feel my heart hurting in my chest, right now."

I thought I was going back and forth between being me and then watching me like I was somebody else. In my mind, I thought I was watching what I was doing and that made me more afraid.

Then, I got the crazy idea that Dad was watching me, too; but I couldn't see where he was. I think I heard myself sobbing, "Oh Dad, I wish you were here. Why don't you come home and help Judge get well?"

"What would Dad do? What would Dad do?" I kept asking myself. Then, I asked, "What could Dad do?"

I've thought of that terrible moment many times, and I believe it really happened as I have remembered it. I'm not sure. I thought of my dad and of all the things he tried to teach me. But they all seemed to race by me, so fast in my mind, I couldn't catch any of them.

"What would Dad do?" Judge's eyes looked quite glazed. "What would Dad do?" Judge wasn't breathing well. "What would Dad do?" Judge's stomach looks all puffed out, and it is tight, like a football. It must have hurt something awful; I could tell. "What would Dad do?"

Then it hit me, "Judge's stomach looks puffed out because it is puffed out, way out. Judge is all stopped up; Judge has been stopped up for three or four days. And he is whining because the gas hurts. Mom told me it was the gas that made me hurt."

If Dad were here, he would say, "Judge needs to have his ashes hauled... so he can pass some gas... or he's going to bust wide open."

Then suddenly, I was running towards the house; ideas were flashing through my mind. I must warm the water first and get the Vaseline. How could I hold the water bag and hold Judge at the same time? I know. I won't use the bag; I'll get Mom's squirter; it's on her top shelf in our bathroom. The Vaseline is in Dad's top dresser drawer.

In a couple minutes, I had gathered up the medical instruments that I needed and was headed back to Judge. I lifted Judge up on the workbench where I had put a pan of warm, soapy water. I had remembered the Vaseline and I smeared some on the open end of Mom's squirter. Then, I sucked up some water and eased the thing into Judge's poor little behind. I was trembling and my heart was pounding like it was going to bust. I asked myself, again and again, "What if I am doing the wrong thing?"

But I didn't stop. I pushed the water in real slow at first. I thought that Judge would just push it right back out, so I stood back. But Judge didn't even try. I guessed he was too weak or tired or something.

I sucked up some more warm water from the pan and slowly pushed it into Judge. Then, I did it again. I knew how it hurt. Boy, did I know how it hurt! But, I knew, too, that I always got better when Mom would make me hold it in. And Judge was holding it in really good. I was settling down a little bit. I remember thinking that I was sweating, but it wasn't that hot. "But am I doing the right thing?" I kept asking myself, again and again.

Then, I did it again to Judge and he started to whine. His little body was shaking something awful and his eyes were looking at mine again, and I was afraid. I couldn't believe how hard Judge was shaking! Dad had said it was okay to be afraid; everybody is afraid at some time.

Judge's belly was really puffed out now. "Of course, it's puffed out," I said to myself, "where else could the water go? There's hardly any left in the pan. I'm running out of warm water; it's all in Judge, and still, he isn't trying to push it out." Why doesn't Judge push the water out? Mom always tried to get me to hold it in for a while. How could Judge know you're supposed to hold the water in for a little while?

Judge really was whining now; maybe he was crying, if dogs cry. Also, Judge was trying to move. I thought he might bust open if I pushed any more water into him, but Mom had said that I never came close to busting. So, I pushed the thing into him and squeezed the bulb. Then, I did it again and again.

All of a sudden, Judge made a funny kind of howling sound and pushed himself off the workbench. He didn't bark... he really was howling. I'll never forget how Judge howled after he had been so quiet for two whole days. I noticed Judge's mouth was round, like a dog cartoon, when he howled.

I jumped back and spilled the rest of the water down my front and I remember I could feel how warm it was. Judge got his front feet out in front of him just before he hit the ashes. (It was one of my jobs to spread ashes on our garage floor too). But Judge's legs folded under him and he skidded on his chin and his chest. I knew the ashes would hurt something awful. He didn't stop though; he just kept right on going with his feet trying really hard to catch up with the rest of him.

A moment before I had thought my dog was really dying. He hadn't moved for hours; now he looked like he was flying right through our half-opened garage door! I was right behind still trying to catch him. I thought I could feel my heart pounding in my chest again, like it did on Halloween when I had tarred Mrs. Oglesby's sidewalks.

I went through our garage door right behind Judge in time to see him making his first turn in our backyard. Judge was starting in a big circle, running as hard as he could go while holding his nose down in the grass as if it were still important to look for a special place to go. I remember thinking that instinct is funny. Judge is about to pop and he's still trying to find a nice spot to go on.

I thought, too, "My poor little friend has gone crazy or wild or whatever dogs do." Then suddenly he tightened his circles and he looked like he was chasing his own tail. No, no, he wasn't chasing his tail he was trying to get at his tail. No, not really at his tail, at his tail end to get it unplugged. Judge is about to bust and he's trying to unplug himself.

Then suddenly it started. At the beginning of his second circle, Judge just plain erupted like a small, fountain. The water arched up and out of his little rear end like pictures I had seen of Yellowstone Park. I remember thinking at the time, "Judge's fountain is twice as high as he is." As he ran faster and faster, it sort-of curved over, farther and farther, making it look like a real rooster's tail.

Suddenly, Judge's rooster tail stopped; it was over. Like Old Faithful shutting down for the afternoon, Judge's little geyser just backed down on itself, hiccuped a couple times, and that was it. I knew it was over. I was sure it was really over; I had been taught well. Boy, did I know when enemas were finally over.

I knew that the ashes in the furnace, like the ashes in our bodies, weren't dirty or nasty; I knew they were just the products of combustion, like Dad had insisted they were. I knew that they could become poisons if allowed to accumulate in our bodies, or in our furnaces. I could see all of my dad's and my mom's ideas now as they raced through my mind. Dad was right about ashes. Mom was right about enemas.

I knew my little companion, who trusted me, wasn't going to die; he was going to live. At first, I couldn't believe it. But Judge was going to live. He was going to live!

My little friend, whom I loved so much, had stayed on his feet while he did his circles. Now, he was still on his feet with both his fore and aft legs akimbo... as akimbo as he could get them, being bowlegged. He seemed to be looking at the carnage he had wrought in our back yard. It wasn't hard to tell where Judge's fountain had started and where his last circle had ended.

I sank to my knees, then to my elbows, and lowered my head to Judge's eye-level so he could see me smile at him. Judge walked over slowly but steadily and licked my face. I picked up my dog and cradled him in my arms. I noticed that he wasn't dirty at all; it was our back yard that had gotten pretty dirty. Dad would have said, "Dick, this place has gotten a tad untidy; let's get it straightened up right away, okay?"

I noticed right away that my dog's eyes were looking like they were looking again... they didn't look blank. And all of a sudden, Judge was hungry again. That is when I was sure Judge was well again; I was so happy. I got some food and water for him and he got right to it. As I watched my dog slurp his food down, I shouted to myself, "My dog is alive; Judge is alive, and he's going to stay that way."

As I settled down, I started thinking about what my folks would think when I told them what I had done to Judge. "You did what with my plunger!" I could hear Mom say. I decided I should tell Dad first and then suggest that he tell Mom, maybe after I had gone to bed.

I looked around and thought it odd that I was alone and there were no sounds. How could there have been no noise with so much excitement? No one had been watching Judge and me. I thought of the question that teachers ask kids to think about. "Is there really a sound if no one is around to hear it?"

This brought to my mind a more serious question, "What if Mom and Dad don't believe me." With this unsettling thought, I set about to examine the evidence like they always did on radio mystery shows, being careful of course "not to tamper with the evidence."

Suddenly, I was surprised to hear our Studebaker as it turned off Castle Street into our alley and drove the short distance behind the Galyon's house to our garage. Dad quickly climbed down and out and walked towards me. "Where is Judge? "He asked, as he looked across our back yard.

Pointing, I said, "Judge is under our maple trees there,

Dad; he's going to be all right. Judge is going to be okay, Dad. I called Miss Webb and she said you were out, Dad, and that she couldn't find you."

"She got worried about you, Dick, and she looked for me and she found me. She said you thought Judge was dying." Dad was looking at Judge and Judge was looking up at Dad, the way he would with his chin resting on his front paws and his belly on the flat cool ground. I knew that Dad could see that Judge's tail was making little circles in the air and that he didn't think Judge looked much like he was going to die.

"I did think Judge was dying, Dad," I said. "I believe Judge would have died."

Dad then looked hard at Judge. Judge wasn't bouncing around; but anyone could see that Judge didn't hurt anymore and that he was smiling like he would do when he was happy. "What do you mean, Judge would have died? What has happened here, Dick? Come straight with me."

That's when I told Dad the whole story. As Dad studied the ground, I showed him where not to step. He listened to me like he was interested in every word. He was very quiet. At the end of my story, Dad had to take off his glasses. He turned away like he always did when he had to wipe off his glasses from crying or laughing.

I was sure Dad thought I had done the right thing and that was why he had to stop talking and cry some. I thought I had never been happier in my whole life. I shouted to myself, "My dad wasn't here to help me, and my dad thinks I did the right thing."

"Dad," I asked after another minute, "do you think I did the right thing? Do you think that I really did save my dog's life today?"

"You may very well have saved your dog's life, Dick," Dad said. "You can be very proud of what you have done here today. Son, Judge was a very sick dog and something sure must have had him plugged up, like you said." Dad then turned away from me to look at Judge.

"I know what it was, Dad," I said.

Then Dad turned towards me. "What was it?" Dad asked quickly with a funny look on his face."I know what made Judge so sick, Dad," I replied, "I know why Judge got all stopped up like he did."

Dad looked curiously hard at me; then he said, "How could you possibly know that? What do you think caused your dog to get all stopped up like he was?"

"I found it, Dad. I looked for it where Judge ran around in circles and I found it. I don't know why Judge stayed in the same circle, like he did. I know Judge went around three times, maybe four. Come over here, Dad, and I'll show you." I led the way, showing my dad where not to step.

"Here, Dad," I pointed, "Here is what had Judge all plugged up the way he was. Judge had eaten this little ball of string."

I will always remember the look on my father's kind face. He really did have a kind face; everybody in Knoxville said my dad had a kind face. He looked in the direction of my finger, and I could see his eyes focusing on the little ball of white string, only slightly dirtied up by Judge. All the water I had squeezed into Judge with Mom's plunger had washed off the little ball of white string.

Dad leaned over and picked up the string on a stick to take a good look at it just like it was real evidence. I knew what Dad was thinking. "I wondered too, Dad, why the string wasn't dirty. The water had washed the string off. I had filled Judge full of an awful lot of water. But, smell it, Dad. Smell the string."

Dad looked at the string then at me. With his head going sideways and back and forth, Dad followed my suggestion. Real quick, he scrunched up his nose... "Hmmm," Dad said. Then he set the string down on the grass and looked over at Judge.

I could see Dad's eyes fill up as he turned towards me. "Oh my, oh my," my dad said. "Dick, you really did save your dog's life today. There is absolutely no doubt about it, Son; the evidence," Dad said, as he started to smile, "is overwhelming. Son, it is irrefutable. Do you know what 'irrefutable' means, Dick?"

I said, "No, sir, I don't know what that word means. What does ir-re-fut-able mean?"

With great, good fun shining from my dad's eyes and also from his glasses, Dad said, "It means the evidence that Judge has provided is mighty powerful." Dad squinched up his nose and smiled again.

Walking towards me and still smiling, Dad reached down and shook my hand like grownups do. Then he said, "I am mighty proud to know you, Mr. Richard Ernest Evans."

I couldn't think of anything to say. Dad would always call me "Mr. Evans" when he thought I had done the right thing. We still had Mom to go, but my dad really did think that I had done the right thing. I had never been so happy in my whole life!

12.1 *Malta harbor after Axis attacks, August, 1942* (Imperial War Museum)

CHAPTER 12
BRAVE AND BEAUTIFUL MALTA

When I first arrived at Valletta, the capital city of the ancient island-nation of Malta, I was immediately briefed on the plans for the invasion of Sicily. I had been ordered to fly to Malta a few days ahead of the invasion (**Operation Husky**) so that I might, as quickly as possible, fly to Sicily, find a suitable landing field for the B-17, and locate the 8th Army command post. I was to get there by whatever means I might divine and report to Monty at his forward headquarters encampment.

Upon landing at the Malta Airdrome, I suggested to my crewmen that they take some time off to look around Valletta's heavily bombarded capital city and check out the beautiful, green farmland that encompassed three-quarters of the island. All agreed this was a good plan and took off quickly, evidencing their bountiful, youthful enthusiasm. They really did have it. I had a little, myself; but after all they were in their high-teens and I was in my low-twenties.

I'm sure my air-crewmen discovered quickly, as I did, that if one is afforded a good view of Malta from one of the island-nation's heights, one could see most of the sights to be seen on Malta on the surface. However, there are prehistoric caves to be visited below the surface; but I wouldn't be able to get it all done during my time on this very beautiful island.

My memory of Valletta is of a stunning, picturesque, ancient city enclosing a small, harbor with damaged vessels lying at anchor around its perimeter. Some were still in full view resting on the bottom with their decks awash a few feet beneath the surface. I was reminded of a similar picture I had seen in Tripolitania that has never left me. That was the vision of a flotilla of half-sunken Axis ships of war in Tripoli's large, wide and surprisingly shallow harbor.

Surrounding Malta's much smaller, but very active harbor, Valletta's historic, ornate an all-white buildings appeared formidable and deeply rooted in the ages. The old San Anton Palace is a beautiful structure that had withstood the ravages of considerable time. I conjectured that proud Maltese citizens had taken extraordinary pains through the centuries to build and preserve ancient Malta and its unique culture.

From talking with older citizens whom I chanced to meet, I inquired about Lieutenant General Robert Baden-Powell, the British Soldier-Statesman. He was a hero of the Boer War in South Africa who had done a tour of duty in 1890 on Malta as Military Secretary and Senior ADC (Aide-de-Camp) to the Governor. Years later I received Baden-Powell's book, *Scouting for Boys*, as a gift from a close friend and neighbor, John LeFevre, a devoted 50-year Boy Scouts of America Scout leader in Los Angeles. I learned that Baden-Powell, an Englishman, was the founder of the worldwide Boy Scout movement. I also learned from John that the first Boy Scout camp outing was on Brownsea Island, off Britain's south coast. Of the 18 Scouts on hand at this first

Boy Scout camp out a century ago, two were named Evans. "Kismet." It was in the stars that the Evans boys became Boy Scouts and one of them an Eagle Scout.

With the notable exception of Valletta, disruption to the island of Malta from sporadic Italian bombings and naval shellings appeared to be superficial.

Malta had a business-as-usual feeling that would stop in its tracks when air-raid warnings were sounded, but then pick up again without losing a beat when the "all-clear" was sounded.

Mussolini must have been fit-to-be-tied when a handful of soldiers from the British Army, a few RAF pilots and the Maltese citizens fended him off, absorbing with impunity all the punishment that the fascist, brutal Italian dictator could bring to bear. Constantly and consistently, the courageous Maltese even refused to return his call when "Il Duce "would proffer terms of surrender.

Beyond the city limits, I remember very well a lush, agrarian countryside with bright green fields, stretching northwest to the water's edge. Blue-green seascapes, topped by massive, brilliant-white cumulus clouds, surrounded the island and completed a picture of serenity that was inconsistent with the scars of battle that abounded in the city. It seemed to me as if the Maltese citizenry and the British soldiers fortunate enough to be stationed there ignored the signs of war.

The scars of war left on Malta were confined for the most part to the capital city of Valletta, in particular to a few government buildings, the docking loading and unloading facilities and marine-repair facilities along the unique circular waterfront.

Il Duce was never able to dislodge the Maltese from their island homeland. The Maltese knights of old, moldering in their graves, must have been proud indeed of the modern-day knights of the 1940s who brought new meaning to the very British word "indomitable."

Mussolini's forces had sunk many British ships in the Mediterranean. These were ships en route to Malta with sorely needed food supplies. Also, Il Duce inflicted substantive damage on Maltese docking facilities in the Valletta Harbor. However, in so doing, Italy's dictator and spoiler sacrificed Italian Navy, Air and Merchant Marine material and resources that he could not afford to lose and could not survive without.

Il Duce's relatively modern armed forces had some early military successes during the Italo-Ethiopian War, during which he devastated, conquered and eventually controlled the Ethiopian Empire from 1935 to 1939. The Italian leader's initial adversary was the emperor, Haile Selassie. Later, faltering against a still powerful British Navy, Mussolini's fate was sealed on the Mediterranean Sea, which he had prematurely proclaimed an "Italian lake."

The people of Malta with all of Mussolini's battering never faltered. The island fortress never fell. Bravery and sacrifice of the highest order by the Maltese and the British were commonplacein Malta in the early stages of WWII.

I remember thinking during the Second World War when flying in the skies over Europe, Africa and later the Pacific, that my country most certainly could not be held accountable for the war. Nor could it be credited with winning it alone. I was proud to be a Yank, but I was aware that there were other countries and peoples besides the USA and Americans who were substantial and timely contributors to the cause of freedom and to the destruction of fascism. The peoples of this island-nation of Malta would forever be on the top of my freedom fighters' list along with some Brits, Canadians, Aussies, and South Afrikaners whom I would meet during the war. But I was certain in my mind that had we Yanks not been a major and timely contributor in men, materials and resolve in the struggle to free the world from fascism, this world which I would inherit and inhabit for the balance of the twentieth century would not, as old timers in the Smoky Mountains would put it, "be a fittin' place to live."

———————

There was much to admire and to like about the Maltese soldiers and the citizens of Malta whom one would meet on the streets of that ancient island-city-country country.

The allied British and American forces were preparing to take the first step towards the invasion of mainland Europe. Winston Churchill's script to expose, attack and weaken the "soft under-belly of Europe" was being followed to the letter.

I would quickly gain a special appreciation for Monty's popularity with the British Military, also for the courage of the pleasant citizens of Malta whom one would meet on the streets.

I quickly became aware that word of my arrival had gone out over the island. The Yank Captain, seen in the map room at the Ops Center, on the flight line at the Valetta Airfield, at the Naval facilities ringing the harbor and at the anti-aircraft gun emplacements ringing the island, was Monty's pilot, a gift from an appreciative General Eisenhower. Everywhere I went in Malta, I felt welcome and was always asked the same two-part question, "I say, Capt'n, you are Monty's Yank pilot, are you not?" and "Fancy 'avin' a spot of tea with us, mate?"

I would answer promptly, "Right you are, laddie; I 'ave indeed been assigned to your 8th Army to fly your General Montgomery about in the B-17 Flying Fawtress that General Eisenhower has turned over to 'im for 'is own personal use. It is a singular 'onor to 'ave been directed by the American Theat'ah Commander to serve your great Field Commander! Yes, I would very much like to join you in a spot of tea... a little milk if you please. Oh, and light on the heat."

My add-on about the heat would always bring smiles and would confirm my position as a loyal ally of the British Commonwealth. During the period of my TDY with General Montgomery, the British never asked me for my ID. I had a US Top-Secret clearance during the course of the war.

Normally, I would be required to show it in classified areas. The British, however, would always seem to know when Monty's Yank pilot was in their area and would wave off any effort on my part to present my ID.

Also, I would also hear quite often, "Why can't you be a Yank, Capt'n Evans; you jes gotta be a blinkin' Welshman. Why, didn't you know, Capt'n, most evry-livin' soul in Wales is named Evans, Capt'n Evans."

I would often let it be known that "actually" I was a product of both the Welsh and Scottish clans, having been born to Ernest Evans and Helen Stewart. I think my heritage helped with Monty, but I thought I shouldn't overdo it. As it turned out, I need not have concerned myself. When I made a point with Monty of our common heritage, I would find it hard to satisfy this proud Englishman. Monty wasn't so sure but would always listen intently, often with his head cocked to one side. When I would shut up, Monty would often smile and ask for more detail.

As I recall Malta now, after passage of half a century, I was surprised to find it a chalky white, except, of course, for the vast green fields and surrounding blue-green water. White, as is commonly understood, reflects thermal energy from the sun, sending it back from whence it came.

I got the notion that if one should happen to be standing erect almost anywhere on Malta, at almost any time during the daylight hours, it would be very likely that one would, indeed, be standing on a white rock. Consequently, one would quickly experience a double whammy as the sun's rays touched one's body, not once, but twice... first heading for and then returning from one's white rock!

I determined to my complete satisfaction that wearing soaking-wet, white clothing was indeed the proper thing to do on Malta to encourage cooling through evaporation. Also, I learned that wearing soaking-wet clothing on Malta was an easy condition to effectuate.

As an Eagle Scout, I understood very well that when perspiration permeating one's apparel evaporates, the evaporative process would cool one's body. On Malta, I would also learn to accept sweat, however distasteful the subject might seem to be.

In the summer of 1943, drinking piping-hot tea to protect one's self from the high temperatures on Malta, was a subject often indulged while standing about in the sunshine. For me, immediately upon raising a hot cup of tea to my lips, fresh perspiration, if there could be such a thing, would burst from my temples and then course down my cheeks... the cheeks of my face first.

Truly, I could feel small streams of water coursing down my body, momentarily damming up above my belt and then streaming down my legs into my shoes. With each forward step, my shoes would make an interesting squishing sound.

"But," I would often ask myself, "had I really gotten cooler as Maltese well-wishers asserted I would?" Actually, I felt that I had not. As a matter of fact, I am quite certain that I never cooled down during my entire stay on that hot, but otherwise delightful, island. In truth, I really wasn't concerned about not being cool. I was just proud to be allied with those brave, enduring, unpretentious people.

While joking about the heat, I gained a profound respect and very real affection for the jovial, pleasant, interested, self-effacing, fearless, Maltese citizens and for the equally fearless, smiling, itinerant Englishmen camping there on the white rocks.

I postulated that King George VI had hoped the George Cross, which he bestowed on the citizens of Malta shortly after his visit with Monty and me in Tripoli, might become a symbol for bravery and loyalty throughout the world. I now understand that it has, indeed.

On the night of the invasion of Sicily, July 10, 1943, the Allied paratroopers were airlifted from Tunisian airfields so as to arrive over their drop zones in southeast Sicily at midnight. This would give them time to jump and locate and recover their equipment that had been parachuted to the ground ahead of them. Also, time to locate each other and get organized into their combat units before sunrise.

The battle for Sicily, the island-state of Italy, was the first WWII battle by the Allies on European soil. It commenced at dawn on July 10, 1943. That morning, I felt some pride as I watched the battle develop on the large wall maps in a British War Room in Cairo. Yanks and Brits were walking on Axis-held Europe for the first time.

At first light, British and American landing craft, led by Patton on the left flank and Monty on the right, headed for the beaches a few miles south and west of the paratroop drop zones in the southeast corner of Sicily.

Monty had asked that I bring his B-17 to Sicily on "**D-Day** plus two-or-three." I remember thinking that "three" sounded about right for a lone B-17 to be making its own invasion of Europe.

My operating orders were straightforward and left me considerable latitude. I was directed to "conduct an air-search for a suitable landing field, land the B-17, inquire as to the location of the British 8th Army Command Post and proceed to said command post without delay by whatever means I might divine, devise, arrange or scrounge." On arriving at the Army Commander's Command Post, I was to "report immediately to the Army Commander himself, General Sir Bernard Law Montgomery."

I grew to like my British Army directives and orders. My British bosses, Monty in particular, never took time to spell out precisely how I should proceed; they simply delineated the results they expected me to achieve.

After a short flight from Malta to Sicily, Syracuse, a Sicilian port city 60 miles south of Mount Etna, was not difficult to spot along the southeastern coast of the triangular-shaped island. Smoke rising from Syracuse's harbor was the first evidence observed by my crew and me that a war was being waged in Europe. For almost two weeks after D-Day, we waited for the General to secure the southeastern corner of Sicily. During that time, we had to fly to Château dun, Algeria, to replace a failing engine on *Theresa Leta*. Finally, we were back in the air and headed for Monty's new headquarters in Sicily

I rejected Syracuse, as well as the coastal towns between Syracuse and Catania, as a place to set down. I could tell, even without a map, where the Germans were stopping to make stands as they withdrew to the north towards Messina, a city about 60 miles northeast of Mt. Etna. It seemed prudent to me to turn away from the smoking cities and fly south.

Very quickly, Staff Sergeant Kennedy's voice came over the intercom: "Waistgun to pilot. Sir, there is a field off to our right that might be worth a look... appears to be a fighter strip, Captain, about 3,500 feet I'd say. Looks to be freshly carved out of a fruit orchard or maybe a nut grove. And, sir, there is a beach close by."

The landing strip Kennedy had sighted did, indeed, have its own beach, which I correctly guessed my men would enjoy while their Captain was hitch-hiking north on very hot, very dusty truck-congested roads toward the first front lines to be contested on continental Europe!

I was delighted at the prospects of my guys having a nice break in a pleasant environment while I was endeavoring to locate the front lines before some non-English-speaking person with a "made-in-Germany" rifle located me. My directive was simply to "find Monty" and "report for duty." My personal plan was to first pin down the location of the front lines then look for the Victor of El Alamein!

I polled my crewmen over our B-17 intercom and found them in agreement with Sergeant Kennedy's suggestion. They thought an airfield with its own sandy beach would be satisfactory.

No fighters or **Gooney Birds** (general-purpose light **cargo aircraft**) could be seen on the quickly hogged-out hard stands scattered about in the nut grove. I circled twice, making a second low-level pass down the single runway. Then I set *Theresa Leta* down "without incident."

Back in those days when we pilots thought we had done an acceptable job of piloting, we would often add the phrase "without incident," usually with a grin and with the intent to draw attention to what we termed "feats of unusual skill and daring." The latter was a tongue-in-cheek expression that we had borrowed from the renowned Ringling Brothers Barnum & Bailey Circus. I was very familiar with the phrase since my dad had taken me to the circus even before I became a Boy Scout.

When landing out of our large formations upon returning from combat missions, we would get our wheels rolling on the runway and immediately add power and drive hard for the far end of the strip, clearing the runway as quickly as possible for other B-17s close on our tails.

This was a straightforward, easily accomplished maneuver for a post-mission, lightly loaded B-17 on a broad, 5,000-foot runway. It would be less straightforward, whatever the load, if attempted on a narrower, shorter 3,500-foot fighter strip like the one I was approaching.

I got my wheels on the ground quickly and was decelerating when my B-17 intercom came alive. I easily recognized the voice of Staff Sergeant Chuck Ward, my tail gunner. On combat missions, Chuck quite literally protected my ass along with his own and those of the eight others in our crew. "Capt'n," Chuck said, his voice conveying some concern, "don't waste any time clearing the runway. There's a B-24 landing right behind us and he's close on our tail. He's touching down right now, Capt'n, and he looks fast. He's looking real fast, Capt'n, I think he's in trouble. I don't believe he's got any brakes at all!"

"Okay, okay, Chuck, "I responded while pushing all four throttles forward to the stops. "Keep talkin' to me Chuck, you're my eyes. What's he doing now? "Before Chuck had time to answer, I had already started pulling off some of the power, which I had just added.

The task suddenly thrust upon me was to race the brakeless B-24 to the other end of our strip without knowing exactly where he was behind me. At the same time, it would be my job to get slowed down sufficiently on the already-short runway so I could make a 180-degree turn onto the taxiway that was just coming into view in front of me on the right.

If the B-24s brakes were shot out, the plane would, without question, over-run the adequate-but-hastily-prepared landing strip. He would be taking everything in his path with him, including me, if I couldn't reach the taxi strip ahead of him and clear the runway by making a tight 180-degree skidding turn from the landing strip onto the narrower taxiway.

"He bounced something awful, Capt'n. Looked like he was standin' on his tail for a moment, but he's down now, and he's rollin'. He still looks fast though, Capt'n... still closing on us. He's com-in' right at us! For sure, Capt'n, he's got no brakes at all."

This was Sergeant Ward's clear, cryptic report. I remember his words as if they were uttered yesterday. There was fear in Chuck's voice but no panic. That B-24 was charging hell-bent right into his face. It would smash into our tail-gun position, cushioning the shock for the rest of us more forward in the plane, but not for Chuck! I will never forget that Chuck did what he was supposed to do. Without being asked, he remained at his station, didn't panic and provided me with a vital "rear-view mirror."

"How far now? How far back is he, Chuck? "I shouted into the intercom. "A football field... half a field? Come on, Sarge, you're my eyes back there! I can't blast out of here; it's too late; we wouldn't get airborne. I've got to make a high-speed, tail-around, 180-degree turn to get off this runway and onto a very narrow taxiway. Is he still closing on us? Give me something to work with, man. This is the real thing!"

"Yes. Yes, he's closing on us, Capt'n; he's slowed some though. He's not as fast as he was. He's maybe 50 yards back; Yeah, he's about half-a-football-field behind us. But he's still gaining on us, Capt'n."

I had the conscious thought, never forgotten, that my youthful tail gunner was being some kind of a man back there. Chuck would be messed up for sure if the B-24 rammed us. Strapped in, as he was in his tail-gun position, he would be looking directly at that B-24 as it kept on coming and slammed headlong right onto his lap!

For sure, Chuck would get it, if I didn't beat that B-24 to the turn off and get turned off the runway onto the narrow taxiway, thereby clearing the runway for him before he caught up and rammed us. We would also wind up in a mess that would get us all if I were going too fast to make it around the 180-degree turn.

"He's slower, Capt'n, but he's still closing on us; for sure he's got no brakes at all, Capt'n."

Normally, the B-17 is taxied on the ground by applying brakes on one side to turn in that direction, then on the other side, to bring the aircraft out of the turn. My big bird would not be able to make the turn ahead of us if we were going too fast. If too fast, we would skid hard to our left, possibly wiping out our main landing gear on our left side. Our left wing would drop, scrape the ground and break at some point. Our left-wing fuel tanks would rupture. There would be an explosion and a fire. And that would be all she wrote.

My turn-off, in view out Johnson's window, was coming up fast on my right. I had inched the plane over to my left as far as I could go; I couldn't take time to look but I knew my left main gear would be just inches from the left side of the runway. Both left engines and practically all of my left wing would not be over the runway; they would be over the grass. Also, at our speed, I knew that hot brakes alone would not get us around the sharp 180-degree right-hand turn. I would have to use the left outboard power all of it, momentarily. Then full right rudder and just the right amount of brakes on the right side to get us turned about. Then brakes on the left to stop our turn and get us straight with the taxiway, after we had gotten around the turn, if we got around it.

I visualized our B-17 leaning precariously over to our left toward the outside of our turn if we attempted the sharp, careening, turn back to our right. Possibly our left-wing tip would drag, and our props would dig in on the left side, forcing us out of our intended turn to the right too soon.

I had only imagined the problem; it hadn't happened yet. Then, quicker than I had expected, it was time. Now or never! I brought power up on No. 1, the left outboard engine, about halfway.

I then started feeding in some right brakes to partially anchor our right landing gear. Immediately, we started turning right, but we were also skidding. We weren't making it around the turn. We had to turn a full 180 degrees. Ninety degrees would just send us off into the trees.

Quickly, but only momentarily, I rammed both left-engine throttles to the firewall. Then just as quickly, I brought them back halfway. After a moment, I pulled them all the way back, attempting to anticipate the delayed responses that the power changes would be having on my lurching, skidding *Flying Fortress*.

We were into a violent, careening, right-hand turn, forcing our airplane to tip to the left toward the outside of the turn, forcing our left wing to drop a frightening angle. Lowering our left-wing tip to a point where it might dig in, then catch, then conceivably flip the B-17 and cause it to roll to the left. I was sure the engine props on the left side would be striking the ground, making instant pretzels out of them.

It wasn't happening that way... not yet. That preamble was only conjecture, a wild picture in my head, which I was trying to sort out.

Well into the turn, I had started pulling power off the left engines, and feeding power in on the right engines, hoping to stop the careening turn to our right in time to keep us on the now straight, and very narrow, taxiway.

I remember clearly, fifty years later, that suddenly I was shouting to myself, "It's working; it's working, oh my God... it is working." Then, thinking of Chuck and the others in the back, I pressed my intercom button and shouted into the intercom, "It's working, we're making it; we're making it, gang; we're going to live through this one."

Then, I did something that is difficult for me to admit. I burst into tears. The water was instantly in my eyes and streaming down my cheeks... and damned if I'm not doing it again... right now as my words are taking form on my computer.

We had careened off the runway onto the taxiway and almost lost control but finally had managed to turn clean around the full curve and get our machine heading in the opposite direction back up the taxiway, which was suddenly straightening out ahead of us. The violent, skidding turn had absorbed enormous amounts of inertial energy in our flying machine and had brought our speed down much faster than I had guessed would be possible.

I tapped the brakes; they were okay. I had not blown our heavy-duty, rubber, expander tubes. But they would be hot to the bursting point. "The brake pucks that the expander tubes were forcing against the brake bands must be red hot," I shouted to myself.

My mind flashed back to Alamogordo, New Mexico a year before. I was practicing **ground loops**, the high-risk, last-resort, emergency procedures like this, out there near White Sands where we had great wide, hard-packed over-runs and plenty of hard, solid ground on either side of our runways. What if I hadn't actually practiced high-speed turnarounds back there where I had the space and hard ground? What if I hadn't learned that you must get the airplane turned sideways on the runway, so it can skid sideways, while still on the runway, and arrive at the turn-off slowed down enough to complete the turn onto the narrow taxiway that's headed in the opposite direction to the runway?

Sergeant Ward had been quiet for a few seconds, but suddenly he came on the intercom again. "We're clear; we're clear, Capt'n. Oh my God, we're clear! The B-24s by us, Capt'n; he was right in my face a few seconds ago. But they're not getting it stopped; it's off the end... it's bouncing like crazy... they've caught a wing... they've got a fire, Captain. A lot of black smoke is starting to boil up!"

I took a backward glance out my left window and was surprised to find that I could see the smoke from the B-24. I had maneuvered my B-17 off the runway and out of the way of the on-coming B-24. I had managed to get on and stay on the narrow taxiway.

"Holy, Moses, we did it, we did it" I shouted to myself. I wouldn't have had a shot at it if Chuck hadn't remained at his post, watching that B-24's flashing blades driving straight for his face and his guts. Fearing that I would tip to the left and drag the left wing, I would never have gone fast enough without Chuck's running report. Nor would I have unlocked the tailwheel and let it castor, without Chuck's continuing reports, telling me where I was in the turn.

It was over in seconds. I couldn't believe that I was taxiing in the opposite direction of our landing roll so soon. I brought the B-17 to a full stop, right where she was, and yelled to Lieutenant Johnson to get Austin, Morris and Kennedy and get out to the B-24 with our fire extinguishers. **"On the double**, Guys. Now!" I could have saved my breath. They were already halfway to the crash-site.

Then I was startled by a British lorry, coming straight for me on the taxiway. It swerved at the last second and careened past me. It, of course, was hell-bent for the B-24 crash site. After it passed, I found a freshly hogged-out revetment, pulled into it and quickly shut down all four Wright-Cyclone engines.

After a moment, I dropped through the front hatch of the B-17 to *terra firma*, to Mother Earth, to the ground.

The sporting way to exit the B-17 from the **forward** crew positions was to drop very carefully through this front hatch. I had performed this feat a hundred times perhaps, counting my B-17 time at Sebring, Tucson, Alamogordo, El Paso, Colorado Springs, Topeka, Salina, West Palm Beach, Georgetown, Belem, Natal, Dakar, Marrakech, Oran, Algiers, Constantine, Navarin, Tunis and Malta. I had never had any trouble before.

On this day, on a small fighter strip, hogged out of a nut grove, on the outskirts of Avola, Sicily, I should have walked back through the fuselage and made my exit through the B-17s rear door. A short, firmly secured, three-step ladder is provided at this rear door for normal B-17 entry and exit. However, hot pilots of the era would say "a lady and a baby" could enter and leave the aircraft from the rear but not from the front of our great Boeing-made flying machine.

Thus, youthful, would-be "**hot pilots**," assigned to bombers and, thereby, denied the opportunity to demonstrate on a regular basis, their "feats of unusual skill and daring," which they thought to be sufficiently unusual and daring to cause them to be mistaken for fighter pilots, might leave the plane through the front hatch. This was particularly the case when a few self-styled, would-be fighter pilots felt they were being abused when selected (compelled) to fly the heavy bombers, the B-17s, B-24s, and B-29s instead of the dashing **P-38s, P-39s, P-40s, P-47s** and **P-51s.**

To make self-evident their masculinity, "with-it" B-17 pilots would enter and exit the aircraft through the forward cargo opening just aft of the bombardier-navigator nose bay instead of walking through the aircraft and stepping out the back door. I was one of those idiot egomaniacs.

The little over seven-foot drop through the opening to the ground could be negotiated successfully by squatting down, bending one's knees, and then leaning forward and grabbing and holding on to the far bottom inside lip of the opening, then swinging one's bent legs down and forward through the opening while straightening one's arms and legs, thereby putting one's feet within a comfortable dropping distance to the uneven ground.

I was momentarily so pleased with myself for standing up to the stresses and strains of probable death and for skillfully man-handling my flying machine out of the way of a second similar machine about to ram mine from behind that I forgot where I was. I was so pleased with myself that I decided to forget the preparatory swing out and back. I just stepped into the seven-foot abyss, wondering why the ground was moving up at me so fast.

I have tried a number of times to reconstruct what I did and why. I've never been able to recall deliberately stepping into that seven-foot hole in the air below all B-17s.

The trip straight down was not forgotten! I remember a moment of vertical flight and trying to get my weight forward so my arms and shoulders were ready to ease the impact loads on my ankles, knees and hips. After crashing to the ground, I was up on all fours very quickly so as not to embarrass myself in front of my crewmen.

However, my crewmen were racing to the crash site. The way I remember it, I was suddenly alone in a field with a large, parked airplane in repose behind me. I had searing pain in one knee and couldn't get on my feet. I crawled a short distance to a nearby tree and eased myself up against it. I thought there would be less of a scene when my crewmen returned if I were sitting up. Standing up for now was out of the question.

The pain in my landing knee, which was forcibly bent the wrong way when my heel absorbed the initial impact load, was the most searing pain that I had ever experienced. It was so bad that I decided that I should go to sleep on the spot.

Soon after my unconscious rest, I became aware of my returning crewmen, who were excitedly discussing their endeavors to help douse the fires on the B-24 that had overrun the runway.

They took no notice of their Captain resting against a tree. When they weren't looking my way, I used the tree to get to my feet. I clawed my way up the trunk of that tree using my fingers and good leg. My knee hurt something awful when I had to put some weight on it for a few seconds at a time.

My crewmen, all talking at once about their efforts to get the B-24 fire under control, did not discern my condition, or so I thought, until Technical Sergeant Morris, my ranking Airman Radio Operator, pushed a glass of cool water into my hands and said in a quiet voice. "Captain, you look a little green; everything all right?"

I drank the water before I said anything; I hadn't realized that I was so thirsty. Then I asked for another glass. The water provided a tremendous lift. The pain in my right knee was throbbing; but with a stick that Morris found and whittled out for me, I was relieved to find that I could get off the ground and, on my feet, and, by grinding my teeth, could handle the pain.

When Technical Sergeant Owens joined us in a few minutes, it became clear that I wasn't fooling my men. Their Aircraft Commander was ailing, and they weren't sure just why. They just got to work, scrounged some food from the near-by service unit that had built the runway, located a few tents and got a welcome fire going.

Later, I met the ranking B-24 pilot and some of his men. He thanked me for getting out of the way on the landing field and was grateful that the entire crew survived. They were part of the two initial B-24 groups that first joined the 9th AF and later the 15th AF and were involved in the invasion of Sicily. As I write and remember that day when the B-24 chased my tail, I would also recall that this group was to be involved later in the unprecedented low-level attack of August 1, 1943, on the Ploesti oil fields in Romania. This was the biggest raid ever on Romanian oil and the most tragic. The toll of men and materials was horrific, and within some weeks later, the Ploesti refineries were producing more oil than before the Allied attack. The Americans returned to the refineries in spring through summer, 1944, and then were successful in the destruction of the Ploesti air defense system and the complex.

After the spring/summer, 1944 Ploesti raids, we would learn from our intelligence officers that fuel oil (the life blood of modern armies) was beginning to be in short supply in Hitler's arsenal. In the words of Winston Churchill, Ploesti was the "taproot of German might."

Most likely the Ploesti raids sent a cold fear, which slowly seeped into Adolph Hitler's psyche. After those daring raids, his war machine was beginning to run out of gas, literally and figuratively. Many years after the war, I would learn through a telephone conversation with a former Aide-De-Camp to Hitler that these raids were indeed critical turning points in the war. From those moments, Der Führer no longer believed that Germany could win the war, the war that he and Germany had started in Poland.

Over Italy, our B-17s would attack most often from around 25,000 feet, our B-24s from around 20,000 feet. Before the Ploesti raid, our "heavies" our 17s and 24s, had never attempted a low altitude attack from 500 to 1,500 feet. And there were problems. Off their course for a period of time, our B-24s lost vital time in the target area, received severe damage and losses from both fighters and ground fire. Occasionally, some suffered damage from their own bombs, which had been released in desperation at unsafe, very low altitudes.

Attacking "on the deck" was an effort to circumvent the early warning net and avoid alerting the fighter and anti-aircraft defenses. The surprise element of this raid was lost, and the formations of heavily loaded B-24 bombers had become a "turkey shoot" for the fleet-winged German Me-109s, attacking from above. They were also easy prey for the 88 mm anti-aircraft batteries firing at point blank range from below.

No one could know in advance just how to best employ the great power that we would bring to the skies over Europe and, in time, over Japan. We had to learn by trial, and in some instances, by error. New equipment, new tactics and new strategies were never fully tested until they had been employed in the presence of a determined desperate enemy. That condition was met in spades at Ploesti. This groundbreaking raid, no pun intended, made it clear that the trade-offs between low and high-altitude attacks required more thinking and more detailed tactical planning.

12.2 "Theresa Leta" crew waiting in Malta for General Montgomery
to set up his command headquarters in Sicily, July 1943.
Captain Evans is sitting in the center

12.3 *B-17 flies over Mt. Etna, Sicily, Italy*

12.4 *B-17 emergency ground loop tracks on a landing field*

13.1 *B-17s drop bombs over Palermo Harbor, Sicily* (National Archives and Records Administration)

CHAPTER 13

PATTON AT PALERMO

Generals Montgomery and Patton on Sicily did land.
Both thought the glory would be simply grand!
Monty went to the right, Patton to the left.
Patton was elated; Monty was bereft!

Richard Eager

General Montgomery was aboard his B-17. Accompanying him was the commander of the Desert Air Force, Air Vice Marshal Harry Broadhurst, and Monty's Chief of Staff, Major General "Freddie" de Guingand, my good friend and protector. These two esteemed leaders of the British brass in the Mediterranean Theater were back in the aft section of the *Theresa Leta*, looking for a place to sit and buckle up. Monty was tucked into his private office in the converted bomb bay. This situation remains scary to this day, as I recall the event of more than a half-century ago.

Monty, securely strapped down in his comfortable chair at his built-in desk in his commodious office in our windowless starboard B-17 bomb bay, was giving little thought to the comfort of his guests. Why, indeed? Was it not his *Flying Fortress*, and had Ike not given it to him in gratitude for his victory at El Alamein? But of course.

I didn't have a problem with this. I thought Monty had earned his perks. His military skills, his resolve and his courage saved many a British neck, not to mention a few Yank necks, and possibly, mine. Monty had won the acclaimed Battle at El Alamein. Whoever picked Monty to be my boss for a while did me a favor.

Lieutenant Vernon, my serious-minded, assiduous, and loyal co-pilot, had posted our B-17 "Form 1" in which we routinely recorded our aircraft's maintenance, service and flight records. All crew members and other passengers aboard for specific flights were also listed in our Form. Typically, before boarding and engine start up, I, as Aircraft Commander, would be giving our B-17 a preflight check. I would be accompanied by my air and ground crew chiefs so I would not always be on hand to greet everyone who climbed aboard our *Flying Fortress*.

On this special day, I wasn't sure just who might have decided at the last minute to join us for Monty's flight from his airfield near Catania to meet General Patton at Patton's "Royal Palace of Palermo." The word being circulated at Monty's field headquarters on the heights above the plains of Catania where Monty and I had spent the preceding six days was that the grateful Sicilians had provided bed and board for General Patton at a facility described variously as a large villa or a mid-sized castle.

Built on the side of a mountain overlooking Palermo and its beautiful cobalt blue, crescent-shaped bay, the Palace of Palermo had a magnificent view. Monty would later describe the view from the sudden world-famous American Lieutenant General's plush digs as "aesthetically mah'velous, but of modest value tactically." I couldn't argue with that.

What Monty thought was of tactical value were his beloved caravans. When Monty brought General Rommel, the Desert Fox, to bay in North Africa and then sent him scurrying back to Hitler for a replacement army, an item beginning to be in short supply in Der Führer's arsenal, Monty helped himself to the two specially fabricated, self-propelled Italian designed caravans. Of course, he was pleased to take them over and put them to the good use they were designed for, a Theater Commander's mobile, battlefield Headquarters.

After the Allied invasion of Sicily, the Royal Navy, on Monty's suggestion, delivered the abandoned matched set of two mobile homes to Monty, their third owner. Monty thought them "smashing" and the army commander smiled every time he passed them.

I, too, thought them smashing, when, on my arrival at General Montgomery's campsite, he pointed to one of them, a WWII Italian-built caravan body remounted on a British Leyland Retriever 6x4 truck chassis and said, "That one was General Annibale 'Electric Whiskers' Bergonzoli, Commander of the Italian 23rd Corps. Bergonzoli was captured at Beda Fomm, south of Benghazi, in February 1941. When I arrived in North Africa, August last year, 1942, it became my home near the battle fields. Now, it makes for an efficient headquarters office."

We stopped in front of the other caravan, which was Italian designed and mounted on a Lancia chassis. Monty mentioned, "Field Marshal Rommel slept here, and when he escaped North Africa, Field Marshal Giovanni Messe, Commander of the 1st Italian Army, benefited from its use until the British 8th Army captured it as the last stages of the North African campaign wore down last May."

Monty had a particular fondness for the Bedroom Caravan, knowing that it once was the quarters for his great adversary, Rommel. He would give it up for only two people, King George VI and Winston Churchill. Other less important visitors were given a nice British tent.

Then, Monty smiled. I thought that the Army Commander enjoyed telling the story of his success and then while studying the listener's reaction, he would rock back in his own pelvic saddle, appearing to defy gravity, and cock his head quite far to one side, reminding me of the roosters we had in the Great Smoky Mountains and whose necks I was hired to wring.

I was delighted to be bedded down in a nice British tent near the caravans; and in appreciation, I showed General Montgomery my perfect set of white teeth, which were the deciding factor in my being selected "the Healthiest Boy in Knoxville," way back when I was going to Park Junior High School. I had thought that I would **RON** but not in such a grand manner near the commander and senior staff, given the circumstances of the war and all.

Monty positioned his command post and senior staff campsite on a mile-high ridge south of the Simeto River, which flows south to Gerbini, then west-to-east across the plains of Catania in the southern shadow of Mt. Etna. He could sit, virtually on his front porch, and observe his 8th Army infantry and tank corps as they methodically fired, moved forward, fired, and advanced again, driving the Germans eastward toward the Golfo di Catania, just south of the toe of Italy in the Mediterranean.

At a critical point in the invasion of Sicily, American pressure from Patton advancing from the west and British pressure from Monty proceeding from the south forced the German Army to retreat north. The retreating Germans were forced around the southeast base of the 10,900-foot Mt. Etna in an effort to reach the Port of Messina, and here they made an orderly withdrawal from Sicily, across the two-mile-wide Stretto di Messina, to mainland Italy. The Allied generals were not too pleased so many German and Italian solders with equipment, ammo and guns made it across the straits... to fight another day.

Aboard Monty's B-17 on a new, recently bulldozed, fighter strip southwest of Catania, Technical Sergeant Owens reported everyone accounted for and ready to start engines. The four Wright-Cyclone "**prop-drivers**" were cranked up and quickly checked out. Everything, as we "**flyboys**" liked to say back in those days, was "great," "hunky-dory," or "copasetic." I still don't understand "hunky-dory" and, as I think of it now, I don't have a full understanding of "copasetic" either.

Turning onto the runway using the port engines (Nos. 1 and 2), I eased the starboard (Nos. 3 and 4) throttles forward to the stops, bringing us out of our turn and heading us down the runway. I also checked the RPM meters and manifold pressure gauges. When moving the yoke (the control column) fore and aft a tad I could feel the pressure of the **airstream** starting to take hold of the stabilizers, our flight-control surfaces that were hinged to the trailing edges of our big bird's wings and the horizontal tail surfaces. This procedure also checked the free movement of the controls.

Bomber airfields in the ETO were typically 5,000 feet; fighter strips were a sparser 3,500. I eyeballed our new 3,500-foot fighter strip **hogged out** of a Sicilian nut grove and deemed it adequate for our light operating weight, i.e., no bombs and limited fuel, albeit loaded to the gunnels with ammo and a substantial load of British brass.

Information about the recently liberated Palermo airfield had been unavailable via the limited telephone resources to which I had access. Monty had advised me, however, that he had signaled (telephoned) Patton himself, had talked directly with the General and learned that the suddenly famous, recently promoted, unpredictable, flamboyant US Army Lieutenant General had inspected the Palermo airfield himself and had, in Monty's precise words, "pronounced it sah-tis-fahc-tory for any type of air-crawft." I thought, "You can't beat that."

I enjoyed Monty's British accent and would often smile (to myself) when Monty would make one of his proclamations. Presumptuously, I believed I would have had my own British accent had my great-grandfathers, Evans and Stewart, not emigrated from Wales and Scotland across the Atlantic to America a few decades before my birth in the Great State of Tennessee.

I had participated in bombing attacks against Axis shipping in Palermo Harbor and recalled a few small fields that we hit, but they certainly were not large enough for a bomber. This would normally have raised suspicions in my mind regarding the Palermo airfield's adequacy for medium-to-heavy military aircraft operations. "Why had it not been on our bombing list?" I wondered. "Why, indeed" as Monty would have put it. "Was it a pasture field of no consequence?" Considering that Patton should know the B-17's requirements, I assumed that Sicily's capital city would surely have an airfield large enough to accommodate a B-17, unencumbered by its usual load of war defense munitions.

Nor did I expect to run into German fighters on the course I had selected, i.e., an east-to-west track along Sicily's median line, well south of where hard-pressed German fighters were operating in limited numbers. As a further precaution, I flew along in the tops of a broken cloud layer with little more than my head poking out above the clouds.

I had discovered that I could leave my B-17 down in the clouds while raising the cockpit up just high enough for me to look across the tops of those beautiful stratocumulus clouds. Of course, if I should see something threatening, I would be in good position to quickly drop back down a few feet, make a small turn, delay a minute or two, then pop back up again for another look.

———————————

Earlier, when visiting with Monty at the British Embassy in Cairo, I had learned the plans for invading Sicily called for landings by Britain and American Army groups on the beaches located on each side of the southeast corner of the island-state. The Sicilian landing beaches were just 60 miles from Malta. Patton, leading the Yank assault, would command the southwestern flank. Monty would command the southeastern flank. Working his way north, Monty would head his 8th Army towards Messina, passing to the east of a very good landmark, the 10,900-foot Mt. Etna, the highest active volcano in the ETO.

From Messina, Monty would have only a short, one-hour boat ride across the Straits of Messina to affect an invasion of the toe of Italy. Although Sicily was a state of Italy, we did not think we would really be invading Europe until we crossed the famous straits. When we each made our personal crossings and eventually put foot on Europe proper, we all congratulated ourselves and glanced back over our shoulders at world famous Mt. Etna, which at that moment in time was itself very active, sending a constant stream of black smoke into the clear skies over the Mediterranean.

Monty very much wanted to lead the invasion Army that would first set foot on Axis held mainland Europe. I couldn't fault the Army commander for this. Had I been in Monty's shoes, I would certainly have wished for the honor as well as the opportunity to run a test of my army's amphibious equipment and my men's amphibious skills.

As the first British Allied Army Commander to defeat an Axis Army in the field, it seemed to me that leading the initial Allied attack on mainland Europe would be an honor Monty and his 8th Army had earned. ROTC at Knoxville High School and University of Tennessee had not made me a "militarist," but I could understand Monty and Patton's interest in being the invasion leader to first set foot on mainland Europe.

Patton, landing in southern Sicily (on Monty's left flank), would head due north for Enna, a moderately sized town in the geographical center of the Italian island state. Patton would then wheel left onto a northwesterly heading and "race" essentially unopposed for Palermo, Sicily's capital city. The Germans, by this time, had departed the northwestern Palermo area and were beginning to make contact with Monty's positions in eastern Sicily.

During the previous week, I had stood on the heights south of Mt. Etna and observed, in the company of General Montgomery, the battle's progress in a valley between Mt. Etna and our position a thousand feet above the valley floor. Intending no humor, Monty pointed out to me that "General Patton need not have raced across Sicily," as was reported, "since there were no German forces of consequence west of Enna with whom General Patton might have had a serious contest."

It occurred to me that just possibly Monty was a little biased in his assessment of Patton's battle skills. So, would I have been had I been in Monty's shoes. Having picked up a bit of a British accent myself on Malta, I responded to Monty with a brisk, "Indeed, Sir, I should think so."

It was quickly made clear to me that the Italian nationals inhabiting Sicily were more at ease with the idea of surrendering to the Yanks, the British, or the South Africans-whoever the commanding general of the forces might be-than remaining hostage to the Germans in their homeland.

Flying west at 800 feet over Sicily, ducking in and out of light cumulus clouds, I was having a very nice day. My introspective, personal flashbacks relating to my arrival in Sicily helped pass the time.

After a few hours, Palermo, a former target but now our destination, could be seen at two o'clock about a hundred miles off our right wing. As we were slightly ahead of our ETA, I chose to continue west, delaying our planned turn to the north towards our destination. Very shortly we were flying over Marsala where I had participated in recent bombing raids on the airdrome there.

Hitler had invaded Africa, in part, to rescue his ally, Mussolini. When the remnants of Rommel's Afrika Corps were suddenly high tailing it out of Africa, Bizerte and Tunis became the principal ports of Axis debarkation. Their principal port of embarkation by sea and air in western Sicily, became Marsala.

The retreating army had shoved off from Bizerte, and Cape Bon, in small, ill-kept boats or anything that would float akin to Dunkirk. Others had been herded into large, clumsy undefended air-gliders, which were towed by aircraft across the short 100-mile Mediterranean crossing from Tunis, to Sicily.

Many of these Axis soldiers never made it to Sicily. Pilots of the US 9th Air Force summarily shot down essentially this entire force. Our fighter pilots termed the massacre a "turkey shoot."

I remember examining my conscience at the time but reminded myself that the people shot down in those clumsy, underpowered, undefended contraptions had buckled under to despots who had conspired to conquer and enslave any and all within reach of their guns and their bombs.

Some Axis troops were able to escape Ike's and Monty's Armies and the 9th and 12th Air Force fighters in Tunisia. A substantial number were able to reach Marsala, only to find themselves on the receiving end of Allied B-17 bombing attacks.

When I would stop for a moment in those days to consider German casualties, I would wonder if any of my German third cousins, whose great-grandmother, Ernst, had also been my great-grandmother Ernst, had been involved.

As I flew by at 800 feet, I was surprised not to see more battle damage to the permanent facilities at Marsala. After a good look to make sure there were no other aircraft in the area, I dropped down and made a few low-level passes. There appeared to be no significant air-support facilities on the field. I could see only great piles of mangled aircraft, bulldozed to the sides of the field, reminding me of the aircraft burial grounds I had viewed on Mussolini's erstwhile Castel Benito Airdrome in Tripoli.

Turning away from Marsala, I headed north for Trapani, on Sicily's western coast, a few-minutes flight from Palermo. After Marsala, I was surprised not to see more carnage at Trapani. I had an even greater surprise awaiting me at my final destination, Palermo.

Approaching Sicily's capital city where General Patton was in residence, I took up a south-westerly heading and made landfall as I passed over a beautiful bay, surrounded on three sides by a crescent-shaped, very attractive Italian city firmly anchored between the steep, nearby heights. Quickly, a large boat, that looked as if it might have been blown clean out of the harbor and up onto the beach below the town, loomed into our view. With no feelings of joy, I speculated, "The shifting of this quite-large Italian vessel from the harbor to the beach was very likely some of our work in our B-17s."

In the *Flying Fortress* in Europe, we attacked our targets, in most cases, from around 25,000 to 35,000 feet. With Monty aboard en route to his meeting with General Patton, I approached Palermo, at just 500 feet above a natural harbor. The scene before me was one of utter destruction. The Palermo Harbor was a vital target for the Allies to dislodge the Axis forces, and the city received severe punishment.

I was not prepared for my first ground level view of the once beautiful Palermo, nor was I prepared for my first viewing of its nearby airfield, which quickly came into focus directly ahead of us.

Dropping down, for a closer look, I flew along its western side. I was afforded an excellent view of a surprisingly small airfield on which a C-47 (DC-3 *Gooney Bird*) was just landing. I watched in disbelief as our wartime, workhorse, air-transport ran the full length of the small field and then crashed headlong into some low trees at the far end. I remember that the actual crash, reviewed from a distance, looked as if it were in slow motion.

The violent scene just witnessed with no sounds seemed unreal. When this *Gooney Bird*, after running out of field finally bounced to a stop, a fire flashed immediately. The ensuing smoke remained low over the field, retracing the just completed flight and ground path of the C-47.

Staying low over the field, the smoke indicated a strong, high-velocity wind into which I might land directly. This was good news.

On the other hand, the clear indication that the field was not long enough for a C-47 to get itself on the ground and stopped was not encouraging. As Monty might have put it, "Actually, the situation was quite disquieting. Quite."

The purpose of our flight to Palermo, was to bring Monty and members of his staff together with General Patton and members of his staff for a powwow on the Allied offensive in Sicily. Rumors had circulated around the world that these Army Commanders, each having great confidence in his own skills in warfare, might not have fully appreciated the capabilities of the other.

British reports in this connection suggested that the situation was disquieting, that Monty was not at all at ease with George, who gave the impression of having some rough edges. On the other hand, Patton appeared to have no objections at all to the bad blood developing between the two Allied Commanders. Some thought Patton gave the impression of loving the unloving relationship.

When we arrived over the Palermo airfield right on time, I was pleased. When I was able to get a good look at our intended destination, some of the joy of the morning left me.

The field was grossly undersized for aircraft of the period. And I could see no runways, taxiways, hangers, or tower, nothing to suggest that it was an airfield except, of course, the burning C-47 that had run off the upwind end of the field. Smoke from this crashed *Gooney Bird* did, however, provide us an excellent indication of wind direction and velocity.

Looking for some positive aspect of the Palermo landing field, I noted that low trees on the periphery of the field might constrain landing aircraft from excessive over-running. These trees had indeed stopped the over-running C-47 at a point accessible to the emergency vehicles seen congregating at the crash site.

When Monty advised me that his people had made inquiries regarding the Palermo airfield and that Patton himself had stepped in and had confirmed "Palermo was satisfactory for all types of aircraft," I should have reminded myself that Patton's much-advertised expertise was tanks. In my mind, I conceded that Palermo was probably great for tanks.

I had endeavored to make inquiries on my own but had quickly discovered that my efforts were to no avail. It was suggested at Monty's mountain camp near Mt. Etna that a direct line had not been established between General Patton's hillside castle and Monty's recently inherited Italian caravans.

In an effort to get a grip on myself, I said to myself, "My God, Richard Eager (I was a closet swearer during WWII… most of the time), there are some airplanes parked down there, but this place can't be called a real airfield. This is a beautiful and tranquil sheep pasture with a few wrecked German and Italian flying machines shoved off to the sides. Also, there is a *Gooney Bird* resting in the trees bordering the downhill end of the field. A vehicle with red crosses on its sides is just arriving, and passengers and crew can be seen running in every direction. And, Oh, my God! The *Gooney Bird* has just burst into more flames!"

As I continued to circle the field, I noted Patton's welcoming entourage waiting below. I envisioned the General himself waiting with his highly polished helmet, flashing Morse code to me. I learned later that Patton was impatiently waiting at the palace with General Keyes, a band, and a company of 15th Infantry to impress the British Commander.

I had already decided that I didn't have the guts to tell Monty that landing a B-17 in that sheep pasture would be a bloody silly thing to do since it was Monty who had set up the meeting and Monty who had "signaled" Patton and determined from George that our "blood and guts" tank man had certified the Palermo airfield "satisfactory for aircraft of all types."

One thing was working for me. As I had observed before, the smoke from the burning *Gooney Bird* was staying very close to the ground indicating a good, stiff breeze, which would shorten my landing run, if I could drive directly into it. I could do this by simply lining up so that I could land diagonally across the field. This would give me a slightly longer run after getting my wheels on the ground. Also, some space on one side into which I might **ground loop** the B-17 would give me some extra room should I have trouble getting it stopped. The impossible was beginning to look possible to me.

On my second circling of the Palermo airfield, I imagined that General Patton was probably-flashing signals to me on every turn, using his well-polished helmet to reflect the sun's rays into my eyes. I said to myself, "This three-star **ground-pounder** has no way of knowing that I flunked Morse code as a Boy Scout and improved only moderately on becoming a Flying Cadet in the Army Air Corps." But I did concede that Georgie had to be credited with devising a unique use for his striking, three-starred headpiece.

It was beginning to get through to me that I was getting myself exercised over the Old Man's choice of head-coverings because I didn't want to face up to my problem: I had no bloody business trying to land one of **Uncle Sam**'s flying machines on that 1,500-foot sheep pasture.

Another thought weighed me down. When my commander, Colonel Upthegrove, first told me that I was going to be Monty's B-17 pilot, he made the point: "And, Dick, don't let those British chaps talk you into something if you don't like the odds." He should also have added, " ...and don't let the American ground-pounders talk you into something if you don't like the odds."

Finally, after completing the second swing around the field, I said to myself, "Okay, Richard Eager, make up your mind; what's it going to be? It's your call. But remember, it's generally understood that General Patton doesn't like to be kept waiting.

"And, probably Monty, strapped in back there in his windowless, makeshift office in our B-17, is getting a little antsy, too. You have a couple of options. You can take Monty back to the nut grove and try to stay out of sight for the rest of the war, or you can try to put this machine on the ground down there where the waiting military welcome committee is watching your every turn."

When, after a few minutes, I had increased the prop pitch, dropped the flaps halfway, brought the RPM and power up slightly and rolled the horizontal stabilizer back a tad to take up the slack, I knew that I had made my decision. I was going to land my B-17.

In a moment, I would be turning onto a base leg, followed by the final approach. The milling group of Patton's aides, motorcycles and escort cars provided a great reference point as I completed my third circle of the field and started my descent for landing.

I had noticed underbrush in the path of my base leg during an earlier circling of the field. Now closer, with the field dead ahead, I could see that this "underbrush" was clumps of small trees, appropriately indigenous, I thought, to this small island state.

I added a little power and rolled the stabilizer back just a tad. My rate-of-descent was more than intended; so was the three-point whap which I felt as my three wheels hit the ground at the same time. I hit harder than intended out of a full stall, a scant couple hundred feet in front of General Patton's welcome party.

"But, so far so good," I thought. I was on the ground and rolling on a corner-to-corner diagonal of the rectangular field. I was angled directly into a brisk head wind. For starters and what I had to work with, I couldn't have done better.

Then I tapped the brakes lightly to determine if my brakes were pulling right or left before I needed them. Not feeling the usual slight surge with my first tap, I tapped again. Nothing.

I came down still harder, still nothing. Then, I "stood on the pedals," as we liked to say back then. Still there was no response. I had no brakes at all, which was a new experience for me in a *Flying Fortress*; I had lost one brake but never both at the same time. "Sabotage!" I thought, but then dismissed the thought as something I could do nothing about.

I yelled to Lieutenant Vernon to try his brakes. There was no response from the pressed pedal. "My God, we don't have any brakes at all! Try yours again," I yelled. Still nothing. "We've got no brakes at all. Our expander tubes were already blown before we tried to use them!" I shouted.

Neither Vernon nor I had any brakes, and we were rolling at a good clip downhill. That is when I was first able to see that the field had a pretty good grade. Flying directly overhead, we were not able to pick up the degree of slope. I shouted to myself, "Oh my god, we're heading into a good wind, but we're also heading downhill on a pretty steep slope and at a pretty fast clip. And our expander tubes have blown on both of our main wheels."

I remember taking a deep breath, and then saying to Vernon, "Don't activate it now, but put your hand on the tail-wheel lock" (a device which prevents the tail wheel from castoring freely but allowing it to swing three degrees right or left of a centerline, thereby helping to keep the plane on a straight course during landings and takeoffs).

"Good, you've got the tail-wheel lock," I said, "Now don't move a muscle until I tell you. Do not disengage it yet; we're all dead if you do. Just press the release and get ready. I'm ruddering our machine over to the right side of the field so we'll have the entire field on our left to groundloop into."

After a few seconds we were still approaching the right-hand boundary too fast and at a slight angle. I yelled as loud as I could, "Not yet, Vernon, but get ready to disengage the tail wheel lock and brace yourself." I remember thinking, "I'm scaring the hell out of poor Vernon, but what can I do? This isn't a motion picture; this is the real thing. And by the way, Richard Eager, if you haven't noticed, you're scared stiff yourself."

I had used full right rudder to angle us over to the right side of the field; then, after a few seconds, I had shifted to left rudder to flatten our angle with the edge of the field. Then, in a moment, I would come on quickly with both right engines and attempt to turn us back across the grade, and, if possible, back up the hill in a looping U-turn."

The time had come. "Disengage, Vernon; disengage the tail wheel castoring lock. Now! Do it now," I yelled; then I came on with a little left rudder. Disengaging the tail wheel lock, allowed the wheel to pivot more than three degrees to the right, causing the tail to swing widely to the right and thereby turning the plane sharply to the left.

"It's working," I thought, "I'm paralleling the right boundary, but I'm not out far enough to swing the tail around and not have it hit that fence, the one that doesn't seem to keep the sheep out."

I delayed for another moment and then yelled, "Hang on, Vernon," as I brought the power up on No. 4, the right outboard engine. The B-17 hesitated and then started turning sharply to the left, "too sharply and too fast," I thought. In my mind's eye, as we careened down and across the field, I could visualize the props on the two right engines striking the ground and bending the tips. But I didn't feel the expected thumps of the props hitting the ground. They weren't striking yet. "The hill is that steep," I remember thinking. My seatbelt was holding my rear-end firmly in the seat pan, but my upper body from my waist up was being forced out to my right, over the aisle, between the pilot's and co-pilot's positions. My right arm was pulled over into Vernon's face, and I was unable to reel it back in.

I had commenced the hard, left turn with the two right throttles firmly gripped in my right hand: I was pressing them forward against the stops. But almost instantly, it seemed the forces were so great that I had to release my right hand to prevent the weight of my upper torso from pulling the power off too soon. When I let go the throttles, my right arm flew past my face in the direction of Vernon. "Honest to God," or, as we said when kids in Tennessee, "Honest Injun," I watched my right palm and my fingers go right by my face, as if in slow motion."

My free arm hadn't hit Vernon as I thought it might; Vernon was out of range, safely pressed up against the co-pilot's window, a foot or two to his right, out of harm's way.

With my left hand still clutching the left throttles and my right arm airborne in Vernon's direction, I was spread-eagle in a semi-vertical, semi-horizontal plane. My upper body had been flung forward slightly and as far right into the space between the pilot and co-pilot seats as my lap belt would permit. I wanted desperately to get my arm back over to the throttle quadrant where I could keep the right throttles from creeping back but I couldn't move anything. I remember thinking, "My arm, fully extended, is a 200-pound pendulum. It just swung by me, but I can't reel it back in!"

Then, I remember clearly that suddenly I was in some kind of dream state that wasn't unpleasant; also, I realized that I was trying hard not to **greyout**. And I wasn't frightened, but I was confused. As wild as it sounds, I knew I was confused. I asked myself what was I trying to do with the airplane controls? Why was I trying so hard to reach the throttle quadrant? Why did I feel like I was dreaming? I had absolutely no idea.

At the same time, in my mind's eye, as if I were watching the scene, not playing a part in it, I could see myself spread-eagle across the cockpit, half in poor Vernon's lap.

Then, as fast as I had lost it, I somehow got some of my brain cells functioning again. I suddenly knew where I was and what it was, I was trying to do. "You have got to get your right arm back over here out of poor Vernon's face, Richard Eager, so you can keep the right engine throttles from creeping back. You've got to get turned back up this bloody hill you've landed on or you're going to run off the downhill end and slam into that burning *Gooney Bird* down there."

Then within seconds, the streak of black smoke from the burning *Gooney Bird* loomed up ahead directly across our path. In a flash, it splashed against our windshield and disappeared. We had flashed through it and now it was behind us. I knew where I was. I said to myself, "You're in mid-field, Richard Eager; you're heading back across the field, great. But you're not getting your flying machine turned back up hill. You're on the ground, but you are heading for the far-left corner. When it was discovered you had no brakes, you angled right to put all of the field on your left so you could ground loop back into it, but you've got to get turned back up the hill."

I had started our ground loop, but I was too fast. I had tried to slow down our rate-of-turn so that we would not skid sidewise, tilt too far to our right, wipe out our landing gear, drag our right wing and engines, and possibly rupture our fuel tanks in the right wing. That would be all she wrote!

I knew that I had been confused for a few seconds, but suddenly I knew I was okay again. My head was clearing, and I was beginning to think again. "We're halfway around, we didn't dig our right wing into the ground. We didn't bang up our props. The downhill grade gave us more clearance for our tipped, right engine than we thought it might. It felt like we were about to catch a wing tip, which might cause us to flip over. But we probably didn't come close to hitting our props; the grade of this airfield is that steep."

We hadn't run off the end into the trees; the violent skidding turn had given us tremendous braking action and had slowed us down. We didn't get turned back up hill, but we still had a lot of field ahead of us to our left.

"We're going to make it; we're going to make it!" I know the words didn't come out of me; they just exploded in my head.

Then, so help me, the Hallelujah Chorus that Mom insisted I learn to sing when I was still a soprano in Knoxville's First Methodist Church choir, came to mind, "hal le lu jah, hal le lu jah, hal leee'-lu-jah!"

Again, I felt some momentary, dream-like confusion in my head; but this time it was different. This time I knew we were going to be okay. My recollection is that I still was desperately trying to muscle the left engines forward again to prevent the B-17 from turning too sharply, which would cause us to skid sidewise and possibly collapse the down-hill right gear, causing the right-wing tip to dig in, breaking the wing spar, and rupturing the wing tank, but it wasn't happening.

The B-17 was slowing down and at last starting to level up. The centrifugal forces pressing me to my right were suddenly gone. I could reach the controls. I could take control of my aircraft again.

Without differential braking and too little speed for the rudder to be effective, the only other way to cause a B-17 to turn right or left is differential power, using the throttles on one side or the other. I gingerly added power on No. 1, our outboard, up-hill engine on our left wing, to increase the radius of our turn across the hill. I needed to use the full-field width to complete our 180-degree turn before heading back up the hill.

Our careening downhill left turn, which I had thought might wipe out our outboard, downhill engine props, had seemed to last an eternity. Suddenly the violent sidewise skidding turn stopped. The downhill wing started coming back up quicker than expected. At last, truly we had it made.

We were not going to wind up in a heap or run headlong into the trees and start a second fire beside the crashed C-47. We weren't going to be slashed up by torn aluminum, and we weren't going to be grilled by a fuel fire. We were going to live. We were going to live! I was able to think again and reel my right arm back in and out of Vernon's face.

Then I saw the parked fighters ahead of us for the first time. "Where did they come from?" I asked myself. "Why hadn't I seen them from the air? Were they camouflaged that well?" When we had circled the field, I had failed to notice two rows of strange looking fighters, Italian, no doubt. I had never seen any Italian planes. They were downhill from the corner where Patton's Aide-de-Camp, Major Codman was waiting.

The excitement was over. We were much slower now; I was settling down. I had no trouble driving our B-17 without brakes using the downhill throttles to bring us around the parked fighters and head us back uphill towards the group of dismayed observers, whom I honestly believe, just wondered why the American pilot was so rough on his airplane. "Probably some show-off at the controls."

My problems, however, were not quite over. I positioned the plane about 50 feet or so in front of Patton's staff.

When we came to a stop, I kept a little power on to keep the B-17 from coasting backwards down the slope that we were on. Sergeant Owens was out in front quickly. He gave me the finger-across-the-throat signal to shut the engines down.

When those "Wright-Cyclones" ground down to a chug or two and stopped, the quiet was so heavy you could feel it. No sound came from Monty's office in the bomb bay, or from the back end of the fuselage where members of his staff were riding, some probably without seat belts fastened, I guessed.

Nor was anyone outside making a sound. For sure, we weren't being welcomed with any band music. There was no sign of life at our end of the field. The smoke from the *Gooney Bird* in view out my left window now was still staying close to the ground as it wafted quickly by. The smoke wasn't making any noise either.

I had unbuckled my seat belt, gotten up but not out of the seat, when, suddenly, I felt light-headed. I was having the illusion that the ground was slowly moving by me. I dropped back on the seat quickly, thinking to allow myself a few more seconds to get settled down before attempting to walk out of the B-17. Also, I gave thought as to just how the matter might be resolved by Patton's staff and Montgomery if I were perceived by all as being intoxicated as I exited a US flying machine after landing it in a circle.

But then, in a flash, it became clear that my head was not playing games; the ground wasn't moving forward; the B-17 was moving backwards, back down the hill from which we had come, and it was picking up speed. I shoved open the window on the pilot's side and yelled, "Sergeant Owens, for God's sake, get the chocks behind the wheels. We're rolling back down the hill we just came up!"

Sergeant Owens, my great top-turret gunner and senior "non-com" on my crew had already caught the movement of the B-17 and was running to retrieve the wheel chocks. In most circumstances the B-17 is parked on a flat surface and needs no chocks. The chocks, which may be needed later, are normally placed ahead of the B-17 to resist forward movement of the flying machine when the engines are being fired up.

After a moment, I exited the B-17, noted that the chocks looked out of place behind the wheels, and said to Owens, "Don't sweat it Sarge, not a problem, and thanks for being Johnny-on-the-spot."

So, what was I going to say when asked why the extraordinary landing? Everyone seemed to be a tad upset.

I was upset that Monty and Patton were insisting on using a bloody *Flying Fortress* for personal convenience and for passing off this nice sheep-grazing hillside as a military airfield. And I was upset with myself for not having the guts to stand up to both of them and refusing to land a B-17 in this beautiful, tranquil sheep pasture. I risked all our necks needlessly, and I am ashamed, damned ashamed, that I didn't have the guts to turn around and fly us back from where we started.

As I walked from the back to the front of General Patton's greeting staff, I noticed there wasn't a sound as Monty's pilot came to attention in front of Major Codman and other notables.

If General Patton had observed our landing, he would have been clearly flushed with anger.

He would not have addressed me or spoken to me directly; he would have spurted at me. "What kind of a landing do you call that?" he would have asked.

Surprisingly in a calm voice, I would have hoped to answer, "Sir, I wouldn't characterize that as a landing. That was a deliberate ground loop to keep from winding up on top of that burning C-47, which can be seen down in the trees below our position. Sir, it was stupid of me to attempt a landing at Palermo. This field is not suitable for B-17 operations. I embarrassed myself. After circling once, I should have headed straight back to the field I had flown out of this morning. I apologize to you, General Patton."

As General Montgomery exited from the plane, I repeated the "apology" that I imagined giving Patton, for not having the fortitude to turn around and fly back to our takeoff point, as I most certainly should have done.

As Patton's welcoming staff began to load up their motorcycles and jeeps, to escort General Montgomery and his staff from the field, I looked in the direction of my boss.

At that moment it took only a glance in Monty's direction to persuade me that The Army Commander was once again out of sorts with me.

I so wanted to just serve General Montgomery and have his respect, his goodwill, possibly his friendship; but I seemed to have a real talent for screwing things up with the 8th Army's Commander, the Victor of Alamein. Then I thought, who is kidding whom; I couldn't think how delighted Monty would have been had I said to him, "Sorry, General Montgomery; this field that you and General Patton selected for me really isn't suitable for B-17 operations. I should have turned around and flown us all, right back to Gela."

I didn't have to worry about Monty, Patton, or Patton's aides for very long. I didn't think any one of them was anxious to hang around the Palermo airfield and talk. Monty looked like he really didn't care to have a talk with his *Flying Fawtress* pilot or even look at him.

Several minutes later with a glaring absence of small talk, Monty and the entourages piled quickly into transport vehicles and could be seen winding their way back down the good-sized hill they had just recently come up, destination Royal Palace of Palermo.

Almost immediately, a war correspondent, who had apparently been part of our welcoming committee, asked if he could have some conversation with me. I said, "Of course," and asked him to give me a few minutes with my crew.

"May I listen in?" he asked. "I am very interested in your rather unique position here in the middle between Monty and Patton, both of whom make no secret of their dissatisfaction with the other."

Smiling at his choice of words, I responded, "Certainly, you would be very welcome; I would be pleased if you would join us and pleased to have you listen in, if you would like."

In a few minutes turning to my crewmen whom Sergeant Owens had corralled for me, I said, "Okay men, listen up. First, I want to apologize to you for that stupid landing. After dragging this field twice, I should have had the guts to make an immediate 180-degree turn and headed us straight back to our home base field. The truth is I plain didn't have the guts to tell Monty that we should not be landing in this very nice sheep pasture.

"If we had not landed, I was sure that Patton would rag Monty at the first opportunity for

Monty's failure to attend such an important meeting. Thus, I was motivated to perform the most stupid act of my flying career to prevent this; I put all our lives into jeopardy. I apologize to you knowing that my words don't mean a damn thing right now.

"Of course, I had no way of knowing that we would lose our brakes, even as I was tapping them to check them out. We did have a good strong wind to land into, but there was no way we could detect from flying directly overhead that our airfield was on a bloody hillside. With this much grade, I should have been landing downwind and uphill. I did it just backwards.

"Some of you with a hole in the B-17 that you can see out of probably realized that since I had no brakes, I used the throttles to get our airplane over to one side of the hill we found ourselves on so I could then ground loop back into the full width of the small airfield and get our flying machine turned around and headed back uphill without wiping out our landing gear.

"One more thing. Some of you have asked if you can go into town and have a look at Palermo, and some have asked if you can run over to the side of the field and look at the wrecked German and Italian aircraft, which we can see have been bull-dozed off to the side of the field. The answer is 'yes', and Lieutenant Vernon will be your point of contact in this connection. General Patton's motorcade that took our generals and staff members into town will be returning in about 30 minutes to take as many of you as would like to go into Palermo to see a very beautiful city.

"You will recall that we hit this small field only once with **frags** and with only modest success. There wasn't much here to hit. Our attacks against shipping were another matter. It appears that we did indeed blow one quite large boat clean out of the water and up onto the beach. Some of you saw it as we were coming in. You might want to take a closer look at it.

"Now, one more thing. We've all heard the stories about booby-trapped aircraft wrecks. I would guess these wrecks across the field have not been booby-trapped, but I have no expertise in this topic and no interest in becoming self-taught.

"Okay, here's the drill, get it straight. I suggest you not get closer than ten yards to these wrecked aircraft on the field, but that's not an order. But listen up, this is an order, do not pick up and bring back to our airplane any keepsakes which you might find at these wrecks. I am dead serious. I will see to your court martial if you disobey this order. Is this clear? We understand each other?"

Everybody agreed that we understood each other and everybody took off in a flash to enjoy some free time. I turned to the war correspondent and asked if he would like to come aboard and have a look at our B-17. He said he'd been working with the ground forces, hadn't been inside a *Flying Fortress* and would very much enjoy getting a first-hand look. When we reached the flight deck, I invited him to take the pilot's seat and I climbed into the co-pilot's seat beside him.

We talked for some time about the B-17, about the kind of missions my group had been flying, and about Monty's bet with Ike, which Ike had told his Chief of Staff he could not recall making.

I volunteered that I thought Monty a great military leader, also a high-strung, tense, hard-working man.

I said that I had been a guest for the past week in Monty's camp pitched atop a precipice, overlooking the plains of Catania, facing the south face of Mt. Etna, the 10,900-foot volcano, dominating the northeast corner of Sicily. I mentioned that I often "**went on recce**" with Monty and one of his aides as they visited his army's front-line positions.

I revealed that on my first "recce" experience with Monty, I had made some inquiries, arrived early at the jeeps and was standing by when Monty arrived. Then, I quickly jumped into the rear seat of the lead jeep. Monty climbed into the front seat beside the driver, looked over his shoulder at me, returned his gaze to the front, and then, without a word, raised his right arm to a point abeam his right ear with his thumb pointing aft at a second Jeep parked behind us.

Thinking this clear enough and requiring no conversation, I extracted myself, along with my red face, from the seat behind Monty and promptly without a word walked briskly to the second jeep, climbed into the front seat beside the driver and awaited further instructions.

Monty turned, looked at me without expression, bent his head forward, raised it quickly, and returned his gaze to the front. Monty's driver released his clutch briskly. Mine did likewise. "This is great," I said, "hang on, Richard Eager; you're up, up and away with the highest ranking 'ground-pounder' in the theater."

Actually, we were "up," but not yet, "away." We had one important stop to make at a supply tent where we picked up two or three-dozen cartons of cigarettes, which I would then watch Monty "toss to the troops," as we drove by.

This upset me; I thought it undignified of a Field Marshal and a put down to his troops. I was sure Yank smokers would agree. They could get all the smokes they wanted at their "ship's store," "commissary," or "**post-exchange**." But, in a short time I decided I was wrong. Monty was surprisingly accurate with his tosses from a moving vehicle and his men were deft catchers. They enjoyed the sport, and everybody was a little happier, including me, after I gave myself a short lecture on "minding one's own business."

At one point, which I judged to be close to the geographic center of the triangular-shaped island of Sicily, the road became very rough. "Very rough, indeed," as Monty would put it. So rough, in fact, that I elected to stand up in my Jeep and hold onto the forward windscreen for support, letting my knees absorb some of the shock instead of my thinly padded buttocks having to absorb the dreadful pounding which I was experiencing.

Suddenly, I realized that our circular path was taking us to the summit of a hill, which at its top formed an almost perfect cone. And suddenly there was Monty in his jeep with his driver just above me at the next level and appropriately... looking down at me.

Since I was already on my feet albeit holding on for dear life in my bouncing jeep and since Monty and I were alone, except for our drivers, I chose to seize the moment. As Monty passed on the level above my jeep, I straightened up, pulled my chin in, smiled, and rendered the hand salute to the Army Commander, British 8th Army, General Sir Bernard Law Montgomery, the Victor at Alamein.

Monty checked that his driver's eyes were on the road and then turned his head to the right and down, allowing his eyes to focus on his Yank Captain who was bouncing along in Jeep No. 2 on the dirt road thirty or forty feet below him.

Monty's eyes softened and his crow's feet deepened with a slight smile. Grasping the jeep windshield with his left hand, The Army Commander straightened his back, released his right hand, and returned his Yank Captain's hand salute.

The war correspondent seemed to enjoy this story, thanked me for my consideration and departed with his notebook. This concluded my arrival in Palermo, but how was I going to fly Monty out of Palermo?

Theresa Leta was in pretty good shape except for damaged brakes. I was confident that the take-off could be managed using the downhill grade and flaps at the right moment; but just the same, I stepped off the field while the Generals were conferring at the castle, and I watched where other aircraft got off the ground and then figuring from that where I could take off.

But once in the air I had to tell the General, his Chief of Staff and Air Marshal, that I couldn't take them all the way home... because the brakes were completely and definitely gone, and I would again have to ground loop the air plane to stop it... and our home station was only 3,000 feet and it was narrow... and it just couldn't be done... but if they wanted to bail out... but they didn't... they were beginning to get very reasonable... they wanted me to do just what I thought best.

So, I picked a roomier field, landed with a good long roll and everything was quite under control. I procured a B-25, passed my passengers into it, and flew them to the base field with very little time lost.

Before the end of the day, I told the General that I was flying back to Navarin Airfield for new brakes and he didn't say, "No." He asked me if I really thought that a B-17 was the ship for him, and I reminded him that I had told him sometime before that it absolutely was not.

Later, after returning from Palermo, a sheepish 8th Army Commander cabled to Eisenhower's Chief of Staff, General Bedell Smith: "Had difficulty with *Fortress* today at Palermo and consider should change it in view of small airfields on which we are now working. Can you send me a C-47 with jeep? Will you have long-range tanks fitted? Grateful if you will send it to Cassibile Airfield near Syracuse."

The Air Marshal aboard the Palermo ship, realizing what took place himself must, have put a bug in the General's ear because Monty frequently referred to me later as "his pilot, to whose skill he owed his life."

13.2 *General G. Keyes shows Sicily map to Generals Montgomery and Patton*
(AP/Shutterstock)

13.3 *General Montgomery says farewell to General Patton at Palermo Airfield, Sicily, Italy*
(National Archives and Records Administration)

13.4 *General Montgomery's caravans move with him from North Africa to Italy, Normandy and later to England* (Crown Copyright)

13.5 *General Montgomery talks with his army and hands out cigarettes in Sicily, Italy* (Imperial War Museum)

13.6 *"Monty" has a habit of rocking backward during casual conversations* (Imperial War Museum)

14.1 *Flight surgeon, "Doc" Hughes*

CHAPTER 14

"DOC" HUGHES OF THE FLYING RINGS

After flying Monty "about" for a few weeks in Sicily, as General Montgomery would put it, I returned to home base Navarin Airfield, Algeria so *Theresa Leta* could get some routine inspections and maintenance. Once the B-17 was brought up-to-snuff again, I put a call into Monty's HQ to advise that his B-17 was ready to fly and inquire if he had any plans for me. I was pleasantly surprised when the voice at the other end of the line interrupted and said, "Would you just hold a moment, Captain Evans? The Army Commander is hereabout, and I believe he would like a word with you."

Very quickly, the voice of the man I was beginning to regard with respect, empathy and affection came on the line. "I say... is that you, Captain Evans? How is our *Flying Faw-tress*? Is it quite ready to fly me about again?" When Monty was happy it showed, even on the phone.

I was pleased to report to my part-time boss that his B-17 was shipshape again. I asked if he had any plans for us. When he responded, "Not immediately," I said that I would like to propose a modification of our plans for future operations.

Monty, clearly in a splendid mood, responded, "Of Cau'se; just what would you like to propose, Captain?"

I had given the matter some thought and was prepared to make my case quickly. "Sir," I said, "I was wondering if the Army Commander would have any objection to my flying combat missions during periods when he does not require my services?" I emphasized that this scheme would make it easier for us to maintain *Theresa Leta* in top condition here at our base where we had first-rate B-17 repair facilities while at the same time keeping her on stand-by for The Army Commander's periodic use.

While Monty was thinking this over, I added that if he would let me know his requirements by dinnertime on any given day, I could be in position and at his disposal by breakfast the following morning at any airfield in the theater. I added that I was sure Generals Eisenhower and Doolittle would endorse this modest adjustment to our arrangement. I had heard that Monty was getting flak from some detractors regarding his highly visible endorsement of the American-made, not British, B-17. This modification of our procedure might prove helpful to him, as well as to my air-crewmen, ground-crewmen and me.

With characteristic linguistic frugality, General Montgomery said, "Splendid," and hung up the phone.

I had not yet become accustomed to Monty's abrupt, if not abrasive, manner. But I was learning as I enjoyed being in the company of the world-famous general and hoped to work for him again. However, I also wished to complete 50 combat missions, return to the States in one piece, visit my family in Tennessee and call on a beautiful, young San Antonio girl whom I had met.

With his acceptance of my proposal, Monty also made it possible for me to spread the Monty boondoggle around among a larger group of deserving crewmen. The Monty TDY was a welcome break in the combat regimen for our B-17 crewmen, including me. And I looked forward to having more regular visits with friends on the base.

Once, on returning to base from a stint with Monty, after briefing Warrant Officer Fogle on *Theresa Leta's* needs and likely schedule, I broke off and walked directly to our 346th Squadron Medical Tent to look in on my squadron doctor.

During the course of a half-dozen months, Doc Hughes and I had become very good friends. This outstanding, youthful MD was a graduate of Ohio State where he had earned his degree in medicine and won national acclaim on the flying rings. "Doc," as he was warmly known, was a fine-looking young man of 28 years or so and would have looked even finer had he done something about his legs at the same time he was building up his massive biceps, triceps, trapezoids and pectorals on the Ohio State flying rings. In a strict, literal sense, our Doc was out of shape.

Upon returning from trips with Monty, Doc would bring me up to date on injuries and losses incurred in my squadron and on the status of recuperating airmen at the regional hospital at Bone Airfield, Algeria. On this particular occasion, my friend Doc announced that he and I were in "deep, serious trouble" with Colonel Upthegrove.

"We're in trouble with Uppie? What have we done?" I inquired. "What have we had *time* to do? You stay in this camp for men and boys; bind our wounds, distribute our **Atabrine**, which makes us turn a nice copper color, and you lace our soup with saltpeter to put our sex lives on hold. Between combat missions, I chase about North Africa with Monty when he calls. I get into a little trouble demonstrating my look-Mom-no-hands, emergency autopilot-landing procedure. So, what kind of trouble are you and I in now, Doc?"

"Well, my friend," the flight surgeon, responded, "some fink has **blabber-mouthed** to the Old Man about my hoisting you up in our arm-to-arm, over-head lifts. Particularly the time when we performed atop the 346th Squadron Ops building."

"Well, that is a **hell-of-a-note**!" Although, that is just what we did. We agreed at the time that, while we must have looked pretty dashing up there, it was pretty damn silly of us. We set a very bad example. "When you think about it, you hadn't had anything to drink, and I'm Mr. Square, who never touches the stuff. Where do you think Uppie got the idea that we would be stupid enough to fall off a bloody roof? You got any ideas on this, Doc?"

"Not really," my all-shoulders-and-arms, stalwart friend responded. "We had done our arm-to-arm lift on the flat a dozen times or so before going up on the roof. What the hell, we couldn't have been more than thirty feet off the ground. I haven't a clue why Uppie would raise so much thunder. By the way, which fink in your squadron do you suppose ratted on us? After Uppie got through chewing me out, would you like to guess what he had to say to me?"

"No, just tell me. What did he say to you?"

My respected medicine man then said, "Captain, don't take this personally. Uppie gave me a little hell. He said, 'Look, Doc, I can spare a pilot or two around here, but you're my ranking flight surgeon and, until now, I thought our smartest. You just better damn well see you stay off roofs, or so help me, I'll see that both your butts are tossed in the brig. You read me, Captain? Am I coming through to you? You can tell that Captain friend of yours, if you like, that I've just put him on the Majors list; but if he'd rather stay a Captain, I can arrange for that, too. Am I getting through to you, Doctor Hughes?'"

I interrupted and said to my Squadron saw-bones, "Okay, okay enough. I've got the picture. I know flyboys are an expendable item around here. Honest to God MDs are in short supply... you don't have to rub it in. Back to our boss, Uppie's really something, isn't he, Doc? He's no more than ten-to-fifteen years older than the rest of us I'd guess; yet a big part of his job is to be a father figure for 500 of us babes in the woods in his Group. He does it very damn well, doesn't he?"

"Absolutely," Doc responded with enthusiasm, "I agree in spades. Our Uppie runs a tight ship around here. I doubt there's a man in the 99th who doesn't know he can come to his Group Commander with most any problem he might run into. I suggest you and I stay off roofs for a spell; how do you feel about it?"

"I'm with you, Doc. I think you're right."

"And, come to think of it," I said, with a grin, "If you dropped me up on top of that roof, I'd be the one who'd have to take the fall, right?"

"Right on," my favorite saw-bones said, smiling. "I vote we stay the hell off roofs for the duration. We can meet in Ohio after the war if you decide you'd still like to continue your lessons, okay? Or we could just shift to the wing of one of our B-17s. Think Uppie would get all tensed up over that?"

Doc Hughes and I grinned at our private nonsense in silence for a minute or so. Then his mood changed, and he said, "You in a hurry, Richard Eager? I've got something else for you."

"Nope, shoot." I answered, "I'm a little weary, but not exhausted yet. What you got on your mind, Doc?"

"Well, I don't think the Old Man is with you all the way, Dick, on your no-hands autopilot-landing scheme. Either that, or he's been running into some flak trying to defend you up in Tunis where General Doolittle and his 12th Air Force staff are just now settling in since making their move from Constantine."

When I didn't comment, Doc Hughes continued, "You know, Dick, I don't know just what you're doing up there with your private test runs, but I'm afraid you've got the whole Group and, very likely, some of the top brass in Tunis spooked. I can imagine how it hit you when you got back here from one of your stints with Monty and learned about the Bizerte crash at Sidi Ahmed Airfield." I inhaled at Doc's mention of this fatal accident in which some of the crewmen I had picked up at Salina, Kansas, and who had flown to the combat zone with me were killed.

"The word I got," Doc Hughes continued, "was that they had flight control problems and were attempting to land using the autopilot system. Some of the guys around here think you're out to prove that the autopilot could make a difference in getting a B-17 down when you've got control problems. It's my guess that most feel the autopilot won't hack it at slow speeds. I'm not straight on what exactly happened on that B-17; but I've heard that they had engine troubles, were low on fuel and may have even collided with another airplane while attempting to land."

I didn't say anything immediately and Doc continued, "I haven't seen the accident report; but from what I've heard, Captain, they were making a straight-in approach on autopilot when suddenly they just stalled out at 200-to-300 feet while still a good half-mile from the runway. There were plenty of witnesses. Apparently, the aircraft suddenly pitched up and then the nose and a wing flipped down as it stalled. There was no possibility for recovery and the fuel exploded when the B-17 hit the ground. There were no survivors.

"I presumed the pilot was gradually raising his nose by entering commands to the autopilot system to ease the control column back. From the pilot's perspective, this would bring the nose up. **SOP** for any landing. Do I have it right?"

"Sure, you do, Doc. You are in the area where I think some procedural changes are in order. I, too, don't know what happened in that plane. I might not have done any better. But, you know, I think Uppie believes I may be on the right track.

"You seem to know, Doc, that I persuaded Uppie to let me make same local flights to test out an idea I've had for some time about using the autopilot as a back-up flight-control system for landings similar to this fatal Bizerte landing. I executed the tests with great care.

"Now, I haven't seen any official reports on the crash and there's been no response from Group or Doolittle's 12th HQ regarding my findings from the recent series of tests, which I flew. But I do think the autopilot scheme might possibly have made a difference. I don't know that and I'm not running around saying that. No one will ever know whether this emergency procedure could have saved the lives of those men. That crash wiped out a full ten-man crew. Several of them, as you know, flew over from the States with me. They were a special crew to me."

Doc Hughes remarked, "I was aware that some of your original crew was lost on that flight. It was my job to run up to Bizerte, recover the bodies and bring them here. I've heard since the crash that your ball-turret gunner, Eldon Austin, tail-gunner, Chuck Ward, are all who are left of your original Atlantic flight nine-man crew... and you are taking it very hard."

"You're right," I confided. "Doc, I wouldn't say this to just anyone. There were a couple of foul-mouthed troublemakers on that crew that I won't miss. I feel guilty now when I think about how I felt about them. But I would shed real tears for Johnson, Kennedy and Morris if I could remember how you do it. I thought they were first-rate gents, who I believe were beginning to think that I knew what I was doing in an airplane."

Doc didn't say anything for a moment; then he asked, "How about telling me just how you use the autopilot in landing the B-17? I'm not qualified to pass judgment, but you know I'm very interested. There has been talk to the effect that the crew on the fatal flight was attempting to use the autopilot to help them get their B-17 down in one piece, but that the autopilot may have actually worked against them."

Responding to my curious, smart Doc, I answered, "We were all just 'making do' as best we could in the desert: experimenting, testing and trying to perfect our crafts. At 18, I learned flight essentials with the Tennessee Air National Guard School. By 21, I graduated as a Second Lieutenant from the Army Air Corp, Kelly Field, and the next day I was teaching my own students to fly and navigate. Tragically, some classmates did not live to see graduation. Three years later I was crossing the Atlantic to the war. It was a lot to take on and quickly. Our B-17s were simply beautifully built airplanes and perfect for our mission. But the handbooks were still being written and the procedures were still being refined. Admittedly, there was a lot of learning as we went. Standing Operation Procedures couldn't account for all flight variables, especially in combat or emergency situations. But experimentation is daunting when the stakes are high.

"Well, okay, Doc. I will explain my theory to you, but you've got to sit still for the whole account because I don't know how to describe it in a few words.

"Okay, first I explained to Uppie exactly what I had in mind. Then, I asked if he had any objections to my running a one-man flight-test program on the QT so that a bunch of our men wouldn't be getting themselves all bent out of shape before they had a chance to fully understand the idea.

"At first, Uppie just looked at me; then he said, 'Well okay, Captain lay it on. But dammit, Dick, keep your head about yourself; I don't enjoy writing these next-of-kin letters back to the States. Don't do something stupid up there. I didn't hire you to be some kind of hotshot test pilot.'"

Neither Doc Hughes nor I said anything for a minute or so. Then my friend asked, "Can you tell me just what you did do with the B-17? What were you able to find out? The scuttle butt around here is that you put your aircraft on autopilot, brought it all the way down to the ground, rolled the wheels down the middle of the runway, then advanced the throttles and took off again... all on autopilot.

"I'm told you flew the B-17 around the field using only the autopilot, the turn-control and the four throttles during the entire flight except the takeoff. You shot a dozen or so **touch-and-go-landings** in something over an hour, and you never touched the rudders, the control column or the autopilot settings. Is this all true? That's a lot to swallow. How did you get the airplane to flare, to level off for the landing?"

"You ask good questions, Doc. You see, I did not flare at any time during the flight, not once. Probably that is the essence of the whole idea I had in mind. I did not use the autopilot controls to raise or lower the nose. I didn't *want* to raise or lower the nose during any part of the entire flight.

"Tell me, Doc, in your words just how does one flare? You've done it a number of times and very well with me sitting beside you. What does the airplane do?

"Okay," my friend said, "I ease the stick back and watch the nose rise slightly above the horizon out front. I roll the elevator trim wheel back, so I don't have to continue to hold back-pressure on the control column, right?"

"Right," I said, "and of course most everybody understands that this is the way you land an airplane. Now, when the nose comes up, Doc, what else happens?"

"The tail goes down?"

"Right," I said, smiling at my bright student's quick responses. "It's like leaning back in a rocking chair, when you think about it. As you rock back farther and farther in a chair or in an airplane, you become more and more unstable. Rock back far enough in an airplane and you'll fall off on a wing.

"As you and I have discussed before, when you've rocked back, you have forced your vertical and horizontal tail surfaces down into the turbulent, hot airflow behind the engines and the props. Let your speed get just a tad low under these conditions and your problem could suddenly become dangerous. Damn dangerous!"

"You like horses, Doc?" I asked and got an affirmative nod.

"A perfect analogy," I suggested. "Haul back on the reins, and your horse's head will come up, ears first. Keep pulling back and his front feet will come up as well; pull some more and his rear end will go down and he'll struggle to keep his balance. You've seen more than one horse sitting almost on his hind end, clawing the air with his forelegs, and trying to get his center of gravity forward again. If a horse delays too long in his effort to recover, like an airplane, he'll fall off on a wing. An aerodynamicist might label a horse inherently unstable. You had enough, Doc? Should we stop? I don't want to sound like I'm preaching."

"No, not yet; I'm not quite there," he answered. "I'll let you go in a minute, but you haven't gotten me back on the ground yet. You do have to get your tail down for God's sake, and you do have to flare to land an aircraft, do you not?"

"No, you do not have to flare; nor do you have to get your tail down; nor is it necessary that you land on three points. You can just drive your flying machine onto the runway with its tail high in the air and set your main landing gear down, not on the first third of the runway, your usual target, but right on the very leading edge of the runway. Now, you are going faster on the approach, but you don't have just two-thirds of the field out ahead of you. At touchdown you have the entire, beautiful runway out ahead of you plus the overrun area at the far end should you need it.

"When you've got the main gear, the two big wheels, rolling nicely on the runway, you could not care less if the elevator surfaces stall out, letting the tail whap down a little hard. On the other hand, you're in big trouble if you've pulled your large wing area up in front of your small tail surfaces a little too soon and a little too far out when you are still two or three hundred feet above the runway. Suddenly, you are not getting a smooth flow of air across your lifting surfaces on the wings or across your principal flight-control surfaces on the tail. Without that smooth flow of air, you will stall."

"This makes a lot of sense to me," Doc interjected. "Fill me in on just a few more things and I'll let you go. That okay?"

"I've always got time for my doctor," I answered. "I'm not stupid. You could put anything you wanted in those pills you give us. What are we missing, Doc?"

"How about just talking me through the final approach? Then we'll drop it. You have set your engine RPM up a tad to 2,000, maybe 2,100, right? You've put your gear down and you've checked it? You've got partial flaps. Right?"

"You're doin' fine, Doc. Are you sure you're a real saw bones... are you a real doctor? Where'd you get the time to get into this aero jazz?"

My doctor smiled; but he wasn't interested in my efforts to be cute. "Okay, okay," I continued, "Assume we've got an engine out and might have other problems that would preclude making jazzy, descending turns onto the landing leg, rolling out of the turn while you're rotating the aircraft or "flaring," as we say, just as you're passing over the end of the runway. All of this is great fun, easy to do and quite safe under normal circumstances. Right?"

Doc Hughes nodded his head up and down in agreement.

I asked, "What do we do now? Or what do I suggest we do that is different from what we normally do?" Answering my own question, I said, "We simply start higher and farther back on a straight-in approach. The first time I tried it, I began a straight-in approach at 1,500-to-1,800 feet, instead of the usual traffic-pattern altitude of 1,000 feet. I was back there, where I could look directly down on our Roman aqueduct.

"Now, our autopilot is on," I continued. "We've made a turn onto our final approach using the autopilot turn control. When we roll out, the runway is straight ahead of us. We are higher than our normal traffic altitude and we're faster, doing 150 mph, our nose is pointing, not at the horizon, as it would be in level flight, nor is it pointed towards our usual landing target, i.e., the first-third of the runway where we would normally intend to land. This time we're pointing our nose at the near, front end of the runway. Right? Nope, wrong again. It is pointed at a point a mile or so ahead and in front of the runway. This is not our standard approach procedure. This is a very different procedure. So what do we do to get on the ground?

"We use only two controls for the balance of the trip. We look out over the nose and add a small increment of power as we advance the throttles. This is the reverse of our usual landing procedure. We're usually pulling power off as we approach the runway.

"We see the nose rise slightly with the increase in power, pointing our B-17 towards a new reference point closer to the end of the runway to keep from hitting the "over-run area" ahead of the actual runway. We continue to add small increments of power, using four throttles at first, then only two when the end of the runway is directly ahead of us and only yards away. If runway alignment has slipped a bit, we use the autopilot turn-control to correct our aim directly for the end of the runway.

"We are not approaching the runway in the usual ways. That is, we are not decreasing power and air-speed as we approach, nor are we heading our *Flying Fortress* for a point where we will pull the throttles back to the stops and at the same time ease the stick back so that we round-out and touch-down in the first third of the field.

"Now, Doc, what's different? What have we done and what have we not done? We have not touched the autopilot. We have adjusted the elevator control, but only to reduce our indicated air-speed, bringing it down to 110 mph. And, by adding power, we have decreased our rate of descent, raised our nose and flattened our glide angle in small easily controlled increments.

"In a short time, our B-17 is skimming over the over-run, with the runway directly ahead of us. We are effectively buzzing the overrun. From this very low perspective, we are able to make very small power adjustments increasing or decreasing airspeed and sink rate. I was surprised to find that with great confidence, I was able to hold the aircraft just a few feet above the over-run, then finally decrease power very slightly, using only the two inboard engines and watching the shadow of the landing gear settling slowly onto the runway. It was beautiful and it was easy to do. I know you could do it, Doc, the first time you tried it with me just talking you through it.

"On my first autopilot touch-down, we were on the ground and rolling so near the approach end of the runway that I pushed the inboards forward halfway, noted the speed, and then pushed them to the fire-wall. Assured immediately of effective rudder control, I quickly brought in the outboards all the way on with the intent to pull them off again halfway down the runway. But then

I thought, 'What the hell,' let's just complete what might be the B-17s first no-hands, autopilot touch-and-go landing. I left the power on and was a hundred feet off the ground before passing the tower.

"Instead of bearing left to avoid the rise where our 346th Squadron is encamped, as I would have done in a normal touch-and-go landing, I was able to continue straight ahead with plenty of speed and ample altitude to clear our squadron OPS building on top of the rise.

"Again, and again, as I practiced this maneuver, the main wheels would make contact with the runway just feet beyond the leading edge. Quite often the wheels would start spinning before the full weight of the B-17 had settled onto them. My crew and I couldn't believe the ease and gentleness of the whole operation."

I had stopped talking, but he was still listening. "Doc," I said, "Your interest is flattering and gratifying. I know that you know I've enjoyed our chat, but I'm beginning to feel a little tuckered out. I don't think you've bought it all quite yet, but you sure have listened. I'm flattered. The key concept, if there is one, is this: We think of pointing an airplane's nose up to go up, and down to go down; and, of course, we often do just that. Suppose we trim up the airplane for straight-and-level flight and then flip on the autopilot switch, effectively putting the airplane in what we might call an airspeed vise.

"We could then make our B-17 go up or down without pulling or pushing its nose above or below the horizon. We would simply add or decrease power to go up or down. The aircraft would be climbing and descending while staying flat the full time. With this technique, we do not pull the nose up to land; we just fly the airplane flat across the over-run and set the front wheels down within a few feet of the front edge of the runway.

"Nor do we stall the airplane as we deliberately do on normal landings. We don't get close to a stall; we're a little fast. We just get low and flat on the approach, grease her on, and then cut power in steps, taking our time to lower our tail.

"The first time I tried this scheme, I touched the wheels on the ground, then in a moment added a few inches of power on the inboard engines only. Observing our shadow on the ground, I could see the wheels lift off the ground. Fascinated, I pulled just a little bit of power off and set them back on the runway gently. I repeated the procedure. I did three touch-and-gos before passing the tower. That first day, I landed a couple of dozen times at 15-to-20 mph over stall speed with plenty of control. All of these landings were smoother than the three-pointers I would normally make.

"My strong suggestion is that we do not target the 'first third' of the field to land nor try for three-point landings when we have an engine or two out. We should strive to put the main gear right on the edge of the field with power on and the vertical tail surfaces high in the airstream, insuring solid, positive control.

"I wrote a full report, Doc. I'm sure Uppie sent a copy up to 15th Air Force HQ. I guess it got shelved somewhere along the line. I haven't been called up to support my case nor been told that I'm on the wrong track. We have not been authorized to check out our lead crew for this procedure; nor have we been invited to demonstrate our findings for the benefit of the 15th AF staff."

Doc Hughes was quiet for a moment and my thoughts wandered into how I might further my theory into standard practice, or if that would be more dangerous. Then, he quite abruptly changed the subject, "Dick, remember the Sergeant who gave you a hard time at Palermo, who defied you and hid some German aircraft parts in the aft fuselage of your B-17, all in spite of your direct and special orders to the contrary? He was a replacement for the day, not one of your original *Theresa Leta* crewmen. I believe you told me once that you were buying table linens for your mom from the sisters at the Palermo Cathedral while one of your Sergeants was busy doing precisely what you had told your crew not to do."

"I remember the stupid jerk! I understood that the risk of running into booby traps on those wrecked aircraft wasn't too great. But I learned from my old man a long time ago that you're stupid if you take unnecessary risks when there is nothing of consequence to be gained."

"Your Old Man told you right, Dick. But I have to tell you, my friend, you missed a chance to save a fellow human being's life."

I wasn't prepared for this challenge from my chum. I hesitated then said, "Are you telling me, Doc, our amateur sapper is dead? That's pretty heavy. This isn't one of your strange jokes, is it?"

"No joke, not this time. If you had thrown him into the **brig** when you got back here, which you had good reason to do, most likely he would still be alive."

I looked hard at my friend. He wasn't smiling. Doc Hughes was an unusual guy... hard to figure at times. He wasn't making a joke of someone's death. I think he thought it his role not to take death too seriously in a war theater. I wasn't going to argue with him. "Doc, did that SOB finally get himself into some real trouble? Just what exactly did he do this time?"

"Well, putting it as succinctly as I can," the good doctor said, "He tried to commit suicide, Dick. This time, he damn well succeeded... in spades."

"Oh my god, when did it happen?" I asked. "And what the hell did he do to himself?"

"It happened about an hour ago just as you were setting down on the runway. I heard the explosion, a sharp bang; I jumped into my wagon and took off in the direction of the noise. I could see other GI vehicles converging on the same general location where our Roman aqueduct is located. Dust hanging in the air took me right to the spot of the explosion. I jumped out of my jeep and almost stumbled on to him, literally. I then gathered him up and brought him here... one of my jobs you know."

"Yeah, I'm guessing that he has been lying here in one of the body-bags that I've been sitting next to while you and I have been chatting. Right? Doc, you know you really are a little strange."

"Yes," he said, "I guess we come off looking like that in my business, trying to take death lightly. I'll tell you; it's pretty hard to get all stirred up when the deceased keeps asking for it the way this character has. I sure can't find any tears for him."

"Okay, Doc, which one of these body-bags that you sat me down between is he occupying?"

"Actually, Captain, he is using both of them. When I arrived at the scene, he was still smoking and he was in two places, about three feet apart. I carry extra bags to crash sites. They were in my wagon when I took off.

"Captain, I didn't intend to set you up. You were a little weary after your flight. Before I could say anything to you, you had plopped yourself right between both of him. The top of him is on your right, the bottom, on your left. You can have a look, if you want. I won't press you, but this will probably be the only time in your life that you will have the opportunity to see a man that you have known in two places at the same time."

I didn't comment. I didn't jump up to look into either one of the bags. Nor did I make a dash for the door. I didn't do anything for a few minutes. Nor did my good friend do anything. I think he thought it part of his job to play a very casual role for the benefit of the rest of us to help us keep the lid on.

"Captain, if you'd thrown his ass in the brig, as I'm sure you considered doing, he'd still be alive. You warned the men and this man in particular, not to take Axis Powers' 'souvenirs' that could blow up in their faces; to stay away from those wrecked planes, bunkers and vehicles. He just didn't listen. No question about it. Your job is no cinch either, Captain. You try to be Mr. Nice Guy once in a while, give a fella a little space and what does he do? He goes out and gets himself blown up."

"That's very nice of you to say, Doc. I know that this man did not intend to kill himself. I think he just wanted to come close to show his comrades that he had some guts, too. He showed us, I guess, the only way he knew how." I felt tired. I looked straight ahead and thought of my crews, the men who were lost and the ones I hoped to bring home. And then I thought briefly on those who never stood a chance.

14.2 *B-17 in trouble, lands at a North African airfield*

15.1 *For many years Dick and his dog, Judge, hike together on the Indian Gap Trail, Smoky Mountains*
(McClung Historical Collection)

CHAPTER 15
GOODBYE TO CHILDHOOD

Most of the times when I got home from school, Judge would be up on our back porch. The minute he would see me turn into our back yard, he would jump to his feet and start making circles in the air with his stub tail. I would dash up our high, wide steps, two-at-a-time, pick up my dog, swing him in the air and let him lick my nose. I didn't really like having Judge lick my nose, but I knew that it made him really happy.

One time I was a little late getting home and Judge wasn't on hand to greet me. Dad often said he thought Judge had a girlfriend down on Linden Avenue, near Ruth Long's house. I told Dad I wanted to have a girlfriend at Ruth Long's house but was afraid to tell Ruth about it.

"Judge will show up in a little while," I thought to myself. "I will get Judge to do a trick and, as always, he will be pleased to oblige me. Then, I will laugh at him and clap my hands, as everybody in our Knoxville High auditorium would do when Judge performed on the stage."

I poured a glass of milk, made a peanut butter and jelly sandwich, and sat down at our break-fast table. Dad had said that my having the milk and peanut butter and jelly after school was an "automatic reflex." I turned my chair so that I could watch for Judge out our back window. From there I could see across the Galyons' backyard and down Castle Street toward Linden Avenue where, a lot of years ago on Halloween, I had tarred Mrs. Oglesby's sidewalks.

Judge would usually come bounding home from that direction, and I wanted to see him before I went out to play shinny street hockey with John Lea, Dick Wayland, I.C. Hewgley, Fred Ford, Jo Brown, Bubba Bean and the gang. Judge would come bounding up so fast I used to think he could smell the peanut butter a block away. Dad had said, "Maybe Judge did smell your peanut butter, Dick. Dogs have a great sense of smell."

If Judge had a girlfriend down on Linden, he was way ahead of me. I thought Ruth Long was keen; but in the Long family, it was only Ruth's mother who seemed to think I was at least okay. Recently, Mrs. Long called Mom and invited me to Ruth's birthday party the day before the party. Ruth must have forgotten how much I liked her. Mrs. Long made me feel at home, even though I was the only one wearing pants that buckled at the knee. So that I might look taller, I had left them unbuckled and hanging to my ankles. Nevertheless, nobody at the party said I looked any taller.

Ruth spent all her time talking to older boys who were all taller and all wearing long pants. I knew Ruth liked older boys and I knew I was getting older. However, I didn't know how to explain to Ruth how I knew I was getting older. I tried to explain to Mom that if I had some long pants, I wouldn't have to explain anything to Ruth or, for that matter, to Mrs. Long, either.

I ran some water in my empty milk glass, left it in the sink, and headed out the back door. From our high and wide back porch, I could see down to where Castle Street crossed Linden, but I didn't see Judge anywhere. "Here Judge," I called. "Come on, Boy, I'll get you something from the kitchen."

As I angled across our lot and the Galyons' backyard towards Castle Street, I noticed that our maple trees were starting to get red again. It occurred to me that I should call John Lea and get some "shinny" going. Shinny was a game like ice hockey; however, we kids played on roller skates in the street. A tin can made a good enough puck, and we fashioned all kinds of sticks with which to flail away at the can. Mom said it was clear to her that we were hitting each other's shins more than the can. She thought it was disgraceful the way my shins bled during the shinny season. I tried to point out to Mom that if I had some long pants, nobody would be able to see the scabs on my shins.

Walking down Castle Street, I very quickly came to the place where it crossed Linden Avenue. Standing in the middle of the intersection, I could see up and down Castle Street. I could look down Linden towards Mrs. Oglesby's house where I had done the tar job or back the other way towards Ruth Long's house. I cupped my hands to my mouth and yelled for Judge in all four directions. Judge didn't show up, so I turned around and headed back up Castle Street towards Magnolia.

On other days when Judge had been close enough to hear me, I would see him running as fast as he could with his chin low to the street. Then, I would see him leap up in the air without stopping to see if he could see me better. It was like he would do in the high grass along Little River in the Smokies when we would go fishing together. He looked funny jumping up the way he did. I would always laugh. He knew when he made me laugh and he would smile to show me he knew. Dad had worked hard to keep me off Magnolia when I was little. I had done the same thing for Judge, so I didn't really expect to find him up on Magnolia.

Suddenly, I stopped in my tracks in mid-street! A wave of awful fear came over me. I thought I had seen something move in the street but there was no wind to make it move. I was looking and running as hard as I could. I did see something in the street. It was trying hard to move. I started shouting silently to myself, "OH please, God, please don't let it be Judge, oh please, please... "

But I already knew it was Judge. I couldn't see well but I could tell it was Judge. He was lying down, and he could not get up. His round eyes showed that he was afraid. He was moving, he was alive, and he was looking at me. His stub tail that usually made circles in the air was flattened out on the street. Judge's whole back end was flat, and he couldn't make it move. He was trying to raise himself with just his front legs, but he was stuck to the street.

"Oh, Judge, please get up," I heard myself say. But Judge couldn't get up and I wasn't helping him at all. I was just standing there above him, looking down at him. He always looked at me like I was the boss and as if I would always know what to do. He looked like he trusted me. I knew he was thinking, "Why doesn't he help; why doesn't he stop the hurt?"

I was afraid at first, afraid to touch the blood and the mess that Judge had made in the street. I thought I was going to throw up. I remember, too, that I was ashamed I didn't know what to do. I was just standing there in the street, looking at my little dog who couldn't get up.

Then, suddenly, I dropped to my knees in front of him and reached out for him. I remember that I thought he looked like he was mashed so flat that he probably was stuck to the pavement.

I worked my hand under his back end and moved him a little bit. He whined and he looked at me because it hurt so much. He could tell I was trying to help. I saw the blood and some of Judge's mess on my hands, but it didn't make me sick. I lifted Judge up slowly and supported him on my chest. I didn't care if some of his mess got on my shirt.

I got up and started across the Galyons' backyard to reach our yard. I didn't know where else to go. My mind flashed back to the time when I had carried Judge this way to our garage, the time when I gave him the enema to get the string out. It struck me that Judge was the same size that he was back then, but that I had gotten bigger. I noticed, too, that some of Judge's hair was getting grey.

When I reached our yard, I had no idea what to do. When I first saw Judge lying in the street, I knew he was going to die. I was sure that this time there wasn't anything I could do to save my dog's life. I started to put him on the grass beside one of our maple trees, but he whined and looked at me so I just sat down and leaned against the tree and held Judge up on my chest so he could see my eyes. I remember thinking that I didn't mind Judge's mess or the blood anymore; nor did I feel sick. I was holding my dog up on my chest so he could see my face and he could see how much I cared.

Judge's eyes looked straight at mine; I could tell they weren't dead. However, I thought Judge's back end was dead; it didn't move at all. His eyes were alive, and they knew who I was. At first, Judge just whined but then he started quivering and he looked so pitifully scared. I thought maybe he was trying to howl or something, but he couldn't get any more sounds to come out. I could hear air blowing in his throat. His eyes looked like I should be doing something to stop the hurt. I couldn't think of anything to do. There was no one around who could tell Judge and me what we should do.

I had already thought of giving Judge something that would knock him out; but we didn't have anything like that in our medicine cabinet. Then, I thought I might find something in the garage and knock him out myself. Strangely, that thought wouldn't go away.

I kept thinking that I knew Judge was going to die. I knew it when I first saw him, and I thought I should do something to stop his pain. I was trying to make the bad thoughts go away by trying to think that Judge could get well. If I knew Judge could never get well, I thought I was a coward for not being able to think of something to do for him.

I saw myself getting up and laying Judge on the grass. I felt like I was watching myself as I walked towards the garage. Our old garage hadn't changed much since the time I had given Judge the enema and saved his life. We hardly ever painted our garage, probably because it sat back on the edge of our alley so far behind our house. I didn't know what I might find in our garage. I didn't know what to look for.

When I think back over so many years, I feel that I can remember everything that happened in those few terrible hours. I remember thinking as I walked to the garage that I already knew when I had laid Judge out on the grass that I had arranged his head so that I could hit him squarely with something flat, something that would knock him out but wouldn't cut his head or hurt his eyes. The fear that filled my mind was... not knowing... if I was doing the right thing.

I saw a piece of pipe in our garage but thought a pipe would hurt too much. I didn't pick it up. Our hammer was on our workbench, but the head was too small and would break the skin and make Judge bleed. Then I saw the driver that Uncle Bob had given me at the Whittle Springs Golf Club where I used to caddy for him. I reached for it.

A strange calm came over me as I walked back to Judge. I knew then that I wouldn't be able to just knock my dog out. How could I hit my dog hard enough but not too hard? But how could I just sit there in the grass and watch him suffer until Doc Smith got home, maybe after dark, and could give Judge something to put him to sleep? Maybe Doc Smith was on a trip. I thought I was being a coward because I was there, and I knew I should put my dog to sleep because he hurt so much.

I decided Judge was too close to the tree. His eyes still looked at me, and he was shivering and whining when I moved him out onto the lawn away from the tree. I knew that I was crying sorrowfully hard, and I felt like a little boy. I didn't care. I remember thinking, "I know why they call it a broken heart... my heart is hurting in my chest... maybe it really is broken."

On my first swing, the flat part of the golf club hit Judge squarely on the flat part of his head just above his eyes, right where I was aiming. The club flipped Judge's little body most of the way around in a circle. I reached down for him, turned his head and looked at his eyes. They were still open, but they didn't look like they were seeing my eyes anymore.

With more confidence and more resolve, I took another swing with the golf club. It caught Judge square on his forehead, and he tumbled backwards across the grass. Again, I lifted Judge up to where his eyes could see mine; they were open, but I could tell his eyes could no longer see mine. Also, the chest of my little, loving, trusting friend of so many wonderful years had given up and had stopped trying to draw air.

I knew Judge's suffering was over, but mine wasn't. "Did I do the right thing?" I have asked myself that question many times, maybe a hundred times. Old memories of wonderful, happy times with my dog would rush back, confused and tumbling over each other.

Judge, standing on our front porch the day we first met, waiting for me to open the door for him. His clipped ears alert and standing straight up and his short tail making little circles in the air. Judge running through the high-grass at Elkmont in the Smoky Mountains when I could see just his head above the grass for a few seconds as he leaped up to check his path through the grass and check my location out in the middle of the stream we called "Little River."

The first times I taught Judge to sit up, to rollover, to speak and to jump back and forth over Grandpa Stewart's cane. Dad said many times that it was remarkable that Judge could remember all his tricks and could do them "on voice command."

The remembrance of Judge's wonderful smile made more wonderful by his wrinkled forehead, his bright eyes and his wide, pulled-back, jowly mouth.

Judge's joy and mine, when the family was finally packed up and on our way to Elkmont, was when we left for the Smokies where Judge and I figured that no little boy would be answering any "lost-dog" ads like the ones Dad made me run in the *Knoxville Journal* for what seemed like such a long time.

––––––––––––––––

We must have had ten years together, maybe more, during which Judge, and I would see each other every day. I can still picture him bouncing along the edge of Little River and Jakes Creek while I was trying to look like Tarzan, diving from some of the high rocks to the deeper pools and running headlong down the middle of the river, jumping from boulder to boulder in my torn shorts, deliberately torn to more closely resemble Tarzan's loin cloth.

Judge would race along the bank and then wait for me while I fished for rainbow trout with grasshoppers. He would help by chasing the grasshoppers through the high grass and making them fly up so I could see them. I would run them down and catch them before they could catch their breath. Judge delighted when we caught a grasshopper together. He wasn't much interested, however, when I would occasionally catch an eight or nine-inch rainbow trout while standing on a big rock in the creek.

Sometimes Judge would wander off. Then later, I would get a glimpse of him as he ran along the edge of the stream in the deep grass bouncing up and down so he could see over the grass and find out where I was. I would get just a quick glance of his white paws, his white muzzle and his white chest as he seemed to hang for a second or two above the grass. I would laugh out loud and think my laugh didn't sound the same when there was no one else out there in the forest to hear it.

At the top of Alum Cave Bluff in the Smokies on the back trail to the top of Mt. LeConte, my fear of high places would keep me well back from the edge. Judge, however, would bounce along the rim, knocking dirt over the lip. It would take a few seconds before I could hear the dirt hitting the ground below. Judge would stop right on the edge, lean forward and look down between his front paws. My skin would feel funny when I looked over the edge, and I would think, "I could never fly an airplane," although this was something I was starting to think I wanted to do.

During the Smoky Mountain summers, Judge was my partner when I earned some extra cash. I would tell people that I was an official "Great Smoky Mountain Guide" and for fifty cents Judge and I would guide them to the top of Chimney Rock, Mt. LeConte, Clingman's Dome or Sugarloaf Mountain. For another two bits, I would carry their gunnysacks full of boxes and canned goods, which they all brought along for their picnics.

My guide uniform consisted of a pair of khaki shorts, socks and well-worn tennis shoes. Mom pointed out that I would be "soaked to the skin" when caught in the frequent summer "cloud bursts." I would argue that there was almost nothing but my skin to soak, and skin dried fast. Dad, not wanting to discourage me, said, "Dick makes a point, Hellie."

I certainly didn't like carrying the gunnysacks full of cans. They made raw places on my shoulders and the lower part of my back. But I was pleased that everybody could see I was building muscles and getting a great tan. I was sure they were saying among themselves, "My, doesn't that young Evans boy look like Tarzan." I thought I probably was a lot like Tarzan, except, being afraid of high places, I had never been very far up a tree. I never had a lady ape for a mother, either.

I couldn't wait until the end of summer when we would go back to Knoxville. I could then run down to Linden Avenue and walk back and forth in front of Ruth Long's house in my shorts, all tanned and all.

President Roosevelt's Civilian Conservation Corps, which on the radio he referred to as "my CCC boys," built wonderful, wide trails throughout the Smokies and marked them with signs that told folks which way to go and where to turn. I didn't want to admit it; but with all those signs pointing the way, I knew that anybody who could read would soon realize they didn't really need a guide in the Smokies. I was in my second season before I realized my customers were paying me six bits a day, not for guiding them around the mountains, but for carrying their gunny sacks full of canned goods up and down those mountain trails.

When I knew a trail sign would be coming up, I would shift the cans on my back, speed up a little, and go ahead of the group. I would place myself so that cans and I would be blocking their view of the trail sign as they hiked by. I would wave my arms to get their attention and point towards the turn we should make up ahead. After they passed, I would fall in behind the line and start working my way back up to the front of the line again. I did this a lot.

At first, I did this as a joke, thinking that most of the time I would be found out and everybody would laugh. I came to realize, however, that most hikers came to the mountains to see the flora, not the fauna. There was practically no fauna to be seen in the Smokies, other than snakes. I found out that most hikers didn't really care to see snakes. Snakes bother them because snakes don't have any legs, slither along the ground on their bellies and stick out their funny-looking, forked tongues.

I discovered that most hikers hiked with their heads down so they could see where their feet were going. The "natural leaders," as my dad would call them, walked at the head of the line where they would always have a good view of the trail, even with their heads down. The "natural followers," Dad suggested, "probably liked to see their own feet." I guessed they also liked to see the backs of the shoes of the natural leaders.

Once in a while, both the leaders and the followers, with their heads down looking at the trail the way they did, would see snakes. We had copperheads in the Smokies, but in all the years I was guiding people, I saw only one. I didn't see him for very long; we were going in opposite directions and neither one of us changed that.

There were, however, more rattlesnakes in the Smokies, but I never heard a single rattle during my entire career as a Smoky Mountain guide. I did see a few rattlers slithering as fast as they could go through the grass or across the rocks. They looked to me like they were always trying to get away and that's what I let them do.

There were also little green garter snakes, which you could pick up and examine. They would hiss at you, but they couldn't bite very much. They weren't poisonous. Dad said he had no idea why they were called garter snakes. He said that he knew their family name was Colubridae.

Dad suggested I tell my customers that the rattlesnakes were of the genera *Crotalus*. I thought this would make me look smart as well as muscular, so I memorized some of the snakes' names and started telling my customers their names. Most of the men thought this very funny and would laugh really hard. Most of the ladies just gave me an odd look and rolled their eyes.

One lady said to me, "They are all vipers, kid." When I told Dad what she said, Dad laughed really hard and then said, "She's wrong, Dick; just poisonous snakes are vipers." Then he added, "And, Son, some women are vipers. We men have to be very careful." Dad thought that this was very amusing, but Mom heard him. She said that Dad "had gone too far this time."

When I would do my trick of trying to block the hikers' views of the trail signs to make my guiding job look more important, Judge would sometimes spoil my act by deliberately pointing towards one of the signs with one of his back legs. Naturally, my hikers would look where Judge was pointing and would see the sign. They would also see what it was that Judge was doing to our National Park signs. The men always thought that this was very funny. Judge seemed to think so, too, the way he would smile and all. The ladies would try very hard not to smile, or even to look.

I did a pretty good business for a few summers. I learned quickly that most hikers thought fifty cents was high for guiding with the signs pointing the way to go. On the other hand, most of them thought that seventy-five cents was dirt cheap for wrestling their canned goods up those trails. When I could get them to notice the raw places their cans were making on my back, they were usually good for the whole buck. Dad said I was conning them and should be happy with seventy-five cents being out there where I could enjoy the beautiful forest and all.

Judge was always worn out when we would get back from one of our all-day, mountain-guiding trips. Not only did he have small legs, but he would also make three trips to my one, what with his pointing at all the signs with his leg and scouting out ahead doubling back to check all the hikers without ever stopping.

What a wonderful life for a boy's happy, carefree dog. What a wonderful life, I have realized since, for the fortunate boy, who for most of a decade, had such a cheerful and loyal little companion.

Eddie May probably hadn't seen me carrying Judge from the street. She must have seen me later, sitting under the tree with my dead dog lying across my lap. She called Dad at school and he came rushing home, as he had done the other time when Judge had eaten the string.

I think I had run out of tears by the time our Dodge turned off Castle Street and into our alley and stopped in front of our garage. The earlier scene when Dad had rushed home to give me support filled my mind. Our Studebaker was long since gone. Instead of climbing down, as he would have from our Studebaker, Dad just stepped out onto our driveway from our "late model" Dodge sedan.

As Dad approached where Judge and I were sitting, I got up and laid Judge on the grass under our maple tree. When I stood up and faced Dad, his arms were turned out and he was looking straight at me. I put my head against his chest for just a moment, but I didn't cry. "I must be out of tears," I thought. I remembered the other time when Dad had rushed home from school to give me a hand and back me up and I had reached around his legs. Now my arms were around Dad's waist. I felt a little funny having my arms around my dad that way.

Dad had put a hand on my head the other time. This time, he put an arm on my shoulder. I remember that I thought my dad felt a little awkward, too. He stepped back and turned to look at Judge. I thought that Dad didn't like what he thought he was seeing. "Tell me exactly what happened here, Dick," as he motioned to the little body by the maples.

I hadn't gone back to Castle Street after bringing Judge over to our yard. I suggested to Dad that we walk back out there where the truck hit Judge and he agreed. When we arrived at the spot, we both looked down and neither of us said anything. Dad said, "It looks like Judge must have been run over by a good-sized truck, Dick which, I guess, just mashed poor old Judge's hind quarters flat."

When Dad said "poor old Judge" it hit me that I had never thought of Judge as being old. To me, "little" had always meant young. At that moment, I realized that while I had been growing up, Judge had been growing old. A picture came quickly to mind. Judge probably had heard me calling him and was running down Castle Street to join me, fast as he could come with his nose near the ground, the way he always did. Dad said he probably didn't even see the truck until it was on top of him. "If I had taken more time getting home from school... If I had just gone to play shinny..." "No," Dad had said to me many times, "Don't waste your time on 'ifs', Dick. We can't roll back the clock."

As we walked back to our yard where Judge was lying on the grass, Dad said, "I can see that Judge had to have been in a lot of pain. I'm so sorry, Dick. I'm terribly, terribly sorry, Son."

"Yes, Dad." I was surprised when my voice sounded okay. I hadn't heard it for a couple of hours. "The truck just ran over Judge's back legs and his belly, Dad. His head, front legs, and his chest weren't hurt at all. I watched him trying to breathe. He had to take a lot of little, short, fast puffs. He was getting air, but he was wearing himself out breathing. His front legs and his head weren't hurt at all, Dad. But his back-end was smashed flat."

"Oh my, oh my," my dad said as he sighed and looked at Judge on the ground in the yard ahead of us, and then back at me. "Did he suffer very long? I mean, did Judge live very long before he died, Dick?" Dad asked looking straight at me.

"Yes, he did suffer, Dad," I said. "Judge hurt something awful. I'll tell you what I did to help Judge after we get back to our yard." I hesitated, then added, "But I don't think you should tell Mom, or Stewart, or Tom and John about it."

While we walked back toward our yard, I could see from the corners of my eyes that Dad had turned quickly to look at me. I thought he wanted to see what he could read in my face. But I turned away. When we reached Judge, both of us stopped and looked down at him. Then I looked up at Dad and I could tell that he knew what I had done to Judge.

For a minute or so, Dad just kept looking hard at Judge. I thought that he was trying to see how I had done it. Without taking his eyes off Judge, he asked me, "What did you do to Judge, Dick?"

"I just knocked him out, Dad."

"Oh my, oh my," Dad said really soft-like. "What did you hit Judge with? It doesn't look as if you left any marks on him, at all."

"I know, I know. I tried not to, Dad. I hit Judge with the old driver that Uncle Bob gave me. I thought I could hit him with the flat part and just knock him out a little bit without cutting him, like putting him to sleep at a hospital."

At first Dad seemed not to understand. He shook his head from side to side as he looked down at Judge. I could tell Dad didn't want to look back at me. Then, he started looking around where we were standing. After a moment he asked where the driver was. I told him that I had put it back in the garage.

"So that nobody would see it?" he asked. Then Dad looked directly at me with a different kind of look on his face.

"No, Dad, so that Mom and Stewart and Tom and John wouldn't see it."

"But you were going to tell me about it?"

"Yes, Dad. I thought you would hear about Judge and would be coming home to help me. I was just sitting here with Judge, waiting for you." I stopped a moment and then went on. "I still want to know, Dad, when you think I've done the right thing. Did I do the right thing this time, Dad? There wasn't anyone here to ask what I should do. I thought I would just knock Judge out a little bit, like at a hospital. But I didn't know how hard to swing and I didn't know how not to swing a golf club hard. I didn't want to just make Judge hurt more. I hit him twice, Dad, as hard as I could. I could tell after the second time that Judge wasn't hurting anymore."

Dad was looking at me, but he didn't answer me. He just shook his head from side to side and looked down at Judge and at the ground near his own feet. Dad knew I wanted to hear him say that I had done the "right thing" when he wasn't here to tell me. Instead, he said, "Son, I think we should let some time go by and we'll talk about Judge later on. We will talk when some of the hurt that you are feeling has gone away."

"Okay, Dad," I said while taking a deep breath. "What do you think I should do with Judge?"

"You and I will bury your dog, Son. Where would you like to have Judge buried?"

After a moment, I asked, "Is it all right, Dad, to bury your own dog in your own back yard?"

Dad answered quickly, "It's all right to bury your own dog in our backyard, Dick. Where would you like for Judge to be? You and I will bury him before the family gets home."

"How about right where Judge is, Dad?"

"Fine, that's a nice spot under one of our maple trees. Later on, it will be nice to remember that this is where you and I said goodbye to Judge. We won't ever forget your little dog, Dick; not for a long, long time." Then Dad looked at me like he wanted to say something else; I waited, and, in a minute, he said, "Dick, I have been thinking. You asked me a question, Son, and I put you off. I don't feel good about that at all."

Dad thought a minute. "Dick, there are situations where the right thing for one person may not be just right for another." Dad, looked at me, wondering if I would understand. "Dick, I don't believe I would have done what I can see you did. But, Dick, I wasn't here... you were. I do believe, Son, that you did the right thing for you, and I am absolutely certain you did the right thing for Judge. His suffering must have been just awful for Judge and for you. With Judge's head and his chest unhurt, he might have lived for quite a few hours well into the night. But it is very clear that Judge could have never, ever gotten well again."

Then Dad was sadly quiet. He didn't say anything or look at me for a few minutes. Then quite suddenly, he looked directly at me and then looked again at the ground where we were going to put Judge. "One thing I am certain of, my son, you did a lot of growing up for one afternoon." Then my dad sighed, took a deep breath and looked at me again. "You won't ever be my little boy again. That hurts, Dick, but that's the way it has to be."

Now Dad was crying a little and I wasn't. I was all cried out. I turned away so that I couldn't see my dad's face, which headed me back towards our garage. I just kept going to find our shovel, to bring it back to Dad.

REMEMBERING JUDGE

When you are a little boy and your dog is dying,
And you're all alone with him,
What can you do?

When his pain is so awful and so terribly grim?
The Galyons have gone away... some place,
And Doc Smith is somewhere else, too.
Doc is our next-door neighbor doctor.
He would know just what to do.

There isn't anything I know how to do,
To help my little dog get well.
Look, look into his eyes.
See? He is dying I can tell!

With my back against our maple tree,
I cradled Judge on my chest
So, he could look into my eyes
And see how I'm bereft.

Oh, what can a little dog be thinking?
When death is so very near?
Would he understand if I took his life?
To end his pain and fear?

Richard Eager

POSTSCRIPT:

In 1952, the Korean War was in progress. A quarter of a century had passed since Judge had died in my arms under our maple tree. As a Colonel in the Strategic Air Command, I had flown from Omaha to Knoxville in the new Lockheed F-80 *Shooting Star*, our first production jet aircraft. My brother, Tom had picked me up at our Knoxville Airport where I had first learned to fly in a Tennessee Air National Guard *Piper Cub* in 1939.

Tom was taking me to his home on the 6th green of the Holston Hills Golf Club for a family reunion. We were driving east on Magnolia when he asked, "Brother, would you like to stop for a look at where we all grew up?"

I answered, "I was thinking about our old homestead on Magnolia while flying down from SAC Headquarters at Omaha. Has it changed very much?"

Tom answered, "It's a liquor store now." In few minutes we stopped, parked, purchased some wine and appetizers, and wandered out behind the liquor store into our old back yard. The big, paired maples were gone, but Judge's tree was still there, older, taller and looking a bit uncared for.

At that moment a thought came to me: the words I would put on paper as I flew back to SAC Headquarters where I was proud to be a member of General Curtis LeMay's new, recently formed Strategic Air Command staff. My thought was to write a short quatrain to my dog, Judge.

TO JUDGE MY CHILDHOOD COMPANION

Developer, spare this tree
Touch not a single bough.
It was here Judge said goodbye to me
It was here I set Judge free.

Richard Eager

15.2 *Dick at the age he had to say goodbye to Judge*

15.3 *Approaching the Chimney Tops on Indian Gap Trail* (McClung Historical Collection)

15.4 *Mt. LeConte from Greenbrier, Smoky Mountains* (McClung Historical Collection)

15.5 *Judge is never scared of heights in the Smoky Mountains* (McClung Historical Collection)

16.1 First Methodist Church, Knoxville, TN (McClung Historical Collection)

CHAPTER 16

GOLGOTHA AT FIRST CHURCH

I will never forget *The Terrible Meek*. The author was Charles Kennedy, and his one-act stage play has remained in my mind for two-thirds of a century. My mother's church friend, young Sarah Broom, a student at the University of Tennessee, directed a production at First Church in Knoxville. Mom said it was more than just a play. Sarah said it was "A Celebration of Easter." Both Sarah and Mom were right. First Church's "Celebration of Easter" turned out to be considerably more than "just a play."

Quite a few people in Knoxville were aware that Mom sang in the choir at Knoxville's downtown First Methodist Church. There were a lot of people in Knoxville who weren't First Church members but who knew by just walking by our church on Sundays that my mom had a strong contralto voice, and who felt she owed it to the Lord to make full use of her talent at First Church. Mom wasn't a deacon or anything, but she managed to have quite a bit to do with the goings on that went on at Knoxville's First Church.

It was spring, 1935, and Easter Sunday was coming on April 21. Mom and some of the church ladies had put their heads together and were talking about having "a very special Easter program" that year. Dr. Paulhamous often said he liked to give the ladies their heads in his church, and he told Mom, "You go ahead, Helen, and work up a nice program for us."

But Dr. Paulhamous, living in Tennessee, must have known that you give a horse his head; and you'd think he would have come up with a better way to tell the ladies at First Church that they had his support and could do whatever they wished to do at their church to celebrate Easter. Mom didn't mind how Dr. Paulhamous put it... head and all; she just wanted First Church to have a very special celebration of Easter that year. Probably it was forgivable that Mom wanted to have a hand in making it happen.

Dad had said to us "Evans Boys" on many occasions, "Your mom is a natural leader among women, and that's not an easy thing to be. We are fortunate that there are a lot of fine women at First Church who are natural followers."

The "Ladies of First Church," as they liked to call themselves, responded to a call from Mom and gathered at the church on a Tuesday. First, they put their heads together and decided that they should organize a special celebration for a special prayer meeting. Prayer meetings were regularly held on Wednesday nights; but this special prayer meeting would be shifted to Good Friday.

The "Church Women," as Dad called them (with no intention of putting them down), hadn't gotten much further than picking the night for their special celebration of the Lord when Sarah Broom suggested to Mom that they should have a play, not in the low-ceiling prayer meeting room downstairs, but in the upstairs vaulted, main church. Sarah, a freshman at the University of

Tennessee, majoring in dramatic arts, said that she knew just the play. Mom gave her okay. Sarah could go ahead, plan the props, assign the parts and direct the play.

Sarah was bright, pretty and very energetic. The church ladies were sure that Sarah would come up with a never-to-be-forgotten evening program. As it happened, they sure were right. I can still recall the event in considerable detail.

Mom was enthusiastic from the very beginning. Mrs. Broom, Sarah's mother, was a special chum of Mom's. Every Sunday at church, the Broom family and the Evans family sat in pews across the aisle from each other. This way, Mother and Mrs. Broom could exchange affirmative nods when Dr. Paulhamous got into esoteric areas of faith that only well-versed believers could fully understand and appreciate.

Mom thought Sarah, Kenneth and Martha Broom were "three of the finest young people one could ever meet." Martha was my age, but we had never made an effort to get very acquainted. Sarah was a little taller. I didn't seem to be catching up to her.

Kenneth was in Troop 12, our church Boy Scout troop, but he was older than I, and I don't believe he noticed when I joined the Troop. Mom was particularly enthusiastic about Sarah and thought my older brother, Stewart, should be, too. Stewart wasn't, but I was. I thought Sarah was keen. It was probably because of my looking at Sarah so much that I didn't always get all that much out of Dr. Paulhamous' Sunday morning sermons. Mom said that she had noticed my interest.

It was right after the benediction one Sunday that Sarah came over to our pew and said to Mom, "Mrs. Evans, I could put on a play for your Celebration of Easter." Sarah added, "I have a part for one of your sons."

Sarah told me later that Mom smiled sweetly, "That's very nice of you, Sarah, but what makes you so sure that Stewart would be right for the part?" Sarah told me that she then smiled back at Mom and said, "The part isn't for Stewart, Mrs. Evans; it's for your second son, Dick."

Sarah, laughing when she told me the rest, said that Mom then asked her, "Do you think Dick will be good in the part? I mean, Sarah, Dick's not very tall, you know."

Sarah replied, "Yes, I know Stewart's taller, but I think Dick is just right." That is when Mom asked Sarah what part she had in mind for me. Sarah said, "I have picked Dick to play Jesus."

At our dinner table, where we got most of our family news, Mom never mentioned this conversation with Sarah. I think Mom must have wondered for a few days if she had heard Sarah right, for I was sure that Mom thought her second-oldest son was her least Christ-like son.

I sure didn't mind. Sarah told me about her conversation with Mom. She thought it was very funny Mom thinking Stewart would make a better Jesus than I would. I was on whatever we called "cloud nine" back in those days when Sarah told me that she told Mom that Stewart just wouldn't work in the part, but that "Dick would be perfect." She took the edge off my delight, however, when she added that she told Mom, "Stewart would be too big for any cross that we could get into the church. "The cross would look bigger with Dick on it."

Since that was the first time I had heard about the cross part, I asked, "Sarah, are you planning to hang me up on a cross in our church in your play... in front of our congregation?"

"Well, I was thinking about it," she answered. "Wouldn't you like to be in my play, Dick?"

That's when Sarah gave me a smile that reminded me that I had thought about her before. I had also thought that I probably wasn't often on her mind.

Then Sarah smiled again, "Do you remember, Dick, that they hanged Jesus and two thieves on three crosses? Well, you're going to help me figure out how we can get three crosses up on our altar in front of the organ pipes and how we can get you on the cross in the center and a couple of your chums on the crosses on each side. We'll clear the pulpit out and scatter a lot of palm fronds around on the floor. We'll do the gambling for Jesus' clothes below the pulpit, down where we take communion. We'll back the three crosses up to the organ pipes and wire them to the structure up there. We'll find some palm fronds to spread around on the stage and in the aisle below. It will give the feeling that the crosses are way back up on a hilltop... on Golgotha."

"Golgotha!" I exclaimed as I immediately felt a wave of goose bumps move across my shoulder blades and a chill down my back. I was respectful of religious people, but I didn't think I was actually very religious. I was just not sure why I got that chill, but I've never forgotten getting it when Sarah said, "Golgotha."

Sarah was already at the University of Tennessee when I was just starting high school. I could tell she knew that I had a crush on her even though I hadn't told her about it. She looked real pretty when she smiled at me that day and said, "Dick, do you think you could learn a few lines?"

The thought that came to me was that a few lines would be about all I could learn. On every Easter that I could remember, Mom had told us what Jesus said on the cross. "Sarah," I continued, "I believe I already know my lines; Mom tells us 'The Easter Story' every Easter."

"Wonderful, now tell me what you can remember."

I answered quickly, "Forgive them, Father, for they know not what they do."

"Good. Anymore?"

Again, I answered promptly. "Father, why hast thou forsaken me?"

Then Sarah smiled, "I'm impressed, Richard Evans, your mom really has trained you very well, indeed."

"There's one more," I said to Sarah, "just before Jesus died, he said, 'It is finished,' and he pronounced "finished" funny. He said finish-ed."

Sarah added, "You're right; he did, and he also said, 'I thirst' when the Roman soldiers taunted him. My goodness, Dick, you already know your whole part. You'll be perfect. All you have to do now is help me figure out how we're going to get three crosses strong enough to hold you and two of your friends up there in the air above our pulpit. Who did you say you would like to have up there with you? I.C. Hewgley and 'Bubba' Bean?"

"Yes," I remarked, "they are my friends and I know they would like to be in a play that you are putting on." I thought for a moment Sarah was going to kiss me on my forehead, but she just gave me a beautiful smile. I think she saw how red my face got and stopped just in time. I don't know what I would have done if she hadn't stopped; however, I did know one thing: If she had kissed me, I couldn't have gotten any redder than I already was.

When some of the church elders heard about Sarah's plans, they thought a portrayal of the crucifix in our church might be too graphic for our congregation. However, Mom and her ladies thought it would "bring religion to the forefront of minds for just a few minutes in our busy lives." Dad predicted she would prevail; and Sarah Broom went to work and so did I as her happy, inspired assistant in charge of crosses.

Since I already knew my speaking part, I started giving some thought as to just how I might get up on my cross, hang there for forty minutes, and then get myself back down again in one piece. I had studied some pictures of the crucified Christ. I thought I could look as He did if I nailed a narrow, downward-sloping seat to the cross, which would support my buttocks and hold me there if I were strapped securely to the cross at the waist. Held to the cross in this manner, I could lean forward at the waist and give the appearance of hanging by my arms.

By positioning a support for my heels at a point on the base of the cross (which would cause my knees to be raised and bent slightly) I could be positioned about as Christ was. I thought that I could be reasonably comfortable for the rather long time that I would have to hang up there. Of course, so would "Bubba" Bean and I.C. Hewgley, who were looking forward to being the two thieves.

Dad helped us find the heavy lumber and the hardware we needed. He personally directed the actual building of the crosses by Bubba, I.C. and me in the Knox High woodworking shop on Saturdays when no one was there. Dad could do that because he was Principal of the Knoxville High School and had a complete set of keys for the whole school. He knew no one would be working there on Saturdays.

We found it easier to get up on our crosses than to get back down. We had strong, enthusiastic handlers and there were no mishaps during our secret dress rehearsal. Sarah had insisted that we be allowed to practice in secret in our church, saying that the "emotional impact" on our audience would be greater if no one had seen us practicing.

Our dress rehearsal was after school on Holy Thursday. The church was quiet and empty. We propped up our three crosses with help from Dad. My two associates and I had clambered onto our positions, one at a time, using two ladders, one in front for us to climb up, the other behind for our helper who would strap our waists to our crosses and then wrap some cloth over the straps. After our waists were secure it was fairly easy to slip our hands into the straps fixed to the ends of our crossbars, about level with our ears. We were helped in placing our feet on our heel supports.

A few days before our rehearsal, I had finally figured out how I could simulate the big spikes that had been nailed into Christ's feet and his palms. "Lincoln Logs," I had silently shouted to myself; "of course, I can cut up some wire hangers, bend one end of a wire around the notch in a 3-inch Lincoln Log, then bend the other end so that it would go between my fingers or toes and clamp to my hands or feet.

At Thursday's rehearsal, Sarah had shouted from the back of the church that the logs looked just like "large, crude spikes jutting from our palms and the tops of our feet." Sarah had inspired me to work for realistic effects, which she later told me with a half-smile, that I had done "very well, indeed." With our knees bent slightly, our upper bodies leaning forward away from the crosses and hanging relaxed on our arms, and with single Lincoln Logs projecting upward from our crossed feet and outward from each of our palms being held in position by the bent hanger wires, we were confident that the effect, as viewed by the audience, would be very realistic.

Sarah "didn't have a clue," as we liked to say back in those days, just how right she was going to be regarding the "emotional impact" her play would have on First Church's congregation when Good Friday night finally rolled around.

During the couple of weeks before Sarah's "Celebration of Easter" was actually celebrated, the excitement at First Church kept growing. Everybody was curious about the upcoming, special "Good Friday Celebration" being planned by "our own Sarah Broom and the young people." The specific nature of the performance had been a well-kept secret from the church members.

The congregation understood that the story was, appropriately, about the crucifixion. No one was prepared for the realism that Sarah and her assistants had planned for them. Sarah had insisted on wiring the curtain up high enough to hide the tops of the three wooden crosses from the church members. As they came in to take their seats, they had no idea what to expect.

Most of the church members said later that they had assumed that the scene would be presented symbolically and, of course, it was. They hadn't stopped to consider just how far Sarah Broom and her three assistants might go symbolically to represent the crucifixion of Christ.

The lights had already been dimmed when our First Methodist Church goers were invited to come in and take their seats. They had been held outside for a considerable time so that our church would fill more quickly than it usually would. The small amount of light from street lamps outside, shining through our stained-glass windows made the windows look more beautiful than they looked in daylight. The ushers had flashlights that they pointed towards the floor as they guided people to their seats. All the regular church lights, which were usually on during evening meetings, were out.

I think everyone was afraid to break the silence after they stepped through the doorway; our church had never been that quiet or that dark before. I had worked hard on the crosses. I was confident that we wouldn't have any trouble getting up there and getting strapped to our small seats. And we didn't. Our handlers had put us up there, one at a time, and we all agreed that we felt secure and fairly comfortable. We also thought that it was clever of us to have noted privately to each other that we had the best seats in the house.

I couldn't wait for the moment when Sarah would open the curtains. I wondered if I would be able see my Mom and Dad and my three brothers in our regular pew, just left of center on the aisle, a third of the way back from the altar. Mom had agreed that she would not tell my brothers what part Sarah had given me. I thought it would be more fun for them if they just suddenly recognized me hanging up there in the middle of our church, on the center and highest cross.

Finally, the curtains started moving. There was some soft beating of a base drum, back in one of our Sunday School rooms. Then, Junior Beaman and a friend of his sounded their trumpets from another room a way off just as the dimmers on the house lights were turned up a little.

Suddenly, I could make out the entire congregation in the dim light, and then I guessed that it was just as suddenly that the congregation got their first glimpse of me on the center cross, and then of I.C. and Bubba on the other crosses. I thought I could hear everybody in our church take a deep breath at the same time. Then one lady started crying as if her heart would break. Others followed her lead.

In a few seconds the curtains were fully parted, and everyone could see on our darkened dais – all three crosses, the Roman soldiers gambling at the foot of the crosses, and Mary, on her knees before Jesus with her head up for a moment (looking up at me), then back down again. I don't think anyone in our church that night dared to take a breath for a few seconds; I didn't.

Hanging up there the way I was with my head almost even with the tops of the organ pipes, I could see the entire congregation without moving my head. I heard or felt a kind of sigh from the audience and then some sobbing; but there was no real outcry... not yet. Things were very quiet, indeed, at Knoxville's First Methodist Church.

Then the story of Christ's death was told again, very softly. I found it easy to hold my position, slumped forward on my arms and hardly taking a breath. I felt more comfortable than I had thought I might be. I knew that Bubba and I.C. would be okay, too.

Some of the details of our reenactment of the Crucifixion have dimmed with time, but I remember very well the Roman soldiers posturing and making noises with their shields and broad swords and the thieves below me arguing over Christ's clothes.

The time was getting close for my first lines and I was excited, and... I felt chilled. I was wearing my shorts with a small torn cloth, hanging from my waist. I decided that I was probably more religious than I had previously thought. I remember clearly that I was trembling and wondered if it was just the cool night. I was also concerned that the cold might make my voice break or tremble, particularly the first utterances of my brief speaking part.

Sarah had said, "Just talk very slowly, Dick; you can hardly be too slow." Suddenly, it was time. I was hearing my own voice, as if I were alone, up in the top of our church. I was saying, "Father... why hast thou... forsaken me?"

For a moment there was no sound in our entire church. In another moment, I heard my voice again, this time saying, "I thirst... "

Then, finally I heard my voice, a little stronger, say, "Forgive them, Father, for they know not what they do."

In the days that followed, people said very little about the Good Friday celebration at First Church. At first, they didn't know what to say. They didn't know what they thought about it or what others might think about it. After a few Sundays passed and our church started to fill up again, they started exchanging viewpoints.

Some, it was clear, had been frightened from the very beginning because it was so dark. When the lights defined the ghastly scene, some got even more frightened, particularly when the base drums and the thunderous clamoring of the large pieces of sheet metal burst upon the room.

A few actually started bolting from the church sanctuary. Then, when Sarah gave the signal for her helpers to flash the house lights off and on and to sweep the ceiling with beams of light from special, high-powered flashlights, a still larger group started for the exits.

I was, of course, getting an extraordinary view and had my own young emotions to understand. I remember very well that I became very cold up there and was shaking when my helpers helped me to unhook myself from the cross. I recall that I was unable to stop shaking for quite a long while from the cold perhaps, but also from the experience, which I took very seriously.

Mom, bearing some of the ultimate responsibility for the realism and frightening aspects of the pageant, noted that there really weren't that many who actually left our First Methodist Church... for good. "Many of the faithful, in hindsight," she conjectured, "thought the portrayal too realistic, but were embarrassed that they had actually fled from the church." Mom suggested to our cast, that most, who left before the curtain closed, were very likely embarrassed by their own performance and not ours. She also mentioned, when remembering what Jesus said to Peter in the Bible, Matthew 26:40, "What, could ye not watch with me one hour?"

In a relatively short period of time, the very nice people of Knoxville's First Methodist Church forgave each other for whatever they thought might need to be forgiven. There were a few who volunteered that they were frightened by the experience. Perhaps the painting, which Sarah Broom had created on an invisible canvas before our eyes, was indeed a masterpiece if reflection and reaffirmation should be important in our lives.

Dad observed with a sly smile, "Unfortunately, there were also a few who were so moved by your performance that they did nothing to quell the momentum, which you in the cast had generated in them. They had just kept on moving until they arrived at another place of worship."

On a more circumspect level, Dad said to his family that he thought that a lot of the church members clearly understood that "they were viewing only a very realistic reenactment of the greatest tragedy of all time. The thunder and the lightning flashes were no more than a stark simulation of what all of us had visualized in our minds might have occurred on that terrible day when Jesus was crucified."

Dad said, "It's really not a bad thing that a reenactment of that day on Golgotha was represented in our church as an awful, monstrous thing. It was, after all," Dad said, "the day when Christ died. It was as ghastly an experience as the world had ever known."

Dad continued, "It was important that we took a moment out of our lives at our small church in Knoxville to remind ourselves of this." I remember that my mom was so grateful to my dad for the points he made in support of the play. And I was proud that Mom never wavered in her full support of Sarah Broom and I think that Sarah was proud of me.

Some who maintained their dignity or perhaps momentarily lacked the strength to bolt from the church themselves said that they thought the thunder (simulated by my friends back stage, flexing and pounding on large pieces of sheet metal), the lightning (simulated by the group that flashed the church lights off and on along with the slashing of the figures on the crosses with the high-powered, hand-held emergency flashlights) and finally the anguished, piercing cries of Mary, Christ's mother, all combined to make a stirring, positive experience for those still in the church at the end of the play.

Dad concluded, "We who created and shared at our own church our own home-grown Golgotha will never, ever forget the experience." Mom said that she agreed with Dad on that point.

———————————————

POSTSCRIPT

Dear Mother and Dad,

I think you were both right. Mom, you thought the word of the Lord should have some fiber in it. Dad, I, for one, have not forgotten the experience or your calming words when a lot of folks at First Church got pretty excited. I remember, Dad, that you stood firm behind Mom and Sarah all the way. You were in it up to your eyeballs, Dad, being the managing director of the building of the crosses at your Knox High Manual Arts workshop.

It hasn't been forever, Dad, but it has been over two-thirds of a century since you predicted that I would never forget "our home-grown Golgotha that Mom and Sarah Broom orchestrated for us."

You were right, Dad. I will never forget you working alongside Bubba Bean, I.C. Hewgley and me, putting those big crosses together in the Knoxville High School woodworking shop on Saturdays. I don't know where Bubba Bean wound up but I.C. didn't get to come home from Europe in 1944 when I did. A.C. Murphy, Fred Ford, Charles Jordan and Dick Wayland, our helpers behind the scenes, didn't get to come home either.

I would like to think my childhood friends live again in the memories of their families.

Your grateful son,
Dick

16.2 *Dick's family ready for church*

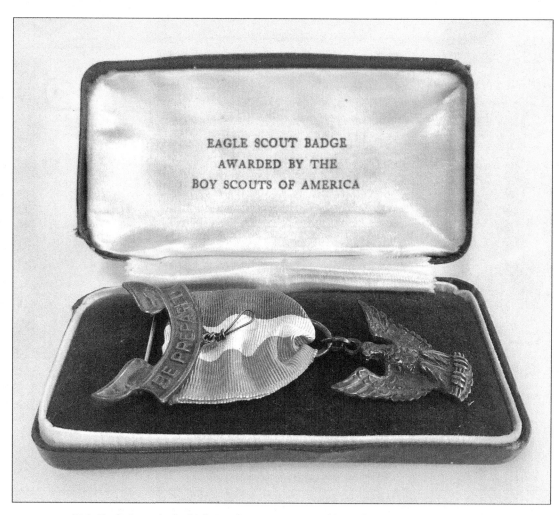

17.1 *Eagle Scout is the highest achievement attainable in the Boy Scouts of America*

CHAPTER 17

NO APPLAUSE FOR EAGLE SCOUTS

CREDO OF THIS EAGLE SCOUT

Life is real. Life is Ernest.
And the grave is not its goal.

Dust thou art, to dust returnest,
Was not spoken of the soul.

Lives of great men all remind us
We can make our lives sublime,

And, departing, leave behind us
Footprints on the sands of time.

With thanks to Longfellow,

Richard Eager

I was told while I was still quite young that a "tenderfoot" was a newcomer to the Wild West, a fellow not yet hardened to the tough life of a rancher, i.e., a greenhorn. I hadn't lived in the West; I live in the East, in east Tennessee... in Knoxville, Tennessee. In the summertime, I lived in The Great Smoky Mountains where a tenderfoot was a Boy Scout who hadn't been a Scout very long.

When I asked my dad about the Boy Scouts, he said, "Fine, Dick. The Scout program will teach you all about the outdoors."

I asked, "Dad, how come our Troop 12 always meets indoors, down in our church basement? How can we learn about the outdoors when we meet most of the time indoors?"

Dad stopped, looked at me and chuckled, "Dick, you meet down in our church basement in the wintertime. You and your fellow Boy Scouts can stay warm and dry and have lots of space to run around when it's too cold to be outside. You can learn your Boy Scout Laws, the Scout Oath, how to tie knots and a lot of interesting things in the wintertime. Then, when summertime comes around again, you can go to camp up in the Smokies and put to good use all the good things you learned in our church basement."

I knew Dad knew that I was better acquainted with our church basement than most of our churchgoers. Some Sundays, I would hang around the door to our auditorium and not go in where Dr. Paulhamous would be getting ready to preach his Sunday morning sermon. If Dad didn't catch me standing around out there before Dr. Paulhamous got going with his Sunday morning service, I would sort of saunter off down the stairs to the furnace room and talk to my friend, Leonard. He would give me lessons in how to "stoke and bank a furnace" with its own ashes.

Sometimes, Leonard would let me help shovel the ashes out of the bottom of the furnace and put them back in the top of the furnace, on the hot coals. Leonard taught me to be careful about the live coals. He said, "Dick, we'd both be in a mess of trouble if I wasn't looking and you set the church on fire."

I liked Leonard a whole lot. For one thing, Leonard wasn't much bigger than I was. Still, Leonard would always talk to me like I was a grown-up, not just a kid. Leonard would teach me lots of things that I should know – how to shovel the ashes out of a church furnace and how to bank a fire to keep it from burning up the coal too fast by shoveling some of the ashes back in again. I was sure that none of my school friends knew how to bank fires in church furnaces.

I remember hearing Mom say to Dad one time when they were having a "private chat" that Dad would have plenty of time to go down to our church furnace room and haul me up to my seat in church where I belonged if he didn't always have to stop and talk with everybody he ushered to their seat.

That's when my dad said to my Mom, "Hellie, it's my job to let folks know that I know when they don't show for church. I talk to them as they walk in, so they'll remember that I'm paying attention. That's my main job. Taking them to their seats is secondary. They know where to sit every Sunday. None of them need help walking... yet." When Dad would talk to Mom that way, he would always smile at Mom and wink at me. This would make me feel like I was going to be a grown-up and maybe pretty soon. I had noticed some changes.

Mom wouldn't smile or wink at Dad; usually she would just shake her head from side to side. Sometimes she would say, "Ernest, I declare." To this day, I have no idea what "I declare" means when you just say it like Mom would and not go ahead and declare something.

I remember Dad told Mom one time there was another reason why he didn't go down to Leonard's furnace room looking for me. He had plenty of time to fetch me out of there okay; but "there wasn't enough time in the whole day to dust off all the ashes that I would get on my hands and trousers from helping Leonard stoke the furnace."

Dad told Mom once with a big smile on his face that he thought, "It was a very nice, Christian act... Dick helping Leonard with the ashes and keeping him company down there in that lonely old furnace room where Leonard worked all day long all by himself."

Eddie May was our housekeeper and Mom's assistant cook. Leonard was our janitor at our First Methodist Church. They were my first black best friends. They were my first grown-up friends in the whole city of Knoxville, outside of Mom and Dad. Sometimes I think of Eddie May and Leonard and say to myself, "They were my friends for a quarter of a century."

Almost everybody in Knoxville, who knew me, called me "the Little Evans Boy." I was called that because of my big brother, Stewart. He came ahead of me and stayed ahead of me. He was always bigger and better at everything I ever did. No matter what it was that I learned how to do, I would always find out that Stewart had already heard about it and learned how to do it ahead, way ahead, of me. I didn't think that was fair.

I would finally learn to do something new like climb a rope at the YMCA. Stewart would always comment that he had done it years before. Often, he would go ahead and show me that he could do something. However, he never did learn how to go hand-over-hand up a rope in the YMCA starting from a sitting position on the floor, holding that sitting position with his legs straight out, all the way to the ceiling and all the way back down to the floor. Stewart was mostly right, though. He could do everything else I could do.

Everything we kids did back then had initials, e.g., PCLS (Park City Lowry School), PJHS (Park Junior High School), BSA (Boy Scouts of America), YMCA (Young Men's Christian Association), KHS (Knoxville High School), ROTC (Reserve Officers Training Corps), UT (University of Tennessee), and the USAAC (US Army Air Corps).

My dad said to me once, "Dick, you sure have gotten yourself tangled up in a mess of acronyms." Dad would say things like that so I would have to go and look up the word. He would say, "Dick, if you look up a word, you may remember it a little longer."

My biggest complaint growing up in Knoxville was that everything I wore and did was second-hand. Everywhere I went, my big brother Stewart, "Pug" as most people called him, had already been. But there was another exception: I learned to fly quite young while still in Knoxville between high school and the university.

Not only did I learn to fly ahead of my big brother, but I also preceded him by a few months into the Army flying school. I was as young as I could be to get in and my older brother was as old as he could be to get in. This was a subject I would never bring up with my big brother but would manage to allude to once in a while. Dad taught us that it wasn't "nice" to say something "in front of somebody" that might embarrass them. He did, however, say, "If you just can't help it, it wasn't too bad if you just alluded to it."

My younger brothers, Tom and John, followed Stewart and me into the Army Air Corps. Stewart, Tom and I were pilots; John was a navigator. All four of Mom's boys served overseas during the second world war; three out of four experienced combat. Happily, all four returned safely.

Besides Leonard at our church and Eddie May, I had another black best friend whose name was the same as Eddie May's, without the May. This Eddie wasn't a girl; he was a boy. I didn't know what Eddie's or Leonard's last names were. I thought I wasn't old enough to ask. Still, we were all best friends.

Eddie, who came along after Eddie May and Leonard, was the cook at our Boy Scout camp, where I was proud to be his assistant. There were 50 Scouts in the camp. Eddie and I fed them all three times a day. I couldn't have done it without Eddie, and Eddie would tell folks he couldn't do it without me either. I was proud when Eddie told people that I was important. Before Eddie, it seemed to me that I hadn't been important at much of anything.

I had quit the Boy Scouts so I could put more time into high school football, high school ROTC and girls, in that order. When I got to the University of Tennessee, I was interested in some of the same things, but I dropped football since the big shoes made me stumble a lot and changed the order to: girls, ROTC and learning to fly airplanes.

Mr. Melvin Hoffeld, my Scoutmaster, got to me one day after church and said, "Dick, I see you have quit the Scouts, too." Then, he went on to say, "Well, you know I wasn't really surprised when you quit. You were just following in your big brother's footsteps. Stewart quit on me, too, just before he could have made Eagle! Your brothers Tom and John are following along after you and Stewart. Maybe I can get one Eagle out of the four Evans boys. What do you think?"

This conversation with my Scoutmaster was causing me to feel some discomfort. That did it. My big brother had always done everything ahead of me, which, I realized in time, was reasonable with him being six years ahead of me in getting born.

I didn't understand a lot of things. For example, I had heard about sex, but didn't have a clue as to its potentialities. I just knew that both Janie Hall and her cousin, Varina Mayo, were "of the other sex." I secretly thought that they were both "keen." My problem was that both of them thought that it was my big brother, Stewart, who was keen.

I shifted back and forth between Janie and Varina. I noticed that my big brother, Stewart, did too. I would have been happy with either one of the Elkmont cousins, if either one had ever looked in my direction, which for them was down. Actually, I thought they might have looked down where I was, if it hadn't been that Stewart was always casually observing that he had become "an even six feet tall." I remember those days as being the most difficult period in my life.

I doubt Varina and Janie ever knew that they were the real reasons I finally made Eagle Scout. I would have traded either one of them for Mel Hoffeld's Scout program in a jiffy. I never told Janie or Varina about me being a Boy Scout; nor did I ever tell Mr. Hoffeld, or anybody else, how I felt about the Elkmont cousins.

Later I learned that Mel Hoffeld was a Scoutmaster for most of his life. Mom said one time, "Mel Hoffeld and his wife, Hattie, probably liked children a lot, but they couldn't ever have any of their own who might have wanted to become Scouts." She said that we Scouts in Troop 12 were the "sons that Mel and Hattie Hoffeld couldn't ever have." That didn't make a lot of sense to me back then, which provides a clue as to how bright I was at that point in my development.

I will never forget, that one Sunday after church, when Mr. Hoffeld sort of cornered me, smiled, looked straight at me and said, "Well, Dick, I'm afraid that I've about given up on you, too."

I remembered that we had had a previous similar conversation, but this one was more pointed. I said something that made it sound like I didn't understand what he had meant by "too." However, I think Mr. Hoffeld thought I understood him, just fine. Still, I went ahead and asked, "Who else have you given up on, Mr. Hoffeld?"

"I think you know, Dick," he said, dropping his eyebrows so he could see me better.

At that moment I didn't have enough "fortitude," as Dad would have phrased it, to tell Mr. Hoffeld that he had just changed my mind. I did, however, start sneaking back to Scout meetings on Friday nights. I didn't tell anybody that I was coming. I would just be in the line-up when the bell rang to start our meeting.

Mr. Hoffeld saw me at the meeting. He knew that I was there, all right. He didn't say anything to me about being back for a couple of Fridays. I know now that this modest, very giving man did a wonderful thing for me. He confronted me and embarrassed me. He did it to see if he could get my attention and get my "motor going." He succeeded in both endeavors.

That's not all Mr. Hoffeld did for me. Dad told me later that what he really did was to "issue a challenge." Mr. Hoffeld told me that I could come to his Scout camp in the summer that was just coming up and pass the Life-Saving merit badge, the only badge keeping me from being an Eagle Scout. "Dick, you're running out of time. This summer will be the last chance you will have to make Eagle Scout, ever!"

"You will have to be some place where you can really work on your swimming every day. You should be around other boys who have already passed their Life-Saving merit badge. They will be anxious to help you."

Mr. Hoffeld knew that I couldn't afford camp. "I can arrange for you to get a job at camp that will pay you enough so you can pay your camp expenses. You will have some time off so you will be able to concentrate on your swimming and on passing your Life-Saving merit badge. Then you will be an Eagle Scout, Dick. Do you really want to be an Eagle Scout bad enough to do a little hard work?"

I never thought of myself as being overly bright, even though I made a "B-average" on my report cards. I was smart enough, however, to ask, "How much would I make in camp?" and "What would I have to do to make it?"

Mr. Hoffeld, who I noticed was beginning to look a little shorter from where I was standing, looked up at me and said, "Dick, what do you think it would be worth to go to Scout Camp in the Smokies for six whole weeks, for the full length of my camp?"

I had been in the Smokies a lot with my family at our cottage at Elkmont, and I had camped out with Mom and Dad on top of Mt. LeConte, but I had never been to a real boys' camp.

"It would be worth a whole lot, Mr. Hoffeld."

"Fine, I'm glad you think it would be worth a whole lot," he said. "That is exactly what I will pay you, Dick... a whole lot. Would you like to sign up? The offer is only good for the summer, which is coming up, which is not far away. Next year you will be too old, Dick, and I may be, too. Your last chance, Dick, to make Eagle Scout."

I had the feeling that my Scoutmaster had tricked me, but I wasn't sure. To give me some time to sort out what kind of a deal I was being offered, I asked, "What would I have to do at camp, Mr. Hoffeld, to make this money that I could use to go to camp?"

Mr. Hoffeld had been fishing. He must have decided it was time to set the hook. He answered with a big smile on his face, "Dick, you will have to do whatever the head cook tells you to do; that's all... nothing more. You will be the assistant head cook for my whole camp."

Mr. Hoffeld hadn't added, "and bottle washer." I had a pretty good idea what my summer job was going to be like. I could see that I wasn't going to be able to date Alice Cox, back in Knoxville, while I was working in Mr. Hoffeld's Scout camp up in the Great Smoky Mountains.

———————————

When I reported for work, in the kitchen, at Camp Murmontis, just a mile from the base of Mt. LeConte, I found my new boss right away. He was short and he was black, like my friend Leonard.

He told me that his name was "Eddie." I told him that I had another black friend whose name was Leonard, who was the janitor at the First Methodist Church in Knoxville, and that Leonard had taught me how to stoke the furnace at our church.

Eddie smiled and said, "That's nice, Dick, and I will teach you how to light a fire in this wood stove. But right now, we've got a little work to do. We've got our first lunch to serve in just thirty minutes. Do you know how to set a table?"

I answered with a grin, "I sure do; I have set lots of tables; my mother taught me how. I know where the plates, the glasses, the napkins and the knives, the forks and the spoons all go."

"Okay," he said, "That's fine. Here's where we keep our clean tablecloths on this shelf and the silver is in those boxes over there under the white cloths. You sure you know where the knives, forks and spoons go on the tables?"

"Yes, sir, I sure do," I said and got right to it. I remember being proud to show my new boss that I would make a good "assistant head-cook and bottle washer." I knew already that I liked Eddie a whole lot. I tended to like people a whole lot when I happened to be a little taller than they were. (I wasn't a lot taller than anybody in those days.)

On that first day in camp, we had fifty campers, ten or twelve camp leaders and workers. Also, fifty or sixty parents who had brought their kids to camp to see where they were going to eat, sleep, swim, hike, bike and play tennis. I was proud to be there helping with the first meal at the first brand-new camp near Gatlinburg with a great view of Mt. LeConte.

They called it "Opening Day" and said the camp's name would be "Camp Murmontis." I couldn't find the word in a dictionary but guessed the name had something to do with the mountains that were all around us. Gatlinburg was nearby. From our camp we could look directly up at the three pinnacles of Mt. LeConte, the third highest peak in the Smokies, behind Clingmans Dome and Mt. Guyot.

The camp that Mr. Hoffeld had built on a shoestring was brand new for him and most of us. It consisted of three or four, old, falling-down, wooden farm buildings and a lot of second-hand, World War I army tents. A new mess hall and kitchen had been built using the "natural" (unpainted) rough lumber, the same as the old farm buildings.

I didn't tell Eddie, but I was sure tired when we sat down to have lunch together after we had cooked, served and cleaned up after what turned out to be the regular Sunday lunch crowd: all of the kids in camp, the camp staff, and most of the parents and brothers and sisters of the campers.

I was proud that Eddie acted like he was proud of me. I was disappointed, however, when I had finished cleaning up the lunch dishes and all the pots and pans. I rushed to get my trunks on and then dashed for the lake to join the other campers. I found that I was just in time to see all the campers and all the visitors, but not at the lake. They were all on the trail, returning from the afternoon swim. I felt embarrassed being the only one on the narrow trail, dressed in a dry swimsuit, who seemed to be heading off in the wrong direction!

Funny thing, it got better and very quickly. Eddie became my friend, just like Leonard. Eddie said that if I worked really hard, he could teach me all I needed to know to be a chef, which he told me was bigger than a cook. Eddie told me that he was getting older. If I could get to be a chef, I could maybe take his job next season.

"But first, we've got to teach you how to be a good assistant cook and bottle washer real fast. Dick, you are spending most of your time drying the silverware. I have other things I need you to do. You're drying one piece at a time; I'm going to show you how we can work together and dry all of the silver at one time. You've been taking over an hour. We'll be done in five minutes, okay?"

I answered, "Okay," even though I already knew that what Eddie was suggesting just wasn't possible. There was no way Eddie, and I could dry all that silver in five minutes. Eddie nodded his head toward the shelves and said, "Now, Dick, you just go over and get those big white sheets that I had you stack on the upper shelf. We're going to use these heavier-than-normal sheets as towels to wipe our silver with. Okay with you?"

I didn't have a clue about what my new boss was talking about. I figured he was pulling some kind of joke on me. In a minute when I had gotten all the sheets down from the top shelf, Eddie said, "Okay, Dick, now spread a couple of our sheets out on the floor one on top of the other. Be careful to keep the topsides of the sheet with the fuzz pointing up."

When I had spread out the sheets the way Eddie asked me to do, he then said, "Okay, Dick, that's fine. Now, you and I are going to put this silver in a pile, in the center of these two sheets." That's just what we did. I still didn't have a clue as to how Eddie was going to do it, but I had stopped doubting him. For sure, I did what Eddie told me to do.

Next, he instructed me to pick up my two corners of the sheet and start twisting them to my right; then he picked up his two corners of the same sheet and started twisting them to his right, the opposite direction to mine. Quickly, the silver was wrapped securely inside the sheets, which now looked like a hammock. Eddie and I held up the two ends so the "hammock" was off the floor.

My teacher, without saying anything, started lifting and then dropping his end of the hammock. He then nodded his head up and down and I followed his example and got the rhythm quickly after just a couple of ups and downs.

We would start the silver up, heading it for the ceiling, and then quickly lower our "hammock" while the silver was still going up, inside the sheets. Then we would both be braced for the moment when the silver heading for the floor was stopped just off the floor by our twisted sheets. When the silver hit our sheets and stopped, the water on the silver kept right on going and was quickly absorbed by the sheets. I remember thinking, "This is a miracle... Eddie is a miracle man."

After no more than six or eight "ups and downs," Eddie slowed down, stopped and set his end back on the floor. I followed his example.

Eddie then instructed me to examine the silver now at rest on the heavy sheeting on the floor. If Eddie had told me that we were going to shake the water out of that silver, I might have smarted off with some wise-apple remark; I was sure glad that for once I hadn't had anything to say. We had done exactly what Eddie said we were going to do. He had said that we were going to dry the silver for the whole camp in just five minutes.

Eddie then picked up his end of the other sheet we had piled the rest of the silver on. We started twisting. When our twisting had quickly formed the second hammock, I didn't need any more instruction. When we would then unroll the sheets on a big table, the silver wasn't damp at all. It was bone dry. Every single time. I couldn't believe it.

Eddie taught me a lot, including how to wring chickens' necks. As we liked to say in Tennessee, I didn't cotton to that job, at first, but Eddie observed that I got "the swing of it pretty fast" for a white kid. In a couple of weeks, I made a significant contribution to the art of wringing chickens' necks.

My first task was to catch those small and under-weight Great Smoky Mountain chickens. I found it extremely difficult to run as fast as one could while leaning over as far as one might and at the same time positioning one's hands close enough to the ground to catch one of these fleet-of-feet, flying fryers. I rated their ability to corner as extraordinary. I believe one of them deliberately ran me into the wire fence, twice.

There had to be a better way to catch these chickens. I got the word out that there would be a weekly "running of the chickens." Eddie responded to my play on words with an instant showing of a mouthful of very nice, white teeth.

I was surprised to discover that there was indeed a chicken "Gordian Knot" to be studied, understood and exploited. I started by simply chasing chickens to see if perhaps there was a pattern in the escape plans being practiced by the more successful birds. I was not able to discover any consistent fowl practices, which I might use in my effort to do them in before I ran clean out of breath.

Suddenly, *voila!* There it was. All the chickens took off vigorously, tired quickly, landed, and reconnoitered at their landing site with much clucking. They would then take off again, repeating their evasion tactics.

There was more. What I had failed to note at first was they all appeared to be right-winged, just as most of us are right-handed. Their course in flight tended to arc to their left. Also, I noted that they tended to make the same number of takeoffs and landings with each sortie, suggesting that they flew until they tired to a specific energy level. I thought who's to know... or to care, if they all keep doing it the same way every time.

I practiced flushing them, making a mental note of the direction of their takeoff run, their course changes, which were always to their left, and their landing direction, also to their left. It was as if they had a stronger right wing turning them to their port side.

The moment my intended prey would become airborne, I would make a 20-degree course correction to the left, thereby shortening my trip to the chickens' point of touchdown. This enabled me to trot, not run, and with minor course corrections at the end, wind up at a point where an exhausted chicken, no longer able to get airborne, would simply be running itself out of air on the ground.

While the exhausted chicken was running, I would easily run along-side it and knock it off its feet with a club which I had fashioned. I would immediately pick up the chicken and wring its neck on the spot, a skill learned at the hands of my new friend, Eddie.

I felt some pride in my scientifically-based discovery. The efficiency with which I would corral chickens, wring their necks, pluck them and deliver them to the camp's super chef, Eddie, was clearly essential. I was particularly proud when, on one occasion, I caught Eddie watching me though trying to stay out of my sight. When I could see him smile and start chuckling, I was sure that he had found me out and approved of my methods.

There was even an easier way I later discovered to process chickens for human consumption... build a fence, which, in time, we did.

I believe the reputation we had down South for eating a lot of fried chicken was probably justified. I know that we had it at least twice a week at Camp Murmontis. The short cuts that Eddie showed me for different "kitchen-helper chores" helped me get through my chores early enough for me to get over to the lake before the whole gang had started back to camp.

Somewhere along the line, I made a breakthrough in my swimming, just as Mr. Hoffeld had said I would. All of a sudden I wasn't afraid of the water at all, nor was I afraid of diving off the 3-meter tower. Very soon, I easily passed all the tests for the Life-Saving merit badge.

I couldn't understand why I had been so timid. Why I had been afraid to grab someone by the wrist in the water, pull him over on my hip, get behind him while keeping his head up, and then swimming the length of the lake with him on my hip, using the side stroke and finally hoisting him out of the water onto the bank.

The camp was in its fourth week when I finished all the requirements for Eagle Scout. I had become a real lifeguard and was very proud to be on duty as part of a three-man team. One of us would stand on our 3-meter, diving tower, while the other two would be stationed on the shore about fifty yards away on each side of the tower. In these positions we had good voice and eye contact between us. Any one of the three of us could yell to the other two at any time to check a swimmer who looked as if he might be having some trouble. From the diving tower, one of us could give directions to the other two. The three of us rotated our positions. I was particularly proud when it was my turn on the tower.

When the campers returned to camp, we lifeguards practiced swimming, diving and lifesaving. Bill Beeler was our swimming and diving coach, our leader, and our soft-spoken boss. I was pleased to follow Bill's instructions and to try anything that Bill suggested I try.

"Okay, Dick, here's what you're going to do. You are going to walk out on our 3-meter board, bringing your hands together and your arms up to a position over your head. You are going to raise your right leg, bending your right knee, on your leap up at the end of the board. You must think to leap up, not out. As you approach the end of the board, your hands and arms should reach straight up, directly over your head, not forward up. Your brisk walk to the end of the board will provide sufficient momentum to position your body over the water beyond the board when you start to descend.

"That's just the preparation part," Bill continued. "Then, when you land, feet first on the end of the board, you are going to bend your knees and let your arms swing down to press the end of the board down as far as you can make it go. As the board starts to recoil and flip back up, you are going to bring your arms almost straight up, letting your hands come together over your head. You will be looking up at a point in the sky about 45 degrees above the horizon.

"At the peak of your dive, you can drop your head and arms forward, tipping you over, so to speak, until your hands and arms are pointing directly toward the water. Keeping your body ramrod straight, you will enter the water with hardly a ripple."

Bill dove beautifully, seemingly without effort. As our coach, he would spend "whatever time it took" to help one of us advance as far as we could. I thought there was nobility in this modest young man.

By the end of camp, I could do a decent swan dive, a fair one-and-a-half, and a poor back dive. Later, after much direction and prodding from Bill, I mastered "the full-twisting-one-and-one-half-forward somersault" off the three-meter board. I learned a dive that I had been sure I could never master.

Might I have learned it without Bill? No way. I complained that the water was smacking my face and my eyes were smarting. Bill wouldn't let me rest. He kept saying that I could "hack it," if I just "hung in there." I improved and, in a few weeks, my headaches started to go away. Even so, nobody ever got me mixed up with Bill when we were up there diving together on the 3-meter boards.

On Saturday nights at camp, we would have an Indian Powwow. We Scouts would sit on the ground in a large circle around a big campfire. The dress was our most roughed-up shorts and no shirts at all. Otherwise, how could a young boy show off his new pectorals, which at last were starting to develop? We would tie a bandana around at the back of our heads and paint black, white and red grease paint on our faces, arms and chests. In the flickering light of the campfire, we really thought that we looked like a bunch of "wild Indians," a common expression in those days used to describe "youthful boys" still short of being "young men."

Parents would drive up from Knoxville for the weekend and be on hand for our Saturday night Powwow. Most would stay over in Gatlinburg, Wonderland Park or Elkmont and be with us for church and Sunday lunch. Eddie and I always served fried chicken.

At our Indian Powwows, our parents would sit in chairs at the edge of the trees; we Scouts would sit on the ground, around a big fire at the center of our camp. It was nice to turn around and have a look at our parents and friends behind our owwows. You couldn't see them too well, but it was nice to see light from the fire jumping around on their faces.

My parents kept saying they were going to come up to see our Powwow. At the last minute I would hear that they weren't able to make it. I knew Dad was always busy getting Summer School going at Knoxville High. I kept looking for my folks to show up in the circle around our fire, but I understood how important it was for Dad to get his high school Summer School going.

One Saturday night I was gazing around the parent circle when suddenly my head stopped, checked back a few faces, and there they were! My whole family... all of them were sitting back there in the trees. My mom, dad and my brothers had all come from Knoxville. They hadn't told me they were coming so I would be surprised. Oh man, was I surprised. Was I ever happy!

The light from the campfire flickered on their faces. Not just Mom and Dad, but Stewart, Tom and John... all of them were there. The whole family had come out to the mountains to see our Indian Powwow, and see where I washed the dishes, washed the pots and pans for fifty campers and on weekends for fifty visitors.

I was so proud that they had come and I couldn't wait until our Powwow was over so I could run up and hug Mom and shake Dad's hand and slap my brothers on their backs.

Finally, Mr. Hoffeld got up to make his announcements about the events planned for Sunday and to invite all the parents to stay for the mid-day Sunday fried chicken dinner.

Mr. Hoffeld began like he always did, saying how much he appreciated the parents "driving out to see their boys and to take part in their campfire activities." Then he said that this was a special night. Something had happened in Troop 12, which had never happened before, and he wanted to "share with the parents."

Mr. Hoffeld said that he had a boy in Troop 12 who he knew could make Eagle Scout, but who had become discouraged and quit. He had reached Life Scout, with one merit badge to go to make Eagle, when he dropped out and stopped coming to Scout meetings.

"Sometimes," Mr. Hoffeld said, "I am pretty sure at the start which boys will make Eagle and which will give up. I told this boy that I needed an assistant cook and bottle washer at my camp and that he could have the job. I would pay him well. I said that I would pay him exactly what it costs me to feed one Boy Scout, bed him down and direct his camp activities."

I was beginning to wonder who the other Boy Scout was that Mr. Hoffeld had made the same deal that he had made with me.

"I like to pin the Eagle Scout badge on my Eagle Scouts myself, but since they're all half-naked here tonight, there's nothing to pin to!" Then everybody laughed like crazy, and we Scouts thought that it was a great joke on us.

As soon as everybody had stopped laughing, Mr. Hoffeld said, "My good friends and fellow parishioners at our First Methodist Church, Helen and Ernest Evans, are here with us tonight. I would like to ask them to come up by the fire with me so that I can pin Dick's Eagle Scout badge on his mother." Then everybody whooped and hollered. My Scout buddies sitting near me got me up and started slapping me on my back and shoulders and doing little Indian dances around me.

Mr. Hoffeld raised his hands over his head and asked, "for some quiet." The parents sat back down, and the Indians stopped whooping it up. Then Knoxville's Troop 12 Scoutmaster began to tell his true story. His story began, "In 1899, just as the 19th century was about to end, a war broke out in South Africa between the natives, the Boers, and the British. The English were trying to establish a colony in South Africa, much as they had done in other parts of the world, including America.

"British Army Commander, Robert Baden-Powell, in charge of the British fort at Mafeking, a rail center and the largest town in North Cape Colony in South Africa, had successfully held this fort which had been under siege for six months. At the conclusion of hostilities and as the 19th century ended, this British Commander was hailed in England as 'The Hero of Mafeking, the Victor in the South African Boer War.'

"A hero and honorable and successful soldier he was," Mr. Hoffeld continued, "but of special interest to us, this same man is remembered perhaps even more importantly as the founder and leader of the Boy Scouts' movement, which was born, spread quickly and became a world-wide organization, during a second career of 'The Hero of Mafeking.'"

Continuing, Mr. Hoffeld said, "To get his Scout program off the ground and going, he personally conceived, developed, sponsored and directed the first Boy Scout camp out. It took place on Brownsea Island, 100 miles southwest of London. It was reached by boat across the Bay of Poole."

After I became an Eagle Scout at Mr. Hoffeld's camp, at his wonderful Powwow, which wouldn't have happened without the help of my fellow-camper and life-long friend, Bill Beeler, I continued to work as Assistant Cook and Chief Bottle Washer for Eddie. I was proud to be so employed.

17.2 Dick trying a new dive

17.3 *Dick, top, never afraid to dive again*

18.1 *Dick holds the tip of the American flag, standing with the Knoxville High School ROTC*
(McClung Historical Collection)

CHAPTER 18

TENNESSEE AIR NATIONAL GUARD

Young Richard once dreamed of flying
Up in the clouds, darting in the azure sky
Not yet encumbered by fears of dying,
"Why" asked the lad of his Dad, "Why not I?"

At first, there was child-like yearning
That twisted and turned in an unsettled mind.
As if something lost that was not returning,
Something, which he alone must find.

Was it an idle youthful whim?
Was it a challenge from the world not known?
Or a call from the future like a chilling wind?
No! Toward manhood it was a course full blown!

Richard Eager

In the spring of 1937, when I was 18, an announcement appeared in the *Knoxville Journal*, the morning newspaper, and also in the *News Sentinel,* the evening one. Both papers reported that the Tennessee Air National Guard would soon be sponsoring ground-school contests in Memphis, Nashville and Knoxville.

Textbooks would be provided, and evening classes would be held twice-weekly for three months. Written exams would be given every Friday and a comprehensive, three-hour examination would be given at the conclusion of the course. The 15 highest scoring participants would be awarded 50 hours of flying-time, including the required dual-time with an instructor-pilot... all at no cost to the winners of the statewide competition. The Tennessee Air National Guard would purchase three brand-new *Piper Cub* airplanes for this forward-thinking, ahead-of-its-time, state-wide, state-sponsored training program. Any contest winner who then completed the 72-hour course successfully would be awarded a Civil Aeronautics Administration (CAA) Private Pilot License and would be qualified to apply for a Land-1 Private Pilot License, which would permit him to carry passengers in Type Land-1 aircraft.

I had always dreamed of being an aviator and gleefully announced to my dad that I couldn't wait to sign up.

I was shattered, however, when Dad responded, "Dick, your older brother is going to register and you probably aren't eligible yet. I doubt you're old enough to fly alone and I would guess that the state would agree with me. Don't you think one Evans is enough the first time? There will be other opportunities for you, Dick. You have a lot of time ahead of you."

It is funny how we remember things that we would rather forget. I recall that I made a big fuss about the unfairness of it all... my big brother, Stewart, getting to do everything first, ahead of me. I remember something else, too, which is hard to admit. I was afraid of heights. I got the "Willies" looking off Alum Cave Bluff and Clingman's Dome in the Great Smoky Mountains. How could I ever expect to learn how to sit in an airplane, look down at the ground and land an airplane on that ground?

Also, like some people described in Mr. Dale Carnegie's then popular book, *How to Win Friends and Influence People*, I was actually relieved that I was already losing before I had even started.

"It isn't my fault," I told myself. "I know I will fail even before I try. Even if I luck out and win, I will probably get washed out. If I learn to fly with an instructor, how can I ever have the nerve to solo... to take off and fly alone in an airplane? How can I ever learn to fly up there in the sky all alone, all by myself?"

Being afraid of heights, I had been told, is a "malady" called *altophobia*. I thought I probably did have this phobia. By considering flying school classes, was I just trying to impress my friends with how hard I had tried? Then I did something unexpected. I told my dad what I had been thinking, wanting to fly, yet so afraid. I asked Dad why he thought I pushed it. Dad just smiled at me and said, "You're a strange kid, Dick, but don't change; you're my son, Richard Evans, and I wouldn't trade you for anything."

I believed my wanting to sign up for the ground school contest confirmed Dad's views of my strangeness. I guess I thought I could never win but my friends would look at me and say, "Look how hard Dick tries." Just like Dale Carnegie said I would.

But then a thought crept into my mind. "Didn't you, Richard Evans, work hard some summers ago to earn the Eagle Scout rank, the highest achievement attainable in the Boy Scouts of America Scouts' program? And didn't you receive just two years ago the **Morgan Medal** for the best-drilled cadet in the Knoxville High School R.O.T.C. Battalion? Yes, it's a leap, but maybe, just maybe... "

When it was time to attend the first meeting to learn about the ground school and register for the class, I forgot when the meeting was scheduled. I rationalized, "Why should I spend my time on something which I already know I won't be able to do very well?"

But then, without registering for the course, I started going to classes anyway. I knew how to find the classes all right; they were held in Knoxville's Park Junior High auditorium where for three years I had "Study Hall," and at the end of my last year, I had stepped out on the stage to receive my Junior High School diploma.

It was also the auditorium where I had played the lead role in a play performed in Latin. After sixty years, a couple of my lines still come to mind. While brandishing a wooden broad sword, which I had made in our school workshop, I beat on a trashcan-lid shield and shouted while being careful to not let my voice wonder into unpracticed ranges, "*Pyrrhus sum, Rex Graecorum!*"

I had shouted to anyone in the student body who spoke Latin, "I am Pyrrhus, King of the Greeks." Miss Duncan, my Latin teacher, beamed and said that everybody in the block could hear me shout it out. In a lower voice, I added, "*Etiam fortes pueri videntur.*" This time, I had declared, "Even the young boys seem to be brave."

My old Park City Junior High School auditorium wasn't just full of memories. I was eager to be there for the classes, which were held in the evening twice a week with a test on Friday. The old auditorium was full with twenty or thirty would-be-pilots.

For the first week of classes, all the seats were taken, and I always stood up in the back or on one side during the entire three-hour session. By the second week, I found a seat in the back. I took all the exams and turned in all my papers, "just for fun," I told myself.

I studied Stewart's books when he wasn't using them. After a couple of weeks, Stewart wasn't using them at all. He dropped out and told me if I wanted his books, I could have them for half price. I told him "fine" and added that I would pay him a dollar a week "til I got him paid off."

He accepted my offer and explained he was too busy going to UT, being drum major of the band and working part-time for TVA. The new Tennessee Valley Authority was just starting to build hydroelectric dams in Tennessee.

I thought, "Yeah, my big brother, Stewart, is also staying busy chasing after the beautiful Elkmont cousins, Janie Hall and Varina Mayo." I never was able to figure out how my brother could pull off dating both of those gorgeous cousins at the same time. I knew that I couldn't date either one, any time.

Janie was blond and had blue eyes; Varina had dark eyes to match her dark hair. I think it was Varina's dark hair that was so appealing to me. Also, Varina was a little shorter than Janie, which I thought would make me look a little taller.

I remember one night at Elkmont, Stewart was sitting with both of the lovely Elkmont cousins in the big, wide swing on their front porch. He had both arms on the back of the swing, an arm behind each of them. I could see from where I was standing, back in the bushes in the dark, that my brother would first put a hand on Janie's shoulder, then switch hands, and put his other hand on Varina's shoulder.

I didn't mind when Stewart put his hand on Janie's shoulder. She was beautiful and blond, but she was also taller than I was so I didn't think she ever noticed me way down there where I was standing.

On the other hand, I really didn't like it when he would put his other arm on Varina's shoulder. Actually, Varina was also taller than I was, but at least, I thought I was gaining on Varina but could never catch up with Janie.

In the third or fourth week of the Tennessee National Guard ground school, the lady who seemed to be the school secretary came back to where I was sitting and asked if my name was Richard Evans.

Feeling some alarm and guessing that I had been found out, I shyly said, "Yes, ma'am, my name is Richard Evans." She then just smiled and mentioned that Mr. Rising would like a few words with me after the meeting. I had to admit to myself I really was frightened. I still hadn't signed up for the classes and couldn't explain what I thought I was doing in the back of the room.

Mr. Rising, whose friends called him "Sunny," which I thought was very clever, was the instructor-pilot, the ground-school teacher and the Director of the Knoxville, Tennessee National Guard ground school. He taught most of the subjects and introduced all of the guest speakers. I figured Mr. Rising probably just wanted to know why someone out there was turning in papers regularly but hadn't taken the time to register for his school.

After the ground school classes, Mr. Rising and some of the instructors would stick around for a while to answer questions from the students who often hung around for another hour or so. I would always hang around with this group and listen until they got talked out. I would then walk or jog the two miles home.

I would never ask a question because Mr. Rising never looked in my direction, although he did look at other people. He probably guessed I was the one who hadn't bothered to register for his classes but still came to hear his lectures and was still turning in exam papers.

Since they hadn't given back any of my tests, I figured they had tossed them out. I hadn't even taken the time to sign-up, so how could I blame them?

The night when I was asked to stay after the meeting, the group that usually stayed to ask questions left quickly. So, there I was alone in the empty auditorium with Mr. Rising.

Mr. Rising turned and looked straight at me, as if he had known all along that I was the one who had been hanging around, listening to those after class questions and turning in the required papers.

I knew my face would be really red this time, but Mr. Rising just smiled and said in a low voice, "Don't tell me; let me guess; you must be Richard Evans. Am I right?" Those were his exact words.

"Yes, sir," I answered, "My name is Richard Evans."

"Well, Richard Evans, we seem to have lost your registration. Would you know anything about this?" I didn't answer right away and my face became even redder. He then continued, "But, we have been getting your test papers right along. And I must say you have been doing quite well." Then he asked me if I happened to know anything about a Stewart Evans.

I said, "Yes, sir, Stewart Evans is my big brother, and he did register for your classes, Mr. Rising. I didn't think I was old enough to register." Mr. Rising looked straight at me for what seemed to be a whole minute, or maybe more. He responded, "You, Richard Evans, never did register for our classes, did you?"

I just shook my head sideways a couple of times, meaning "no" and then just continued to look at him, knowing that my face was getting very hot.

"Still, you came to classes regularly and turned in papers with quite good drawings attached. Your brother, on the other hand, did register with us but hasn't turned in a single paper. I presume, by now, he has dropped out. Does this seem at all strange to you, Mr. Richard Evans?"

I must have nodded "yes" because Mr. Rising just went right on and said, "Your brother is not the only one, by the way, who has dropped out on us. Guess what? We now have room for you, and I can put your name on our roster right now, tonight, Mr. Richard Evans. That is, if you are interested enough in our school to sign up this time. Would you like me to write in your name,

Mr. Richard Evans? I know how to spell it. If you would like me to do that, I can do it tonight before I go home."

I was so surprised that my mouth must have just fallen open. Catching my breath, I said that I sure would like to have my name written into his roster. I don't know how I looked but must have looked pretty funny because Mr. Rising grinned, and then he laughed. But I could tell he was not laughing at me. "Okay, I'll see you in class, Mr. Richard Evans... and good luck to you." Mr. Rising gave me a real big smile, disappeared behind the old curtain that years before had been pulled back to reveal a younger, just-as-nervous, Richard Ernest Evans, playing the lead part in a play written in Latin, a language that was already dead when Miss Duncan, our Latin teacher, was directing us.

Again, I saw myself on the Junior High stage, brandishing my wooden broadsword and shouting: "*Pyrrhus sum, Rex Tennesseans*... Pyrrhus I, King of Tennesseans. "I'm going to learn to fly; I'm going to fly, away up high in the sky like 'Lucky Lindy' and Admiral Richard E. Byrd have done."

In those days, multiple-choice tests were not that common. We were expected to write out most of our answers in detail. That is just what I did on all of the questions, on all of the tests. During the last big three-hour Tennessee National Guard test, I wrote pages and pages of detailed answers, including gratuitous diagrams and sketches. In those days, people would say I was a pretty good "drawer."

The final exam was on a Saturday morning. I was still writing and drawing diagrams well beyond lunchtime and I wasn't alone. Those of us still working were not told to hurry it up. Mr. Rising was a wonderful, kind and pleasant man. He told all of us to take as much time as we liked and mentioned several times that he would stay through the whole afternoon if anyone of us needed the extra time.

Announcement of the winners was scheduled the following Friday afternoon. That week became one of the longest weeks of my life. When Friday finally came around, the auditorium filled up as we waited for Mr. Rising to walk to the stage and start the meeting.

Boy. Was I ever excited! Mr. Rising started our meeting by introducing someone from the Tennessee National Guard Headquarters in Nashville, who told us that Tennessee was the only state that had a program like ours. As I recall, a few other states quickly followed the Tennessee example over the next few years.

Mr. Rising then added a few more comments and finally said, "Okay, the moment you have all been waiting for is at hand. We will start right from the top." The top scorer's name was called. I hadn't heard it before. It wasn't mine. I didn't think it would be mine.

Mr. Rising called out some more names including a lady's name and then very quickly got to number 5, which didn't happen to be mine either. Neither was number 10. I wasn't surprised because I could see that everyone whose name had been called was a lot older than me. I decided on the spot that, sure enough, I probably wasn't going to win one of those 15 spots.

I was concentrating on being number 13 so I could tell myself that I was just unlucky if I wasn't number 13. As it turned out, I was not number 13, just like I had told myself I wouldn't be.

While Mr. Rising was calling number 14, I gave up. I had worked hard. Dad had always said that working hard is what really counts. If I was persistent, someday I would win... something... sometime... maybe.

I tried not to listen to Mr. Rising anymore. But he said something about the youngest student. Did he say, "Our last winner, number 15, is the youngest... by three or more years and his name is... Mr. Richard E. Evans."

I flew out of the Junior High School auditorium, running towards home. When I reached the porch, Dad met me at our front door and Mom was right behind him. They had heard me yelling from the time I passed Dr. Smith's house. "I won, Dad; I won, Mother," I shouted, "I'm going to learn to fly. I won 50 hours of flying time. I'm going to be a pilot, Dad. I'm going to be an aviator... like 'Lucky Lindy' and Jimmie Doolittle."

———————————

I couldn't have known then, but I would later fly the Atlantic, like "Lucky Lindy," only I would fly it in both directions. My flights were from the States to South America, Africa, Egypt, the European War Theater and England. Most of those flights were combat missions out of North Africa and Italy, attacking targets in Germany, France, Sicily, Italy, and Austria. I would fly the great Boeing Company's B-17 *Flying Fortress* and later, near the end of the war, the Boeing B-29 **Superfortress** across the Pacific from California to General LeMay's bases on Guam, Tinian and Saipan. Even later I would fly B-29s over Japan from General Doolittle's bases on Okinawa until the war came to an abrupt conclusion.

———————————

"Calm down, calm down," Dad said, with a smile. "Tell us what all the excitement is about."

Today as I write these words, my mind flashes back to those early days more than a half a century ago. Tears come to my eyes and tightness to my throat. How many times did my nice dad say to me, always with that smile, "Calm down, calm down, Dick? Now, what's all the excitement about, Son?"

"I won, Dad, I won! I'm going to learn to fly; I'm going to be a pilot," I shouted, still huffing and puffing after my two-mile run. "I was number 15, Mom. I was the last one to win 50 hours of flying time! I didn't think I could win, but I'm going to be a flyer, Mom." I looked right at Mom. I noticed that she did not look at me. Mom was looking at the floor.

Dad put his arm around Mom's shoulder and glanced at me. "Remember, Helen, what we have always said... what we must always do. We must help them learn to do the things they want to do, Helen."

Mr. Rising had instructed me to report at "0730 hours" the following Monday to the flight line at Knoxville's new Municipal Airport. This airport was well positioned to serve Knoxville and the growth-area contiguous to the city. It was located just twenty minutes or so from downtown Knoxville, next door to Maryville, and practically on top of Alcoa, a small, new community named after the Aluminum Company of America. The aluminum company just completed new facilities just across the highway.

"I'll be in my office, just inside the new hangar. You and I will roll our airplane onto the tarmac together. Richard Evans, you will be the first in our first class to fly our new *Piper Cub*. You will be the first in Tennessee to participate in our first-of-a-kind statewide program. I know that you will do very well for I know how hard you have worked to get this far."

Mr. Rising chuckled and added, "I'm counting on you not to go busting up our brand new airplane on its first official flight, okay? You would go down in Tennessee history as being the first student to fly our new aircraft, the first to crash it and, predictably, the first to get washed out of our first training program. Now, you wouldn't want this to happen, would you?"

"Yes," I assured my first IP. "I sure don't want to be first to do any one of those things."

I was the first to arrive at Knoxville's new airport on that Monday morning. However, I failed to arrive at the appointed hour. I was an hour early. I had decided to give myself a little margin since I hitchhiked to the airport from home.

I took the time to look around our new airport. There were a few **Aeronca, Taylorcraft**s and a single **Beechcraft Model 17** *Staggerwing*. The Beechcraft was distinct from the others because it stood much higher off the ground, had two cockpits in tandem, a large radial engine and distinctive staggered wings. The lower wing was attached to the bottom of the fuselage, a foot or so in front of the upper wing.

The *Piper Cub* that I found in a hanger was brand new, a gift from the Department of Aviation of the State of Tennessee. I was proud to help Mr. Rising push it out of the hanger for its first official flight.

My first lesson was "the walk-around inspection," the final visual inspection before climbing aboard. Then, I was checked out on my first pre-flight check list. I read the checklist very carefully item by item. Mr. Rising would do the actual checking and report to me the condition or the setting of each instrument, the controls or whatever it was we were checking. This was my first "checklist"; a few thousand would follow in the years ahead.

Next was the start-up procedure. On the *Piper Cub*, the visual inspection and operating control procedures were quite simple, but those basics were the important starting places for the larger more complex systems I would encounter later. I was on my way. I was going to be a flyer, or, as we later liked to jokingly refer to ourselves... "A fly-boy."

After I soloed and had logged a few hours in the *Piper Cub*, I tackled the Taylorcraft, the Aeronca, the exciting Beechcraft *Staggerwing* and the beautiful, all-metal Luscombe, expanding my horizons with each step.

I wasn't a smart aleck or a wise guy in an airplane. Mr. Rising saw to that. Mr. Rising, whom I never called "Sunny," taught me the full meaning of the word "respect," particularly as it applied to aircraft.

At some time during my USAAC pilot training days, I heard Winston Churchill proclaim in a radio broadcast, "Never in the field of human conflict was so much owed by so many to so few." I have never forgotten England's war-time Prime Minister praising the relatively few British fighter pilots who, initially outnumbered, engaged Hitler's well-trained **Luftwaffe** over the British homeland and eventually turned them about and chased them back to Germany.

We in the United States can never thank Britain enough for giving us the time that we needed to get ourselves trained, equipped, positioned here and "over there." "Over there" was a well-known World War One expression meaning across the Atlantic where all the fighting was taking place. "Over there," as we would all eventually learn, was the origin of perhaps the greatest threat to the civilized world since the beginning of time.

I was always short on the money I needed to rent airplanes to accumulate the required number of flight hours. I soon discovered, however, that chums of mine at the University of Tennessee were very willing to pay the rental fees on the *Cubs,* Aeronca, Luscombe and the Beechcraft *Staggerwing,* which were available to me for training, if I would take them sightseeing over Knoxville, Mt. LeConte in the Smokies and other interesting places.

On one such flight in the 2-seater Luscombe, I embarrassed myself. And, I learned a valuable lesson... very early.

My best chum in those days was Joe Brown, who said he would buy the gas if I would fly him from Knoxville to Tri-City, an airport in the northeast corner of Tennessee serving Bristol, Kingsport and Johnson City. It would be my first "cross-country" flight and my first crack-up.

Joe and I had a great trip up the Tennessee Valley, following the Tennessee River and the Appalachian Mountain chain. I found the Tri-City Airport to be quite close to Bristol and made a small course correction in that direction to take us to the airport.

Good-buddy Joe, at that moment, advised me his business was actually in Kingsport, which was coming into focus directly ahead of us.

Full of confidence (actually, over-confidence, plus a generous helping of bravado), I boasted, "Not to worry, Joe, my man, I will locate a place to land down there somewhere near Kingsport. I will land, let you out and will continue on to the Tri-City Airport, which is in view northwest of our present position, right now. At Tri-City, I'll have lunch and await your arrival. We can take off for Knoxville at 1400 hours." Joe was delighted.

I advised Joe that we were in luck. We were directly over the Kingsport Country Club, there were no golfers in view on the entire course at that hour in the morning, and I would be able to land on the No. 9 fairway towards the clubhouse into a good breeze that would shorten our landing roll. I would have room and time to taxi back and takeoff into the wind before any golfers showed up on the fairway. Joe thought this was a great plan.

On landing, I noted I was getting a rather strong cross wind from my left. I deftly lowered my left wing, turning the Luscombe into the wind, keeping me aligned with the No. 9 fairway with the expectation of quickly straightening out and leveling off at the moment of landing. What can I say? It was a superior landing. I had done a perfect job.

Joe jumped out of the airplane and headed for the clubhouse. After taxiing back to the far end of the 9th fairway, turning around and again facing the clubhouse, I "gave her the gun" and was accelerating nicely, and expecting to lift off, at any second.

My luck was holding; still no golfers in view on the fairways. The Luscombe was a delightful, two-place aircraft with side-by-side seating and plenty of power for its size. Heading into a quite-stiff breeze, it jumped quickly into the air. It also just as quickly started sliding to my right across the fairway as the just-noted stiff breeze was pushing it.

No problem for the experienced aviator I had decided I was. I just steepened up my turn into the wind. However, I had not yet learned that this maneuver would cost me some lift. Suddenly, I realized that I was rising at a slower rate than expected because the fairway was sloping upward ahead of me.

I did not panic and I did not stall out. *Au contraire*. Exercising great skill, I was thinking to myself, I got over the hill in a flash. I had failed however, to take note of the good-sized tree that was coming over this same hill from the opposite direction to greet me.

This tree's branches caught my right wing, causing the Luscombe's left wing to tilt upward. Quickly losing the little altitude that I once had gained, the plane bounced to the ground not as a smooth ride. My unusual landing would be recognized by the torn and gashed fairway surface from the "three-pointer" tricycle landing gear. The branches of the tree cushioned the shock of the tree-assisted landing, which the aircraft made on its own, on the fairway, without any help from its fearless, youthful, and stupid jerk-of-a-pilot!

My lap belt held my lap in position. It did not keep my forehead from swinging to my left, towards the "whisky compass," which in those days was suspended on wires above the instrument panel where the pilot could glance up and see it easily. Also, where an adventuresome pilot might in emergency circumstances try to knock it out of his line-of-sight, with his head.

My initial emotion was not fear but gross embarrassment. I realized immediately that I had made a complete jerk of myself. The damage to the fairway was far more than a divot. The injury to the Luscombe was minor, and I was able to get it back to a position for take-off without further incident.

The damage to my head was not serious, but the blood on my shirtfront could only be described as unequivocal evidence of my hubris. Good pilots don't bleed and approach for landing at the same time. The major damage was to my ego. The word "disastrous" comes to mind. But, it may have saved my life. I would never be so foolish and stupidly cocky again. Flying was a huge responsibility, and the rules were to be followed... always.

The lesson learned, "follow aviation rules to the nth degree" remained with me during all the twenty years that I would continue to fly airplanes during World War II, the Korean War and the Cold War. Those learned lessons were the basics that supported the wisdom, experience-based intuition and flight precautions that helped me survive 54 missions over German-occupied territory, one mission over Japan and my flying career as a jet pilot. There was some luck, too, but some say, "You make your own luck."

I had successfully combined my first real cross-country flight, my first landing on a golf course, and my first tree-assisted landing and my first bleeding head wound—all in a single morning. I believed this achievement had not been equaled in all of aviation history. What can I say?

Surprisingly, my slight miscalculation did not destroy my flying career, nor did it wipe out my list of student passengers at UT, who wanted some "stick-and-rudder time" at reduced rates regardless of the obvious risks of flying with me. Actually, Joe became my first, regular half-fare-paying-passenger to venture back into the sky with me.

The incident made me famous. Actually, infamous in the small valley in Tennessee where I grew up, which was rapidly becoming identified with The Tennessee Valley Authority (TVA), and the then newly-designated "Great Smoky Mountains National Park." The incident humbled me, and I would never take those chances again.

January 19, 1939 was not an important date to Robert E. Lee, the celebrated Commander of the Confederate Army in the US Civil War, although it would have been General Lee's 132nd birthday. Of course, he was not on hand to celebrate. General Lee had been dead for the last 69 years.

Still, many young men born and raised in the South would want to remember and honor the great Civil War Commander on the 132nd anniversary of his birth. I, too, being a proud son of the South, was particularly pleased and proud to celebrate General Lee's birthday, as it was also mine, but only my 20th.

I had determined that January 19, 1939 would be my personal **D-Day** (decision day) for deciding to volunteer immediately for flight training in the then-new Air Corps of the US Army or to delay until my junior and senior years were completed at UT.

Thousands of my contemporaries were facing this same decision, which would have an enormous effect on the rest of our lives. I opted to apply immediately for flight training in the Army Air Corps' "Flying Cadet" program.

In mid-year of 1939, I reported, as ordered by the War Department, to the Army Flight Surgeon's Office at Candler Field in Atlanta, Georgia, which was easy hitchhiking distance from Knoxville.

The word was out that one would be a shoe-in if he passed his "Schneider," an essential heart test given by an Army flight surgeon. Prospective recruits had to run for a specified time at a specified rate on a treadmill and a few minutes later were given the test.

My first reading after running the specified rate for the specified time caused a very nice, fatherly-type flight surgeon to put his hand on my shoulder, look me in the eyes and say, "Son, I know you have a good heart. Otherwise, at the rate it is now beating, it would burst. It is going so fast; I can't get a decent reading with my instruments. So, here's what we're going to do. I am going to lunch. You are going to pass up lunch, stay here in my office, spread yourself out on this bunk and have a nice rest. It would be great if you could just go to sleep. Don't worry about a thing. I will wake you up after I get a good reading on your heart, which I already know is just fine."

It was rumored, back in those pre-WWII days, that medical authorities were arguing over the authenticity of the "Schneider Heart Test" as employed by the Army Air Corps medics. I learned that my story was typical.

Thanks to the Atlanta doctor, I was accepted and was ordered by The War Department to depart my home in Knoxville on December 26, 1939, signed a contract December 27 at Fort Oglethorpe, Georgia, and reported for duty in the US Army Air Corps at Love Field, Dallas, Texas, on the afternoon of December 28.

As I remember those days before the end of 1939, I realized that joining the USAAC was truly a pivotal time in my life. I could have continued my education and graduated from the University of Tennessee, but I wanted to be part of the war in defense of the long-standing principles of freedom. Maybe, too, the Eagle Scout Oath: "Duty to God and country, Duty to other people and Duty to self" had some influence on my being.

18.2 *Dick first learns to fly the "Piper Cub", McGhee Tyson Airport, Knoxville, TN*

18.3 *Dick marches in the Armistice Day Parade, 1936, Knoxville, TN*

18.4 *Dick wins the Morgan Medal for best-drilled cadet*

18.5 *McGhee Tyson Airport, Knoxville, TN*

18.6 *Dick flies the Beechcraft Model 17 "Staggerwing"*

18.7 *ROTC
training exercises
are not easy*

18.8 *Dick enjoys
a rest during
ROTC training*

19.1 *Knoxville High School* (McClung Historical Collection)

CHAPTER 19

KNOXVILLE'S PRINCIPLED PRINCIPAL

My dad was a tad strict; some folks would say.
But it wasn't Dad's fault that he grew up that way.
Dad's dad, you see, was an itinerant minister,
It was preordained that Dad be just a tad sinister!
My dad became the Principal of "Old Knox High."
Still, to his four sons, Dad was an all-right guy.
Why, before Dad would swat us, he would always say?
"Son, it hurts me to whap you on the rear this way."
On just such an occasion, I once risked an affront.
I chortled, "Better, dear Dad, the rear than the front."
"Not-to-worry," Dad responded, "Your dad's not daft.
He understands the difference between fore, and aft."

Richard Eager

This book is dedicated to a giving dad, who knew how to dole out nice things, like an occasional character-building thump on a son's lower backside. My dad, bespectacled, church-going, scholarly and soft-spoken, was by all accounts a gentleman. He could, of course, have lapses. Periodically he might say to one or more of his four sons, "I see that it has become necessary for me to exercise some discipline around here."

Dad would, indeed, exercise some discipline around our house by causing an old razor strap to swing a few times in the direction of one or more of his errant sons. Dad always had some nice comment to make. He would pat the head of his wayward son, smile and say, "In the exercise of discipline, we have a balanced program. My sons get the discipline... I get the exercise."

Dad would most always end his "disciplinary sessions" with a smile. His sons, however, would not fully appreciate, as Dad put it, his "propensity for pleasantries and light jocularity."

Dad did not have to exercise his razor strap on my brothers or me all that often. I am certain the family gentry was never in jeopardy. When Dad took a few swings in the direction of one of his bent-over sons, it might have appeared that he was swinging quite hard, but he really wasn't. Proof? That's easy... Dad never left scars, as he might put it, "of any significance." I once borrowed Mom's hand mirror to check out Dad's work. No blood, no scars. But some red stripes? Well, yes, I'm afraid so. There was considerable residual heat.

What Dad did do with some effectiveness was to keep that old strap handy above the door in the room my brother Stewart and I shared for a number of years. It was always within Dad's reach and never out of Stewart's and my sight. We could see it residing there above the door when we got up to carry our papers in the morning, when we returned to dress for school, and, yes, when we went to bed at night.

I don't recall, however, that Dad's old strap was ever moved to Tom and John's room. I think the punishment of choice during the formative years of my two younger brothers shifted from some never-that-bad derriere swats to a prohibition against driving the family car. Younger brother Tom opined that, in his view, Dad's up-dated "more humane" procedure was just as effective.

———————————

In his early '20s, Dad became the principal of Woodstock High in Woodstock, Illinois, just 30 miles north of where Chicago's O'Hare Airport would later be built. Dad told me that the first time he saw Mom, she was singing contralto in the choir of Woodstock's First Methodist Church. The first time Mom saw Dad was three days later at choir practice.

Dad said that he was sitting quietly and facing forward in the seat beside Mom when the choir director tapped his music stand with his baton and said in a strong, clear voice, "I am pleased to announce that we have a new tenor, whose name is Mr. William Ernest Evans. Mr. Evans, by the way, is also the new principal of our Woodstock High School. Would everyone please rise and welcome, Mr. William Ernest Evans."

Dad told me later that Mom's welcome was particularly welcome. He and Mom were beginning to sing along together quite nicely at the Woodstock Church and elsewhere. But Grandpa Stewart, without warning, packed up his family members and moved them lock, stock and Mom to the Tennessee Valley and the Great Smokies. "Considerably before the Smokies became great or even started smoking," Dad added with a smile.

Dad said to me, "Dick, I quite suddenly ceased to find the Woodstock choir challenging. Without your Mom's booming contralto voice, it just wasn't the same around Woodstock." Dad then went on to say that his solution to the problem was to transfer his musical affiliation from Woodstock's Methodist Church to Knoxville's First Methodist Church. Dad had made some inquiries. The Knoxville church was, coincidentally, as was the case in Woodstock, in need of a tenor.

"You should have seen your mother's face, Dick," Dad continued, "when she glanced around at choir practice and again found me in the seat beside her. She was radiant. If I had waited until Sunday, the folks down in the front row would have felt the heat from your mother's beautiful, blushing face."

I asked Dad how he could afford to give up his new principal job at Woodstock and come to Knoxville. He looked at me with his eyes shining and then laughed that he had always wanted to be the Principal of Knox High and he preferred to sing in church choirs that had strong contraltos.

"But, Dad," I questioned, "You have always told us that when you got to Knoxville, they already had a principal for their high school." Dad answered, "Well yes, that's true, Dick. I signed up, mid-term, to teach Chemistry and Woodworking at Knoxville High School to give them a second chance to hire me when the fall semester came around. Actually, they didn't appoint me Principal until the following semester when my first full year as a Chemistry teacher was concluded. When it looked as if they were going to keep me around for a while, and after a few more choir practices, your mother decided to keep me around for the rest of our lives."

(Dear reader, my eyes seem to be leaking again and the image on my computer screen is becoming quite blurred. One moment, please, as I regain my composure and confess that this problem of mine seems to be reoccurring with greater frequency as I grow older and look back through the years and recall the very good judgment exercised by me in selecting my dear mother and my thoughtful and considerate father.)

Dad continued his story. "In a short time, I bought our old place at 3036 Magnolia Avenue in Knoxville where my sons, all five of you, were born." Dad smiled and then added, "After the first year I gave up singing in our church choir, became an elder in Knoxville's First Methodist Church and remained on the job for life at your mother's side."

That's how my dad came to be known as the "Perennial Principal" of Knoxville's firsthand, for many years, only senior high school. Dad was content and happy to be retained in his job for 40-plus years. I remember that the people in Knoxville referred to Dad as "an institution," which I also remember I didn't understand until I enrolled in Dad's institution myself.

Come to think of it, my mom also became an "institution" in Knoxville. In short time, she became the choir director at "First Church" and remained so for about the same period of time that Dad was the Principal at Knoxville High School. Dad opined that neither Mom nor he ever received a stipend for their various church responsibilities during all the years that they were singing and working together.

Given an opening, Mom would always add wistfully, "During that period of time, I also gave your dad five sons." I think Mom also gave Dad the full responsibility for never giving Mom a daughter for whom she would have made lovely dresses on the same dining room table where she made all of her own dresses. My mother told me once that she made her own clothes because she did not consider sewing up the knees of her four boys' trousers once a week "as being very creative."

I never learned exactly why Mom did it. But one Sunday she announced while we were eating Sunday dinner that she was going to make a suit for one of her sons... the one named Richard Ernest. I was stunned! I still do not know just why Mom wanted to sew a suit for me. What would my friends say when they learned that I wasn't wearing a "store-bought" suit and when they learned that I was wearing a "home-made" suit that my mother had made for me at her sewing machine on our dining room table?

Dad understood. He tried to talk Mom out of it. Then he told me his efforts on my behalf were to no avail. He then tried to talk me into it. He said that I wasn't getting a "homemade" suit; I was getting a tailored suit, by a very professional tailor.

I never did learn who tipped them off. The first time I wore my new suit to church, every woman in the place was feeling the cloth and commenting on the fine stitching that held my suit together. Mother stayed longer than usual after church to respond to questions. I thought I would die. I was never so embarrassed in my whole life.

Dad saw what was going on. He didn't make a move to help me with all those ladies who wanted to feel my new suit. After our regular Sunday lunch, which was really Sunday dinner at lunchtime in those days, Dad took me aside and said he wanted to have a talk with me. What Dad told me was that I should not be talking about "my homemade suit," but about my "tailor-made suit." I followed his advice and was soon bragging about my new suit that my mom, who was a tailor, had made for me.

After thirty years, the people in Knoxville would say, "Why, you know, practically every livin' soul in the City of Knoxville has gone to school under Prof Evans." Most everybody has heard his wife, Helen's, deep, arresting, contralto voice on Sundays in the First Methodist Church choir." Dad would often add, depending on his audience, "Actually you wouldn't have to be in the church. You could hear 'Hellie' if you were in the neighborhood."

When I have allowed my thoughts to stretch back three-quarters of a century, my mom and my dad always come to mind. I am sure a few folks in Knoxville perceived my dad as being a tad stiff and proper. I don't believe, however, that anyone in his family ever thought of him that way.

I believe Prof Evans's family knew him as being warm, fair, friendly, sympathetic and very big on Christian principles as characterized by the Ten Commandments, the Golden Rule and the Twelve Boy Scout Laws. Otherwise, Dad was a perfectly normal fellow... not square at all.

———————————

Miss MacDougal, my towering, controlling, spinsterish, Biology teacher, was my favorite teacher in high school. But there was a point when I was not her favorite student. It wasn't a youthful crush or anything like that, but I really liked and respected Miss MacDougal very much. I looked forward to going to her classes and enjoyed learning biology a whole lot.

An unusual thing happened in Miss MacDougal's biology class, related in a way to her subject. Now, it is not that difficult, really, to discuss what happened in Miss MacDougal's class once you get what happened there out into the open. As I think of it now, it was out in the open right from the start.

Everybody knows that you're not supposed to do the thing that actually happened in Miss MacDougal's classroom if you can help it. Particularly when the doors and the windows are closed tight to keep out a heavy rainstorm that happened to be in progress one day in Miss MacDougal's Biology class. Sometimes things "just happen." A boy who still claims that he was innocent of wrongdoing will be caught up in a nasty situation.

Nobody in class actually heard anything. But everybody in class, including Miss MacDougal... particularly Miss MacDougal, had no doubt that somebody in our hermetically-sealed biology classroom had inadvertently, I presumed, passed a *modicum of flatus.*

It was very likely not the quantity, but the quality, of the disturbance that caused a small problem to be blown out of proportion and in the direction of Miss MacDougal.

Funny thing, everybody in class except Miss MacDougal knew exactly who it was. And, very likely, many also thought that if it was absolutely necessary and couldn't be avoided, where better than in a biology class?

Whatever. Suddenly, Miss MacDougal seemed to leap up from her chair, come around from behind her desk and immediately start sweeping her biology class with her eyes. I guessed that she was looking for a clue. Whatever it was she thought she was looking for, she was sure she had found it in the third row from the front on the window side where I usually sat and was, in fact, sitting on that particular morning.

My classmates told me later that Miss MacDougal was actually pointing towards the door before she could get the words out. What she was finally able to say was, "Richard Evans, you get yourself up and out of that seat, through that door and on your way to the Principal's Office without any delay or small talk. Now. Move! Immediately!"

Ignoring my pleading eyes, Miss MacDougal again shouted, "No. No discussion! I don't want to talk to you. I just want you on your feet, through that door, and out of my classroom... now!"

When Miss MacDougal found her voice and had yelled, "out of here," I had already gotten up and gotten started to get out of *there*. When I found myself alone in the hall, I was the one who was speechless. I was dumbfounded.

I still am unable to remember the trip down the long hall and down the wide stairs to the Principal's office. To this day, I am unable to remember how I got down there. I am certain that I was in shock for the first time in my life. I had heard about shock in the Boy Scouts and understood that at first your face gets really red, then it quickly turns white. I couldn't see myself; so I couldn't be sure.

I sort of came to, I think, when I got to Dad's office and first saw Miss Webb, Dad's secretary. "Dick, why aren't you in class? Dick, you look as white as a ghost. Is there something wrong with you? Are you feeling all right, Dick? You don't look very good to me! Say something, anything... Dick what has happened to you?"

I remember very clearly that my mouth opened with each of Miss Webb's questions, but I wasn't able to get in sync with her questions to get any sound out at all. She finally slowed down, "You look a little pale, Dick; come into my office and sit down. I'll get you a glass of cold water. You can tell me what's going on."

I remember how very nice Miss Webb always was to me. I had just come to KHS, mid-term, and had just started classes. But I had been in her office many times, waiting to catch a ride home with Dad. I think my problem was that I had never used the word "fart" when ladies were present, and as I recall, Miss MacDougal hadn't told us about "flatus" yet. I flat didn't have the vocabulary to explain to Miss Webb just what had happened in Miss MacDougal's Biology class.

When I finally was able to get across to Miss Webb what had happened in class, she very quickly left the room, using the door into Dad's private office. I could hear her talking to Dad, and in a few minutes, I could tell that both Miss Webb and my dad were trying hard not to laugh. At that moment, I didn't think that what had happened in Miss MacDougal's Biology class was at all funny. It was a few more minutes before Miss Webb was able to come back through her private doorway to tell me that Dad wanted to talk with me right away.

Dad didn't waste any time. I closed the door to my father's office behind me, like I had done many times. Dad got right to the point. "Just one thing, Dick. Did you or did you not actually fart in Miss MacDougal's Biology class? If you did, why didn't you try to hold it back? Or bolt from the room? Or something? Why under the sun did you just sit there and let it go?"

When I didn't answer right away while trying to figure out which question to tackle first, Dad added" ...and how much noise did it make?" (Funny the things we remember for half a century. I believe I sort of stalled out, while wondering how come my dad could be so interested in the specifics of a fart... him being a principal and all.)

Finally, I was able to get out a partial answer, "Dad, I didn't do it. I would die before I would fart in Miss MacDougal's Biology class, Dad. I would 'hold it back' for the full hour. I like Miss MacDougal and Biology is my best subject."

Dad didn't seem able to talk for a minute, so I went on, "Dad, Miss MacDougal is my favorite teacher. I'd burst before I'd fart in her class. Dad, everybody in class knew who farted except Miss MacDougal. She didn't ask me or anybody else who did it; she just pointed towards the door and said for me to see how fast I could get through it. Dad, she declared that I shouldn't stop until I got to your office. Here I am, Dad."

Dad smiled and then chuckled a couple times before saying, "Okay, okay, I believe you, Son. I know you couldn't make this story up. If someone really has to fart, I would presume a Biology class might be as appropriate a place as any." Dad chuckled at his own joke; and I chuckled back, so that Dad would know that I got his joke.

"Okay, Dick, here's what we're going to do. We are not going to embarrass Miss MacDougal. Miss MacDougal has made a mistake; but, Son, she is one of my finest teachers. I've heard you say, Dick, that you like her and that you like her classes." I responded, "Yes, Dad, Miss MacDougal tries very hard to make Biology interesting for all of us."

"Okay, okay." Dad resumed. "So as not to embarrass Miss MacDougal, Son, I suggest that you just disappear; get out in the halls and wonder around, which all you kids seem to want to do. When the next bell rings, go to your next class. This is your opportunity. Have a good time."

"When you go back to your Biology class on Monday, don't bring up the subject of farting. Do you understand?" Dad smiled, tried hard not to laugh, then gave up. He laughed so heartily that he had to get his handkerchief out and wipe his glasses off.

I remember how Dad would sometimes have to get his handkerchief out to wipe off his glasses when one of us had done something boyishly funny. I recall how happy his four sons were when Dad would laugh really hard at something. Particularly, as Mom would say, if it was "a little off-color." To the best I can recall, nothing around our house was ever very much off-color.

With my dad's plan in mind, I did not return to Biology class and did enjoy "hanging around" in the halls just like Dad said I would. When I went back to Miss MacDougal's class the next Monday, I didn't bring up the subject of farting nor did she. Neither did any of my classmates, all of whom knew exactly who it was that actually let go... on that rainy day.

I'm sure that Miss MacDougal learned, in time, that she had made a mistake and that Dad had let her off the hook. I liked Miss MacDougal and Biology even more than before. I could tell that she liked me, too.

Years later, in 1955, when Dad finally retired, the City of Knoxville did a nice thing for a tired, but happy, old man. They declared a city wide "Honor Evans Day" and planned a "This Is Your Life, Professor Evans" program. Dad was "front page" in both Knoxville's morning *Journal* and its evening *News Sentinel*, both of which I had "carried papers" for for many years.

"This is Your Life" programs were just being aired on radio for the first time and were very popular. We heard a lot of them on our Atwater Kent radio. I recall hearing that Assistant Principal, Johnnie Walker, was very pleased to learn that Dad was going to retire.

Mr. Walker offered his full support to the celebration of Dad's retirement, at last.

Dad and Knoxville High School ran out of steam about the same time. The tired old building was itself retired about four years or so ahead of Dad. I visited our old school one other time when the last class had marched out. The vacant halls, the empty, dusty auditorium and the gym... all seemed smaller than I had remembered those spaces. Remembering the school brought back a flood of memories... and a few tears.

Although Knoxville had several new high schools, the City Council decided that a "This Is Your Life" program, honoring Dad should be held in the old combination study hall-and-auditorium in the unoccupied old facility. This old hall with a balcony and two-story windows was where Dad had held "Assembly" every Wednesday for forty-one years.

Mom said, "There isn't much we can do for that old hall of ours except give it a good dusting and drape some blue and white, twisted paper across the windows and the balcony." That's exactly what a group of KHS alumni did.

On "Honor Evans Night," the old auditorium looked quite spiffy. With the opening of the curtain and some music from the KHS band, the Master of Ceremony walked Dad up onto the stage and sat him down, facing the audience in a beautiful leather chair in the middle of the stage.

Observing the scene from the front row, Mom exclaimed, "Most of the folks living in Knoxville have walked up on that old stage to get their diplomas from Pop; now it's Pop's turn. He's up there now to receive his diploma... from everyone who was crowded into the auditorium."

Special guests, whom Dad would be asked to identify by their voices, were seated backstage behind the curtain. They would greet Dad from back there; then Dad would try to guess who they were. In practically all cases, Dad could identify them correctly.

I recall that Paul LeBailey had come down from Ohio. Dad hadn't seen Paul for half a century, not since they had played basketball together at Oberlin College. Dad, in his senior year, had been both the team captain and the coach at the small college. Dad recognized his old college chum's voice immediately; then, promptly lost his own. Mom said later, "When Paul came out from behind that curtain, things were starting to get a little sloppy all over Dad's old study hall."

Another visitor backstage was a Colonel who had served in the Army's Second World War Flying Corps and who had "re-upped" for the Korean War in the then newly established, US Air Force. Serving on General Curtis LeMay's Strategic Air Command (SAC) Staff in Omaha, this visitor had flown alone to Knoxville in a Lockheed F-80 *Shooting Star*, the first military jet aircraft produced in quantity in the United States.

When this visitor's turn came, the announcer said, "Professor Evans, your next visitor wanted so much to be here tonight that he flew to Knoxville from Omaha after work, arriving just an hour ago at our McGhee-Tyson Airport. He tells me that he must fly back to Omaha tonight... something about briefing General LeMay the first thing in the morning on the B-58 program. He told me the B-58 is a delta-winged, Mach 2 aircraft being manufactured by General Dynamics in Fort Worth, Texas."

This happy visitor then said from behind the curtain, "Good evening, Professor. I am honored to be a part of this distinguished group, gathered here from different parts of the country, to be on Knox High's old stage with you tonight. Funny thing, I keep getting this déjà vu feeling that I have been here on this stage before."

My dad chuckled and said, "I know that voice... that's one of my sons, the one whom his friends call 'Richard Eager.'"

A few more surprise visitors greeted Dad. When there were no more smiling, eager faces to greet the professor from behind the curtain, the program continued with the cheerleaders leading the audience in a few "yells."

Just before everybody stood up to sing the school fight song to end the program, George Dempster, Knoxville's mayor for many years and also the inventor of the world-famous "Dempster Dumpster," got to his feet to say a few remarks.

His Honor, the Mayor, spoke of his personal association with Dad through the years... how he had visited the Evans' family cottage at Elkmont in the Great Smokies, had hiked up Mt. LeConte, had fished for rainbow trout in Jakes Creek and Little River. He described the camaraderie they enjoyed, pitching horseshoes for many happy hours in front of the old Evans cottage, which our dad had built "with his own hands" in the early '20s.

With a straight face, His Honor, the Mayor, told Dad that it would be necessary for him to delay a few minutes after the celebration to help clean up the stage. Dad looked a bit unsettled, but His Honor continued, "In particular, Ernest, you and your four sons are going to have to haul this leather chair, which you have been occupying the entire evening, off this stage and to your car. You're going to have to load it on your car and take it home with you."

Observing Dad's puzzled expression, his good friend, the Mayor, smiled and added, "Ernest, this leather chair is yours. A gift from a lot of very nice Knox High kids, whom you and I have watched grow up... kids whom you, Ernest, have helped many, many Knoxville families bring up."

While everyone in the auditorium was observing Dad's confusion and reaching for their handkerchiefs there was dead silence. Suddenly they were all on their feet clapping and cheering... making more noise than Dad would ever have permitted in his assembly hall.

Then everyone in the old Study Hall stood and sang the Trojan fight song.

Suddenly it was all over. The forty-one-year reign of Professor Evans at Knoxville High School, including four years as Principal at the new East Hight School, had come to an end. This time the venerable professor had, indeed, as Mom had suggested earlier, received his diploma.

Professor Evans and the lady, whom he had stalked in Woodstock, Illinois, and had then followed to Tennessee almost fifty years ago, walked, arm-in-arm, out of Knox High's "Assembly

Hall" accompanied by their four sons. The old hall had held its last assembly, its last student play and last graduation ceremony. The old KHS auditorium and study hall was empty and silent. It would never be put to its intended use again. It would soon be knocked down, its bricks arranged in stacks and sold.

The KHS auditorium was at the north end of the school, a city-block from the school's front door. This section of the building had not been occupied since the school's closing one year earlier and it was a rather long walk for Dad, down the dusty old hall to the front door. He wasn't thinking of the walk; he couldn't get over his beautiful, new leather chair.

I recall thinking at the time, I would never, ever forget this moment, Mom and Dad, with their four sons, all of whom had participated in World War II, walking arm-in-arm silently down that long, darkened hallway. Yes, together Dad, Mom, Stewart, Tom, John and I walked arm-in-arm down that darkened hallway... full of memories.

Large, clean spaces on the otherwise dingy, time-darkened walls marked the positions of the portraits of the US Presidents that had hung there for four decades. This image of the darkened, picture-less hallway would remain with me forever.

I was sure that each member of our family was thinking that this would be our last walk together down this squeaky old hallway in the company of Knox High's respected, enduring principal... and it was.

As we neared the front door of the building, brothers Tom and John moved out ahead of us to block Mom and Dad's view. Normally, one could look down the broad front steps to a curved driveway that stretched to the street corners on either side.

This semi-circular drive enclosed a wide, grassy area with a statue at its center, an imposing, twenty-foot, cast-iron likeness of a World War I "Doughboy" (an enduring nickname for American soldiers) with his rifle in his left hand and his right, clenched fist raised over his head. This 1921 doughboy, portraying the spirit of Tennessee, "The Volunteer State," stood before a 55-foot obelisk of East Tennessee marble, which looked as if it might be about a tenth-scale copy of the Washington Monument in Washington DC.

As my younger brothers, Tom and John, held open the large double, front doors, my older and taller brother, Stewart, and I maneuvered Dad into a position behind Mom where Dad could not see out front.

Mom and Dad, now alone, were a dozen steps above a scene unfamiliar to Mom, but one that Dad had seen many times at periodic fire drills.

Mom and Dad's audience of KHS students, teachers, families and friends had not gone home. They were waiting for Dad and Mom to arrive at the large landing at the top of the steps. When my brothers and I guided Mom and Dad through the large, wide doors and out onto the landing, it was clear to them that the audience that had filled our school auditorium had not gone home.

They were all gathered together in front of the school to honor their old principal... one more time.

Dad was the first to notice a lone automobile parked in front of the crowd near the bottom of the stairs. Dad quickly recognized his old, horse-shoe-tossing friend, Knoxville's Mayor, standing beside an open door on the driver's side. His Honor was beckoning Dad to come down the steps and take a drive in Mom and Dad's brand-new Buick sedan, a graduation present from the City of Knoxville to Professor Evans and his wife, Helen, the beloved mother and father of Stewart, Dick, Tom and John Evans.

Wouldn't you know! It was one of those, brand-new, spiffy, two-toned jobs. The two tones were, you guessed it, blue and white, Knox High and Dad's old school colors.

19.8 Dick and his mother, Helen

19.7 *Dick and his father, "Pop"*

19.4 *Dick's father moves to Knoxville to follow his future bride, Helen*

19.5 *Helen, Dick's mother, the future bride*

19.6 *Helen, the expert seamstress, modeling one of her own creations*

19.7 *The Knoxville High School alums and friends gather to honor Principal, William E. Evans, 1955*

19.8 A gift to the principled principal for "Honor Evans Day"

20.1 *Cold mornings before a mission, Foggia, Italy*

CHAPTER 20
MERRY CHRISTMAS VENEZIA

SALUTARI VENEZIA

Our target the wharf, on the Lagoon of Venice.
Its use by the Nazis had made it a menace.
Supplies for the Axis intercepted here,
Could shorten the war... bring an end to fear.

On a southwest axis, I started our run.
It wasn't for glory; it was a job to be done.
Axis bombs and bullets, flowing south from this place,
Yanks and Brits in the south would face.

But, it wasn't to be, at least not on this day,
No bombardiers would shout that their bombs were away!
The words transmitted from the bombardier's bay
Were that clouds obscured the target that day.

The formation leader, with much to remember,
Remembers well the day... twenty-five December.
Venice was not bombed that Christmas Day,
It's been nice to remember, it happened this way.

Soon the thrust of the War was quickly shifted,
And, Venezia's name from the bomb list was lifted.
I will never forget how Fate dealt its hand.
No bombs on Venice did ever land.

Richard Eager

It was 0530 hours. It was bleak, cold and just beginning to get light at San Severo, Italy, 25 miles north of our recently acquired air depot at the Foggia Main Airdrome. San Severo is 85 miles north of the pleasant Adriatic town of Bari, where General Doolittle had wisely chosen to locate his seaside military headquarters following the move of the B-17s and B-24s from North Africa to Italy.

At San Severo, the crews of the 99th Bomb Group promptly got to their feet as Colonel Upthegrove entered the briefing tent. Despite the early morning wake-up call and morning chill, I was sure most who were on hand were pleased to rise from their seats to show their respect for their esteemed Group Commander.

Colonel Upthegrove quickly announced the "Target of the Day." Everyone assigned to today's mission had earlier received preliminary briefings in smaller groups, comprising their own special ties, and already knew the target for that winter day was Udine and the alternates, harbors near the timeless city of Venice.

Venice... *Venezia*! The ancient, beautiful, and exotic Italian city of canals with its fabled history, its monumental, irreplaceable relics and works of art had not been on our target list before. I was not sure why the aircrews of the 99th Bomb Group, which had assembled for this early morning briefing, had a sentimental objection to bombing Venice but clearly, we did.

Was it because so many Americans were natives of Italy before coming to America? Was it because so many of us, who were Welsh, Scottish, or German, had found their Italian neighbors in the states to be such family-loving, hard-working, and pleasant people? Was it because Italian girls were so exciting and had such beautiful dark eyes, exotic, ebony-black hair and more?

"Listen up, Richard Eager. You are the bloody formation leader today. There just might be some questions for you. You are to lead a force of 370 flight crews in 37 B-17s, armed with 13 Browning M2 .50-caliber machine guns per plane with a total of 148 tons of high explosive bombs. And you are going to lead them wherever you are told.

"Your mission is to knock out the extensive port facilities at Udine and further down the coast near Venice, which have been commandeered by Hitler's logistic types who are transporting men, guns, ammo and fuel from Austria to the Italian front through the Venice seaport."

Our formal briefing was completed and those of us scheduled to make the trip were trucked to our assigned aircraft. We stowed our personal gear at our respective combat stations and performed final inspections of our flying machines and our on-board equipment.

When everyone was aboard and the doors secured behind them, we all took our respective positions in the pilot's compartment, in the bombardier's office (forward and downstairs), in the radio compartment (aft of the side-by-side bomb bays) and midship where the ball turret, waist gun and tail gun operators were stationed.

The top turret gunner and ranking enlisted airman aboard also served as our chief in-flight engineer. He would position himself on the flight deck, between the pilot and the co-pilot positions for startup and takeoff, making himself available to assist the two pilots in the operation and control of the many different aircraft systems.

Upon entering the combat zone en route to the target, the gunners would methodically unstow their weapons, re-check the loading of their ammo belts, position boxes of spare ammo close by, secure themselves at or inside their respective stations, and fire a few rounds to "check their action."

With all the necessary maintenance, servicing, briefing, loading of fuel, oxygen, bombs, ammo, maps, food, water, and equipment accomplished, the flight crew with their doors secured behind them had nothing to do, but to watch their wrist watches as the seconds ticked away.

Finally, the big hand on the formation leader's watch would reach the specified "start-engine time." He would then raise his left thumb visible to both his co-pilot beside him and his ground crew chief in view out his left window. He would then nod his head, up and down, one time.

The co-pilot would then activate the start-engine switch on the No. 1 engine. With No. 1

driving the on-board power generator, the pilot would signal his ground crew chief to disconnect ground power.

Engine startup was always a special never-to-be-forgotten moment for my fellow combat air crewman and for me. I was always impressed when the B-17s roared to life preparatory to a combat mission.

The silence that had pervaded the airfield would suddenly be shattered, as first the formation leader's single engine, then another and another would roar to life. In a very few minutes, the entire area would be overwhelmed by the sound of Wright Cyclone Model R-1820-97 9-cylinder engines. Only when a combat mission is beginning, will all four aircraft squadrons, constituting a B-17 group, fire up their engines together and then quickly start taxiing toward the takeoff end of the runway.

It was an unforgettable experience. Some sight. Some sounds. Some goose bumps! No matter how many times I experienced it, I never became so jaded to think the event commonplace. My heart would beat faster when I was just one of the pilots in one of those large formations, which we routinely put into the air many, many times during the war.

I was even a tad more excited when I was the lead of a large formation. When it was my job to start firing up those engines. When then it would be my job to guide the procession to the takeoff end of the runway. When, as the big hand on my wristwatch reached the specified 0925 position, the take-off time that day, I would release my brakes and advance the four throttles on my B-17 for take-off. Behind me followed 36 other *Flying Fortresses* headed for Udine, Italy and alternates following the coastline to Venice.

But that was long ago, a half century ago, and this is now, today, and Century 20 is about to shut down for all time. I am at my computer writing about the mid-century wars, World War II and Korea, in which affairs I was aboard... along with many thousands of my contemporaries.

Every year on Memorial Day, this aging wartime jock watches on TV the starter at the Indianapolis Motor Speedway as he watches his watch tick off the seconds and finally drops his flag and thus starts another closed track, 500-mile auto race.

On just such an occasion I was on hand in Indianapolis, at the track with my lifelong friend, Colonel Russell E. Schleeh. Russ was the pilot of General Curtis LeMay's B-17 in the European air offensive, staged from the UK. It was the toughest World War II Theater.

Russ had flown side-by-side with our esteemed wartime Army Air Corps leader, LeMay, who was destined from the beginning to be the Chief of Staff of our US Air Force. Russ and I had great seats in the B-17s, B-24s and B-29s of World War II and later in the jet powered B-47s, B-52s and Mach 2 B-58s of the Korean War and Cold War.

On one day in May, Russ and I had great seats at the then newly refurbished Indianapolis Motor Speedway. We could look directly down on the starter as he stepped to the microphone to make his annual, stirring, starting send-off of the top racecar drivers of the world.

Stoic, never flustered, modest, iron-man Russ handled the situation very well. On the other hand, I made a plain, damn fool of myself. When I heard the starter's voice, as it boomed out over the racetrack, "Gentlemen, start your engines," tears filled my eyes, blurring the whole extraordinary scene.

At that moment at Indianapolis, I began recalling other times and other places when Russ and I had watched the big hand on our wrist watches, clicking their way towards the straight-up position, towards the twelve o'clock position: Tick, tick, tick, TICK. Suddenly, I was fantasizing. I was sure the starter had shouted loud and clear over the racetrack public address system, "Flyboys, start your Wright Cyclone engines on your B-17 *Flying Fortresses*."

Every major mission is a great undertaking with many small, carefully timed tasks executed flawlessly until the selected enemy target was reached, bombed, and destroyed. En route to the target, it was the formation leader's responsibility to fly the Lead Aircraft of the Lead Squadron of the Lead Group of the Air Division through the flak fields and through the flashing, slashing enemy fighters wherever they might be lurking.

After assembling the entire formation just south of the *Promontorio del Gargano*, the land spur on the back of the Italian boot which projects into the Adriatic Sea, I turned to a northwesterly heading, paralleling the Yugoslavia coastline, heading our formation toward the northeasterly corner of the Adriatic. To conserve our precious petrol, we would climb slowly and would arrive at our **IP** (initial point) for our bomb run – in just over two hours.

We expected no air opposition on the run up the Adriatic and got none. By this time in the air war, the Italian air arm was effectively out of business; and their German allies were beginning to have more business than they were able to handle.

Arriving in the region of Trieste, in the extreme north-east corner of the Gulf of Venice, I started a slow left-hand turn, which would enable individual squadrons (of 6-to-7 aircraft each) to cut across my radius-of-turn, as necessary, to tighten up our formation and thus tighten up the bombing pattern that we would place on the ground. With few exceptions, it was our intent to smash our enemy's war-making capabilities while taking care to protect his art, his churches, and religious symbols.

The Italian sky had been clear of clouds as we flew north over the beautiful Adriatic Sea; but now, after making landfall and establishing our bomb run towards the marshalling yards of Udine, we were above and, part of the time, in broken clouds, with the breaks between the clouds becoming smaller and smaller and fewer and fewer.

With the cloud build-up in the area and the inability to establish a clear view of the target, we could not drop our cargo at that point. We turned south following the coastline to pick off our alternates, namely Italian commercial docks, and refineries around and near Venice.

Rolling out of the turn away from Udine we now headed to our next specified southern axis-of-attack and initiated our bomb run.

Out my left window, I could see the Adriatic Sea in the clear with no clouds to the distant horizon. Off to my right to the north, I was looking into broken-to-solid clouds, building up along the Italian Alps and spilling over and down the south side of the mountains towards us. Even while flying toward the alternate bomb run, I thought it a beautiful scene and Italy a place I would like to visit someday. Italians were a people I would like to get to know better.

Lieutenant James Markiewicz, a top-rated bombardier, respected comrade, and friend, clutched his bombsight, activating a left-right needle on my pilot's panel. My task, from that moment, was simply to hold a precise, pre-determined altitude and airspeed, and in responding to this needle, make small, left-right corrections as required to keep this needle centered.

On the bomb run, I worked for Lieutenant Markiewicz. At this critical juncture in the combat mission, the lead-bombardier was the de-facto aircraft commander. James, during that critical sixty seconds, was the 99th Bomb Group-Leader-Commander-Pathfinder for the entire group of flying squadrons.

Looking forward and down toward the target, the same view that the bombsight and bombardier would be getting, I could see the northern point of the *Laguna Veneta* only intermittently. We would be in the clear for a few seconds, but then the darkening cumulus clouds, hanging low over Venice, would block our view completely. I could see substantial shipping activity in the *Laguna Veneta* as we paralleled its course below, but I was beginning to question whether James was going to be able to see down and sight directly on our **AP**.

James advised that periodically he would have good vertical visibility, but that he could get only brief looks out ahead where the target was. I said, "Do not let them drop, James, unless you are right on target. We want to deprive Hitler the use of the Murano docks and associated shipping facilities without hitting anything or anyone else. Make no mistake of it."

In a moment James said, "It's lookin' better, Major." Then he came back online. "Nope, it's gone again. We're flying in and out of stratocumulus build-ups, Major, and I'm not able to see very far out front where my bombsight is looking."

The bombardier sees his target as an illusion, driving into him at a faster and faster rate. So long as he can see the target he can effectively "track it," making finer and finer adjustments, as it seems to accelerate and drive towards him. The small, fine corrections made in the last few seconds of the bomb run are always critical.

"How much time before 'bombs away', James?" I asked. "Thirty-five... make it thirty... seconds," he answered.

After fifteen seconds of searching out ahead, finding no breaks in the clouds, I immediately gave the order to abort this run. I said, "Close the bomb doors, repeat, close the bomb doors." Then immediately, I started a slow left-turn off the target, an unspoken but very clear visual signal to the formation that the leader is aborting the bombing attack. I could hear our bomb doors slam shut and knew that the bombardiers in our other aircraft, visually keying on my doors, would be immediately closing theirs.

I had deep respect for most of my bombardiers. Another, Lieutenant Bjork, flew regularly with me when I led Colonel Upthegrove's 99th Bomb Group. Bob was a pleasant, quietly courageous young man. He knew his business and was never distracted from his bomb sight, even when his partner navigator, Captain Helms, my good friend, who also flew often with me, was standing beside him firing away with our forward .50-caliber machine guns while under attack by German fighters. Carl's work as navigator required unusual precision and concentration to know the exact position of the plane at all times. When the B-17 was attacked, he used that same precision and concentration to take deadly aim and defend us against the incoming enemy fighters.

Based on mutual respect, the three of us had become the best of friends despite Bob and Carl both being a full inch taller than I. We clearly understood and appreciated our dependency upon one another.

A second run forty minutes later, (it takes time to swing a large formation around a complete 360-degree, racetrack turn) made it clear to me that the local weather at Venice was not improving. Clearly, it was deteriorating. We had fuel enough for a third pass, but I saw no point in it. I hit my intercom switch and said, "Button 'er up, James, and replace the safety pins in our bombs; we'll take 'em home and turn 'em in this time. It is not going to happen today."

I hit my formation intercom button and almost shouted into my hand mike, "We are aborting the run. This is no day to be bombing anyway. For God's sake, this is Christmas Day, Christmas, 1943! Merry Christmas, Venezia, Our best wishes from the 99th Bomb Group."

First Lieutenant Blakemore, my able, highly experienced Squadron Navigator, came online indicating his approval, "Sounds like a good plan to me, Major. I suggest a heading of one three five (135 degrees). This will take us down the middle of the Adriatic, giving us plenty of time to get set if German fighters should come at us from either side; okay with you, Major?"

"Fine, Lieutenant, good plan. We have plenty of fuel; I'll keep the cruise power throttle settings and descend en route a couple-hundred feet-per-minute as we go. We'll be moving right along at about 200 miles-per-hour. Give me an ETA, if you will, for a position abeam Pescara. We'll be south of the German lines, by the time we get there. I'll make a small course correction at Pescara, angling us to the right and heading us inland directly for our airfield."

I then called to our ball turret gunner, "Staff Sergeant James Boswell, you still down there, protecting our soft underbelly?" I could see in my mind's eye this young man's usual boyish smile, tousled hair, and very alive eyes.

Responding with typical enthusiasm, one of my favorite people in the world said, "It's fine down here, Major; no sweat; I'm in good shape. A ball turret is a great place to round out the day, wouldn't you say, Major?"

"Very good," I said, chuckling in response to Sergeant Boswell's pun, "Why don't you plan to round out your day in your specially-equipped round house. Say, about an hour from now, we will be abeam Pescara. When we pass Rimini, and Ancona, take a good look around. If you can, pick up any German Navy activity that our intelligence types might like to hear about, okay?"

"Right-on, Major," Sergeant Boswell answered, "I'll keep an eye out. I've got a map down here; I'll be able to pinpoint our location most of the time. If I see anything move, anything at all, you'll be the first to know. Okay if I wake you up, sir?"

Smiling to myself, I hit my intercom button and responded quickly in an unsmiling voice saying, "Watch your language, Sergeant Boswell." The intercom switch at our crew positions would make a clicking sound when activated. I heard no voices, but a chorus of clicking switches mirrored the smiles that I imagined were visible at all stations in our B-17.

On this mission, Boswell and Robert McKeeman were my B-17's ball turret and tail gun crew. They reminded me of two other live wires who flew with me across the Atlantic and with Monty. Staff Sergeant Austin, ball turret gunner, and Sergeant Charles "Chuck" Ward, tail gunner, would not relax until our wheels were back on the ground at some base. Even when there was no longer anything to shoot at, they were always alert and checking. I would have enjoyed telling them that I thought them great young guys. Their deft use of their paired guns in Austin's ball turret under our center-section and Ward's equally lonely and cramped compartment in our tail section were very good reasons why I was still alive. I have never forgotten the debt and never will.

I guessed that Ward and Austin were 19 or 20. I recall saying to myself, "Richard Eager, when you were 19, you were a junior at University of Tennessee, flying a *Piper Cub*. At UT, you would watch Gene McEver run and Bobbie Dodd pass and kick… up and down the Tennessee "Vol's" Shields-Watkins Field.

"In your freshman year, you sold peanuts in the stands. In your sophomore year, you applied for admittance in the US Army Air Corps. In your junior year, you were accepted, and you left UT to become a Flying Cadet. My recollection is that you sure weren't ready to go to war when you were Austin's and Ward's age or Boswell's or McKeeman's."

We were seeing less and less of Hermann Göring's Luftwaffe. It was becoming clear to us in the air that Hitler was not going to be able to put out the fires, which he had himself kindled, in North Africa, Europe, the Balkans and Russia. The next step, sure to follow, would be the invasion of Europe from the west… from the UK. Many military leaders, including the Germans, thought the best place to cross would be from the White Cliffs of Dover areas over the 20-mile Strait of Dover, to France. The invasion would be some sight to view, from those White Cliffs, and we heard the Germans thought so, too, and were preparing for that possibility.

Invasion from the east, from Russia, was already a threat, because of the weakening German battle line extending 1,800 miles from Leningrad to Smolensk to Kiev.

It was becoming more certain every day that Hitler's troops and tanks would never see Baku (**Operation Edelweiss**). They entered the oil fields of Maikop, Russia, in the summer of 1942, but were stopped by the Russian Armies before taking over the oil resources of Grozny. Der Führer's legions were 400 miles south beyond Stalingrad, but they were still another 400 miles short of Baku, the processing plants, oil fields and transport facilities in the southeast corner of Eurasia, on the Caspian Sea.

Landings at Foggia, Italy, in our new B-17Fs and B-17Gs, the latter equipped with new "chin" turrets, were "routinely uneventful." Our Aussie cousins, who shared our base, equipped with British *Wellingtons*, would have very different experiences, however.

As I approached our field when returning from the *Laguna Veneta*, Venice, target, a tired, well-used *Wellington* was having a "different experience" at that very moment, just ahead of my B-17. As I turned onto my landing leg, the *Wellington*'s right main gear collapsed at mid-field, causing it to veer off the runway to the right. Almost immediately, I could see a small fire quickly becoming a larger fire.

The plucky *Wellington* wound up clear of the runway, enabling me to continue my approach. Within a few seconds, I streaked through the smoke, angling towards me on the left side of the runway. In another second, I flashed by the upended *Wellington*.

I have retained a picture in my mind of the crew scrambling to get clear of their wrecked flying machine, scattering in all directions like the chickens whose necks I used to wring at Boy Scout camp in the Smokies. I remember, too, seeing the fire wagons, promptly on the scene, quickly bringing the fire under control. I said to myself, "Those fearless Aussies will have that ancient machine of theirs ready to fly again tomorrow night."

Later, I visited my Australian counterpart who shared the Foggia base with me and inquired about his *Wellington* crew that had experienced some difficulty ahead of me. His crewmen, he said, "were shaken up a bit, but were otherwise unhurt." The *Wellington*? "Oh," he said, "we shall just have to wreck another one to get the parts we need for this one, you know." Then with a smile, he added, "A **piece of cike**, Major. You know, a piece of cike, as we say Down Under."

We met a few times and talked about Australia and America. I think we both realized that we looked quite a bit alike. I suggested, as I'm afraid I often did with Britishers from throughout the Commonwealth, that we were probably distant cousins. My family names, Evans-Stewart, certainly reflected a family heritage from Scotland and Wales. I'm sure we would have become good friends, but we were both so busy with our jobs that we had little time to relax and jawbone.

Also, the Aussies flew the night shift in their *Wellingtons*, while we flew the day shift in our *Flying Fortresses*.

On returning to base, I roughed out a poem to remind me of the unusual circumstances and how I felt about the situation at the time. I had not aborted a mission before, nor did I abort a mission after the Venice mission. The title of my poem was, "Salutari Venezia."

During the period of the occupation of Italy by the Allies after my 99th Bomb Group and Monty's 8th Army had moved to Italy, Monty would still call on me from time to time for a ride in his *Flying Fawtress*. I would simply advise Uppie of Monty's request, get on the tele to locate the Army Commander's present HQs, and then fire up *Theresa Leta* and head out to find my part-time boss. The ride depended, of course, if the landing field in mind was of sufficient length.

Uppie would advise Doolittle, and General Jim would let Ike know my plans for picking up Monty. Neither Ike nor Jimmie ever called back to tell me to stay when my **ETD** rolled around. I would climb aboard "Monty's B-17," take off, and head out for the liberated airfield near to the Army Commander's last known position—on the active Italian battlefield.

On one such occasion, I picked up General Montgomery about "mid-boot" to fly him to North Africa, for a meeting with General Eisenhower and Prime Minister Churchill and then on to England, where he would start preparing for the long-expected invasion of Europe, across the channel. We flew his American C-47 when I picked up Monty in Italy, and on to Marrakesh. He was in very good spirits, which I took to mean that he and Ike were, for the time being, at peace with each other, and that Patton and his overbearing manner towards Monty was somewhere else.

After returning Monty and his staff in a borrowed B-25 to their HQs after the Palermo flight, Monty had not bothered to check in with me. Our understanding was straightforward: "Don't call me. If I want to go someplace, I will call you." This seemed straightforward enough to me. I did call once to let him know how some engine repairs were going. Monty had a keen interest in keeping those B-17 props spinning. He wasn't one to forget our first flight to Cairo, from Tripoli, when I feathered No. 3 engine to save oil, and he anxiously focused on the non-spinning prop just outside his co-pilot window. I didn't forget, either!

I was aware, after the invasion of Italy, that Monty was staying busy clearing the east side of Italy, of Germans, while our US General Mark Clark was seeing to the west side.

Monty no longer had reservations about occupying the co-pilot's position in the B-17 or the C-47, during flight. He would stand between the pilot and co-pilot positions during engine start-up, run-up, and takeoff. Then, he would watch attentively as the landing gear and flaps were withdrawn from the airstream after takeoff. When everything was "up and locked" and "climb-power had been set up," the Army Commander would ask, "I say, Major Evans, would it be quite all right for me to fly co-pilot for a time?"

I would respond that it would indeed be quite satisfactory. In a moment Monty would be in and my co-pilot would be out.

My flight engineer would usually help Monty adjust his seatbelt and get him settled in. The Army Commander would then very quickly "check out the landscape."

Monty would soon be talking with some excitement. "I say, Major Evans," he might start off...

"I see you have been promoted. My congratulations." The Army Commander would smile, pleasantly and warmly. We had come a long way.

When Monty smiled, I would, of course, smile back. I remember saying, "Thank you, General; thank you very much. I am pleased that you noticed my promotion. I was recently made a Squadron Commander, which warrants the rank of Major. In the air, I fly as a Group Leader, sometimes as a Division Leader. I must put in a little more ground-time before I can expect to move up to Lieutenant Colonel."

"Yes, yes, I understand, "Monty responded. "I know a few of your superior officers, General Eisenhower and General Doolittle in particular, but I am not just sure to whom you report directly." "Sir, my immediate senior officer is my Group Commander and recently promoted Division Commander, Brigadier General Fay Upthegrove. General Upthegrove is a dedicated 'old line officer' and a father figure for the young men in his command. General Upthegrove is a quiet, very fair, and caring Commander, General Montgomery. I have great respect and affection for him. I have told General Upthegrove quite a bit about you. He has great respect for you. I'm sure you would enjoy knowing each other, should the opportunity arise.

"I am also acquainted with General Doolittle, having met with him on occasion at his Head-quarters at Constantine, and a few times at my 99th Bomb Group Headquarters. I have made visits to General Eisenhower's Supreme Allied Headquarters in Algiers, working with his staff, but I have had no direct contact with our Theater Commander."

Then I shifted gears and said, "General Montgomery, I have had more contact of late with you and your senior staff than with my own leaders. You probably remember I met General de Guingand in Tripoli, just a few minutes before he introduced me to you. General de Guingand introduced us in front of your Headquarters tent near Mussolini's erstwhile Castel Benito Airport.

"General Montgomery, I think your Chief-of-Staff is an elegant gentleman and a great credit to you and to his country, South Africa, which he has told me he loves very much. I think you must know, General, that General de Guingand holds you in the highest regards."

When Monty didn't respond right away, I continued. "General Montgomery, I also met your General Wilson, General Eisenhower's deputy, whom you call 'Jumbo.' General Wilson introduced himself to me. I was very flattered. It was the day King George VI traveled to Tripoli, to visit you and to thank you for your victory over General Rommel. Most Americans realize, I am sure, that battle started at El Alamein, and ended near Tunis. I'm sure that history will call the second El Alamein battle a turning-point battle of World War II.

"General Wilson was most kind to me. He briefed me on some kingly protocol and just in time – a few minutes before you, General, presented me to your King."

When General Montgomery again did not respond, I said, "While we were awaiting the arrival of King George VI, General Wilson took the time to introduce me to your Corps Commanders. I was flattered to meet those wonderful men on your battle staff, the youthful Generals who helped you drive General Rommel out of Egypt, Cyrenaica, Tripolitania, and Tunisia. In the States, General Montgomery, we would call your North African operation a clean sweep."

Monty smiled, looked pleased, and then was quiet for a few minutes. Then he embarked on a different subject, as if he had something on his mind. "Major Evans, I notice when I got aboard that you have a different crew. Not the men we have had before. I looked for some familiar faces to greet. Do you change crewmen often? When you fly combat missions, do you try to stay with one crew, or do you shift about a bit?"

"General Montgomery," I said, "I do shift crewmen on every combat mission I fly. I have become a Squadron Commander since we were together, General, and I schedule myself with different crews so that I can be familiar with the strengths and weaknesses of all of the men under my modest command, in particular, the 'comers,' who are working hard to excel, to push ahead of their contemporaries."

When the Army Commander just smiled and waited, I added, "General Montgomery, I am very pleased that you remembered my men and inquired about them. General, most of the B-17 crewmen with whom you were familiar, in fact, four were killed in a B-17 crash, flying with another pilot."

General Montgomery then turned quickly towards me, "I am so terribly sorry. I was afraid when I didn't see them right off that something might have happened. They were a fine body of young men." There was genuine sadness in The Army Commander's voice.

"Indeed, they were," I responded. "Thank you, General Montgomery, I know you mean that; I'm sorry they are not here, to hear you say that you regarded them highly. Lieutenant Johnson, my co-pilot, who often turned over his seat to you, was killed. So was Technical Sergeant Owens, my enlisted crew chief and top-turret gunner, who was with us here in the forward cockpit most of the time. Sergeant Owens was a leader who, quite literally, led. I don't recall ever hearing Sergeant Owens giving orders to his men. I remember him as always just taking off right away to get going on an assignment. I remember his men were immediately on the run to catch up and keep up with him.

"General, I doubt you noticed Technical Sergeant Morris, our radio officer. He was a fine, quiet, thinking man. He was tucked into the small radio operator's compartment, just aft of your office in our bomb bay. I thought of Sergeant Morris as a father figure for the younger enlisted crewmen in my ten-man force. My heart aches when I think of my crewmen as they were falling to their deaths. I shall never forget them, General Montgomery. Our ever-vigilant waist gunner, Staff Sergeant Kennedy, also died in a B-17 accident. He was brought on as one of your crew for he had already flown many missions and had more than his share of "kills."

I was seeing a very different side to General Montgomery. He was truly saddened to hear about my *Theresa Leta* crew, no question about it. "General Montgomery," I continued, "I wish that I could tell my men that you remembered them and inquired about them. They would have been very proud. Sergeants Austin, Ward and Second Lieutenants Beringsmith and Carver, my ball turret, tail gunner, bombardier and navigator survived. They've pretty much fulfilled their missions and will be on their way home soon. I'm sure you remember Austin and Ward; they were our youthful eager beavers. Beringsmith was the serious one that always had our backs, and Carver was well respected for plotting the safe routes through enemy territories for our *Flying Fortress*. They were flying a separate mission when the accident, killing four of my original crew, took place."

While General Montgomery and I were getting reacquainted, I flew south over the Mediterranean, just offshore Naples, the Pompeii ruins, and Mt. Vesuvius. I asked General Montgomery if he had ever seen the inside of the famous volcano. When he answered that he had not, I asked if he would like to have a look. His answer assured me that our friendship was being re-established at a level higher than we had previously achieved. He said, with an interesting smile, using a phrase I'm afraid he had heard me use. General Montgomery said, "But of couse."

On my first pass, I flew by the volcano, just high enough for Monty to see over the side and into the very large, round hole. When the General evidenced no fear at all and asked if we might have a second "closer look" into the bowl of Vesuvius, I was delighted, and pleased to comply. I didn't get close to the sides, but I did drop down into the bowl on a second run so that he might, for a few seconds, be looking up, at the rim, and daylight.

After "just one more" requested look into the mouth of the famous volcano, we rolled out on to a southerly course that pointed us down the western shin of the boot of Italy, past the Isle of Capri. I then asked Monty if he would like to look at the Salerno beachhead, where our American General Mark Clark and his troops had recently come ashore.

"General Montgomery, this was following your earlier arrival in Italy. You had wasted no time in coming directly across the Strait of Messina well ahead of our forces."

The Army Commander responded that he would like, very much, to have a look at Salerno. He remembered, indeed, when the attack was launched. He was pleased with the Americans' final success, though the first three days the US Army was in desperate straits. The Germans were well prepared and had far outmaneuvered the US invading forces and the battle was in the Germans' favor.

I retold the story that General Clark and his Army were in danger of being forced back toward the beach by very experienced German divisions. On the fourth day, as more and more US military equipment was brought in, the Americans (with steady assistance from their British partners) were able to make progress off the beachhead. The Germans were hit with army artillery on land, naval bombardment from the USS *Boise* and USS *Philadelphia* at sea and aerial bombing from the B-17 heavy bombers.

Monty asked if I had been involved in any way with the invasion. I told him that our B-17s were often used to "soften up" areas where known heavy enemy artillery was positioned.

As we looked down on Salerno's broad and very deep beach, I told Monty that I flew a few missions with the 5th Bomb Wing, primarily against various highways and bridges in support ofthe American advance at Salerno.

I was pleased to relate this story to General Montgomery, one of the world authorities on ground tactics. I thought he might enjoy it and clearly, he did. When you had Monty's attention, he would lean towards you, cupping his ear to get it all. It was a pleasant, flattering eccentricity.

Occasionally, when we were refueling and delayed on the ground, Monty could be quite gregarious. While standing beside his B-17 or C-47, he would talk endlessly with my airmen, to their delight and to mine.

At the same time, Monty, without warning and with comparable verve, might suddenly "go off the air." I had learned not to be surprised when he would suddenly become quiet. At first, I felt his ego had been ruffled a tad, but I would say to myself, "Monty really isn't the stuffy, withdrawn individual that some might think. When one is afforded the opportunity to get acquainted with England's most illustrious and most successful Army Commander, the title Monty enjoyed the most, one finds that he is sociable, enthusiastic and very pleasant to be around." Ending my soliloquy, I said to myself, "What's the harm if Monty doesn't bother to announce his mood swings in advance? I don't have a problem with this. Monty is just being frugal with his enthusiasms."

Glancing in his direction, beside me in the co-pilot's seat, I noticed that he suddenly seemed lost in his own thoughts. I said to myself, "What did I tell you, Richard Eager? Monty is being frugal this very minute with his enthusiasms. Why don't you just bug off, clam up and leave the Army Commander to his own thoughts. Pay attention to your driving his plane, the C-47, on this journey."

The silence did not persist as long as I had thought it might. In past trips, Monty and I had enjoyed many very pleasant hours together in the pilots' compartment of the *Theresa Leta* and which Monty enjoyed calling, "My *Flying Fawtress*, which Ike gave me to fly about in." Suddenly, the Army Commander broke the silence, to which I had been a willing participant. I was not prepared for what followed.

Monty had turned towards me, while allowing his gaze to remain fixed on the distant horizon in front of our flying machine. With no warning, six short words came tumbling from Monty's voice box so fast that at first, I was not able to grasp their meaning. General Montgomery hesitated and then repeated his words in an even voice: "I could have been your father."

I turned quickly towards Monty, intending to make eye contact. The Army Commander, however, was still looking straight ahead towards the horizon. After a moment, I did catch his eye and said, "Thank you, General Montgomery. Thank you, sir. I too have had this very same thought. General, I would have been very proud."

———————————

Yes, I would have been proud... for Monty had many of the fine, personal characteristics I so admired in my father. Bernard Law Montgomery and William Ernest Evans shared a highly principled confidence in the way they led their lives, a confidence born of strong convictions. Each was loyal to his country and concerned with his fellow man. Both used their God-given intellect to become wise in their professions. Part of that wisdom was the belief to only take risks if there was true clarity that something of great consequence would be gained. Monty followed that belief though others misunderstood him. For example, he held back his troops on certain war fronts until he knew they could win. Ernest Evans taught generations of students and families to carefully weigh all risks before making serious life decisions. Dad though, had a patient heart, profound humility, and demonstrated leadership in his own quiet way. Monty was much more direct in his demeanor but no less sincere.

When I look back to remember that particular conversation during the flight across the Mediterranean on our way to Marrakesh, I also recall the few days I spent as Monty's guest at his headquarters in Sicily, above the Plains of Cantania, where we watched the British 8th Army, as they pursued the Germans from around Mt. Etna and eventually out of Sicily. He frequently referred to me and introduced me to others as "His Pilot." Years later in a reference in his diary as to our flight to meet General Patton at Palermo, where the slope and insufficient length of the landing area demanded the unconventional and dangerous ground loop, General Montgomery acknowledged, " ...I escaped a nasty accident in *Fortress* only by skill of pilot and might have been killed."

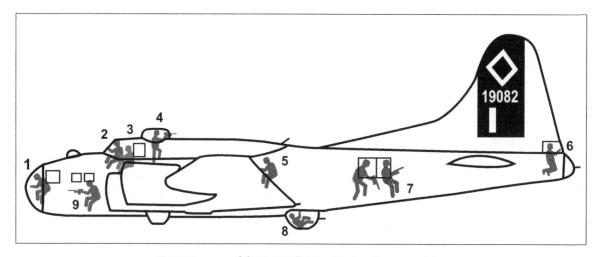

20.2 *Diagram of the B-17E "Flying Fortress" crew positions*
(Diagram inspired by one given by Gary Staffo, 99th BG Historical Society)

This is a drawing of the B-17E.

The *Theresa Leta* had only the number 19082 placed on her tail.

The diamond with the off center Roman numeral I is the tail design for the B-17s flown by Captain Richard Earnest Evans' 356th Squadron, 99th BG, Diamondbacks.

Theresa Leta was transferred from England with the 92nd BG to the Mediterranean Theater of Operations and loaned to General Bernard L. Montgomery, Commander of the British 8th Army.

Crew positions included:

1 Bombardier	**4** Flight Engineer	**7** Waist Gunners
2 Co-Pilot	**5** Radio Operator	**8** Ball Turret Gunner
3 Pilot	**6** Tail Gunner	**9** Navigator

20.3 *The original "Theresa Leta" crew with General Montgomery, far left;*
and Captain Richard E. Evans, far right

20.4 *B-17 waist gunners* (World Conflict Images)

20.5 *B-17s line up for mission take-off* (World Conflict Images)

20.6 *B-17 ball turret gunner* (World Conflict Images)

20.7 *B-17 top turret gunner* (World Conflict Images)

V-238-H (99ᵗʰ B.G. 346ᵗʰ Sq.)(Ship 416)(1302 Hrs.-8-31-43)(12"-18,600')(120° Pisa M/y, Italy)

20.8 *A target covered quite well, Pisa, Italy*

20.9 *Major Evans is lead ship on a Padua, Italy, mission*

20.10 *Major Evans, lighter military coat, watches General Montgomery cut the ceremonial ribbon,*
opening the new "Bailey" bridge over the Sangro River (Imperial War Museum)

20.11 *Flying over Mt. Vesuvius, Italy*

21.1 *B-29 bombers fly near Mount Fuji, Japan* (United States Army Air Force)

CHAPTER 21

ESCAPE FROM OKINAWA

On the heights above a bay, just named "Buckner"
On an island for centuries called "Okinawa"
I was there in late summer of '45,
A witness to Pacific phenomena.

Our B-29s were faced into the storm,
Tied fast to their pads
The monstrous power, the typhoon, to contain.
We had taxied them about and into the wind,
Their urge for flight was to constrain.

Suddenly, the heavens burst!
And the eye of the storm was born.
It was a writhing, undulating hole, within clouds

Overhead. Winds that had been
thrashing and crashing about,
Were suddenly silent... and quite dead!

Then, in a moment, the eye passed us by,
And again, the fury of the tempest was relentless.
Some comrades, who had braced their tents to the wind,
Were suddenly quite chagrined... and tent less!

Richard Eager

Buckner Bay, 200 feet straight down and below our GI tents, had been named in honor of US Marine Corps Commander, Lieutenant General Simon B. Buckner, Jr., who was killed in action on Okinawa on June 18, 1945. That was just a few months before World War II ground to a halt, hesitated and was then suddenly over. Many were killed just a few months before the battles were over.

The war that some thought might end all wars was over. It had effectively been over for a few weeks for me. I was flying out of Guam, Saipan and Tinian and coming on top of the tragic but successful Marine assaults on Iwo Jima and Okinawa. General LeMay's B-29 firestorm strikes on Tokyo and the Atomic Bomb attacks on Hiroshima and Nagasaki had been the final, fatal blows. The War Lords of Japan had not served their nation well. They had no place to go, no place to hide. They were through. World War II was history.

With 54 bombing missions under my belt in the European Theater of Operation, I had ample combat credits to depart Okinawa at any time. My US Army **ASR Score** was well over the 80 points needed for officers. If I could get away promptly, I could be home for Christmas; but time was running out for me.

My bosses, Generals Doolittle and LeMay, were already home. They had flown record-breaking, great circle flights from Tokyo to the US, via the Aleutians, Southern Alaska and Canada, in B-29s stripped of bombs, combat equipment and heavy gear, but loaded to the gunnels with auxiliary fuel.

I had written to my young wife, my beautiful JoAnn, and asked her to tell our dear baby, Bobbie, that, "I'll be home for Christmas, you can plan on me," an expression I had lifted from Bing Crosby's then popular carol. But time was slipping by and I reminded myself that Bing had added in the song's second verse: "I'll be home... if only in my dreams."

————————————

Early in 1945, I had flown from Alamogordo, New Mexico to Colorado Springs to look in on my big brother, Pug. He had become Assistant Director of Training and Operations at 2nd Air Force Headquarters. Also, he had made Lieutenant Colonel ahead of me. In a short time, however, I would catch up with him. Later he would make Colonel and pass me by again! Still, I liked the guy.

We met for lunch at the 2nd Air Force Officers' Club and were joined by Colonel Tommy DuBose. The Colonel was not yet an "old-timer," but he was a respected member in good standing of the pre-1939 Army Air Corps aviators, the title for the experienced men in the early USAAC. Joining late in 1939, I had straddled that time line with one foot in the past in the USAAC (United States Army Air Corps) and the other in the future USAF (United States Air Force).

As with many of his contemporaries, Colonel DuBose had not gone overseas. His skills, which were needed in the ZI to help plan, develop and direct the largest, most complex flying-training organization the world had ever known, had prevented his securing an overseas assignment. There were a lot of great guys who wanted to get overseas to have a part in the war but were hung up indefinitely in the States in "The Training Command."

Before going overseas, I understood and appreciated that I had been well-trained by hard-working, dedicated people. Before I had joined the Army Air Corps in 1939, a lot of work had gone into the training program, which I had received under the direction of men like Tommy DuBose. They had developed the flying training curriculum. Many of us were able to build proficiency, gain experience and learn self-confidence before meeting our country's enemies in the air over Africa, Europe, the Pacific and China-Burma-India Theaters of War.

I did not have an excess of self-confidence when I arrived at Love Field in Dallas from Knoxville in December 1939 to commence Primary Flight Training in the then relatively new, undeveloped Flying Corps of the US Army.

I would meet men like Colonel DuBose who were already "well out on the power curve" before I had gotten off the ground. You can believe I was respectful and grateful.

When the Colonel sat down to have lunch with my older brother and me, he was ebullient. "Well, it's set. As of today, I am the new Commander of the 316th B-29 Bomb Wing. Lunch is on you, Pug, my friend. Pug, I have people like you who are tied down here in the 2nd Air Force to thank for my promotion and my release from the Air Training Command. The training program of my 316th Bomb Wing in B-29s is almost complete. I will be taking this new wing to the Pacific to join Curtis LeMay in a very few weeks. I am a Wing Commander, and I am raring to get going."

The small group of us at the table was delighted for Colonel DuBose. I must have been delighted. I immediately applied for a job in Colonel Tommy DuBose's new 316th B-29 Bomb Wing.

I had been in Europe and felt that I should also see what it was like in the Pacific. I had come this far; I should get over there to help finish things up. Then, I could go home, assured that I could stay.

Colonel DuBose, in response, looked over the top of his glasses without speaking, a characteristic gesture to which I would become accustomed. Then quickly, he asked what aircraft had I been checked out in? What aircraft was I current in? What was my current duty assignment? Who was my present boss, and would he let me go without a big fuss?"

"Colonel DuBose, I'm current in B-17s, B-24s, B-29s, B-25s and A-20s. I'm an Instructor Pilot in these machines and a few more. I'm not current on paper but have recently flown P-47s and P-51s. My most recent flight in a P-51 was a couple hours ago when I took off from Alamogordo to fly up here and look in on my big brother. My present assignment, Colonel DuBose, is Director of Fight Operations at the Alamogordo Training Center."

"So, you are Pug's little brother. Apparently, you beat your older brother into the Army Air Corps. How did that happen?"

I was surprised the Colonel mentioned my brother, Stewart, by his nickname. "Pug had a good job, Colonel DuBose, with the TVA. Also, there were some young ladies in East Tennessee that he felt obligated to look after. I was in my junior year at the University of Tennessee, broke most of the time and always looking for a part-time job so that I could take girls out like my brother, Pug, did on a regular basis. I figured the Army Air Corps was steady work with a war coming and all."

When Colonel DuBose didn't respond, I raised my eyebrows and continued, "Also, Colonel, I've been 'Little Pug' most of my life, and I've been trying for years to put it behind me. I never really cared for the name even though my big brother, Pug, provided me with employment for years as his assistant on his early-morning paper routes and his late-night Curtis Publishing Company magazine routes. I did cut grass on my own, Colonel. I never swept floors nor washed windows, however, until I went to Randolph Field for Basic Flight Training in the USAAC."

Colonel DuBose shook his head from side-to-side, laughed pleasantly for a few seconds, then lunged for his lunch. In a short time, he glanced at his watch, stood up quickly and said, "I gotta scram out of here, gotta be wheels-up by 1400 hours. You'll hear from me, Little Pug. See you, Big Pug."

That afternoon, I returned to Alamogordo, a shortflight from Peterson Field, Colorado Springs. When I taxied to the line at Alamogordo, the **AO** met my plane and said, "Welcome home, Major. I have a TWX for you from HQ 2AF."

I opened an unsealed envelope, withdrew the wire and read, "You're on Little Pug! Pack your bags, DuBose."

"Well, what do you know," I said to myself. Colonel DuBose wasn't in a hurry to get to Peterson Field after all. He must have decided during our lunch to drop by the 2nd AF Personnel Records Section and have a look at my file. Then it appears he marched straight over to the assignments people and had me transferred, effective immediately, to his new 316th Wing's staff.

I said to myself, "Wow, Richard Eager, Colonel Tommie DuBose had you reassigned to his new B-29 Wing before you were off the ground and wheels-up at Peterson Field." I turned and asked the AO what time the TWX had arrived Alamogordo.

"1330, on the nose," he said.

"What do you know?" I exclaimed to myself, "I was a dues-paying member of the 316th B-29 Bomb Wing before my brother Pug and I had finished lunch."

After landing and closing out my flight plan at Alamogordo Base Ops, I got on the phone immediately and reached a beautiful Texas lady whom I often referred to in those days as, "my darling, my darling, my life and my bride."

"Hey, honey," I yelled into the phone, "Guess what? We are getting out of here. We are going to be transferred to Colorado Springs. Sweetheart, it's beautiful and wonderful up there at 'The Springs.' You can look right up at the peak of Pikes Peak. There's a great resort where we can light and hole-up until we find more permanent lodging. The place is called 'The Broadmoor.' How is my beautiful pregnant wife, the light of my life, Mrs. JoAnn Nelson Evans, feeling?"

"I'm just fine, thank you. Incidentally, I probably know more about the Broadmoor than you do," she continued. "Connie and I have stayed there many times with Mom and Dad on our way to Estes Park. I was probably playing tennis and skating on the Broadmoor ice rink before you joined The Army Air Corps. You can make my reservations at the Broadmoor just any time you like. If my choices are Alamogordo and the desert or the Broadmoor and The Springs, I'll go with the Broadmoor every time." Then she asked, "Did you have a good flight back?"

"I sure did," I said, "But I almost fouled-up. With a short flight and no weather, it was nice to just fly VFR (Visual Flight Rules), stay down on the deck and watch the sights go flashing by my window. It's particularly pleasant to fly low in a P-51. You can move right along in that machine. Guess what your new hubby forgot all about?"

"I can't imagine. What did you forget to do while I was sitting around down here?"

"I almost flew right into the Alamogordo classified area just north of our field. I was on the deck, flying south and was in the Albuquerque-Santa Fe restricted area when I decided to pull up and have a look around. Realizing where I was, I got back down on the deck pronto, hoping that no one had seen me. I turned west, got myself over on the other side of the Rio Grande and headed south again straight down the river. I flew very carefully above the river.

"At the ground speed I was making, I knew I could hold course for 35 minutes, then turn to 150 degrees and in another 8 minutes White Sands would pop right up in front of me. I would then check in with the tower, pick up the active runway, pull up to traffic altitude, set that flying machine down and call my girl. You do know don't you, Sweetheart, that your husband's not just chasing about banging into things up there, don't you, Honey?"

"Yes, I know," she said, but I could tell she was smiling at her new hubby's ego trip. "I know you know how to drive around in airplanes. I want to hear more about our going up to The Springs.

Shall I come out to the line and pick you up?"

"I'm sorry; I do get carried away, don't I? Yes, I would love to be picked up. I could get a ride, but if it is not too much trouble, I'll be standing out in front of Base Ops."

———————

Forty-eight hours later my wife and I were on our way to Colorado Springs. We had decided to drive to Cloudcroft, a short 20-mile run up onto the Sacramento Range, and rent a cottage for the night. It didn't seem like we had driven very far up into the mountains when it started getting cooler. We were into the trees, a pleasant change after living on the New Mexico desert for several months.

Living near the Broadmoor Hotel at Colorado Springs was heaven. I thought things couldn't be better, but they were. Unexpectedly and without warning, my promotion to Lieutenant Colonel came through. Wow! I had thought that I should be on the promotion list when I had moved up to leading our Group and Division combat formations across the Mediterranean and up into France, Germany, Austria, Italy, Romania and Greece. I hadn't been a Major too long, so I was surprised and delighted when my promotion to Lieutenant Colonel caught up with me at Colorado Springs.

After only a couple of weeks, Colonel DuBose called me into his office. He asked if I would like to fly out to General LeMay's Headquarters on Guam, fly a few missions over Japan and get some first-hand experience in the on-going B-29 operations in the middle of the Pacific. My new boss also thoughtfully inquired, "What plans do you have, Dick, for your wife, whom I know is pregnant?"

I answered, "Thank you for asking. JoAnn and I have discussed her going home to San Antonio for a few weeks. I don't think she would mind going a little earlier. Florence, her mom, would love having her at home knowing she is pregnant."

A few days later I was off to the Pacific. I flew a B-25 across the Rockies and the western desert to Travis Airfield, located between Sacramento and San Francisco. A spare pilot went along to return my B-25 to The Springs. I was told at the Travis Air Transport Command Base Ops that I could get a ride out that night to Oahu in a couple of hours if I liked. I was told also that a Mr. Boris Karloff would be making the trip with me if I had no objections."

I laughed and said, "Please convey to Mr. Karloff that I would be pleased to make the flight to The Islands with him." My time with Monty had afforded me the opportunity to get acquainted with some special Englishmen: King George VI, Bernard Montgomery of Alamein, Ike's deputy, General "Jumbo" Wilson, and Monty's Deputy and Chief-of-Staff, General de Guingand of South Africa came to mind. I thought that Dr. Frankenstein's monster might provide some balance to this group of Englishmen, who had become good friends, albeit in Monty's case only after some growing pains.

I was of course, very pleased. My having this world-famous actor to myself for an entire evening enhanced the prospects of a pleasant flight to Guam, Saipan and Tinian with a stopover in Hawaii. Back in Knoxville at our Riviera Theater, I had watched Lon Chaney play *The Phantom of The Opera* and Douglas Fairbanks play *The Man in the Iron Mask*. But I had missed out on *Frankenstein*, the monster played by Mr. Boris Karloff, whose acquaintance I was about to make on the long flight from Sacramento to Hawaii. If Boris and I hit it off, perhaps he would show me the scars on his neck where the bolts were attached and tell me how they removed them after the film shooting sessions.

I went aboard ahead of schedule and was surprised to find that Mr. Karloff was also ahead of schedule. The great actor was engrossed in the San Francisco evening paper; so, I wisely chose not to introduce myself immediately. When his glasses looked over the top of his newspaper without giving away any interest he might have had in my arrival, I elected not to attempt to engage him in conversation. "Not yet," I thought to myself, "Don't tense up, Richard Eager. There will be plenty of time for you to have a nice chat with the Mr. Karloff. It takes a while to cross the Pacific Ocean."

Heavy with fuel for the 2,075 nautical-mile flight to the islands, our climb-out after takeoff in the C-54 was, as might be expected, quite slow. Our pilot put us quickly on a heading straight for the Golden Gate Bridge, straight into a setting sun. It was an extraordinary picture: in the background, a brilliant sun, low in the western sky and slowly sinking into the Pacific Ocean and in the foreground, San Francisco's Golden Gate Bridge appearing to be bouncing along as it flew directly towards us.

Later, our MATS pilots would jokingly tell me, "Oh, we always miss the bridge by a good 20-to-30 feet. We take a look outside from time to time as we approach it to see whether the bridge, which looks like it is flying directly toward us, will be flying just above or just below us."

I wasn't a bonafide "old-timer" in the pre-war Army Flying Corps, but I had enlisted well ahead of the massive, tidal wave build-up of military pilots required for the Second World War. My timing put me with a group of flyboys who would typically checkout in new aircraft at the rate of one a week when the aircraft were available. We would then be made Instructor Pilots in these same aircraft the following week. That is when one really learns to fly, up there in the sky, trying to teach someone else how to do it in an airplane they've just been checked-out in. As a group my contemporaries and I were very confident, probably even cocky, Aircraft Commanders except when we flew via the Military Air Transport Service. The MATS pilots were the acknowledged professionals.

As Mr. Karloff and I approached the Golden Gate Bridge, I wasn't sure whether it was the MATS pilot's intention to fly over or under it this time. It looked a little close as it loomed up ahead of us. It did, indeed, seem to be flying directly towards us.

I knew it would miss us. I was pleased when it did!

Mr. Karloff appeared to be as intrigued as I to observe the bridge as it came bouncing along towards us at a good clip and then pass very quickly directly beneath us.

After the bridge was safely behind us, we took up a new course heading that would advance us in the direction of Hawaii, a few spotty islands almost 2,100 nautical miles from San Francisco – way out there in the broad Pacific.

Mr. Karloff and I were both apparently so excited about the prospects of our trip across the broad Pacific and our expectations of meeting each other that we were both sound asleep at about "bridge plus-twenty" minutes.

It had not been my intent to drop off right away. However, when I had closed my eyes for just a few seconds after the Golden Gate Bridge disappeared in the mist behind us, somebody must have hit me from behind. Who was lurking back there behind me? Right. Frankenstein's monstrous monster was back there in the back of that MATS C-54.

Upon awakening after an hour of restful repose, I noticed that Mr. Karloff was not just awakening. The great English actor of the period looked very much like an Englishman just refreshed after his regular afternoon nap. He was reading his evening paper and waiting for someone to bring him hot tea and his evening meal, both of which were about to arrive.

Even as I was giving the matter some thought, his "batman," who was also my "Staff Sergeant," arrived with his hot tea. Noting that I had come to life, my Staff Sergeant quickly returned with a second cup of hot tea for me.

Mr. Karloff was again immersed in his reading. I sighed, "If this imported Hollywood-type doesn't come off this hot tea and reading jag very quickly, I will fall asleep all over again. I will never find out what it's like to get acquainted with a monster."

Bingo, my lone, fellow passenger got up, stretched, glanced around the cabin area and allowed his eyes to focus on me. He walked directly over to my seat. I saw him coming and was on my feet when he arrived. He was smiling and I matched his with one of my own.

In a wonderfully cultured English voice, my fellow passenger said, "Good evening, Colonel. I noticed you early on when we came aboard but I am afraid that I was a bit weary. I have just come from our UK, you know, and have not yet adjusted myself to your time clock. I had thought we might say "hello" before we left the ground, but I am afraid that I dozed off before we took off, you know." Mr. Karloff looked directly at me and smiled.

I acknowledged his clever play on words with a smile of my own. "Mr. Karloff, I was told earlier this afternoon that we were on the same passenger list. I was looking forward to meeting you. I had no idea that just the two of us would be sharing the airplane. Sir, as I think of it now, perhaps this flight was set up for you, and I am an interloper."

"Not for me," Mr. Karloff said, "I have not had military training of any kind. I perceive that this flight was set for you; indeed, you have had considerable military training. I had never before noticed the star above the shield on your American pilots' wings, Colonel. May I ask, just what does the star signify?"

I responded, "Our Air Corps pilot insignia comes in three configurations. The wings that we are awarded on graduation from flying school consist of only the paired wings, mounted on each side of a shield that is adorned with stars and bars. When we meet the requirements for Senior Pilot, a single star is added above the shield. Should we advance to Command Pilot status, the star is then enclosed in a wreath."

"I say, Colonel Evans, shall we order our evening meal? Our batman said early on that with a few minutes warning, he might serve us quite any time we wished. By the way, what do you Yank chaps call your batmen?"

I hesitated, got a screwball idea and then responded with a "Sir, we call our batmen often."

Mr. Karloff looked puzzled but for only a moment. He looked for a confirming smile on my face, found it and then slapped his thigh just once and too hard. He didn't laugh aloud, but it wasn't necessary. You could hear this able actor's broad grin. "All right, Colonel, tell me. Just how do you address your batmen?"

"Sir, we call them 'Orderlies.' I have no idea where the term came from. I think it's probably an English expression, passed down to us from our forefathers."

Picking up the freshly printed menu, I glanced at it and said, "Well, let's see what they have for us. Sometimes it is Spam, sometimes steak. This is my first flight on MATS. I've heard that the chow is often very good."

It turned out to be steak. It was indeed very good. When a VIP is expected and when there is enough time to run down something special, the MATS crews make the extra effort. Our steaks were nicely broiled. Mr. Karloff had recognized that a special effort was being made for him. I was pleased that he let our batman know that he understood and was appreciative.

At one point during our jovial, airborne meal, Mr. Karloff quite suddenly asked, "Colonel Evans, what do you Americans think of Boris Karloff? How do you feel about an Englishman who thinks of himself as being quite literate but who actually is quite shy, yet plays quite sinister roles in motion pictures?"

Choosing my words with some care, "I would guess that Americans would say this man must be something of a dichotomy. I would venture that thoughtful Americans would think of Boris Karloff as a well-educated, soft-spoken Englishman with a penchant for surreal roles in motion pictures. I am sure that your work is respected and enjoyed in the States. I believe that most Americans have read and understand that serious theater is your forte, but that you also enjoy the comedy aspect for which you have become known. Probably, you remind American audiences that your Mr. Shakespeare can poke fun and provoke laughter as well as bring pathos and tears. Am I right? Wasn't he interested in comedy as well as tragedy?"

In response, Mr. Karloff said, "Of course he was and I'm sure he enjoyed both."

"Sir, I believe that you are probably better known in the States than you may realize. I will confess that when I learned we were scheduled to fly to Hawaii together, I had a few extra minutes, so I decided I would make use of the time and 'check you out' as we Yanks like to say."

"I am speechless, and I am flattered that you were interested in 'checking me out.' If I were to do the same on you, Colonel, I'd think at first because of your name that you are a Welshman, are you not?"

"Yes, my heritage is half Welsh, a quarter Scottish and a quarter German. My surnames are Evans, Stewart and Ernst. I was recently in your British Isles just a short time ago, flying personnel from Foggia, Italy, while I awaited transportation orders to the States. I had flown 54 missions over German-occupied territory and was ready to transfer out of the Mediterranean Theater. Before that time, I flew your General Montgomery to Marrakech where he spent a pleasant New Years' with Eisenhower and Churchill. The plan was for us to continue in his B-25, which was fitted out with extra fuel tanks, to the UK, but Eisenhower insisted he fly on the regularly scheduled larger American four engine C-54 *Skymaster* transport plane, flown by the Air Transport Command. I felt honored to be assigned to fly your General Montgomery 'about' as Monty liked to put it. I flew with Montgomery off and on for most of six months."

"Were you flying combat missions out of England, Colonel?"

"No, I was not. I had been flying combat out of bases in North Africa and Italy. General Eisenhower was my regional or Theater Commander, and Lieutenant General Doolittle was our 12th Air Force Commander in Africa.

Mr. Karloff asked again, "You had an unusual assignment. What, in heaven's name, did you think about it? How did you get along with our Monty? He could be a bit brittle, actually quite crusty, could he not?"

"I had a few problems with your Monty, and he didn't hesitate to make it clear that I was on occasion a bit of a problem for him. I am confident that he would agree when I say that we got along very well most of the time. I am proud to be able to say that we parted quite warm friends. I have great respect for your Monty, Mr. Karloff. He is a dedicated, professional soldier, very much in control of himself. He is equally cool under fire whether the heat was coming from the Germans or from General Patton."

Mr. Karloff smiled and then said, "I would be interested, Colonel Evans, to hear of some of your experiences with our Monty if it would not betray a trust or embarrass you."

"Not at all. I admit that I found Monty to be a little short and defensive, even abrasive on a few occasions. General Montgomery was a hero of mine, even before we got quite well acquainted. Both General 'Jumbo' Wilson, who succeeded General Eisenhower at Allied Forces Headquarters as the Supreme Allied Commander in the Mediterranean, and General de Guingand, Monty's Chief of Staff, briefed me in some detail on Monty. General Wilson from the UK and General de Guingand from South Africa became my good friends, along with your General Montgomery.

"Monty, beside me in the co-pilot's seat of Ike's B-17 flying over the El Alamein battlefield, would tell me how Rommel was attempting to flank him from the southwest and other pertinent battle stories."

After blowing off so much smoke of my own, I paused to give Mr. Karloff an opportunity to get back into the conversation, but he was still listening.

"Mr. Karloff, Monty was a very proud man and at times he was quick to assume a defensive posture and attitude. I figured I could take a lot from the man who took command of the British 8th Army, stood on the Libyan Plateau above the Qattara Depression, and said in effect, 'They shall not pass.' He then made sure that they, by damn, did not pass. The 'by damn' was mine, Mr. Karloff, not Monty's. Monty didn't swear. I never heard Monty swear during the entire six or so months I flew with him."

It was a long flight, but most comfortable with the conversations that ensued between the two of us.

The last I saw of Mr. Karloff was across the airline baggage loading area on Kauai, north of the main island. He was about 60 feet away. I raised my right arm, with a bent elbow and cupped hand, and then straightened my elbow in a "soft" military salute. I caught his eye, smiled and shouted "Goodbye." He seemed to enjoy my soft salute and smiled a goodbye in reply.

My new boss, good friend and Wing Commander, Colonel Tommy DuBose, was sending me to Guam, Okinawa and Tinian for a few weeks TDY to look in on General Curtis LeMay's 20th Air Force operation. I met with his Wing Commanders, Generals "Rosie" O'Donnell, Jr., Thomas E. Moore and Thomas S. Power, as well as the top men on his Ops staff, Generals William H. "Butch" Blanchard, John B. Montgomery and Jack J. Catton.

I couldn't know then, but in ten years in another war, I would return from civilian life to active duty to work again with all of those great gents. I would be afforded the opportunity as the **DO** of SAC's B-47 test programs. These programs were to test the first jet bomber, the B-47, and to set the 25, 30 and 35-hour flight records using midair refueling techniques to stay aloft.

It would be my job as Wing DO to lead the first full group (24 B-47s) to England for a 30-day stay. My group made a single, ground refueling stop at Loring AFB, Maine, en route.

On our return flight from the UK to Tampa, we would fly a great circle course from RAF Fairford AFB, our UK base, to MacDill AFB. We would deviate from course moderately to meet our Boeing KC-97 *Stratofreighter* tankers over Scotland to replace the considerable fuel for takeoff, climb out and course digressions required to assemble the formation. As planned, we would have sufficient fuel to deviate again from our great circle course to conduct a 4th of July fly-by at precisely high noon over Wright-Patterson AFB, Ohio. It would then be all downhill from Wright-Patterson to MacDill AFB, our operating base in Tampa.

All of these men that I met in Guam, Okinawa, Saipan and Tinian gave me the same message to take back to my Wing Commander, Tommy DuBose. It was easy to see that his contemporaries held Colonel DuBose in high esteem. They said, "Tell Tommy that we're pleased to welcome him and his 316th Wing to the **PTO**. Tell him he'd better get on his horse and get his butt out here. Things are going to be winding down now very quickly."

At General LeMay's headquarters and in each wing that I visited, the Commander would tell their Ops people to discuss in detail with "Tommy DuBose's Spy" any maintenance and operational problems which they were having and to "let him study" their strike photos of the Tokyo fire-bombings.

Before departing Guam for the States, an officer approached me and said, "Hey, Dick, want to put this in your report?" He handed me a newspaper from home. The entire front page was a picture of Tokyo engulfed in flames. How ironic. The very forces that Japan itself had set in motion effectively destroyed Tokyo. Not in 1941 against our World War II Allies but against its own pre-World War II neighbor, China, back in 1931 with the "Manchurian Incident" and 1937, the "Second Sino-Japanese War," two years before I would apply for acceptance in the US Army's new Army Air Corps.

When I returned to Colorado Springs, I reported immediately to Colonel DuBose, "Sir, I'm sure you are already aware. My trip to the 8th Air Force can do little more than confirm that the 316th is going to be a tad late getting to this war. I know that under the circumstances, you will greet this news from your many friends on Guam, Tinian, Saipan and Okinawa with mixed emotions. I can only verify it for you."

"Yeah, I know, Dick," he said with a sigh and a look that I could well understand, "But don't bother to labor the point with the troops yet. Write up your report but hand-carry it to me. I'll put it in my safe for the time being, okay?"

"Of course, Colonel," I said, understanding the irony of my new boss' situation. All military men wanted the destructive, murderous war to end, but not until they themselves had some direct involvement in its ending.

Then, my new boss with his usual broad smile, asked, "How much flying were you able to get in while you were over there?"

"Sir, I told everybody I met that I was a personal friend of Tommy DuBose. They were ready to give me anything I wanted to fly, Colonel."

"They put a B-29 IP with me to keep me out of trouble and let me fly a few reconnaissance runs up to Japan. It was nice driving that big bird around in the sky again."

"See anything interesting, during your runs over Japan?" continued Colonel DuBose.

"The really exciting thing to see, Colonel, was that there wasn't much for me to see. I really mean that. I didn't see a single burst of flak at our altitude. There was some exploding a couple-hundred feet below our altitude, but they didn't seem able to reach us with their anti-aircraft guns.

"I did see some fighters scramble as we approached the Tokyo-Yokohama area. Their immediate climb rate was impressive; but when they got close to our altitude, they did not have enough steam left to mount an attack. On both flights the few fighters that I was able to see broke off before reaching our altitude. I got the idea that we had probably already destroyed much of the industrial might of Japan.

"I've been reminded more than a few times during this war, Colonel, just how much I owe to the guys and gals at Boeing, North American, Douglas, Lockheed and Northrop and some others whose machines I may still get a chance to fly. I know they've often worked long, hard, monotonous shifts to put our planes together for us."

"Yeah, you're right, Dick," he said, "Could you see anything when you overflew Tokyo?"

"Actually, not very much. We had scattered to broken clouds over the Tokyo–Yokohama region on the runs that I made. I could see all of Tokyo Bay, but only glimpses of the cities through breaks in the clouds. I could make out some bombed out and burned-out areas, but I had already seen their pictures in the War Rooms on Guam, Tinian and Saipan.

The most unusual thing I saw, even though we have all seen pictures and been forewarned, was us flying sideways alongside Mt. Fujiyama. The **jet streams** that we've been hearing about are for real! In my case, I started picking them up around 30,000 feet right over central Japan. Often, they are over 100 mph, and unless your course is in line with the jet stream, you really do fly sidewise.

"Colonel, you sit up there with your flying machine cocked so far into the wind, that sometimes you look out your side window to see what is straight ahead of you, to see what you're flying towards. It is an amazing flying sensation. We'll take it, it is clearly harder on the Japanese pilots than it is on us.

"Returning from my second mission to Japan, Colonel, we stopped off to deliver some parts at Iwo Jima. I was glad for the opportunity to have a quick look around. I grabbed a jeep and wheeled around the island while the parts we brought were being unloaded and some fuel on-loaded. The impression that I got was we all owe much to our Marines."

Colonel DuBose was fully aware of the significance of the Marine invasions of Iwo Jima and Okinawa and agreed we owe the Marines a great deal. I said I would prepare a written report for him as requested.

At this point I said, "If it's OK with you, Colonel DuBose, I think I'll be taking off. But before I go, I want you to know you sure have a lot of fine friends out there. They went out of their way to make my fact-finding mission informative and pleasant. I have a list of names who asked to be remembered to you, which I will provide with my report."

I was then on my way; but could not help imagining what it would have been like to have been a Marine in the South Pacific.

I had been shot at, but unlike the Marines at Iwo Jima. I said to myself, "Richard Eager, you were never a sitting duck; you were always a moving target usually moving at a couple hundred miles per hour. You were once afraid of flying. But imagine, if you had been a Marine Sergeant with your feet planted firmly on the ground at Iwo Jima when the order came to advance up this hill and you turned to your men and said, 'Okay, you soldiers, follow me.' Do you think your legs might have turned to jelly? Luckily, Richard Eager, you will never know.

"The men who stood on the beach at Iwo Jima faced real fear. You have been spared that, Richard Eager. Go back and climb into your B-29 flying machine and relax. Fly back home in considerable comfort and don't you ever be too stuffy about what you were required to do in the war."

———————————

As I was writing this book, I looked at the numbers. The tally in human suffering in the 36-day hell at Iwo Jima exceeded 47,000 soldiers. 26,000 American casualties including 6,800 dead were listed. Out of 21,000 Japanese soldiers, only 216 survived. The Japanese directives were simpler than ours. The young men in Japan were directed to win or to lose completely... to prevail or die.

Iwo Jima would provide an immediate fighter base for P-51s, putting them within range of Tokyo. They would be able to provide cover for our attacking B-29s. Also, crippled B-29s unable to make it back to their base in the Marianas could often reach Iwo Jima from Japan. Iwo would shorten the war, and, ironically, would save Japanese lives as well as British and American ones.

The story at Okinawa was similar; the 82-day Battle of Okinawa was the largest beach landing in the Pacific Theater. There were over 100,000 Japanese casualties and 50,000 Allied casualties. When "Oki" was freed and in a matter of days quickly readied for B-29s, I was on the island to see it happening. Our Navy had some work to do but the flyboys' war was almost over.

———————————

Several weeks later after seeing my baby daughter, Bobbie, for the first time and spending a few days in San Antonio with JoAnn and the baby, I returned to Okinawa with Colonel DuBose and our 316th B-29 Wing. On August 6, as we were preparing our unit for its first mission over Japan, Colonel Paul Tibbets and his crew on the *Enola Gay* dropped the atom bomb on Hiroshima. That event was followed three days later by another atom bomb dropped on Nagasaki. Japan surrendered six days later. The war was over.

———————————

The Army Air Corps had a "point system" for demobilization of U.S. Armed Forces after the war. The system implemented what was known as the ASR Score or Advanced Service Rating Score. Its purpose was to be as fair as possible about where you stood in the lineup with all the others who had put in their time and had the required points to ship out and go home, or in military language, to "return to the ZI." Everybody overseas was given points for military duty time, out-of-country duty time, each battle star or decoration, dependent children and additional points for combat time. A total of 85 points was needed to be eligible. I had accumulated enough points in the European Theater of Operations to be well up on the Okinawa list, actually at the top of it. The actual plans and process to return the military men and women to the States when the war ended was called "Operation Magic Carpet." When I checked in every morning with Lieutenant Colonel Dave Christianson's office, our Wing Director of Personnel, he would greet me with the same smile. He would have no travel orders sending me back to the States.

"Don't sweat it, Dick," he would say, "You're probably top man on our list here in Okinawa. There just isn't any transport to get you on and out of here. You might see if Colonel DuBose would authorize a B-29 training flight to the Philippines. You could fly down there and get in their line."

"Wouldn't I just be starting all over again in a longer line?" I asked.

"Probably, but I understand they have a troop ship coming in from Indo-China."

"A troop ship," I gasped, "Ye gods, Dave, I've done my time on troop ships, that's how I got back to the ZI from the ETO. Can you believe it? I volunteered; I wanted the experience. Never again will I want that experience if I can avoid it. I'm a bloody Army Air Corps aviator. I told my bride, my mom, and my dad that I'd be home by Christmas. My new daughter, Barbara Lynn, is going to have her first birthday without her dad if I don't hurry it up and get out of here pretty soon."

My friend cocked his head to one side, "Oh you'd make Christmas, Dick, I'm sure." Then he cocked it still further and said, "Come to think of it, it might not be this Christmas."

"I'm not in the mood for your smart remarks, Colonel; I'm getting worried. I've got a new wife who hasn't seen that much of her husband, a daughter who has seen her father even less, and a mom and a pop who feel they have been patient with me and the Army Air Corps."

Colonel Christianson then pulled a paper from his files, floated it across his desk to me and gave me a couple of minutes to get the gist of it.

"What am I reading? It looks like somebody's travel orders. What are all these numbers about? What do they mean? Why are you showing me somebody else's travel orders?"

"Lieutenant Colonel Evans, if you really want to move around the world in our system, you must have numbers on your travel orders like this fellow has on his. I can look up these numbers that are on his orders. I can tell you where he's from and where he is allowed to go and what form of transportation, we must make available for him. In this particular case, I would guess that this Brigadier General probably worked pretty close to General Hap Arnold, you know the fellow who's been running our Army Air Corps. I would wager, this BG very likely worked long and hard hours for Hap during the war. The General, wishing to reward him for his loyal service, directed that these orders be written for him.

"General Arnold has had some special orders written for this one-star general that are the rough equivalent of a signed blank check with the place where you put in the amount left blank. This piece of paper gives this man authority to go anywhere in the world he might like and to use any aircraft that's flyable wherever he might happen to find himself. Guess where he wants to go from here and what he wants us to fly in."

My good friend said with a smile, "Calcutta and a *B-29 Superfortress*. If you would like to be on the ramp to wave him off, takeoff is scheduled for 0800 hours tomorrow morning. I would be glad to pick you up in my jeep and we could ride out to the end of the runway together."

"No, thanks. A B-29 takeoff doesn't do that much for me anymore. You were right when you said I should have worked harder and made BG, or at least full Colonel; then maybe I could get off this lousy island and return home to my gals for Christmas." I remember heaving a big sigh and saying, "Well, hell, Colonel, keep your ear to the ground for me. Let me know if something turns up where they'll let a Light Colonel ride in their baggage compartment. I'll take it."

When I left the Quonset hut that housed Wing Personnel, I was even more dejected than before. I had always tried to be patient. Dad had often said "Remember, Dick, you're not the only pebble on the beach."

I smiled inside and said to myself, "Richard Eager, you're smiling again, you damn fool. Your old man can make you smile even when you feel like sitting in a corner and crying, even when he's 7,700 miles away on the other side of the Pacific." Dad was right though. There are a lot of POWs and guys in hospitals who have had a lot tougher war than I have. I know I'm not the only bloody pebble on the beach. I thought how I used to hate to hear Dad tell me that.

I decided that I would not go back to the tent and read. I would grab a jeep and find my way down to the bottom of the 200-foot promontory that for a couple of months had been like an over-sized front porch for my friends and me. There was a small Navy Seabee installation down there and a very nice beach. There was not a soul around. I figured I'd drive a jeep down there and take a look so I could tell Dad that there really was a time when I was the biggest pebble on a blinking beach. It was on Buckner Bay, Okinawa.

On my way, I dropped by Kadena Air Base Ops and checked the schedule. Sure enough, a B-29 was set up to fly to Calcutta the next morning. That didn't help me feel any better.

It didn't take long to find my way down to the bottom of our private cliff. When I looked up, I could see the edge where my neighbor, Colonel Rogers, watched his tent and worldly goods fly out to sea during one of the typhoons that thrashed the islands. Okinawa was located in what was called "Typhoon Alley." Many of the typhoons were destructive with winds from 73-91mph, severe typhoons clocked winds at 92 mph, and the super typhoon winds would be at least 120 mph. Planes, ships, shelters and supplies were often times severely damaged, leaving the soldiers, sailors and flyboys without protection until tents and huts could be raised again. Those natural forces of nature seemed to assist the enemy. We lived in hastily built tents that had no resistance to the Pacific cyclones. Yes, many belongings flew off the cliff and out to sea. It will be hard to forget watching those shirts and shorts leading the way, dancing and flying as if an invisible, very excited whirling dervish wore them.

I found a Navy crate on the beach, sat down on it and looked out across the Philippine Sea.

Home was the way I was looking. I was homesick. The men of the 316th Wing would do a tour of duty on Okinawa. Because of my prior overseas service, I had already been relieved and replaced. About 955 miles from where I was sitting, the USS Missouri, anchored in Tokyo Bay, became the historical site for the Japanese delegation to sign the "Japanese Instrument of Surrender," after General MacArthur signed first.

It was over for me and I could go home if I could just get my butt off this bloody island. My dad came to mind and I thought, "Here I go again, Dad, feeling sorry for myself. What can I do, Pop? I really am trapped this time and I feel very helpless."

I don't know when I got the idea. I think it might have been when I was driving back up the steep hill from the beach. "You're nuts, Richard Eager. It won't work. You might really get in a jam in India. On the other hand, it might work. How bad do you really want to go home? What do you have to lose? With the war over and all, do you really think they are going to throw the book at you? You even have a couple of medals that might help your case.

"Could I get Colonel DuBose in trouble?" I came to the conclusion that I probably wouldn't; but I sure wasn't going to take the chance. Why shouldn't I ask Colonel DuBose and let him decide? He's my boss."

At chow that night I tried again to sort it out. I had cooled off, but I could feel that I was sweating. "I can't do something that could get Colonel DuBose in trouble, something that could block his promotion. He's overdue from being hung up in the States so long. This might be his last shot at getting his star. Damn!" I silently swore to myself.

After dinner, I wandered over to Personnel, thinking I might talk to Dave and sound him out. Nothing was locked up on Oki; there was nothing to take and no place to go with it. I opened the door and walked in. Colonel Christianson wasn't there; nobody was there. It occurred to me that nobody would be there. There's nothing to do. Didn't I know the war was over?

I walked over to Dave's file cabinet. I had seen which drawer he had opened. It took only a couple of minutes, and there it was. There was the piece of paper that directed anybody and everybody who saw it to let the bearer fly wherever he damn well pleased, anywhere in the whole bloody world.

I was very nervous and sweating. I had put a piece of paper into the typewriter and I was already half through the letter I was typing. I remember thinking about Miss Ferguson, my homeroom teacher in high school, who persuaded me that typing wasn't just for sissies. She had said I would someday thank her for practically forcing me to take a half-semester of typing at Knox High. She said, "Dick, it's not going to hurt your football." I remembered that I said, "Miss Ferguson, it couldn't hurt my football."

I had made an exact copy of the letter and was careful to get all the reference numbers correct. Actually, it wasn't an exact copy. I had substituted my name in the places where I had left out the Brigadier General's name. Then I rolled off a half dozen copies on the mimeograph, thinking it might be a long trip with a lot of stops.

I hadn't thought the whole process through yet. It was no surprise to me when I found myself heading for Colonel DuBose's quarters, a single Quonset hut, not very far from my tent. When he opened his door, I said to myself, "Thank God, he's alone."

"Come in, Dick," he said, "What hair-brained scheme have you thought up now? Where do you want me to sign? How come you're working? Don't you know this war is over?"

"Thanks, Colonel, and thanks for the way you put it. It just so happens that I have brought along a hair-brained scheme for you to consider. It's very possible that you won't like it. Would you, please, just read this piece of paper? Then we'll talk."

My wing commander read it quickly and then dropped his head so that he could look directly at me over the top of his eyeglasses with his eyebrows raised. He often did this. He read the paper that I had handed him. Then he smiled and said, "This is great, Dick, I'm glad for you. I know how much you want to go home, and I'm glad your orders finally came through. I'm glad, too, that you wanted to come in and tell me about it. You ought to be out of here by the end of the week."

He paused and then said, "Something's wrong, isn't it? Why are you bringing these orders to me? Why didn't I receive your orders first?"

He stopped for a second, and I figured I'd better jump in. "Colonel, those orders are like the orders the Brigadier General from Washington has. As a matter of fact, they're identical except where you see my name instead of his."

My boss and friend took a good look. "By damn, they sure are the same orders; Colonel Christianson showed them to me... said they authorized travel any way the BG wanted to go to anywhere he might like to go. We have to set up a B-29 to take him to the Kalaikunda Air Force Station, near Kharagpur, India. Why anybody would want to go to Kalaikunda I can't imagine."

"Well, that's where I come in. Colonel Christianson showed me the orders, told me about the flight. I thought you might let me fly the Brigadier to the Kalaikunda Air Force Station, in the B-29. I'm current in the B-29, test-hopped one yesterday, Colonel. I'm an instructor pilot on the B-29, or did you know that?"

"I'm missing something. You would be back here in the next couple days. How the hell is that helping you get to Texas or Tennessee or wherever it is you're from or want to go?"

"I would take another pilot along, Colonel. He would bring the B-29 back to you here at Okinawa in the next day or two. I would then head on home, heading west, not east."

"Good God all mighty, Dick; you're serious. Don't you know you'd be going the wrong way; you go east for Christ sakes to get from Okinawa to the States. You know that? You don't turn around and head for India when you're trying to get to San Francisco. Kalaikunda is the end of the bloody line."

"Colonel, you are right. That Air Force Station near Kharagpur, India, is also the beginning of the line. You just head west instead of east. You see, Sir, the Earth is like a basketball... it's..."

"Don't get smart with me, Colonel," he said. His words were sharp, but his eyes were grinning at me as he peered out over the top of his glasses.

"Colonel, I thought I could hitchhike on the ATC (Air Transport Command system) out of the Kalaikunda station. That's why I would need the orders. That is why I typed them."

"I know; I heard you, Colonel, but would you please repeat that last part again? No, don't. I don't want to hear about it. For God's sake, Dick, you really copied that BG's orders. Everywhere his name used to be, yours is now? Well, I'll be gone-to-hell; you've lost your bloody mind, Richard Eager. Is that what I hear them calling you?"

"Yes, sir; I picked that name up at Randolph and Kelly Field back in San Antonio in 1939 and 1940. My classmates seemed to think that I was too eager. I think it was because I was their Cadet Commander, Colonel."

My boss was now staring at me as if he was really thinking about what was going on. My dad had taught me a good thing. I remember he once said, "Don't jump to the conclusion, Dick, that you've lost before it's made very clear that you really have. Sometimes it's a good idea to just sit tight and wait." That's exactly what I did that evening on Okinawa in my Commander's Quonset hut.

After a minute of complete silence, I decided that Colonel DuBose's dad must have taught him the same thing. He was just sitting there waiting me out.

Finally, he got up out of his chair and hit his fist in his other hand and said, "Damn, Dick, I think you might just pull this off. The traffic to the States from here is east straight across the Pacific. The traffic goes the other way out of Kalaikunda, India. It flows west to New Delhi and Karachi across the Middle East, North Africa and the Atlantic. The dividing line is China. You came out here with enough points to get back home when the war ended but you're stuck here because we're at the end of the line. Come to think of it, you're at the end of both lines. As I think of it, you had enough points to stay home. Why the hell didn't you? No, don't answer that. Just tell me how you figure on pulling this off?"

"Well, sir, I thought the same way you're thinking right now. I know I'm taking some risk; I could run into some hard-nosed type who would insist on checking out my orders, but I thought most of them would be too damn busy, what with everybody heading home to the States and all."

When I taxied to the end of the runway the next morning it was 0755 hours. I could relax a few seconds, take a deep breath and run through the checklist. That's when I noticed the Wing Commander's staff car parked on the side of the taxiway. And there was my boss, Colonel DuBose, and my good friend Colonel Christianson, standing beside the car. Both of them gave me a kind of half-salute and half-wave goodbye.

Men don't cry, of course; but sometimes tears come to their eyes, which is what happened to mine on the end of that Okinawa runway. For a few seconds, it didn't seem like they were going to stop. The war was really over for me; I was finally going home, this time to stay. I was sitting in a B-29 in the driver's seat hoping that others standing on the taxiway waving hadn't noticed the excess of water coursing down my cheeks.

My radio crackled and the tower operator said, "You are cleared for takeoff, three-zero-six." There was a pause; then he came on again. "Hope you make it, Colonel," he said.

"Thanks, Sarge," I answered, "I'll drop you a card."

As I turned onto the runway and advanced the throttle, the engines roared in response. The big steel and aluminum monster shuddered, started rolling and picked up speed. We had a full load of fuel, but no bombs. We were off quite quickly. The landing gear was grinding up. Moments later it clanked as the up-locks embraced it and the covers closed securely.

I was level and accelerating as I passed to one side of our tents perched out on the end of our pleasant promontory. As expected, the ground dropped away rapidly at the end of our cliff. Straightaway, we were three or four hundred feet over Buckner Bay.

I relaxed the slight back-pressure I was holding on the control column and allowed the right wing to drop, putting us into a gentle, descending right turn toward the south tip of Okinawa, where some of the last fighting of World War II had taken place, where the US Marine Theater Commander, General Buckner, had died in the last weeks of the war.

With the elevator control, I flattened the angle at which we were approaching the surface of the Pacific. I had plenty of time to notice the shades of green in the shallows and the cobalt blue in the depths.

I thought of General Simon Buckner who was alive just weeks ago. I remembered all the fine men who had been with me in Africa, Sicily and Italy who weren't going home, either. Why was I getting to go home... and they weren't?

The B-29 picked up speed in the shallow descent towards the bay and I was now rolling the elevator control back to level us up and start our climb to cruise altitude. Also, I had commenced a 180-degree turn back to my right that would head us in the direction of China and India where I would find Kalaikunda. "You're going the wrong way, Richard Eager; but if you can manage to just keep going west from Kalaikunda, follow the sun over the Atlantic, you just might make it to Texas, your home, for Christmas."

Then I shouted silently to myself, "You're going home, Richard Eager, you're going home to your family and to those you love and who love you. You are on your way to see your lovely wife and baby daughter."

My thoughts raced. "Never forget Frank Roberts, your flight crews, and all the others who aren't making the trips home. You're on your way; but many of your comrades are here to stay... forever, somewhere on the other side of the world. Richard Eager, you are a very lucky man. Don't you ever, ever forget Technical Sergeant Francis Morris... Staff Sergeant Victor Kennedy... your co-pilot, Second Lieutenant Fred Johnson and Technical Sergeant Dale Owens, the men who didn't return home from Europe when you did."

Don't forget your special friend, Doc Hughes of the flying rings, or King George VI. And always remember Monty, who wasn't demonstrative with praise and affection, but when he would say, "My pilot," I knew he meant me.

The war was over for me, but my friend from Air Corp Cadet School, Major Frank A. Roberts, who pinned the name "Richard Eager" on me, would not be on his way back home. He did, indeed, put everything he had to give... on the line. My friend for life, for just a few fleeting years, would not see his family again. He would not be making that trip of which we all dreamed. Frank would never be recovered from his B-29... from the bottom of the Pacific Ocean near Tokyo Bay.

21.2 *Major Frank A. Roberts, B-29 pilot, never made it home*

21.3 *Cadet Frank A. Roberts coined the name, "Richard Eager," for Cadet Richard Evans*

21.4 *Dick with his "special girl," JoAnn Nelson, who is attending The University of Texas*

21.5 *The newlyweds,*
Major and Mrs.
Richard E. Evans

21.6 *Dick and JoAnn's*
wedding trip to Knoxville, TN

21.7 *USAAF Matts C-54 "Skymaster" flies to Hawaii* (National Archives and Records Administration)

21.8 *What it is like to fly (B-17) over the Golden Gate Bridge, San Francisco*
(National Archives and Records Administration)

*21.9 Fond memories with Field Marshal Bernard Law Montgomery,
1ˢᵗ Viscount Montgomery of Alamein*

E.1 *Colonel Richard E. Evans, Command Pilot*

EPILOGUE

"To Dick,
Who directed our B-47 & B-58 ops suitability test programs, flew
our first 25, 30, and 35-hour multi-refueling B-47 missions, planned
and lead our full B-47 wing deployment to the U.K. and directed our
MAD & SAC B-70 source selection boards. With thanks for your help
in building SAC into the world's mightiest force for peace."

Curtis E. LeMay
General Curtis E. LeMay's personal autograph
in Colonel Richard Evans' copy of LeMay's biography,
Iron Eagle, by Thomas M. Coffey

At the end of the war, Richard E. Evans, informally called Dick, settled into a new life with his bride, JoAnn, and infant daughter, Barbara, in Pasadena, California. After six-and-a- half years in the US Army Air Corps, he, along with millions of Americans, left the military. Dick embarked on a new career as an insurance representative and very quickly became a top agent for Massachusetts Mutual Life Insurance Company. During that time, in 1948, his son, Donald, was born.

Dick's love of flying never waned, so he joined the California Air National Guard, the Air Reserve Component of the US Air Force. He continued to fly and broaden his experience in the newest aircraft as soon as they were deployed. He remained in the Air Force Reserves until 1951, when he returned to active duty in the US Air Force during the Korean War. The Korean War was a serious escalation in the Cold War, which would shape international relations for over forty years.

The Cold War, a period of intense geopolitical tension between the Soviet Union and the United States and their respective allies, emerged in the late 1940s. The conflict was based around the ideological and economic struggle for global influence by the two powers. Of critical importance was the doctrine of Mutually Assured Destruction (MAD), which discouraged a pre-emptive attack by either side. The United States created NATO (North Atlantic Treaty Organization) in 1949 in anticipation of a Soviet attack; and the Soviet Union formed the Warsaw Pact in 1955 in response to NATO.

At this time, the main deterrent against Russian aggression in Europe was the Strategic Air Command (SAC). This branch of the now-called US Air Force had at its disposal older B-29 bombers and some nuclear weapons. The US made it clear that SAC could and would drop nuclear bombs on Soviet cities if the Soviet Union attacked and overran Europe. SAC was responsible for Cold War command and control of two of the three components of the US military's strategic nuclear strike forces, the so-called "nuclear triad": the land-based strategic bomber aircraft and intercontinental ballistic missiles (ICBMs).

Being outnumbered in army size, the threat of nuclear annihilation was one of few options available to the US; and soon the Soviets developed a similar arsenal of weapons. By mid-1950, the US was embroiled in the defense of South Korea, in what would become known as the Korean War (June 25,1950 – July 27,1953).

Sometime early in the Korean War, Dick received a phone call from an old friend, Colonel Don Hillman, who casually asked, "How would you like the best job in the US Air Force?" Known in the Air Force for his leadership and flying skills in WWII, Dick had been recommended for the position of Deputy Director of Operations, HQ 306th Bomb Wing, MacDill AFB, FL. His new assignment would be to run the operations suitability tests for the Strategic Air Command's first jet bomber, the B-47 *Stratojet*. He said, "Yes, I'll take the job." He knew he could handle the challenge and believed he could make a difference. He was thirty-two years old.

On March 24, 1951, Dick was recalled to active duty. Although Lieutenant Colonel Evans had the "points" and seniority to avoid service and was well on his way to wealth in his civilian job, he chose to reenlist. Reflecting on that decision, Dick's son, Don, later asked his father, "Why? Why did you go back into service? After all, you had spent six-and-a-half years of your life defending our nation. Wasn't that enough?" In response, Dick told his son that he could not look his fellow reserve officers in the eye if he did not enlist, and he knew that SAC's mission was one he wanted to support. He reported for duty at MacDill Air Force Base in the fall of 1951.

The Commander of SAC was General Curtis LeMay, a legend in the Air Force. As the 4th Bombardment Wing Commander, he personally led the important Schweinfurt-Regensburg mission task force over Germany, ordered the dropping of the atomic bombs on Japan, and ran the "Berlin Airlift." LeMay planned to build SAC into such a powerful organization that no power would dare to attack the United States or invade its European allies. His first goal was to acquire a fleet of jet bombers and refueling aircraft that could strike the Soviet Union directly and still return to the safety of US bases. LeMay would later become the Head of the Joint Chiefs of Staff under Kennedy during the Cuban Missile Crisis. It is said that, even today, within the US Air Force, when there is a hard decision to be made, the question is "What would LeMay do?"

Having served under General LeMay at Tinian, Evans had the good fortune of serving once again under the command of the iconic general. Moreover, Evans would report directly to the legendary Colonel Michael N. W. McCoy. Both Evans and McCoy were possibly hand-picked for these coveted positions because of their WWII experiences working with the British Royal Air Force. McCoy had joined the Royal Canadian Air Force to fight in the early phases of the Battle of Britain prior to the U.S. entering the war; and Evans had earned recognition for his special assignment as Field Marshal Montgomery's trusted B-17 pilot in North Africa and Southern Europe. The US-UK relationship remained strong long after V-Day; and at this point in the Cold War, British bases were once again essential to the success of long-range missions. To reach the Soviet Union successfully, the B-47 aircraft had to be refueled in flight by fuel tankers based in Britain.

Upon his SAC appointment, Lieutenant Colonel Evans, his wife and two children moved immediately to MacDill Air Force Base in Tampa, Florida, where the first B-47 bombers were delivered, and where the leadership was busy testing the bombers and training crews for military duty with the new equipment.

Key to this training was the ability to refuel the aircraft in flight. Even though it was very fast, the B-47 needed to be refueled multiple times to strike anywhere in the Soviet Union and then return to a friendly base. As part of this training, Lieutenant Colonel Evans set Air Force jet bomber refueling records for maintaining a B-47 in flight for 25, 30, and 35 hours. For his longest world-record mission, Evans was awarded the rank of Colonel in 1954. His reviewers reported: "His performance of duty is characterized by imagination, persuasiveness, ability to speak on his feet, and a complete grasp of the operational significance and problems of the jet medium bombardment field."

The journal of the US Air Force, *Air Force* magazine, documented the strategic importance of the 35-hour mission by featuring Colonel Evans and his crew on the magazine's cover commemorating the 10th anniversary of Strategic Air Command. Though the B-47 never saw significant combat, the program made the Soviets sit up and take notice. They never invaded Western Europe and the threat of mass retaliation by US nuclear weapons helped de-escalate the tensions of the Cold War.

The B-47 program attracted some of America's best military leadership to MacDill AFB. A group of officers had a small, informal club on nearby Lake Carroll where they could relax and water ski with their families and colleagues. Many Air Force legends passed through Lake Carroll: Colonel Don E. Hillman, who flew the first B-47B deep-penetration flight over the Soviet Union years before the famed Francis Gary Powers U-2 flights; General Paul Tibbets who dropped the atomic bomb on Hiroshima; and Colonel Patrick Fleming, who was the number four Naval Ace in WWII. There was also a major who was reputed to be the only American to shoot down a four-engine bomber (German Focke-Wulf 200 *Condor*) with a four-engine bomber (B-24 *Liberator*) and a Colonel whose exploits were the basis of the book and movie *Twelve O'Clock High*. Also, during his frequent visits to MacDill, General LeMay was often an honored guest at Lake Carroll.

On a lark, Dick Evans, Don Hillman and Pat Fleming joined forces and would water ski in the famous aquatic shows at Cypress Gardens, Florida, where they became known as "The Three Flying Colonels." Dick told his family that he and his Air Force buddies were really a foil for the better skiers in the show. Dick, Don and Pat would go over the ramp together and fly 50 to 60 feet. They would then be followed by the Cypress Garden pros who would soar 120 feet. Also, water skiing legend and airman at the time, "Barefoot Stew" McDonald, participated. They all had a great time.

Another celebrity visitor to Lake Carrol was Jimmy Stewart, who was at the time filming the highly acclaimed Paramount Pictures film "*Strategic Air Command*." Most of the extensive flying scenes were shot on location at MacDill Air Force Base and Evans personally flew the multiple B-47 scenes depicting Jimmy Stewart as an Air Force B-47 pilot.

Lieutenant Colonel Henry Deutschendorf, Sr., or "Dutch" as he was called by friends, was a trusted flying buddy of Colonel Evans during his B-47 days. Dutch would go on to set several world speed records in the B-58 and his "Air Force Brat" son would grow up to be John Denver, the popular singer. Dick's children would remember the junior Deutschendorf fondly, recalling John's guitar playing on the porches of many airbase residences.

In 1955, Colonel Evans was again offered the job of his dreams. He was asked to run another operations suitability test program, this time as Deputy Chief Requirements Division Director, HQ SAC, Offutt AFB, Bellevue, Nebraska, for the Convair B-58 *Hustler*, the first operational bomber capable of Mach 2 flight. Since the B-58 had a range comparable to the B-47, the young officer was charged with developing it as a weapon system for SAC. The Air Force needed to determine if the B-58 could be refueled in flight and thereby become an ultra-fast weapon able to rush into the Soviet Union, drop a payload of bombs and return. Evans, a record holder for in-flight refueling endurance, was perfectly suited to the job. Upon his transfer, Evans and his family moved to Offutt AFB.

Now a full "Bird" Colonel at the age of thirty-six, Evans continued his pilot duties and learned to fly the B-52 *Stratofortress* as well as the F-102 *Delta Dagger*. While at Offutt, Colonel Evans served under then Colonel Jack J. Catton. Catton was the youngest Air Force Officer at the time to make Brigadier General and later was the Commander of SAC's 15th Air Force. Evans was also assigned to take charge of SAC's procurement board for the B-70 *Valkyrie*, which the US Air Force intended to compliment or replace the B-52. In an "Officer Performance" report, Colonel Catton stated, " ...Of particular note, and in my consideration his very strongest point, is his extremely good character. This man is the servant of his own very high ideals. He will not subordinate his ideals under any circumstances. He is completely honest, thoroughly trustworthy and dependable."

In 1958, Dick and his family moved to Carswell Air Force Base in Fort Worth, Texas, home of the B-58 *Hustler* and its manufacturer, Convair. At Carswell, Colonel Evans became head of SAC's suitability test program for the new B-58A *Hustler*, a medium bomber capable of Mach 2 speed. After training in the supersonic Convair F-102 *Delta Dagger*, Evans became the first Air Force pilot to fly the B-58. Prior to this, all B-58s were flown by the manufacturer's test pilots.

The B-58, a cutting-edge but aero-dynamically unstable aircraft, was way ahead of its time. Tragically, 26 of the 116 B-58s built, crashed. Those who survived flying the B-58 loved it; but the aircraft enjoyed but a brief Air Force career, never seeing combat.

Colonel Evans' career was progressing smoothly until he made a serious mistake. In 1959, he was selected to serve on a promotion board at the Pentagon in Washington, DC. While there, he went to visit his old friend and then Chief of Staff of the Air Force, General Curtis LeMay. During their meeting, LeMay naturally asked Colonel Evans what he thought of the B-58A. Evans said he considered it a dangerous aircraft and did not think it would be a successful addition to the SAC arsenal. Evans had shared his honest opinion but had jumped up the chain of command.

While Evans considered the discussion with his old friend and the leader of the US Air Force to be an innocent aside, his boss, four-star General John Paul McConnell, was furious that he had discussed the B-58 "behind his back." McConnell considered this a betrayal of the Chain of Command and removed Colonel Evans from his job of leading the B-58 operations program. General LeMay did not intervene. Evans had been in the Air Force for 16 years and could retire after four more. But knowing he would now probably never achieve the rank of General, Colonel Evans decided to leave the Air Force. He retired from active duty July 14, 1959, but continued military service in the US Air Force Reserve. Dick subsequently moved his family to Los Angeles, California.

In Los Angeles, Dick became a lobbyist for what was then North American Aviation. Among those aircraft built by the company was the B-70 *Valkyrie*. On behalf of North American Aviation, Dick continued to represent the B-70 and later was a consultant to Northrop Grumman in its competition to build the B-1 *Lancer* and to Douglas Aircraft in its competition to build the C-5A *Galaxy*. General LeMay and Colonel Evans remained close friends until LeMay's death in 1990.

Dick Evans died June 16, 2006. He outlived most of his Air Force buddies. He was a bit of a "Man of La Mancha." This comes through repeatedly in his book, as he expresses the many pleasant associations and friendships he enjoyed while participating in an organization so much larger than himself. He was a man who deeply valued the US Air Force and its mission, a man motivated by love of country and not money, and a man who would tell you the truth instead of being political. He was representative of so many good Americans who live their lives in the service of their nation. To this day, Dick's children, Barbara and Don, call themselves "SAC Brats" with great pride in knowing first hand the accomplishments and hard work of their father, Colonel Richard E. Evans.

E.2 *A long day's work, flying the B-58*

E.3 *Replica of AAF & USAF insignias and medals worn by Colonel Richard E. Evans*
(Gift from Colonel Frank J. McKeown, DMD)

Colonel Rank Insignias
Command Pilot Wings

Distinguished Flying Cross
Air Medal with two silver Oak Leaf Clusters

Presidential Unit Citation
Air Force Outstanding Unit Award with bronze Oak Leaf Cluster
American Defense Service Medal

American Campaign Medal
European-African-Middle Eastern Campaign with four bronze Stars
Asiatic-Pacific Campaign Medal with one bronze Star

World War II Victory Medal
National Defense Service Medal
Korean Service Medal

Air Force Longevity Service Award with three bronze Oak Leaf Clusters
Armed Forces Reserve Medal with Hourglass Device
United Nations Korea Medal

E.4 *Colonel Evans in the B-47 pilot seat*

E.5 *B-47 "Stratojet" takes off*

E.6 *B-47 "Stratojet" is refueled by a Boeing KC-135 "Stratotanker"*

E.7 *B-47 makes drogue parachute landing*

E.8 *B-52 "Stratofortress," is the icon of the US Cold War*

E.9 *Colonel Richard Evans flies the B-58 "Hustler"*

E.10 *B-58 "Hustler"*

E.11 *B-58 "Hustler" is refueled by the Boeing KC-135 "Stratotanker"*

E.12 *Artist drawing of the B-70 "Valkyrie," of which only two are built*

E.13 *B-70 "Valkyrie" model is admired by Richard Evans and Jimmy Stewart*

E.14 *The "three flying colonels" ski-jump the ramp*

E.15 *Colonel Don and Lois Hillman, JoAnn and Colonel Richard Evans
(left to right) enjoy skiing at Cypress Gardens, FL*

E.16 *Daughter, Bobbie, skis with her father, Dick Evans*

E.17 *Dick's family, young son, Don, daughter, Bobbie and wife, JoAnn, enjoying Lake Carroll, FL*

E.18 *JoAnn and Dick water skiing on Lake Carroll, FL*

ACKNOWLEDGEMENTS

As I look back and remember all the people who helped me bring my father's book to the world, I am humbled. A book starts as the creation of one individual. It then evolves from a wonderful, imaginative idea and is supported and realized by many caring and talented individuals.

First, I want to thank Colonel Richard E. Evans for putting his stories in writing for others to read. Dad, your life, your family, and your friends live on within your narratives.

Family is the first group to acknowledge. My husband, John C. Kinnear, my daughter, Katherine H. "Katie" Kinnear, brother-in-law, Colonel Frank J. "Mick" McKeown, brother, Donald N. "Don" Evans, and my mother, JoAnn N. Law, were all involved in very special ways. Our family loved hearing our father/grandfather recount his poignant stories. My brother, Don, is to be thanked for suggesting to our father that he write down his stories. Don also contributed details to the Epilogue which helped summarize Colonel Richard Evans' post-war career in the Strategic Air Command. My mother, JoAnn, shared valuable family knowledge that filled out some of the accounts of Richard Evans' youth, as her memories reach far back to the years before my brother and I were born. John and Katie were fellow copy editors through the entire evolution of the book. Many an evening was filled with discussions of factual details, concerns, and exciting discoveries. We shared the joys of historical fact-finding within museums like the Imperial War Museum and the American Air Museum in Britain and the National Archives and Records Administration in the United States. A vast range of primary sources provided the historical backbone for this book, and the discovery of each new military record, General Montgomery's photo or a crew member's name, was a precious victory for my family.

The historians who worked and researched for this project are another remarkable group. I'll never forget the day Mick McKeown introduced me to Yvonne Kinkaid, Research Historian, Archives Section, USAF Office of History, Bolling AFB. She found many fundamental military reports that clarified Colonel Evans' movements and missions through North Africa and Italy and helped to knit the military memories together. Yvonne encouraged me to contact Dr. John A. Arnold, PhD, President and Co-Founder of NICOM, Inc. for further research needs. With that fine recommendation in hand, I contacted Dr. Arnold, whereupon he and his staff began locating Colonel Evans' entire Air Force personnel records, numerous 99th BG mission descriptions and most of his flight records. Later, when we met in person, I asked him to be my line editor. His literary expertise and military knowledge were invaluable to bringing disparate chapters together into a cohesive story of my father's early life. Steve Hunnisett, author of the "Blitzwalkers Blog" and Associate Member of the Guild of Battlefield Guides, was my British counterpart historian. He found indispensable information about Field Marshal General Bernard Montgomery's B-17 *Theresa Leta* flights. Steve spent countless hours in the Imperial War Museum archives and various British WWII airdromes to check flight records and more. He also assisted in securing the IWM licenses so that iconic IWM photographs could be printed in this book.

Treasured family photographs add to this book's resonance with readers. I am very grateful for the Evans family Tennessee members, Tom Evans, Jr., Lynda Evans, Dana Huskey, Nancy Pelfrey, and Leslie Evans, who shared their personal family photos. Old photographs need restoration and Santa Barbara's Letitia Haynes, photographer and restoration artist, brought life and light to many of the photographs in this book. Early in the editing process, Donna Dayton, Cate School Director of Technology, found a special group of "techies" who were able to convert my father's old computer floppy discs to a readable format where more history of his life was uncovered. Bud Hoyt from World Conflict Images, Joanna Bouldin from McClung Historical Collection, Knoxville Historical Society, and William Hunnewell and Gary Staffo, from the 99th Bomb Group Historical Society, all contributed impactful photos to the project.

As historical research continued, connections were made with families who were linked to the B-17 "Flying Fortress," *Theresa Leta*. I am very indebted for photos and background stories from Lee and Alan Beringsmith, sons of Second Lieutenant Albert L. Beringsmith, *Theresa Leta* bombardier, and Wesley J. Hudson, son of Captain James W. Hudson, the photographer who took most of the pictures of General Montgomery as well as those of Captain Richard E. Evans when they flew together in the *Theresa Leta*.

Early in the editing process, when I was searching the London IWM photo archives, a new name jumped out. Among the first images taken of General Montgomery and his borrowed American B-17 in North Africa, was a picture labeled: "The General is introduced to the crew by the Captain of the plane." Surprisingly, the captain pictured was not Captain Richard E. Evans. It took weeks of additional research, but I learned that "Monty's" first *Theresa Leta* pilot was Lieutenant Frank B. Evans. His second pilot was my father, Captain Richard E. Evans. I am indebted to Lieutenant Frank B. Evan's children, Carolyn Evans, Steve Evans, John Evans, Mary Evans, and my contact Tom B. Evans, for sharing their father's unpublished memoirs and providing important photos for this book. They must be very proud of their father, a fine B-17 pilot who was awarded the Distinguished Flying Cross.

A special group of "readers" added inspiration and excellent comments. They were Joan Jackson, Carol Newman, Natalie Myerson, Mick McKeown, Don Evans, Gary Staffo (99th BG Historical Society, Vice President), First Lieutenant, John A. Clark (WWII B-17 pilot), and personal pilot friends, Frank Robinson, and Chuck Thornton. A dear friend and an amazing academic, John Caldwell, author of *Anatomy of Victory*, could always be called upon for immediate historical perspective, and his wife, Karen Sketch, cheered the project onward. Joan Lentz and her husband, Gib, Gina Janotta and her husband, Joe, were also part of the cheering section when some parts of the book seemed particularly challenging. Frank Drain and Allan Moller introduced me to knowledgeable groups within the 390th Memorial Museum, Tucson, AZ, who assisted my research.

Once the book's front matter, body and back matter were in place, who was going to design the book with well-chosen type styles, photo placements, front/back covers? Who would do the tedious job of final proofreading? And who would bring it to the public through print? For these tasks, I was fortunate to find book designer, Anna Lafferty of Lafferty Design Plus, proofreader, Amanda de Lucia, and publisher, Erin Graffy of Kieran Publishing. As any writer knows, the last mile to publication is often the hardest and these three professionals provided incredible support.

In summary, there were many who helped bring Colonel Richard E. Evans' book to print. We care that Colonel Evans is remembered; but importantly, we also learned from his stories. As Bud Hoyt, photograph contributor to this book, profoundly noted: "There were countless other young men and women doing heroic things on a daily basis during World War II when our country's very existence was in peril." And so lastly, I acknowledge and thank those who served alongside my father and lived a piece of incredible history.

Barbara "Bobbie" Evans Kinnear
April 25, 2021

LIST OF PHOTOGRAPHS

FRONT COVER
General Montgomery and Captain Evans, standing in front of the B-17E, "Theresa Leta"

MAPS
M.1 *Captain Richard E. Evans keeps his own record of his Atlantic Ocean crossing to North Africa and his first 25 MTO missions*

Chapter 1: ORDERS FROM IKE
1.1 *B-17s cross the great Atlantic Ocean to North Africa*
1.2 *Richard first trains in PT-3, Love Field, Dallas*
1.3 *Roosevelt and Churchill meet at the Casablanca Conference* (Imperial War Museum)
1.4 *General Fay Upthegrove, 99th BG Commander*
1.5 *Ground crewmen load the bombs for a mission* (99th Bomb Group Historical Society)
1.6 *B-17s roll out on steel Marsden Matting in Tunisia, 1943* (National Archives and Records Administration)
1.7 *Flying cadets, Frank A. Roberts, left end of third file, "Richard Eager," far right with sword, Randolph Field, TX*
1.8 *Frank Roberts is left of flying cadet roommates, Kelly Field, TX*
1.9 *Flying cadet "Richard Eager" buys his first car*
1.10 *Pilot training in Boeing "Stearman" biplane*
1.11 *Consolidated PT-3s are first primary flying school trainers built in quantity*
1.12 *AT-6 training maneuvers*
1.13 *Flak looks like white puffs of cotton when reflecting the sunlight*
1.14 *Flying into the sun, flak is backlit and looks like ominous black clouds* (99th Bomb Group Historical Society)
1.15 *B-17s fly in combat formation to drop their bombs* (99th Bomb Group Historical Society)
1.16 *"Theresa Leta" is Monty's future B-17* (Imperial War Museum)

Chapter 2: FORCED LANDING IN AFRICA
2.1 *Tight B-17 formations fly through storm clouds* (99th Bomb Group Historical Society)
2.2 *B-17s fly tucked in elements of three in formations* (99th Bomb Group Historical Society)
2.3 *B-17 looks like a windmill in the dark*

Chapter 3: MONTY, THE VICTOR AT ALAMEIN
3.1 *General Montgomery is the Victor of Alamein*
3.2 *General Francis de Guingand stands in front of one of Montgomery's caravans* (Imperial War Museum)
3.3 *B-17 contrails alert the enemy to their presence* (World Conflict Images)
3.4 *B-17s join with other flights for a long mission* (Captain Joseph J. Merhar Jr. Collection, AFHRA)
3.5 *99th BG B-17s fly over the Swiss Alps*
3.6 *Contrails fill the sky as a 99th BG squadron of B-17s flies toward its mission*
3.7 *Captain Richard Evans teaches navigation students*

Chapter 4: "I'M SORRY, MRS. OGLESBY"
4.1 *Big brother, Stewart, and Dick, second from left, sit with their mother and brothers, Tom and toddler, John, in front of their home, 306 Magnolia Avenue, Knoxville, TN, during the 1920s*
4.2 *A Knoxville home like Mrs. Oglesby's* (McClung Historical Collection)

Chapter 5: SMOKY MOUNTAIN LOGGING TRAIN
5.1 *Stewart and baby Bobby, Dick's elder brothers, play with their parents in the yard*
5.2 *Dick, left, at the age of his first trip to the Smokies with his mother and older brother, Stewart*
5.3 *Engine 105 takes families to the great Smoky Mountains* (McClung Historical Collection)
5.4 *Dick's parents, to the right, sit on the observation car that travels through the Smoky Mountains*
5.5 *Bath in the big sink is a special memory at "Osocozy"*
5.6 *Dick's mother, left, and his Aunt Marian enjoy the front porch of "Osocozy"*
5.7 *Dick, left, and friends play in Jakes Creek*

CHRONOLOGY
RICHARD ERNEST EVANS AND THE EVENTS
THAT MARKED HIS LIFE AND
IN WHICH HE LEFT HIS MARK

"There is a tide in the affairs of men
Which, taken at the flood,
can lead to fortune"

Julius Caesar

REE - Richard Ernest Evans (professional name), Dick (family/casual name)
#0-397378 (USAAC ID Number)

HWS - Helen Wylhemien Stewart, mother, (HWS)

WEE - William Ernest Evans, father, (WEE)

JN - JoAnn Nelson, future wife, (JN)

FBE - First Lieutenant Frank Burton Evans #0-438428, 301st GB, 353rd Squadron, is the first USAAC pilot assigned to fly British Field Marshall Bernard Law Montgomery in the B-17E, *Theresa Leta* (4/15/43 – 6/14/43). REE is the second USAAC pilot assigned to fly "Monty" in the *Theresa Leta*

TL - *Theresa Leta* - General Montgomery's B-17E "Flying Fortress," #41-9082, also identified as #19082, printed as 19082 on the airplane's tail

Where no initials are indicated, the world events recorded in this chronology give context to set the stage for Colonel Richard E. Evans' life

NOTE: When needed, sources are identified within parentheses ( ). Further details of the sources are found in the "Chronology Source Notes," immediately following this Chronology

---

Apr 4, 1885
WEE - William Ernest Evans "Willie" or "Pug" is born in Fremont, OH. Dies 1957

Nov 17, 1887
Bernard Law Montgomery "Monty" is born in Kennington, Surrey, England. Dies March 24, 1976

Feb 1, 1890
HWS - Helen Wylhemien Stewart is born in Lincoln, NE. Dies 1983

Jun 25, 1912
WEE and HWS marry in Knoxville, TN

May 27, 1913
William Stewart Evans "Pug" is born Knoxville, TN. He is REE's oldest brother. Dies 1999

Jul 28, 1914
The Great War (World War I) begins

1915
Robert Monteath Evans "Bobby" is born in Knoxville, TN. He is REE's older brother, dies

1917, while family is summer vacationing at the cabin, "Osocozy," in the Great Smoky Mountains

1917
WEE - Serves as Principal for Knoxville High School from 1917 – 1951. The high school's buildings become inadequate, so the city builds three new high schools. WEE becomes the principal of the new East High School until his retirement in 1955

Nov 11, 1918
The Great War (World War I) ends

Jan 19, 1919
REE - Born in Knoxville, TN. Dies 2006

Summer 1921
REE - Family spends the summer in the Great Smoky Mountains (Chapter 5, "Smoky Mountain Logging Train")

Dec 15, 1922
Tom Hamilton Evans, REE's younger brother is born in Knoxville, TN. Dies 2018

Sep 4, 1924
John Albert Evans, REE's youngest brother, is born in Knoxville, TN. Dies 2016

1925-1931
REE - Attends Park City Lowry Grammar School (Chapter 10, "School Daze")

Jul 2, 1926
The United States Army Air Corp (USAAC) became the aerial warfare service component of the United States Army

Oct 1926
REE - Gets in trouble with the neighbor (Chapter 4, "I'm Sorry, Mrs. Oglesby")

1931-1934
REE - Attends Park Junior High School

1931
REE - Joins Knoxville's Boy Scouts of America (BSA) Troop 12

1932
REE - Advances quickly to BSA Life Scout

Jan 30, 1933
Adolf Hitler becomes Chancellor of Germany

Summer 1934
REE - Becomes BSA's highest rank, Eagle Scout

1934-1937
REE - Attends Knoxville High School and graduates, taking Second Honors in the Honor Roll. While in the ROTC at KHS for 3 years, REE becomes the Lieutenant Colonel in Advanced Military. Wins the "Wiley K. Morgan Medal," which is given by *Knoxville News Sentinel* General Manager Wiley K. Morgan

Apr 19, 1935
REE - Performs as Jesus in the play, The Terrible Meek (Chapter 16, "Golgotha at First Church")

May 22, 1936
REE - "Dick Evans is Neatest, Best Drilled Cadet. Dick, son of Principal and Mrs. W. E. Evans, 3036 Magnolia Avenue, is a member of the high school rifle team, Knoxville High School ROTC battalion, a director of the 1937B class, treasurer of the Senior Hi-Y, and an Eagle Scout. He represents B Company and competes with Joe Johnson, A Company and Alvin Smith, C Company, for the medal, which is presented to him by the donor, Wiley K. Morgan." ("Dick Evans is Neatest, Best Drilled Cadet." May 22,1936, 14:32)

Nov 11, 1936
REE - Leads Knoxville High School ROTC company in the downtown parade to celebrate Armistice Day (Photograph: 18.2)

Spring 1937
REE - Graduates from Knoxville High School

Spring 1937
REE - Takes ground school classes and wins one of 15 places for 50 hours of flying instruction awarded by the Tennessee Air National Guard

1937-1939
REE - Attends University of Tennessee. He participates in the ROTC, Reserve Officers' Training Corps

May 1939
REE - Poses with *Piper Cub*, single engine airplane, McGhee Tyson Airport. This was the first plane he flies (Photograph: 18.5)

Jul 28, 1939
REE - Attends ROTC training camp at Fort McClellan, AL. Photos of REE holding military shells and drinking from a canteen (Photographs: 18.7, 18.8)

Aug 15, 1939
REE - Applies for appointment as flying cadet, signed in Knoxville, TN. Contract states, "If I successfully complete the course of instruction as a flying cadet, I will accept a commission as Second Lieutenant, Air Corps Reserve, if such a commission is tendered me, and I agree to serve for three years on active duty as such unless sooner relieved by competent authority"

Aug 23, 1939
Nazi Germany and the Soviet Union sign the German-Soviet Nonaggression Pact, in which the two countries agree to take no military action against each other for the next ten years

Aug 31, 1939
REE - War Department sends orders advising REE of his acceptance to Flying Cadet School. He is accepted in the San Antonio Aviation Cadet Center (SAACC), TX. He is ordered to report for duty at Love Field, Dallas, TX for the Primary training. REE is a junior at University of Tennessee

Sep 1, 1939
Adolph Hitler invades Poland, and WWII "bursts" on to the eastern European horizon

Sep 1, 1939
As Germany invades Poland the US Army's air arm has barely embarked on its new program of expansion. At the close of 1938, the statistics show a first-line combat aircraft strength of less than 500 planes (not including observation planes) and personnel of 2,337 officers, 29 warrant officers, and 19,301 enlisted men (including flying cadets) ...At the end of August 1939, on the eve of war, the Air Corps has strength of 2,720 officers, 27 warrant officers, and 23,779 enlisted men (including 860 flying cadets). Of the approximately 1,500 tactical aircraft, only about 800 are classified as standard or first line, and of the 59 "skeletonized" squadrons, 3 are balloon and 10 are observation squadrons. The 26,526 officers and men in the Air Corps represented some 14% of the total strength of the Army. By contrast the German Air Force in September 1939, has personnel strength of over 500,000 and a first-line aircraft complement of 3,750 planes, supported by a 10 to 25 per cent reserve of first-line planes. The Royal Air Force at the same time has over 100,000 officers and men and at least 1,750 first-line planes. (Cravens, W.F./ Cate, J.L., Eds., 173)

Sep 3, 1939
Britain declares war on Germany

Sep 5, 1939
United States proclaims neutrality

Nov 1939
REE - Is dressed in civilian clothes standing by nose of a Beechcraft Model 17 *Staggerwing* (Photograph: 18.6)

Dec 27, 1939
REE - Officially enlists in the "Regular Army of the United States for the period of three years." Signs contract on 27 December 1939 at Fort Oglethorpe, GA. Accepts Flying Cadet position for Army Air Corps (AAC)

Dec 28, 1939
REE - Travels by train to Love Field, Dallas, TX. This is his first day in the military service, in the new "Corps of the US Army." It will later be called the US Army Air Corps (USAAC). Following WWII, it will be elevated again, becoming the US Air Force (USAF). The War Department is then divided logically into Land, Sea and Air

Dec 28, 1939
REE - Arrives Love Field, Dallas, TX and is "sworn in"

Dec 30, 1939
REE - Checks out in the "ancient" Consolidated PT-3, the AAC's primary training aircraft (Photographs: 1.10, 1.11)

Mar 23, 1940
REE - Graduates from Primary Flying School, Love Field and departs Dallas, for Randolph Field, San Antonio, TX. While at Randolph REE trains in Boeing-Stearman biplane. Becomes the Cadet Commander Company "C" of the Army Air Corps Flying School Class of 40-E, Randolph Field Army Air Corps. For his "gung-ho" enthusiasm, he earns the nickname Richard Eager, given to him by fellow Air Corp Cadet, Frank A. Roberts (Photograph: 1.8)

Mar 27, 1940
REE - Evaluation by his commander: "His character is Excellent. Efficiency rating as soldier Superior." (REE's Official Military Personnel File (MPF)

Apr 9, 1940
Nazis invade Denmark and southern Norway

May 10, 1940
Hitler launches a *Blitzkrieg* against Netherlands, Belgium, Luxemburg and France

May 19, 1940
British troops are pushed back to the beach at Dunkirk and rescued by British boats

May 26 - Jun 4, 1940
Dunkirk evacuation. Some 338,000 British Expeditionary Force and other Allied troops are evacuated from Dunkirk to England as German forces closed in on them ("Battle of Dunkirk" 2019)

May 1940
REE - Flying Cadets Frank A. Roberts, left end of third file, and Richard E. Evans, Cadet Commander, far right, are practicing military drill commands at Randolph Field, Texas, the Army Air Corps "West Point of the Air" (Photograph: 1.7)

Jun 10, 1940
Italy declares war on the United Kingdom and France

Jun 11, 1940
Italian Air Force launches first air attacks against Malta

Jun 14, 1940
Germans enter Paris

Jun 22, 1940
France surrenders to Nazi Germany

Jun 23, 1940
REE - Transfers to Advanced Flying School at Kelly Field, San Antonio, TX (Photograph: 1.13)

Jul 10, 1940
Battle of Britain begins, as the Luftwaffe vies unsuccessfully with the Royal Air Force for control of the skies over southern England. The last bombing is October 31, 1940

Aug 1940
JN and REE meet for first time at friend, Lois Daubert Dawsons' home, across the alley from the Nelson home, San Antonio, TX

Aug 20, 1940
Winston Churchill speaks in the House of Commons and states, "Never in the field of human conflict was so much owed by so many to so few" as he reflects on the bravery of the Royal Air Force crews and the fleet air arm of the Royal Navy to defend the United Kingdom from air attacks from the German Luftwaffe. This is a battle fought entirely by the air forces of each nation from July 10 – October 31, 1940

Aug 30, 1940
REE - Graduates at Kelly Field (Class of 40-E). "Honorably discharged as a Flying Cadet." Rated "Airplane pilot Excellent." REE completes cadet training and is sworn in as Second Lieutenant USAAC and an Instructor Pilot, Kelly Field (OMPF)

Sep 3, 1940
REE - writes a description of graduation ceremonies, Class of 40-E Air Corps Advanced Flying School, Kelly Field, TX. He mentions movie stars who are in attendance because they are in town to film the movie, "I Wanted Wings" (Appendices: 9.3.40, Cadet Graduation)

Sep 7, 1940
First German air raids, The Blitz, on Central London begin. Air raids end May 11, 1941

Sep 13, 1940
Italian forces invade Egypt from Cyrenaica, the eastern province of Libya

Oct 1940
The British Western Desert Air Force is formed under the command of Air Vice-Marshal Arthur Coningham to conduct operations in North Africa

Nov 5, 1940
Roosevelt is re-elected as US president

Nov 8, 1940
REE - Is stationed at Southeast Air Corps Training Center, Maxwell Field, Montgomery, AL.

Nov 29, 1940
REE - Transfers to Flight #8 Advanced Training Group 1, Squadron II, Southeastern Training Center, Maxwell Field Montgomery, AL. Training in plane BC-1A (OMPF)

Feb 7, 1941
General Annibale "Electric Whiskers" Bergonzoli, commander of the Italian 23rd Corps, is captured in the battle of Beda Fomm, Libya, by the 6th Australian Division, Western Desert Force

Feb 14, 1941
First units of the Deutsches Afrika Korps commanded by General Field Marshal Johannes Erwin Eugen Rommel start to arrive in Libya, during Operation Sonnenblume to reinforce the Italians, who are forced back into Libya, by British troops

Early 1941
US General Headquarters Air Force is subdivided into four air stateside districts (Northeast, Northwest, Southeast and Southwest) in 1940, which now are designated as First, Second Third and Fourth Air Forces. Each numbered air force is organized to contain the wings and combat groups

Mar 11, 1941
President Roosevelt signs the Lend-Lease Act

Mar 20, 1941
REE - Efficiency Report: "A rather boisterous, likeable officer, aggressive and eager but rather scatter-brained and apt to act before thinking. Officer needs more experience before suitable for duty with civilian components. He has a high present value and an excellent potential value" (OMPF)

Apr 6, 1941
Nazis invade Greece and Yugoslavia

May 24, 1941
Sinking of the British ship, *Hood*, by the German ship, Bismarck

May 27, 1941
Sinking of the *Bismarck* by the British Navy

Jun 20, 1941
US Army Air Corps (USAAC) becomes the US Army Air Forces (USAAF)

Jun 22, 1941

Germany attacks Soviet Union as Operation Barbarossa begins, after conquering Yugoslavia, Greece and Crete, in April and May. Hitler sends three million soldiers and 3,000 tanks into Russia. The Russians are taken by surprise as they had signed a treaty with Germany in 1939. Many Russian cities fall to Germany, but Hitler is not expecting the conquest of Russia to last into winter. The German soldiers are far from their supply lines and do not have food, fuel and winter clothing and many freeze to death (Operation Barbarossa, 2019)

Jun 1941

Nazi SS *Einsatzgruppen* (mobile killing units) begin mass murders

Jul 31, 1941

Herman Göring instructs Reinhard Heydrich, chief lieutenant in the paramilitary corps known as the SS (Schutzstaffel), to prepare for the "Final Solution to the Jewish question," giving him authority to do all that is necessary to exterminate the Jews

Sep 5, 1941

TL - Boeing B-17E (5th edition of Boeing's famed *Flying Fortress* series) takes first flight. 512 B-17Es are built. The bomber has a crew of 10 (Pilot, Co-Pilot, Bombardier, Navigator, Radio Operator, Flight Engineer, Ball Turret Gunner, Tail Gunner and two Waist Gunners). The specifications are wingspan 104 feet, length 74 feet, maximum speed 318 mph, cruising speed 226 mph and maximum range 3,200 miles. There are four Wright R-1820-655 engines (1,000 HP each). The maximum bomb load is 4,200 pounds and the defense armaments include ten .50-caliber machine guns, one .30 caliber machine gun. "The rugged B-17 heavy bomber was developed as a strategic bomber in the 1930s. Legendary for its ability to sustain heavy damage in battle and bolstered by its nearly self-sufficient firepower, B-17s were most often used for daytime raids over Germany." ("B-17E *Flying Fortress*, Historical Snapshot" 2021)

Oct 5, 1941

REE - Describes training Air Corp student navigators in all weather conditions. He is transferred to Turner Field, Albany, GA. He flies twin-engine ship for navigation school, training about eight students in flight at a time. (Appendices: 10.5.41, Navigation Instructor)

Oct 16, 1941

REE - Efficiency Report: Flying Instructor, excellent. Pilot, excellent. Ten other characteristics rated "4 very satisfactory" or "5 excellent" (OMPF)

Dec 7, 1941

Japanese attack the US naval base at Pearl Harbor, bringing America into the war. In the following weeks, Japan also attacks British territories in the Far East

Dec 8, 1941

United States and Britain declare war on Japan

Dec 10, 1941

REE - Letter describes the poignant emotions of why he wants to go to war (Appendices: 12.10.41, Going to War)

Dec 11, 1941

Germany declares war on the United States

Dec 16, 1941

Rommel begins a retreat to El Agheila, Libya, in North Africa

Dec 19, 1941

Hitler takes complete command of the German Army

Jan 26, 1942

First American forces arrive in Great Britain

Jan 28, 1942

The US 8th AF is established, and a small group of officers move to England to study the methods of the RAF and plan for future operations from English bases

Feb 1, 1942

REE - Awarded First Lieutenant rank

Feb 15, 1942

Japan takes Singapore from the British

Mar 2, 1942

US Army is functionally reorganized into three autonomous forces: The Army Ground Forces, the Service of Supply and the Army Air Forces, each commanded by a general who reports directly to the Army Chief of Staff

Mar 8, 1942

REE - Writes JN about student navigation techniques and his requests to be transferred to the war front (Appendices: 3.8.42, Navigation Techniques)

Apr 3, 1942

REE - Swears Oath of Office as a First Lieutenant,

Hendricks Field, FL. Becomes a B-17 Instructor Pilot at Seabring Air Base, FL. Also, IP for A-20, B-25 and B-24 at Tucson, El Paso, Alamogordo, and Salina Airfield, Kansas

Spring 1942
Increasing merchant shipping losses to German U-boats puts Britain's survival at stake

Apr 1942
The Luftwaffe subjects Malta, to an intense blitz. The Royal Opera House and many buildings in Valletta are destroyed. Malta is left with only a few serviceable fighter aircraft

Apr 1942
The Royal Air Force begins its systematic "area bombing" of German cities

Apr 7, 1942
TL - *Theresa Leta* (B-17E tail number 41-9082) is assigned to 419th Bomb Squadron, 301st Bombardment Group. Delivered Geiger Field, Spokane, WA (American Air Museum in Britain)

Apr 8, 1942
REE - transfers from his instructor position in the Navigation School at Turner Field, Albany GA to the Air Force Combat Crew School, Hendricks Field, Sebring, Florida, as the flight instructor on a B-17 (Photograph: 3.6)

Apr 14, 1942
REE - Describes to JN the use of "our famous U.S. bombsight" and time-off for a B-17 pilot instructor (Appendices: 4.14.42, Norden Bombsight)

Apr 15, 1942
From London, King George VI awards the George Cross to the people and defenders of Malta. The island country bravely resists the German siege from June 11, 1940 – November 20, 1942

Apr 18, 1942
Major James Doolittle leads an attack from the aircraft carrier, USS *Hornet*, with 16 B-25s to Japanese targets in Tokyo, Kobe, Yokohama, Osaka, and Nagoya

May 12, 1942
TL - First American 8th AF units arrive in Great Britain. *Theresa Leta* assigned to the 8th AF

May 30 – 31, 1942
The first time in defense of Great Britain, one thousand British RAF bombers attack Cologne, Germany ("Haunting Photos – the Bombed-Out Ruins of Cologne in WWII" 2020)

May 30, 1942
B-17F takes first flight. 2,405 are produced. This is the B-17 model that REE flies to Africa from Salina, Kansas ("B-17 Bomber *Flying Fortress* – The Queen of the Skies." 2020)

Jun 1942
Mass murder of Jews by gassing begins at Auschwitz

Jun 4-7, 1942
The US Navy gains a vital victory over the Japanese at the Battle of Midway, giving it naval superiority in the Pacific

Jun 7, 1942
TL -*Theresa Leta* lands at Teague Field, BW1, Greenland, on way to England (American Air Museum in Britain. 2014)

Jun 15, 1942
V-Mail service begins

1942
Major General Dwight D. Eisenhower is appointed Commander of the European Theater of Operations

Jun 17, 1942
REE - Reports to commander of Tucson Air Base, AZ

Jun 24, 1942
Rommel begins pursuit of British 8th Army from Tobruk to Mersa Matruh in North Africa

Jun 30, 1942
Beginning of the first part of the Battle of El Alamein

Jul 1942
Eisenhower becomes Lieutenant General and named to head Operation Torch, the Allied invasion of French North Africa

Jul 1942
Brigadier General Jimmy Doolittle is assigned to US 8th Army

Jul 1942
TL -*Theresa Leta* is transferred to 97th Bomb Group. Later she is fitted out with an office in the bomb bay for General Carl Spaatz. April 1943, she is used to transport Field Marshal Montgomery (American Air Museum in Britain. 2014)

Aug 1, 1942
Two American B-17 heavy bomb groups arrive in England. They successfully fly their first mission on August 17, taking no casualties

Aug 4, 1942
Prime Minister Churchill spends time in Cairo with his staff. He departs for Tehran (August 10) and on to Moscow (August 12) to meet Stalin for the Moscow Conference

Aug 7, 1942
Lieutenant General William Gott is appointed Commander of the British 8th Army, August 6. Before he takes command, he is killed when flying to Cairo, from the battle area. He is traveling in a British Bombay transport plane when German *Messerschmitt* Bf-109 fighters attack them. The plane makes a successful crash landing but is strafed on the ground by pursuing German fighters. Out of 21 personnel on board only 5 survive, including the pilot. Lieutenant General Bernard L. Montgomery is then appointed Commander of British 8th Army ("Squadron Leader, Hugh 'Jimmy' James Obituary." 2015)

Aug 12, 1942
Stalin and Churchill meet in Moscow for the Moscow Conference. It is a very difficult meeting. Stalin takes issue at every point with bluntness, almost to the point of insult, with such remarks as "You can't win wars if you aren't willing to take risks and you must not be so afraid of the Germans." This phase of the discussion ends by Stalin stating abruptly, but with dignity, that he cannot force action (by the Allies) but he does not agree with the arguments… (later, Churchill brings the discussion back to the Second Front. He explains the decision regarding "Torch," the invasion of North Africa, which begins on 2 Nov 1942, and its tactics, emphasizing the need for secrecy... About this time the Prime Minister draws a picture of a crocodile and points out that it was as well to strike the belly as the snout. ("Crocodile Underbellies." 2020)

Aug 13, 1942
REE - Is assigned to 330th Heavy Bomb Group, Alamogordo Air Base, NM. Upon activation July 6, 1942, the 330th Bombardment Group is assigned to Second Air Force as a Consolidated B-24 *Liberator* Replacement Training Unit (RTU). The Group performed this training at Alamogordo Army Airfield in NM, then later at Biggs Field near El Paso, TX

Aug 13, 1942
General Sir Harold Alexander installs Montgomery as Commanding General of the British 8th Army

Aug 15, 1942
Monty takes command of the British 8th Army

Aug 17, 1942
First all-American air attack in Europe

Aug 19, 1942
Operation Jubilee, the Allied assault on the German-occupied port of Dieppe, France, is a failure. Of the 6,086 men who made it ashore, 4,397 are reported missing, taken prisoner, wounded, or killed. Tragic lessons are learned but helped to prepare for the invasion of North Africa and Normandy ("Dieppe Landing: Operation Jubilee and the Origins of the Normandy landings." 2020)

Aug 19, 1942
Churchill visits Montgomery in his new office at El Alamein

Aug 20, 1942
US 12th Air Force is activated at Bolling Field, District of Columbia. The group initially trained in England and then participated in Operation Torch, the three-pronged invasion of North Africa

Aug 23, 1942
Churchill, on his second visit to the western desert, meets Monty

Aug 23, 1942
Battle of Stalingrad begins. The 6th Army of the *Wehrmacht* begins its assault. The battle is infamous as one of the largest, longest, and bloodiest engagements in modern warfare. It is over February 2, 1943

Aug 30, 1942
Rommel begins his offensive at El Alamein with a thrust toward Cairo and the Suez Canal

Aug 31, 1942
Montgomery successfully repels Rommel's attack against Alam el Halfa by predicting the high ground as a likely target and prepares its defenses before the attack commences. Montgomery does not take the offensive until his troops are ready and there are enough supplies

Sep 1942
Montgomery receives great quantities of supplies from the US

Sep 1942
TL -*Theresa Leta* is transferred to 92nd BG

Sep 15, 1942
Major General Dwight D. Eisenhower appoints

Major General W. Bedell Smith chief-of-staff at Allied Forces Headquarters

Sep 23, 1942
Brigadier General James H. Doolittle is named Commander of the US 12th Air Force

Oct 15, 1942
REE - Is awarded the captain rank

Oct 16, 1942
REE - Transfers to 450th Bomb Squadron, Biggs Field Army Air Base, TX

Oct 18, 1942
REE - Writes to parents from Allis Hotel, Wichita, KS, about the dangers of pilot training (Appendices: 10.18.42, Training Pilots)

Oct 23 - Nov 4, 1942
Second Battle of El Alamein is fought near the western frontier of Egypt. This is the first large-scale, decisive Allied British land victory of the war. This victory was a boost to British morale and to Lieutenant General Bernard Law Montgomery's fame ("Second Battle of El Alamein." 2021)

Nov 1942
Doolittle is promoted to Major General and during March 1943, becomes Commanding General of the Northwest African Strategic Air Force, a unified command of US Army Air Force and Royal Air Force units

Nov 8, 1942
Operation Torch is the British-American invasion of French North Africa during the North African Campaign of WWII. The USAF Air Transport Command uses the Maison Blanche Airport, Algiers

Nov 8, 1942
General Spaatz is promoted to three-star rank and assumes command of all-American air forces in the European Theater. The general often flies in the B-17 *Theresa Leta*, which had a special office built in the plane's bomb bay

Nov 9, 1942
Doolittle leads the US 12th AF into North Africa. US 97th Bomb Group was part of the group and 17 days later the 301st Bomb Group would follow

Nov 11, 1942
General Bernard Montgomery is awarded the Knight Grand Cross of the Order of the Bath

Nov 19, 1942
The Red Army launches Operation Uranus, a two-pronged attack targeting the weaker Romanian and Italian armies protecting the German 6th Army's flanks. The Axis forces are overrun, and the 6th Army is cut off, surrounded and surrenders. The Battle of Stalingrad is the battle that turned the tide in the war between Germany and the Soviet Union ("Soviets Launch Counterattack at Stalingrad." 2020)

Dec 6, 1942
REE - Writes letter to JN about transfer to Army Air Base, Sioux City, IA. "Then I ran into Major Dawson, the number one instrument pilot. He said I could join his special group. I have around 2,000 hours in the air, well Bunny Dawson, formerly of Eastern Airlines, has just 13,000 hours" (Appendices: 12.6.42, Mentors)

Dec 7, 1942
REE - Moves to Salina, KS to teach "the boys the technique of landing an airplane completely blind ... by the instruments alone"

Dec 25, 1942
REE - Is stationed at headquarters, 21st Wing Army Air Base, Salina, KA

Jan 4, 1943
General Williams, a commander 2nd Air Force Combat-Crew Training Program, requests Captain Evans to write a letter, describing his suggestions to improve training methods and policies (Appendices: 1.4.43, Combat-Crew Training Program)

Jan 9, 1943
FBE - First Lieutenant Frank B. Evans is awarded "the Distinguished Flying Cross for extraordinary achievement while participating in a bombing mission on 2 January 1943. First Lieutenant Evans brought his badly crippled plane back safely although the plane had no tail wheel nor rudder control and two engines were shot out. This extraordinary achievement reflects great credit upon himself and the Military services of the United States." This award is given in the name of the Commanding General, North African Theater of Operations, by Command of Lieutenant General Spaatz (Evans, First Lieutenant Frank B. n.d.)

Jan 14 – 24, 1943
The Casablanca Conference is held at the Anfa Hotel in Casablanca, French Morocco, from January 14 – 24, 1943, to plan the Allied European strategy for the next phase of World War II. In

attendance are United States President, Franklin D. Roosevelt, British Prime Minister, Winston Churchill, and representing the Free French forces, Generals Charles de Gaulle, and Henri Giraud. Premier Joseph Stalin had declined to attend, citing the ongoing conflict in Stalingrad, which requires his presence in the Soviet Union. A notable development at the Conference is the finalization of allied strategic plans against the Axis powers, and the promulgation of the policy of "unconditional surrender" ("The Casablanca Conference." 1943) (Photograph: 1.3)

Jan 19, 1943
REE - Turns 24 years old

Jan 20, 1943
REE - Meets Colonel Fay Upthegrove who is taking the 99th Bomb Group to North Africa, and then on to England to join the US 8th Air Force. Evans asks Upthegrove if he can join the 99th BG as a pilot, because another pilot who was supposed to fly with Upthegrove is hospitalized. The B-17F, *Able Mable* #25477, is assigned to Evans (Chapter 1, "Orders from Ike")

Jan 21, 1943
As part of the Soviet counter-offensive, the last of the airports held by the Germans fell to the Soviets, completely cutting off the Germans from supplies. The Germans are forced to surrender at Stalingrad, February 2, 1943. In July Germany is defeated at Kursk... its last offensive in the east

Jan 21, 1943
Tripoli falls to the Allied forces

Jan 21, 1943
REE - The 99th Bomb Group with 35 aircraft (B-17F) "departs by air from Smokey Hill Army Air Base, Salina, KS for DeRidder Army Air Base, DeRidder, LA" ("War Diary, 99th BG." Jan 1943)

Jan 23, 1943
TL - *Theresa Leta* is transferred to Mediterranean Theater of Operation (Photograph: 1.15)

Jan 23, 1943
British Army takes Tripoli, Libya. The airfield is renamed RAF Castel Benito (Tripoli-Castel Benito Airport) and is used by several Allied operational squadrons involved in the desert war and in the Tunisia battles

Jan 25, 1943
REE - Writes a difficult letter to his parents on why he is ready to go to war (Appendices: 1.25.43

Flying to Africa

Jan 30, 1943
REE - "99th BG departs by air for West Palm Beach, FL, Morrison AF Field" (99th BG Area Action Plan. 1943)

Feb 2, 1943
Operation's Orders to the 99th BG: "Under authority contained in letter from the Adjutant General to the Commanding Generals, all Armies, G.H.Q. Air Forces, Departments and Corps Areas. Etcetera, dated June 5, 1941, File A. G. 320-2 (6-3-41) NR-N Subject: 'Constitution of the Air Corps Ferrying Command' and verbal instructions Commanding General, Air Transport Command, Washington D. C. The following named personnel will proceed in aircraft as indicated from Morrison Field, West Palm Beach, Florida to England, reporting upon arrival threat to Commanding Officer, Headquarters 8th Air Force for duty and assignment" ("Operation's Orders Number 37." 1943)

Feb 5, 1943
REE - "99th BG Departs by air for Puerto Rico, Borinquen Field" (99th BG Area Action Plan)

All thirty-five aircraft fly to Borinquen Field, Puerto Rico ("War Diary 99th BG," Feb 1943)

Feb 10, 1943
REE - All aircraft fly to Atkinson Field, Georgetown, British Guiana, now Guyana ("War Diary 99th BG," Feb 1943)

Feb 11, 1943
REE - Last ship is cleared to fly to Belem, Brazil ("War Diary 99th BG," Feb 1943)

Feb 12, 1943
REE - Last of remaining ships is cleared for Natal, Brazil ("War Diary 99th BG," Feb 1943)

Feb 17, 1943
REE - All except four ships had cleared to Yundum Field, Bathurst, Gambia. "Left Natal at 2142 hours. Turbulent. Most of us sweat out the takeoff for the long ocean trip. No one has flown across the ocean before – from our group. Slept most of the night on spare parts box with parachutes for pillows. Hot cocoa and sandwiches just before dawn ... Landed Jeswang Field. It was the wrong airdrome, and we proceeded to Yundum Field nearby. Native blacks surrounded the airplanes as we landed. Also, our first landing on a steel runway strip. Slept on rope beds in Nissen huts. Toilets are pails with wooden covers. It took us

11 hours and 45 minutes to fly across the Atlantic and we traveled 1,852 miles." ("War Diary 99th BG," Sheet 6) (Photograph: 1.1)

Feb 14, 1943
Massive attack through gaps in the eastern dorsal range of hills, eastern Tunisia, catches American forces by surprise. Thousands of GIs are killed, captured, or routed near Sidi Bou Zid by forces commanded by Field Marshal Rommel and Gen Hans-Jurgen von Amim

Feb 22, 1943
REE - B-17F from Marrakesh to Oran (Individual Flight Record (IFR))

Feb 23, 1943
Official date that the 99th Bomb Group headquarters is stationed at Navarin Airfield, Algeria

Feb 24, 1943
REE - "On this date three squadrons, 346th, 348th and 416th depart for Oran (La Senia) while the remaining squadron receives a hold on order ("War Diary 99th BG," Feb 1943)

Mar 1943
Major General J. Doolittle, commander of the US 12th Air Force becomes commanding general of the Northwest African Strategic Air Forces

Mar 3, 1943
REE - "The flight echelon of the 99th Bomb Group (H) less two airplanes complete the trip from Marrakesh to Oran (La Senia). All aircraft are receiving a final check-over here before proceeding to the operational base. In the meantime, personnel are attending lectures on the various phases of combat given by experienced instructors" ("War Diary 99th BG" Mar 1943)

Mar 6, 1943
REE - "All life rafts are taken from the aircraft to supply a 'first-line' organization, thereby immobilizing the 99th when over-water missions are concerned. The commanding officer is now at our future operational base inspection facilities. We will expect to receive orders 'to the front' any day now." ("War Diary 99th BG," Mar 1943)

The 99th BG is not joining the US 8th AF in England. The 99th BG flies B-17Fs. The earlier B-17E model (*Theresa Leta*) heavy bomber is flown to North Africa by the 97th and 301st BG from England. The 99th, 97th and 301st are attached to the 5th Wing of the 12th Air Force stationed in North Africa (Lauer III, Ford J. n.d.)

Mar 6, 1943
REE - Parents have not heard from him for over three weeks. They do not know of the strategic change of plans for the 99th BG to remain in North Africa and strike Hitler from the "underbelly" of Europe. They think that their son is in England (Appendices: 3.6.43, Worried Family)

Mar 6, 1943
Rommel attacks British 8th Army at Medenine and is successfully repulsed. This is Operation Capri, Battle of Medenine

Mar 15 - 28
"Navarin Airfield, Algeria. The 99th BG finishes the preliminary training at La Senia, Oran and moves eastward, two squadrons to 97th BG Base and two to the 301st Base" ("War Diary 99th BG." Sheet 7)

Mar 16, 1943
REE - 99th Bombardment Group enters combat zone. The squadrons are: 346th Squadron, 347th Bombardment, 348th Squadron and 416th Squadron. Their aircraft tail insignias are Diamond Y I, Diamond Y II, Diamond YIII and Diamond Y IV. Captain Evans is in the 346th Squadron

Mar 18, 1943
FBE - "I was assigned to give a talk to the 99th Bomb Group on bailing out ... what to do and most of all what not to do" (Evans, 1st Lieut. Frank B.)

Mar 19 – 31, 1943
Battle of the Mareth Line is an attack by the British 8th Army against the Mareth line, held by Italo-German 1st Army. The Mareth Line had been constructed by the French in Tunisia as a defensive position in case of Italian aggression from Tripolitania prior to WWII

Mar 23, 1943
Battle of El Guettar fought. US 1st Infantry Division repels an attack by the German 10th Panzer Division in south central Tunisia

Mar 25, 1943
Work is partially completed on the base for the 99th and all airplanes were brought in and made ready for the first mission ("War Diary 99th BG," Sheet 7)

Mar 31, 1943
"Eisenhower comes to visit me in Tunisia, 31 March 1943." (Montgomery, Bernard Law, 1st Viscount Montgomery)

Mar 31 – Aug 6, 1943
99th BG missions (#1 – #60) are flown from
Navarin Airfield, Algeria

Mar 31, 1943
99th BG flies its first combat mission against an
enemy airdrome at Villacidro, A/D Sardinia with
Colonel Upthegrove leading and the largest number of B-17s to be used in the war to that date. The
99th comes to be referred to as the Diamondbacks,
due to a diamond insignia painted on the vertical
stabilizer of their B-17s. Ninety-four are employed
with the 99th and two other groups join the force.
As Allied ground forces force the German Afrika
Korps to retreat into Tunisia, the 99th continues to
fly missions to cut off German supplies coming
from Italy and Sicily. For the rest of 1943, the 99th
flies missions primarily across the Mediterranean
to bomb targets in Sicily and Italy. In June, news
of a possible Arab uprising makes the men of
the 99th nervous and they resort to wearing a
sidearm at all times. Although a major uprising
does not occur there are acts of sabotage (Lauer
III, Ford J., n.d.)

Mar 31, 1943
REE - Flies Mission #1 Villacidro, Sardinia:
Cagliari A/D. This is the first combat mission
Captain R. E. Evans flies. He lists his first 25
Missions on a map, labeled M.1 within this book
(Combat Mission 346th Squadron)

Apr 2, 1943
"He (General Eisenhower) came to visit me at my
Army HQ shortly after the Battle of Mareth; it
was April 2nd and I was busy preparing to attack
the Akarit position, and then to burst through
the GABES Gap out onto the plains of Central
Tunisia. I told General Eisenhower that when
I had captured SFAX there would be need for
considerable coordination between the Allied
armies in Tunisia, and this might mean a good
deal of traveling about for me. I asked him if he
would give me a Fortress; the splendid armament
of the aircraft make escort quite unnecessary, and
I would be able to travel at will and deal easily
with enemy opposition. I said I would make him
a present of SFAX by mid-April, and if he would
give me a Fortress it would be magnificent. He
agreed" (Hamilton, Nigel 1983: 224)

Apr 4, 1943
REE - Flies Mission #2 Naples, Italy Port Area
(Combat Mission 346th Squadron)

Apr 4, 1943
REE - Writes to JN, describing tent living in
Navarin, Algeria (Appendices: 4.4.43, Africa Tent
Living)

Apr 5, 1943
REE - Flies Mission #3 Trapani, Sicily Milo A/D
(Combat Mission 346th Squadron)

Apr 5 - 27, 1943
RAF and USAAF are ordered to conduct operations against Axis air power by day and night
to prevent their resupply or withdrawal. Owing
to bad weather and the need to gather intelligence, Operation Flax did not begin until 5 April.
During those twenty-two days, the German
transport fleets suffer huge losses; one day in
particular, April 18, fifty-two German transports
are destroyed. At the same time shipping lanes
between Sicily and Tunisia are disrupted. The
aerial and shipping links between Axis-held Sicily
and Italy are destroyed. German transport fleets
suffer heavy losses from which they are unable to
recover ("Operation Flax," 2011)

Apr 10, 1943
REE - Flies Mission #4 LA Maddalena, Sardinia
Naval Base (Combat Mission 346th Squadron)

Apr 10, 1943
"We captured SFAX at 0800 hours. I at once sent
a message to General EISENHOWER asking for
a *Flying Fortress* to be sent over to me at once; his
Chief of Staff, General Bedell Smith, had promised me a Fortress when I captured SFAX. It was
to become my personal property for the duration
of the war. It will be interesting to see when it
arrives." (Montgomery's Diary Notes, BLM 34)

Apr 10, 1943
"On the morning of the 10th April I sent a message
to Eisenhower asking for the aircraft. It arrived
on the 16th April, a B-17 (a *Flying Fortress*). It
made me a thoroughly mobile general. Later, I got
properly ticked off by Brooke, the C.I.G.S. for my
action in the matter. He said that it was all a joke
on the part of Bedell Smith and that Eisenhower was furious when I demanded the aircraft. I
explained that it was very far from a joke on that
day at Tripoli when the statement was made. I
don't think Bedell Smith had ever told Eisenhower
about it and was suddenly confronted with having
to pay. Brooke added that the R.A.F. could well
have provided me with an aircraft; they certainly
could but didn't in spite of my repeated requests.

Eisenhower produced it at once. And being the great and generous man he is, he arranged that I was provided with an aircraft from American sources for the rest of the war." (Montgomery, Bernard Law, 1st Viscount 1958, 184)

Apr 11, 1943

General Montgomery visits Sfax after its capture by the 8th Army. He inspects a guard of honor of the Black Watch (Photograph: 8.1)

Apr 11, 1943

"I received a message from General SPAATZ, Commandeer of NW African Air Force under General EISENHOWER, saying that a B-17 (Fortress) with crew would be sent to me and asking where it was to be delivered. I replied it should be sent to GABES. It will be a great thing to have my own aeroplane!" (Montgomery's Diary Notes, BLM 34)

Apr 11, 1943

REE - Flies Mission #5 Marsala, Sicily Harbor (Combat Mission 346th Squadron)

Apr 15, 1943

FBE - First Lieutenant Frank B. Evans is told, "to report to British General B. L. Montgomery as his flight crew, flying the plane that had been used by General Spaatz." Frank B. Evans' description of the special B-17: "the plane to be used was a B-17E on which the bomb bay had been converted for long range flights by the installation of an auxiliary fuel tank on one side and a desk, worktable and chair on the other side for the General. Air Corps General "Tooey" Spaatz had used this B-17 until now. The plane was still equipped with a normal complement of defensive guns for protection, so our assignment included my entire crew, even a bombardier." (Evans, 1st Lieut. Frank B.)

Apr 16, 1943

FBE - "Our orders read to report to the General at Gabes, Tunisia. The nearest landing place we knew of was at Tripoli, Libya. So that is where we first flew (from 12th AF Training Station, Navarin Airfield) on April 16. Personnel at the airport did not know the exact location of the General's headquarters but told us there was a British Spitfire landing area near the battlefront in Tunisia, north of Tripoli. We took off and flew until we found the field, a pasture (Evans, 1st Lieut. Frank B.)

Apr 17, 1943

Montgomery is presented with a B-17 *Flying Fortress*, which he duly inspects on 17 April; here he is looking out of the window of the pilot's cockpit. First Lieutenant Frank B. Evans is the command pilot (Photographs: 8.2, 8.3, 8.4, 8.5)

Apr 17, 1943

Extract from 417th Squadron Operations Record book, "General Montgomery visits our dispersal where his aircraft is kept and chatted informally with our pilots and ground crew" ("Operations Record Book." April 1943)

Apr 18, 1943

British 8th army is still fighting in Tunisia

Apr 18, 1943

REE - Flies Mission #6 Palermo, Sicily Port (Combat Mission 346th Squadron)

Apr 19, 1943

TL - "It was urgently necessary that we should meet with Eisenhower and reach decisions on certain vital matters. This was agreed at once and I flew to Algiers in my recently acquired *Flying Fortress* on the 19th of April" (Montgomery, Bernard Law 1958, 153)

Apr 20, 1943

FBE - Montgomery and his B-17 relocate in Sfax, Tunisia, where the 12th medium bomb group, flying B-25s, had their base (Evans, 1st Lieut. Frank B.)

Apr 21, 1943

Extract from letter to Sir Harold Alexander from General Montgomery, "On Friday 23 April I will go to Cairo. Spend 24 and 25 April in Cairo, Return to my HQ on 26 April" ("Alexander Papers WO 214/18." 1943)

Apr 26, 1943

Extract from letter to Mrs. Phyllis Reynolds, "I have my own *Flying Fortress* aeroplane now, won by me from the Americans. The story of how I got it is very amusing, and I will tell it to you one day. It is a great thing to have your own aeroplane, to start when you like, and go where you like. It is an enormous affair and I understand they cost about £100,000 each!! A part of it has been fitted up as a very comfortable little study for me, with two armchairs and a table for writing, etc. You can fly at 200 miles an hour for eleven hours, without a stop. When the situation here allows, I shall fly home for a 10-day rest." (Montgomery, General Bernard L. 1943)

Apr 28, 1943

99th Bomb Group's ground crewmen were "ferried to Staten Island where the men and equipment were bundled and crammed aboard the U.S.S. Edmund B. Alexander, staying overnight in the docks, and pulling out early in the morning, the 29th of April." (Bruno, James F. 131)

Apr 30, 1943
REE - Writes a poem to his parents about the rain and mud conditions that ground the planes and the long wait for clear weather (Appendices: 4.30.43, Greetings from Africa)

May 3, 1943
REE - Flies Mission #7 Bizerte, Tunisia, shipping, no bombs dropped (Combat Mission 346th Squadron)

May 3, 1943
"Today the group flew Mission #11 and the target was shipping in Bizerte Harbor, Tunisia. 28 ships took off at 1555 and one came back immediately because of mechanical trouble. Later 2 more ships came back due to crew members being sick. The rest of the evening turned out to be one of the worst which this group has experienced and probably ever will experience" ("War Diary 99th BG," May 1943)

May 3, 1943
REE - Flies his B-17 away from 346th Squadron formation because of dangerous flight conditions and makes emergency landing in a field about 20 miles north and east of the Germans, who were withdrawing to Tunis. Met British artillery brigade near field where he landed his B-17 for the night (Chapter 2, "Forced Landing in Africa")

May 3, 1943
REE - "Special Account" describes in detail one of the worst events for the 99th BG (Appendices: 5.3.43, Tragic Night Lives Long in Memory)

May 6 – 13, 1943
These dates are the culmination of Operation Vulcan, with the British army taking Tunis, (deep water port) and American troops reaching Bizerte. By May 13, all the Axis forces in Tunisia surrender. Alexander cables Churchill, "All enemy resistance has ceased. We are masters of the North African shores." By the close of the operations, nearly 240,000 German and Italian troops are captured. Axis forces officially surrender in North Africa

May 7, 1943
"I visited ALGIERS on 7 May and saw BEDELL-SMITH" (Montgomery, Bernard Law. 1943, 37/1)

May 7, 1943
FBE - "On May 7 we (Monty) went back to Algiers for more meetings. We were to return to his headquarters that evening, but due to bad thunderstorms and weather over the mountains, I told his aides I would not fly" (Evans, 1st Lieut. Frank B.)

May 9, 1943
REE - Flies Mission #8 Palermo, Sicily (Combat Mission 346th Squadron)

May 10, 1943
REE - Flies Mission #9 Trapani, Sicily Milo A/D (Combat Mission 346th Squadron)

May 10, 1943
"On 10 May I went to CAIRO and saw my staff there and had conferences with them. I returned to Army HQ near SOUSSE on 13 May. Resistance in North Africa had ended on 12 May and Field Marshal MESSE (the Italian Commander in the field) had surrendered to 8th Army on 13 May; he dined with me at Main Army HQ on 13 May and we discussed various aspects of the battles we had fought against each other." (Montgomery, Bernard Law. 1943, 37/1)

May 10, 1943
FBE - "We (Monty) returned to Cairo. On this flight the #3 engine burned 31 gallons of oil. This dictated that we take the plane to a US Air Corps maintenance base up near the Suez Canal to have the engine changed." (Evans, 1st Lieut. Frank B.)

May 11, 1943
REE - Flies Mission #10 Marsala, Sicily (Combat Mission 346th Squadron)

May 12, 1943
99th BG ground crew arrives Oran, Algeria, and is moved to bivouac area at La Senia (*The Diamondbacks* 9)

May 13, 1943
FBE - "The plane was repaired, and we went back to Cairo, picked up the General and flew back to his headquarters." (Evans, 1st Lieut. Frank B.)

May 13, 1943
REE - Flies Mission #11 Cagliari, Sardinia (Combat Mission 346th Squadron)

May 14, 1943
REE - Flies Mission #12 Civitavecchia, Italy shipping (Combat Mission 346th Squadron)

May 16, 1943
FBE - "We took off for London with an overnight

fuel and rest stop at Gibraltar for England" (Evans, 1st Lieut. Frank B.)

May 16, 1943

"On 16 May I sent my Army HQ back to Tripoli, and in my *Flying Fortress* for England. I arrived in London afternoon of 17 May." (Montgomery, Bernard Law. 1943, 37/1)

May 16, 1943

"I left Tripoli in my *Flying Fortress* on the 16th of May, arriving in England on the 17th. I enjoyed the visit, and especially my time with Davie (son)." (Montgomery, Bernard Law, 1st Viscount Montgomery. 1958 164)

May 17, 1943

FBE - "We continued our flight to England. After we left Gibraltar for England we were not within sight of the coast of France, but we did see a German 4-engine patrol bomber. Not being sure whether or not they were aware of our VIP passenger, we increased our speed to make sure they could come no closer to us. As we hit the coast of England, four RAF spitfires escorted us to our landing field at Northolt on the outskirts of London." (Evans, 1st Lieut. Frank B.)

May 17, 1943

"General Montgomery, 8th Army, arrives in Fortress Aircraft." ("Operations Record Book, AIR28/601." 1943)

May 17, 1943

Montgomery uses his B-17 to fly home to England where he receives an enthusiastic welcome on arrival at RAF Northolt, London Borough of Hillington, West London

May 18, 1943

REE - Flies Mission #13 Trapani, Sicily (Combat Mission 346th Squadron)

May 19, 1943

REE - Flies Mission #14 Sciacca, Sicily, L/G, no bombs dropped (Combat Mission 346th Squadron)

May 24, 1943

REE - Flies Mission #15 La Maddalena, Sardinia, shipping (Combat Mission 346th Squadron)

May 25, 1943

REE - Flies Mission #16 Messina, Sicily (Combat Mission 346th Squadron)

May 30, 1943

REE - Flies Mission #17 Naples, Italy Capodichina A/D (Combat Mission 346th Squadron)

May 31, 1943

REE - Flies Mission #18 Foggia, Italy (Combat Mission 346th Squadron)

May 31, 1943

99th BG flew 25th mission, bombed Foggia A/D in Italy, for the longest Mission to date, and the bombs destroyed many enemy aircraft grounded on the field (Bruno 1995, 132)

Jun 1, 1943

King George VI visits Malta

Jun 2, 1943

"General Montgomery leaves station by Fortress." ("Operations Record Book, AIR28/601 1943)

Jun 2, 1943

FBE - "We headed back to North Africa and flew all the way to Algeria non-stop, a flight of 9 hours and 50 minutes. The General now had his headquarters based on the outskirts of Tripoli" (Evans, 1st Lieut. Frank B.)

Jun 2, 1943

"I returned to 8th Army via Algiers and met the Prime Minister and the C.I.G.S (Chief of the Imperial General Staff) there on 2nd June; I did the journey from London to Algiers in one day in the *Flying Fortress*, in daylight." (Montgomery, Bernard Law, 1st Viscount, 165)

Jun 5, 1943

REE to JN - "I am writing you on what may prove to be one of the greatest air battles of all times... and it may be a dud." (Appendices: 6.5.43, Bombing Pantelleria #1)

Jun 5, 1943

REE - Flies Mission #19 La Spezia, Italy Harbor (Combat Mission 346th Squadron)

Jun 7, 1943

REE - Flies Mission #20 Pantelleria Island town (Combat Mission 346th Squadron)

Jun 8, 1943

REE - Flies Mission #21 Pantelleria Island gun positions (Combat Mission 346th Squadron)

Jun 8, 1943

FBE - "We again took him (Monty) to Cairo" (Evans, 1st Lieut. Frank B.)

Jun 9, 1943

REE - Flies Mission #22 Pantelleria Island Gun Position #7 (Combat Mission 346th Squadron)

Jun 9, 1943
REE - Sends an interesting V-Mail to JN, regarding important bombing mission (Appendices: 6.9.43, Bombing Pantelleria #2)

Jun 10, 1943
REE - Flies Mission #23 Pantelleria Island gun position #7 (Combat Mission 346th Squadron)

Jun 10, 1943
REE - Flies Mission #24 Pantelleria Island gun position #7 (Combat Mission 346th Squadron)

Jun 11, 1943
REE - Flies Mission #25 Pantelleria Island gun position #4A & #5. In Captain Evan's handwriting "25 more in Italy, Yugoslavia, Greece, Germany and Austria" (Combat Mission 346th Squadron)

Jun 11, 1943
Allied forces capture Pantelleria, Operation Corkscrew. B-17s and B-24s are part of Allied bombardment of island

Jun 13, 1943
FBE - "We returned to Tripoli and the General invited me to stay at his headquarters to continue to recuperate" (Evans, 1st Lieut. Frank B.)

Jun 13, 1943
REE - Special orders, Number 99, by Command of Major General Doolittle, through Brigadier General, Hoyt S. Vandenberg, GSC, Chief of Staff to command Captain Richard E. Evans and eight crewmen to fly Field Marshal Bernard L. Montgomery in an American B-17. "3. Following named O (Officers) and EM (Enlisted Men), 99th Bomb Group (H) are placed on DS (Defense Support) with NAAF (North African Air Force) until further orders, WP, reporting upon arrival to CG (Commanding General) threat for day. Restricted Document Headquarters Northwest Africa Strategic Air Force (Appendices: 6.13.43, Orders to Pilot General Montgomery's B-17)

Jun 13, 1943
REE - Colonel Upthegrove tells Captain Evans about his "Monty" assignment. Evans is stationed at the Navarin Airfield. His tent mate is 346th Squadron Commander Major Leon Lowery (Chapter 1 "Orders from Ike")

Jun 13, 1943
REE - Writes letter to JN, describing the temporary and unusual assignment to fly the British Field Marshall B. Montgomery in an American

B-17 wherever he needs to travel (Appendices: 6.13.43, Monty's B-17)

Jun 13, 1943
"The King arrives in North Africa on 13 June and was to visit Tripoli, and see units of 8th Army" (Montgomery, Bernard Law. MF, June 13, 1943)

Jun 14, 1943
'Pointblank' directive is issued to improve Allied bombing strategy. Orders are given for the RAF Bomber Command and the US 8th Air Force to bomb specific targets such as aircraft factories to disable German aircraft fighter strength thus drawing it away from Allied frontline operations and ensuring it will not be an obstacle to the invasion of NW Europe (Carey, Brian Todd 1998)

Jun 14, 1943
King George VI flies to Oran ("King George VI Visit to Oran," 1943)

Jun 14, 1943
FBE - "We received word from General Spaatz's headquarters that another crew had been assigned to this duty. I was somewhat relieved as my crew was getting restless... as long as we were here all promotions, and all hope of finishing our missions were on hold" (Evans, 1st Lieut. Frank B.)

Jun 15, 1943
FBE - "We were relieved from the General Montgomery assignment, and were turned to our Group (301st BG) at St. Donat. We took the plane back to (Château dun-du-Rhumel Airfield) Algiers, for the other crew, and then went back to our own bomb group where we were reinstated to resume flying our bombing missions" (Evans, 1st Lieut. Frank B.)

Jun 15, 1943
FBE - "Lieut. Evans, Captain of my B-17 Fortress. 1. I would like to thank you, and your officers and Sgts., for the splendid way in which you have performed your duties while you have been with me. You have a magnificent team under your command, and I have much enjoyed our association together. 2. Now you are to return to combat work, and I am to have a new crew. I shall miss you all very much. We have had a good time together, and I hope you have enjoyed your time with me. 3. The very best of luck to you all." Signed by B. L. Montgomery, General 8th Army." Letter given to First Lieutenant Frank B. Evans (Evans, 1st Lieut. Frank B.)

Jun - Aug 1943
REE - USAF Summary Report from November 1942 to February 1944: Report mentions "Pilot for General Montgomery" between June and August. Also mentions flying hours in B-17, B-25 and checked out in C-47 (OMPF)

Jun 15, 1943
"Today the vacation ended at 0320 hours in the dark of the night. Briefings for the 34th mission were held at 0435. The target for today was Bocca di Falco Airdrome at Palermo, Sicily. 28 of our aircraft were off the ground at 0600 hours. Five of these returned early, 3 as spares and two with mechanical trouble. 23 airplanes were over target and dropped 431x120 frags and 65x300 demobilizing bombs for a total of 35.61 tons. The target was well covered, and considerable harm was caused. Flak was very heavy and intense and accurate. Me-109s were observed quite away from target but had no desire to mix. All our planes returned at noon. The remainder of the day was free. This morning a storm blew in from the west bringing dust, then rain to settle the dust" ("War Diary 99th BG," Sheet 27)

Jun 17, 1943
REE - B-17E Navarin Airfield, Algeria to Tripoli. On this day Captain Richard E. Evans meets Field Marshal Bernard L. Montgomery (IFR)

Jun 19, 1943
King George VI at 1000 hours arrives Gromballia. 1030 hours depart Gromballia. 1300 hours arrive Castel Benito 8th Army Programme, 2200 hours depart Tripoli, Libya ("King George VI NA Tour," 1943)

Jun 19, 1943
On the morning of 19 June his Majesty arrived at Castel Benito Airport, Tripoli, Libya on a visit to the British 8th Army. While waiting for the King's arrival, General Montgomery introduces Captain Evans to General Maitland Wilson (Photographs: 6.3, 6.4)

Jun 19, 1943
His majesty shakes hands with Captain Richard E. Evans during introduction of officers and meets *Theresa Leta* crew (Photographs: 6.5, 6.6)

Jun 19, 1943
TL - "On June 19, 1943, when King George VI visits the British 8th Army, Montgomery decided to show his highness his new American toy (B-17E *Theresa Leta*)" (Moser, Pat, 1993)

Jun 19, 1943
REE - General Bernard L. Montgomery introduces his new pilot, Captain Richard E. Evans, to King George VI (Chapter 6, "The King and I")

Jun 19, 1943
"He stayed with us in our camp on the seashore some miles from Tripoli." "On the day he arrived, the 19th June, he gave me the accolade of Knighthood in the lunch marquee near the airfield" (Montgomery, Bernard Law, 1st Viscount 165)

Jun 19, 1943
REE - B-17E Tripoli to Cairo. Montgomery flies to Cairo in the *Theresa Leta* (IFR)

Jun 19, 1943
REE - Writes to his father about his bombing experiences, flak, and meeting King George VI (Appendices: 6.19.43, Flying Through Flak)

Jun 20, 1943
"King 0830 hours arrives in Malta. 2200 hours departs Malta" ("King George VI NA Tour," 1943)

Jun 20, 1943 "Admiral Cunningham was present when the King visited North Africa in June 1943 and accompanied him on a historic trip to the Island of Malta on 20 June. King George VI personally awarded the George Cross to the Island, a symbolic recognition of their collective bravery and endurance" (World War II Today 1943)

Jun 21, 1943
King returns to Tripoli, Libya, 0830 hours. Stays night with 8th Army ("King George VI NA Tour," 1943)

Jun 21, 1943
"HM King George VI rides with General Montgomery in a staff car between lines of cheering troops during his second visit to Tripoli" ("King George VI Visits North Africa," 1943) (Photograph: 6.7)

Jun 22, 1943
King George VI continues his visit with General Montgomery at 8th Army HQ Tripoli, Libya

Jun 23, 1943
REE - B-17E, Tripoli to Cairo (Chapter 8, "The Engine's Stopped!") (IFR)

Jun 25, 1943
99th BG flies Mission #36 to Messina, Sicily

Jun 29, 1943
TL - *Theresa Leta* is in Cairo having all four

engines replaced. "He (Monty) had left it in Cairo on 29 June to have new engines fitted; 'I have done so much traveling in the fortress that it now needs 4 engines,' he boasted to Phyllis Reynolds on 30 June. This will take some little time, as the new engines will have to be flown over to Cairo from Algiers. So, the RAF has given me a Hudson aircraft, and I am using that till the Fortress is ready again" (Montgomery, Bernard Law, BLM 37/1)

Jul 1943

The Military Database (99th BG) is complete after July 1943. Prior to that most of the reports are missing. So, most of the 99th BG Mission reports from March 1943 until mid-July 1943 are missing. Captain Evans kept his own list of combat missions before this date (Photograph: Maps M.1)

Jul 3, 1943

"On the afternoon of 3 July, I left NORTH AFRICA by air and flew to MALTA, arriving there 1700 hours" (Montgomery, Bernard Law, BLM 37/1)

Jul 5, 1943

99th Bomb Group bombs an airfield at Gerbini, Sicily, led by Colonel Upthegrove. Mission #41 was successful in the amount of damage done to the enemy target, but it also was heavy in casualty losses to the 99th (Bruno, James F. 133)

Jul 5, 1943

99th BG receives the first War Department Citation for "outstanding performance of duty in armed conflict with the enemy on 5 July 1943" (Drain, Richard E. 17)

Jul 5, 1943

Narrative Statement Indicates Basis for the War Department Citation, honoring the 99th BG (Appendices: 7.5.43, 99th BG Citation)

Jul 10, 1943

REE - Personal message from the army commander to his troops, autographed by General B. L. Montgomery, "… Now ready to carry into Italy… Good luck and good hunting in the home country of Italy" (Appendices: 7.10.43, Monty Enters Sicily)

Jul 10, 1943

The Allied invasion of Sicily (Operation Husky) begins before dawn with a naval and air bombardment and the landing of airborne troops. The 99th BG flew mission in support of this invasion of Sicily (Bruno, James F. 133)

Jul 10, 1943

On July 10, 1943, Allied ships deposit Patton's 7th US Army on the beaches along the Gulf of Gela, on Sicily's southwest coast. Montgomery's British 8th Army went ashore to the east, south of Syracuse. The Allies target the city of Messina, at the northeast tip of the triangular island. Capturing Sicily would eliminate persistent Axis attacks on nearby Mediterranean supply routes, and if Messina could be taken quickly, the invaders would snare thousands of Axis prisoners and gain a convenient jumping-off spot for the upcoming invasion of Italy (Ethier, Eric, 2021)

Jul 12, 1943

REE - Writes a letter to JN, describing the fascinating city of WWII Cairo. He is waiting for the TL B-17E engines to be repaired (Appendices: 7.12.43, WWII Cairo Description)

Jul 13, 1943

REE - Flies B-17E around Heliopolis Airfield (IFR)

Jul 14, 1943

REE - Flies B-17E from Heliopolis, Cairo to Tripoli (IFR)

Jul 15, 1943

REE - Flies B-17E from Tripoli to Navarin Airfield, Algeria to Malta (Chapter 13, "Brave and Beautiful Malta") (IFR)

Jul 18, 1943

The 99th BG makes a special accounting of the 50 missions completed, which describes, enemy aircraft destroyed, bombs on enemy objectives, miles traveled by combat crews, damaged planes, crew losses and other pertinent facts (Appendices: 7.18.43, 99th BG Celebrates first 50 missions)

Jul 18, 1943

"A new threat lies over the Catania Plain and over Gerbini and its eight satellite aerodromes. With the British 8th Army surging across the plain to the outskirts of Catania itself, Mt. Etna, which dominates the region, has started to erupt for the first time in recent years. A British war correspondent in Sicily reports that the great volcano has begun to belch columns of lurid smoke and flames from its lower crater" ("Mt. Etna Joins in Sicilian War," 1943)

Jul 18, 1943

REE - B-17E Malta to Navarin Airfield, Algeria (IFR)

Jul 19, 1943

"History was made today, history which drew comment from the four corners of the Earth. Today's events may alter the entire war program of the Axis as well as the Allies. For the first time in many years, warfare was carried to Rome. It was the initial air bombardment of the Holy City. The 99th Bomb Group was first to drop bombs on this city. In preparation for this event, H-Hour was at 0515 hours. Forty of our aircraft took off at 0807 on the start of Mission #54. Two aircraft returned early to this base due to mechanical failure and a third landed at Bizerte with two engines out. Thirty-seven of our planes went over the target, the Lorenzo Marshalling Yards and dropped 432x500 bombs (108 tons), the heaviest load we have ever dropped on any one raid. The target was well covered, and many hits were observed on the yards and on surrounding railroad buildings. The neutrality of the separate Vatican State was carefully observed, and no stray bombs fell therein. Flak over the target" ("War Diary 99th BG," Sheet 36)

Jul 20, 1943

REE - Receives a V-Mail from his mother describing how many friends and family enjoy his letters to home (Appendices: 7.20.43, Richard's Stories Home)

Jul 20, 1943

TL - "The aeroplane (*Theresa Leta*) had been located at Château dun by RAF Air Marshal Arthur Tedder on 20 July. One of its new engines had failed, and it had been sent to Syracuse as soon as it was ready" (Hamilton, Nigel, 333)

Jul 21, 1943

REE - B-17E Navarin Airfield, Algeria to Malta (IFR)

Jul 22, 1943

99th BG Flies Mission #56 to Foggia marshalling yards where the group encounters severe opposition (Bruno, James F. 133)

Jul 22, 1943

Truscott's Division enters Palermo, Sicily after covering an astonishing 100 miles in just 72 hours. Wild celebrations and ebullient Sicilian greeted the Americans. Support for Italy's Fascist Dictator Benito Mussolini was nowhere to be seen

Jul 23, 1943

REE - Flies from Malta to Cassibile Airfield (near Syracuse, Sicily) (IFR)

Jul 23, 1943

REE - Flies to Cassibile Airfield, near Syracuse, Sicily. Orders to bring B-17, *Theresa Leta*, to Monty from Château dun. Monty is located at field HQs, Catania, Sicily. Monty invites REE to stay at HQ. "During the previous week (before the Palermo flight) I had stood on the heights south of Mt. Etna and observed in the company of General Montgomery, the battle's progress in a valley between Mt. Etna and our position a thousand feet above the valley floor" (Chapter 13, "Brave and Beautiful Malta")

Jul 23, 1943

Patton marches into Palermo, Sicily

Jul 24, 1943

"Mission #57 took up today where it left off last night at the advance base. The target was the Marshalling Yards at Bologna, up in Northern Italy. The planes took off at 0620. Five of them returned early. Twenty-four went over the target and dropped 288x500 bombs (72 tons). The target area was well covered. Many fires and explosions were seen, including and ammunition train. Flak was heavy, very slight, and inaccurate and no fighters were encountered. Consequently, all our planes returned to the home base, with the exception of 482, which was left at Djeidieda, Tunisia, for supercharger repairs" ("War Diary 99th BG," Sheet 37)

Jul 25, 1943

King Victor Emmanuel III, supported by leading Italian political figures, deposes dictator Benito Mussolini, and Italy begins to negotiate peace terms with the Allies. As German commanders planned to evacuate Sicily, Patton and Montgomery began squeezing Axis defenders into the island's northeast corner (Ethier, Eric 2021)

Jul 25, 1943

Patton flies across the island of Sicily to Syracuse to meet Monty. When Montgomery visits Palermo a few days later, Patton sends an escort to meet him at the airport and greeted him at his headquarters with a full band. "I hope Monty realized that I did this to show him up for doing nothing for me on the 25th," Patton wrote in his diary (Ethier, Eric 2021)

Jul 27, 1943

REE - Flies the B-17E from Cassibile to Malta to Cassibile (IFR)

Jul 27, 1943

"Patton and I arrange further details of co-operation between our two armies. I now had the *Flying Fortress* in SICILY and was glad to have it back again; it had been away having new engines put in" (Montgomery's Diary Notes, BLM 39 1943)

Jul 28, 1943

REE - Flies Montgomery and his staff in the *Theresa Leta* to Palermo (Chapter 14, Patton at Palermo)

Jul 28, 1943

REE - Flies B-17E Cassibile to Palermo to Comiso, Sicily (IFR). Flies B-25 Comiso to Cassibile, Sicily (IFR)

Jul 28, 1943

"I flew over to PALERMO with my Chief of Staff and AOC to see General Patton, GOC 7th American Army. We had a great reception. The Americans are most delightful people and are very easy to work with. I discussed plans for future operations with General Patton" (Montgomery, Bernard Law, BLM 39) (Photograph: 14.2)

Jul 28, 1943

General Bernard Montgomery says farewell to Lieutenant General George Patton at an airfield near Palermo, Sicily, after Montgomery's visit (Photograph: 13.3)

Jul 28, 1943

A sheepish 8th Army Commander cabled to General Bedell Smith: "Had difficulty with Fortress today at Palermo and consider should change it in view of small airfields on which we are now working. Can you send me a C-47 with jeep? Will you have long-range tanks fitted? Grateful if you will send it to Cassibile Airfield near Syracuse" (Montgomery's Diary Notes, BLM 39)

Jul 27– 28, 1943

Allied air raid causes a firestorm in Hamburg that destroys nearly half of the city

Jul 29, 1943

REE - Flies B-17E from Comiso to Notary Airfield (IFR)

Jul 31, 1943

"My new aeroplane, a C-47 with a Jeep inside, arrived. The Fortress is too big for the smaller air-fields which we now have to use, and I was nearly killed trying to land in PALERMO on 28 July. So General EISENHOWER has exchanged it, giving me the C-47 instead – with a Jeep inside" (Montgomery, Bernard Law, BLM 39)

Jul 31, 1943

Montgomery wrote to Bedell Smith, "C-47 has arrived. Thank you very much. Am glad to have it. I escaped a nasty accident in Fortress only by skill of pilot and might have been killed. Am sending C-47 to Maison Blanche to be fitted with seats and have other minor adjustments made. Grateful if you will tell depot at Maison Blanche to do this work" (8th Army HQ War Diary 1943)

Aug 1, 1943

Ploesti, Romania, raid when American B-24 bombers fly out of the Libyan Desert, across the Mediterranean Sea to target and return a two-thousand-mile journey that did push the abilities of both planes and crews to their limits. 178 attack planes fly into a fiery hell that will be remembered as "Black Sunday"

Aug 1, 1943

REE - Flies Notary, Tunis to Cassibile (IFR)

Aug 1, 1943

"Hour this morning was 0500 for mission number 60. 28 airplanes took off at 0737 to bomb the dock area at Naples, Italy. There were 5 early returns, leaving 23 to go over the target, dropping 276x500 bombs (69 tons). The dock area was well covered. Two vessels in the harbor were probably hit. Many hits were made on buildings and maritime installations on the waterfront. Flak over the target was moderate, heavy and inaccurate. 25 fighters of the enemy attacked our formations. Three of them escaped. Two were damaged, six probably destroyed and 14 destroyed for certain. Our aircraft, 42-3129 of the 346th Squadron, was badly hit by fighters, but made its way to Djeidieda, where, in attempting to make a landing it crashed, killing Lieutenant Howard B. Ebbers and his entire crew. Two of our aircraft were damaged by flak. All the planes returned by 1430. We gained one new crew with plane 42-30474, which was assigned to the 346th Squadron and another plane 42-5856, assigned to the 347th Squadron" ("War Diary 99th BG," Sheet 42)

Aug 1, 1943

"I moved up and joined TAC Army, situated near HQ 30 Corps just south of RAMACKA. It was a lovely site, high up on a mountain with a superb view. We acquired a Peacock this day. We already have some canaries, with a hen sitting on three eggs" (Montgomery, Bernard Law, BLM 39)

Aug 3 – 4, 1943
REE - Flies a B-17E Cassibile to Tripoli to Cassibile to Tripoli (IFR)

Aug 3, 1943
Lieutenant General George S. Patton visits a hospital in Sicily. He slaps a soldier who is hospitalized for psychoneurosis, accusing him of cowardice. It later emerges that the soldier has malaria and a high fever

Aug 4, 1943
99th BG moves headquarters to Oudna Airfield, Tunisia

Aug 5, 1943
"Early this day we captured CATANIA, MISTERRBIANCO and PALERMO. This was very satisfactory. The thrust of 5 Division left Division of 13 Corps directed on BELPASSO and once we secured that place the enemy lateral road would be cut ... I decided to visit CENTURIPE to look into operations on the left flank. It is difficult to describe CENTURIPE; it is a large town built on a very high mountain crag and the only road leading up to it is one mess of hairpin bends. Its capture by 78 Division was a truly amazing affair and only good troops could have done it... From CENTURIPE the enemy positions on the line BIANCAVILLIA – ADRANO are completely dominated, and observation is possible over the whole enemy area. On the left I saw the Canadian troops advancing, infantry and tanks covered by artillery fire; it was a perfect view of a battle episode, and I doubt if one will ever see such a good scene again... it was possible only because of the superb viewpoint. From my viewpoint and ADRANO I could see the leading troops of 78 Division enlarging their bridgehead over the Simeto River" (Montgomery, Bernard Law, BLM 39)

Aug 5, 1943
REE - Autographed letter to the B-17 *Theresa Leta* crew, " ...Good-bye and the best of luck to you all, always... " Major Evans and his crew continue to make bombing raids in other B-17s. Monty left the B-17, *Theresa Leta*, and crew. (Appendices: 8.5.43, Monty writes a letter of thanks to the *Theresa Leta* crew)

Aug 5, 1943
REE - Is given an autographed photograph by General Montgomery (Photograph: 3.1)

Aug 6 – Dec 8, 1943
99th BG flies missions (#61 – #113) from Oudna

Airfield, Tunisia, near Mohammedia, a few miles from Tunisia (Bruno, James F. 134)

Aug 1943
The 99th Bombardment Group is now based in Oudna Airfield, Tunisia. The 346th Bombardment Squadron is a B-17 *Flying Fortress* squadron, assigned to the 99th BG, 15th Air Force

Aug 6, 1943
"On the left 30 Corps captured BIANCAVILIA and ADRANO" (Montgomery, Bernard Law, BLM 39)

Aug 7, 1943
REE - Flies B-17E Cassibile to Malta (IFR)

Aug 9, 1943
REE - Flies B-17E Malta to Tunis (IFR)

Aug 10, 1943
12th Air Force is stationed at Tunisia

Aug 10, 1943
REE - Writes to JoAnn: "I am once again back in my old outfit, carrying on with the work I really came over for to do" (Appendices: 8.10.43, Back with 99th BG)

Aug 11 – 17, 1943
The Italian and German Armies are successful in withdrawing across the Straits of Messina

Aug 12, 1943
REE - Writes a 20-page V-Mail to his parents, describing the entire Monty story, the B-17 repairs in Cairo, Malta, and the Palermo landing (Appendices: 8.12.43, Monty Story from V- Mail)

Aug 13, 1943
REE - Flies a B-17F for his Mission #26 to Rome, 5:55 hours (IFR)

Aug 17, 1943
REE - Flies a B-17F for his Mission #27, 7:30 hours (IFR)

Aug 17, 1943
99th flies Mission #64, first mission to France, Latube A/D at Marseilles (Bruno, James F. 134)

Aug 17, 1943
Americans fly daylight air raids on Regensburg and Schweinfurt in Germany

Aug 17, 1943
Patton arrives in Messina hours ahead of the British, completing the capture of Sicily

Aug 19, 1943
REE - Flies a B-17F for his Mission #28, 5:50 hours (IFR)

Aug 25, 1943
99th BG Mission #66 targets Foggia. 41 enemy aircraft on the ground and 28 others in the air (Bruno, James F. 134)

Aug 25, 1943
REE - Flies a B-17F for his Mission #29, 5:30 hours (IFR)

Aug 29, 1943
REE - Flies a B-17F for his Mission #30, 5:45 hours (IFR)

Aug 31, 1943
REE - Flies a B-17F for his Mission #31, 8:00 hours (IFR)

Aug 30, 1943
REE - 99th BG, 346th Bomb Squadron reports a holiday. General Atkinson presented Colonel Upthegrove with the Distinguished Flying Cross and the Silver Star. Several others received the DFC ("War Diary 99th BG," Sheet 46)

Aug 31, 1943
REE - Flies a B-17F for his Mission #32, 8:00 hours (IFR)

Aug 31, 1943
REE - Combat Photo, number V-238-H, 99th BG 346th Squadron taken from Ship 416, 1302 hrs. 12"- 18,600 ft. Pisa, M/Y Italy (Photograph: 20.3)

Aug 31, 1943
REE - "This morning the aircraft of the group participated in our #71 Mission. At 0945, forty-two aircraft took off to bomb the Pisa M/Y in Italy. Two of these returned early. Forty aircraft passed over the target and dropped 472x500 bombs (119.75 tons), covering the target quite well. The airfield outside of the target area was covered, causing considerable damage. Flak was heavy, moderate, and inaccurate. All the aircraft returned at 1600 hours to the home base except for #477, which landed at Palermo, Sicily with two engines out. The gunners destroyed one enemy, Me-109, aircraft" ("War Diary 99th BG," Sheet 46)

Sep 2, 1943
99th BG mission #72 over Bologna, Italy. The 348th lost a crew and ship (Bruno, James F. 135)

Sep 3, 1943
Representatives of the Italian government sign an armistice with the Allies. The Allies begin the invasion plans to capture the Axis forces within Italy's borders

Sep 5, 1943
REE - Flies a B-17F for his Mission #33, 7:30 hours (IFR)

Sep 6, 1943
REE - Writes to his father about the ground loop landing to save the B-17 from crashing at Palermo Airfield before meeting General Patton (Appendices: 9.6.43, Monty-Palermo Story)

Sep 8, 1943
99th BG Mission #77 to Frascati, Italy A/D near Rome

Sep 9, 1943
British 8th Army and US 5th Army main invasion forces land on the mainland of Italy. Allied invasion of Italy begins at Salerno on the western coast in Operation Avalanche, while two supporting operations took place in Calabria (Operation Baytown) and Taranto (Operation Slapstick) further south at the "toe" and west at the "heal"

Sep 9, 1943
150 B-17s from the 5th Bomb Wing attack the German High Command HQ in Frascati. The next six missions flown by the 5th Bomb Wing are primarily against various highways and bridges in support of the American advance at Salerno. 5th Bomb Wing consists of battle groups, 97th, 99th and 301st, and later 2nd, 463rd and 483rd

Sep 10, 1943
REE - Flies a B-17F for his Mission #34, 5:50 hours (IFR)

Sep 14, 1943
REE - Flies a B-17F for his Mission #35, 6:50 hours (IFR)

Sep 15, 1943
REE - Writes to his mother how he met, pursued, and loves JoAnn Nelson (Appendices: 9.15.43, The Story of JoAnn)

Sep 17, 1943
REE - Flies B-17F Oudna to Oran to Oudna (IFR)

Sep 18, 1943
REE - Becomes new squadron Operations Officer ("War Diary 99th BG," Sheet 50)

Oct 1943
Foggia Airfield Complex is heavily bombed by the US Army Air Force and Royal Air Force in 1943, before being seized by the British 8th Army in October 1943, during the Italian Campaign. By

mid-1944, about two dozen airfields are in operation in the Foggia area supporting strategic bombing missions; escort missions; tactical fighter operations; reconnaissance and air defense missions

Oct 1 – 21, 1943
REE - During this time period contributes meritorious achievements in aerial flight while participating in sustained operational activities against the enemy from October 1 – 21, 1943. For this period of activity the Citation: Oak-Leaf 7th Cluster is later awarded (Appendices: 10.1 – 10.21.43, Oak-Leaf Cluster)

Oct 1, 1943
REE - Flies a B-17F for his Mission #36, 9:30 hours (IFR)

Oct 4, 1943
REE - Flies a B-17F for his Mission #37, 8:35 hours (IFR)

Oct 5, 1943
REE - Flies a B-17F for his Mission #38, 7:35 hours (IFR)

Oct 9, 1943
REE - Flies a B-17F for his Mission #39, 8:35 hours (IFR)

Oct 9, 1943
REE - 99th BG Mission #93 bombs Salonika and Mission #94 bombs Larissa, Greece. "The group split up today for a double mission, and for the first time in our history we raided targets in Greece. Fourteen ships led by Lt. Col. Thurman took off at 0731 to bomb Sedes A/D at Salonika, Mission #93, while 16 planes led by Capt. Evans took off at 0816 to bomb Larissa A/D, Mission #94. There were four early returns in the Evans group and 12 planes went over the target at 1225, scoring bomb hits extending across the field. There were no fighters, moderate flak and all planes returned safely at 1715" ("War Diary 99th BG," Sheet 55)

Oct 12, 1943
REE - Tells his mother that he can't come home for Christmas. "I'm leading a fine bunch of young men and they really need me..." (Appendices: 10.12.43, Not Home for Christmas)

Oct 12, 1943
REE - Flies a B-17F for his #40 Mission, 2:00 hours (IFR)

Oct 19, 1943
REE - Flies a B-17F for his Mission #41, 1:45 hours (IFR)

Oct 21, 1943
REE - Flies a B-17F for his Mission #42, 4:30 hours (IFR)

Oct 23, 1943
REE - Flies a B-17F for his Mission #43, 3:30 hours (IFR)

Oct 24, 1943
REE - Flies a B-17F for his Mission #44, 7:00 hours (IFR)

Oct 25, 1943
REE - Flies a B-17F for his Mission #45, 3:40 hours (IFR)

Oct 29, 1943
REE - Father asks his son to come home. That, "Of course if you feel it's your duty to stay, I know you will do it, you have gone the second mile always." (Appendices: 10.29.43, Father's Request "Come Home")

Oct 29, 1943
REE - Flies a B-17F for his Mission #46, 8 hours (IFR)

Oct 29, 1943
REE - "Captain Richard Evans, deputy commander and operations officer, received his Majority this day Congratulations" ("War Diary 346th Squadron" Sheet 24)

Oct 30, 1943
99th BG Mission #100 is a flop because of complete overcast over Turin, but credit is given for 100 missions (Bruno, James F. 136)

Nov – Dec 1943
REE - Monty on occasion calls Major Evans to fly him in "his" B-17, *Theresa Leta*. Monty recognizes that Evans is promoted to a Major. Monty also has access to an American C-47 with a jeep for small airfields, which Evans can fly (Chapter 20, "Merry Christmas, Venezia")

Nov 1, 1943
Doolittle takes command of the US 15th Air Force in the Mediterranean Theater of Operations. The 15th Air Force results from a reorganization of Doolittle's 12th Air Force. The strategy is for this group to operate when the 8th AF in England is socked in by bad English weather. As bases around Foggia, Italy, became available, the 15th can reach targets in southern France, Germany, Poland, Czechoslovakia, and the Balkans, some

of which were difficult to reach from England ("Second Bomb Group, 15th Air Force")

Nov 2, 1943
Four B-17 groups (includes the 99th BG) of the 5th Bomb Wing and two B-24 groups of the 9th Air Force were combined with two fighter groups to form the new 15th Air Force. On its first day of existence, the 15th flew a 1,600-mile round trip to bomb the Messerschmitt aircraft factory at Wiener Neustadt, Austria ("Second Bomb Group, 15th Air Force)

Nov 2, 1943
99th BG targets Wiener Neustadt, Austria, A/C Factory, Mission #98

Nov 3, 1943
REE - Flies a B-17G, 3:50 hours (IFR)

Nov 3, 1943
99th BG approved motto, "Sight with Might"

Nov 4, 1943
"Today was the day for our big celebration of the100th group Mission ...All personnel gathered around the huge barbecue pits to eat steaks and drink beer. There was music by the 301st BG orchestra. Then at 1730 Col. Upthegrove went to the microphone and reviewed our first 100 missions, paying tribute to flying and ground personnel alike. He then introduced distinguished guests for the occasion including Lt. Gen. Spaatz, Chief of the new 15th Air Force and Maj. Gen. Doolittle, Chief of Strategic Operations. Gen Spaatz said our group was destined to play a leading role in the forth-coming operations of the 15th, which he said would be devoted largely to targets in Germany ("War Dairy 99th BG," Sheet 59)

Nov 6, 1943
REE - Flies a B-17G for his Mission #47, 6 hours (IFR)

Nov 6, 1943
REE - Flies bombing run, 99th BG Mission #103, Orbatello, Italy, RR Bridge - Ship 23026, *Roger the Lodger* (99th BG Historical Society Database)

Nov 6, 1943
REE - "3 B-17s and 4 B-17s took off jointly at about 0850 from Oudna #1 on a bombing mission. Target: 3 to bomb railroad bridge 5 miles north of Orbatello, Italy, and 4 to bomb railroad bridge of Orbatello on the Fiora River. Formation took off together and split near target and after bombing, joined and returned safely to base at

about 1415. Mission accomplished though no direct hits on bridges were observed. Tracks and approaches were hit. Near misses near bridge. Bomb load was 6x1000 and bombing altitude was 3,000 feet. No flak, no fighters, no mishaps" ("War Diary 99th BG," Sheet 60)

Nov 8, 1943
REE - Flies B-17G for his Mission #48, 8:30 hours (IFR)

Nov 8, 1943
REE - flew bombing run to Turin, Italy - Ship 230313 (99th BG Historical Society n.d.)

Nov 8, 1943
REE - "12 B-17s took off at about 0917 from Oudna #1 on a bombing mission. Target: Turin-ball bearing factory. Aircraft 856 and 026 returned early. Mission accomplished and target believed destroyed by excellent concentration of hits. Aircraft 343, 383, 918, 129 and 313 landed at Alghero (Sardinia), Italy to refuel and returned in evening. 407 turned back 20 minutes from target and returned at 1846. 477 landed at Decimomannu, (Sardinia) Italy, and to return to base 11-9-43. 026 landed at Alghero, to return tomorrow. Bomb loads 12x500. No flak. 6 Me-109s are around target but no hostile action taken. All but three dropped bombs on target" ("War Diary 99th BG," Sheet 60)

Nov 10, 1943
REE - Becomes Commanding Officer of the 346th Squadron, 99th BG, Title was Squadron Commander ("346th Squadron Unit History 99th BG, 1943)

Nov 12, 1943
Colonel Upthegrove addressed all officers under his command at the Officers' club. In a well-constructed speech, he covered military social, economic, and political problems as they affect the soldier and the welfare of the nation. Fighting this war is but the beginning of our problems to keep America strong and provide her with leadership and farsighted action. His unexpected topic of discussion proved stimulating and found much praise amongst those of his audience ("War Diary 346th Squadron" Sheet 28)

Nov 16, 1943
REE - Flies a B-17G for his Mission #49, 7:10 hours (IFR)

Nov 16, 1943
REE - Flies 99th BG Mission #106 to Istres Le

Tube, France – Ship 229513, *El Diablo*. 22 aircraft took off, 2 returned early. "Observations, FLAK, heavy, intense and accurate. Five aircraft holed. 12 to 15 Me-109s and Fw-190s" (99th BG Historical Society. n.d.)

Nov 16, 1943
REE - "6 B-17s took off at about 0845 from Oudna #1 on a bombing mission. Target: Le Tube Airdrome, France. 026, 407, 477, 513, 526, 856 all hit the target. Mission successful and fair results obtained. Bomb load: 12x500. Flak was heavy, intense, and accurate.10 to 15 enemy fighters attacked the formation. Me-109s and Fw-190s. Our gunners claimed two destroyed. S/Sgt. Titus killed in action by fighter fire. S/Sgt. Brennam wounded. Both were gunners in 477. Our planes returned at about 1610" ("War Diary 99th BG," Sheet 62)

Nov 20, 1943
REE - Flies a B-17G, 5 hours (IFR)

Nov 21, 1943
REE - Flies a B-17F, 3:30 hours (IFR)

Nov 25, 1943
99th BG says good-bye to Colonel Upthegrove who left the group for USA (Bruno, James F. 36)

Nov 26, 1943
REE - Flies a B-17F, 2:15 hours (IFR)

Nov 27, 1943
Monty's Battle of the Sangro River commences

Nov 28, 1943
The Tehran Conference convenes, Roosevelt, Churchill, and Stalin

Nov 30, 1943
REE - Flies a B-17G, 3:10 hours (IFR)

Dec 1, 1943
German line on the Sangro River is broken

Dec 1, 1943 – Jan 7, 1944
REE - During these dates, 1 December 1943 to 7 January 1944, contributes meritorious achievements in aerial flight while participating sustained operational activities against the enemy. For this period of activity the Citation: Oak-Leaf 9th Cluster is later awarded (Appendices: 12.1.43 – 1.7.44, Oak-Leaf Cluster)

Dec 1, 1943
REE - Flies a B-17G for his Mission #50, 8:30 hours (IFR)

Dec 1, 1943
REE - "The following aircraft took off from Oudna Airfield, Tunisia #1 at about 0905 on a bombing mission: 229513 *El Diablo* (Evans), 75, 526, 407, 856, 470, 223, 418, 396, 026, 477, and 338. Target: Aero Engine works at Turin, Italy. Mission very successful, bomb load: 12x500. Flak was heavy, moderate, and accurate. About 8 Me-109s were observed over the target and these were engaged by our P-38s. Planes stopped at a staging area to refuel and returned safely to the base. 470 and 418 were early returns. No mishaps" ("War Diary 99th BG," Sheet 65)

Dec 9, 1943
REE - Flies a B-17G, 5:45 hours (IFR)

Dec 11, 1943
REE - Flies a B-17G, 2:45 hours (IFR)

Dec 11, 1943
346th Bombardment Squadron, 99th moves from Oudna Airfield, Tunisia, and is based in Tortorella Airfield, 6 miles from Foggia, Italy. Living conditions at Tortorella are very harsh. The summers are hot and dusty, the winters cold and wet. Buildings are few, and airplane maintenance crews work out in the open. The men live in tents using homemade gasoline stoves for heat. The men constantly struggle through mud and water, snow, and ice, or choking dust, depending on the season ("99th BG in Action During WWII" DVD 2014) (Photograph: 20.1)

Dec 12, 1943
REE - Flies a B-17F, 3:00 hours (IFR)

Dec 13, 1943
Changes of Station to Tortorella Field, Foggia, Italy: The air echelon and part of the ground departed on December 13 and arrived the same day (346th Squadron Unit History 1943)

Dec 14, 1943
General Montgomery cuts the ceremonial ribbon to officially open the bridge made with "Bailey" bridge panels constructed over the Sangro River on December 14, 1943 (Photograph: 20.10)

Dec 14 – Apr 26, 1945
99th BG flies Missions (#114 – #395) from Tortorella, Foggia, Italy

Dec 16, 1943
REE - Flies a B-17G for his Mission #51, 5:30 hours (IFR)

Dec 16, 1943

REE - "Thirty-two of our planes took off at 1037 today for Mission #118 to the RR yards and bridges at Padua, Italy. With Major Evans of the 346th leading (ship 124396, *Eight Ball*), all 32 planes went over the target at 1300, dropping 384 500-pounders. ...Flak was slight, inaccurate, and heavy, while three fighters appeared but did not engage. All planes returned safely at 1500. On a raid that would have consumed seven or eight hours if sprung from NA, our bombers made it from here in four hours and 23 minutes, thus proving the utility of our new base, Foggia #2" ("War Diary 99th BG," Sheet 68)

Dec 16, 1943

Combat Photograph number V-406-B, 99th BG 347th Squadron, Ship 340, 1307 Hrs., 12"- 23,000 ft., Padua M/Y, Italy (Photograph: 20.9)

Dec 23, 1943

REE - Flies a B-17G, 1 hour (IFR)

Dec 24, 1943

"Very early in the morning of the 24th December, I was woken up to be given a signal from the War Office to say I was to return to England to succeed General Paget in command of 21 Army Group, the British Group of Armies preparing to open a 'second front' across the Channel" (Montgomery, Bernard Law, 1st Viscount 182)

Dec 25, 1943

REE - Flies a B-17F for his Mission #52, 4:40 hours (IFR)

Dec 25, 1943

REE - "Christmas, 1943, and we attempted to send our respects to the Axis with Mission #119 to the M/Y at Udine, Italy. With Major Evans of the 346th (Ship 229513, *El Diablo*) leading 37 of our planes [we] took off at 0925. Five were early returns. But the target was closed in and so were all the alternates. Frustrated, our ships brought their bombs back at 1420. Meanwhile a cold snap set in as the group celebrated Christmas as best it could. Church services were crowded. The Quartermaster came through with another big turkey dinner with most of the trimmings... ("War Diary 99th BG," Sheet 70) (Chapter 20, "Merry Christmas, Venezia")

Dec 27, 1943

"I flew to Algiers on the 27th December to see Eisenhower and Bedell Smith, who was going to

go with Eisenhower as his Chief of Staff. ...I got back to Tactical H.Q. in Italy on the afternoon of the 28th December." (Montgomery, Bernard Law, 1st Viscount 184)

Dec 28, 1943

REE - 99th BG - 416th Bomb Squadron, Aircraft 472. "Twenty-nine of our planes took off at 0945 for Mission #120 to M/Y at Rimini, Italy. Two were early returns. Led by Captain Bransom of the 348th 27 planes went over the target at 1230, dropping 311 500-pounders. Undercast spoiled the aim and most bombs landed in the southwest part of the city. No flak or fighters and all planes returned safely at 1415." ("War Diary 99th BG," Sheet 70)

Dec 30, 1943

At TAC HQ I gave my farewell address to the 8th Army at Vasto, 30 December1943. "I had asked my Corps Commanders to attend, Dempsey and Allfrey, and of course Freyberg of the New Zealand Division, and Broadhurst of the Desert Air Force." (Montgomery, Bernard Law, 1st Viscount 186)

Dec 30, 1943

REE - Flies a B-17G for his Mission #53, 4:45 hours (IFR)

Dec 30, 1943

REE - Twenty-six of our planes took off at 1022 for Mission #122 to M/Y at Rimini, Italy. There was one early return. Led by Major Evans of the 346th, 25 ships went over the target at 1317, dropping 300 500-pounders, which really plastered the target. The entire M/Y was covered with hits causing heavy damage. There was one large explosion, believed by crewman to have been an ammunition train. RR bridges and many shops and warehouses were hit. There was slight flak and five fighters engaged, but all our planes returned safely at 1445 ("War Diary 99th BG," Sheet 71)

Dec 31, 1943

On 31 December I handed over to my successor, Lieutenant General Sir Oliver Leese, and took off from the Sangro airstrip for home (Montgomery, Field Marshal Viscount 130)

Dec 31, 1943

"The next morning, the 31st December, I took off in my *Dakota* (C-47) aircraft from the air strip near my Tactical H.Q. We had a heavy load, as besides myself and my A.D.C.s there were de Guingand, Graham, Williams, and Richards.

We also had with us five soldiers, quite a lot of luggage, and a full load of petrol. The airstrip was small, and I asked the pilot if we would get off. (The airstrip was an unimproved airfield near the Sangro River, Adriatic Coast) He said he thought we should just manage it; and we did, but only just" (Montgomery, Bernard Law, 1st Viscount 187)

Dec 31, 1943
REE - Flies 8:00 hours and 5:00 hours (IFR)

Dec 31, 1943
REE - Flies Monty from a base north of Naples, across the Mediterranean to Algiers and on to Marrakesh to meet with Eisenhower and Churchill. This is their last flight together (Chapter 21, "Escape from Okinawa")

Jan 1944
Doolittle takes command of US 8th AF in Britain, which he controlled until V-E Day

Jan 1, 1944
"The PM and EISENHOWER both refused to let me fly to England in my own aeroplane, which only had two engines. So, I transferred to the routine C-54 (my pilot), a four-engine ship and reached PRESTWICK at 0900 hours on 2nd January. My own C-47 followed, full of oranges" (Montgomery, Bernard Law, BLM 72)

Jan 2, 1944
"I flew on to London, which I reached at 1300 hours" (Montgomery, Bernard Law, BLM 72)

Jan 5, 1944
REE - Efficiency Report: Foggia (Tortorella), Italy Flight leader, 346th Bomb Squadron, Excellent. Operations Officer, 346th Bomb Squadron, Excellent. Commanding officer, 346th Bomb Squadron, Excellent. Comments: "Exceptional ability as a pilot. A very likable individual with a mind of his own: lacks experience in administrative duties but has proven himself in combat. In comparing this officer with all officers of his grade known to me, I would place him among the middle third" (OMPF)

Jan 7, 1944
REE - B-17G, Mission #54 4:25 hours (IFR)

Jan 7, 1944
REE - Flies bombing run to Maribor, Yugoslavia - Plane 229775, *Wongo*. "Nine B-17s took off on a bombing mission. Target: Weiner Neustadt, Germany. Take off at 0735. Participating: 396, 470,

477, 026, 338, 520, 263, 775 and 407. Numbers 396, 477, 263 and 775 returned early and en route home 775 bombed Split Harbor, Yugoslavia, at 16,000 feet. Bombs fell on small merchant vessels. Bomb load carried: 12x500. Others did not hit target or alternates because of weather and returned at 1223. No flak or fighters" ("War Diary 346th Squadron," Sheet 42)

Jan 8, 1944
REE - Flies a B-17G, 2:00 hours (IFR)

Jan 10 – 11, 1944
REE - Flies a B-17G, 2:00 hours and 1:45 hours (IFR)

Jan 19 – 20, 1944
99th BG fly softening attacks on Airdromes and around Rome, targets Ciampino and Centocelle (Bruno, James F. 138)

Jan 21, 1944
REE - Flies a B-17F, 6:40 hours (IFR)

Jan 22, 1944
Anzio invasion, Operation Shingle

Jan 22, 1944 – Feb 15, 1944
REE - Flies a B-17F on ferrying missions to deliver fighter pilots to England so they can pick up new fighter planes to fly back to Italy

Jan 26, 1944
REE - Flies a B-17F, 7:20 hours (IFR)

Jan 28, 1944
REE - Flies a B-17F, 10:45 hours (IFR)

Feb 2, 1944
REE - Flies a B-17F, 2:20 hours (IFR)

Feb 2, 1944
REE - Father almost pleads with his son, "Hurry up boy, we're really getting anxious" (Appendices: 2.2.44, Come Home)

Feb 11, 1944
REE - Flies a B-17F, 6:00 hours (IFR)

Feb 12, 1944
REE - Flies a B-17F, 3:10 hours (IFR)

Feb 13, 1944
REE - Flies a B-17F, 4:25 hours (IFR)

Feb. 13 – 26, 1944
"Big Week" - 3,300 planes from 8th AF and 500 from 15th AF dropped 10,000 tons to destroy Luftwaffe factories in central Germany

Feb 14, 1944
REE - "... Major Evans returned to this base (Tortorella Field, Foggia) from England yesterday and was seen by us today. He is again in command. Captain Helms returned with him" ("War Diary 346th Squadron," Sheet 53)

Feb 15 – 19, 1944
REE - Is waiting transportation to US. Checks out in B-26, P-38, and P-47, 6:50 hrs. flight time (OMPF)

Feb 16, 1944
REE - " ...Major Evans buzzes the field in a P-38 this noon and later at around 1600 buzzes in a P-47. He is checked out in both" ("War Diary 346th Squadron," Sheet 53)

Feb 17, 1944
REE – " ...Major Evans left this day. A grand officer and man. He was well liked, and we shall miss him much" ("War Diary 346th," Sheet 53)

Feb 17, 1944
REE - Distinguished Flying Cross citation is recorded (Appendices: 2.17.43, Major Richard E. Evans' Citation)

Feb 19 – Apr 10, 1944
REE - "Awaiting transportation & enroute US (21 days ship travel)" (OMPF)

Mar 2, 1944
REE - "...Awards came through for some of our personnel: DFC for Lieutenant Kline, Major Evans, Captain Helms, Lieutenant Bjork..." ("War Diary 346th Squadron," Sheet 56)

Mar 15, 1944
99th BG attacked Monte Cassino, a stronghold for the Germans and our Mission #161 was highly successful (Bruno, James F. 139)

Mar 17 – 23, 1944
Mount Vesuvius erupts and destroys the towns, Sans Sebastiano, Massa di Somma. A black "snowstorm' of ash spouts from the volcano and causes severe damage to the planes from 340th BG based at Pompeii Field (Muller, Richard R. 2021)

Mar 18, 1944
British drop 3,000 tons of bombs during an air raid on Hamburg, Germany

Mar 27, 1944
REE - To parents - "We will be married on Uncle Bob's birthday. I'm delirious. Be home for Dad's birthday. Get the family together. Let's celebrate..."

Apr 1, 1944
REE - Marries JoAnn Nelson at Alamo Heights United Methodist Church, San Antonio, TX. They travel to see Dick's family in Knoxville, TN, April 4, and honeymoon in FL, at the Pacific Hotel in Miami, an Army Redistribution Station for military men returning from battle. Men reunite with their wives, are debriefed about enemy positions, rest and relax before being released or reassigned (Photographs: 21.4, 21.5, 21.6)

Apr 10 – 25, 1944
REE - And JN enjoy R&R at Miami Beach, FL (OMPF)

Apr 13, 1944
REE - Is given the Distinguished Flying Cross citation from the Decoration and Awards Branch, Military Personnel division, AGO. This is a Record of Award of Decoration by Agency other than War Department (Appendices: 4.13.44, Distinguished Flying Cross)

Apr 23, 1944
99th BG bombs an aircraft factory at Weiner Neustadt, Austria. The 99th is the lead group on this mission. The group receives another Presidential Citation for the mission (Bruno, James F. 139)

May 4 - 25, 1944
REE - Reports to 202nd AAF Base Unit (IIU), GAAF, Galveston, TX, as a student in the four-engine B-29 pilots instructor course (OMPF)

May 31, 1944
REE - Is ACU Attaché, 231st AAF Student Instructor, B-29 Class AO-8-1. (B-17, 10 hrs. & B-29 10 hrs.) (OMPF)

May 14, 1944
Final D-Day briefing is at St. Paul's School, Chiswick, England

Jun 6, 1944
REE - Is awarded Oak-Leaf Clusters AM number 7th. Citation: "For meritorious achievements in aerial flight while participating in sustained operational activities against the enemy from 1 October 1943 – 21 October 1943" (Appendices: 6.6.44, Oak-Leaf Cluster 10.1.43 – 10.12.43)

Jun 6, 1944
REE - Is awarded Oak-Leaf Clusters AM number 9th. Citation: "For meritorious achievement in aerial flight while participating in sustained operational activities against the enemy from

the dates December 1, 1943, to January 7, 1944."
By command, Major General Twining (Appendices: 6.6.44, Oak Leaf Cluster 12.1.43 – 1.7.44)

Jun 6 – Aug 19, 1944
D-Day Normandy is successful with landings of Operation Neptune, (Beaches: Utah, Omaha, La Pointe duHoc, Gold, Juno, Sword). Operation Overlord is the code name for the Battle of Normandy, Allied invasion of northwest Europe

Jun 13, 1944
First V-1 flying bomb is launched against Britain

Jun 19 – 22, 1944
A great storm damages much of the two artificial harbors (Arromanches & Omaha Beach), which are used for Allied invasion of northwest Europe

Jun 30, 1944
REE - Transferred to 231st Army Airfield Base Unit, Army Air Base Alamogordo, NM. He is assistant Director of Training

Jul 1944
REE - REE and JN live in Alamogordo, NM

Jul 7 – 9, 1944
Liberation of Caen, Operation Charnwood

Jul 18, 1944
Liberation of Saint-Lo, Normandy, Operation Goodwood

Jul 24 – Aug 1, 1944
"Battle of Tinian," the Americans take Island and build largest airbase during WWII. Designed to accommodate the entire 313th Bombardment Wing of Boeing B-29 *Superfortress* bombers. Tinian Island is launching point for the atomic bomb attacks against Hiroshima and Nagasaki

Jul 25 – 30, 1944
Operation Cobra leads Americans into Coutances, Granville, and Avranches, France

Aug 4, 1944
US Army Air Corps, 316th Bomb Wing VH (Very Heavy) is constituted this date

Aug 14, 1944
316th Bomb Wing is activated, assigned to the 8th Air Force, and plans are underway to move to Okinawa

Aug 21, 1944
Falaise Pocket is closed. The area of Falaise, Calvados within the region of Normandy, France, is where the defining battle to conquer the German

Army, is fought. The Western Allies encircled the German Army Group B, 7th Army and the 5th Panzer Army

Aug 25, 1944
Liberation of Paris

Oct 14, 1944
Allied forces liberate Athens; Rommel "commits suicide"

Oct 30, 1944
Last use of gas chambers at Auschwitz

Dec 3 – 31, 1944
REE - Joins HQ 316th Bomb Wing VH originating at Peterson Field, Colorado Springs, as the staff operations and training officer (OMPF)

Dec 16, 1944 – Jan 27, 1945
Battle of the Bulge in the Ardennes and the Germans fail with their offensive

Dec 25, 1944
REE - Visits family in San Antonio

Dec 26, 1944
Patton relieves Bastogne

Jan 1945
REE - And JN move to Colorado Springs

Jan 23, 1945
Major Frank A. Roberts MIA (Major Evans' very good friend). "...while over the target, the formation was aggressively intercepted by enemy fighters. An attacking fighter believed to be a Ki-61 *Tony* made a vertical dive and opened fire on his B-29, hitting the bomber's No. 4 engine, causing it to explode. Damaged, the B-29, *Homing De-Vice*, turned on its back and spun into the sea... no one was believed to have survived" ("B-29-50-BW 'Homing De-Vice' 1945) (Photographs: 21.2, 21.3)

Jan 27, 1945
Soviet troops enter Auschwitz, Birkenau, Monowitz, and liberate more than 7,000 remaining prisoners, who are mostly ill and dying ("Soviet Forces Liberate Auschwitz" 2020)

Feb 4 –11, 1945
Roosevelt, Churchill, and Stalin meet at Yalta

Feb 13 – 14, 1945
Dresden is destroyed by a firestorm after Allied bombing raids

Feb 13, 1945
REE - is a member of the 316th Wing and en route

to Guam, from Peterson Field, Colorado Springs. He flies a B-29 to visit General LeMay, commander of the 21st Bomber Command, Guam Territory. He also travels to visit commanders of the 73rd Bombardment Wing, Saipan, and Tinian (Photograph: 21.1)

Mar 9 – 10, 1945
REE - On the night of the first B-29 low-level incendiary raids over Japan, Evans arrives in Tinian with his B-29. Evans is present with LeMay throughout the evening of the raid. This is the beginning of a long-term friendship with General Curtis LeMay (Chapter 21, "Escape from Okinawa")

Mar 26, 1945
Battle of Iwo Jima is won

Apr 1 – Jun 22, 1945
Battle of Okinawa takes place against the Japanese Army. This is the last major battle of World War II. The Kadena Air Base was needed for the planned invasion of the Japanese home islands ("Battle of Okinawa" 2020)

Apr 12, 1945
Allies liberate Buchenwald and Belsen concentration camps, President Roosevelt dies. Harry S. Truman becomes President

Apr 18, 1945
German forces in the Reims surrender

Apr 18, 1945
REE - Daughter, Barbara Lynn Evans, "Bobbie," is born. He visits San Antonio, to be with his wife and new baby for a short time. Several weeks later Major Evans flies to Okinawa, with Colonel DuBose and the 316th B-29 Wing

Apr 21, 1945
Soviets reach Berlin

Apr 21, 1945
Major John William Poston, Field Marshal Sir Bernard Law Montgomery's Aide-de-Camp, is killed in an ambush by German forces, returning to Montgomery's tactical headquarters at Luneburg Heath, from London, thirteen days before Germany surrendered. General Montgomery writes Poston's obituary, "There can be few young officers who have seen this war from the inside as did John Poston; he knew everything that was going on; he was in possession of much information that is secret and must remain secret for all time: I trusted him absolutely, and he never once failed me... I was completely devoted to him, and I feel very sad;

something has definitely gone out of my life." (Montgomery, Field Marshal Sir Bernard, 7)

Apr 28, 1945
Mussolini is captured and hanged by Italian partisans; Allies take Venice

Apr 29, 1945
US 7th Army liberates Dachau

Apr 30, 1945
Adolf Hitler commits suicide in Berlin, as Soviet troops storm his capital

May 2, 1945
German troops in Italy surrender

May 4, 1945
Montgomery accepts formal surrender of the German military at Luneburg Heath, east of Hamburg, Germany

May 7, 1945
Unconditional surrender of all German forces to Allies

May 8, 1945
V-E (Victory in Europe) Day

Jun 18, 1945
Lieutenant General Simon Buckner Jr. is killed in action at Okinawa just four days before the Japanese surrender the island

Jun 22, 1945
TL - *Theresa Leta* is written off inventory (American Air Museum in Britain 2014)

Jun 22, 1945
Japanese surrender Okinawa

Jun 1945
REE - Flies back to the Pacific end of June 1945, with commanding officer, Colonel DuBose and the 316th B-29 Wing. The war is close to ending (Chapter 21, "Escape from Okinawa")

Jun 30, 1945
REE - Efficiency Report: Operations and Training staff, HQ 316th Bomb Wing VH. "This officer's attention to duty and desire to do a job well is outstanding. He is a superior officer in all respects. In comparison with other officers of the same grade known to me I would place him in the upper third." "I concur in the foregoing report. Colonel Thomas J. DuBose" (OMPF)

Jul 6, 1945
The United Kingdom general election is held. Clement Attlee becomes Prime Minister

Jul 16, 1945
First atomic bomb test is successfully exploded

Aug 6, 1945
Nuclear bomb "Little Boy" is dropped over Hiroshima. The plane based on Tinian Island, is the *Enola Gay*. The pilot is Colonel Paul Tibbets, who later became Brigadier General Tibbets

Aug 9, 1945
Nuclear bomb "Fat Man" is dropped over Nagasaki. Major Charles W. Sweeney pilots the B-29, *Bockscar*

Aug 10, 1945
REE - Is given the grade status of Lieutenant Colonel (OMPF)

Aug 15, 1945
The unconditional surrender of Imperial Japan is announced by Japanese Emperor Hirohito

Sep 2, 1945
Japan formally surrenders aboard the battleship U.S.S. *Missouri* in Tokyo Bay, ending the Second World War

Oct 1, 1945
REE - Flies a B-29 from his base in Okinawa, to the Kalaikunda Air Force Station, near Kharagpur, located in the state of West Bengal, India. He begins his return home, hitching a ride on aircraft heading for Florida, via the Middle East (Chapter 21, "Escape from Okinawa")

Oct 2 – 22, 1945
REE - Returns to the USA, flies as a command pilot on a B-25D from Kharagpur to Pandaveswar, Karachi, and as a co-pilot on a B-24M to Abadan, Cairo, Tripoli, Marrakech, Dakar, Natal, George-town, Puerto Rico, Morrison Field, FL (IFR)

Nov 8, 1945
99th Bombardment Group is inactivated at Marcianise Airfield, Italy

Dec 1945
REE - Is home for Christmas

Dec 31, 1945
REE - From July 1 to December 31, 1945, is an MTO returnee on TDY while en route to next station. San Antonio District, AAF Personnel Distribution Command (OMPF)

Jan 19 – Dec 31, 1946
REE - No flying time is accomplished (OMPF)

Feb 1, 1946
REE - Is on terminal leave until relief from active duty (OMPF)

Mar 21, 1946
Strategic Air Command (SAC), Tactical Air Command (TAC) and the Air Defense Command (ADC) are established within the Army Air Force. The idea of continuously maintaining a combat-ready force in time of peace has never been attempted in the history of the nation. With the three combat commands the US Air Force can provide security through airpower, to deter threats from communist nations, prevent nuclear warfare and wage the cold war

1946 – 1951
REE - Departs active duty and joins the California Air National Guard. He continues to fly and broaden his experience in the newest aircraft, as fast as they are developed (OMPF)

May 31, 1946
REE - Date of relief from active duty, HQ 316th Bomb Wing, 6th AF, Okinawa. Lapel Button issued. ASR Score 174 points. Colonel Evans flies 54 combat missions (325 combat hours) over German-occupied territory including 1 combat mission over Japan (OMPF)

Major Evans leaves US Army Air Force and becomes a financial planner in Pasadena, California. He meets John Yates of Yates Agency, which is associated with Massachusetts Mutual Life Insurance Company of Springfield, MA. They meet when sharing a table at a crowded Los Angeles restaurant. From that meeting, he enters the life insurance business and becomes a "Life Estate Analyst"

Jun 1– Nov 9, 1946
REE - Is in inactive reserve status

Nov 10, 1946 - Aug 11, 1948
REE - Joins the California Air National Guard and serves as an operations and training staff officer and group commander (OMPF)

Nov 10, 1946
REE - Is given the USAF rating specialty or designation as Senior Pilot (OMPF)

1947
REE - Becomes a member of the Million Dollar Round Table (established 1927), which helps insurance brokers and financial advisors establish best business practices. Dick Evans writes

over 4 million dollars of life insurance policies. Additionally, Evans develops an estate-planning and life-underwriting business, not limited to the military, but specifically designed to acquaint military personnel with life-underwriting vehicles, available to them while in the service and after their retirement from the service

1947
REE - JoAnn and Dick live in a small apartment in Los Angeles, CA, and later purchase a home on Brigdon Road, Pasadena, CA

1947 – 1991
The Cold War date, according to most historians, runs from the time of the Truman Doctrine to the collapse of the Soviet Union

Feb 14, 1947
REE - Is a member of the 62nd Wing, California National Guard, 246th Service Group. Stationed at Metropolitan Airport, Van Nuys, CA. His Individual Flight Record resumes on this date. To maintain his Air Force pilot status while serving in the reserves, he flies the following airplanes: North American T-6 and T-6C *Texan*, North American P-51D *Mustang*, Douglas A-26B *Invader*, A-26C *Invader*, Republic P-47A *Thunderbolt*, Douglas C-47A *Skytrain* and Martin B-26 *Marauder* (IFR)

Sep 18, 1947
The US Army Air Force becomes the US Air Force under provisions of the National Security Act of 1947

Oct 14, 1947
US Air Force Captain Charles "Chuck" Yeager makes the first supersonic flight on record. He breaks the sound barrier in the Bell X-1 aircraft

Jul 1, 1948
General Curtis E. LeMay is the commander of the USAF Europe, heading operations for the Berlin Airlift, in the face of a blockade by the Soviet Union, and its satellite states that threaten to starve the civilian population of the Western occupation zones of Berlin

Aug 12, 1948 – Oct 20, 1949
REE - Is in inactive reserve status (OMPF)

Oct 19, 1948 – Jun 30, 1957
General Curtis LeMay is the SAC Commander- in-Chief. He builds from the remnants of WWII, an all-jet bomber force, manned and supported by professional airmen dedicated to the preservation of peace. His leadership brings forth plans for the development and integration of an intercontinental ballistic missile capability

Oct 29, 1948
REE - Son, Donald Nelson Evans, "Don," is born

Apr 4, 1949
NATO (North Atlantic Treaty Organization) is organized to be an intergovernmental military alliance between, when founded, twelve (now thirty) European and North American countries

Oct 21, 1949 – Mar 23, 1951
REE - Given a mobile assignment, department of the army, active-duty tour (OMPF)

Aug 29, 1949
Soviet Union secretly conducted its first successful nuclear weapon test at the Semipalatinsk test site in Kazakhstan

Jun 25, 1950
The Korean War begins. Armed forces from communist North Korea, invade UN-backed South Korea, setting off the Korean War. The US, acting under the auspices of the United Nations, quickly comes to the defense of South Korea

March 15, 1951
Using a Boeing KC-97A *Stratofreighter* tanker, the Boeing Airplane Company successfully refuels a B-47 jet bomber in flight ("Chronology of American Aerospace Events," 1959)

Mar 24, 1951
REE - Is recalled to active duty (OMPF)

Mar 25 – Oct 17, 1951
REE - Is attached to HQ 15th Air Force, March Air Force Base, CA (OMPF)

Jun 1951
The B-47, the world's first swept-wing bomber, enters service with the USAF's Strategic Air Command (SAC). It has never seen combat as a bomber, but is a main stay of SAC's bomber strength during the late '50s and early '60s and remains in use as a bomber until 1965

"The Strategic Air Command aircrews who flew the B-47 loved it and feared it. The Air Force's first jet-powered bomber allowed SAC commander General Curtis LeMay to build a formidable nuclear force during the 1950s. He used the planes for reconnaissance missions and electronic warfare jamming, too. SAC veterans believed that they prevented World War III. The B-47 had an atrocious safety record. Of slightly more than 2,000 built, 203 crashed. Four hundred and thirty-six SAC crew members died aboard B-47s." (Liewer, Steve, 2018)

Oct 18 – Nov 1, 1951
REE - Serves as Deputy Director of Operations, HQ Squadron 306th Bomb Wing, MacDill Air Force Base, FL (OMPF)

Feb 12, 1952
REE - Top Secret clearance is granted to REE (OMPF)

Aug 6, 1952
REE - USAF Effectiveness Report (Dec 27, 1951 to Jun 19, 1952), "The title and grade of the primary duty assignment of subject officer as reflected on the Manning document (monthly manpower report) is Deputy Director of Operations in the authorized grade of Lieutenant Colonel. Working with this officer daily, I have had many opportunities to observe the outstanding qualities of leadership, mature planning and constructive thinking demonstrated by Colonel Evans. He is not prone to make snap decisions but correlates all facts in his mind to arrive at a logical conclusion. Colonel Evans is completely capable of working at any organizational level. He formulates plans well into the future but does not overlook the day-to-day details. He exhibits sound managerial techniques, and because of this effective leadership, inspires subordinates to greater efforts. I feel that this officer should be promoted ahead of his contemporaries." Colonel John C. Thrift and Colonel Michael N. W. McCoy (OMPF)

Oct 15, 1952
Colonel Donald E. Hillman participated in the first deep-reconnaissance mission against the Soviet Union when he commanded a B-47 *Stratojet* over Siberia (*Veteran Tributes*, 2021)

Jan 13, 1953
REE - USAF Officer Effectiveness Report (Jun 20 – Dec 31, 1952). REE is Deputy Director of Operations HQ 306th Bomb Wing, MacDill AFB, FL. "Through daily observation of Lt. Col. Evans, I have found him to be an unusually versatile officer in that he handles any assignment with a minimum of confusion, and always with exceptional results. As project officer for Operation 'SKYTRY,' he has been responsible for complete planning of missions to be flown, acts as the representative of the Commanding General of the Air Division at conferences between A.M.C. (Air Mobility Command), A.P.G. and S.A.C. He is thorough in his daily work and plans the activities well into the future. He works very well with both subordinates and superior officers and is well liked by all. He exercises outstanding judgment in the economic management of personnel and resources under his supervision. He is completely capable of working as a staff officer in any planning level of the Air Force. He uses a common sense, logical approach to any problem, which ensures his planning to be feasible and logical." Colonel John C. Thrift and Colonel Michael N. W. McCoy (OMPF)

Jun 4 – Sep 6, 1953
REE - Serves in England (Foreign Service) with the 306th Bomb Wing. This is the first SAC unit to equip with the B-47B and is the first unit to deploy to the United Kingdom, for a ninety-day tour of duty. The wing (45 B-47s) is stationed at RAF Fairford Air Base, Fairford, Gloucestershire, England (OMPF)

Spring 1953
"A USAF B-47 *Stratojet* bomber set a transatlantic speed record in completing a 2,925-mile flight from Limestone AFB, Maine to Fairford, England in 4 hours 43 minutes, an average of 618 mph" ("A Chronology of American Aerospace Events" 1959)

Jul 1, 1953
REE - Leads a flight of 15 B-47s over Paris-Le Bourget Airport for the Paris Air Show. Established in 1909, it is a large trade fair, demonstrating military and civilian aircraft

Jul 8, 1953
REE - Writes a letter to his mother about flying the B-47 (Appendices: 7.8.53, Flying a B-47)

Jul 21, 1953
REE - Writes a humorous letter of being interviewed before flying from Limestone, Maine, to Fairford Air Force Base, United Kingdom in a B-47 in record time (Appendices: 7.21.53, B-47 Atlantic Crossing Record)

Jul 27, 1953
Korean War ends

Aug 4, 1953
USAF B-47 *Stratojet* bomber set a nonstop distance record for jet aircraft in making a 4,450-mile flight from Fairford, England to MacDill AFB, FL, in 9 hours 53 minutes" (A Chronology of American Aerospace Events, 1959)

Aug 12, 1953

REE - USAF Officer Effectiveness Report (Jan 1 – Aug 11, 1953), REE is Director of Operations. "Lt. Col. Evans is a calm, mature officer who not only monitors day-to-day operations, but makes effective plans into the future. He displays excellent organizational effective plans well into the future. He displays excellent organizational ability, which is evidenced by the way his directorate functions. He is tactful in his dealings with both subordinates and superior officers and is extremely loyal to the Wing and its Commander. He is calm and very effective under pressure, quickly reviewing a problem and providing an excellent and workable decision. He readily assumes responsibility. He exercises excellent judgment in the economic management of personnel and resources under his supervision. A typical example of this officer's performance is the way he has planned and monitored the training of B-47 combat crews. His personal efforts have resulted in increased combat-ready capability of the Wing at a much earlier date than was believed possible. Colonel Evans is well qualified to function as an operations officer at division level or higher. This report is based on daily contact." Col. Michael N. W. McCoy, MacDill AF Base (OMPF) (Photographs: Epilogue E.4, E.5, E.6, E.7)

Sep 5, 1953

REE - "*Stratojet* Sets Record in Flight Across Atlantic. Lt. Col. Evans flies B-47 group. Tampa, FL, Sept. 5 – A California colonel flew his B-47 *Stratojet* bomber from England, to Florida, today in nine hours and seven minutes, smashing a Transatlantic record less than 24 hours old" ("*Stratojet* Sets Record on Flight Across the Atlantic" 1953)

Jan 4, 1954

REE - USAF officer Effectiveness Report (Aug 12 – Dec 31,1953). "I consider Lt. Col. Evans as an extremely well qualified officer who has continually done an outstanding job in his routine duties. The supervision of the operational aspect of the 306th rotation to the UK left nothing to be desired. His briefings are always thorough and well presented. He is intelligent, cooperative, and uses very sound judgment. Lt. Col. Evans is exceptionally well qualified and recommended for promotion to the grade of Colonel." Colonel Richard N. Ellis, Deputy Wing Commander, and Brigadier General Hewitt T. Wheless, Wing Commander 306th Bomb Wing (OMPF)

May 14, 1954

REE - Is promoted to grade Colonel (OMPF)

Jul 9, 1954

REE - USAF Officer Effectiveness Report (Jan 1 – Jul 8, 1954): "This officer's typical performance of duty is characterized by imagination, persuasiveness, ability to speak on his feet, and a complete grasp of the operational significance and problems of the jet medium bombardment field. A typical example of his capabilities in the operational and planning field was provided recently in the monitors and leadership evident in the thoroughness of planning and accomplishment of an extremely long-range jet medium bomber mission. The degree of success of this very important milestone in jet aircraft accomplishment was largely due to Colonel Evans' planning foresight." "...Colonel Evans at very infrequent internals is slow to accept an idea or requirement which is contrary to his own. He does not give in easily to direction or directive, which is contrary to his own opinion, which at times makes him appear rather dogmatic in his approach to problem solution. However, when he understands he has been given a directive and his appeal for change or relief has been denied, he puts forth his wholehearted support in accomplishing the job." "I have noted the outstanding ratings in Section III and concur with the overall report as changed by the endorsing officers." Signed by Colonel Richard N. Ellis, Deputy Commander, Colonel Kenneth O. Sanborn, Wing Commander, Major General Frank A. Armstrong, Commander, and General Curtis E. LeMay, Commander HQ Strategic Air Command, Offutt AFB, Omaha, NE (OMPF)

Aug 1954

REE - Is the pilot with crew members Major Anton Ungstad (Observer) and Lieutenant Colonel Glenn McConnel (Aircraft Commander) of the 306th Bomb Wing from MacDill AFB, who sets a B-47 Jet endurance record for 35 hours of continuous flying

Sep 6, 1954

REE - Is the B-47 pilot for the General Electric ad, "SAC Flies a mission." The sub-title states, "Strategic Air Command Maintains Peace with Hand-picked Men, 600-MPH Boeing Bombers Powered by G-E Jets." Colonel Evans flies the B-47 in all aircraft photographs, and is shown in the next page, involved in a briefing session, and checking the engine with his co-pilot (Appendices: 9.6.54, "SAC Flies a Mission")

Sep 22, 1954
REE - Letter to his mother on reasons why he wants to "spend my life perfecting a fighting force" along with poignant thoughts of the leadership he admires who have been dedicated to American defense (Appendices: 9.22.54, American Defense)

Aug 31, 1954 – Mar 10, 1955
REE - Stationed Harmon AFB, Newfoundland, (Foreign Service) as the SAC Liaison Officer. During the period, January 15, REE was also stationed in Greenland as the SAC Liaison Officer, Thule AFB, Greenland (OMPF)

Mar 11 - Apr 17, 1955
REE - Travel leave and processing, takes time to travel with his family and move from MacDill AFB to Offutt AFB. He becomes Deputy Chief Requirements Division Operations Director, HQ SAC, Offutt AFB, NE (OMPF)

Mar 25, 1955
REE - The movie, "Strategic Air Command," is released. In August 1954, Colonel Evans flies all the B-47 aircraft scenes for the movie starring Jimmy Stewart, at MacDill AFB

Jun 2, 1955
WEE - In honor of Dick's father, Mayor George R. Dempster, proclaimed Thursday, June 9, 1955, as "Honor Evans Day" in the city of Knoxville, TN (Appendices: 6.2.55, "Honor Evans Day" Proclamation for Dick's father)

Jun 9, 1955
"Honor Evans Day," Knoxville, TN. City celebrates their highly respected Knoxville High School principal, Dick's father, William Ernest Evans, for serving for 41 years as an educator with the city of Knoxville Schools System (Chapter 19, "Knoxville's Principled Principal") (Photographs: 19.1, 19.7, 19.8)

Aug 30, 1955
REE - Becomes USAF rating specialty or designation, Command Pilot (OMPF) (Photograph: Epilogue E.1, E.3)

Sep 6, 1955
REE - USAF Officer Effectiveness Report (Jul 9, 1954 – Aug 11, 1955) - Colonel Evans transfers to HQ SAC, Offutt AFB, NE. A summary of a very detailed report for Evans is: "Promotion - should be promoted ahead of his contemporaries;

Potential - unlimited potential in either staff or command assignments; Examples - Part of Colonel Evans' varied background experience was participating on the scene in SAC's Cold Weather Test during the past winter at Thule. After being assigned to this headquarters, he has organized and put into effect a program to give the SAC force a true cold weather capability. This program encompasses new concepts of aircraft equipment, ground handling equipment, clothing, training, etc. Working with R & D people from the Air Force and industry he showed himself to be an effective "idea" man as well as an organizer... This is a fine active young officer whose effectiveness, I anticipate, will soon equal that indicated by the Reporting Officer. Reports from Colonel Don E. Hillman, Brig. General W. H. Blanchard, Deputy Director, Operations and noted by General Curtis E. LeMay, Commander in Chief, SAC (OMPF)

Apr 1956
REE - Is on the cover of *Air Force* magazine, April 1956. He is pictured center with his crew, discussing flight plans in front of the B-47A. The article within this magazine, "Breaking in the *Stratojet*" by Colonel Michael N. W. McCoy, Commander of the 306th BG, refers to the tremendous time and military energy to test the B-47 and crew to quickly reach England and Europe if needed for defense. The strategic goal for the B-47's presence in England is as a counter to Soviet power over European countries (Appendices: 4.56, "SAC Pilots Test the B-47")

Mar 10, 1956
REE - Is awarded the AFLSA with 2 Bronze OLC AFR 900-10. Award translated: Air Force Longevity Service Award with two bronze oak leaf clusters for successful completion of an aggregate total of four years of honorable active service in North Africa (OMPF)

May 18, 1956
REE - Annual Report Officer Performance evaluation (Aug 12, 1955 – May 15, 1956) regarding promotion, potential, problem solving, speaking, etc. Some of the highlights describe his ability to attack a problem in a well-organized thorough manner and then effectively explain and give briefs about the problem. An example is: "during the past several months he perceived that the role of the air to surface missile was not completely clear or firm to others. He made a detailed study of the problem, injecting considerable original

thinking into the solution. He carried his recommendations thru the SAC Staff and the Air Staff. They were subsequently adopted and formed the framework for development planning in this field for the Air Force." Reports from Brigadier General W. H. Blanchard, Deputy Director, Operations, SAC, Colonel Donald E. Hillman and General Curtis LeMay, Commander in Chief, SAC (OMPF)

Oct 11, 1956
REE - Annual Report Officer Performance evaluation (May 16 – Sep 30,1956). In summary several comments were: "I have flown with Colonel Evans and have been impressed with his outstanding ability as a pilot and his enthusiastic approach to flying. He has a wealth of experience in modern tactical jet bombers and maintains currency therein. He is of great value to the Air Force in his rated capacity. Another of this officer's exceptional points is his ability to express himself orally and in writing. The many requests for Col. Evans to speak are testimony to his ability in this regard. The following example is typical of Col. Evans's duty performance: At the request of the Commander-in-Chief, Col. Evans prepared a briefing for presentation to the Air Council to justify this command's position on all future strategic weapons systems. This was a difficult and important task that was accomplished quickly, logically, and capably. The presentation has since been given to the Commander-in-Chief, SAC, and to the Air Staff. Many complimentary remarks were issued with respect to the method of presentation and the sound logic continued. ...I consider Col. Evans to be among the top ten percent of all colonels with whom I have been associated." Reported by Colonel Jack J. Catton, Chief, Tactical Requirements Division, Director of Operations, SAC (OMPF)

Nov – Dec 1956
REE - Attends B-52 school at Castle Air Base, California the last three weeks of November and the first week of December. He checks out in the B-52 (Photograph: Epilogue E.8)

Nov 11, 1956
The Convair B-58 *Hustler* is the first operational supersonic jet bomber capable of flying above Mach 2. But during its first 10,000 hours of flight time, the B-58 bomber logs only 500 hours at speeds above Mach 1. The aircraft's first flight occurred on 11 November 1956. A difficult and

protracted flight test program involving 30 aircraft continued until April 1959, and the aircraft is retired from service in January 1970. It uses a delta wing and has two General Electric J79 engines mounted in pods under each wing (total of four engines). It carries nuclear weapons and fuel in a large pod mounted under the fuselage. ("Weapons of Mass Destruction," 2020)

1956 – 1957
REE - Colonel Evans directs SAC's procurement board for the B-70 (Mach 3 bomber) at Offutt AFB in Bellevue, NE (OMPF)

Feb 16, 1957
The Convair B-58A *Hustler, Mach-in-Boid*, made her first flight on this date and first inflight, refueling test June 11, 1958 (Miller, Jay 1985)

Jul 1957
General LeMay is named Vice Chief of Staff of the U.S. Air Force, General Thomas S. Powers becomes Commander-in-Chief of SAC. General Powers assumes its well-known motto, "Peace Is Our Profession" (Wishart, David J., Ed. 2021)

Oct 21, 1957
REE - Officer Performance report (Oct 1, 1956 – Sep 30, 1957) is very detailed and positive. Several examples of outstanding achievement are the following: a) "On his own initiative he undertook to develop a different type of test program for the B-58, the Air Force's first supersonic bomber. This was done in recognition of concern of CINCSAC (Commander in Chief, Strategic Air Command) with respect to SAC's operating a supersonic bomber and the fact that an unusually large number of test aircraft is being procured. A detailed study of the problem by Colonel Evans resulted in comprehensive recommendations, which have subsequently been approved by CINCSAC and Commander ARDC (Air Research and Development Command). Colonel Evans aggressively continues the necessary follow-up actions to ensure that a test program will be established that will provide the greatest amount of knowledge to the Air Force and (SAC). As a result of nearly over-powering budgetary limitations. ...Col. Evans managed to ferret out all the necessary information from HQ AMC, USAF, OCAAMA and SAC. With this basic information he caused a detailed study to be made so that specific recommendations could be made to the Staff and the Commander-in-Chief. This very difficult task

was accomplished in a minimum of time with the resulting withdrawal of requirements for modifications valued at approximately $140 million."

Another exemplary comment for Colonel Evans, "Of particular note, and in my consideration his very strongest point, is his extremely good character. This man is the servant of his own very high ideals. He will not subordinate his ideals under any circumstances. He is completely honest, thoroughly trustworthy and dependable." Colonel Jack J. Catton, Chief, Requirements Division, Major General Robert H. Terrill, Director of Operations, SAC (OMPF)

1958 – 1959
REE - Is placed as head of operations for the 3958th Operational Test and Evaluation Squadron, the (SAC) Air Force suitability test program for the new B-58A Hustler medium bomber, which is capable of flying Mach 2. This program is based at Carswell AFB, Ft. Worth, TX. Colonel Richard E. Evans regularly flies the supersonic Convair F-102 *Delta Dagger*, which prepares him for his training to fly the B-58 *Hustler* (OMPF)

Mar 10, 1958
REE - The Air Force Outstanding Unit Award (AFOUA) is given to Colonel Evans and his unit, 3958th Operational Test and Evaluation Squadron (OMPF)

Jun 8, 1958
REE - Commander 3958th Operational Evaluation & Training Squadron, Carswell AFB, Texas (OMPF)

Jul 3, 1958
REE - USAF Officer Effectiveness Report (Oct 1, 1957, to Jun 8, 1958). Some standout comments are: "Suggested Assignments or type of Duty: Colonel Evans has just been assigned as Commander of the SAC unit, which will conduct evaluations and initial training program associated with bringing the B-58 into our combat inventory. This is part of the 19th Air Division, Carswell AFB. I consider him ideally suited for this assignment and recommend his retention for at least two years. Colonel Evans is exceptionally well qualified for duty as a SAC Combat Wing commander." ...Flying Proficiency: I have met no other officer in the Air Force who considers maintenance of flying proficiency more important than does Colonel Evans. He is currently fully qualified in the F-102. This qualification he achieved on his own initiative in preparation for his duty in the

B-58 program. He is an excellent pilot and very highly motivated. ...Last February, after a decision had been reached to procure B-58s for the SAC inventory, a configuration review was conducted jointly by Air Research and Development Command (ARDC), Air Mobility Command (AMC) and SAC operational concepts would be provided. Again, Colonel Evans was selected to head SAC's participation and again he achieved our purpose in an outstanding manner. The spirit of cooperation and singleness of purpose now existing among ARDC, AMC and SAC is testimony to Colonel Evans' leadership, understanding and devotion to SAC and the USAF." Signed by Colonel Jack Catton, USAF and Major General James V. Edmundson, Deputy Director of Operations (OMPF)

Fall 1958
REE - Checks out in the B-58 (OMPF) (Photograph: Epilogue E.9)

Dec 16, 1958
B-58A first accident, crashes near Canon AFB. One out of three crew die

Jan – Feb 1959
REE - Colonel Evans participates in a US Air Force "Promotion Board" meeting at the Pentagon; he makes a "friend" courtesy call to General Curtis LeMay, then Chief of Staff of the US Air Force. When asked about the B-58A, Evans states in summary, it is a very difficult plane to fly, and that he does not see that it has an important function at SAC

Spring 1959
REE - General John Paul McConnell, Evans' Commander, is furious that Evans spoke to LeMay about the B-58 stability issues. The chain of command is General McConnell to General Thomas S. Power, Commander in Chief of SAC, who reports to General LeMay. Colonel Evans is "canned" from the B-58 test program. Knowing he will never make General, Evans decides to leave the Air Force despite the fact he could hold a lesser position for four more years and retire with full pension. Instead, Evans leaves the Air Force and becomes a spokesman in Washington, DC for North American Aviation's XB-70 *Valkyrie* program. Only two B-70s are produced in the USA. Evans' official civilian business address and title is B-70 Weapons Systems, Manager, North American Aircraft Co., Inc.

Jun 11, 1959
"The Air Force began to plan the production and delivery schedules of 185 B-58Bs, which counting the B-58As, would increase the total to 290 aircraft. ...While working at SAC, General LeMay does not like the B-58A bomber, and as Vice Chief of Staff (Pentagon), he still holds to his opinion. The new model (B-58B) looks to be too expensive, its automatic equipment for low-level flight too complex" ("Weapons of Mass Destruction" 2020)

Jul 1, 1959
REE - The order for release from active military service is July 1, 1959. Colonel Evans is honorably discharged from the Air Force (OMPF)

Jul 7, 1959
"The Air Staff eliminates the B-58B from the program and the B-58A again appears to be in serious jeopardy" ("Weapons of Mass Destruction" 2020)

Jul 14, 1959
REE - Official date that Colonel Evans is "separated" from the Air Force (OMPF)

Jul 14, 1959
The Pentagon informs General Thomas Power that there are insufficient funds to satisfy all of SAC's needs. SAC scales back plans to purchase 290 B-58s ("Weapons of Mass Destruction" 2020)

Jul 31, 1959
REE - USAF Officer Effectiveness Report (Jun 9, 1958 – Jun 8, 1959): "Colonel Evans is instrumental in establishing a training program to support the B-58A weapons system. In the fall of 1958, he attends a course on the B-58 at Convair and subsequently becomes the first SAC pilot to check out in the aircraft. His knowledge of the airplane and related problems thus gained was of great value in highlighting to higher headquarters the peculiar requirements of this new system, and in monitoring the crew-training program being developed for use by combat Crew-Training School. He has done an excellent job on tasks that are of interest to him. Certain aspects of his responsibilities in bedding down the B-58 force at Carswell have presented formidable problems, but by and large satisfactory solutions have been achieved in all major areas. ...he has actively participated in TF-102 flying and is proficient in the T-33. The fact that he is the first SAC pilot to check out in the B-58 attests to his great interest in the flying business." Brigadier General Nils

O. Ohman, HQ 19th Air Division Commander (OMPF)

Aug 24, 1959
REE - General McConnell evaluates Brigadier General Ohman's review of Colonel Evans: "I do not agree with the report as written by the evaluating officer. Colonel Evans has left the service to accept employment with North American Aircraft Company and, therefore, the report is of no consequence as far as any future career development might be involved. Nevertheless, an accurate portrayal of his effectiveness as a matter of record is required in his interest and in the interest of the United States Air Force. I have indicated by my initials in the appropriate boxes what I consider to be an accurate evaluation of his performance of duty during the period covered by the report." General McConnell did rate Colonel Evans outstanding for flying knowledge; excellent for job initiative, competent and efficient for job adaptability and other consistent and excellent adjectives were used for job characteristics. Lieutenant General J. P. McConnell, Commander, HQ Second Air Force (OMPF)

Evans tells his family that General McConnell "fired" him from the B-58 Test Squadron position for having a frank, unguarded discussion with a friend, General Curtis LeMay, who was General McConnell's superior, without first talking to General McConnell

LeMay never defends Evans. Air Force "chain-of-command" policies demand that Colonel Evans is relieved of duty with the B-58A Test Squadron program. Evans and LeMay remain fast family friends until LeMay's death October 3,1990, and Helen Maitland LeMay's death in 1992

Nov 25, 1959
REE - Reserve assignment for Colonel Evans is with the 4306th Support Squadron, 15th Air Force, USAF March Air Force Base, CA (OMPF)

1960
REE - lives in Rolling Hills Estates, California

May 1, 1960
Francis Gary Powers, a U-2 pilot, is shot down, parachutes to safety and captured while on a reconnaissance flight deep inside the Soviet Union. His capture is known as the U-2 Incident. He admits to working for the US Central Intelligence Agency ("U-2 Incident, United States-Soviet" 2021)

Aug 1, 1960

The B-58 *Hustler* enters operational service. In all, the Air Force acquired 116 B-58As. "Like many of the early delta wing aircraft, the *Hustler* was a monster to fly. The plane had eccentric landing, takeoff, stall, and spin characteristics, which pilots often struggled to master. The *Hustler* also had an ambitious set of controls that did not always accord with the experience and capabilities of its pilots. The maintenance demands of the aircraft, which had many specialized systems, were also extremely high. All of this led to a startling accident rate. 26 (36 crewman died) of the 116 *Hustlers* were lost to accidents, resulting in a total loss rate of 22.4 % over a service life of ten years." (Farley, Robert 2016)

Aug 1, 1960

"SAC's 3958th Operational Employment Testing and Evaluation Squadron is a most important member of the now extinct Air Research and Development Command (ARDC), which supervises the B-58 testing. The 3958th is responsible for the proper development of a combat crew-training program. It selects and educates B-58 maintenance personnel and to creates a cadre of flight crews that will serve as instructors in forthcoming combat crew training classes. In addition, the 3958th puts together standard operating procedures for the future B-58 wings. SAC's 65th Bombardment Squadron finds no fault in the 3958th performance" ("Weapons of Mass Destruction" 2020)

Nov 7, 1960

REE - Reserve Officer Training Performance Report (Sep 24, 1959 – Oct 31, 1960): "Colonel Evans has shown an intense interest in his assignment as mobilization Director of Operations and his previous experience in command and staff positions in strategic operations has adapted him particularly well for this assignment. Being extremely enthusiastic and energetic, he has displayed a high degree of interest in all operational functions. Through his civilian occupation, he promotes better public understanding of the mission systems with both the public and the Air Force... Suggested assignments: continue as a staff officer at any level in the Operations field or command of a tactical unit. He actively participates in flying at every opportunity and is extremely interested in maintaining proficiency in the T-33 and B-58 aircraft." Colonel Jean B. Miller, Director of

Operations, endorsed by Colonel Pinkham Smith, Chief of Staff, HQ 15th Air Force (OMPF)

Dec 1960

The Air Force reaches a final decision. The 1961 purchase was retained, but the fiscal year 1962 procurement was deleted. SAC would receive 2 wings of B-58As and no more. ("Weapons of Mass Destruction" 2020)

Jan 12, 1961

Lieutenant Colonel John H. Deutschendorf and his B-58 crew set six world speed records

Aug 1961

East Germany's communist government builds the Berlin Wall to stop its citizens leaving the city for the West

Mar 1962

REE - Reserve Officer Training Performance Report (Nov 1, 1960 – Jan 31, 1962). "Colonel Evans has maintained an outstanding level of professional ability and interest during this reporting period. He has voluntarily, at his own time and expense, sought opportunities for increasing his military knowledge and value." "...Flying proficiency, Colonel Evans displays a greater than normal interest in maintaining a high level of proficiency in his assigned aircraft." Colonel Jean B. Miller, Director of Operations 15th Air Force. "I concur. Colonel Evans has made many contributions to the Air Force mission, both during his active-duty training periods and in civil life." Colonel Robert V. De Shazo, Chief of Staff, 15th Air Force, March AFB, CA (OMPF)

Oct 1962

The US challenges the Soviet decision to site nuclear missiles in Cuba. The resulting crisis is the closest that the world has come to nuclear war

Oct 31, 1963

REE - Officer Military Record states the following: Colonel Evans is Command pilot, who flies 55 combat missions, 135 combat hours. As of Dec 31, 1961, he flies a total of 5,335:25 hours (OMPF)

Sep 21, 1964

First flight of the XB-70A *Valkyrie* built by North American Aviation

Nov 30, 1964

REE - Field Grade Officer Effectiveness Report (Feb 1, 1962 – Oct 31, 1964): "During the period covered by this report Colonel Evans was largely concerned with Project Blue Dart. His broad background and understanding of military history and strategic thoughts and concepts contributed greatly to that study. He is most skillful in communicating complex concepts and has demonstrated an outstanding ability to get ideas across to diverse audiences with a minimum of fuss and delay. His views on increasing the flexibility of our offensive force have served as a reservoir for numerous conceptual adaptations, which have increased the general understanding of air power, strengths: His obvious strengths are his understanding into workable concepts, and then present these concepts clearly and concisely." H. S. Judy, Dep. Dir. of Plans for Advanced Planning, and Major General Arthur C. Agan, Jr. Director of Plans & Operations (OMPF)

Feb 21, 1968
"General McConnell, Air Force Chief of Staff, since February 1965, reaffirms before the Senate Armed Services Committee that the entire B-58 fleet would be phased out before June 1970" ("Weapons of Mass Destruction" 2020)

Jun 6, 1969
REE - Officer Military Record, Colonel Evans is Information Staff Officer, 15th AAF, March AFB, CA (OMPF)

Dec 31, 1969
"The Convair B-58 *Hustler* is our major deterrent to nuclear war until the emergence of the space program and the advent of missile technology. These programs are instrumental in winning the 'Cold War.' Unfortunately, politics resulted in its early demise after a short 10 years of operation. The *Hustler* was phased out on December 31, 1969" (The B-58 *Hustler* Association 2021)

1970s
REE - Is a consultant to Northrop Grumman in the B-1 competition. He is also a consultant for Douglas's C-54

Aug 3, 1970
REE - "Appreciation Letter" Colonel Evans receives a letter of appreciation for his efforts to completely revitalize the 15th Air Force command-briefing program. "Just as important, however, as both a 'blue suitor' and civilian, you provided the perspective and insight needed to get us on the proper track." Lieutenant General Paul K. Carlton, USAF Commander, 15th Air Force, March AFB, CA (Appendices: 8.3.70, Appreciation Letter 15th AF)

Aug 30, 1970
REE - "Is relieved from assignment, removed from reserve status, assigned to the Retired Reserve Section and placed on the USAF Reserve Retired List effective as indicated below" (OMPF)

March 24, 1976
Field Marshal The Viscount Montgomery of Alamein dies in his country home, Isington Mill

Dec. 9, 1987
Iron Eagle: The Turbulent Life of General Curtis LeMay by Thomas M. Coffey is published. General LeMay autographs the book for his long time Air Force friend, Colonel Richard E. Evans

Oct 3, 1990
General Curtis Emerson LeMay dies

1990 – 1993
REE - Begins writing his book. Dick enjoys retirement with family, good friends, non-profit projects, and travel

Jun 16, 2006
REE - Colonel Richard E. Evans (87 years old) dies and is buried with full military honors. He is interned at Green Hills Memorial Park, Rancho Palos Verdes, California

CHRONOLOGY SOURCE NOTES

"A Chronology of American Aerospace Events." Air Force Pamphlet, NO. 210-1-1. Jul 1, 1959.

"Alexander Papers WO 214/18." UK National Archives, Apr 21, 1943.

American Air Museum in Britain. Object number FRE-1014. Sep 27, 2014.
http://www.americanairmuseum.com/aircraft/1148

"Battle of Dunkirk." *History.* Oct 11, 2019.
https://www.history.com/topics/world-war-ii/dunkirk#section 2

"Battle of Okinawa." *History.* Mar 30, 2020.
https://www.history.com/topics/world-war-ii/battle-of-okinawa

The B-58 *Hustler* Association. Fort Worth, Texas, May 2, 2021. http://www.b58hustlerassn.net/

Bruno, James F. *Beyond Fighter Escort.* Milwaukee: Ken Cook Co. 1995.

"B-17 Bomber *Flying Fortress* - The Queen of the Skies." *B-17 Data Base.* B-17 41-9082, Nov 8, 2020.
https://b17flyingfortress.de/en/

"B-17 *Flying Fortress*: Historical Snapshots." Boeing, n.d.
https://www.boeing.com/history/products/B-17-flying-fortress.page

"B-29-50-BW 'Homing De-Vice' Serial Number 42-24785." *Pacific Wrecks.* 1945.
https://www.pacificwrecks.com/aircraft/b-29/42-24785.html

Carey, Brian Todd. "How Allied Air Attacks Evolved During World War II." *Historynet,* Nov 1998.
https://www.historynet.com/how-allied-air-attacks-evolved-during-world-war-ii.html

"The Casablanca Conference." *Bureau of Public Affairs, Office of the Historian, US Department of State,*
1943. https://history.state.gov/milestones/1937-1945/casablanca

Combat Mission 346th Squadron. Photograph, "M-1 Captain Richard E. Evans keeps his own record of
his Atlantic Ocean crossing to North Africa and his first 25 Mediterranean Theater of Operations
missions." *Richard Eager*, June 11, 1943.

Cravens, W. F. and Cate, J. L. Eds. "The Definitions of Policies, Section II Equipment and Services: The
Air Corps in 1939." *The Army Air Forces in World War II: VI Men and Planes.* May 15, 2021, 173.
https://www.ibiblio.org/hyperwar/AAF/VI/AAF-VI-5.html

"Crocodile Underbellies." *The Churchill Project*, Hillsdale College. Nov 8, 2020.
https://winstonchurchill.hillsdale.edu/soft-underbelly-fortress-europe/

"Dieppe Landing: Operation Jubilee and The Origins of the Normandy Landings." *D-Day Overlord:
Encyclopedia of Normandy Landings.* Dec 26, 2020. https://www.dday-overlord.com/en/d-day/ori-
gins/operation-jubilee

The Diamondbacks: The History of the 99th Bomb Group (H). Paducah, Kentucky: Turner Publishing
Company, 1998: 9.

"Dick Evans is Neatest, Best-Drilled Cadet." *Blue and White*: *Knoxville High School's Weekly Newspaper.*
Knoxville, TN, May 22, 1936, 14: 32.

8th Army HQ War Diary WO169/8994. PRO, The National Archives, UK, Jul 31, 1943.

Ethier, Eric. "General George S. Patton's Race to Capture Messina." May 3, 2021. https://www.historynet.
com/world-war-ii-general-george-s-pattons-race-to-capture-messina.htm

Evans, First Lieutenant Frank B. *Memories and Missions of World War II.* Unpublished memoirs. 301st
Bomb Group, n.d.

Farley, Robert. "The B-58 Hustler: America's Cold War Nuclear Bomber Blunder." *The National Interest.* Jun 10, 2016. https://nationalinterest.org/feature/the-b-58-hustler-americas-cold-war-nuclear-bomber-blunder-16547

Hamilton, Nigel. *Master of the Battlefield: Monty's War Years, 1942-1944.* New York: McGraw-Hill Book Company, 1983: 244.

"Haunting Photos - The Bombed-Out Ruins of Cologne in WWII." *War History Online.* Dec 26, 2020. https://www.warhistoryonline.com/world-war-ii/bombed-outcologne-m.html

Hudson, Captain James W. *Victory Mail of World War II.* USA: Xlibris Corp., 2007.

Individual Flight Record (IFR), (Colonel Richard E. Evans), Air Force Officer Flight Records. National Archives and Records Administration. National Personnel Records Center, St. Louis, MO.

"King George VI Visits North Africa and Malta." *World War II Today,* Jun 20, 1943. http://ww2today.com/20th-june-1943-king-george-vi-visits-north-africa-and-malta

"King George VI Visit to Oran," *5th US Army Programme.* Imperial War Museum, London, 1943.

"King George VI NA tour." *British 8th Army Program.* Imperial War Museum, London, 1943.

Lauer III, Ford J. "History of the 99th Bombardment Group." 99th BG Historical Society, n.d. http://www.99bombgroup.org/history.php

Liewer, Steve. "SAC Vets Who Flew Sleek, Dangerous B-47s Gather for the Last Time in Omaha." *World-Herald*Sep 21, 2018. https://www.omaha.com/news/military/sac-vets-who-flew-sleek-dangerous-b-47s-gather-for-last-time-in-Omaha/article_0baf751b-83da-57f8-9b3d-5946afa45b6e.html

Miller, Jay. "Disposition of B-58 Hustlers." *Aerograph 4 Convair B-58.* 1985.

Montgomery, Bernard Law. 1st Viscount Montgomery. *The Memoirs of Field-Marshal, the Viscount Montgomery of Alamein.* K.G. New York: The World Publishing Company, 1958: 184.

Montgomery, Bernard Law. *Papers.* MF (Microfilm). Imperial War Museum, London, Jun 13, 1943.

Montgomery, Bernard Law. "Diary Notes." BLM 34, Imperial War Museum, London, 1943.

_____ "Diary Notes." BLM 37/1, Imperial War Museum, London, 1943.

_____ "Diary Notes." BLM 39, Imperial War Museum, London, 1943.

_____ "Diary Notes." BLM 72, Imperial War Museum, London, 1944.

Montgomery, Field Marshal Sir Bernard. "Major J. Poston, M.C." *The Times* (50128) Apr 27, 1945: 7.

Montgomery, Field Marshal Viscount Bernard Law of Alamein. *El Alamein to the River Sangro.* London: Hutchinson, 1952: 130.

Montgomery, General Bernard L. "Letters to the Reynolds." Imperial War Museum, London, Apr 26, 1943.

Moser, Pat, "B-17 Gunner Had the Job of Covering Monty's 'Tail' - General's Crew Was the Ticket to Allied Big Time." *Tri-City Herald,* Jun 6, 1993.

"Mt. Etna Joins in Sicilian War." *The Advertiser.* Adelaide, South Australia, Jul 18, 1943: 1. https://trove.nla.gov.au/newspaper/article/48760650

Muller, Richard R. "First Mount Vesuvius, Then the Nazis." *Historynet,* May 15, 2021. https://www.historynet.com/first-mount-vesuvius-then-the-nazis.html

"99th BG Area Action Plan (AAP) Summary Document." Air Force Archives, United States Air Force Historical Office. Bolling Air Force Base, Washington DC. Jan 30, 1943.

99th BG Historical Society, n.d. https://www.99bombgroup.org

"99th BG in Action During WWII." *Military Cinema.* Archival Film on DVD, Military Cinema, Inc. 2014.

Official Military Personnel File (OMPF), (Colonel Richard E. Evans). National Archives and Records Administration (NARA). National Personnel Records Center, St. Louis, MO.

"Operation Barbarossa," *History*, Jun 7, 2019. https://www.history.com/topics/world-war-ii/operation-Barbarossa

"Operation Flax," *World War II Database*. Apr 2011. https://ww2db.com/nattlespec.php?battle_id=24

"Operation's Orders Number 37." Confidential ATC 14, Headquarters, 15th Ferrying Group, Caribbean Wing, REE's Personnel file, February 2, 1943.

"Operations Record Book, Document AIR27/1818/19." UK National Archives, Apr 17, 1943.

"Operations Record Book, AIR28/601." RAF Northolt, UK National Archives. 1943.

"Second Battle of El Alamein," National Army Museum. May 15, 2021. https://www.nam.ac.uk/explore/battle-Alamein

"Second Bomb Group, 15th Air Force, United States Army. 1943-1945." May 15, 2021. http://www.2ndbombgroup.org/15thAirForce.htm

"Soviets Launch Counterattack at Stalingrad." *History*. Nov 18, 2020. https://www.history.com/this-day-in-history/soviet-counterattack-at-Stalingrad

"Squadron Leader Hugh 'Jimmy' James. Obituary." *The Telegraph.co.uk*. Jan 14, 2015. https://www.telegraph.co.uk/news/obituaries/11345480/Squadron-Leader-Hugh-Jimmy-James-obituary.html

"Soviet Forces Liberate Auschwitz." United States Holocaust Memorial Museum. Dec 27, 2020. https://www.ushmm.org/learn/timeline-of-events/1942-1945/soviet-forces-liberate-Auschwitz

"*Stratojet* Sets Record on Flight Across Atlantic" By *United Press*. Tampa, FL. Sep 5, 1953.

"346th Squadron Unit History," 99th BG (Sep 1943 to Jan 1944 inclusive), NARA. Nov 10, 1943.

"U-2 Incident, United States-Soviet History." *Encyclopedia Britannica*. Mar 2, 2021. https://www.britannica.com/event/U-2-Incident

"Veteran Tributes: Honoring those Who Served: Donald E. Hillman." May 15, 2021. http://veterantributes.org/TributeDetail.php?recordID=1639

"War Diary 346th Squadron," Sheet 24, Oudna #1, NATO USA, NARA. Oct 29, 1943.

"War Diary 346th Squadron," Sheet 28, National Archives and Records Administration (NARA). Nov 12, 1943.

_____ Sheet 42, NARA. Jan 7, 1944.

_____ Sheet 53, NARA. Feb 14, 1944.

_____ Sheet 53, NARA. Feb 16, 1944.

_____ Sheet 53, NARA. Feb 17, 1944.

_____ Sheet 56, NARA. Mar 2, 1944.

"War Diary 99th Bombardment Group" Station Oudna, Sheet 5, NARA. Jan, Feb, Mar 1943.

_____ Station Oudna, Sheet 6, NARA. Feb 17, 1943.

_____ Station Oudna #1, Sheet 7, NARA. Mar 15 - 28, 1943.

_____ Station Oudna, Sheet 16, NARA. May 1943.

_____ Station Oudna, Sheet 27, NARA. June15, 1943.

_____ Station Oudna, Sheet 36, NARA. Jul 19, 1943.

_____ Station Oudna, Sheet 37, NARA. Jul 24, 1943.

_____ Station Oudna, Sheet 42, NARA. Aug 1, 1943.

_____ Station Oudna, Sheet 46, NARA. Aug 30, 1943.

_____ Station Oudna, Sheet 46, NARA. Aug 31, 1943.

_____ Station Oudna, Sheet 50, NARA. Sep 18, 1943.

_____ Station Oudna, Sheet 55, NARA. Oct 9, 1943.

_____ Station Oudna, Sheet 59, NARA. Nov 4, 1943.

_____ Station Oudna, Sheet 60, NARA. Nov 6, 1943.

_____ Station Oudna, Sheet 60, NARA. Nov 8, 1943.

_____ Station Oudna, Sheet 62, NARA. Nov 16, 1943.

_____ Station Oudna, Sheet 65, NARA. Dec 1, 1943.

_____ Station Oudna, Sheet 68, NARA. Dec 16, 1943.

_____ Station Oudna, Sheet 70, NARA. Dec 25, 1943.

_____ Station Oudna, Sheet 70, NARA. Dec 28, 1943.

_____ Station Oudna, Sheet 71, NARA. Dec 30, 1943.

_____ Station Oudna, Sheet 1, NARA. Jan, Feb, Mar 1944.

"Weapons of Mass Destruction, B-58 Final Construction." Global Security Organization. Nov 8, 2020. https://www.globalsecurity.org/wmd/systems/b-58-fc.html

Wishart, David J., Editor, "Strategic Air Command." *Encyclopedia of the Great Plains*. May 15, 2021. http://plainshumanities.unl.edu/encyclopedia/doc/egp.war.046.xml

GLOSSARY

SECOND WORLD WAR YANK AND BRITISH VERNACULARISMS & PERSONALITIES 1939–1945

AA: Anti-aircraft guns, especially German 88 mm, were employed effectively as artillery.

AC: The Army Air Corps; also, the USAAC, which became the USAAF during WWII; then the USAF post-WWII, joining the Army and Navy as an equal partner, reforming a 3-part land-sea-air Department of Defense. My period of service spanned this interesting and historic period of transition.

abort: A canceled mission (noun), or the act of canceling a mission (verb). A ground abort: to cancel before becoming airborne. An air abort: to cancel while in-flight, signaled by radio or by flares fired from the aircraft or the ground.

AC, Aircraft: Principal aircraft in WWII USAAF:
- Trainers - PT-3, PT-17, BT-9, BT-14, BC-1A, AT-6, AT-7
- Bombers - B-17, B-18, B-24, B-25, B-26, B-29
- Fighters (Pursuit) - P-38, P-39, P-40, P-47, P-51
- Ground Support (Attack) - A-20
- Cargo - C-47, C-54

AC Aircraft: Principal aircraft in WWII UK RAF:
- Spitfire, Lancaster, and Wellington

AC: Aircraft: Principal German AC: Ju-88, Me-109, Fw-190, Me-110 and Me-262 jet. I saw very few German jets zinging by and wasn't anxious to see more.

A/C: Aviation Cadet, in USAAC, USAAF and later USAF. The period of Aviation Cadet Training was eight months and a few days.

ack-ack or flak: (German Acht-acht for "eight-eight" the size of the ammunition). Shell bursts at altitude from anti-aircraft guns, round in shape becoming elongated vertically, resembled white tufts of cotton when sun was behind attacking bombers, inky-black shadows when back-lit, i.e., when bombers were flying head-on into the sun and the flak. The latter reminded me of miniature thunderheads, appropriately black.

AD: Air Division, a tactical entity, a flight formation; usually three or four 18-aircraft groups of three to four squadrons each.

AFT: Advanced Flight Training, at Kelly Field, TX. The third level of Cadet Training after Primary and Basic training at Love and Randolph Fields in Dallas and San Antonio, 1939–40.

AEF: Allied Expeditionary Force, organized in the UK, commanded by General Eisenhower, mostly British Commonwealth and American military that invaded Europe. The fateful message: "This is London, June 6, 1944; the Allied Expeditionary Forces have landed on this morning on the northern coast of France." (I have never reread those lines without goose bumps and fogged glasses).

AF or Air Force: An Administrative and air-tactical organization made up of divisions, groups and squadrons:
- 8th AF (strategic) B-17s and B-24s in the UK and North Africa
- 12th AF (strategic) B-24s in Libya
- 9th AF (tactical) B-25s and A-20s in Egypt and Libya
- 20th AF (strategic) B-29s in India, China, Guam, and Okinawa

aft: The back end of a B-17 where the tail gunner sat; the other end where the pilots sat was forward. Of course, aft is where everyone is when they are behind something or somebody.

airborne: The state of being after taking off "into the wild blue yonder," the same as getting "up, up and away."

aircrew: Also known as flight crew. I had an exceptional B-17 crew, each trained for his position. They flew with me as we escorted Field Marshal Bernard Law Montgomery to wherever he needed to go. Johnson, Kennedy, Morris, Austin, Ward, and I also flew together from the ZI across the Atlantic to the war zone in North Africa:

- Captain or Pilot - Commander in charge of the aircraft. Captain Richard Ernest Evans
- First Officer or Co-Pilot - Backup to pilot, handles ground maneuvering. Second Lieutenant Fred L. Johnson, Jr.
- Second Officer or Flight Engineer - Engine health monitoring and top gun turret. Staff Sergeant Dale E. Owens
- Navigator - Determines plane position relative to Earth, targets, and enemy territory. Second Lieutenant Thomas H. Carver
- Bombardier or Bomb Aimer - Delivers the payload on the target. Second Lieutenant Albert L. "A. L." Beringsmith, who was aptly named after all, he had to keep his "bearings" as a bomb aimer
- Radio Operator - Communicates with the formation and headquarters. Technical Sergeant Francis "Frank" R. Morris
- Waist Gunner (usually 2) - Defends the aircraft against enemy attacks at midsection of the plane. Staff Sergeant Victor J. Kennedy
- Ball Turret Gunner - Defends aircraft against enemy attacks from below. Staff Sergeant Eldon B. Austin
- Tail Gunner - Most important defense to defend aircraft from enemy attacks from behind. Staff Sergeant Charles "Chuck" W. Ward

airhead: A lame brain, jerk, or dull tool; stronger definition would be a stupid ass. There were few honest-to-God airheads in the wartime Army Air Corps. I knew just one, but his qualifications were outstanding; he accidently killed himself.

airman: An enlisted grade, non-officer, air crewman. In B-17s and B-29s, it was a good idea to "not leave home without a few of them."

airstream: The relative stream of air flowing over an aircraft, its wings, and its stabilizing and control surfaces resulting from the aircraft's forward movement.

Aldis lamp: A hand-held signal light, employed in the air traffic control towers, a backup to normal radio communication. A tower operator could point an Aldis lamp at an aircraft taxiing on the airdrome or flying in the local area, a green light indicating, "okay to taxi, land or takeoff;" a red light, warning, "hold, do not taxi, takeoff or land."

Colored flares were available in control towers; red indicating, "do not taxi or land," green, "okay

to taxi, takeoff or land." Flares were also available in aircraft; red, to signal "emergency injured crewmen aboard." Signal lights and flares were backup for ground-to-air and air-to-ground radio communication systems.

alert: A condition where fully-serviced aircraft and combat crews are standing by for immediate engine-start-up and takeoff. A crew in this status is "On Alert." "Alert" was also the mental state that a flying cadet was supposed to be in... at all times.

Algiers: North African Theater Headquarters for General Eisenhower.

ammo: Ammunition for B-17s, .50-caliber, belt-loaded ammo, fired from Browning machine guns, mounted usually in pairs. There were eleven to thirteen guns on B-17 series "D" through "G" aircraft. The *Theresa Leta* had nine machine guns.

angle of attack: The angle above or below the horizontal plain, at which the airfoil (aircraft wing) is meeting the airstream during flight. Pulling back on the "stick," or control column, of course, increased the angle at which one's wing was "attacking" the air.

anoxia: Literally a total deprivation of oxygen. Often used incorrectly as a contraction of anoxemia. In any event, very few Army Air Force flyboys could spell, pronounce, or wanted to think about anoxia.

anoxemia: Partial reduction of oxygen content in the arterial blood, resulting in impaired mental and physical responses. At 25,000 feet, crewmen not on oxygen would become unconscious in one minute and dead in twenty. Before becoming "oxygen-qualified" (authorized to fly above 12,000 feet) pilots were required to take an "oxygen check-out flight" with a special instructor, an Air Corps doctor when available .

Oxygen masks would be donned at 12,000 feet. At 18 to 20,000 feet, masks would be removed from one "student" at a time. In less than a minute, as I recall, the subject would pass out. The instructor would then replace his mask, and in a few seconds the subject would be fully recovered. And in most cases the subject could not believe he had just passed out. The point was well made when one watched one comrade after another lose it completely, then in seconds swear that he had not been off oxygen.

AO: Airdrome Officer co-ordinates work of all airdrome personnel and supervises the safety and movement of air traffic.

AP: The aiming point, on which the bombardier positions his vertical and horizontal crosshairs. It can be the target or a point near the target easier to identify, which can be used for sighting by "off-setting" distance and direction data into the bombsight equipment.

APO: Army Post Office, overseas regional post offices serving the military forces.

approach: The landing leg of a standard flight pattern established at all airbases; also, final approach, the last part of an approach, when one making an "instrument approach" is hopeful of breaking out of the clouds and seeing a well-lit runway directly ahead. Interest in breaking out is heightened at night, particularly in severe turbulence, freezing rain or snow and when one is tired after a long flight or has a case of the trots.

Arnold, General Henry H. ("Hap"): 1886-1950. FDR's Chief of the Army Air Corps in World War II.

arse: British for ass, typical usages were: "That flyboy couldn't find his arse with both hands" and "get your arse in gear, laddie," a suggestion frequently made to a rare, inept, slow-moving pilot.

ASAP: As soon as possible, often employed by senior officers addressing junior officers or non-coms. e.g., "Get going, men, ASAP; Stop wasting time; Desist from flubbing the dub; Quit farting around; Get your asses in gear." (I am sorry, but there were times, a few times, when language like this was used).

ASR Score: Army Air Corps used the Advanced Service Rating scoring system during World War II for the demobilization effort to send the troops home. It was designed to return individual servicemen back to the U.S. based on time served, family status and honors received in battle. It worked, but the time to reach home was painstakingly slow.

ass: Often "stupid ass." See "arse" above.

ass-in-gear: An explicit expletive, usually preceded by, "Get your... meaning, Get yourself organized and moving."

Atabrine: The drug of choice to protect the troops from malaria. Was the drug of choice for the docs but not for the army? The little yellow pills were bitter and appeared to impart a sickly hue to the skin. Side effects were headaches, nausea, and vomiting, and in a few cases, it produced a temporary psychosis... just what pilots and crew did not need.

Auchinleck, General Claude: The towering British 8th Army Commanding General, preceding General Montgomery. "The Auk," larger than life, was a popular and famous Army Commander with many years of duty in India before and after World War II.

Aussies: Australia's great, courageous people! Following my TDY with Monty and while commanding a B-17 squadron, I shared a flying field with an Aussie *Wellington* squadron near Foggia, Italy. The British-made medium bomber was nicknamed the "Widow Maker." I had great respect and affection for my Aussie counterpart; I was sure it took more guts to fly Wellingtons than to drive our beautiful, reliable, well-armed B-17s around in the sky. I would say, "Thank you, God, and thank you Boeing Aircraft Company, at Seattle, for your great, ahead-of-its-time B-17."

autopilot: Automatic Flight Control System, which when activated by pilot would maintain flight-altitude and course. Turns and small corrections could be made without disengagement. The formation leader would often put the lead aircraft on autopilot control on the bomb-run, with other pilots maintaining position in formation, flying visually and manually.

Avalanche: The code name for the Invasion of Italy (September 3–16, 1943), Gulf of Salerno, south of Naples, by American US 5th Army and Canadians. The operation was led by General Sir Harold Alexander's 15th Army Group (comprising Lieutenant General Mark Clark's US 5th Army and General Bernard Montgomery's British 8th Army).

AWOL: (Pronounced awahl) Absent Without Leave, a serious oversight, which could turn to desertion in the Army, particularly when a war is going on.

A-20: The two-engine Douglas Aircraft Company light attack bomber, a versatile ground-support aircraft, a delight to fly.

AT-6: A single-engine North American Aviation Advanced Flying Trainer, which came into service in 1940. Kelly Field received its first AT-6 while I was finishing cadet flight training therein the summer of 1940. Length 29 ft., wingspan 42 ft., wt. 5,200 lbs., max speed 200 mph, ceiling 24,000 ft., range 750 miles. On my initial flight in the AT-6, I performed a difficult 720-degree ground loop (two complete turns) in the new aircraft. Observers, expecting a new student to climb out, were aghast when it was a new instructor who emerged.

AT-7: A two-engine Advanced Navigation Trainer, manufactured by Beech Aircraft Corporation. I flew AT-7s at Turner Air Base, Albany, GA, as a navigation instructor-pilot and teaching six student navigators at a time, working at individual workstations in the airplane.

While flying on a navigation-training mission over Georgia, I recall hearing FDR over my AT-7 airborne radio declare war on Japan. I would soon be transferred to Sebring, Florida for checkout training in B-17s. Checkout training in B-24s at Tucson, Arizona followed. I was overseas in B-17s the following year.

B-17 heavy bomber: The *Flying Fortress* built by Boeing Aircraft Company. Wingspan 104 ft., length 75 ft., tail hgt. 19 ft., max gross wt. 40,000 lbs., takeoff speed 110 mph, approach speed 140-150 mph, max speed at 30,000 ft. 280 mph. On more than one occasion, Monty proclaimed the B-17 a "re-mahkable aircrawft... an absolutely re-mahkable aircrawft."

B-24 heavy bomber: The *Liberator* built by Consolidated Aircraft. It was larger, heavier and had greater payload and longer range than the B-17 and had more hydraulic, fewer electrical systems. There were fewer B-24s in the UK and North Africa, but the B-24s were dominant in the pre-B-29 Pacific Theater where its greater range was a vital over-water requirement. My brother, John, was a youthful B-24 navigator stationed in Guam. He ranged all over the vast central Pacific. B-24 pilots were proud to fly the somewhat harder-to-fly B-24s. B-17 pilots were happy the B-24 pilots were happy in their B-24s. I was happy to be an Instructor Pilot in both.

ball turret, B-17: Two .50-caliber machine guns, mounted in a steel and glass rotating ball, protruding from the bottom-center of the B-17 fuselage. Young, trusting, smaller, gunners entered the turret from the aft-fuselage compartment after crossing themselves. They then strapped themselves into their rotating compartment with help from fellow crewmen.

The ball turret gunner could point his paired .50-caliber machine guns in every direction, except up where the B-17 was. Upon leaving the combat zone, B-17 waist gunners would lift half-frozen ball turret gunners back up into the aircraft and stretch them out to thaw out in the radio compartment. Most were able to walk from the aircraft unassisted after a three-to-four-hour return flight back to their home base.

Barbarossa: Code name for the invasion of Russia by Germany on June 22, 1941, coincidentally the same day of the year that Napoleon invaded Russia years before. Hitler, in delaying Barbarossa to first neutralize Yugoslavia and Greece and perhaps to best Napoleon, shot himself in the foot, so to speak. When his Army Groups advanced through the Baltic States towards Leningrad, through Belorussia towards Moscow and through the Ukraine towards Kiev, his *blitzkrieg* tactics, refined in Poland, Belgium, France, Yugoslavia, and Greece, were successful... at first.

At the beginning of his campaign against Russia, Hitler put Leningrad under siege; but he was unable to take and occupy this port city on the Baltic. German soldiers, perhaps in Company strength, entered Moscow. However, within a few days, they were driven out of the city and back into the sub-zero Russian winter.

Later, Hitler's vaunted 6th Army entered Stalingrad, only to find itself surrounded and cut off. Hitler's decision to attack his Russian ally, early in the war but late in the year, was a death sentence to millions of German soldiers who did not live to meet the American and English soldiers on the French beaches at Normandy. I always felt we owed a debt of gratitude to the Russians.

base leg: A part of a standard USAAF, left-turning, rectangular flying pattern around an airfield. The base leg is the last leg before making a 90-degree turn onto the "final" landing leg. The pilot, normally in the left seat in multi-engine aircraft, views the runway easily out of his left window as he descends on the base leg and prepares to turn onto the landing or final approach leg.

Base Ops: Base Operations, the tent, shack, or Quonset hut where pilots filed flight clearances before local or cross-country flights and where they closed out their flight clearances ASAP after landing.

Base Wx: Base Weather, next door to Base Ops, was where regional weather information was collected and plotted on Wx maps for study by pilots before "taking-off into the wild, blue yonder," into "ice and snow," or into "the blackness of night," or all three.

batman: The personal servant of an officer, especially in the British armed forces.

Battle Ax: Code name for Invasion of Cyrenaica, Libya (June 14, 1941) by the British Army under Commander in Chief (C in C), General Archibald Wavell. Churchill subsequently replaced General Wavell by appointing General Sir Claude Auchinleck C in C, who also was unable to contain General Erwin Rommel, Hitler's "Desert Fox."

Baytown: Code name for the invasion (September 3, 1943) of Italy by General Montgomery's British Army at Reggio Calabria, on the toe of the boot of Italy.

been had: Taken advantage of, e.g., "I've been had." Sometimes, accompanied by an appeal for divine assistance, e.g., "My God! I've been had. Where'd she go?"

BG: A Bomb or Bombardment Group, e.g., Colonel Upthegrove's 99th BG. The BGS were groups or units of bomber aircraft, made up of three to four squadrons. Our B-17 group consisted of approximately 72 aircraft with 96 crews. Each crew contained 9 to 11 crew members. To support the BG, there were hundreds of army personnel involved in the daily operations as if supporting a small town. The Bombardment Group Categories are:
- Very Heavy - B-29 *Superfortress*, B-32 *Dominator*
- Heavy - B-17 *Flying Fortress*, B-24 *Liberator*
- Medium - B-25 *Mitchell*, B-26 *Marauder*
- Light - A-20 *Havoc*, A-26 *Invader*

Biskra: An Algerian town, south of the Atlas Range on the northern rim of the Sahara Desert where B-17s from the UK operated in the closing months of 1942. Before better-located airfields

could be built, supplied, and manned, blowing sand at Biskra was a serious problem for parked B-17s.

Bizerte: An Algerian coastal city 70 miles NW of Tunis and near the ruins of ancient Carthage. Until near the end of the African campaign, Bizerte and its airfield, Sidi Ahmed, was well protected by flak and German fighters. Flying with another pilot, several members of my initial ten-man B-17 crew were killed in a crash landing at that airfield. I have never forgotten these men and never will.

blabbermouth: One who blabs or shoots off his mouth, particularly in connection with classified information or information that might put a giving girl's honor at risk. Blabbermouths risked being "slapped into the brig" or being slapped by a distraught giving girl.

Boche: Name in World War I for a German soldier, also a Kraut or sometimes a Kraut-head (demeaning form); or in World War II, a Jerry.

Boeing: (The Boeing Company) The leading WWII large bomber aircraft design, development and manufacturing company located near Seattle, WA.

bomb-aimer: British for bombardier, the air crewman who is responsible for arming the bombs before release, locating the target, operating the bombsight and releasing the bombs. Positioned in the nose of the aircraft with the navigator. The bombardier also shares in the manning of the .50-caliber machine guns located in the nose of the B-17G Model aircraft.

bomb bay: Also called weapons bay on some military craft, is a compartment, usually in the aircraft's fuselage, to carry bombs. In Monty's *Theresa Leta*, the bomb bay doors were sealed tightly shut and covered by a rug upon which were placed a desk and lamp for Monty's use.

bombers: US Army Air Corps, all of which I had the honor of flying:
- B-17 *Flying Fortress* - Boeing, 13,000 manufactured, wingspan 103 ft., length 66 ft., loaded weight 55,000 lbs., max speed 300 mph, max alt 30,000 ft. A sound aircraft
- B-17E - First ordered on August 30, 1940, and the first prototype took to the air on its maiden flight on September 5, 1941. The previous B-17D had a severe blind spot immediately to

the rear, making it almost impossible to direct defensive firepower against any enemy fighter approaching from that direction. The B-17E introduced a new rear fuselage with a manually operated turret, housing two .50-caliber machine guns fitted in the extreme tail. Normally a crew of 10 flew the B-17: Pilot, copilot, bombardier, navigator, flight engineer, radio operator, tail gunner, belly gunner, and two waist gunners. Either the navigator or the bombardier operated the nose gun when they were not occupied by their primary duties. The flight engineer normally operated the dorsal or top turret

- B-24 *Liberator* - Consolidated, 20,000 manufactured, wingspan 110 ft., length 66 ft., loaded weight 65,000 lbs., max speed 300 mph, max alt 25,000 ft., higher payload than the B-17 but a little more difficult to fly. Also called the "Flying Coffin" because it had only one exit, located near the tail

- B-25 *Mitchell* - North American Aviation, 9,816 manufactured, wingspan 67 ft., length 52 ft., loaded weight 41,000 lbs., max speed 272 mph, max alt 25,000 ft. Very reliable and great to fly. Lieutenant Colonel Jimmy Doolittle and his team flew B-25s off the deck of the USS *Hornet*.

- B-26 *Marauder* - Martin, 5,288 manufactured, wingspan 65 ft., length 58 ft., loaded weight 37,000 lbs., max speed 282 mph, max alt 23,507 ft. A heavier "feel" than the B-25, but a "tough bird to knock down," I was told. It was a little "goosey" flying solo on one's initial flight. Not for novices

- B-26 *Invader* - Douglas, wingspan 70 ft., length 50 ft., loaded weight 35,000 lbs., max speed 354 mph, max alt 22,100 ft. It was a much lighter feel than the initial B-26. It was a great aircraft for "light bombardment" and a reliable cross-country aircraft for crew-training flights

- B-29 *Superfortress* - Boeing, 4,300 manufactured, wingspan 141ft., length 99 ft., max gross weight, 135,000 lbs., cruising speed 350 mph, alt 30,000 ft., range 5,400 miles. The B-29 felt heavy, particularly on takeoffs out of Guam, Saipan, and Tinian. After bombs away over Japan, however the *Super Fortress* could operate at altitudes beyond the reach of the Japanese defenders. The B-29, designed for high-altitude operation, was also found by General Curtis LeMay to be very effective flying at low altitudes at night dropping incendiary bombs

bombs B-17: 1,000, 500 and 250-pound GP (general purpose) demolition bombs; 2000-pound armor-piercing bombs; fragmentation and fire-bombs, carried in "clusters" or "bundles"; most common B-17 load: 12 500-lb GP bombs. All bombs or bomb clusters had safety pins attached by cables to the bomb bay. When released, the bombs cleared the bomb bay before the safety pins were pulled from the bombs, allowing a small propeller to spin off, thereby arming the bombs. Thus, the bombs were safely disarmed until they had cleared the bottom of the B-17 by about twenty feet.

Bone: An Algerian town on Mediterranean; the site of a tactical airfield and a joint US-British hospital (loaded with patients when I visited). I was surprised, pleased and proud to see German POWs bedded down close by to American and British patients. The hospital was located quite close to a dramatic cliff that afforded an extraordinary view of the blue-green Mediterranean Sea, three hundred feet or so almost straight down below.

BOQ: Bachelor Officers Quarters, an on-base facility where female visitation rights were restricted to full Colonel and General Officer ranks (just kidding).

brig or "th' brig": Where uncooperative, unrepentant airmen and soldiers were detained until they "straightened up and flew right." Old timers will remember a war-period song by the same name.

BS: A farm product, also any unsupported, often self-serving, exaggeration.

BSer: One given to excessive BSing.

B-4 Bag: The well designed, well made, WWII, all-purpose, GI suit bag; one did not leave home without his B-4 bag.

BTO: A "big time operator," is a flyboy who leaves the airport with his date within fifteen minutes after an unscheduled landing.

BT-9: The early North American Aviation Basic Trainer aircraft; it was standard equipment at Randolph Field, TX. I distinguished myself by being the first on record to land a BT-9 inverted on a Texas ranch. The real story is how I then faced and survived Lieutenant Luper's wash-out board, and then, with Lieutenant Cunningham's support, effectively implemented a flying safety modification of the BT-9 aircraft and graduated with my class still as Cadet Captain of "C" Company.

cannibalize: To remove usable parts from a Category "E" aircraft for use in repairable aircraft.

canteen: A foot soldier's water supply, which, in WWI hung around his neck, and in WWII, hung from his "web belt" on his hip. Also, in WWII a canteen was a place where a soldier could get a drink, a dance, sometimes a girl and sometimes all three. At a particular canteen in Hollywood, a few motion picture people would drop by and contribute personal time and effort to make a soldier's leave a little less lonely. Gary Cooper took my crew and me to one in Hollywood one evening. Coop had met my B-29 at Mines Field (now LAX) and invited me to dine with him and his beautiful wife, Veronica Balfe, nicknamed Rocky. And was she ever wonderful and beautiful, and kind, and nice.

Cargo Aircraft:
- C-47 *Gooney Bird* - The highly successful 2-engine, medium range, workhorse, all-purpose, lightweight Douglas transport aircraft. Also, called the *Dakota* or *Skytrain*. It was developed from the civilian Douglas DC-3 airliner. The reliable C-47s were everywhere and always on the move
- C-54 *Skymaster* - The equally successful 4-engine, longer range, medium weight air transport with larger cargo capacity than the C-47. I flew these great, early workhorse aircraft a few times.

carryall: A 3/4-ton GI truck used as a weapon and/or personnel carrier; it was a step between the 1/2-ton jeep and the standard 2 1/2-ton all-purpose truck.

Casablanca Conference: January 14-23, 1943, was the first of a series of Roosevelt and Churchill wartime meetings at which a policy of "no negotiated-surrender" was agreed upon and never modified. My 99th Bomb Group, having departed the ZI, was in route to Casablanca at the time of this meeting of the two Great War Leaders

It was rumored that Churchill and FDR had journeyed from their meeting place on the Atlantic coast to a villa near Marrakesh, where the 99th was delayed, pending completion of its new operating base in central Algeria, a few miles from ancient Constantine. This was the first of

the "Summit Meetings" by the two Allied leaders, which continued throughout the course of the war. Their mutual friendship and respect for each other, which was developed in Morocco, became a powerful plus factor in the winning of WWII by the Allies.

Cat E: Category E, a designation given aircraft damaged beyond economical repair. Parts would be quickly removed from Cat E aircraft and used to get other aircraft back into the air.

CAVU: (Pronounced "caa-voo") This acronym stood for "ceiling and visibility unlimited," i.e., "clear skies; weather clearance not required."

CG or Commanding General: Of a division, wing or higher. General Upthegrove or "Uppie" became one just as I was leaving to return to the States.

chandelle: An aircraft control maneuver, employed in WWII, in which the pilot combines a narrow 180-degree turn with a climb and ends up facing his enemy. Basic fighter maneuvers (BFM) were developed in WWI and became more complex with the development of faster, stronger aircraft. Often used by fighter pilots to remove the enemy from his tail, just in time.

Châteaudun-du-Rhumel: A small Algerian town in a broad valley directly below Constantine high in the pleasant green mountains. Nearby was the airfield (nicknamed Château Dun), home base for both our 87th and 301st sister B-17 Bomb Groups. Colonel Upthegrove's 99th Bomb Group, based at nearby Navarin, two to three miles to the west, had a newer, well-equipped base to itself; but we didn't have the cool, green mountains and the Red Cross girls nearby.

chin turret: The gun turret, only on B-17Gs, with two .50-caliber guns, mounted forward in the aircraft nose and operated by the bombardier or the navigator.

Churchill, Winston Leonard Spencer: Prime Minister of the UK during WWII. Born 1874, he became Prime Minister at age 65 in 1940 to '45, and again from 1951 to '55. Queen Elizabeth II knighted him on April 24, 1953. He died in 1965 at age 91. I had no direct contact with Churchill but had pleasant conversations with King George VI in Tripoli.

Classifications of Classified Material, oral or written:
- Confidential - For military personnel only, usually pertaining to aircraft and specialized equipment
- Secret - For individuals with "secret" clearances as pertaining to specific equipment and operational plans
- Top secret - For individuals with "top secret clearances" and "need-to-know" with respect to specific equipment and plans
- Eyes only - Highly classified, sealed material, to be opened and read only by addressee

clear ice: Smooth, transparent ice that forms on the leading edge of an aircraft wing in clouds or freezing rain; potentially dangerous in that it can effectively change the shape of a wing's leading edge, destroying lift and, in severe cases, may cause the aircraft to stall.

C in C: Commander in Chief, the Supreme Commander in Chief of all the armed forces of a nation.

CO: Commanding Officer of a squadron, group, or base. I was CO of the 346th Squadron. Colonel Upthegrove was CO of the 99th Bomb Group. General Jimmie Doolittle was CG (Commanding General) of our 12th Air Force. Later, following our move from North Africa to Italy, Doolittle would become the first CG of the new 15th Air Force.

contrails (or vapor trails): Visible moisture, condensed from cold air at high altitude (not by hot exhaust from our aircraft engines). Strikingly beautiful, white streaks against the clear blue skies at 25,000 feet, they were a great show, but also, they were great multi-formed white flags blowing in the breeze for German Me-109 and Fw-190 pilots to pick up at great distance.

cross-countries: Relatively long flights, usually with landings away from home base.

crack silk: To parachute out of a damaged plane. Parachutes were originally made from canvas and later silk. When silk became unavailable because of the Japanese War, parachutes were made with a newly developed material, nylon.

C/S: Chief of Staff: Highest ranking Air Corps officer (General Hap Arnold) in WWII. C/S is also the third ranking officer after the commander and deputy commander at specific echelons of command, above Group level.

Cyrenaica: The eastern portion of Libya, on the Mediterranean Sea, abutting Egypt to the east. During 1942 and 1943, extensive military engagements between British and Axis forces led by Monty and Rommel, respectively, took place in Cyrenaica, at Tobruk, Benghazi, El Agheila and Surt. Cyrenaica is roughly the eastern half of Libya; Tripolitania is the western half.

D-day: Military definition, the day, usually unspecified, set for the beginning of a planned attack. Usually a well-kept secret .

dead ahead: A navigation term meaning straight ahead of an aircraft or boat on its present heading.

deadbeat: a bum, who doesn't pull his own weight, i.e., do his job. We had very few actual deadbeats in the WWII Army Air Corps.

deadhead: An unflattering designation given an air crewman on board an aircraft as a passenger without flight duties.

De Guingand, Major General Sir Francis Wilfred: Better known as "Freddie de Guingand." He was General Montgomery's combo Deputy Commander and Chief of Staff for both Administration and Operations. He was also my advisor, warm friend, and protector. He would often patch things up for me with Monty. He was able, loyal, courageous and always pleasant: a delightful human being. Sir Francis would be Monty's second-in-command until the end of the war. I heard that, in the post-war period, General de Guingand had traveled to Rhodesia for business. I had hoped to visit him someday but never made it to that part of Africa.

demos: High-explosive, demolition, and general-purpose bombs, 500, 1,000 and 2,000-pounders. 500-pounders were carried by B-17s 50% of the time.

Dempsey, General Miles: CMDR, XIII Corps, British Army was one of Monty's three Corps Commanders. He was pleasant, reserved, business-like and very cordial with me.

Deputy or Dep: No. 2 in command, e.g., Deputy CO of a Base, a Group, Wing, an Air Force or a Theater.

DFC: Distinguished Flying Cross - Military decoration awarded to any officer or enlisted member of the USAF who distinguished themselves in support of operations by heroism or extraordinary achievement while participating in an aerial flight. And there were many in WWII. I humbly received one February 17, 1944, recognizing Richard E. Evans for "His aggressive undertaking and initiative under difficult conditions, his superior leadership and devotion to duty throughout his outstanding record of over fifty combat missions against the enemy" together with "his extraordinary achievements while participating in an attack on an important rail center in Italy, in which he led a formation of thirty-two *Flying Fortresses*, merited Evans the DFC."

dimwit: A wartime airman cadet or officer falling somewhere between a screwball, idiot, or flibbertigibbet.

ding-a-ling: A balmy, worthless individual, without redeeming features. We had a few, fully qualified ding-a-lings with us overseas.

DO: Director of Operations, a hell of a job. Oversees an organization's daily business activities and implements an operational plan. It's a "buck stops here" job.

dodos: A bird that can't fly, also an "airplane driver" who can't, either.

don't sweat it: A verbal directive from a senior officer to the effect, "Don't worry about it, Son; just do what you're damn well told to do."

Doolittle, General Jimmie: Early American flyer, established many personal aviation "firsts," i.e., first US cross-country flight from Pablo Beach now Jacksonville, FL to Rockwell Field, San Diego, CA; first extensive flights at high altitudes; first extensive night flights. April 18, 1942, then Lieutenant Colonel Doolittle lead his team of sixteen B-25 crews to successfully bomb Tokyo, Kobe, Yokohama, Osaka, and Nagoya. At the end of WWII, Generals LeMay and Doolittle made separate great circle B-29 *Superfortress* bomber flights from Japan to the US, via the Aleutian Islands, Alaska, Canada, and Great Lakes, landing short of Washington in Ohio.

downdraft: Descending column of air which can destroy lift on upper aircraft wing surfaces, causing loss of altitude of aircraft in flight, or loss of lift required to get an aircraft airborne off the runway and "up, up, and away."

DR, or dead reckoning: Navigation without visual ground reference, radio, radar, celestial or ground control assist, using magnetic headings, applying wind direction and velocity information, and making time and distance calculations.

dry run: A practice bomb-run in which no bombs are dropped.

DS: Detached Service is a temporary assignment to another unit similar to TDY, temporary duty.

eager: A term enjoying wide use at the USAAC flight schools of the '30s and early '40s, particularly at Randolph, Kelly, and Brooks Fields in San Antonio, TX. It was intended to describe a state of mind required of all flying cadets. In a particular 1940s class, 40-E, one cadet, unsure of himself and no doubt trying too hard, was actually named "Eager" by classmates, who in point of fact thought him "too blinking eager."

Eisenhower, General Dwight David: "Ike" The Commander in Chief who directed the invasions of North Africa and Sicily before leading the conquest over Hitler's army in France and Germany. Eisenhower and Monty did not always agree, but they did respect each other's strengths.

El Alamein: Shortened to Alamein. A small insignificant Egyptian coastal railway station on the Mediterranean Sea, 65 miles west of Alexandria, 150 miles northwest of Cairo, 30 miles north of the Qattara Depression. The Qattara (pronounced gi-tarra) to the south and the Med to the north, formed a 30-mile-wide land bridge providing the only access to Cairo by an invading army driving east. South of the Qattara lies 1,000 miles of Saharan sands.

The British Army, under Lieutenant General Bernard Law Montgomery, defeated the German Africa Corps led by General Erwin Rommel, Hitler's celebrated "Desert Fox." The Fox could not out-flank his foe using his favorite tactic. Attacking west to east, he could not make a wide left end run because of the Mediterranean to the north nor a right end run because of the Qattara to the south.

When unable to pierce Monty's left flank on the south, he could only turnabout and retrace his steps, taking a heavy toll in tanks as he withdrew. The battle at El Alamein, Operation Lightfoot, lasted just 13 days, from October 23 to November 4, 1942.

The German forces withdrew 1,500 miles to the west, to Tunisia, with Monty's army following. Subsequently, the British and US Operation Torch landing forces and the Free French forces in North Africa joined the battle, attacking Rommel from the west.

In the early part of 1943, the pincers closed, trapping, and defeating the Axis Armies in Tunisia. On March 9, to keep from being captured, General Rommel left the area on "sick leave" in his private two-seated *Fieseler Storch* aircraft, flying alone, first to Rome and then to Hitler's winter quarters near the Baltic.

El Aouina (pronounced El "O-ween-ah"): The airport at Tunis used in WWII by the French, Germans, British and Yanks in that order.

elements: A flight formation of three aircraft, forming as viewed from above or below, a "V." Jimmie Doolittle and other early flyboys picked up the concept by watching migrating geese. Two elements of three aircraft each, flying in tandem, one behind the other and stepped down, formed a six-aircraft squadron. A seventh aircraft might be flown in the "slot" behind the trailing element.

empennage: The tail structure of an aircraft, including the vertical and horizontal stabilizers and vertical and horizontal flight control surfaces (rudder and elevators). The tail gunner's position and his gun mounts, or turret, are located in the empennage.

Enigma machine: a super-secret, German-developed radio transmission, enciphering/deciphering machine, used to scramble and un-scramble top-level communications between the German high command and its army and naval field forces. An Enigma machine with vital techniques, developed by the Polish Cipher Bureau, was secreted out of Poland to French and British military intelligence just five weeks before the German attack on Warsaw. The British, in turn, established the Government Code and Cipher School (GC&CS) at Bletchley Park.

The British eventually cracked the frequently-changing codes for properly setting the machine to "read" the messages, thereby making it possible for their radio operators to pick up and decipher many of Hitler's directives to and from his field generals. Great care was exercised by the British to avoid tipping their hand to the Germans. Hitler never understood why the Allies were making some smart moves. The complete "Enigma" saga was not released to the world until 1974, 29 years after the end of WWII.

Enola Gay: The name of the B-29 that dropped the first A-Bomb on Hiroshima, Japan. Pilot, Colonel Paul Tibbets, the Commander of the special group organized to deliver the weapon, named the aircraft in honor of his mother. Paul and I became friends as flying school classmates at Randolph and Kelly Fields in '39 and '40.

Our paths crossed again on Guam when I was flying through to Okinawa and Paul was preparing to deliver the world's first atomic bomb. During the Korean War period, we saw a lot of each other while contributing to the development testing of the B-47, our first strategic jet bomber.

I was stationed at MacDill Air Force Base, as Director of Operations of the 306th Wing, the first to be equipped with the new jet bomber. Paul was a short flight up the Gulf of Mexico to Eglin Air Force Base, where he was Director of Flight-Test Operations. I was delighted when invited to RON for a few days with Paul, at his home, on the water at Eglin Air Base. Paul's family was away, except for Enola Gay, a lovely, quiet, genteel lady who insisted on preparing and serving three meals a day for her son and his friend.

escape kit: A package containing implements, medicines, food, currency, and foreign language messages that could be helpful to airmen downed in enemy-held territory.

ETA: Estimated times of arrival, i.e., at a TP (turning point) at the IP (initial point or start of a bomb run), at a target or at an intended landing base. One could not leave Base Ops without one. After arrival at a destination, Base Ops would receive an ATA (actual time of arrival) from the local tower and then advise the Base Ops at the point-of-departure, of mission completion.

ETD: Estimated Time of Departure or takeoff. If a soldier missed this, he or she was AWOL.

ETO: European Theater of Operations including the UK, the Mediterranean area, North Africa, Italy, France, Germany, USSR, etc. The MTO, Mediterranean Theater of Operations, was the part of the war when Allied forces attacked Churchill's "soft underbelly" of Europe, which was German-held North Africa and Italy.

eyeball or eyeballed: To estimate or guess, e.g., "I would eyeball that distance at fifteen miles." Employed also in specific goal-oriented social activities, e.g., "Captain James has been eyeballing that lassie for the last hour."

farted up: A deplorable term used to describe an operation not brought to a successful conclusion. A slow-witted formation leader, for example, might fart up an entire mission for 100 or more aircraft.

farting around: Wasting time, failing to seize the moment or the opportunity when it was at hand.

FC: Flying Cadet undergoing flying training at primary, basic and advanced flying schools in the early Army Air Corps flying days from 1939 through WWII.

FEAF: Far East Air Force, the military aviation organization of the US Army in the Philippines formed in 1941. This brave force in defense of the Philippines was almost destroyed by the Japanese advances.

feather an engine: Propeller blades are turned so that their mid to outer section is aligned with the airflow (turned edge first to the air stream), creating minimal air resistance. The engine is shut down and at rest. Best to warn your passengers before feathering an engine.

feather merchants: Civilian workers at military installations presumed by inconsiderate and disrespectful military types as being lightweights. Often, I noted that it was the name-callers who were the lightweights.

field grade officer: Senior officer from Major, Lieutenant Colonel, Colonel up to and including Five-star Generals.

Fighters: Known as pursuit aircraft in WWI. The British fighters were *Supermarine Spitfires* and *Hawker Hurricanes*; the German fighters were *Messerschmitt* Me-109s and *Focke-Wulf* Fw-190s; the better-known Japanese fighters were Ki-43

Hayabusa, Mitsubishi J2M, Nakajima Gekko, Mitsubishi A6M Zero; the USACC fighters were:

- P-38 *Lightning* - twin-engine, twin-boom (two tails), fighter interceptor. Enjoyed early success in all theaters; a delight to fly
- P-39 *Airacobra*- the principal American fighter in service when the US entered World War II. Inefficient turbocharger prevented the plane from performing high-altitude work
- P-40 *Tomahawk*- the standard single-engine fighter in the Pacific early in the war. It successfully fought the Japanese *Zero*. It was one of the few military aircraft that I was not checked out to fly during the war
- P-47 *Thunderbolt* (also "The Jug") - single-engine fighter and fighter-bomber. I thought it rugged and heavy on the ground, but powerful and maneuverable in-flight; a joy to fly. My good Knoxville friend, A. C. Murphy, was killed in a P-47 during the air war over Britain
- P-51 *Mustang* - long-range, escort fighter. It was very successful in ETO after being re-equipped with new engines and the ability to jettison the fuel tanks. Major Ellis, a 40-E Flying School classmate and good friend in command of the Foggia Repair Depot, "arranged" for me to check myself out by simply studying the technology orders, climbing aboard a parked aircraft, starting it up, taxiing it to the end of the active runway and pushing the throttles forward. I developed some proficiency by putting airtime on newly-repaired A-20s, P-47s, P-51s, B-25s and B-26s. I never had it so good

firewall: A metal partition aft of the aircraft engines in early single-engine airplanes, providing fire protection to the cabin area aft of the engine. A more-recent verb form of firewall means to push all the throttles forward as far as they can go, e.g., "Okay, guys, let's push 'em to the firewall and get our butts out of here." (out of the combat zone).

flak: Anti-aircraft explosions at altitude; also unwanted discussion and argument at an inopportune time, e.g., "Don't give me any flak; just get your butt in gear and get your flying machine off the ground."

flares: Pyrotechnic devices fired from aircraft; red to indicate injured crewmen aboard or damaged aircraft attempting a difficult landing; used also for "friend-or-foe" identification in flight.

flyboy: A youthful pilot, particularly one who is "gung-ho," a "good jock" or an "eager beaver."

flight crew: Same as aircrew, brave folks.

Flying Fortress: The name given the B-17 by a *Seattle News* reporter, describing the rollout of the first B-17 at the Boeing, Seattle plant on July 16, 1935, four years before WWII started. Monty referred to his B-17, appropriately I thought, as "my (his) Flying Faw'tress." I was pleased to be Monty's driver on quite a few trips.

Foggia Airfield Complex: Series of WWII military airfields located within 25-mile radius of Foggia, Italy. After capturing the fields from the German and Italian military, they were used by heavy bomber operations. Life was not easy there... cold and wet or hot and dry, tents, dirt, or hay strewn floors and, for relaxing, wooden cots. Foggia Airfields included: Amendola, Bari, Canne, Castelluccio, Celone, Cerignola, Giulia, Lesina, Lucera, Madna, Pantanella, Salsola, San Giovanni Ramitelli, San Severo, Spinazzola, Stornara, Torretto, Triolo, Venosa and Vincenzo.

for the duration: Oft-used phrase referring to something very likely to continue for a long time, like a war, like THE war.

forward (noun): The front of large aircraft where the Pe-lots sat. The word, Pe-lots, is a disparaging term rarely used by Pe-lots themselves.

Fortnight: Brit's pronunciation is fortnit. Quite a long time, 14 nights, as I recall.

frags: Fragmentation bombs, designed to break into many small metal shards when detonated; effective against ground personnel and early, cloth-covered aircraft.

frog: In WWI, Frenchmen were called "Frogs." In WWII, an amphibian, abounding in Algeria and Morocco, who's fried hind legs provided a most-suitable substitute for Spam.

frogmen: In WWII, Navy specialists in under-water reconnaissance, ship repairs and military operations; a highly trained and skilled, coura-geous bunch of guys who were proud to be called "Frogmen," I was told.

fuselage: The body of an aircraft, everything but the wings, the tail and the empennage.

GCA: A ground-controlled approach, a letdown through weather and an approach-to-landing by an aircraft, receiving flight instructions from a ground-based operator who is observing the landing aircraft on a radarscope.

Gaggle: An assemblage of airborne aircraft, usually fighter aircraft, adapted from "gaggle of geese."

General: A General Officer:
- Brigadier General – one-star
- Major General – two-star
- Lieutenant General – three-star
- Full General – four-star
- Commanding General – five-star

There were nine US five-star general officers called to duty in the Second World War:
- Fleet Admiral William D. Leahy
- General of the Army George Marshall
- Fleet Admiral Ernest King
- General of the Army Douglas MacArthur
- Fleet Admiral Chester Nimitz
- General of the Army Dwight D. Eisenhower
- General of the Army and Air Force Henry H. Arnold
- Fleet Admiral William Halsey, Jr.
- General of the Army Omar Bradley

get with it: Usually a command, e.g., "get with the program" or often used, "get off your butt and... "

GI, Government Issue: GI clothing, equipment etc.; also slang for a starting grade or low-ranking soldier or airman. e.g., "Who's that knuckle-headed GI trying to make a move on Mary Jo?"

go-around: An order "not to land" given by the airdrome control tower operator to a pilot making an approach. The procedure is then to hit the throttles, climb promptly straight ahead to traffic altitude and remain in the traffic pattern and request another try for the runway.

GPs: The General-Purpose bombs, usually 500 or 1,000-pounders, which were carried probably 75% of the time by the WWII B-17 *Flying Fortress* and the B-24 *Liberator*.

Greyout: A partial loss of sight, dimming of color, light, and peripheral vision, which is caused by a drop of blood pressure and lack of oxygen to the brain. Pilots and crew are subject to forces (cen-trifugal and gravity) when their airplanes soar or dive in altitude, turn and twist as they fly through dangerous skies or make rough landings.

ground loop: With flying machines, a ground loop is a rapid rotation of a fixed-wing aircraft in the horizontal plane (yawing) while on the ground. Aerodynamic forces may cause the advancing wing to rise, which may then cause the other wingtip to touch the ground. In severe cases (particularly if the ground is uneven and soft), the inside wing can dig in, propellers grind through the landing surface, causing the aircraft to swing violently or even cartwheel. Pilots did not want to ground loop if they could help it.

ground-pounders: Non-flying personnel. An unflattering term not normally used when addressing ground crewmen who are working on the aircraft one is scheduled to fly.

Group: Name given for the basic USAAC and later, the USAF administrative entity and combat organization during WWII and thereafter. The typical Group organizational structure consisted of:

- Al-Personnel and Administration
- A2-Intelligence (enemy information)
- A3-Flight Operations
- A4-Supply and Maintenance (aircraft and equipment)
- A5-Plans, which were required and developed at higher, command echelons

The B-17 combat group consisted of three to four squadrons, each comprised of 6 to 10 B-17s, plus flight crews, maintenance crews, supply, administration, and medical personnel as required for specific group organizations.

guff: Unsolicited feedback and chatter from a junior officer following receipt of a specific order. The senior officer might follow up with, "I don' wanna hear any more guff out o' you, Soldier; you hearin' me all right? You got my meanin'? We understand each other, Soldier?"

gun: as a verb, to rev-up or advance the throttles on an aircraft on the ground, with the wheels chocked or the brakes set for the purpose of testing engine performance. After prolonged, slow taxiing to the end of the runway, one might rev-up one's engines to make a final check before gunning the engines for takeoff.

gung-ho: From the Pacific Theater, a Chinese expression. The mentality and cooperative attitude of an individual or group, ready to take on a tough mission or difficult task anytime, anyplace, and most anywhere. Most of the flyboys and air-crewmen that I knew in WWII were gung-ho most of the time.

Hangar Queen: An aircraft in questionable state of repair, spending most of her time in the hangar. Hangar Queens were often cannibalized, their special parts removed to keep other AC in the air.

head up: A vulgar expression (head up his a--) in general use in wartime Army Air Corps conveying the idea of a total black out of intelligence (smarts) due to careless positioning of one's head.

head up and locked: A more defining and limiting form of "head up his etc." adapted from co-pilots' routine announcements, following take offs, "Gear up and locked."

hell-no and hell-yes: Watered-down expletives which non-swearing types who waited too long to learn, might employ without fear of recrimination.

hell-of-a-note: A softened, watered-down expletive, usually preceded by "that's a." I found it helpful in dealing with acute disappointment, as when on R and R in the UK, one's date failed to show up.

Hirohito, Michinomiya: Emperor of Japan from 1926, until his death at age 88 in 1989; the last to die of the seven wartime leaders, Churchill, Roosevelt, Kai-Shek, Hitler, Mussolini, Stalin, and Hirohito.

Hiroshima: The Japanese city, devastated by the first nuclear bomb (nicknamed *Big Boy*) on August 6, 1945. The bomb was dropped by a B-29 (509th Bomb Group), named *Enola Gay*. An all-clear signal had been inadvertently sounded at Hiroshima. Practically the entire population going to work in the morning was exposed to the bomb's concussion forces and fall-out.

Hitler, Adolph: Born in 1889, an infantryman in WWI became Der Fuhrer of Germany at age 50 in 1933. He was 12 years in office, died by suicide in 1945 at age 56, was the shortest lived of the seven wartime leaders, Roosevelt, Churchill, Stalin, Hitler, Hirohito, Kai-Shek and Mussolini.

hot pilots: Skilled pilots, very good "stick-and-rudder men."

hogged out: Dug out, e.g., a runway "hogged out" of a nut orchard in Sicily, by bulldozers... for Monty's B-17.

HSA: Referring to the joy of flying a plane, "She climbs like a homesick angel."

hunky-dory: A slang term describing something, or anything that was great, fine or all right.

Iceberg: Codename of the Okinawa Invasion, closely following the Iwo Jima invasion. Japanese Kamikaze (suicide) attacks on US and British naval vessels off Okinawa during "Iceberg" were the most effective of the war. Attacking US forces came ashore quickly but required weeks to rout out desperate native Okinawans at the south end of the island. Even though fighting continued in the southern part of the island, B-29s were brought to Okinawa with essentially zero risk to the aircraft and aircrews. I arrived at Okinawa during this later period.

inboard engine: On a four-engine aircraft the two inside engines, numbered #2 on the left nearest to the fuselage (port inner) and #3 on the right nearest to the fuselage (starboard inner). Normal sequence of engine start-up procedures was #1, #2, #3 and #4.

info: Information, usually military, technical, or tactical; often "classified info" when related to equipment, tactics, targets, and force disposition.

in gear: Often used in connection with an order or strong suggestion, e.g., "Get your butt in gear and get over here, Mister, now!" It was hard to believe things were said like that! Actually, I didn't unless it was absolutely necessary.

intercom: The on-board, hard-wired, aircrew radio communication system, connecting crewmen with the aircraft commander and with each other. During attacks by enemy fighters, gunners in the aft sections of the aircraft would make extensive use of the intercom system to forestall any suggestion of over-confidence on the part of aircraft commanders not able to see "what the hell" was going on back there.

in the soup: Flying in inclement weather in clouds, on the gauges, with no visual contact with the ground or with Planet Earth.

in-trail: A squadron formation in the air arranged with six three-ship elements, one behind the other and stepped down to the rear.

IP (Initial point): A visual navigational checkpoint ahead of the target, usually also a turning point from which the formation would make a straight in run to the bomb-release point. The IP is the beginning of the bomb-run. As would be expected, flak was most often heaviest during the bombing run from the IP to the "bombs away" release point.

Jeep: WWII all-purpose vehicle. Without the Jeep, the war might have been lost.

Jerry: A German flyer or airborne German aircraft, a carry-over from WWI.

jet streams: Fast flowing, narrow and meandering air currents in the atmosphere of Earth. The strongest, Polar Jets, are found 30,000 to 39,000 above sea level. These were a joy to ride if you were flying away from Japan, but not heading toward Japan from Okinawa. General LeMay instructed his pilots to fly at 5,000 feet when attacking Japanese military targets so as not to run out of gas.

jock, usually "A jock": A hot pilot, one having great aptitude for his work. Also, a ladies' man, or would-be ladies' man.

Jug: The fighter pilots' name for the Republic P-47 *Thunderbolt*; it had a heavy, jug-like, lumbering appearance on the ground but was a delight to fly. I checked myself out in the P-47 after studying the tech-order for a few hours in the cockpit of a P-47 at the Foggia Main Depot in Italy.

Junior Birdman: A name awarded a pilot judged to be less-than-fully-qualified, often used as a disparaging reference to a pilot who was most likely not present.

Kai-shek, Chiang: After the Pearl Harbor attack and the opening of the Pacific War, China became one of the Allied powers. Kai-shek was named Supreme Commander of Allied forces in the China war zone. He died at the age of 87 on April 5, 1975, in Taiwan.

Kamikaze pilots: Japanese suicide pilots who attacked Allied warships in the Pacific Ocean. They flew one-way trips.

Kelly Field: Airfield in San Antonio, and the Army Air Corps' only Advanced Flying Training Field in 1939 when I "joined up." Brooks Field, also in San Antonio, became a second Advanced Flying Training field. My brother, Tom, was stationed there a couple of years after me.

Kiev: A major Russian city in the Ukraine south of Moscow where a key German-Russian tank battle was fought. Neither side claimed victory at Kiev, but the Russians suffered significant losses. Although not considered so at the time, Hitler's eventual fate was probably sealed at Kiev.

King George VI of England: With whom I had a notable conversation at Mussolini's Castle Bonito Airdrome in Tripoli. His Majesty was en route to Malta, to award The Maltese Cross to the citizens of Malta, for bravery and sacrifice in the defense of the small island nation. His Majesty stopped off in Tripoli, to honor Monty's decisive 8ᵗʰ Army victory over General Rommel in North Africa and to meet General Montgomery's new American *Flying Fortress* pilot.

KP: Kitchen Police, post-meal cleanup duty. I developed great skills in KP at Boy Scout camps in the Smoky Mountains but never washed a dish in the Army Air Corps.

Kursk: The 13-day, longest, practically continuous day and night tank-battle of all time. It did not end the war in Russia, immediately; it did, however, make clear to General Erich von Manstein, if not Hitler, that Nazi Germany's bloody, inglorious moment in history was effectively over. The losses in manpower, trucks and tanks on both sides were horrendous. There was no clear winner at Kurtz, but there was a clear loser, Nazi Germany.

laid on: Something planned in connection with future combat missions. The word is, "they've laid on another run up to the German AC manufacturing facilities at Augsburg."

latrine: A utilitarian, wooden building, usually erected about the time that the intended users are "moving up" to their next base of operations. The usual progression is: (1) slit trenches, a degrading experience; (2) frag crates (empty fragmentation bombs crates) with round holes cut in the top, deployed on a hillside. Actually, quite pleasant on a few memorable moonlit evenings; (3) a new full-blown inside latrine; and finally (4) orders to "move out and move up again" ad infinitum.

Leese, Lieutenant General Sir Oliver: Commander XXX Corps, British Army under Monty in Africa, Sicily and subsequently in Italy. Commander Leese, unlike Claude Auchenleck and Maitland Wilson who were bigger than life, was down where I could eyeball him straight on. Leese was not tall, but he was youthful, handsome, modest, hardworking, and I was sure he had earned Monty's respect and loyalty and was Monty's favorite. General Leese replaced Monty as Army Commander in northern Italy, when Ike directed Monty to return to the UK, to participate in the invasion of Europe (Operation Overlord).

Leningrad: It was the first crack in Hitler's armor. "Der Fuhrer" quickly put Leningrad under siege when he attacked Russia; but he was never able to take the city, thereby preventing him from moving east and north of Moscow. Also, German forces were tied down indefinitely at Leningrad, which conceivably could have made a difference at Moscow with respect to force structure and timing.

LeMay, General Curtis E.: a general who was a force behind the US Army Air Force (USAAF). He perfected strategic bombardment techniques in the ETO and the PTO during the Second World War. They called him "Iron Ass" for his very strict training policy. When his men were not flying a mission, they were training for a mission.

Lieutenant Colonel: the army rank above Major and below full Colonel. I made Lieutenant Colonel after returning to the States from Europe. Shortly thereafter I rejoined General Doolittle's Air Force, which at the time was being transferred from the UK to Okinawa.

Lightening: The twin-boom fuselage Lockheed P-38 fighter plane that I ached to fly. Finally, at the Foggia Main Depot without an instructor pilot available, I read the "instruction book" and took off from Foggia Main, Italy, very carefully. Lovely machine!

loop: A well-known aerobatic maneuver in which the airplane dives to pick up speed, is then pulled up and over on its back, effecting a vertical loop in the sky.

Love Field: The Dallas Municipal Airport in 1939-40. There was also an Army Air Corps detachment established on its north perimeter for Primary Flight Training. The training area extended as far north as the delightful school for young ladies at Denton, where Flying Cadets from Love field could spend pleasant Sunday afternoons but with no opportunity for follow-up activities.

Luftwaffe: The German equivalent of the wartime US Army Air Corps. The principal Luftwaffe aircraft of interest to B-17 pilots were:

- Me-109s *Messerschmitt*
- Fw-190s *Folk Wolf*
- Me-262s *Schwalbe* Jet, which was startling to see as they quickly, circled our formations on occasions. Their speed was unbelievable for the period, but we realized very quickly that they did not exist in large numbers. They did not appear to be anxious to attack our large formations and expose themselves to our concentration of gunfire

Maison Blanche Aerodrome: The principal airfield at Algiers, (seized November 8, 1942), serving as General Eisenhower's Supreme Allied Headquarters. I would sometimes make over-night flights to Maison Blanche to get quick repair service for Monty's B-17. I had only one opportunity to have a look at the Kasbah of Algiers, which was plenty. I remember it as being similar to other Kasbahs... all up hill.

making time: Achieving romantic ends. Not to be confused with "marking time" i.e., getting nowhere, achieving nothing.

Marauder: The Martin B-26 bomber, which I found to be my most challenging solo checkout at Foggia. I learned very quickly on my first landing when I perceived that I was very quickly running out of airfield that the *Marauder* could be ground-looped without any effort at all!

In fact, I practiced ground looping the B-26, as a technique for quickly reducing speed while still in the narrow but slightly larger turn-around areas at the end of most WWII airfields. Approaching the end of the runway, I would ease my machine over to the right edge, unlock the tailwheel and then at exactly the right moment tap the left brake.

The B-26 would castor on its left wheel, doing a quick 360-degree non-violent turn, in place! When on occasion the B-26 on its own initiative chose to exceed 360 degrees, I would let it, and bring my steed to a halt after 720 degrees of turn. I had perfected this technique on semi-wild horses in the Great Smoky Mountains.

Maxwell Field, Montgomery, AL: I also trained there and was proud to know that the field was once called the Wright Flying School, where the Wright Brothers set up one of the earliest flying schools in the world.

meathead: A title awarded to a very few select senior officers by unappreciative junior officers, intending to suggest only a few, if any, active brain cells. I had personal experience with just two genuine meatheads during the entire WWII period: one Staff Sergeant and one Brigadier General. Their qualifications for deserving the title were... outstanding.

Messerschmitts: German fighters, most often Me-109s with wing-mounted high-caliber machine guns; also 2-engine Me-190s, slower and less maneuverable, but with a capability to lob rockets into our formations from some distance, albeit with modest accuracy.

Mfg: Manufacture or Manufacturer

- B-17 and B-29 Mfg was Boeing
- AT-6, P-51, and B-25 Mfg was North American Aviation
- C-47 and C-54 Mfg was Douglas Aircraft Company
- P-12 Mfg was Lockheed

Mess Hall, also Mess Tent or plain Mess: Dining facilities where military personnel ate military chow, which was never actually a mess. I heard lots of squawks but cannot recall cases where the chow was sent back.

Montgomery, General Bernard Law: "Monty," Army Commander of the British Army, victor over German General Erwin Rommel at El Alamein, the first major Allied victory of WWII; also victorious in Sicily and Italy. Commander, 21st Army Group, under General Eisenhower, in Operation Overlord the invasion of mainland Europe across the English Channel.

Monty sought to persuade Ike to remain in the UK as over-all commander of all the Allied forces, giving Monty total command of all allied ground forces on the continent. Ike, however, had presumed this to be his job and, indeed, it was.

Morgan Medal: Army Junior ROTC high school program; I won the Morgan Medal as the best-drilled second-year cadet.

move out: An old US Army command, meaning, "Get yourself organized Soldier and get going." Abbreviated form is "Off your butt and on your feet, Soldier!"

Mussolini, Benito Amilcare Andrea: "Il Duce" (The Leader) of Italy during WWII was born in 1883. He took office in 1922, and was in office for 21 years, the longest of the principal war leaders. Mussolini died at age 62 in 1943. Il Duce and his mistress were killed, not by the Allies but by his own countrymen. An Italian mob confronted Mussolini and his mistress, when they tried to cross over to Switzerland, hid them in a farmhouse for the night, and shot them the next day in the small village, Giulino di Mezzegra, on the shores of Lake Como. Later they were hanged upside down in the "Square of the Fifteen Martyrs," Milan.

I thought most American soldiers, ground-pounders, and flyboys alike, had a warm feeling for Italians but hated Mussolini as a posturing, blustering, hard-drinking, womanizing SOB. (Otherwise, we had nothing against the guy).

Navarin: An Algerian village between Setif and Constantine that was the home base of the 99th Bomb Group. It had a single main road, few wooden structures, a community of males only bathhouse and an ample amphitheater for observing the fine points of springtime: equestrian, stud-farming operations. The Arabian horse flesh we saw in the area was beautiful.

Non-commissioned officers, NCO: The youthful, ranking Airmen, Staff, Technical and Master Sergeants, who not only serviced and maintained the aircraft and the operating bases but also manned the B-17's machine guns in the air. Thinking commissioned officers' assessment of noncoms: "One could not function nor live very long in the war zone without them!"

nose guns, B-17: Various configurations were used, ranging from two individual guns manned by the bombardier and navigator to a four-gun set on the B-17G with individual guns on each side of the nose, plus a two-gun, center-mounted, chin turret.

not with the program: Said of someone dragging his feet, "not carrying his weight," sometimes a non-conformist, who might be described as an "uncooperative, no-good SOB." (Actually, I met only one SOB who fit the mold throughout the entire period. His qualifications for the title, however, were exceptional).

Numbered Air Forces: Wartime organization of the US Army Air Force services quickly evolved as WWII progressed. My 346th Squadron was part of the 99th Bomb or Bombardment Group, which functioned under the 5th Bomb Wing, operating under the 12th Air Force fighting in the European-African-Middle Eastern Theater.

- Stateside Air Forces: First, Second, Third, and Fourth
- Asiatic-Pacific Theater Air Forces: Fifth, Seventh, Tenth, Thirteenth, Fourteenth, and Twentieth
- European-African-Middle Eastern Theater Air Forces: Eighth, Ninth, Twelfth, and Fifteenth
- Panama Canal Air Forces: Sixth
- Alaska Air Forces: Eleventh

OD: Officer of the Day, an officer designated to stand in for the CO (Commanding Officer of a unit or a base) for the duration of a specific day.

Okinawa, Oki: large Japanese sland 960 miles south of Tokyo, Japan. It was the site of a major (and costly) naval invasion and ground battle in June 1945, involving the US Navy, Marines and Seabees. The Japanese *Kamikaze* suicide attacks reached their peak (also their terminus) at Okinawa.

The 8th Air Force, commanded by Jimmie Doolittle, was transferred from England to Okinawa following the end of the war in Europe. So also, was I, arriving a few weeks ahead of General Doolittle and just one week before General Buckner, the ground-force US 10th Army Commander, who was killed, down the road just a mile south of my campsite.

I was once again working for Doolittle, albeit for only a few weeks. WWII was winding down and almost over when I arrived on the island.

General LeMay's firebombing raids out of Guam, Saipan and Tinian were shutting Japan down at a faster rate than anyone could have guessed possible.

Olympic: The code name for the invasion of Japan, which was never undertaken and was never necessary. General LeMay's B-29 nighttime firebombing raids and the two atomic bomb drops persuaded the Japanese leaders that tens of thousands of Japanese lives could be saved but only by a Japanese unconditional surrender.

on the double or OTD: Hurry it up, e.g., "Get your butt up here, Richard Eager, the Commander wants to see you, OTD."

Ops: Operations, as in Base Ops and Flight Ops, where pilots received weather information, filed flight plans and obtained flight clearances so they could take off, and go "up, up and away" and chase around in "the wild blue yonder."

Operation Centerboard: The code name for the world's second atomic bombing. This was the strategic atomic bombing of Nagasaki on the western side of Kyushu Island in the Japanese Home Islands on August 9, 1945. A Boeing B-29 *Superfortress* named *Bockscar*, piloted by Major Charles W. Sweeney, dropped the Nagasaki bomb, codenamed "Fat Man."

Operation Husky: The codename for the invasion of Sicily, that began before dawn on July 10, 1943, with combined air and sea landings involving 150,000 troops, 3,000 ships and 4,000 aircraft, all directed at the southern shores of the island. This massive assault was nearly canceled the previous day when a summer storm arose and caused serious difficulties for paratroopers dropping behind enemy lines that night. However, the storm also worked to the Allies' advantage when Axis defenders along the Sicilian coast judged that no commander would attempt amphibious landings in such wind and rain. By the afternoon of July 10, supported by shattering naval and aerial bombardments of enemy positions, 150,000 Allied troops reached the Sicilian shores, bringing along 600 tanks. This was an invasion of the south eastern corner of Sicily by the British Army, commanded by Lieutenant General Bernard Law Montgomery, and by the US 7th Army Commander, Lieutenant General George S. Patton.

Operation Overlord: The long expected, highly contested invasion of Normandy, France on June 6, 1944, by Allied Armies launched from England.

Operation Silverplate: The codename for the preparations to deliver the first atomic bomb, "Little Boy," which was dropped on Hiroshima on August 6, 1945. The bomb was carried by the B-29 *Enola Gay*, which the pilot, Colonel Paul W. Tibbets, named after his mother.

Operation Torch: The Allied landings from ships in the Atlantic and the Mediterranean onto the beaches in NW Africa on November 8, 1942, following the second Battle at El Alamein by just four days and preceding my arrival in the combat theater by a few weeks. The German armies in North Africa were trapped and defeated in Tunisia by the British forces, commanded by Monty, coming from the east and by US forces, commanded by Ike, from the west.

outboards: On a four-engined aircraft, the two outside engines, numbered #1, farthest left from the fuselage (port outer), and #4, farthest right from the fuselage (starboard outer). On a wide desert runway, only the outboards would be used for taxiing to keep the dust down.

piece of cike: The Yank equivalent of this Aussie expression is "nothing to it."

An Aussie Squadron Commander, sharing a base with our 99th Bomb Group, crash-landed his British *Wellington* (said by inconsiderate Yanks to be held together by bailing wire) on our common runway. He managed to get clear before the explosion. Excited and proud of my fellow English-speaking counterpart and grateful that he had escaped, I greeted him after he jumped out onto the ground and ran from the plane with, "Smashing, Old chap, simply smashing." To which my friend responded without emotion, except for a wry smile, "A piece of cike, Laddie." (Since then, I have often speculated that my Aussie friend was very likely Crocodile Dundee's dad).

Poston, Lieutenant John: Dearly respected Aide-de-Camp to Field Marshal Sir Bernard Law Montgomery in North Africa, Sicily, Italy, and Northern Europe. John served with distinction and won the Military Cross while still a lieutenant. He was an officer in the 11th Hussars and was quickly promoted to Captain and then to Major by December 1944. He was killed by a Nazi ambush, April 21, 1945, returning to Field Marshal Montgomery's tactical HQ at Luneburg Heath... so very close to the end of the war.

Primary training aircraft, US: Consolidated bi-plane PT-3 (phased out in 1939-40), replaced by the Stearman PT-17 bi-plane, which became the standard "Primary" or starter trainer during the war period. My first flight in an army aircraft was in the PT-3. My second army aircraft to fly was the BT-9; the third was the BC-1A, which was soon after replaced by the AT-6, even as I was graduating.

pronto: A one-word military command having essentially the same meaning as the oft-used,

"Off your butt and on your feet, Soldier."

prop-drivers: Aircraft engines.

prop wash: Disturbed air aft of an aircraft, which can be upsetting to a pilot landing behind another airplane and trailing too closely. Prop wash was also loose talk uttered by a blabbermouth.

PTO, Pacific Theater of Operations: Theater of Operations title for the war between US forces and the Japanese military leadership, from December 7, 1941 to August 14, 1945. By attacking Pearl Harbor, the Japanese thought they could deter the US from interfering with their plans for take-over actions in Southeast Asia against overseas territories of the United Kingdom, the Netherlands, and the US. We showed them!

PX: Post Exchange, an on-base general store; later, in the USAF, "The Base Exchange," often a very nice facility in the Z1; usually less elegant in a war theater where they were often housed in a tent or Quonset hut. Still, they were well-supplied and appreciated. The Navy had Base Exchanges too, on board ships and on shore, which they called, "Ship Stores."

Qattara Depression: Pronounced guh-tah'-rah, was and still is a narrow canyon, 300 feet deep, in Egypt, located 35 miles south of the Mediterranean and the small railroad town of El Alamein, located on the Mediterranean.

It was the Qattara that made Alamein significant militarily and historically. Land armies, Italian and German in WWII, seeking to approach Cairo from the west, would have to cross this narrow 30 to 50 mile wide "land-bridge" bordered on the north by the Mediterranean Sea, and on the south by the Qattara.

The British Army, under Lieutenant General Auchinleck, stopped German General Rommel at this Alamein choke point. Then Lieutenant General Montgomery, a few months later, dislodged Rommel from Alamein and drove him west along the Med to Tunisia where British, French, and American forces completed the destruction of Rommel's Army, forcing his surrender and quick and final exodus from North Africa.

Quonset hut: Transportable, quickly-erected structures resembling "stretched igloos," typically used for temporary housing, flight-line storage and maintenance facilities. The above-mentioned Base Exchanges and Ship Stores were often-housed in Quonset Huts.

Q-Up: British for "line-up" and short for "queue-up." During WWII, British citizens Q-Up for long periods for most everything they did, gaining respect from the world for their patience, forebearance and bravery. When German fighters Q-up, off to one side (usually to the right of our B-17 formations), this would be step one before an assault, which would follow quickly with courageous and disruptive, head-on, frontal attacks directly into our bomber formations.

QT: "On the QT" in connection with unofficial and/or surreptitious activity, e.g., "I have a date with Betty Sue; Betty Sue is the General's Red Cross girlfriend; Betty Sue suggested that I keep our date on the QT."

RAF: The British Royal Air Force, a gallant, tough, able, soft-speaking group of guys that I will be proud to salute the rest of my life. They did talk funny though. After every mission, especially from those who lived through the "Battle of Britain," they would always say, "T'was a piece of kike, laddie."

Randolph Field: The Army Air Corps' "West Point of the Air." It is in Texas, 20 miles NE of San Antonio. In the '40s, Flying Cadets took their "Basic Training" in North American BT-9s, and later, just as my 40-E Class was going through, BT-13s were added. At Randolph Field, Cadets "sweated-out" being "washed-out."

RAP or a bum rap: A situation resulting from false, unsupported allegations that could negatively affect one's reputation, performance of duty and career... or all three! I received just two genuine bum raps during the course of my entire military career, both from Generals. I reasoned, "If you're going to get yourself bounced around a bit, pick a General Officer for the job. The more stars he's got, the more sympathy you'll get from contemporaries."

ROA: Radius of Action, e.g., the B-17s ROA with a combat load was 800 to 1,000 miles from bases in the UK and NA. B-24s could carry more weight a greater distance but were thought to be more vulnerable to flak (ack-ack) and fighter attacks because of their greater dependency on hydraulic systems, which were thought to be more vulnerable than electrical systems.

RON: Remain Over Night, something WWII soldier-boys and flyboys alike tried very hard to do with limited success in North Africa, Italy, and England, early on, and even less in Guam, Saipan, Tinian, and Okinawa, as the war was shutting down.

Rommel, General Erwin, the "Desert Fox": Hitler's favorite general, who at the end, Hitler ordered killed by a lethal pill, which Hitler later used in the killing of his wife and himself. Knowledgeable soldiers and airmen alike the world-over saluted General Rommel for his courage and loyalty to his country even though it was Germany.

Roosevelt, Franklin Delano: "FDR," the respected, revered, patriarchal, US President during WWII. He was the Commander in Chief of the US Armed Services. Born in 1882, he became President at age 51 in 1933, was reelected three times, and died in office in 1945, at age 63. The wartime President teamed up with Winston Churchill, British Prime Minister, and George Marshall, US Army Chief of Staff, in defeating Fascism.

Rosie the Riveter: A WWII expression, applied good-naturedly and with affection to patriotic, brave American women who replaced men in the war industries. At the war's end, returning from the ETO and PTO, I visited the Boeing Company and told the "Rosies" who riveted for us that I loved them.

rpm: Revolutions per minute. It is the speed of an airplane prop in a propeller aircraft and is typically under 2400 rpms. A runaway propeller is out-of-control and runs at a very high rpm, which could cause engine failure.

sack: One's bed. A typical morning call, "Okay, you flyboys in here outa-tha-sack, off your butts and on your feet! Chow call in ten minutes."

Screw-up (or fowl-up): To perform unsatisfactorily at most any undertaking. Also, foul-up, flub-the-dub and bomb-out were in common use during WWII. May be used as a noun or verb, e.g., "That fowl-up fowled" or "That screw up screwed-up, in spades, when he sloshed his beer on the General's new medals." Strangely, a flyboy might report, after a date with Mary Jo, that he "bombed out," which made no sense at all.

Sea Lion: Code name for Hitler's planned invasion of England, which he was never able to pull off. The Royal Air Force and the stout Royal "ack-ack" gunners shot the German attackers out of the skies over their own homes in Britain. Hitler hesitated, canceled, and then turned back towards the Balkans and then east towards Russia. Never again did he have the stomach to turn west, across the 20-or-so miles straits that separated Europe from the UK. The Brits were noble partners. Could I take a little guff from Monty? "But, of cause."

Shavetail: A second lieutenant, also from WWI Army Quartermaster days, an unbroken mule whose tail was shaved to tell it apart from an experienced one.

Sidi Ahmed Air Base: The German airfield at Bizerte, 50 miles NW of Tunis, where the 99th Bomb Group experienced its first serious challenge in the air. I can still visualize the Me-109s and Fw-190s, rising over Sidi Ahmed, resembling bees, intent on stinging us out of the skies! I remember with pain that Sidi Ahmed was also the crash site where several of the ten-man crew with whom I had flown from Salina, KS to the combat theater... died.

slot, the: The position in a flight formation where "Tail-end-Charlie" flies. A fourth aircraft added to a flight of three or six planes, filling out a diamond formation by flying below and behind an Element Leader.

SNAFU: "Situation Normal, All Fouled Up" was an oft-used wartime expression employed to describe a specific flying mission where things got a little out-of-hand. A stronger "F-word" (e.g., "farted up") might be substituted, depending upon the severity of the particular SNAFU.

SOP: "Standard Operating Procedure," "The Only Way to Fly!"

Spring of '44: A period of international fear and apprehension, particularly in the US and the UK. And, I am sure, in Germany as well. Everyone was expecting the invasion of France and Germany by Allied Forces from the UK. Everyone clearly understood the potential costs in blood to both sides, which would constitute a great and terrible disaster on a global scale.

squadron: The basic administrative and tactical Army Air Corps flight-operations organization.

A B-17 squadron was equipped with 7 to 10 B-17s, each with 10 to 12-man crews. A B-17 Group was formed by assembling 3 or 4 squadrons under a Group Commander who led with relatively small intelligence, administrative, maintenance and operations staffs reporting to him.

Stalin, Joseph Vissarionovich: Russian Premier during WWII. Born in 1878. Stalin would become Premier at age 63 in 1941; he was in office twelve years until his death in 1953, at age 75. Reportedly he was a hard, tough, customer, but he was one of the Allies' "Big Three" (Roosevelt, Churchill, and Stalin).

Stalingrad: A major Russian city, 600 miles SE of Moscow, located on the Volga at a point where the river, flowing SW, makes a 90-degree turn to the SE towards the Caspian Sea. The Don River, just 40 miles NE of Stalingrad, flows SE, then makes a 90-degree turn to the SW.

German General Friedrich Paulus' 6th Army became trapped between the two rivers (the Volga and Don) in midwinter when Russian pincers, closed on him from the NE and the SE at the same time.

At this point in the war, Hitler moved Field Marshal Erich von Manstein, his premier Field Marshal, from the Leningrad front to take command of the Don Army Group and attempt to free Von Paulus' trapped 6th Army. Hitler summoned the very able, highly respected Marshal Manstein too late in the year. He had no chance for success fighting both the better-positioned Russians and the deadly Russian winter. Oil became like grease; marching men became like half-frozen sloths.

The Russians believed that they had trapped 100,000 men when the dead-of-winter battle at Stalingrad was finally concluded. When the Russians were able to make a headcount, the Germans captives numbered 300,000.

These were the best-of-the-best of Hitler's *Wehrmacht* that American "ground-pounders" and "flyboys" would never have to face. Thank you, Mother Russia. I hoped we in America would never forget that debt to Russia.

At Leningrad in the north, near the Baltic, the Germans had been stopped but were not driven off or back for a thousand days. At Moscow in central Russia, the Germans were stopped again, but this time they were driven back, and driven away from the warmth of the Russian capital city in the dead of the Russian winter.

At Stalingrad, an entire German Army was stopped, surrounded, defeated and marched off to oblivion beyond the Ural Mountains that separate Europe from Eurasia.

Stalingrad would be the linchpin; there would be no turning back for Adolph Hitler. After Stalingrad, he could not even disengage! His armies, in defeat, raced west across Russia and Poland for Berlin with increasing momentum, ironically retracing the earlier German attacks.

standing down: No flying scheduled, most likely to "let some weather pass through," or to "bring our B-17s up to combat-ready status," or both.

Storch: Was a small, 2-place, light, single engine German observation aircraft, larger but comparable to the US Piper Cub. Rommel, who had been a youthful WWI pilot, kept a *Storch* close by while operating in North Africa against Monty.

Often General Rommel would fly alone to reconnoiter the disposition of his troops and also with some nerve, Monty's troops. Upon his defeat by Monty, Rommel escaped from North Africa in his personal *Storch*.

straight-in approach: A landing approach without entering a standard, rectangular approach pattern. Returning crippled aircraft or aircraft with injured crewmen aboard would be directed by radio to make straight-in approaches; others would delay entering the traffic pattern until the damaged, returning aircraft had cleared the runway.

strip: A short runway, usually a "fighter strip," typically 3,500 feet in length. B-17 and B-24 fields were longer, 5,000 to 6,000 feet to accommodate the longer takeoff runs needed to lift the bombs and fuel required for the long-distance-heavy-bombing requirements.

sweat-out: To worry, to fret, the act of being highly concerned about an impending outcome. B-17 air crewmen would sweat-out a scheduled mission, also a postcard, letter, anything from a stateside sweetheart.

tad: A very small amount of something, i.e., "Give it a tad more throttle" or "Keep an eye on No. 3-engine oil pressure; it's running a tad low."

Tafraoui Airport: An airbase at Oran, Algeria, formerly a French Foreign Legion Base, a fuel-stop for the 99th Bomb Group in route from Marrakesh to Navarin.

The beds of rough, tough Legionnaires at Oran consisted of straw mats on flattened spring-steel bars. My knees, elbows and all kinds of things slipped between those dreadful steel bars. The pain was not to be believed. Sleep was not to be had. Vows against service in the French Foreign Legion were made by Yanks forced to submit to these tortures.

Tail-end Charlie: The pilot of an aircraft assigned to fly the trailing position, required to complete a "diamond" formation or a seven-ship squadron formation. The pilot of the trailing ship, filling the "slot" was warmly referred to as "Tail-end Charlie."

I requested this position on my first few combat missions to observe the entire formation. Then I worked my way forward in the formation to the Group and Wing lead positions.

tail turret: Paired .50-calibar machine guns are located in the airplane tail, providing nearly 160 degrees field-of-fire, aft of the B-17 both vertically and horizontally. Nose turrets first appeared on late B-17 Model Gs, and no one disapproved of this important modification.

TDY: A temporary-duty assignment to another organization, e.g., I received orders placing me "on TDY to the British Army, until otherwise notified," to fly General Sir Bernard Law Montgomery "about" in the skies over North Africa, the Mediterranean Sea, Sicily and Italy.

Telergma Airfield, Algeria: A major 12th Air Force logistics base, 30 miles south of Constantine. Also, of historical interest, the recovery field for General LeMay's Air Force B-17 shuttle raid from the UK to the *Messerschmitt* fighter assembly facilities in Regensburg, Germany, before returning to the UK the following day.

The ONLY way to fly: A joyous exclamation exclaimed by 1940s aviators intending to convey to all within range of their voices their complete acceptance, satisfaction, and joy of whatever was happening to them in their lives at that particular moment in time... and an early Western Airlines slogan.

Theresa Leta: The B-17E, tail number 41-9082 used by Field Marshal B. L. Montgomery. "My plane," as Monty called her, was equipped with the normal complement of defensive guns for protection. This required a full crew, even a bombardier. The bomb bay had been converted for long-range flights by the addition of an auxiliary fuel tank on one side and a desk, worktable, and chair on the other side for the General. The plane, given to Monty, had earlier been fitted out for and used by General Carl "Tooey" Spaatz, Commander of the 8th Air Force.

The *Theresa Leta* was first assigned on April 7, 1942, to the 419th Squadron, 301st Bomb Group and delivered to Geiger Field, Spokane, WA before being flown to Great Britain. In July she was transferred to the 97th BG. During her time with Monty, First Lieutenant Frank B. Evans flew her from April 16 to June 15, and Captain Richard E. Evans was her pilot from June 15 to August 11, 1943. Monty and his army invaded Sicily and Italy. During that time Captain Evans was occasionally called by Monty to fly him in the *Theresa Leta,* as long as the field was adequate. General Montgomery and Captain Evans last flight together was the end of the year, 1943. *Theresa Leta* was "written off" in inventory on June 22, 1945.

The Terrible Meek: A one-act stage play for three voices, performed in darkness and usually presented in churches during Easter. Published by Charles E. Rann Kennedy, 1921. I had risen to uplifting heights in this play.

Thunderbolt: The Republic P-47 "Jug," which I checked myself out in during the week before returning to the states from the European Theater of Operations, the ETO.

tin can: In Navy jargon, a destroyer in the old Army Air Corps, any old boat in which one might be required to make a cross-Atlantic trip.

top turret, B-17: Or dorsal turret is a gun position directly aft of the pilots' compartment, manned by the ranking non-com officer on-board. The gunner sitting in a rotating saddle and manning two .50-caliber guns had 360 degrees of fire laterally and 140 degrees vertically.

The thumping, rapid-fire noise, directly behind the pilot and copilot's heads was admittedly distracting. I had no recollection, however, of any complaints from any B-17 pilots. During air attacks by German Me-109s and Fw-190s, I found the nerve-wracking thumping just behind my head... a calming, very pleasant experience.

Touch-and-go-landings: Practice landings in which contact with the runway is made but lift-off is then immediately affected without allowing the aircraft to slow-to-a-stop on the runway. The British, using a language not always understood by Yanks, called their "touch and gos" "circuits and bumps."

Training Aircraft, Civilian (Pre-War):
- *Piper Cub* - Initial solo and flight-training aircraft for Private Pilot training and licensing in the Tennessee Air National Guard. I won free lessons for flight training in a competitive contest in 1937
- Aeronca - Flown by me as I continued private pilot flying in 1937
- Beechcraft Model 17 *Staggerwing* - A joy to fly when I continued training in a larger biplane in 1937
- Luscombe - I continued private pilot flight instruction in 1938 in the then new, all-metal Luscombe
- Taylorcraft - As popular an airplane today as it was when I flew it

Training Aircraft, Military Flying and Navigation Training:
- BT-9 and BT-13 - Basic Flying Training, North American Aviation at Randolph Field, San Antonio, TX
- BC-1A and AT-6 - Advanced Flying Training, North American Aviation at Kelly and Brooks Fields, San Antonio, TX
- AT-7 Navigator Training, Beachcraft - Turner Field, Albany, GA. I flew the first four of these aircraft under license as a Land-1, Private Pilot; the last four, as a Flight and Navigation Instructor in the Army Air Corps Flight-Training Programs of '40 and '41

Turning points of the war in Russia:
- **Leningrad** (Saint Petersburg), put under siege for an extended period but was never occupied, which was an embarrassment to Hitler but not strategically critical
- **Moscow**, capital of Russia and Hitler's obvious principal objective in his Operation Barbarossa. Hitler's forces were able to enter the outskirts of

Moscow but were then very quickly repelled by the Russian Armies and stalled for many weeks by the ensuing Russian winter. When Hitler delayed his attack on Russia by at least two months while he detoured south to neutralize possible pressures from the Balkan Peninsula, fighting in winter was the result. The ensuing delays very likely saved Moscow and possibly Russia. This was a psychological disaster for Hitler and perhaps the psychological turning point of the War in Europe.
- **Stalingrad** (Volgograd), a mortal blow to Germany, with the total loss of an entire army and an immediate requirement to withdraw from the Caucasus, where the Axis flanks and rear were suddenly exposed. Hitler stalled, short of Baku (south and east of the Caucasus) when he was at the very door to the Russian oil fields, which he coveted and could not stay alive without.

TWX: abbreviation for Teletypewriter Exchange Service. AT & T began TWX November 1931. It was invaluable for military communications if the telephone lines were intact.

Ultra: A British security classification assigned to enemy intelligence information, acquired through the Enigma decoding machine and processed by the British "Golf, Cheese and Chess Society," GC&CS, an acronym for the long-standing "Government Code and Cipher School."

This super-secret British Intelligence Group, based in the UK near London, reported directly to Churchill. Monty credited King George VI with special initiative and substantive, direct personal interest and support to the British intelligence gathering system.

Uncle Sam: Uncle Sugar, the provider of all good things flowing from the States to the war zones throughout the world.

Upthegrove, Colonel Fay: A Colonel at the beginning of WWII, but he was rapidly promoted to Major General. "Uppie" was the quiet, unassuming, totally in charge 99th Bomb Group Commander, during the 1943-44 period of my service in the European Theater of Operations. The occasional twinkles observed in Uppie's friendly but often tired, overworked eyes were reward enough for most of his men. I thought my commander and mentor during most of my active combat service was the epitome of the often-referenced expression, "An officer and a gentleman."

When we said goodbye, I saluted my revered commander. He didn't return my salute. He just smiled, extended his hand, and shook mine warmly. Then he added, "Major, my Squadron Commanders and formation leaders have earned for me my general's star and I thank you. And Richard Eager, I am pleased that I was smart enough that night when you challenged me in the hanger at Salina, Kansas to hire you on the spot. I presume you will agree; it was a great night for both of us."

I was aware that excess moisture, accumulating around my eyeballs, was beginning to course down my cheeks, drip from my chin and mess up my personally-ironed shirtfront. General Upthegrove, observing the damage I was doing to my uniform, gave my hand another two quick up and downs and released it ahead of the flood. Then, backing up out of harm's way, he smiled again.

Up, Up and Away: Phrase used often by WWII pilots, probably borrowed from the Superman comics and radio series of the early '40s.

USO Tours: Organized to bring entertainment personalities and public figures in contact with military personnel, the USO tours were tremendously helpful to the morale of soldiers, sailors and flyers. I caught Bob Hope's evening outdoor show, sitting on the side of a hill near Tunis.

V-Mail: Letters between home and the overseas bases, which were censored, cut up as necessary, delivered to and sent from the APO's in the ZI and overseas. The letters arrived as 4 x 5-inch, photo prints. The service was usually excellent bringing some comfort to families in the States and to service personnel overseas in the combat theaters.

way to go: Enthusiastic approval, a contraction of "Atta-way-to-go," followed by the name of the individual receiving the approbation.

waist gun, B-17: Two, swivel-mounted, .50-caliber manually aimed and operated guns, fired through the open, left, and right hatches in the aft fuselage section of the aircraft. The firing envelope was restricted forward by the B-17's wings and aft by the horizontal stabilizers, which the waist gunners

were instructed to take pains not to shoot off.

wave-off: The signal from a "Landing Safety Officer" responsible for the safe landings of incoming planes. They are stationed in the airfield's control tower. In case of emergencies, they may direct a pilot to go around and start the final approach again. Flags and flares are used to signal. Pilots are always prepared for a wave-off or two by calculating to have enough fuel on board in case of wave-offs.

went on recee: Short for reconnaissance, visiting a place to become familiar with it. Moving to a spot where one can spot the enemy, but hopefully where the enemy can't spot you.

Wing: Higher up the US Army Air Force command the Wings were the administrative headquarters to control the Groups (bombardment, fighter, tactical, training, reconnaissance, antisubmarine, troop carriers and replacement, etc.) The 99th Bombardment Group served under the 5th Bomb Wing, which was supervised by the 12th Air Force.

with it: A reference to a soldier of any rank who is trying very hard. He is "with it," or with the program; in FEAF (Far East Air Forces), a fellow who was "with it" was "gung ho." I knew many who worked very hard to be "with the program," but when they went to the Pacific near the end of the war, it took only a few days for them to shift and tell their men that they were "gung ho."

WWII, Sept 1, 1939 – Sept 2, 1945: Six years of war (2,194 days); over 70 to 85 million deaths including civilians, untold millions missing and displaced from their homes, their families... and their countries.

Wright Cyclone Model R-1820-97: 9-cylinder 1200 hp (horsepower) engine; the B-17E, F and G bombers were powered by four of them.

WX: Weather, "Base WX" was the place on all airbases where WX clearances were obtained pre-flight and closed out post-flight.

Yalta: A city in southern Russia, where the Allied leaders met for the last time—however, without FDR.

Yank: British for an American, particularly a US soldier, a carryover from WWI.

ying-yang: A euphemistic slang term for a penis never mentioned in mixed company.

zapped: What B-17 gunners sought to do and often did to destroy German Me-109s and Fw-190s and Japanese *Zeros* (Mitsubishi A6Ms).

***Zero*, Mitsubishi A6M:** The principal Japanese fighter plane. It had a wingspan of 39 ft., length 29 ft., empty weight 3,704 lbs., max speed 332 mph, ceiling 10,000 ft., range 1,929 miles.

The B-29 at 34,000 feet was effectively above the reach of the Japanese fighter interceptors near the end of the war. I found this very reassuring. In the letters to my young wife, I wrote, "The war is over!" When subsequently queried, I said, "The war is effectively over, they can't reach our altitude!"

ZI or The ZI: The Zone of the Interior, the USA and the place everybody wrote letters to and wanted to get back to. My letters would reach home and I would follow them. With the war behind me, I did get home in time for Christmas 1945.

zinger: A German Me-109 or Mw-190 or a Japanese A6M (*Zero*) that would on occasions go "zinging" through our formations at substantial risk to their fearless German and Japanese pilots and, as I thought at the time, at considerable risk to us as well.

APPENDICES

CONVERSATIONS WITH HOME

September 3, 1940 - Air Corps Advanced Flying School, Kelly Field, TX
Cadet Graduation (p.1) - Dick Evans to JoAnn Nelson

AIR CORPS ADVANCED FLYING SCHOOL
KELLY FIELD, TEXAS

3 September 40

Hello Gorgeous !

    The fish weren't biting, so you wrote me a
letter. By heck, I'm certainly glad that they weren't hungry.
You know what that means? It means that I'm competing with
a _fish_ now. Well anyway, I wone, but it was _too_ close.

    I was delighted--and not a bit surprised--
to discover when I read your letter that your stay in the
mountains was proving to be a source of a whole lot of fun
for you and your good fably. You know, my friend, you're very
lucky to have your folks so near that they seem to be in your
way once in awhile. Like everything we run across in life,
we don't really appreciate good parents until they're out of
our reach. But I'm not saying anything new--I guess I was
just thinking of me own mammy an' pappy. You asked about 'em.
Yep, they're gone--in fact, they're once again holding down
"Ol' 3036 Magnolia." Ah, my dear, it's a humble dwelling--
right--but what Little Dicky Bird wouldn't give to get just
one good glimps of it !

    For the past five or six classes, the graduation
ceremony from the Air Corps Advanced Flying School has amounted
to little more than the passing out of wings and diplomas.
They usually threw in a speach or two. But not so with 40-E.
The big wigs got to thinkin'--"Now there's a bunch of fine
young men if ever we've seen any fine young men. Maybe we
oughta sorta line up a pretty-fair graduation for them." So
what did they do? Why they dropped a line to a bunch of movie
stars and told 'em how things were. Well, you know what happened--
Ray milland, Constance Moore, Wayne Morris, Brian Donlevy, Bill
Holden and a new one, Veronica Lake, just couldn't stay away.
Of course, the fact that they spent part of their time here in
San Antonio shooting scenes for the new picture, "I Wanted Wings"
--of course, that had _something_ to do with their dropping in on
us, but you understand it was mainly to see the class of 40-E
graduate. And did we graduate ! But wait until I get another
sheet of "writin'" paper, and I'll tell you about it....

September 3, 1940 - Air Corps Advanced Flying School, Kelly Field, TX
Cadet Graduation (p.2) - Dick Evans to JoAnn Nelson

-2-

It was a big day when 40-E graduated--all San
Antonio turned out--for a glimps of Ray Milland and Constance
Moore. The band played and in we marched. Everybody clapped,
and of course we all blushed. The big shots marched in and
got comfortable on the grand stand. The movie stars took their
seats up front, amid many a "oooo" and "ahhhh." The chaplain
gave us a few words and we were ready to go. A dull roar was
heard from the east. Everybody looked and a very impressive
sight met their gaze. Ninety-six planes in close formation were
winging their proud way thru the Texas sky. As they approached
the field they seemed to be coming faster and faster. They roared
passed the reviewing stand, a bare hundred feet off the ground.
In a few seconds they disappeared in the west. The post commander
chinned a while, and finally the flying cadets known as the
Class of 40-E marched across the stage, received their wings
and diplomas and became lieutenants in Uncle Sam's Air Corps.
It was all over but the shoutin', so everybody started shoutin'.
Sweethearts pinned shiny silver wings on proud ex-flying cadets
and proud mammies and pappies congratulated their sons. Well,
my mammy and pappy were already Tennessee bound, and the girl
who I like to think of as my sweetheart was vacationing deep in
the mountains of Colorado. So I just stuck my wings in my
pocket and sauntered back to my little hole in the Cadet Barracks.

That night we put on our full dress monkey suits,
shined up our patent leathers, hauled out the lovliest lass
available, and climbed up onto the Gunter Roof for a little
dining and dancing. All the glamour boys and glamour girls were
there for our little party. Milland was kinda bored, but Morris
smiled for all the girlies. Constance Moore was just what you'd
expect--just too too something 'er other. Veronica Lake looked
aenemic. The guy that everybody liked was Harry Davenport--
remember him? He played the part of the old house man in "All
This and Heaven Too." He tried in vain on several occassions
to warn Bette Davis of the impending danger. Surely you remember
that old codger.

A lot has happened since then. Me an' my three
buddies have set up house-keeping over on Fulton Avenue. We
got us a black boy who does our cooking, cleans up after us,
washes our cars, shines our shoes and spoils us in general.
His wife does our laundry--between the two of 'em, they take
good care of us. Our little home is very comfortable. Nothing
splendiferous, but very very adequate.

Tell your pop that we can't wait to see his soup
strainer. Tell your mom that my mom thinks that she is a "very
lovely and gracious lady"--unquote. And you had better check
on Connie and see if we're still good buddies.

My dear, don't tell anyone--they might get the idea
that I'm in love with you--but I've had a sorta lost feeling for
the past week or so. Do hurry back and brighten up San Antonio
for an old man, won't you..........

October 5, 1941 - Turner Field, Albany, GA
Navigation Instructor (p.1) - Dick Evans to JoAnn Nelson

TURNER FIELD
ALBANY, GEORGIA

5 October 41

Hello Little Gorgeous !

          Right now I am very lonely for
you. I would whisper words of love and romance if I
listened to my heart. But I'm afraid--afraid to
listen to my heart. And then too, the thoughts that
hearts in love think--while they may <u>sound</u> all right--
look very silly on paper.

          For a long time I put on my uniform
and reported to the flight line in the morning much
the same as a civilian mechanic dons his greasy over-
alls and checks in at the garage. I really wasn't
in the <u>Army</u>. I just went to work with some army
people in the morning and returned home again in the
evening. "When the day was done and the shadows
were falling," I was for all practical purposes just
another young "feller" who perhaps should oughta still
be in college. But...

          The story has changed. Today,
I'm singin' with the rest of 'em: "I'm in the army
now." Yep, they got me at last. One day last week
about noon o'clock, I found in my box a copy of
Special Orders # 227, fresh from Washington. Paragraph # 20, among other things, stated that one
Lt. R. E. Evans, A. C. would report immediately if
not sooner to Turner Field, Albany, Georgia (pronounced
"All-Benny, Geow-Ja" down here). The next day, bright
and early, Richard and Whiffle were once again on the
high road, Whiffle groaning from the load that Richard
had piled on'im.

          When we reported for duty here
at Turner Field---I'll tell you on the next sheet..

October 5, 1941 - Turner Field, Albany, GA
Navigation Instructor (p.2) - Dick Evans to JoAnn Nelson

TURNER FIELD
ALBANY, GEORGIA
-2-

       As I was saying, when we reported
for duty here at Turner Field, we found to our
sorrow that temporary quarters--you know, for-the-
duration buildings--were available. So now I'm living
--not in my little ten-room house on the hill--but
in the B.O.Q. I'm in the army all right--I eat,
sleep and fly it 26 hours every day. The mosquitoes
are terriffic. I can remember only one instance
where they troubled me more.....

       At last I'm out of the back seat.
I won't be flying students around anymore, anytime
soon. I'm a pilot on a twin-engine ship in the Navigation School. We fly student navigators about the
country, permitting them to control the flight path
of the airyplane by verbal order only in order that
they may get practical experience in navigating thru
the blue. If, after following the student navigators
directions for a couple hours or more, it is evident
that both pilot and navigator are completely and
thoroughly lost, it is up to the former to bring both
the former and the latter back to terra firma in one
piece. Many of our problems take us out over the
Atlantic and Gulf of Mehhico. There are very few
highways and railroads out there, making it a little
difficult at times to accomplish the afore-mentioned
feat. Half of the work is done at night. All kinds
of weather conditions are encountered, affording excellent experience for the pilot. I'm eating the
stuff up.

       I want _so much_ to see you again,
JoAnn. But I can see now that it's going to take
another sheet to tell you about that. This dainty
stationery erks me..

December 10, 1941 - Turner Field, Albany, GA
Going to War (p.1) - Dick Evans to JoAnn Nelson

Turner Field, Ga.
10 December 1941

Hello Sweetheart !

These are momentous days. Yesterday we heard
on our radio the startling news that the Impire of Japan had
attacked without warning U. S. positions in the Pacific. Today
while winging our way from Turner Field to Barksdale, we heard
on our radio compass Franklin Roosevelt's speech to both houses
asking Congress to declare a state of war in existence between
Japan and the U.S. We heard the governmental machinery of our
great nation swing into action--pass on the president's proposals
in one hour and twenty-nine minutes.

Tuning from one station to another for maximum
volume and minimum interference, we picked up amazingly fresh
news concerning the new conflict. A radio announcer perched on
a roof top in Manila tells us that he is, at this moment, an eye
witness to Manila's first air raid. "A great fire has been started,"
he says, "believed to be in the vacinity of Nichols Field, headquarters for the U.S.A.A.C. in the Phillipines." Later he tells
us that it is under control, that the anti-aircraft guns have been
able to bring down a couple enemy ships, that it is midnight there
with a large half moon although it is midday here in America.
Washington says that Guam, Midway, and Wake islands have also been
subjected to enemy bombs.

Then we hear the Prime Minister of the English
Commonwealth tell us that at last the democracies of the world have
joined hands in their fight against the scourge of Nazism which
if our way of life is to prevail, must perish from the earth. We
are reminded that "our side" constitutes 4/5 of the world's
population, that we have the advantage of superior recources,
that we should and will win this war but that it will take time,
time, time. That of course means personal sacrifice for all of us.
Already, it is hard to purchase certain commodities. Later on it
will become increasingly difficult. But these inconveniences we
quickly accept and forget when we stop to realize that the real
cost of war is blood. Before this dastardly business is completed,
many many Americans will have made the greatest of all sacrifices.

And that's where we come in, Jo Ann. Your
current favorite--if I still retain that enviable distinction--
is a charter member, as you know, of Uncle Sam's fighting forces.
His post at present is however in one of the large Air Corps Training Centers, a non-combatant group. It is probable that he will
be forced to serve his country in this capacity for some time to
come, and then it's just as probable that he will be yanked out
when he least expects it and placed in a combat outfit.

December 10, 1941 - Turner Field, Albany, GA
Going to War (p.2) - Dick Evans to JoAnn Nelson

-2-

In either case, in order that I may be more
certain myself, let me tell you exactly where I stand on this
subject. Roosevelt says that he and Eleanor and James all hate
War and Sir Richard is in complete agreement with the three of
them. But, Roosevelt--no doubt with Eleanor and James standing
firmly behind him--although he hates war, has seen fit to ask our
representative body in Washington to declare that such a state of
affairs exists. The afore-mentioned legistative bodies agreed
to the man (but not to the woman) with our president and again
I'm right with the lot of them. I guess everybody is--there
doesn't seem to be any other alternative.

So we've decided to fight and I'm all for it.
Fine so far. Now a very personal question arises; the country,
yes; but how about ME. I may be able to stay out of this thing.
In the last war lots of men did their "fighting" right here in
the U.S. They did their part by training the personnel necessary
to cary the fight to the enemy. And don't misunderstand me, they
did do their part--their work was indespensable.

I guess you know what I'm driving at, Sweetie,
--if they give me the opportunity, I'll volunteer.for a fighter
squadron. You'll see it as Mother does. I know--it's foolishness,
it's asking for it, worst of all it's nothing more than false pride
that makes me want to act in this way. You're both probably right.
But somebody must do the job--we've already established that fact--
just who the heck am I to be left out. Mom says that I won't be
the one to suffer--it'll be the folks who love me that it will hit
the hardest. Well, I guess that includes my immediate family and
you I believe. But really, who are you to be exempt from any little
mental anguish that my departure from life on this terrestial
sphere might bring about? The battle's on--we're all in on it.
I am not without a full realization of the possible--perhaps
probable--consequences, but, Ye Gods, I'm not afraid to die.
And then too, Gorgeous, lots of bird men are going to fall out of
their nests here in this country while teaching others how to
climb and glide and soar and dart. That's one death I would hate
to die.

Again, don't get me wrong--I'm not brave.
The first time I meet some bird up there who violently objects
to my presence, I'll be scared stiff. I actually tremble right
now at the thought. Usually I back my policies with some attempt
at sound logic--this time I just feel that it's what I oughta do.

Two days have passed. We landed at Barksdale;
I placed your letter (this one of course) in my map case. Planned
to type it sos you could read it when I returned to Turner. The
flight back that night was uneventful. Again we listened to the
news, looked at the moon, wished it weren't so....

December 10, 1941 - Turner Field, Albany, GA
Going to War (p.3) - Dick Evans to JoAnn Nelson

-3-

       Things are at last coming home to us.
Always it's been some awful business way across the water someplace.
Today fifteen of our navigation instructors--non-flying scholarly
gents who know how to get around by the stars--have been given
just 24 hours in which to settle their affairs and be on their way
to the west coast, jumping off point for the Pacific.

       Our commanding officer has told us that we
can expect a call for experienced pilots any <u>hour</u>. My buddie,
Young Tom Weldon, and I have asked that our names be placed at
the head of the volunteer list.

       As I read back thru this mess, now that I'm
planted frimly on the ground again, I seem to note a "touch" of
the dramatic. It's probably overdone, but I'm sending it along
anyhoo because it's exactly what I felt when I wrote it.

       There's something else I feel that you may
be interested in....... Words are poor expression for this feeling.
I do love you, JoAnn. Sometimes I think that I always shall.
This is one of the times....

Dick

D

March 8, 1942 - Turner Field, Albany, GA
Navigation Techniques (p.1) - Dick Evans to JoAnn Nelson

TURNER FIELD
ALBANY, GEORGIA
8 March '42

Jo Ann, My Sweet,

        I love you. I don't prove it
by writing every day, but it's a fact. I do think of you
all the time but of course you couldn't know about this
unless your psysic, could you?

        I've written a couple letters
recently that you won't get--they didn't sound a bit
clever when I read them over. Sometimes I get very dis-
couraged--I'm afraid that I'm not much of a lover on paper.
Perhaps I could do better in person. Do you think perhaps
I could?

        The last time you wrote you said
that you loved me--you always say it in fact. Even so,
when I start to write, I have misgivings. You are so
sweet and lovely and lovable that I feel certain there
are at least an even dozen cadets, lieutenents, aggaies,
etc. (I could go on for days) that are falling all over
each other in their individual attempts to be first on
your hit parade. Since I am unable to show my devotion in
any way other than the field of correspondence--and I fail
horribly here--it seems only natural to me that with the
passing of time my enviable position will be filled by
someone else perhaps better qualified for the job. If the
situation is unchanged at the present time, do write and
tell me as much--I love to hear it over and over again.

        Guess where I yam. I'm 7000 feet
over the Florida Gulf Coast. It is a most be-u-tiful day--
scattered white, fluffy, cumulus clouds, bloooo sky, glaring-
white beaches, sudsy surf, and green, green water. We're
heading south over the Gulf. About 100 miles out we'll
turn west and fly towards San Antonio for awhile. We
could spot a sub 50 feet under the water today, but we
couldn't do any more than throw our shoes at him. We have
our life belts on while we're over water, but we don't have
our rubber boat along today. If we were forced down out
here, we'd radio our position while gliding down, make a
belly landing, stay with the ship 'til she sank then start
swimming. --But we don't plan on doing this..

March 8, 1942 - Turner Field, Albany, GA
Navigation Techniques (p.2) - Dick Evans to JoAnn Nelson

TURNER FIELD
ALBANY, GEORGIA
-2-

We just dropped a bomb—not an
explosive bomb, but a smoke bomb. When it strikes the water,
it ignites and issues smoke for two or three minutes. The
navigators take readings on it; determine our wind drift.
The motors just stopped—I had forgotten to switch gas tanks
and we ran one dry. When you switho over they start right
up again but your heart skips a couple when they first go out.
Oh well..

We've turned now. Our present
heading if we held it long enough, would take us to Corpus
Christi. We've just received information by radio that a
train has left the town of Brundage, Georgia, headed towards
Montgomery, Alabama. We are given his ETA at two towns on
his route. From this information we are able to determine
roughly his speed. Our problem is to intercept this train,
starting from our present position way out here in the middle
of nowhere. We have turned again and are now flying in a
northerly direction. The navigator has just passed up the
final heading. He says if we turn to 350° at 1549E we'll
be heading for the nearest point of interception on the railroad track. He will now determine the ETA, or the time at
which we will arrive at the track. Usually we figure the
train a little faster than it could possibly be so that
we hit <u>up</u> the track a little way. Then we turn and fly down
the track until we see him steaming around the bend. We
pull off the track, circle and approach the train from the
rear. (Then the fun !) We zoom over him at about 50 feet,
flap our flippers and fly away. If it were the real thing,
we'd be droping parachute bombs as we fly over. The small
parachutes delay the bomb action just long enough to let
the low-flying airplane get out of range of the explosion.

Yesterday my student navigator
missed by about 15 minutes. By my own calculations, the
train was just pulling out of a little town south of us
when we arrived at the track. I flew to another position
on the track, followed the track a couple minutes, located
the Chattanooga Choo Choo and let him have it—both barrels.

For sometime, I've been endeavoring
to get reassigned to tatical duty with an overseas garrison.
Four times, my formal written requests have been returned.
I don't guess they figure I can shoot straight. In the
process of trying to talk my requests thru regular military
channels, I have had occassion to speak and become acquainted
with a number of big shots in the SEACTC, including the
General himself..

April 14, 1942 - Turner Field, Albany, GA
Nordon Bombsite - Dick Evans to JoAnn Nelson

TURNER FIELD,
ALBANY, GEORGIA

Hendricks Fld, Sebring, Fla.
April 14th. 1942

Hello Gorgeous !

Do you mind if I sorta talk to you
for a little while? I must admit I'm pretty lonely, and-a
it helps some I think to sit and peck at this sheet of paper
with San Antonio foremost in my mind.

Today, we studied the famous U.S.
bombsight. Everytime we take it out of its safe, we carry
side arms. Anytime, you see someone sporting a 45 automatic
on their hip, you can stand by to watch America's Hope being
carried gently to its post in the bombardier's compartment
in the nose of the Flying Fortress. It's not too complicated;
because with much effort they were finally able to teach me
to sight it in properly. Right now I couldn't hit the
Everglades from 5000 feet, but I've got the idea I reckon.
We just made dry runs today--your flyin' dad can tell you
what dry runs are I betcha. Very soon now, we'll drop bombs
and see just how good we really are. If you're interested
in this bird we're flyin' now, refer to Life Magazine, April
6th issue.

The first part of this beautiful
day your No. 1 Florida admirer spent studying the oxygen
system in the B-17 airplane, preparitory to making a lecture
on same. I found it more of a task than I had anticipated,
but surprising enough very interesting. I'd tell you about
it, but it's a secret..

So you see, we don't just fly these
big clunks around in the blue. Sometimes we really work hard.
For example, the other day we had trouble with the landing
gear on our pride and joy. While the mechanics were slave-
ing to check the gear on every ship on the field, we had a
day off. (It's not as bad as it sounds. Remember, the
mechanics are free every hour we're in the air, and sometimes we go out for ten hours at a stretch.) Well, about
this day we had off,,,we're just two an' a half hours from
Miami here; so I got three of my flyin' buddies and we
climbed aboard Whiffle just as he was pulling out for the
playground city of the woild. The highway cruises right
thru the edge of the Everglades, and there are indians in the
Everglades. We found an old Seminole by the name of Chesnut
who said he'd do anything for the boys who were fighting for
<u>his</u> country. He really said that, and it sounded mighty
good even though we weren't actively engaged in the conflict
to date. He said he'd give us the shirt off his very back
--for a slight consideration--which gave me an idea...

October 18, 1942 - Kansas City, MO
On Training Pilots (4 pages) - Dick Evans to his mother

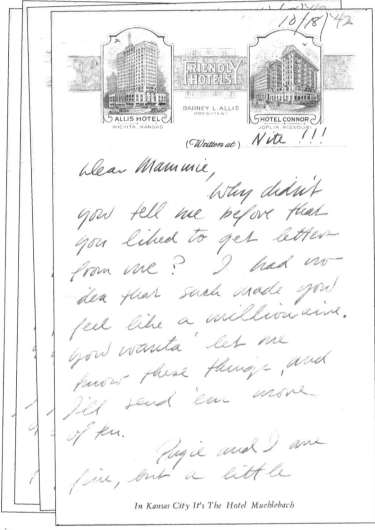

In Kansas City It's The Hotel Muehlebach

Dear Mammie,

Why didn't you tell me before that you liked to get letters from me? I had no idea that such made you feel like a millionaire. You wanta' let me know these things and I'll send 'em more often.

Pugie and I are fine, but a little unhappy about recent accidents in our outfits. Mine was first—four or five days ago—his next a couple days ago. My boys crashed when landing. The ship caught on fire and was completely destroyed. We had 13 on board. All were saved but one.

I covered the accident with my camera. I'll send you some releases when I get time to print up some. (This crash at El Paso) Stewarts was worse than mine. His kids flew into a mountain at night. There were nine aboard and all perished. The ship was scattered all over the mountaintop.

Both accidents can be contributed to inexperienced pilots. It's a shame we don't have more highly trained men for these big ships.

My boys came in with one motor out and feathered. That gave them two on one side and only one on the other, which is plenty if you use your head. They thought that they had overshot the field—decided to "pour on the coal" and go around. The pilot jammed on full throttle!! The two motors on the right wing just rolled the one motor on the left right into the ground.

December 6, 1942 - Army Air Base, Sioux City, IA
On Mentors (p.1) - Dick Evans to JoAnn Nelson

Army Air Base
Sioux City, Iowa
December 6th, 1942

Well Young Lady,

      Things have been poppin' since last we were together.
When I left you with big tears in your eyes, I proceeded first to
the telegraph office with big tears in my eyes. I wired your folks
and told them that their oldest was on her way home. Then I drove
to the field, picked up some of my dudds, grabbed a bite to eat and
started for Alamogordo. The drive was uneventful. Arrived Alamogoogoo
0300 the next morning. My airplane was packed and ready to go. Our
timing was practically perfect. Takeoff was delayed a while due to a
little weather at Topeka. Come the dawn, however, we were in the air
and headed in the right direction. After delivering our load, we
returned to Alamo and arrived that station by supper time. The next
day they flew me up, and that night I settled down in the Topeka
BOQ.

      Then things started happening sure 'nough. Headquarters,
2nd Air Force, put out a call for Senior Flight Commanders--your
friend falls into that catagory. At first I thought that this might
mean an immergency call for some replacements in the field, and I was
plenty tickled. But, upon inquiry, I found that this call was for
some experienced flight commanders to be used as such in the organization of new groups of combat men, which would mean that--should I
be chosen, and I already was--I would have to accompany these men
threw the 3-months training that I had just gotten out of.

      Then I ran into Major Dawson, the No. 1 instrument
pilot in the country. He was organizing a group of select men to act
as instrument instructors and check pilots for the whole 2nd Air
Force. I had known him in Florida which was a break for me. When
he learned of my situation, he honored me by offering me a chance to
work with him. He flew with me and said I'd do, so he got on the phone,
called 2nd Air Force Headquarters, told 'em he had a man that he'd
like to use with him in his instrument work. (He's pretty well known
up there.) They said, "Sure, Bunny, do whatever you want with him."

      You've heard me mention that I have something like
2000 hours in the air. Well, Bunny Dawson, formerly of Eastern
Airlines, has just 13,000 hours....

      After a couple days at Topeka, we flew over to Salina.
After a couple days there, we flew up here to Sioux City. That was
last night. When we tookoff, it was snowing, the runways were icy,
the airport lights were reflecting on the clouds hanging directly
above the field and snow and low ceilings had been reported all along
our intended route. We flew instruments threw the stuff for about an
hour or so; broke out before we got to our destination. Ice formed on
the leading edge of the wings and tail surfaces and covered the windows,
slowing us down a little bit and making it difficult to see what was
going on outside.

        1.

December 6, 1942 - Army Air Base, Sioux City, IA
On Mentors (p.2) - Dick Evans to JoAnn Nelson

-2-

These conditions--just refered to--are generouly
considered dangerous, which indeed they can be, but the only real
flyers in the country--the airline pilots of over ten years ex-
perience--know the tricks to penetrating all types of bad weather.
Consider the break I've gotten in getting to understudy the best in
the business in the whole dern country and probably the world.

If you were desirous of becoming an actress of
reknown and you were told that you could understudy Helen Hays
if you dared to the anology would be perfect..

My home now is my suitcase. We leave here tomorrow
night, December 7th--that's monday night I think. I cannot be
certain where 'tis I'll wind up, but I'll let you know when I do.
I expect to do allittle work at Salina, teaching the boys there
the technique of landing an airplane completely blind--by the use
of instruments alone. I don't know where Christmas will catch
me, and that's just what it is going to do. I seem to be in an
airplane all the time.

I won't forget for sometime the hours that the two
of us had together. Maybe someday, if we are then as mutually agreed
as we seem to be now, maybe we will make our happiness a lifetime
proposition.

Richard

January 4, 1943 - Army Air Base, Sioux City, IA
Combat Crew Training Program (p.1) - Captain R. E. Evans to General Williams

4 Jan 43

CONCERNING 2ND AIR FORCE COMBAT-CREW TRAINING PROGRAM

Following a brief discussion concerning the current problems encountered in the present 2nd Air Force Combat-Crew Training Program in which General Williams permitted the undersigned to air his views, the former requested that the latter put into writing his suggestions for the general improvement of training methods and policies. The following is respectfully submitted:

Time, availability of supplies, availability of experienced personnel, transportation problems, the natural confusion that necessarily accompanies any large scale mobilization of manpower—all these elements make difficult the organization and training of competent combat crews for war. Training commands, operating under 2nd Air Force direction, are sending into the combat theaters today valuable replacement crews, some well qualified for their job.

With due regard for the difficulties just mentioned, it is the opinion of the undersigned that more and better-trained crews could be produced from these commands if existing policies of the 2nd Air Force were, in some cases, modified, stream-lined or discarded, to be replaced by more efficient and simpler means of accomplishing the task.

With three years as a pilot in the Air Corps, one year of which included work as a combat-crew first pilot, four-engine instructor, flight commander, operations officer, and Wing instrument check pilot, the undersigned feels qualified to make suggestions as regards the combat-crew training program. Ideas submitted do not represent solely the view-point of one man, but, on the contrary, are the combined thoughts of many pilots, navigators and tail-gunners, group and squadron commanders, flight commanders and operations officers—in short, the men who, being on the actual flying line are necessarily better qualified—as opposed to those not so strategically located—to observe that which is being actually accomplished and offer suggestions accordingly.

Complete standardization of all combat-crew training and clarification of basic aims of program is in order. Stress and keep stressing to every individual in the Air Force our basic aim—namely, to produce combat crews to the highest point of efficiency possible, utilizing the time, materials and manpower within our immediate grasp. Supply all organizations with charts similar in idea to attached Chart No. 1, showing general—not specific—program. In addition to this, distribute complete breakdown by phases of the basic chart, stating definitely, training to be accomplished by individual crew members. (This is being done at the present time.) For success, strict adherence to minimum requirements as shown on Chart No. 1 would be essential.

Recognition of the fact that parent organizations are training and not tactical organizations. By this recognition, make possible liberal overages in table of organization to properly account for instructors needed in training organizations and not needed in tactical organizations. (This is being accomplished only in part at the present time.)

January 4, 1943 - Army Air Base, Sioux City, IA
Combat Crew Training Program (p.2) - Captain R. E. Evans to General Williams

-2-

Sack "Flight-Commander-Instructor" system of training. "Back around the horn" usage of flight commanders is a constant plowing under of our most experienced personnel. A man qualified to lead men on a flight across the ocean and into the face of our enemys' guns should not be at Tucson teaching "circuits and bumps." Morale among these men, our "first-line" leaders, reaches a new low when they prepare to return to first phase again!

Make flight commanders flight commanders. After experience abroad, send these men, not to first phase, but to third phase to organize a new team, to give the crews the benefits of his experiences, to be directly responsible for and charged with the thorough briefing of these crews for their flight across.

Supply training squadrons with instructors to replace flight commanders and assign them to the squadron. (Practical immediate application of this idea would necessitate utilizing present flight commanders as instructors in their present positions.) The quality of training would be "upped" considerably as the instructor—not being passed around from one field to the other—became a specialist in his phase.

Understudy the instructors in first phase with "less-than-500-hour" men, passing along the first-phase instructors to replace second, who in turn move up to third phase. The third phase instructors, when replaced, will make an excellent pool of green flight-commander material, and will be right on the same base with the experienced flight commanders whom they would understudy. They can either continue to understudy the more-experienced flight commander right on across the ocean or, if necessary, they can be thoroughly briefed by the "man who's been there" and sent out on their own.

The lack of elasticity to present policy of keeping the combat crew intact "come hell or high water" is not conducive to increased production. This policy should, and rightfully is, the basis of our whole system of training, but when it interferes materially with our combat-crew production, it is obscuring our clear vision and our true goal. Rarely do the crews ever get to combat intact—just as they started in first phase—anyway. (Who are we kidding?) The essence of the integrity-of-the-combat-crew-idea is the creation of a team which will function more efficiently as a result of a well defined esprit de corps. Since this is the "ultimate," genuine effort should be made at the start and right on thru the phases to get the crew members together and keep them together, but this is not always possible nor is it always practicable! Friction between crew members rarely is caused by so-called personality clashes. It results, in 95% of the cases, from the apprehension and knowledge among crew members regarding the abilities of other crew members to successfully hold up their side of the job. If our program is altered to the point where unqualified crew members are no longer passed along from phase to phase irrespective of their abilities, then the crew that is minus a navigator and is forced to accept a stranger in a hurry will be confident of his qualifications; because, they would consider mentally: "if he didn't know his stuff, he wouldn't be here."

January 4, 1943 - Army Air Base, Sioux City, IA
Combat Crew Training Program (p.3) - Captain R. E. Evans to General Williams

-3-

The part of a man's hair is not of much concern to eight average American young men if the party in question merits respect. After they've been thru fire together just once, they'll be fast friends; and "fire" may only mean riding out a thunderstorm together.

Return incompetent individuals to other phases or schools for additional training when necessary, but do not return eight men primed for combat to the field of endeavor from which they just graduated simply because one of their number failed to stack up in the final analysis. This is poison and certain death to morale. (Consider how happy two crews, now in training with the 505th Bomb Squadron, are going to be with their first pilots when they discover themselves back in third phase because--in this case--the undersigned found their respective first pilots unqualified as weather pilots?) There is a school of thought which be-leaves that sending the complete crew back for additional training is the answer, that it will cause organization commanders "down the line" sufficient distress such to "place them forever on the ball", insuring the quality of crew personnel in the future. This is the negative approach to the solution. On the contrary, it would more than likely cause borderline cases to be treated with unwarranted leniency to prevent sending a good crew back because of one man.

There is no discipline among the combat crews. The Army in the eyes of the typical combat crew member may be likened unto a Boy Scout organization, and nothing was ever said with more serious intent! The men are not getting the initial training in their respective schools prior to graduation. This is unfortunate. Time does not permit extensive training of men in the face of constant calls from overseas to "pass the ammunition" and the men to handle it. But the situation can be helped considerably. The parent organizayions should have the authority within themselves to render quick decisions and administer "quick justice." aA speedy Court Martial within the Group, giving group officers full authority would help. Make it as simple to reduce officers (ie. to the grade of flight officer or warrent officer) as it now is to reduce enlisted men.

Do whatever is necessary to provide an incentive among the crew members to "put out" and feel bigger because of personal denials and inconveniences evoked by virtue of the fact that they are in the Army, instead of eternal "bitching." (And I do not advocate complete removal of a fine old Army tradition.)

By establishing some system to the "passing out" of promotions (such as suggested by Chart No. 2) create the desire in every crew member to accomplish with dispatch the work necessary to get from one phase to the next. Let the men know that they will not go on to the next phase (more rank and more money) unless they are fully qualified. Let them know this by showing them cases that did not go on. The recommended system of promotions or something similar, besides materially helping morale and discipline, would be providing a definite system and a just system.

January 4, 1943 - Army Air Base, Sioux City, IA
Combat Crew Training Program (p.4) - Captain R. E. Evans to General Williams

---

-4-

The above suggestions and recommendations, complaints and reprisals, are not to be construed as the answers, but it is believed by the undersigned that these, flavored with the experience of the more-experienced might evolve the answer.

Many of us have not yet been priviliged to settle any of our personal disputes on the other side, but, with the information afforded us by those who are there and have been there, we find that conditions over there are not beyond the realm of our imaginations, and that we can easily transplant ourselves in our mind's eye to the theaters of war and imagine with what degree of excitement we would receive replacement crews not competent for the job they were sent to do. Quality, not quantity, must now become our primary consideration. With fair trial, the undersigned is confident that a system evolving from the above recommendations would not only increase the efficiency of the crews and definitely improve morale, but it would also increase production.

RICHARD E. EVANS
Captain, Air Corps

Copy to:
Miss Joan Nelson

I'm sure you got a bang out of the above--if you even read it. Not quite sure just why I sent you a copy; except that in a conversation with General Williams of about an hour's duration, he asked me to put my ideas on paper--that he was interested. Many of the big dogs and the little dogs here on the post agree with me. If the big boys in 2Nd Air Force see it my way, then there will be some changes made for the better, and I will have the satisfaction of knowing that I provoked the move. You couldn't understand much of this--with no knowledge of the situation as it now exists--but I just wanted you to know that your young friend, name of Richard, was hard at work.

When I returned to Salina, I found a Christmas gift from the No. 1 gal. Honey your choice was perfect. I can't imagine how you found out that I was in dire need of such a kit--not much! In showing off my handsome leather bag to some of my friends, I was assured by them that I had just received the best available in this field of merchandice. One Lieutenant produced one that he had had for three years--somewhat similar to mine--it was still in good shape and he had used it continuously. (Did you ever try to type with crozed fingers?) I am grateful to you, Darling--the little gift and the love I know accompanied it mean an awful lot to me........

January 25, 1943 - DeRidder Army Base, DeRidder, LA
Flying to Africa (p.1) - Dick Evans to his parents

DE RIDDER ARMY AIR BASE

OFFICERS' MESS

DE RIDDER, LOUISIANA

January 25, 1943

To the Professor and the Mrs, my beloved "mom an' pop,"

For about five days now, I've had some relatively important news to communicate to you, but I've been flubbing the dub, trying to decide just how I should best put it. Usually, I put things just as they are, and straight from the shoulder; and this will prove no exception...

As you perhaps have guessed from the tone, I have at last succeeded in getting Captain Richard transfered to a combat outfit. My job with Major Dawson was a success--I learned much and I made many friends. My letter to the General brought me considerable favorable comment, and a personal letter from the General himself which I shall send to you. But it's never been a secret--particularly to you two-- that I have felt and will continue to feel that everything I do is incomplete until I have done a little of the dirty work on the other side of the ocean.

23 &24¢

I've been here in DeRidder a couple days, will more than likely leave within the next couple days. My address will then be: 99th Bombardment Group, Army Air Base, West Palm Beach, Florida. I'll call you on the telephone when I get over there. I will not be able to divulge my time of departure when I learn myself when it is, but I shall continue to keep in touch with you, and I will mail a letter to you telling of my departure, the day I leave.

I have left my automobile with Major Dawson, 21st Wing, Salina, Kansas. When I call I'd like to be able to find out if Tom or John can get out and drive it home. If such is possible, I will write particulars. It's in good hands--there's no particular rush. Things are a little off the beam because I left Salina just about 48 hours after the change was made.

I can tell you just this much: we do not know exactly where we are going, but we do know within certain bounds. We will leave Florida for Natal, Brazil. There will be a couple stops before reaching this point. The next jump from there is to the African coast. More than likely we will land somewhere in Dakar. From there we will go north......and that's about it. We have studied this route very carefully. The weather, the available landing fields, the distances, the gasoline necessary to make the hops and lots of other particulars. Our airplanes are the very latest B-17F's--the Flying Fortress's. They have no peer in the WORLD. Today, six of us were flying in close formation over the Gulf at 20,000 feet, testing our guns and turrets. It's some sight to see one of those airplanes flying only feet from you, spouting lead in all directions...

January 25, 1943 - DeRidder Army Base, DeRidder, LA
Flying to Africa (p.2) - Dick Evans to his parents

-2-

I'll just use the back of this sheet if you don't
mind. The man that let me have this piece of paper and permitted
me to use this foul typewriter acted as though he was departing
with his pants when he made the gesture. And he's still here to
see that I don't get another sheet. I'm sweating out an envelope.

In my next letter, I will send you my foreign
address. It constitutes a definite APO number and I do not have
it with me right now.

I talked to Joan the other night over the phone.
Gosh, I bought fifteen minutes worth of Tel and Tel, and I s'pose
only five minutes was actually spent talking. Both of us wanted
to say things that we knew would have sounded silly even to each
other. ~~We both just looked into the telephone and thought of each~~
other. Touching, isn't it? She wrote me not long ago and mentioned
that Tom had written. She says she intends to look him up if I run
off with some Egyptian dame. Tell the ol' boy he better take advantage of this trip I'm makin', 'cause it'll be too late for anybody to do any good just about a week or so after I get back into
the States....That's if she hasn't already done the running off
herself. I'm dead serious about Joan. If we ever break up because
of some third party, I sincerely hope that the change of plans is
her idea and not mine. Always, I have contended that I was still
looking, and I have been, but I've pretty well made up my mind now.
It would make me happy to know that you and Joan were keeping in
touch with ~~eachother~~ while I'm away. Drop her a line sometime.

I may not come out of this fracas alive, and I well
know that before starting; but believe me I wouldn't want to live
after this unless I had a chance to do something about it myself.
I never felt better about anything before in my whole life. And
just between us, I don't think you need give much concern about my
~~neck~~--just ask God to forgive me for those necks I'm going to break.

No matter where in this world I go, I shall always
~~be thinking of you and my conduct will~~ be tempered and controlled
by the principles that you laid so deeply into my very soul the
the twenty years that I lived with you in the same house. I am
a very stubborn person, and, as my Mother so readily agrees, I am
a rather cocky person, but I am not completely without religion.
I will not fail you on this score. I will learn to know God better
because the stress or circumstances will cause me to look more
earnestly to him for guidance and help. It's true that I have never
gone out of my way to pay homage to him during the days of my life
when I considered myself more or less independant and in need of
very little assistance; but--although it does not look sportsman
like on the surface--if God is like I feel he is, I will not seek
him in vain. If they live in cleanliness and play fairly with
their fellows, I believe God feels okay about young men who do not
spend much time on their knees.

My experiences will be tremendous, including my
religious experiences. I shall look forward to the day when I
can sit down with you and tell you all about them. If you worry
yourselves to death over your sons, that day will never come.

March 6, 1943 - Knoxville, TN
V-mail from Worried Family - W. E. Evans to Captain R. E. Evans

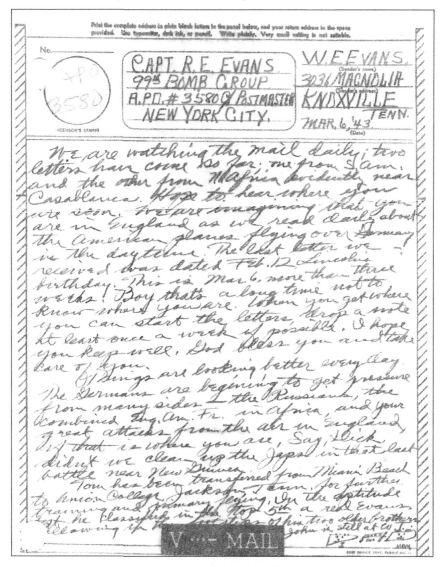

We are watching the mail daily; two letters have come so far. One from S. Am. and the other from N. Africa ___ near Casablanca. Hope to hear where you are soon. We are imagining that you are in England as we read daily about the American planes flying over Germany in the daytime. The last letter, we received was dated Feb. 12, Lincoln's birthday. This is Mar 6, more than three weeks. Boy that's a long time not to know where you are. When you get there, you can start the letters, drop us a note at least once a week if possible. I hope you keep well. God bless you and take care of you.

Things are looking better every day. The Germans are beginning to get pressure from many sides – the Russians, the combined England, Fr in Africa and your great attacks from the air in England if that is where you are. Say, Dick didn't we clean up the Japs in that last battle near New Guinea.

Tom has been transferred from Miami Beach to Union College, Jackson, Tenn. for further training and primary flying. In the institute (?) he classified in the top 5th a real Evans following on the footsteps of his two older brothers. John is still at CO ___ Field   DAD Mom

April 4, 1943 - San Antonio, TX
Africa Tent Living - Captain R. E. Evans to JoAnn Nelson

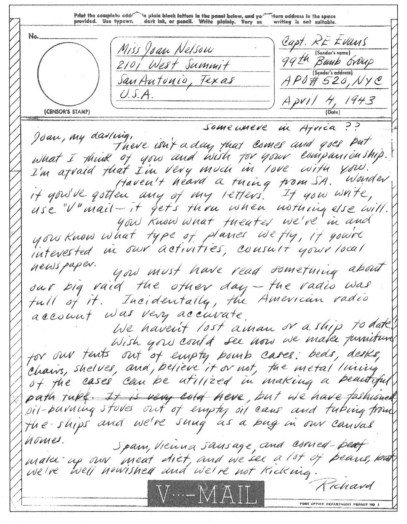

Joan, my darling,

There isn't a day that comes and goes but what I think of you and wish for your companionship. I'm afraid that I'm very much in love with you.

Haven't heard a thing from SA. Wonder if you've gotten any of my letters. If you write, use "V" mail—it gets thru when nothing else will.

You know what theater we're in and you know what type of planes we fly, if you're interested in our activities, consult your local newspaper.

You must have read something about our big raid the other day—the radio was full of it. Incidentally, the American radio account was very accurate.

We haven't lost a man or a ship to date!

Wish you could see how we make furniture, chairs, shelves, and, believe it or not, the metal lining of the cases can be utilized in making a beautiful bathtub. It is very cold here, but we have fashioned oil-burning stoves out of empty oil cans and tubing from the ships and we're snug as a bug in our canvas homes.

Spam, Vienna sausage, and corned beef make up our meat diet, and we see a lot of beans, but we're well-nourished and we're not kicking.   Richard

April 30, 1943 - Navarin Airfield, Algeria
Greetings from Africa, Captain R. E. Evans to his parents

Print the complete address in plain block letters in the panel below, and your return address in the space provided. Use typewriter, dark ink, or pencil. Write plainly. Very small writing is not suitable.

4/43

No. _____

R. E. Evans,
Captain, AAF

(CENSOR'S STAMP)

To
Prof. and Mrs. W. E. Evans, ACIV.

3036 Magnolia Avenue

Knoxville, Tennessee

U. S. A.

From
Captain R. E. Evans, AAF
(Sender's name)
99th Bomb Group, APO# 52
(Sender's address)
New York City, U. S. A.

April th' 30th, 1943
(Date)

Hello Ma, Hello Pa,
Greetings to you from Africa.
It rained all night the night before
And rained last night a little more.
The weather's wet, the ground is too;
The mud is deep and just like glue.

This morn from my tent I stepped for a stretch--
The wind was light and the air was fresh.
I took a deep breath, presumably of air,
So deep was the mud it got in my hair.
With strong, swift strokes I retraced my way,
I closed the flaps and shut out the day.

Tonight sometime, when the moon is high,
I'll sneak out again and give 'er a try.
If the mud at this time is too deep for wading,
I'll back in my tent and continue the waiting.
For days and days it's been like this
With never a letup, never a miss.

It can't go on--it just ain't coiture.
The inactivity is worse than torture.
We came this way to deal out thunder:
Weather permitting, we will not blunder.
The sky is clearing, the sun is shining.
Watch out Nazis, you're just before dieing!

------Evans

(Editor's note: The above proves conclusively that, contrary to popular belief, they do have corn in Africa!)

V·--MAIL

U. S. GOVERNMENT PRINTING OFFICE : 1942   16-28143-4

May 3, 1943 - Navarin Airfield, Algeria
Tragic Night Lives Long in Memory - 99th B.G. Files

SPECIAL ACCOUNT

The night of May 3, 1943, was one to live long in the memory of
the 99th. The target was Bizerte, the weather terrible. Nobody could
find the target. Reluctantly the ships turned back with their bombs, crews
hoping they'd be able to find their home field. Only three ships did;
others landed at alternate fields; but from four ships came tales of
heroism, courage and death.

Two whole crews--20 men--"cracked silk" after they were unable to
find a place to set down. The pilot of one, 1st Lt. Edward P. McLaughlin,
Richmond, Cal., caught a brief glimpse of a North African town, made a
perfect bombing run and dropped most of his men down the main street.
The pilot of the other ship, Capt. Max E. Davis, of Pasadena, Cal.,
scattered his men over the North African countryside. But by truck, mule,
donkey or foot all 20 men made it back to their base. One suffered a
broken leg, another five broken ribs from the parachute jumps.

A third ship had a tougher time. The pilot, 1st Lt. Sidney E. Buck,
of Kensington, Md., and his crew decided not to bail out, but to ride
down their ship laden with 12 500-pound demolition bombs. They flew
around until the gas was almost gone. Once they touched a mountain slope
and part of the horizontal stabilizer was clipped off. Then a lightning
flash brightened up the only safe landing place in miles around. Lt.
Buck started to let down. His landing lights wouldn't work. Vaguely he
saw a mountain in his path, managed to zoom over it. The landing was
hard--two engines caught fire and the plane began to burn. The crew
scrambled out, started to run from the plane, had to return to help a
man who was injured and couldn't walk. They reached the safety of a
sand dune 300 yards away when the bombs let go.

A fourth ship, piloted by deputy commander Lt. Col. Leroy Rainey,
crash landed in the Mediterranean. Col. Rainey let down about 15 miles
offshore after first radioing Airsea rescue, which promised to send two
boats. They never showed up. The crew survived the landing, then
assembled in and hanging on a five-man life raft (the other raft could
not be pried loose.)

Several hours later the raft capsized and could not be righted. The
men hung on grimly. Drained of strength, the radio operator finally let
go and went down. The assistant radio operator set out to swim to shore.
He was never seen again. Then the co-pilot, supported by two others,
died by the boat and slipped ~~interthacouxinx~~ away.

In mid-afternoon of the next day the bombardier and engineer decided
to swim for it when the life raft was about 600 yards offshore. There
was a strong offshore current; they disappeared. At dusk the raft swept
by a reef. Col. Rainey and three others jumped and grabbed for the reef,
managed to hang on. The navigator and tail gunner failed to reach the
reef and were swept out to sea. Weak, sick, half-dead, the four
survivors came back home to tell about it.

June 5, 1943 - North Africa
Bombing #1 Pantelleria, Italy - Captain R. E. Evans to Miss JoAnn Nelson

My Darling,

I am writing you on what may prove to be one of the greatest air battles of all time—and then it may be a dud. If it is as we expect it to be and if we meet with the success we intend to have, tomorrow's forthcoming engagement will make day-after-tomorrow's headlines all over the world.

When the bombs start falling and the flack is flashing all around, and airplanes with wings aflame with gunfire go screaming by the cockpit windows, you, my sweet, will be there—in my heart and on my mind.

The touch of drama penned above is not meant to alarm or impress you. The flack and pursuit bullets really aren't too terrifying after you've been "amongst" them for a while. The thought—that you are there—isn't just prop wash. Wherever I go you are there and you always will be... Never doubt it. RE

June 9, 1943 - North Africa
Bombing #2 Pantelleria, Italy - Captain R. E. Evans to Miss JoAnn Nelson

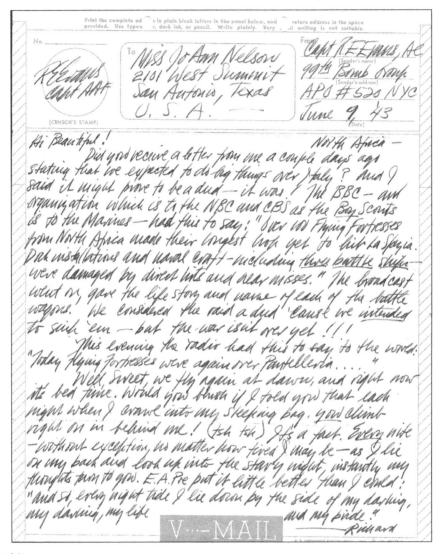

Hi Beautiful!

Did you receive a letter from me a couple of days ago stating that we expected to do big things over Italy? And I said it might prove to be a dud—it was! The BBC, an organization which is to the NBC and CBS as the Boy Scouts is to the Marines—has this to say: "Over 100 Flying Fortresses from North Africa made their longest trip yet to hit La Spezia Dock installations and naval craft—including three battle ships—were damaged by direct hits and near misses." The broadcast went on gave the life story and name of each of the battle wagons! We considered the raid a dud 'cause we intended to sink em—but the war isn't over yet!!!!

This evening the radio had this to say to the world: "Today Flying Fortresses were again over Pantelleria..."

Well, sweet, we fly again at dawn, and right now it's bedtime. Would you blush if I told you that each night when I crawl into my sleeping bag, you climb right on in behind me! (tsk, tsk) It's a fact. Every nite—without exception, no matter how tired I may be—as I lie on my back and look up into the starry night, instantly my thoughts turn to you. E. A. Poe put it little better than I could: "and so every night tide I lie down by the side of my darling, my darling, my life and my bride."   Richard

June 13, 1943 - North Africa - Strategic Air Force, Northwest Africa
Orders to Pilot General Montgomery's B-17 - Major General Dolittle to Captain R.E. Evans

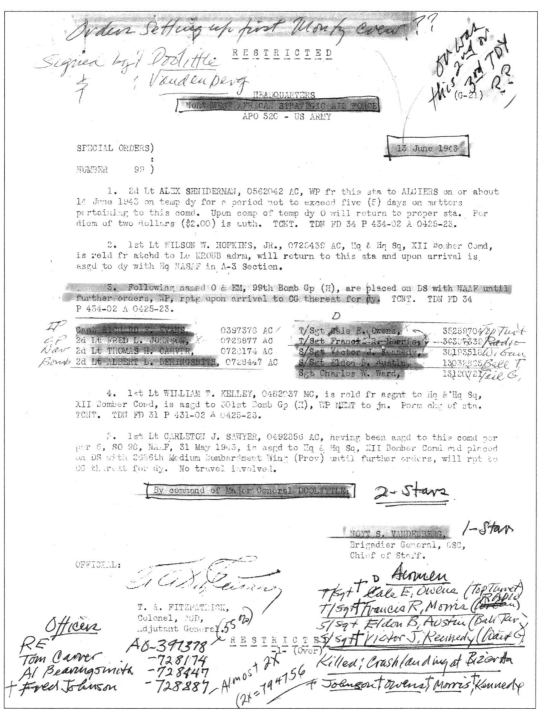

Note: This original order reflects Colonel Evan's annotations as he worked on early drafts for his books

June 13, 1943 - North Africa
Monty's B-17 - Captain R. E. Evans to JoAnn Nelson

To My Beautiful Joan, Hi!

    I was wondering—does the fact that my present form of employment might possible expose me to a certain amount of danger, cause you any particular anxiety or concern? It would be avoiding the truth if I implied that I do not earnestly desire that you give some thought to my safety—for obvious reasons—but I do hope that you do not actually worry very much. The idea, received from your letters, that I am once in a while in your thoughts, is cause for great personal comfort and satisfaction, but I would—for a fact—be exceedingly unhappy if I thought that you were saddened whenever the image of Richard Eager passed before your mind's eye.

    If, never-the-less, such is the case, more or less, then you might be interested to know that I have an assignment for the next few weeks or so which will not require my active participation in the current Mediterranean Air War. Orders have just been written by Wing changing me from combat duty to "chauffeur" duty.

    This afternoon or tomorrow morning a brand-new airplane of the type that I currently fly will land here at our base and be immediately turned over to me. It will be the latest "thing" in this type of equipment and it will incorporate into its design certain additional features not included in the standard models. It will have its full complement of guns for protection against possible attack, but in the bomb bay where the bombs are normally carried, certain changes have been made in order that certain high officials can view the war from above and, at the same time, enjoy the comfort their position of authority and responsibility merits. As yet, I have not seen the interior of this lounge car de-lux, but they tell me it's something!

    My new boss, you have heard if you have read the papers during the last couple of years. He's a British subject. His rank—a well-known make of auto tire. His name—that of the place to which I was sent a after tearing myself from your arms in front of your algebra class. He is famous for his work in the world, in which even I had a small part.

    My crew has been hand-picked by me—we're packed and eager. If he turns out to be a nice man, I'll show him your pictures, and tell him about my beautiful sweetheart in Texas. --Dick

June 19, 1943 - Tripoli, North Africa
Flying Through the Flak - Captain R. E. Evans to his father

From Tripoli 6/43
North Africa
June 19, 1943
Day King Geo in Tripoli

My dear Professor,

   I am - was recently- in receipt of your letter of May 10, 1943. Much obliged.

   To date I have told you practically nothing concerning our activities. You have
learned from my letter that I live in a tent, that I live very comfortably considering
the circumstances, that I am currently in the best of health physically and mentally,
and that all this happens in an agricultural valley "somewhere in North Africa" that
is similar in climate to Elkmont, of about the same altitude as Sevierville, and about
the same latitude as Chattanooga. I haven't mentioned it before, but after you read
this you will know that this valley I speak of is literally aflame in the springtime
with red poppies -- the sight has no parallel in the Tennessee Valley or the whole
of the United States so far as I know.

   You know practically nothing -- I repeat -- of my activities in the air because
to date I have told you nothing, and I have told you nothing -- not because I do not
hold you in the highest regard -- but because I am conscious about the censoring of
my own mail, and I wanted "to do the right thing". A recent conversation with our
intelligence officer revealed a new field of things not verboten. Generally, as I
have previously mentioned, you can actually get a better, more accurate picture of
the war from British and American radio than I could give you anyway -- I can speak
authoritatively only on what can be seen from one cockpit. Refer to your copy of
Time Magazine which, when introduced into your field of vision, will bring "spots"
before your eyes -- It is verboten to mention by name anyone above the rank of full
colonel-- and we will find a map of this theatre of activity which will give you a
very comprehensive insight into the activities of your son -- me!

   But you would like to know more about my own personal experiences; you would
like to look at a spot on the map and say "My son was there when they blasted hell
out of that place"(You would not say "hell", of course). I use the term only when
there is no alternative. "Heck" does not carry the punch of a good "hell". So,
listen and you shall hear -- now it can be told!!!
         20 Missions by 6/19/43 (30 to go)   20 or 24?
   Since I arrived in this neck of the woods it has been my pleasure to participate
in as many air battles as you have children plus two score and ten, divided by three,
with an additional couple of couples thrown in, and two more. (This will, of course,
be easy for you because you are a professor.) Always we come in contact with the
enemy either in the form of bullets, flack, or aerial bombardment. There is always
flack, although it is so inacurate and so mild that it is necessary after the
engagement to reflect carefully for some time in order to bring to mind whether or
not it was actually up there. (These cases are rare -- rare indeed!) We do not
always encounter pursuit. The missions are frequently planned so that we will arrive
over the target area at siesta time, thereby insuring the absence of all pursuit
opposition. You can readily see, (because you are a professor), that it is practically
impossible for the pursuit ships to be up in the air, bombing and shooting us, with
their pilots in the middle of their afternoon siesta. (This does not stop the flack
boys because it is common knowledge that you have to lie flat on your back to shoot
straight up.)

   The most awe-inspiring flack barage of flack barages used to exist over a town
in these parts whose name starts -- coincidently -- with the same letter as that of
the name of my favorite uncle. This town has a sister town only a few kilometers
distant, the name of which starts with the letter which also starts my oldest younger
brothers' name. Now when we fly over these towns, we receive no opposition at all.

               Tunis

June 19, 1943 - Tripoli, North Africa
Flying Through the Flak (p.2) - Captain R. E. Evans to his father

Palermo

Strange! It is rumored that the present occupants are friendly. At the present time
the stuff is thickest over a seacoast town in this part of the world. (The letter --
same as my older brother's nickname)P located on the northern coast of Sicily --
it is no longer verboten to mention localities. Once we hit this town in force,
and the flack bursting ahead of us was so thick and so "many" that the bursts collective
look like a big black cloud hovering over the city. We waded on in -- found it pretty
dark inside --, but after what seemed about three hours and thirty minutes time, we
were out and in the clear. Later, we noticed for the first time lots of new places
in our ships where the light of day penetrated the interior. Reference to the "G"
file proved conclusively that these apertures were not included in the original
design. We concluded that we were attacked, while passing through that dark cloud,
by some very large and vicious form of flying termites. I recall that my plane,
name "Nazi Nemesis", normallyas gentle a lady as you will find, jumped quite
violently when one ripped a large hunk out of her tail.

As I mentioned before, we always have flack, but we cannot always count on
pursuit to make the trip "really"interesting. Not long ago the BBC -- which is to
the NBC and CBS what the Boy Scout organization is to the Marines -- had this to
say, and I quote, "Over a hundred Flying Fortresses attacked the hey city of
Messina. While enroute to the target the heavy bombers were attacked by a large
number of ME-109's." (They gave the number at around 40 -- I couldn't tell).
"A running battle ensued." The radio account continued -- said we inflicted
"considerable damage" on the enemy,(conservative). Said," A number of Messer*schmitts*
were shot down -- only one of our aircraft is missing". It will stay missing --
we saw it explode on the impact with the water. I might quote from the Berlin
broadcast, but their reports are usually a little obscure -- rather inclined to give
the wrong picture. They wouldsay that "fifteen Fortresses went flaming into the sea."
Incidentally, this was our first and only ship lost to combat since beginning
operations in this theatre.

First Combat Loss

The battle accounts that you get in America are fundamentally correct, -- I used
to wonder about that. On the other hand, we have talked with German and Italian
prisoners,(EM and officers), who thought that prior to their capture that all of
North Africa was in their hands, and that eastern coastal towns in the United States
had been bombed. (They haven't, have they?)

Well, Pop, we've hit him in the shins a number of times, we've dern near
deflated his football, we raised a little hell -- if you please -- in "plane"
view of his very heart -- the place they won't let us bomb -- and that little
spot across the Tyrrhenian Sea promises a good crop this year for the plowing
we've done.

Rome

Once I saw the birthplace of Napoleon, and before we were home from that trip
I had seen the birthplace of Columbus and the snow-capped Alps Mountains in the
distance. A number of times I have seen the Isle of Capri and thehome of Ceri
Beri Bin; Another time the site of Napoleon's famous100-day exile could be dimly
made out on the horizon, while the Isle of MonteCristo slid beneath my wing.
I saw Vesuvius placidly blowing smoke rings, I have seen Mt. Etna belch forth more
than twice, and I have watched Stromboli give forth with a small burp!

Yes, I have done some swimming in the blue Mediterranean and it is delightful.
I visited a couple of our hospitals and talked to the boys. In three beds lined up

June 19, 1943 - Tripoli, North Africa
Flying Through the Flak (p.3) - Captain R. E. Evans to his father

-3-

One after the other were American, British and German! All three received exactly
the same treatment and care, (This makes me think our side has basically the right
idea.) I visited some prison camps and I have looked in on most of the big cities
in North Africa. I have been surprised to find more than a few times beautifully
and wonderfully developed agricultural valleys; I have travelled through mountainous
country very similar to our Smokies. I have stood on wind-swept, rock-bound coasts
and watched the blue-green waters of the Mediterranean crash on the base of a craggy
cliff -- hundreds of feet below -- breath-taking beauty! -- All this I have seen
in dark (?) Africa.

Employed by the United States Government, now loaned temporarily to the British
Government, I am no longer a fighting man -- I am a chauffeur. At the present time,
I am geographically in an X Italian city which was once famous for its pirates. I
believe "Old Ironsides" once pulled up in front of this harbor.

Yesterday, I spent the day with my new boss. We were joined by a British air
marshal with his complete set of ribbons. Today, Britain's Na.1 was arrived here
and my boss,(who was featured in the April 5 Life - to his delight and everlasting
happiness), presented me! Tsh! Tsh! The King was just as he appeared on the
silver screen; not large, pleasant, genteel, a little weary from constant over-
attention, and never quite sure of himself -- not wanting to look you directly in
the eye. He asked me a few conversational questions, shook my hand -- which I
still use as before -- and took his leave. Lots of pictures -- including movies --
were taken. Perhaps I can get you one.

These experiences with the brass hats are unusual, Pop, and as such, interesting,
but know ye, they are not the real thing! I am these days in the company of generals,
air marshals and kings only because of circumstances, not because of anything
meritorious that I have accomplished.

My boss had a bet with one of our generals that he would get into Sfax first.
He won, as you know. A Fortress, complete with crew,-- was the pay-off. He is
proud of his bet and his prize, not of me. He would have presented his airplane
instead of me to the King, but he could order me to be there, and he would have
had to roll the airplane over. Well, are you weary of so much reading? I wish I
had more time to "talk over things" like this with you. While I

While I am on this detail I'll not be hearing from you and Mom, but when I return
to the outfit there will be -- I know -- lots of pleasant literature for me to wade
through -- making possible many happy hours. Don't ever think that I do not know
that "you all" are writing. I tell you when and how the letters arrive only for your
general information. If the service isn't too good, remember they are planning big
things over here, and mail isn't first on the priority list any more.

                                                    DICK

July 12, 1943 - Cairo, Egypt
WWII Cairo Description (p.1) - Captain R .E. Evans to JoAnn Nelson

<pre>
                                           North Africa
                                           July 12, 1943

My dear,

        In an atmosphere colored by fifteen languages and dialects,
camels, pyramids, and date palms, arab markets and dancing exotic
dusky women, it is strange that the predominant thought among my
thoughts should be you--and yet, such is the case. Yes, it's
strange--exceedingly strange--that a mutual attraction--not a phy-
sical thing, but rather a cosmic thing which exists only in the minds
and hearts of two individuals--should be so powerful. Indeed, so
potent that its effects are felt a third of the way around the globe.
That, My Darling, is our love.

        Tonight, I walked home from a "picher show" in a North
African city surprisingly modern and up-to-date in some parts.
Tonight, I did not find myself in one these parts. The dimly lit
streets and alleeys all looked alike. Except for the stars, I was
lost. By keeping the North Star to my right and at right angles
to my course, I knew that I would be heading generally west, would
                        be able to determine the
most direct route to the sight of my lodging. So, I wasn't particu-
larly worried about not knowing just where I was, and the jaunt
thru the darkened avenues gave me an excellent chance to observe
the swarthy Arab and his mid-night activities. To my surprise, I
found considerable activity for this time of day. Filthy little
shops and stands--lit by flickering oil laterns and candles, tended
by noisy, excitable arabs--were despensing bread, camel meat, water
mellon, and certain delicately prepared bits which a white man finds
it hard to even look upon. The taxi cabs are now quite absent,
being lined up in front of the night clubs, but horse-drawn carrages
frequently rattle by. Twice we encountered camel carravans. Fifteen
or twenty camels quietly flowing by on their padded feet is some
sight. Actually they do flow. Homely, grotesque, impossible in
appearance, they, never-the-less, give evidence to some sort of
grace in their slow and methodical walk. On the back of 'bout every
third camel a small oil latern dangles--probably the first tail light!

        The walk thru the twisting streets goes on and on.. I
remove my wallet from my hip pocket, place it in my shirt pocket,
and button the flap. I begin to look anxiously for   . A
small Arab boy has been walking at my side, singing in the usual
Arab monotone. I pause to inspect something of interest--he pauses
too, not noticing me at all, his song always on his lips. Off we
go again and my companion is right with me, still singing. I wished,
at the time that I could somehow bring the complete picture of this
strange world back with me to the states that my friends might ex-
perience it too, that they might see the camels and the dirty little
people, that they might smell the unusual orders, that they might
hear the throaty grumbling voices, the high-pitched cries and the
boys song, that they might feel whatever it was that I was feeling
</pre>

July 12, 1943 - Cairo, Egypt
WWII Cairo Description (p.2) - Captain R. E. Evans to JoAnn Nelson

-2-

in that atmosphere that gathered so close about one.

     Finally _____ arrived and it was not until then that my bright young companion of the melodious voice departed. I paused on the bridge, looked to the moonlight, flickering about on this ancient and reknown river, watched the single-sail native craft glide slowly by. Yes, I thought of you, Darling. But I had been thinking of you for sometime. Once again I tortured myself and imagined you beside me,,leaning on the rail, breathing the cool night air, your eyes dancing and smiling at me, and you cracking wise about this and that...

     Some of the things I see I shall never forget. Recently, a scene presented itself before my questioning eyes that I can only attempt to describe to you. (It's significance to our future life as husbaand and wife will be obvious.) The sun was high, bright and hot, hot, hot. The air was dry, and the ever-present nostalgic oders of the Arabian city were heavy in the atmosphere. One could not tell whether the Arab smelled like his goats as he drove them along the streets or whether it was the goats that smelled like the Arab--neither smell quite like the camel. My attention rested for a time on an Arab funeral procession across the square. The processioners, on foot behind the much decorated horse-drawn carrage in which rested the deceased, seemed to be in the best sperits possible as they jabbered and jabbered and walked and walked. Then my interest was transfered to another part of the square. It is not uncommon to see an Arab astride his donkey as his wife skips hurridly along side to keep up, no is it an uncommon sight to see an Arab riding triumphantly along in what resembles a donkey-drawn ox-cart with the whole back end loaded down with his wives. So the sight that cought my eye probably went entirely unnoticed by the people who had been around these parts longer than I, but there were some very interesting aspects to this little scene in particular and to me they were quite unique. There was the inevitable, long-eared, sad-faced jack ass, the same funny little two-wheel cart, the Arab and a couple wifes--both measuring two ax handles across the beam--both exposed to the scorching rays of the mid-day Egyptian sun. But what about his nibs and the sun--a different story, entirely different. Somewhere he had procured, by some means known only to himself I suppose, a parasol of the kind used by tight-rope walkers, can can girls, and Betsy Ross. It was pink, it had flowers, and it was frilly-- it was a very lovely parasol. And by his austere expression the head of the house was undoubtedly fully cognizant of this fact. But that's not all--one of the women was standing up in the back of the lurching cart and leaning forward so that she might hold the parasol over the head of her lord and master.... Well, JoAnn, My Darling, my requirements will more-than-likely not be so exacting, but let this be a lesson to you--don't ever get cocky--I got a lot of ideas from our Arab cousins.....

July 20, 1943 - North Africa
Richard's Stories in North Africa - Mrs. W. E. Evans to Captain R. E. Evans

Hey there!

Where are you any way and watch ya doin? Is your new job and your new boss going to change our date? That was once going to be Aug. and not too far along in it. Was I thrilled to get the cablegram definitely! When Dad received your long letter, he was supposed to make a speech before the "Y men's" club so instead of writing a speech he read your letter. The men had fits over it. He carries it around with him all the time. I made him loan it to me to take to a meeting at Mrs. Broom's. The women went crazy over it. Nice combination! Any way everybody enjoyed it. Miss Laskey made copies for Stewart, Tom & John. It was wonderful!! Everybody says to Dick "keeping a diary? He should! He could publish and sell it." Judge Jennings says "Dick's a better man than the king. I'm delighted to represent him! "It's not as exciting at 3036 as where you are. ___ less your darling like your ___ right. I'd love to know. Mommie

August 10, 1943 - North Africa
Back with the 99th BG - Captain R. E. Evans to JoAnn Nelson

Hi Sweetie!
   What would you like to hear from Africa? Would you like to hear that after a very successful two months
with the pride of the British people, I am once again back in my old outfit, carrying on with the work I really came
over here for-to-do? Would it mean anything in particular to you if I told you that we've moved from our original
location—we're a little closer to 'em now? Would you like to hear that I think you're a beautiful liar—as regards the
comparison you drew between the King and me? (Keep right on wearing those rose-colored glasses Sweetheart) And,
oh yes, would you care to be reminded that you belong to me and me alone—just as I belong to you?   *Dick –*

August 12, 1943 - North Africa
The Monty Story (20 pages) - Captain R. E. Evans to his parents

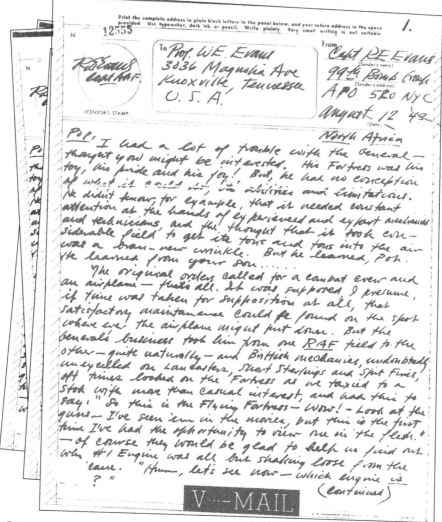

Pop,

    I had a lot of trouble with the General. Thought you might be interested. His Fortress was his toy, his pride and his joy! But he has no conception of what it could do; it's abilities and limitations. He didn't know for example, that it needed constant attention at the hands of experienced and expert mechanics and technicians and the thought that it took considerable field to get its tons and tons into the air, was a brand-new wrinkle. But he learned, Pop, and he learned from your son...

    The original orders called for a combat crew and an airplane... that's all. It was proposed I presume if time was taken for suppositions at all, that satisfactory maintenance could be found on the spot wherever the airplane might put down. But the General's business took him from one RAF field to the other, quite naturally, and British mechanics, undoubtedly excellent on Lancasters, Stuart Sterlings and Spit Fires, oft times looked on the "Fortress" as we taxied to a stop with more that casual interest, and had time to say, "So this is the "Flying Fortress, wow! Look at the guns... I've seen them in movies, but this is the first time I've had the opportunity to view one in the field." Of course, they would be glad to help us find out why #1 engine was all but shaking loose from the plane. "Hmmm, let's see now, which engine is #1?"

(Continued)

August 12, 1943 - North Africa
The Monty Story (20 pages) - Captain R. E. Evans to his parents

Page #2

The General had been operating in this manner for two months when I took over the job. He had experienced considerable mechanical difficulty. We had actually accomplished only three flights. He wondered why???

After a ground run up, which revealed nothing, I took off from Tripoli with his nibs bound for Cairo, with full confidence. An hour out, over a section of the Mediterranean, before Bengasi, #1 engine began shaking violently. I referred to the instruments, watched it very closely. Then the oil pressure on #3 started "acting up." I thought, "What is this!!!" The pressure on #3 started falling off... and engines just won't run without oil. I feathered it. Then the pressure on #2 began to oscillate, and I began to sweat. We were about 4 ½ hours out of Cairo. Should I go back??? With a conference of generals awaiting the arrival of The General in Cairo, the final before the invasion I was soon to find out... I would look pretty silly on the ground at Tripoli if nothing further developed. It was just as close to Bengasi. I decided to go ahead as long as I had three engines... put down at the closest field if I had to feather either #1 or #2.

I started navigating in earnest, figuring to the minute at what time I would pass all fields including the small auxiliary fields. From information I had gathered at Tripoli I started plotting the distance of these fields on my map.

(Continued)

Page #3

Bengasi looked darn good as it slid beneath my wing. At least we weren't going to have to swim the Gulf of Sidra, but the Cyrenaican Desert looked very hot and dry for a Sunday afternoon stroll! Straight ahead, right on course, constantly checking position by dead reckoning, so that at any time a course for Darnah or Tobruk could be assumed immediately if necessary, and the cold sweat kept pouring off my troubled brow. Once by Sidi Barresi we had a highway to the north, which I felt would make a satisfactory landing ground.

The General came forward, took over the co-pilot's position, pointed out to one of the desert battlefields below. Burned out tanks and lories and tracks scarring the "face" of the desert were all that was left, mute evidence of the struggle that had been waged up and down the Libyan Desert. I could not help but think "what a blessing that most of the fighting should take place way out here where no body but the actual participants could be hurt. What a pity that whole question couldn't be decided right here on this perfect battlefield, this God-forsaken land of sand and sun."

At El Alamein, the General became very excited. This is where, as you will recall, Montgomery relieved "the Auch", "reorganized the VIII Army and started Rommel the other way. "See that black hill over there?" He would say see that wadi over there..."

(Continued)

Page #4

"Well Rommel was over there, and I was over there... see the trenches? He started for Cairo around my left flank, but that was as I had expected. I was waiting for him..."

I was again breathing... for the first time in four hours. Cairo was now the closest field. I had committed myself... will she hold out? Probably!

The General noticed the feathered motor after sitting right by it for hours. His countenance darkened, "are we in trouble?" he asked. I showed him all my beautiful white teeth and said, "I think not, sometimes we turn one off and give it a rest." He was satisfied. Indeed, he was delighted... what an airplane! Marvelous! Magnificent! Astounding! Never intending to be flippant, I thought he would grasp the humor, but concluded that everything was under control. But he swallowed the whole thing, and I just let it ride. I was beginning to get acquainted with my new boss. Indeed, if we were going to continue life on this terrestrial sphere, there would have to be a change in bosses... as regards the airplane... so from that moment on, I took over. I began telling instead of asking... and we lived...

(Continued)

Page #5

On the ground at Cairo, I found I had sufficient strength to stand by the side of this great man and receive his gracious thanks for a" splendid trip down" and the smoothest landing etc., etc. in front of a news camera.

I was instructed to be ready to take off in three days. I said, "I'll call the Embassy tonight and let you know, General, after checking the oil consumption, and the condition of the spark plugs and magnetos whether I will need one or four new engines." I really fainted at my own audacity... and so did he!!!

No help was available at this field. There were Americans near Suez. I had to make my decisions in a hurry. I'll go over there! Two superchargers ran away on take-off, recall that three engines were all that I had in the first place. (Stewart will tell you what it means to have Superchargers run away). The power was cut, back on the ground

August 12, 1943 - North Africa
The Monty Story (20 pages) - Captain R. E. Evans to his parents

immediately, brakes and then aground loop at the end of the runway. Back to the line we taxied. "The airplane can't go to the mechanics. Bring the mechanics to the airplane!" "New engines, tools and pats! Pronto! First priority! This is General Montgomery's airplane!"

So, we got a new engine on #3, and the Superchargers were "looked at" the spark plugs we changed throughout" an hour's test flight before the General rides," I said, so up we went, the morning of the third day!

(Continued)

Page #6

She flew but people in Cairo wondered what the long black streak of smoke of #1 engine meant. Three gallons of oil an hour per engine is excessive, maximum allowable!! Engine #1 used 12 gallons in forty-five minutes, #2 used 6 in the same length of time, #3 was Okay and #4 used 4½... I made the General's acquaintance on the trip down. Now I knew his airplane!

He arrived the same morning at 0800 hours Cairo time, ready to take off for Tripoli. I was now glad as I confronted him that I had warned him properly, not covering up a thing. "Sir, I began." I was even a little mad because of his dogged insistence that the airplane would "somehow" be ready to go when he was. "Sir, if you are determined to take off in this airplane, I and my crew will fly you. We will be in our respective positions, but before we do I insist on telling you the exact status of this aircraft resulting, I think, from criminal negligence! (You will recall your son always leaned a little towards the dramatic...) "You will not be killed," I bragged "but you may find yourself in one of the airports between here and Tripoli, you may find yourself on the desert highway you know so well and it's very possible that you might spend the latter part of the afternoon, paddling a small rubber boat on the beautiful blue Mediterranean.

(Continued)

Page #7

There is no reason to believe, although I could get no information as regards its history, there is no reason why #3 engine shouldn't function beautifully for an indefinite period of time. However, based on actual flight test, I know for certain that #4 engine will last just 8 hours before refueling will be necessary (sufficient for the trip) that #2 will be good for an even 6 hours, and that #1 will function for 3 hours. The trip requires 6 hour's time with normal power output." The old man stroked his chin and looked at his new pilot out of the corner of his eye. He took another airplane for the journey and I spent the next two weeks in Cairo getting new engines "throughout." Engines can be changed overnight, but the English have been having tea five times a day for centuries and habit is a bad thing to break.

I saw the Sphinx, climbed the pyramids, visited the rug and perfume shops, took in the night clubs, brushed up my diving at the Gayela, no its Gezira Club, met Gordon Baskill and Ott Lyons and generally acquainted myself with Cairo and Egypt.

The General invaded Sicily...

(Continued)

Page #8

Let's go back just a bit... while the General was in Cairo, I was on three different occasions, his guest at the British Embassy. I respectfully brought to his attention the need for trained "and experienced B-17 mechanics aboard the airplane. Have them on hand the moment the airplane hits the ground," I suggested. Permit the men to remain with the plane over a period of time, so that they can become "familiar" with it, know its quirks, know where its strong and where it is weak. (Believe me, Pop, a B-17... each and every one of them has a personality all its own). "On the other hand," I said, "There is really no need for all the gunners and the bombardier, who of course do absolutely nothing, replace them with mechanics. Combine the Pilot and Navigator" (and I explained that he was fortunate in having just the man) I even outlined the whole thing on paper and submitted it to him, showing how... if picked men were utilized... he could have both mechanics and gunners aboard, since many can shoot, and few can trouble shoot. But I was a fool, and I had had little experiences with Generals before. I got wise and saw the errors of my ways.

(Continued)

Page #9

(If you're tired, you can take this thing to Elkmont and finish it, Pop and Mom and Stewart and Joan...)

Sooo, I took the General's ADC aside and sold him on views. (I was a good salesman 'cause I was very much interested in my work) I begged him to present the plan to his nibs in the quiet of the evening... as it were... in any fashion he should see fit to utilize. He did just that and before the General left, he accosted me, said "Evans, I've been thinking (wonderful thought I) I've been thinking that we should make a few changes in the crew set up and maybe

August 12, 1943 - North Africa
The Monty Story (20 pages) - Captain R. E. Evans to his parents

take some mechanics right along with us. What do you think of that?" With a completely sober countenance, I assure you, I told the General that I thought his idea was superb. Heck, it was!

He was going to take it up with Eisenhower, but he never did. However, when he met us in Sicily, I introduced him to a brand-new crew with myself the single exception. Again, he cocked his head and wondered... but that's another story and I think I'll tell it to Mother – Dick   (Continued)

Page #10

Dear Mother, O'mine,

I was just telling Father O'mine, husband o'yourn, about the trials and tribulations of your son Richard, back in the days when he was a General's "driver-arounder." We got as far as Cairo and I got tired of Pop, decided to talk to you for a while...

"Report to Malta via Tripoli" read the orders; so off we went, the pyramids sinking into the desert sands behind us.

Arriving at Tripoli just before dark, I then knew that the engine installation work had been bad and that the new #3 was an old one that had been "picked up someplace." In short and I won't bore you with the boring details lest you be... er... bored. The ship was in no condition for work in Sicily, a combat zone.

There was no help to be had in Tripoli and no one to turn to for official instruction. It was for me to decide. We threw our cots under the wings and went to sleep. At 0200, I woke up the crew... before 0300 we were in the air flying over the Mediterranean heading for Malta? ??? heading for the 99th Bomb Group... Home! After riding out a storm with everybody aboard, including the co-pilot... asleep... everybody except me.

(Continued)

Page #11

To repeat... everybody asleep but the pilot, we in due time busted into the clear and just as the sun was breaking the horizon, we rolled to a stop on the very familiar runway of our home port.

I got very busy, very fast. In less than one hour's time I had genuine American B-17 mechanics swarming over the airplane, adjusting, and readjusting, inspecting and generally rebuilding this bucket of bolts. I won't alarm you with a description of the condition upon my arrival, but when asked to describe the condition of #2 engine, one of the ground technicians who was working on the ship said, "No, Sir, it doesn't seem to be very rough, but while taxing the ship, I had to reach out the window every once in a while, and push the engine back on to the motor mounts..."

There is no liquor around Navarone, the place where we were stationed, but Cairo is known for it. Of course, I had promised everybody that I'd bring 'em a bottle, but I only had five when I got there. One for the Sqdn. CO, one for the Group CO, and the boys drew for the rest... In very short order, I was a jolly good fellow...

(Continued)

Page #12

I tell you this because it paved the way for a few requests that I had in mind. I wanted some new men, some mechanics, and some mechanics who could also shoot if it became necessary. In fact, I wanted to take away from the Sqdn. some of the best men they had and leave some dead wood in return. For authority, I said the General had given me a verbal Okay, but that paper confirmation had not had time to catch up. I got the men. (Orders haven't been written to this day, but we got the job done)

That night under a beautiful Mediterranean moon, we landed in Malta. It was now evident that #3 was a dud and would have to be changed. No orders were awaiting me in Malta, so off we went... again on our own hook but acting in the "best interests of the war effort" ... this time to Algiers. (At Algiers, I wrote you and Pop and Stewart and Joan.) My new crew turned out to be pure gold. In 48 hours, the new engine had been installed, a carburetor changed, and we were actually in the air bound for Malta. Come what may from the big boys, I knew that I had made the only decision under the circumstances and now I was flying an airplane fit for a General!

(Continued)

Page #13

But there was no word for us in Malta. I went to the field CO, told him my story, told him that I was going to take my crew, a highly trained group of men, back to my outfit so that we could be accomplishing something, contributing something toward the war effort. I told him that we were very little over two hours away, and that we'd come immediately when called.

August 12, 1943 - North Africa
The Monty Story (20 pages) - Captain R. E. Evans to his parents

But he got cold feet, and just before I was ready to take off, he wanted to see me. He insisted that we try again to reach the General. I insisted that we had tried and tried and that I was a bit weary of trying. He said, "one more signal." (They "signaled," we wired") I said okay... under the condition... that you permit me to deliver the message in person. (He was only a full colonel...) "How will you get there? Was his question. My answer was "I'll get there, you just say it's okay as far as you're concerned." It was...

Now Mother dear, you will remember that I am a hitchhiker of some fame... or ill fame more or less. My first hitch was in an airplane, from Malta to a spot near Syracuse. From there on it was trucks. Whenever I was stopped, I told the stopper that I was the Generals' pilot,   *(Continued)*

Page #14

and I told 'em that the General had sent for me. When I arrived at the Army's commander's hdqts, in time for supper that evening, I told him that "they" in Malta had sent me...

None the wiser, he was delighted to see me, made me the guest of honor at dinner, talked to me at length, inquired about "his Fortress." I told him that it was in the best condition it had ever been in. "Only one more thing I want to do," I said, "I'd like to change those wheels and get a new break unit... the breaks are the only things that keep the airplane from being in first class condition" ... but he didn't seem to hear me.

After three days at his Hdqts, much time being spent inspecting the battlefield and assault beaches, I returned to Malta... this time with passage all arranged... gathered up my crew and flew to Sicily.

For the first time, I experienced a bombing raid with me underneath! Just like the 4th of July, only more so! Sometimes the whole sky lit up like day... sometimes the ground quaking beneath your feet. Once an airplane, theirs, crashed into a nearby mountain, blew up, then burned for hours. It was terrific. We flew the old boy around Sicily; we were always ready, but we never got jumped.   *(Continued)*

Page #15

It was at this time that the General kept goading me into bringing the Fortress into this and that field... not really adequate for this type of equipment. Our home base was only 3,000 feet and we normally use 6,000. Many times, I flatly refused to accommodate him knowing full well that he was mentally calling me a coward and a poor pilot. On one particular flight I had occasion to clear this point up in his mind.

He announced that we were going to Palermo. (It had just been taken) "What's the field like," I said. I had bombed it but never had the opportunity to really look it over. With a little contempt in his voice, he said, "It's plenty big enough. I anticipated you. I signaled General Patton and he said, 'the same. The field's big enough for anything.'"

At this meeting, I was actually embarrassed, Mother. So knowing this, you can understand, my feelings when I tell you that I was glad when I got to Palermo and found the field not completely adequate for pursuit planes. I could see from the air that it was the shortest field I had ever seen... I couldn't see that to land into the wind was to land downhill!   *(Continued)*

Page #16

I am ashamed Mother, that I did not tell him out right that the field was too small, that a landing would endanger his life and the lives of my crew... not to mention a half million bucks worth of airplane.

Before I describe what took place let me give some figures... some comparative values. The airport at Salina is 10,000 feet long more than enough for any airplane in existence at the time. McGhee Tyson is about a mile, around 5,000 feet. This is more than enough for commercial equipment... adequate for heavy bombers if not fully loaded. 3,500 feet is the shortest runway I ever used in the US. Palermo was just 3,300 feet with an additional 500 feet, which was rough ground slopping off an easy 10% grade. Trees and buildings made it impossible to get on the ground right at the edge of the field. And here's the payoff: A transport (DC-3), which normally needed only a third of the space required by a bomber... cracked up right ahead of me. He just ran right into the trees at "the other" end.

I told the co-pilot Lt. Vernon, to tighten his safety belt... that I was about to show the General what could be done   *(Continued)*

August 12, 1943 - North Africa
The Monty Story (20 pages) - Captain R. E. Evans to his parents

Page #17

by an average pilot with a B-17 if it was necessary. (I could see General Patton's retinue of "lesser ites", newspaper correspondents, and newsreel photographers, patiently awaiting the arrival of General Montgomery and his Fortress, and it seemed necessary.) Down we went. I lined up with a place where there were no buildings at the near edge, just trees. It was my intention to brush through the trees (You can't brush through buildings!) We brushed 'em alright, and we were soon on the ground, but rolling 90 miles per hour and downhill! (This I had not counted on). Immediately, I had the co-pilot cut the two in board engines and called for the tail wheel to be unlocked. (Later he said he thought at the time that I was crazy) I headed the big ship for the right-hand corner of the field saving what breaks I dared (I dared use 'em all!!!) Just before we hit the downhill slope that I mentioned I gave her full gun (throttle) on the outside, right hand motor. Before the vessel (? Word) taut ground loop to the left had started, I had already reversed the process, using #1 engine to slow up the

(Continued)

Page #18

ground loop before it started. In this manner I had partial control of the careening, screaming Flying Fortress. The tire should have blown out, breaking the wheel. (It did in South America with one of the boys) The right gear should have folded up. The right-wing tip should have hit the ground. Both of the propellers on the right-hand side should have dug into the ground. But none of these things happened and soon we were rolling up in front of a throng of people who - I honestly believe - just wondered why the American pilot was so rough on his airplane. "Probably some show-off at the controls...."

Between you and me, Mommie, I'll give God full credit, but why he wanted to help such a fool I do not know. Again, my knees were strong enough for the newsreel camera, but this time the General had to send up into the ship for me. General Patton probably beamed... hadn't he said the field was big enough for anything. Well, most anything, because this pilot could have smashed his landing gear trying to ground loop his airplane at the end of the field...

(Continued)

Page #19

I was confident that the take off could be managed using the downhill grade and flaps at the right moment, but just the same I stepped off the field while the Generals were conferring and I watched where the DC's got off the ground, figuring from that where I could get off.

But once in the air, I had to tell the General his Chief of Staff and an Air Marshal, that I couldn't take them all the way home... because the brakes were completely and definitely gone and I would again have to ground loop the air plane to stop it... and our home station was only 3,000 feet and it was narrow... and it just couldn't be done... but if they wanted to bail out... but they didn't... they were beginning to get very reasonable... they wanted me to do just what I thought best. So, I picked a more roomy field, landed as a good long roll and everything was quite under control. I got a B-25, passed my passengers into it and flew them to the base field with very little time lost.

I told the General that I was flying back to Navarone for new brakes and he didn't say "No." He asked me if I really thought that a 17 was the ship for him, and I reminded him that I had told him sometime before that it absolutely was not. I told him in leaving that it meant curtains for me...

(Continued)

Page #20

and I did enjoy working for the old man. Felt that a blank type of airplane would be more appropriate for his needs. He wired Eisenhower and ordered a blank type of airplane. He now has a blank type and he's very happy. (The blank is obviously for security reasons.)

Before I left his services, he invited me "up" for a few days. Together we watched battles and looked over battlefields. Between you and me... again... ????, the Air Marshal aboard the Palermo ship realizing what took place himself, must have put a bird in the General's ear; because he frequently referred to me later as "his pilot" to whose skill he owed his life." Tch, tch...

Finally, I bid him adieu and took my leave and an autographed photo of the old man. This story is known only to you and Pop and my crew and General Monty. Because of the need for continued personal reference the story I quite naturally of interest only to some one very much interested in me. I believe you qualify...

Now, I am once again back in the old grind. As I mentioned before to you it was an interesting "mile post in my career."

As you have gathered, we have moved. We are no longer at Navarone (now it can be told). We're a bit closer to him... we can smash him a little quicker from here...

Your son, Richard

September 6, 1943 - North Africa
The Monty-Palermo Story - Captain R. E. Evans to his father

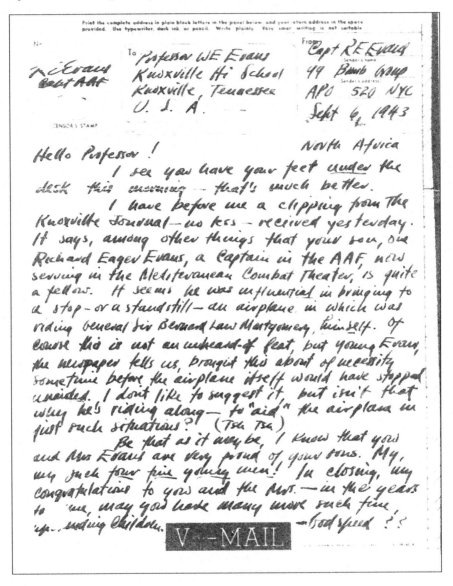

Hello Professor!

I see you have your feet under the desk this morning –that's much better.

I have before me a clipping from the Knoxville Journal—no less—received yesterday. It says, among other things that your son, one Richard Eager Evans, a Captain in the AAF, now serving in the Mediterranean Combat Theater, is quite a fellow. It seems he was influential in bringing to a stop—or a standstill—an airplane, in which was riding General Sir Bernard Law Montgomery, himself. Of course, this is just an unheard-of feat, but young Evans, the newspapers tell us, brought this about out of necessity sometime before the airplane itself would have stopped unaided. I don't like to suggest it, but isn't that why he's riding along—to "aid" the airplane in just such situations? (Tsk Tsk)

Be that as it may be, I know that you and Mrs. Evans are very proud of your sons. My, my such four fine young men! In closing, my congratulations to you and the Mrs. in the years to come, may you have many more such fine upstanding children. –God speed ??

September 15, 1943 - North Africa
The Story of JoAnn - Captain R. E. Evans to his mother

15 Sep 43

North Africa (Naturally)
September th' 15th, 1943

Dear Air Corps Mommie,

Enclosed you will find a poem written by your
son, name of Richard Eager. In order for the reader to gain all that
is to be had from the poem, it is essential that the story of JoAnn
and Dick be made quite clear in his or her mind. For this reason, we
have asked the poet to honor us with a brief account of the events
that took place in San Anton' during the time covered by the poem.
He has consented and his brief account follows--on the next five pages!

Young Richard was at Randolph Field when the
story actually began. For sometime he had been working very hard,
trying to learn how to fly. So eager was he to learn to fly and fly
well, that he frequently remained on the post during his time off,
studying his airplanes and generally trying to get ahead (or better,
to keep from getting behind). It was at this time that he realized
that there were no women in his life (a most deplorable state of affairs).
Now Randolph is considerable distance from San Antonio, and it was
rumored that there was some excellent hunting to be had in this great
city. So, the question of transportation arose immediately and it was
dealt with with just about the same speed that it arose---with...

Soo, having supplied himself with a shiny new
convertable automobile, our eager cadet accomplished the first step
towards winning over some damsel's heart. (In this regard, it was easy
to get cars in San Antonio, especially if you were a Flying Cadet.
Any care made could be had for a consideration--the consideration being
about $2500. Of course, if you were stationed at Randolph, you could
get a substantial discount of--say--about $1500, which, by the way,
ain't hey. If you didn't have the cash on you, 'twas no matter "just
sign here, here, here, here and here, Buddy, and the car's yours.
That's the idea--right on the dotted lines. Step right up, Gentlemen.
Who'll be next?" But of course, all this is beside the point...

His next move was to divide the City of San Antonio
into districts. Then he started a street by street canvas--each weekend
he would check off another district.

Having completed his Basic Flying Training, he
was transfered from Randolph to Kelly Field where he studied Advanced
Flying, and continued his search. But--Alas!--he cruised up the last
street of San Antonio, and not one pretty little girl had come rushing
out of her house to throw her arms about our hero's neck. He decided
that love was fore-ordained anyway, as he had heard someone say; so he
started gaining a little weight back.

Now, he spent his weekends diving and swimming,
and he was quite happy. Then one day, while executing a beautiful swan
dive, he spotted across the pool "the most beautiful girl I've ever
laid my eyes on"--his own words! Dumfounded, he stopped right in the
middle of the dive, returned to the board and just staired. Shortly,
she took her leave, but she also took his heart.

October 12, 1943 - North Africa
Not Home for Christmas - Capt R.E. Evans to his mother

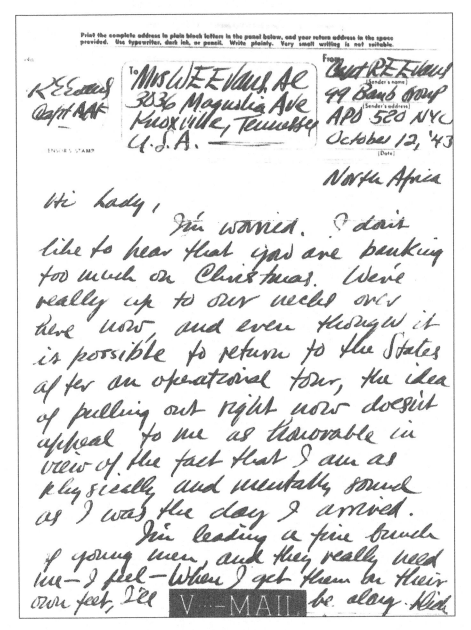

Hi Lady,

I'm worried. I don't like to hear that you are banking too much on Christmas. We're really up to our necks over here now and even though it is possible to return to the States after an operational tour, the idea of pulling out right now doesn't appeal to me as honorable in view of the fact that I am as physically and mentally sound as I was the day I arrived.

I'm leading a fine bunch of young men and they really need me – I feel – when I get them on their own feet, I'll be along. Dick

October 29, 1943 - Knoxville, TN
Father's Request to Come Home, W. E. Evans to Capt. R. Evans

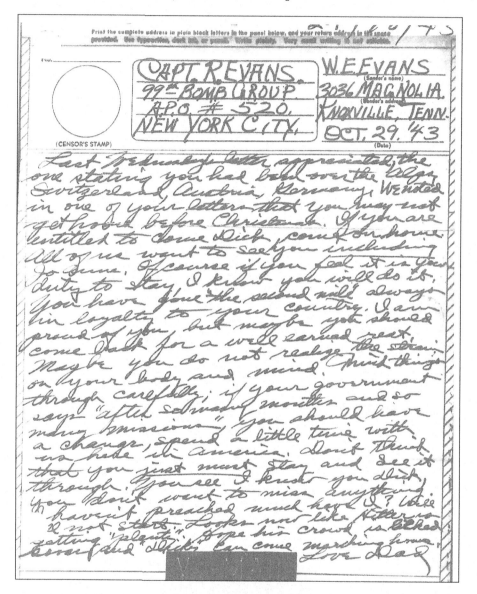

Last ___ letter appreciated, the one stating you had been over the Alps, Switzerland, Austria, Germany. We noted in one of your letters that you may not get home before Christmas. If you are entitled to leave Dick come on home. All of us want to see you are including JoAnn. Of course, if you feel it is your duty to stay, I know you will do it you have gone the second mile always in loyalty to your country. I am proud of you, but maybe you should come back for a well-earned rest. Maybe you do not realize the strain on your body and mind. Think things through carefully; if your government says "after so many months and so many missions" you should have a change, spend a little time with us here in America. Don't think that you just must stay and see it through. You see I know you Dick. You don't want to miss anything. I haven't preached, much have I? I'll now not start. Looks now like Hitler is getting "plenty". Hope his crowd is ___ and Dick can come marching home. Love Dad

February 2, 1944 - Knoxville, TN
Not Coming Home, W. E. Evans to Major R. E. Evans

MOM'S birthday has passed and no Dick. Gosh, my birthday seems terribly far away. You know, I have a sneaking feeling that you want to be there for the fall of Rome. That will be a classic event – Rome the Imperial city, the home of the Pope. Dick be sure that you do not stay too long. Come back in good health; don't depend on your feelings. You have been on a great nerve strain, come back when you are entitled to and rest up and see your mom and pop and brothers and the girl. What more appeal do you want? Hurry up boy, we're really getting anxious. Gen. D…. Jr. is here from Alaska. We were at their home out on Maryville Pike Sunday, and they were at our home last night for dinner. Mr. D… is ___ Mgr. now.   Dad

July 8, 1953 - Fairford Air Force Base, United Kingdom
Flying a B-47, Colonel R. E. Evans to his parents

8 July 53

FAIRFORD AIR FORCE BASE
United Kingdom

8 July 1953

Dear Mom and Dad:

Possibly you heard of our tragic accident. I thought it might mean something to you to know how it happened. Flying a relatively new airplane, too often we blame the airplane when something goes wrong. Another reason for blaming the airplane—it's unsporting to blame a dead man. Still another reason—with explosions, fires and impact damage, the evidence is often destroyed—there is nothing with which to refute the man-made assumption that the machine failed the man.

In the case of this accident, there were many qualified observers and considerable evidence. The airplane was seen making a normal 90° turn into the field. It overshot the turn. Instead of going around or making a second pass, the pilot attempted to make the turn by putting the airplane into a near-90° bank. The steeper the bank, the higher the stall speed. The B-47 stalled, visibly shuddered, whipped back in the other direction and hit tail first in a field, rolled and bounced 500 feet and stopped dead at a railroad embankment. It is little more than your trying to turn too sharply, the auto stalling out of the turn, sliding sidewise into the ditch.

Of course I tell you this because I want you to understand that my chances of flying a B-47 and surviving are above average. The first time I landed in England, I overshot the runway twice, but it didn't bother my pride any to give 'er the gun and go around for another try. From the standpoint of the airplane, I've never flown a safer one. When we came across the Atlantic, we were in clear skies all the way, the storms were all beneath us. We go like the wind, but we can slow down when we get there, and our landings are only a little hotter than conventional airplanes.

Flying home, we'll be going against the wind, but with the sun and the clock. It will take about six hours to cross the Atlantic and three and a half to get on down to Tampa. We'll take off about 0700 in the morning (Brittish Daylight Time), land at Limestone at 0700 EST. Fuel and eat for a couple hours, get off for Florida about 0900 and land just thirty minutes after noon, in time for a quick lunch, and —you guessed it— some water skiing.

Had a fine experience the other day. Lead a flight of 15 B-47's over Le Bourget airport, a Paris airshow. Made this old insurance salesman feel pretty good to sit out in front of a $45,000,000.00 Airmada.

All my love to you both.

July 21, 1953 - Fairford Air Force Base, United Kingdom
B-47 Atlantic Crossing Record, Colonel R. E. Evans to his parents

---

```
                    FAIRFORD AIR FORCE BASE
                         United Kingdom

                                              21 July 1953


Dear Mom:

Many, many thanks for your fine letter.  It's always fun to get a letter
from you, but overseas, it is doubly enjoyable.

It's a shame you didn't get to hear me over the radio.  Everyone says I
was absolutely terriffic.  In all modesty, I am forced to agree with them.
It went something like this:
```

Announcer: And now we take you to Limestone, Maine, where Lt. Colonel
            Dick Evans is preparing to lead the second group of B-47's
            across the North Atlantic. Colonel, do you expect to beat
            the record for the crossing?

Evans: Certainly not. You understand, it was my boss who yesterday
            set that record.

Announcer: Heh, heh. Will it be difficult, Colonel, for you to find
            your way across the ocean at night?

Evans: Well, I wouldn't say . . .

Announcer: I see. Now, Colonel, just how many men do you have to help
            you fly this great jet aircraft?

Evans: Why, we have a crew of . . .

Announcer: Splendid. Colonel, do you have any comments which might be
            of interest to the thousands of listeners from coast to coast
            who are bidding you "bon voyage" this historic night?

Evans: As a matter of fact, I do. I would like to thank . . .

Announcer: THANK YOU, Colonel Evans. Ladies and gentlemen, you have been
            listening to the voice of Colonel Dick Evans, United States
            Air Force, from Limestone, Maine. I return you now to New
            York.

```
The TV coverage on the UK arrival was really something.  They filmed the
B-47's touching down and deploying the drag chutes, an unusual sight
for many, a beautiful sight for any.  And, of course, they cought the
formation leader as he climbed down out of his B-47 and accepted the
welcome of the 7th Air Division Commanding General.  This was Colonel
McCoy--I lead the second group in the next day, had difficulty finding
a jeep to get off the flying field.
```

September 6, 1954
Life Magazine Article (p.1) - Colonel R. E. Evans is Pilot for Featured B-47

DEDICATED TO AMERICA'S DEFENSE

REFUELING IN MID-AIR A SAC B-47 APPROACHES BOOM, EXTENDING FROM TAIL OF BOEING KC-97 "FLYING TANKER."

SAC FLIES A MISSION

Strategic Air Command Maintains Peace with Hand-picked Men, 600-MPH Boeing Bombers Powered by G-E Jets

One of the great powers that deters enemy aggression is the Air Force's Strategic Air Command. For aggressors know that in case of attack on this nation, SAC is ready to deliver the counterblow which can, in Air Force words, "destroy the enemy's means and will for making war." Thus SAC is at the heart of our defense. Our lives, our freedom may some day depend upon its success.

SAC's success depends upon the competence of its men and reliability of its equipment. To achieve the former, the Air Force hand-picks its men, gives them up to nine years intensive training, keeps them constantly alert by "fire alarm" simulated bombing missions.

SAC's planes, engines, electronic equipment are the joint responsibility of the Air Force and the manufacturers who produce them. The top performance of the six General Electric J47 jet engines, which power SAC's Boeing B-47 bombers, and much other equipment of a classified nature, is the result of years of teamwork between Air Force and G-E specialists.

So carefully engineered is the J47, it actually operates longer than piston engines between overhauls, is easier to service and maintain. With mid-air refueling, these engines power the B-47 for as long as 20 hours at a time—covering a distance equivalent to halfway around the world—at speeds in excess of 600 mph. Yet, the jets must be capable of being so smoothly controlled that the B-47 can fly linked together with a flying tanker miles above the earth.

G.E. built the first American jet engine 11 years ago, and since that time has produced more jet engines than any other company in the world. In making this contribution to U. S. defense, General Electric has built new plants, trained thousands of specialists, and in many cases pulled top engineers and scientists off other important projects so that their thinking might be utilized to the country's best interest.

General Electric is proud that it shares the Air Force's grave responsibility: that of keeping peace and keeping America free. *General Electric Company, Schenectady 5, N. Y.* 230-28

ENGINEERS: G.E. constantly adds to its staff of engineers and scientists. If you have a background of successful engineering, and are not in defense production, send your qualifications to Technical Personnel Service Dept., Section B, Schenectady 5, N.Y.

Progress Is Our Most Important Product

GENERAL ⊛ ELECTRIC

September 6, 1954
Life Magazine Article (p.2) - Colonel R. E. Evans is pilot for featured B-47

SIX NEW G-E JET ENGINES are being installed by skilled maintenance crews in this Boeing B-47. Often B-47s fly more than 600 hours before a single engine is changed. G-E research and development have doubled life of engines, saving taxpayers over $100,000,000.

TARGET FOR TODAY is the subject of an intensive briefing session between B-47 and tanker crews. All of these SAC men are carefully screened for their important jobs, many are highly trained in not one, but in several different intricate operations.

PILOT LOOKS UNDER THE HOOD, with his co-pilot and maintenance chief. More than 300 separate items on plane are carefully checked before the bomber may take off. Jet engines get rigid inspection, must be in perfect order before pilot will sign check-out sheet.

TAKE OFF! With powerful jets roaring, the 92-ton bomber skims down the runway. At approximately 135 miles per hour, it clears the ground, climbs swiftly to flight altitude. Superb pilot training plus natural coordination and skill make this difficult performance look easy.

FILL 'ER UP! Refueling in the air enables SAC planes actually to fly around the world non-stop. As pilot keeps his eye on the tail of the flying "gas station," a Boeing KC-97, the refueling boom neatly spears the opening in the B-47. Fuel for the six jet engines is pumped

under pressure at about 600 gallons per minute. Absolutely smooth operation of engines and equipment makes this one of the most fabulous trapeze acts on earth. With tanks full, the B-47 can proceed to its target, drop simulated bombs, refuel in mid-air, and return home.

HOME FOR DINNER! The B-47 saves its brakes with a huge parachute, which it pops after landing. Now crew must report fully on flight, operation of equipment, success of mission. SAC crews travel all over the world, spend 90 days or more each year in foreign countries. To the alert young, college or high-school graduate, the United States Air Force offers one of the most satisfying, rewarding careers possible.

September 22, 1954 - Comments about the *Life* Magazine Article's Title,
"Dedicated to America's Defense" - Colonel R. E. Evans to his Mother

.... *If you had your speckles on you possibly caught my physiognomy in the front of the B-47, shown in the refueling position in the GE ad in 6 Sept issue of Life. I flew the B-47 for the aerial shots and some of the pictures made while we were getting ready to go, also appears in the ad. (When I look at the pictures, its hard to realize it's me--seems a long way from the Life Insurance business and in such a relatively short period of time.)*

Over our pictures they have printed: "Dedicated to America's Defense." I believe most of the leaders in SAC, along with being what we usually call "worldly types," are really and truly motivated finally by just such an idea as this. It bothers me sometimes to think that I have settled down, and I guess I'm well committed to spending my life perfecting a fighting force. Sometimes, I just hate it, and ask myself "what are you doing here?"

And then I think about Billy Mitchell – one man. And I think how he, in peace time, got himself thrown out of the business, which was his livelihood because he was absolutely and entirely "dedicated to America's defense." He realized when World War I was over that we would have to start there and not just keep up but stay ahead it we wanted to survive.

And I think of Edward Teller, and inspired person who has put his country "above self." We wouldn't really use an H Bomb, I don't believe, unless the Russians had one. We can thank God and Edward Teller that we have one. We almost didn't. And they did, and we just got ours really in time ...in time to still hold the world in balance.

We can be inspired by their leadership and their example, and we can be reassured when it seems that we are exiled to a lesser task. And when we are tired and bored and lonely, we can get up and do it again, because we think we have something worthy of our devotion and dedication.

What a speech. What a fancy way of saying I hate the Air Force yet find a way to think I love it sometimes.

Anyway, I love you, and Pops and JoAnn and Bobbie and Donnie—and oh how I miss you.

The one called Dick

June 2, 1955 - City of Knoxville, TN
Honor: Evans Day Proclamation for Dick's Father

CITY OF KNOXVILLE
TENNESSEE

GEO. R. DEMPSTER
MAYOR

P R O C L A M A T I O N

WHEREAS, William Ernest Evans is retiring from active service after 41 years as an educator with the City of Knoxville Schools System; and

WHEREAS, because of his kindly, dignified and inspirational manner in dealing with young men and women, William Ernest Evans has greatly influenced the lives and careers of many thousands of people who studied under his supervision, and is held in high esteem - a personification of the ideals of the teaching profession - by the citizenry of Knoxville; and

WHEREAS, the graduates and patrons of Knoxville High School and East High School, the two institutions where William Ernest Evans served as principal during his long service, have organized to pay tribute to Mr. Evans on the occasion of his retiring from active service; and

WHEREAS, this organization has made plans to hold special events in honor of Mr. Evans on Thursday, June 9, 1955, designating that day as "Honor Evans Day",

NOW, THEREFORE, I, Geo. R. Dempster, Mayor of the City of Knoxville, do hereby proclaim Thursday, June 9, 1955, as "HONOR EVANS DAY" in the City of Knoxville as a token of the esteem that the people of Knoxville hold for their beloved educator, William Ernet Evans, and I urge the citizens of Knoxville to participate in the events designed to honor Mr. Evans on this day.

WITNESS my hand and the Seal of the City of Knoxville this 2nd day of June, 1955.

George R. Dempster
Mayor

Chandler
Printers

April, 1956 - MacDill AFB, FL
SAC Pilots Test the B-47

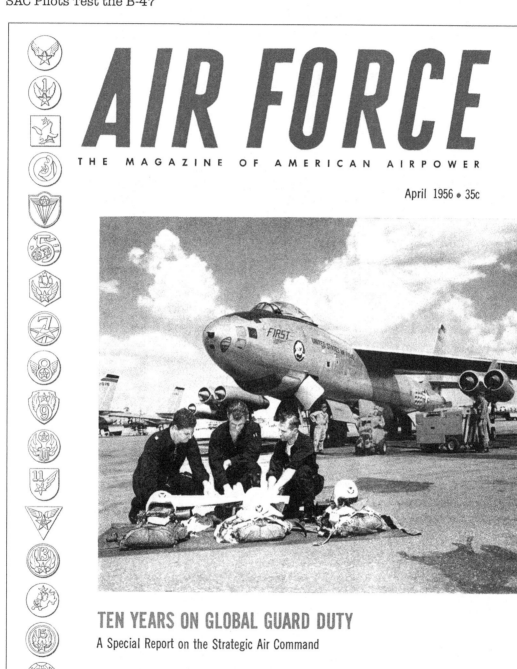

Colonel R. E. Evans (center), and his crew prepare for a test flight

APPENDICES
AWARDS AND CITATIONS

July 5, 1943 - Gerbini Airfield, Sicily
99th BG Award Citation Narative (p.1)

U.S. CONFIDENTIAL EQUALS BRITISH CONFIDENTIAL

NARRATIVE STATEMENT INDICATED AS BASIS FOR CITATION

On 4 July 1943, an order was issued directing three groups of heavy bombers to attack and destroy enemy aircraft on an airdrome in Sicily, aircraft that might be a severe hindrance to our invasion efforts scheduled for only five days hence. The battle order which reached the 99th Bombardment Group (H) on that day, directed that it should lead two other Bombardment Groups, the 97th and 301st on a mission to Gerbini Airdrome, Sicily on the morning of 5 July 1943. Fragmentation bombs were to be dropped by the 99th Bomb Group with the purpose of destroying enemy aircraft on the south half of the main airdrome and on the adjacent area. This target was of prime importance because at that time, the main airdrome and satellities at Gerbini constituted the principal Sicilian bases for fighters which had to be destroyed before the invasion.

Although only twenty-four (24) planes required for the mission, the ground personnel put forth strenuous efforts and early on the morning of 5th July 1943, twenty-eight (28) Flying Fortresses of the 99th Bomb Group lifted their cargo of men and bombs and headed into the northeast on their missions to destroy the enemy. Shortly after rendesvous with the other two groups one of our bombers was forced by mechanical trouble to return to its base. The remaining twenty-seven (27) Forts of the group, under the leadership of Colonel FAY R. UPTHEGROVE, the Commanding Officer, bored steadily onward toward the target.

As the formation drew near the target area it was observed that the enemy was preparing to prevent the destruction of its principal airdrome and the aircraft on it if that were at all possible. Swarms of enemy 109's, FW 190's, and Macchi 202's were sweeping up to reach the bombers as they went steadily on toward the target at an altitude of twenty-one thousand (21,000) feet. About fifteen (15) minutes before reaching their target the group was suddenly attacked by the enemy fighters which now number at least one hundred (100) aircraft.

Fierce and aggressive encounters took place as the enemy formed up in a co-ordinated series of attacks. Some of the enemy pressed attacks in groups of four (4) to sixteen (16) from ten o'clock to two o'clock in line astern and line abreast. Many of these were very determined, continuing their flight entirely through our formation with machine guns and cannon blazing. Other groups of four (4) to six (6) made continuous passes from the rear while still others were attacking singly and in two's from all angles. Two large formations queued up in line astern parallel and on each side of our formation them peeled off one at a time, first on one side and then on the other, attacking our group from three (3) and nine (9) o'clock. The evident purpose of the attackers was to break up our formation, knock out as many bombers as possible and so disrupt the group that its bombing would be entirely ineffectual. But in this they failed miserably.

Fighting back with cool and steady nerves our crews continued relentlessly to the target. Enemy fighters were streaming down enveloped in flames while others exploded in mid-air as our gunners put their bullets into gas tanks and other vital parts of the planes. The enemy too scored against our group as three (3) of the 99th bombers fell to the sustained attack. But in spite of the fury of the battle, in spite of the loss of the bombers, and ignoring the heavy, accurate flak that was bursting among our aircraft, the group remained in perfect formation and dropped its load of bombs with devasting results.

July 5, 1943 - Gerbini Airfield, Sicily
99th BG Award Citation Narative (p.2)

U.S. CONFIDENTIAL EQUALS BRITISH CONFIDENTIAL

(narrative statement continued)

The whole of the area assigned as a target to the 99th Bomb Group was covered thoroughly and completely with an excellent pattern of hits. Of the twenty-eight (28) enemy aircraft on the ground in the south half of the airdrome and adjacent dispersal area, official interpretation of photographs credited this group with the destruction or serious damage of twenty (20) of these aircraft on the ground. In addition, building, installations, storage pits, revetments and previously damaged hangars in the target area were heavily hit. The enemy had been given a crushing blow. The aerial battle continued for nearly a full hour and when the last of the enemy planes broke off the attack his numbers had been out in half by the deadly accurate fire of the 99th Group's gunners. Officially verified claims of this group were thirty-eight (38) enemy aircraft destroyed, eleven (11) probably destroyed and one (1) damaged; a total of fifty (50) in the air. Up to that time this was the greatest number of enemy aircraft ever destroyed by one Group in aerial battle. Added to those knocked out on the ground the total reached seventy (70) aircraft destroyed or badly damaged by twenty-seven (27) bombers of the 99th Bomb Group in an hour's time.

Out of all the furiousness of the battle a number of outstanding feats were recorded. One waist gunner was officially credited with the destruction of seven (7) enemy aircraft, which was at that time was an unsurpassed record in any theater and since has reputedly been surpassed by only one man in another theater of operations. The Fortress from which this gunner sent his deadly hail of lead carried others too who were dealing death and destruction to the enemy fighters. The crew of this one airplane accounted for a total of twelve (12) officially credited enemy aircraft destroyed and one (1) damaged which is still a record for one bomber. Crews of our bombers who observed their three (3) sister ships go down claimed that one of them alone knocked at least six (6) enemy fighters from the sky, although these play no part in the official totals.

The top turret gunner of one of our lost Forts, S/Sgt. ALLEN B. HUCKABEE, who parachuted to safety and was captured only to later escape and rejoin the group, had this to say about the enemy fighters destroyed that day. "The Italians told us we shot down fifty-one (51) of their planes in that fight."

When the 99th Bombers returned to base it was found that in addition to the three (3) bombers and their crews who went down near the target, two crew members had been wounded and nine (9) of our aircraft damaged by flak and enemy fighters.

It had been a terrific struggle and our losses were severe but the enemy had suffered a blow which made him incapable of dominating the skies when our troops landed on Sicily in the invasion which started just five (5) days later.

For their part in the successful accomplishment of this important mission a number of awards were made to those who contributed outstanding acts in the fulfillment of their duties.

Such heroic deeds and outstanding results obtained in the accomplishment of a dangerous and important mission reflect great credit upon the 99th Bomb Group (H) and the Air Forces of the United States Army.

July 18, 1943 - Navarin Airfield, Algeria
99th BG Celebrates 50 Missions

CONFIDENTIAL

SPECIAL ACCOUNT

  On July 18, 1943, the 99th Bombardment Group celebrated an anniversary--
of its first 50 missions completed against the enemy. The saga of the
first 50 was one of individual and collective courage and skill in times
of stress, but it was also an impressive collection of statistics.
  The 99th combat men looked at the records as of July 16 and
- discovered:
  1. Of 518 enemy fighters encountered, they shot down, probably
destroyed or damaged 162 or 31.27 percent. 114 of these were destroyed,
28 probably destroyed and 20 damaged. They have destroyed or damaged
433 enemy planes in the air and on the ground.
  2. Their bombs had destroyed 271 enemy aircraft on the ground.
  3. They had dropped 3,089,740 pounds of bombs on enemy objectives,
shot 704,995 rounds of .50 caliber ammunition.
  In 50 missions the combat crews traveled 44,886 miles to and from the
target--nearly twice around the world. It took them 292 hours or more
than 12 days and nights of combat flying to pile up this mileage.
  Naturally the Fortresses didn't always come out with whole skins.
Flak damaged 107 airplanes and enemy fighters managed to put holes in
31 of them. Up to July 5 only one plane had been lost in actual combat.
On that three more were lost when more than 100 enemy fighters ganged up
on the group. But many of these crews were seen to bail out and one ship
was observed to crash land on the beach. And for revenge the gunners
blasted down 38 enemy planes, with 14 more probables and one damaged.
  Throughout the 50 missions the group had the inspired leadership of
Col. Fay R. Upthegrove, commander, and Lt. Col. Leroy A. Rainey, deputy
commander.

February 17, 1944 - Foggia #2 Airfield, Italy
Major R. E. Evans' Distinguished Flying Cross Citation

	ECORATIONS AND AWARDS BRANCH, MILITARY PERSONNEL DIVISION, AGO.		Initials glm	
			Date 4/13/44	
RECORD OF AWARD OF DECORATION BY AGENCY OTHER THAN WAR DEPARTMENT				

Last Name	First Name	Middle Initial	Serial No.	Grade
EVANS	RICHARD	E	O-397378	Maj.

Organization	Foreign	Others
365th Bomb. Squadron, 99th Bomb. Group		

Headquarters	Station or APO	G.O. No.	Section	Date
FIFTEENTH AIR FORCE	520	55	I	17 Feb.44

Type of Award	Posthumous	DO NOT WRITE IN COLUMN BELOW
DFC	no	

Oak-Leaf Clusters	Number	Posthumous	

By Command of	Amended	Revoked	
Maj. Gen. TWINING			

CITATION

For extraordinary achievement while participating in aerial flight in the Mediterranean Theatre of Operations as group leader and pilot of a B-17 type aircraft. On an attack upon the marshalling yards at Padua, Italy, on 16 December 1943, Major Evans led a formation of thirty-two (32) Flying Fortresses, and despite prohibiting weather conditions as evidenced by poor visibility and heavy undercast, Major Evans exercised sound judgment and great skill so as to reach the target with the entire formation. Unable to follow the scheduled plans, Major Evans regrouped his flight and by entering upon a second method of attack took full advantage of a cloud opening to make possible the outstanding fullfillment of his mission which resulted in grave damage to this highly important enemy rail center. By his aggressive undertaking and initiative under difficult, perilous conditions, together with his superior leadership and devotion to duty throughout his outstanding record of over fifty (50) combat missions against the enemy, Major Evans has upheld the highest traditions of the Military Service and has reflected great credit upon himself and the Army Air Force of the United States. Residence at appointment: Knoxville, Tennessee.

June 6, 1944 - Foggia #2 Airfield, Italy
Major R. E. Evans' Oak Leaf Clusters 7th

DECORATIONS AND AWARDS BRANCH				Initials pb	10
MILITARY PERSONNEL DIVISION, AG				Date 6/17/44	
RECORD OF AWARD OF DECORATION BY AGENCY OTHER THAN WAR DEPARTMENT					

Last Name	First Name	Middle Initial	Serial No.		Grade
EVANS	RICHARD	E	O-397378		Maj
Organization			Foreign		Others
346th Bomb Sq 99th Bomb Gp					
Headquarters		Station or APO	G.O. No.	Section	Date
15th AF		520	879	I	2 6 Jun 44
Type of Award			Posthumous		DO NOT WRITE IN COLUMN BELOW
Oak-Leaf Clusters		Number	Posthumous		
AM		7th	NO		
By Command of			Amended	Revoked	
MAJ GEN TWINING					

CITATION

    For meritorious achievement in aerial flight while partici-
pating in sustained operational activities against the enemy from
1 October 1943 to 21 October 1943. Home address: Knoxville, Tennessee.

June 6, 1944 - Foggia #2 Airfield, Italy
Major R. E. Evans' Oak leaf Cluster 9th

DECORATIONS AND AWARDS BRANCH				Initials _____ mbl	
MILITARY PERSONNEL DIVISION, AGO.				Date 16 August 44	
RECORD OF AWARD OF DECORATION BY AGENCY OTHER THAN WAR DEPARTMENT					

Last Name	First Name	Middle Initial	Serial No.		Grade
EVANS	RICHARD	E	O-397378		Maj
Organization			**Foreign**		**Others**
346th Bomb. Sq., 99th Bomb. Gp					
Headquarters		Station or APO	G.O. No.	Section	Date
15th Air Force		520	880	II I	6 June 1944
Type of Award			**Posthumous**		**DO NOT WRITE IN COLUMN BELOW**
Oak-Leaf Clusters		Number	Posthumous		
AM		9th	NO		
By Command of			Amended	Revoked	
Maj. Gen. TWINING					

CITATION

For meritorious achievement in aerial flight while participating in sustained operational activities against the enemy from the dates 1 December 1943 to ~~XXXXXXXXXXXXXXXXX1942~~ 7 January 1944.

Home address: Knoxville, Tennessee.

August 3, 1970 - DAF, Fifteenth Air Force, (SAC) March Air Force Base, CA
Appreciation Letter Upon Retirement
Lt. General Paul K. Carlson, Commander to Colonel R. E. Evans

---

DEPARTMENT OF THE AIR FORCE
HEADQUARTERS FIFTEENTH AIR FORCE (SAC)
MARCH AIR FORCE BASE, CALIFORNIA, 92508

3   AUG 1970

Colonel Richard E. Evans, AFRes
Executive Director of Marketing
North American Rockwell Corp.
1700 East Imperial Highway
El Segundo, California 90245

Dear Dick

I want to express again our appreciation for your efforts
in completely revitalizing our Fifteenth Air Force command
briefing program. As you are well aware, we have a vital
and interesting story to tell, and we are anxious to present
it in the most effective manner possible.

Your professional and technological abilities certainly
contributed immeasurably to the outstanding revision. Just
as important, however, as both a "blue-suiter" and a civilian,
you provided the perspective and insight needed to get us on
the proper track. These abilities, combined with the necessary drive to get the job done under severe time limitation,
resulted in what everyone agrees is a highly refreshing and
professional presentation.

I hope we will be able to learn and profit from your service
again before your retirement, and that we continue to see you
often after that.

Sincerely

P K

PAUL K. CARLTON, Lt Gen, USAF
Commander

Peace . . . . is our Profession

APPENDICES

LETTERS FROM GENERAL MONTGOMERY
TO CAPTAIN R. E. EVANS

July 10, 1943 - North Africa
Monty Enters Sicily

B. L. Montgomery
General
Eighth Army.

EIGHTH ARMY

PERSONAL MESSAGE FROM THE ARMY COMMANDER

To be read out to all Troops

1. The time has now come to carry the war into Italy, and into the Continent of Europe. The Italian Overseas Empire has been exterminated; we will now deal with the home country.

2. To the Eighth Army has been given the great honour of representing the British Empire in the Allied Force which is now to carry out this task. On our left will be our American allies. Together we will set about the Italians in their own country in no uncertain way; they came into this war to suit themselves and they must now take the consequences; they asked for it, and they will now get it.

3. On behalf of us all I want to give a very hearty welcome to the Canadian troops that are now joining the Eighth Army. I know well the fighting men of Canada; they are magnificent soldiers, and the long and careful training they have received in England will now be put to very good use—to the great benefit of the Eighth Army.

4. The task in front of us is not easy. But it is not so difficult as many we have had in the past, and have overcome successfully. In all our operations we have always had the close and intimate support of the Royal Navy and the R.A.F., and because of that support we have always succeeded. In this operation the combined effort of the three fighting services is being applied in tremendous strength, and nothing will be able to stand against it. The three of us together—Navy, Army and Air Force—will see the thing through. I want all of you, my soldiers, to know that I have complete confidence in the successful outcome of this operation.

5. Therefore, with faith in God and with enthusiasm for our cause and for the day of battle, let us all enter into this contest with stout hearts and with determination to conquer.

The eyes of our families, and in fact of the whole Empire, will be on us once the battle starts; we will see that they get good news and plenty of it.

6. To each one of you, whatever may be your rank or employment, I would say:

GOOD LUCK AND GOOD HUNTING IN THE
HOME COUNTRY OF ITALY

B. L. Montgomery.

General,
Eighth Army.

10 July, 1943.

August 5, 1943 - Sicily, Italy
Thank You and Goodbye - General Montgomery to *Theresa Leta* Crew

Capt EVANS,
  U.S. Army,
Pilot of my Fortress Aircraft.
----

1.   On the occasion of the departure of you and your crew I

   would like to thank you all, each one of you, for the good

   work you have done whilst with me.

        It has been a very great pleasure to have had you

   serving with me, and with the Eighth Army.

2.   Good-bye and the best of luck to you all, always.

                              B. L. Montgomery.

                                      General,
SICILY   Eighth Army.
5.8.43.

July, 1943 - Sicily, Italy
General Montgomery Explains his Bet (p.1) to Captain R. E Evans

The Fortress aircraft was given to me by General Eisenhower in April 1943, after I had captured SFAX. He came to visit me at my Army H.Q. shortly after the Battle of MARETH; it was the 2nd April and I was busy preparing to attack the AKARIT position, and then to burst through the GABES Gap and out into the plain of central Tunisia.

I told General Eisenhower that when I had captured SFAX there would be need for considerable co-ordination between the action of the Allied armies in Tunisia, and this might mean a good deal of travelling about for me. I asked him if he would give me a Fortress (B.17); the splendid armament of these aircraft makes an escort quite unnecessary, and I would be able

July, 1943 - Sicily, Italy
General Montgomery Explains his Bet (p.2) to Captain R. E Evans

to travel at will and to deal easily with any enemy opposition. I said I would make him a present of SFAX by the middle of April; and if he would then give me a Fortress it would be magnificent. He agreed. I captured SFAX on 10 April and the Fortress was sent over to me a few days later.

I have travelled many miles in it and it has saved me much fatigue.

I have no hesitation in saying that having my own Fortress aircraft, so that I can travel about at will, has definitely contributed to the successful operations of the Eighth Army. I cannot express adequately my gratitude to General Eisenhower for giving it to me; he is a splendid man to serve under, and it is a pleasure and an honour to be under his command.

The crew of my Fortress are a fine body of officers and men, and their

July, 1943 - Sicily, Italy
General Montgomery Explains his Bet (p.3) to Captain R. E Evans

comfort and well-being is one of my first considerations.

It is a very great honour for a British general to be flown about by an American crew in an American aircraft, and I am very conscious of this fact.

B. L. Montgomery
General
Eighth Army.

Made in the USA
Las Vegas, NV
19 October 2021